ENCYCLOPEDIA OF REVOLUTIONARY AMERICA

VOLUME I

ENCYCLOPEDIA OF REVOLUTIONARY AMERICA

Volume I
A to G

Volume II
H to R

Volume III
S to Z

ENCYCLOPEDIA OF REVOLUTIONARY AMERICA

VOLUME I

Paul A. Gilje

Foreword by
Gary B. Nash, Consulting Editor

Facts On File
An imprint of Infobase Publishing

To Ann

Encyclopedia of Revolutionary America

Copyright © 2010 Paul A. Gilje

Facts On File, Inc.
An imprint of Infobase Publishing
132 West 31st Street
New York NY 10001

Library of Congress Cataloging-in-Publication Data

Gilje, Paul A., 1951–
Encyclopedia of revolutionary America / Paul A. Gilje ; foreword by Gary B. Nash.
v. cm.
Includes bibliographical references and index.
Contents: v. 1. A to G — v. 2. H to R — v. 3. S to Z.
ISBN 978-0-8160-6505-9 (hc : alk. paper) 1. United States—History—Revolution, 1775–1783—Encyclopedias. 2. United States—History—1783–1815—Encyclopedias. [1. United States—History—Revolution, 1775–1783—Encyclopedias. 2. United States—History—1783–1815—Encyclopedias.] I. Title.
E208.G55 2010
973.3—dc22   2009013596

Text design by Erik Lindstrom
Illustrations by Dale Williams
Composition by Hermitage Publishing Services
Cover printed by Sheridan Books, Inc., Ann Arbor, Mich.
Book printed and bound by Sheridan Books, Inc., Ann Arbor, Mich.
Date printed: July 2010
Printed in the United States of America

10 9 8 7 6 5 4 3 2 1

Contents

List of Entries

Acknowledgments

I would like to acknowledge a number of people who have helped me in producing this encyclopedia. First, I want to thank Gary B. Nash, who served as consulting editor. Gary reviewed the headword list, insisting on additional entries on several important African Americans, Native Americans, women, and others. He has also read every entry and made invaluable suggestions for improvements in style and content. I also must acknowledge the many authors who wrote entries. Without their expertise and research, this encyclopedia would have been impossible to produce. These individuals are recognized by name after the entries they wrote (any unsigned entry was written by me). On numerous occasions I have relied upon the efficiency and kindness of the staff in the Department of History at the University of Oklahoma, especially Barbara Million, Kelly Guin, Rhonda George, and Tanya Miller. I have also been fortunate in having a number of research assistants at the University of Oklahoma who have aided me in compiling and organizing the material for the encyclopedia. These assistants were Patrick Bottiger, Mike Barnett, Dan Flaherty, and Billy Smith. My daughter Karin Gilje also provided crucial help early in the project by putting together the selection of documents. Owen Lancer and the copy editors at Facts On File have also been great to work with. Owen has encouraged and guided me in a long process. And the copy editors caught errors of style and fact, vastly improving the encyclopedia. Finally, I want to acknowledge the continued support of my wife, Ann Gilje. I dedicate these three volumes to her.

Foreword

Two hundred and thirty-five years have elapsed since the minutemen at Concord and Lexington exchanged fire on April 19, 1775, with the red-coated British forces that had trooped from Boston to capture American arms. This ignited the American Revolution, which had been brewing for a decade. From that year to the present, historians have studied the Revolution and written about it—passionately, argumentatively, and often brilliantly. How does our understanding of the American Revolution, in all of its many dimensions, stand today?

Thomas Jefferson and John Adams, exchanging thoughts in 1815 on how those who followed them would understand the American Revolution, wondered if the full story would ever be remembered. "Who shall write the history of the American Revolution?" Adams asked of Jefferson. "Who can write it? Who will ever be able to write it?" Pondering these queries from his perch at Monticello, Jefferson answered: "Nobody except merely its external facts . . . The life and soul of history must be forever unknown." Both men knew that Charles Thomson, secretary of the Continental Congress for its entire duration from 1774 to 1787, had burned his thousand-page account of the war, afraid that he "could not tell the truth without giving great offense" to many of the nation's founders. It was better that the American people cherish a mythic version of the Revolution, Thomson argued, and in this way they would learn to venerate the founding fathers without knowing of their foibles and their many missteps. Thus disappeared one of the most important insider accounts of the course of the Continental Congress as it directed the war for independence.

Yet at the same time, hundreds of participants were scribbling in their diaries, pouring out their thought to each other in letters, reporting to Congress, and passing on stories to their children and grandchildren. The detritus of the revolutionary era began to accumulate.

Adams, Jefferson, and Thomson misjudged the ability and determination of those who followed them to mine the archival ore of the revolutionary generation. Historical societies founded after the Revolution, from the mighty Library of Congress to citizen-run local organizations, began collecting materials of every imaginable sort, and they have not abated their quest for new materials to this day because the American Revolution continues to fascinate the public as well as specialists. Hardly a year goes by without new materials surfacing, often from long-hidden sources. We now possess a rich and multistranded archival treasure house of primary sources on the American Revolution. Utilizing this ever-growing documentary record, historians have filled our libraries with engaging biographies; explorations of America's greatest explosion of political thinking; local narratives; blow-by-blow battle accounts and annals of military strategies and tactics; and discussions of the economic, diplomatic, religious, intellectual, and social dimensions of what was then called "the glorious cause." This is why this new encyclopedia on the American Revolution should be a welcome addition to every library and at the elbow of every student of the Revolution who knows the importance in a democracy of examining its past, especially its seedtime.

Giving special value to this new encyclopedia of the American Revolutionary era is the scholarship of this generation of historians that brings forward for our consideration the involvement and contributions of individuals and groups of people who were much involved in the tumultuous events of the late 18th century but heretofore have been largely neglected. Scanning the list of entries in this three-volume set, the reader will see names of Native Americans, women, African Americans, and individuals from the lower and middling echelons of society who never made it into the pages of earlier encyclopedias and are still seeking their place in the history books read in the schools. Consulting these entries, readers will see how the Revolution swept into its coils people of every region, every walk of life, every political persuasion, every religious commitment. It is the hallmark of scholarship in recent decades to show how many stepped out of the shadows of their communities to participate in winning a war of independence, to help fashion the contours of postwar society, or to resist the revolutionary movement as those loyal to the British king and parliament or as seekers of freedom and unalienable rights who saw their future of life, liberty, and the pursuit of happiness possible only by enlisting under the banners of the British king. This encyclopedia, then, presents American society in the whole, addressing its many parts as the American Revolution ushered in an age of democratic revolutions in the Western world.

—Gary B. Nash

Introduction

The American Revolution was the most important event in U.S. history. Not only did it create a new government, throw off monarchical government, and mark an end to colonial rule, it also revamped both the society and the economy of what had been British North America. Out of a colonial rebellion there emerged a new egalitarian and capitalist order that has come to mark the United States. Although this ideal of equality was not extended to all Americans in this period, the American Revolution was both affected by and had an effect upon all groups within the new nation, including women, African Americans, and Native Americans. This encyclopedia has entries capturing the Revolution in all of its diversity. There are entries on all the so-called Founding Fathers, including significant army officers, major politicians, Supreme Court justices, and cabinet members. But there are also entries on notable women, African-American leaders, and important Native Americans, as well as lesser known, yet significant, European-American males who left an indelible mark on the period. Because of the comprehensive view of the American Revolution employed by the editor, the encyclopedia also has a broad chronological range that begins with the opening of the French and Indian War in 1754 and continues to the end of the War of 1812 in 1815. The reader interested in military developments will find entries on both major and minor battles within this period. But there is also a host of other entries covering a wide variety of broad topics ranging from illegal activities such as smuggling and prostitution to the ideals of liberty and citizenship.

This encyclopedia has an expansive geographical perspective, demonstrating the interaction between developments in what became the United States with the Atlantic world and including developments within the greater North American continent. This emphasis reflects the increased scholarly interest in placing American history in a broader context. As a result, there are entries on Great Britain and France as well as on Africa and several of the earth's oceans. The idea behind these entries was not to provide a full history of these distant locations but to explore the relevance of these regions to North American history.

The editor has been careful in the use of some terms. The reader will note the near absence of the word *patriot* for supporters of the Revolution and the sparse appearance of the term *American*. Although used at the time, the term *patriot* implies that those who did not support the Revolution were somehow traitors to their nation—an assumption that is difficult to sustain in an era when nationhood was undergoing a dramatic shift and loyalties were often ambiguous at best. (For an explanation of this ambiguity, see the entries on nationalism and citizenship.) Likewise, to call revolutionaries "Americans" implies that their opponents, even those born in North America, were somehow un-American. Moreover, using *American* for the European Americans in conflict with Native Americans suggests that indigenous people were also un-American. To avoid this bias, the encyclopedia uses different terminology, referring to those who supported independence as Revolutionaries and Whigs, and relies on *European American* as a term in contrast to Native American or African American. There are some exceptions to this practice. In a few instances, especially in dealing with diplomatic entries, the term *American* was unavoidable. In some other entries, the term is used to include all Americans—Loyalists, Revolutionaries, African Americans, and Native Americans.

This encyclopedia builds on and extends Volume III of the *Encyclopedia of American History,* produced under the general editorship of Gary B. Nash. Although there is some overlap with that shorter book, this encyclopedia has entries of greater length and many new articles that reflect its increased time span, larger geographical content, and greater depth. This encyclopedia also has a set of documents at the end that seek to provide a sample of the many different voices of the American people from the period. There is also a bibliography organized topically, with a commentary highlighting the most useful books. This bibliography should be especially helpful to students looking for guidance on further reading.

ENTRIES
A TO G

A

Abercromby, James (James Abercrombie)
(1706–1781) *British general*

A general who had command of the British forces in North America in 1758, James Abercromby is best known for a disastrous attack on Fort Carillon (later FORT TICONDEROGA). Abercromby was born in Scotland to an aristocratic family; he was only 11 when he entered the British army as an ensign. His early military career was during a time of peace, and advancement was slow. Using his family connections, he obtained a seat in Parliament in 1734 and was appointed lieutenant governor of Stirling Castle in 1739. The outbreak of war in 1744 created opportunity for promotion, and by the end of King George's War (1744–48), Abercromby was a colonel. The Seven Years' War (known in the North American colonies as the FRENCH AND INDIAN WAR, 1754–63) brought him out of retirement and further promotions. He was appointed second in command to JOHN CAMPBELL, FOURTH EARL OF LOUDOUN, in 1756. For two years Abercromby and Loudoun hesitated to take any major military action as they dealt with undisciplined provincials and chaotic conditions on the FRONTIER. They contemplated an assault on LOUISBOURG but decided against that move in the winter of 1757–58. Abercromby spent most of this time in Albany and northern New York, organizing supplies and his troops.

When Loudoun was recalled to England in 1758, Abercromby became commander in chief. The British planned a multipronged assault on the French in North America, and Abercromby was ordered to capture Fort Carillon. He amassed a huge force of 16,000 men, 6,000 of whom were British regulars. By early July he had his army at the northern end of Lake George, only a few miles from their objective. On July 6 his capable second in command, George Augustus, Lord Howe (elder brother of RICHARD, LORD HOWE and SIR WILLIAM HOWE, British commanders during the REVOLUTIONARY WAR), was killed by NATIVE AMERICANS in an ambush. This loss dispirited the British troops who had no faith in Abercromby, whom they referred to as "Granny." Without Howe's council, Abercromby was at a loss and took two days to advance the four miles to the French lines. He then made a terrible tactical decision. Relying on the advice of a junior engineer, and without scouting the situation himself, Abercromby decided that the French, who numbered 3,500 and had entrenched themselves in breastworks before the fort, could be beaten with a frontal assault without artillery support. Leaving their cannon at Lake George, thousands of British soldiers massed for the attack on July 8. The result was a disaster of epic proportions. The advancing columns of redcoats were disrupted by felled trees and mowed down by a withering fire from the French. In four hours the British suffered almost 2,000 casualties, including large numbers of the famous Black Watch regiment from Scotland. Compounding the catastrophe, Abercromby, who had not witnessed the attack, ordered a precipitous and demoralizing retreat. Subsequently, he was recalled to GREAT BRITAIN, where in retirement he was later promoted on the basis of seniority. He never again held an active command and died on April 23, 1781.

Further reading: Fred Anderson, *Crucible of War: The Seven Years' War and the Fate of Empire in British North America, 1754–1766* (New York: Vintage, 2000).

abolition

Fueled by the ANTISLAVERY sentiment that accompanied the AMERICAN REVOLUTION, several states supported the abolition of SLAVERY during the REVOLUTIONARY WAR (1775–83) and the first years of the early republic. In retrospect, it is clear that the states that emancipated slaves were northern and that the states that did not free slaves by legislative action were southern. Of course, it was easier for these northern states to free their slaves since African-American slaves formed only a small proportion of the total

Logo for an early abolition society *(New York Public Library)*

population: All of the northern states had 10 percent or less of their population as slaves, while several southern states had as much as 50 percent of their population as slaves. Moreover, larger and more central portions of the southern ECONOMY relied upon slavery than in the North. Despite this demography, the North-South division was not as evident at the time, and the movement toward freeing slaves was fitful and not obviously tied to one region. Even some states in what became the South considered emancipation of some sort, and several southern states passed laws to facilitate private manumission. However, by 1815, although some slavery still existed in northern states, the stark division between the North and South on slavery, which would eventually lead to civil war, had begun to emerge.

Vermont was the first state to free its slaves. Although not admitted into the union as a state until 1791, Vermonters drew up a constitution in 1777 that boldly opened with a declaration of rights:

> THAT all men are born equally free and independent, and have certain natural, inherent and unalienable rights, amongst which are the enjoying and defending life and liberty acquiring, possessing and protecting property, and pursuing and obtaining happiness and safety. Therefore, no male person, born in this country,

or brought from over sea, ought to be holden by law, to serve any person, as a servant, slave or apprentice, after he arrives to the age of twenty-one Years, nor female, in like manner, after she arrives to the age of eighteen years, unless they are bound by their own consent, after they arrive to such age, or bound by law, for the payment of debts, damages, fines, costs, or the like.

This provision could be viewed as allowing a person to be held as a slave until he or she reached the age of majority—21 for men, 18 for women—but was interpreted as freeing the state's slaves while still permitting bound apprenticeships for European Americans. Although rhetorically important, Vermont's attack on slavery had a limited impact since in 1770 the Green Mountain region—the area that became Vermont—had about 25 slaves.

Two other New England states did away with slavery without any direct legislative action. Massachusetts had a history of court cases and petitions challenging slavery that stretched back to the colonial era. During the 1780s there were several more court cases that ultimately led to the end of slavery in the state. In particular, the QUOK WALKER CASE, which began as a civil suit over an assault and battery, ended with a judge in 1783 asserting that slavery ran counter to the state constitution, which had stated that all men were free and equal. Although the precise timing of Massachusetts slaves' actual emancipation remains unclear, because of the Quok Walker case and others—like the suit of Mum Bet (see ELIZABETH FREEMAN)—slavery had ended in Massachusetts by 1790. New Hampshire probably followed a similar path in emancipating slaves, but the exact details of slavery's abolition in the Granite State remain obscure. New Hampshire courts might have interpreted the state's 1783 constitutional declaration of rights as establishing the freedom of all men, but a 1784 law included a provision for taxing slaves. A 1789 tax-code revision did not mention slaves, and there are several sources from the late 1780s asserting that slavery had ended in the state. Yet there remained a few AFRICAN AMERICANS who were enslaved (150 in 1792), and only in 1857 did New Hampshire's legislature officially abolish slavery. By that time there had been no slaves in the state for decades.

All of the other states that abolished slavery followed a different course by passing gradual emancipation laws. Abolition challenged two crucial values of mainstream European-American society. First, ending slavery destroyed the investment that the slaveholder had in the slave. This destruction of property—even though it was property in persons—was antithetical to the sanctity of private property that was a hallmark of Anglo-American society. Second, few European Americans looked at African Americans as their equals, and most European Americans believed that African Americans were not ready for freedom. By delaying the abolition of slavery, gradual emancipation offered a compromise to these challenges: Gradually emancipating slaves compensated the slaveholder for the loss of his investment by the labor of the slave up to a certain date, and the years of continued bondage required by gradual emancipation before freedom could serve as a transitional period to prepare the African American for an independent life, at least theoretically.

Pennsylvanians were the first to pass a gradual emancipation law. Inspired by the revolutionary rhetoric of LIBERTY and building on a Quaker antislavery tradition, both the state's executive council and its assembly began seriously considering freeing slaves in 1778, despite being concerned that African Americans would be "scarcely competent for freedom." The final bill to emerge in 1780 freed all slaves born after the law's passage, but it made them bound servants until they reached the age of 28. It also insisted that slaveholders register their slaves by November 1, 1781, or their slaves would immediately be freed. Although the law guaranteed the eventual end of slavery in the state, it had the strange consequence of creating an indentured African-American labor force bound out for the most productive years of their lives. A market for these indentured servants emerged that actually encouraged the importation of African Americans into Pennsylvania from elsewhere in the United States. Slaveholders from neighboring states, including the Chesapeake area, could send their slaves to Pennsylvania, free them, and then sell their indentures at a profit. Slave owners made less MONEY than they would if they sold a slave for life, but they also could salve their consciences by disassociating themselves from what many considered an evil institution. During the 1790s, WEST INDIES refugees escaping the revolutionary and racial warfare of places like Saint Domingue (HAITI), sold as many as 5,600 slaves into indentured servitude following the provisions of the 1780 law. Despite the halfway status that indentured servitude represented for African Americans in Pennsylvania, the 1780 law, combined with increasing private manumissions, had almost completely extinguished slavery for life in the state by 1800. In 1820 there were only 211 slaves in the state.

Two other states—Rhode Island and Connecticut—passed gradual emancipation laws as a result of the experience of the Revolutionary War. During that conflict, led by Quakers, many people in Rhode Island came to see the inconsistency of fighting for liberty while also living in a state that accepted slavery. Newport merchants, however, were deeply involved in the SLAVE TRADE. Early in 1784 the Rhode Island assembly compromised by agreeing not to interfere with the slave trade but declared all slaves born after March 1, 1784, apprentices serving until age 18 for females and age 21 for males. By 1810 there were 108 slaves in the state, although a few slaves were recorded in the census as late as 1840.

Some people in Connecticut urged the end of slavery as early as 1776, and in 1777 the state passed a law making it easier to manumit slaves. Attempts in 1779 and 1780 to end slavery in the state failed. However, early in 1784 Roger Sherman and Richard Law submitted an omnibus bill revising the state laws which included the statement that "sound Policy requires that the Abolition of Slavery should be effected as soon as may be." They then included a provision that all children of slaves born after March 1, 1784, would be freed when they turned age 25. When the legislature accepted the omnibus revision without amendment, either intentionally or unintentionally, they set slavery in the state on a course toward extinction. In 1797 another law reduced the age of freedom to 21. By 1810 there were only 310 slaves in the state, and in 1848 Connecticut passed a law that ended all slavery in the state.

Slavery was more deeply embedded in New York and New Jersey, and it therefore took longer for the antislavery forces to gain a gradual emancipation law. Some New York leaders, such as GOUVERNEUR MORRIS, had argued against slavery during the writing of the state constitution in 1777. Morris's views did not gain much support; however, during the mid 1780s there was a much more concerted legislative effort, which ultimately failed when opponents saddled a gradual emancipation law with a number of provisions limiting the rights of any freed African Americans. During the 1790s there were several more attempts to pass an abolition law, but it was not until 1799 that the measure succeeded. Modeled after the Pennsylvania law, the measure freed slaves born after July 4, 1799, but bound them to their mother's owners until the males reached age 28 and the females reached age 25. The legislature revised the law a couple of times thereafter. The original law allowed the owners to surrender an infant to the community, which would then pay to have someone care for the child. Since ex-owners would often agree to raise their freed slave child, the state ended up compensating them for emancipation. In 1804 New York introduced a clause limiting the state's commitment to pay for the upkeep of the freed slaves. The state legislature also passed laws to prevent the exportation of slaves from the state as a means of avoiding emancipation, and finally, in 1817, the state created a new timetable that freed all of New York's slaves on July 4, 1827.

New Jersey was the last of the states to embrace gradual emancipation in the early republic. Pennsylvania's 1780 law triggered an extensive debate over slavery in New Jersey in the 1780s, but any effort at freeing slaves made little headway. Attempts to pass a law during the 1790s were also futile. However, in 1803 the state legislature accepted gradual emancipation by an overwhelming margin. After July 4, 1804, all children born to slaves would be free and bound out to their mother's owner until age 25 for males and age 21 for females. Like the New York law, the New Jersey bill included a provision for state support of children abandoned to the overseers of the poor—a measure that became a form of compensation to the slave owners who would then be paid to raise the children. In 1805 the state legislature decided that it would no longer pay such compensation to children born from that point forward, but continued to pay for children already surrendered and then rebound to the parent's master. In 1811 the state passed another revision, which ended all such compensation. There would be some slaves in New Jersey into the 1850s.

The national government also acted against slavery with the NORTHWEST ORDINANCE of 1787, which prevented the importation of slavery north of the Ohio River. As states in the Northwest entered the union they included provisions abolishing slavery in their constitutions. Thus, by 1815 the distinction between a free North and a slave South, while not absolute, had begun to emerge.

See also SLAVE TRADE, DOMESTIC.

Further reading: Gary B. Nash and Jean R. Soderland, *Freedom by Degrees: Emancipation and its Aftermath* (New York: Oxford University Press, 1991); Arthur Zilversmit, *The First Emancipation: The Abolition of Slavery in the North* (Chicago: University of Chicago Press, 1967).

Acadians

The Acadians were French CATHOLICS from NOVA SCOTIA, most of whom were exiled in 1755 during the FRENCH AND INDIAN WAR (1754–63) and dispersed throughout the British North American colonies. Many of the Acadians eventually resettled in LOUISIANA and became the ethnic group called *Cajuns*.

The Acadians traced their origins back to the 17th-century French settlers who populated the French colony of Acadia. They lived mainly by FISHING and farming. A combined force of British soldiers and colonists from New England conquered Acadia in 1710. In 1714 the territory, centered mainly on the Bay of Fundy around the settlement of Port Royal (later Annapolis Royal), became Nova Scotia. Few English-speaking colonists came to the region until the 1750s, and Acadians, who numbered about 9,000–10,000 by then, retained ambiguous loyalties.

Around 1750, British officials made a concerted effort to colonize Nova Scotia, establishing Halifax and encouraging Protestants from other North American colonies, Germany, and GREAT BRITAIN to settle in the area. The hope was that the newcomers would intermingle with the French Catholics (the term *Acadian* only came into common usage after the expulsion) and encourage them to assume a British identity and Protestant religion. Upon the outbreak of the French and Indian War, the Acadians appeared to present a problem for the British officials. For several years the British had been warring with the Micmac, a conflict in which the Acadians had acted neutral at best and at times seemed to support the NATIVE AMERICANS. Once fighting with FRANCE began, the Acadians' loyalties became even more unclear. Most French Catholics continued to insist that any loyalty oath to the British king include the condition that they did not have to serve in the military. Moreover, some French Catholics appeared to support France rather than Great Britain. The British therefore decided to expel all French-speaking Catholics from Nova Scotia. But rather than sending them to France, the British dispersed the Acadians throughout the North American colonies in the belief that when spread out they would lose their Gallic identity and become British, while simultaneously abandoning their Catholicism.

The means of expulsion were harsh. British and colonial troops would occupy a village or town, seize all the men, and imprison them, while the women and young children worked to finish the harvest. Then the women and children would join the men, and they would be shipped to the other British North American colonies. Once the Acadians left, their houses and farm buildings were burned. Over the next couple of years, any Acadians not taken in 1755 were tracked down and also expelled. The British removed about 7,000 people from Nova Scotia. A few Acadians escaped to establish settlements on the St. John River in what is now New Brunswick, and some made it to other French colonies. The treatment of the exiles in their new homes was often bleak, and the Acadians frequently had to depend on charity from the local governments—a fact that did not endear them to the other colonists. Many Acadians, rather than assimilating, only developed a stronger sense of group identity from the ordeal. After the TREATY OF PARIS (1763), Acadians were allowed to leave the British colonies. Some illegally returned to CANADA; others went to the two French islands of St. Pierre and Miquelon off the coast of Newfoundland. By the end of the 18th century, encouraged by the Spanish, many Acadian exiles settled around the mouth of the Mississippi River to become the Cajuns of Louisiana. In 1847 Henry Wadsworth Longfellow immortalized the story of the Acadians in his romantic epic poem *Evangeline*.

Further reading: John Mack Faragher, *A Great and Noble Scheme: The Tragic Story of the Expulsion of the French Acadians from their American Homeland* (New York: Norton, 2005); Geoffrey Plank, *An Unsettled Conquest: The British Campaign Against the Peoples of Acadia* (Philadelphia: University of Pennsylvania Press, 2001).

Adams, Abigail (1744–1818) *First Lady*

Abigail Adams is best remembered as the wife of one president and the mother of another. She was born on November 11, 1744, in Weymouth, Massachusetts, the daughter of William Smith, a Congregationalist minister and his wife Elizabeth Quincy. Abigail Smith did not receive any formal schooling but was well educated at home. She was an avid reader and letter writer throughout her life. In fact, as demonstrated by her letters, she had a powerful and nimble mind, quick wit, and broad base of knowledge.

When she was 15 years old, Abigail Smith met JOHN ADAMS, a lawyer nine years her senior from nearby Braintree (now Quincy), Massachusetts. After a long courtship, they married in 1764 when Abigail was 19. It was a happy marriage that lasted 54 years until Abigail's death in 1818. John and Abigail Adams were separated for many years during their marriage because of John's activities in support of the AMERICAN REVOLUTION, first as a congressman in Philadelphia between 1774 and 1777, and later when he served abroad as a diplomat between 1778 and 1788. In 1784 Abigail joined her husband in FRANCE. During their years apart, Abigail raised four children: Abigail, John Quincy, Charles, and Thomas Boylston. Another child died in infancy. Although, like most married women in this period, Abigail could not sign contracts in her own name, she acted in her husband's stead, buying real estate and selling goods while she also managed the family farm and sustained the family's financial resources.

Owing to their frequent separations, Abigail and John Adams carried on an extensive correspondence, which is an invaluable source for how this famous couple coped with the domestic challenges posed by the Revolution. In her letters Abigail did not simply discuss domestic matters. She also expressed political opinions—for example, condemning SLAVERY and advocating improved EDUCATION for women. Famously, on March 31, 1776, Abigail wrote to John that she longed "to hear that you have declared an independency," and she cautioned him that "in the new code of laws which I suppose it will be necessary for you to make, I desire you would remember the ladies and be more generous and favorable to them than your ancestors." She made this request in the context of criticizing the legal authority of husbands over wives. Her comment has sometimes been portrayed as one of the first statements of feminist thinking in the United States. This interpretation is tempered by virtue of the fact that Abigail made her statement in the form of a request in a private letter.

When Abigail joined her husband in Paris in 1784, she quickly became good friends with THOMAS JEFFERSON. In 1785 she and John went to London, where he served as the first U.S. minister to GREAT BRITAIN. In 1788 the Adamses returned to the United States. When John became the first vice president, Abigail divided her time between the nation's capital (first New York and then Philadelphia) and the family home in Braintree. Abigail befriended the First Lady, MARTHA CUSTIS WASHINGTON, and became involved in the official social scene.

Abigail Adams was more than a wife to John Adams; she was his close friend and political confidant and advisor. Like her husband, she reacted negatively to the radicalization of the FRENCH REVOLUTION (1789–99) during the 1790s and resented the intense partisanship it created in the United States. As First Lady from 1797 to 1801, she entertained government officials and representatives from other nations. But she also encouraged John to oppose the French in the QUASI-WAR (1798–1800) crisis. She enjoyed the popularity she shared with John as the nation flirted with war. The ELECTION OF 1800, however, left a bitter taste in her mouth. Like John Adams, she felt a deep personal wound from the invective heaped upon the president by the DEMOCRATIC-REPUBLICAN PARTY newspapers, especially since the opposition was led by Thomas Jefferson. It would take many years before both Adamses could put their sense of injury aside.

After 1801, John and Abigail retired to their farm in Massachusetts. In 1804 she wrote a letter of condolence to Jefferson on the death of his daughter Mary Jefferson Eppes, whom Abigail had taken care of for several months when she was in England. Abigail and Jefferson exchanged letters for about a year in which they discussed the political breach between the two families, only to have Abigail end the correspondence despite Jefferson's appeal for friendship. (John Adams would begin his famous retirement correspondence with Jefferson in 1812). In her later years she was a staunch supporter of the political aspirations of her eldest son, JOHN QUINCY ADAMS, who would be elected president in 1824. Abigail Adams died on October 28, 1818.

See also WOMEN'S STATUS AND RIGHTS.

Further reading: Charles W. Akers, *Abigail Adams: An American Woman* (Boston: Little, Brown, 1980); Edith B. Gelles, *Portia: The World of Abigail Adams* (Bloomington: Indiana University Press, 1992).

—Francis D. Cogliano

Adams, Hannah (1755–1831) *author*

Faced with POVERTY and the need to support her father and family, Hannah Adams became one of the first authors to try to earn a living by writing in the United States. Born to a well-to do family on October 2, 1755, in Medford, Massachusetts, Adams received her EDUCATION from her father, who tutored "rusticated" Harvard students (those who were sent to the country for disciplinary reasons). Eventually, Adams became a tutor herself. Her mother died when she was 12, and her father lost most of his fortune while Adams was still in her teens.

Adams read broadly, and in 1778, disgusted with the bias she found in the written accounts of different religions, she began her own study of comparative religions. This effort led to the publication of *An Alphabetical Compendium of the Various Sects Which Have Appeared in the World from the Beginning of the Christian Aera to the Present Day . . .* in 1784. This book would undergo several revisions and be republished throughout the United States and GREAT BRITAIN. Although it did not quite provide the financial security Adams had hoped, it earned her an income and, perhaps more important, an international reputation as a scholar and intellectual. The book strove, as Adams explained in the first edition, to "honestly and impartially" collect "the sense of the different sects, as it is given by the authors" she cited. In other words, she sought to understand the world religions, including Islam, Judaism, Paganism, and DEISM on their own terms. This study, however, only increased her commitment to liberal Christianity, and she eventually became a Unitarian. She published other books, including a history of New England that led to a legal dispute, ultimately decided in her favor, with the conservative minister and writer JEDIDIAH MORSE. Despite her break from traditional female roles—she was an unmarried author with a trans-Atlantic reputation—she did not become a spokesperson for women's rights. She did, however, assert that if women were given an equal education to men, women might "admit a measure of improvement, that would at least equal, and perhaps in many instances eclipse, the boasted glory of the other sex." She died in Brookline, Massachusetts on November 15, 1832.

See also RELIGION.

Adams, John (1735–1826) *first U.S. vice president, second U.S. president*

Revolutionary leader John Adams was born on October 30, 1735, in Braintree (now Quincy), Massachusetts. His father was a farmer who had held office as a selectman and militia officer. In 1751 John Adams gained admission to Harvard, becoming the first of his family to attend college. When he graduated in 1755, he accepted a position as a teacher in Worcester, Massachusetts. The life of a provincial schoolmaster did not appeal to Adams, and he began to read law with James Putnam, a prominent Worcester lawyer. In 1758 he returned to Braintree to practice law. During the years when he established his legal practice, Adams began to court Abigail Smith, the daughter of a minister, William Smith, from neighboring Weymouth. They were married on October 25, 1764. John and ABIGAIL ADAMS enjoyed a long, loving, and happy marriage that lasted for 54 years until Abigail's death in 1818.

Adams's legal work frequently took him to Boston, where he became involved in the movement against British imperial regulations. In 1765 he penned a series of anonymous articles for the *Boston Gazette* in opposition to the STAMP ACT (1765). These articles, which were collected and published as *A Dissertation on Canon and Feudal Law*, traced the origin and rise of freedom. Britons derived their rights, Adams argued, from God, not from the Crown or Parliament. Adams also opposed the Stamp Act more explicitly when he drafted the Braintree Instructions, in which he asserted the Stamp Act was unconstitutional because colonial Americans had not consented to it. Through these writings, Adams established himself as an articulate and intelligent critic of British imperial regulations.

As a lawyer, Adams believed in the rule of law. He demonstrated this commitment in 1770 when he agreed to defend the British soldiers tried for murder as a result of the so-called BOSTON MASSACRE (March 5, 1770). Adams, along with JOSIAH QUINCY, secured acquittals for the accused soldiers except for two who were convicted of a lesser charge of manslaughter. Radicals criticized Adams in the Boston press for his role in the trial. His defense of the soldiers revealed a willingness to challenge popular sentiment, a position that would characterize much of Adams's later public career.

In the wake of the adoption of the COERCIVE ACTS (1774) in the aftermath of the BOSTON TEA PARTY (December 16, 1773), Adams concluded that reconciliation between Britain and the colonies was unlikely. In 1774, when he represented Massachusetts in the FIRST CONTINENTAL CONGRESS, Adams went to Philadelphia as one of the foremost radicals in the revolutionary movement.

Between 1774 and 1777 Adams served in the First Continental Congress and the SECOND CONTINENTAL CONGRESS in Philadelphia. This was probably the most productive and important period in his long public career. In 1775, under the pseudonym *Novanglus* (New Englander), he published a series of newspaper essays in which he argued that Parliament could only regulate the external TRADE of the colonies and, therefore, its revenue acts were illegal. He contended that colonial Americans had sought to preserve the British constitution, but it was the British government that had acted in an unconstitutional manner. When fighting broke out in spring 1775, Adams worked tirelessly within Congress and made crucial contributions to the war effort as chair of the Board of War and Ordnance. In June 1775 he successfully advocated the appointment of the Virginian GEORGE WASHINGTON as commander in chief of the CONTINENTAL ARMY. Washington's appointment indicated that the rebellion would be a united colonial effort rather than just a New England affair. Adams was also an early and forceful advocate of the creation of a navy to challenge British dominance at sea. By 1778, when he left Congress, he had served on more congressional committees—90—than anyone else, chairing 25 of them. His myriad efforts led the New York congressman JOHN JAY to describe Adams as "the first man in the House."

Adams also contributed to the debate over independence. In January 1776 he published *Thoughts on Government,* a pamphlet that set out a design as to how the colonies could govern themselves if independent; he recommended republican legislative and executive forms for the state governments. In May 1776 he helped to draft the resolutions debated by Congress that would declare the colonies independent, and in June he served on the committee that assisted THOMAS JEFFERSON in drafting the DECLARATION OF INDEPENDENCE. On July 1 he delivered a speech in favor of independence, which played a crucial role in the next day's congressional vote to declare the colonies free of British rule.

Adams spent most of the decade from 1778 to 1788 abroad on diplomatic missions on behalf of the fledgling United States in FRANCE, The NETHERLANDS, and GREAT BRITAIN. As a diplomat he secured loans from the Dutch to help finance the REVOLUTIONARY WAR (1775–83), chaired the commission that negotiated the TREATY OF PARIS (1783), and served as the first ambassador from the United States to Britain between 1785 and 1788. Despite these achievements, Adams found his years as a diplomat trying. For much of his time abroad he was isolated from Abigail and their children. Combative, blunt, and sometimes abrasive, Adams was ill-suited for diplomacy. Soon after his arrival in France, he fell out with BENJAMIN FRANKLIN and offended his French hosts.

During Adams's service abroad, significant constitutional developments occurred in the United States, including ratification of the ARTICLES OF CONFEDERATION and the writing and ratification of the U.S. CONSTITUTION, to which he was an indirect contributor. In 1779 he had been the major author of the draft of the relatively conservative constitution for Massachusetts that was eventually adopted in 1780. That constitution created a bicameral legislature, strong executive and judiciary branches, a limited franchise, and a bill of rights. It served as one of JAMES MADISON's models when drafting the federal Constitution. Adams also contributed to the debate over the Constitution when he published *Defense of the Constitutions of the Government of the United States* in three volumes in 1787 and 1788. The work—a wide-ranging (and occasionally rambling) commentary on the history, structure, and functioning of political systems—presented Adams's arguments in favor of a centralized bicameral system such as the one he had designed for Massachusetts. *Defense of Constitutions* signaled that Adams, the radical of 1776, was, by 1788, more

John Adams, second president of the United States. Painting by E. Savage in 1800 *(Library of Congress)*

closely identified with the conservative wing of the revolutionary movement.

As early as 1770, when he defended the British soldiers accused in the Boston Massacre, Adams had expressed skepticism about placing too much faith in the will of the common people. He believed that the public, whose will must be consulted in a republic, could also be fickle, passionate, and unstable. By 1788 he feared, as did many supporters of the Constitution, that excessive democracy was as much a threat to LIBERTY in the United States as royal tyranny in 1776 and parliamentary high-handedness (the Stamp Act) in 1765. Adams believed his concern about popular upheaval was confirmed by the outbreak of the FRENCH REVOLUTION (1789–99). In response to civil disorder in Europe and North America, he published a series of essays called *Discourses on Davila* (1791), which reflected his increasingly conservative views on politics.

Owing to this outlook, Adams was associated with the FEDERALIST PARTY (though he was not close to the party's leader, ALEXANDER HAMILTON). In 1789 he was elected vice president to serve under George Washington. Although he described the vice presidency as "the most insignificant office that ever the invention of man contrived," Adams served two terms as Washington's deputy. Unfortunately, his years as vice president are most remembered for the debate he initiated over the proper way to address the president. This concern with the dignity of the executive office brought derision as Adams was charged with "noblemania"; referred to as the "Duke of Braintree"; and even ridiculed, because of his weight, as "His Rotundity." During the 1790s, sharp partisan divisions emerged between the Federalist Party, led by Washington and Hamilton, and the DEMOCRATIC-REPUBLICAN PARTY, led by Jefferson and Madison. In the first openly contested presidential election in 1796, Adams defeated Jefferson in a narrowly sectional vote by 71 to 68 votes in the Electoral College.

The most urgent issue confronting Adams when he became president concerned relations between the United States and France. Great Britain and France had been at war since 1793. Although the United States pursued a policy of neutrality, JAY'S TREATY (1794) had established a close trading relationship between Great Britain and the United States. The French interpreted Adams's victory as an endorsement of the Federalist Party's pro-British policy. In 1796 the French began seizing ships, and in early 1797 they expelled the U.S. ambassador at Versailles. The two nations engaged in an undeclared naval war (the QUASI-WAR, 1798–1800), and both sides felt that an open declaration of war was inevitable. Indeed, there was tremendous clamor in the United States for war with France in 1798. In anticipation of the conflict, Congress appropriated MONEY to strengthen the nation's defenses and adopted a series of bills known as the ALIEN AND SEDITION ACTS (1798) to restrict citizenship for immigrants, take any necessary punitive measures against enemy aliens, and stifle internal dissent. Despite a brief surge in his own popularity and the pressure to declare war, Adams hesitated. Always one who preferred to be right rather than popular, he pursued long and complex negotiations with the French, which eventually prevented an open breach between the two former allies. However, his policy alienated many within his own party, especially Alexander Hamilton, who supported a war with France.

Adams stood for reelection in 1800 without the full support of his party. When he first assumed office, he had kept most of Washington's cabinet, but these men were more loyal to Hamilton than to Adams. In spring 1800, hearing of Hamilton's schemes to replace him with another candidate on the Federalist ticket, Adams dismissed some of the disloyal cabinet members. Hamilton then openly broke with him by writing a pamphlet declaring that Adams was unfit for the office of the president. Hamilton had intended the essay for private distribution, but it soon was published publicly, much to the joy of the Democratic-Republicans. In the controversial ELECTION OF 1800, Adams finished third in the Electoral College behind Jefferson and AARON BURR. Repudiated by the public and his party, he was bitterly disappointed. One of his last official acts was to fill a large number of lifetime judgeships with party jurists. The appointment of these so-called midnight judges angered the Democratic-Republicans because they were made after the election. Adams departed WASHINGTON, D.C., without attending the inauguration of his old friend, colleague, and successor, Thomas Jefferson.

Thirty-six years after the Stamp Act crisis, John Adams left public life in 1801. He spent the next 25 years on his farm in Massachusetts, where he also wrote newspaper articles reviewing the AMERICAN REVOLUTION and his presidency. In 1812 BENJAMIN RUSH mediated the rebirth of the friendship between Adams and Jefferson. The two men carried on a long correspondence during their old age which remains a monument in the history of American letters. Adams lived to see his oldest son, JOHN QUINCY ADAMS, elected president in 1824.

John Adams died on July 4, 1826, the 50th anniversary of the passage of the Declaration of Independence. His last words were "Jefferson still survives." Yet Jefferson had died several hours earlier on the same day.

See also JUDICIARY ACT OF 1801; POLITICAL PARTIES; REPUBLICANISM.

Further reading: Lester J. Cappon, ed., *The Adams-Jefferson Letters,* 2 vols. (Chapel Hill: University of North Carolina Press, 1959); Joseph J. Ellis, *Passionate Sage: The Character and Legacy of John Adams* (New York: Norton, 2001); John Ferling, *John Adams: A Life* (New York: Owl Books, 1996); David G. McCullough, *John Adams* (New York: Simon and Schuster, 2001); Peter Shaw, *The Character of John Adams* (Chapel Hill: University of North Carolina Press, 1976).

—Francis D. Cogliano

Adams, John Quincy (1767–1848) *sixth U.S. president*

Born in Braintree (now Quincy), Massachusetts, on July 11, 1767, John Quincy Adams was the most gifted American diplomat during the early republic and served as the sixth president of the United States. Adams was uniquely qualified for a life of public service. He was the son of the revolutionary leader JOHN ADAMS and ABIGAIL ADAMS. John Quincy Adams received his earliest education from his parents. At the age of 10 the younger Adams accompanied his father to Europe on his diplomatic missions. He learned French fluently and was educated in a private school in Paris and at the University of Leiden. In 1782–83 he served as secretary and interpreter for an American diplomat, Francis Dana, on a journey to the Russian court in St. Petersburg. They traveled by way of The NETHERLANDS, the German states, and Scandinavia. When Adams returned to the United States in 1785, aged 18, he was extraordinarily well-traveled; an accomplished linguist; and well-read in the classics, history, and mathematics. Adams completed his EDUCATION at Harvard College. He graduated in 1787 and read law in Newburyport, Massachusetts, under the supervision of THEOPHILUS PARSONS, a distinguished and conservative Massachusetts jurist. In 1790 he was admitted to the bar and settled down to practice law in Boston.

Like his father, Adams was independent-minded and identified with the emerging FEDERALIST PARTY. He came to the attention of President GEORGE WASHINGTON as the author of newspaper articles defending the administration's neutrality policies during the wars of the FRENCH REVOLUTION (1789–99). In consequence, Washington appointed the younger Adams as the U.S. minister to The Netherlands (1794–97). After serving in The Hague, Adams represented the United States at the Prussian court from 1797 to 1801. While on diplomatic business in London, Adams met and courted Louisa Catherine Johnson, daughter of Joshua Johnson, a U.S. diplomat in GREAT BRITAIN. He and Louisa were married on July 26, 1797.

President John Adams recalled his son from Berlin after he lost the bitterly contested ELECTION OF 1800. The younger Adams returned to Boston to pursue his legal career. Public life continued to exert a pull on him, and in 1803 he was elected to represent Massachusetts in the United States Senate. Although a member of the Federalist Party, Adams was independent-minded. To the dismay of the Massachusetts Federalist Party, Adams supported two crucial Jeffersonian diplomatic initiatives: the LOUISIANA PURCHASE and the EMBARGO OF 1807. After the state legislature named his successor six months before his term was to expire, Adams resigned from the Senate. Once again, Adams returned to Boston to resume his legal career and to serve as Boylston professor of oratory and rhetoric at Harvard.

By this time, Adams's political allegiances had shifted toward THOMAS JEFFERSON. As a result, his return to Massachusetts was brief as President JAMES MADISON appointed him to be the first U.S. ambassador to RUSSIA, a post he held from 1809 to 1814. Adams left the Russian court to act as the chief of the mission at Ghent during the negotiations to end the WAR OF 1812 (1812–15). In those negotiations, he and his delegation held out against immense pressure for an agreement that would end the conflict without any loss of territory or concessions of any kind. The treaty also did not gain anything for the United States, but just maintaining the status quo against the most powerful nation on earth was seen as a victory. When the TREATY OF GHENT (1814) was concluded, Adams served as the U.S. ambassador to Great Britain (1815–17), a post his father had held 30 years before. Between 1794 and 1817, Adams represented the United States for more than 15 years in the Netherlands, PRUSSIA, Russia, and Great Britain. During that period he was an astute observer and reporter of the wars of the French Revolution and NAPOLEON BONAPARTE. He had become the most experienced and skilled U.S. diplomat of his era.

President JAMES MONROE recalled Adams from London to serve as his secretary of state, a post Adams held from 1817 until 1825. Adams became one of the country's most successful secretaries of state. Schooled from a young age in European ways and experienced in European affairs, he believed strongly in Washington's doctrine that the United States should remain isolated from Europe's conflicts. He articulated this view as the chief architect of the Monroe Doctrine. As secretary of state, Adams was responsible for negotiating the Adams-Onís Treaty (1819), by which the United States acquired East and West FLORIDA and recognized the border of the United States as extending from the Gulf of Mexico to the Rocky Mountains and thence along the 42nd parallel to the PACIFIC OCEAN. He also negotiated the Convention of 1818 with Great Britain, which set the border between the United States and British Canada along the 49th parallel to the Rockies. Beyond that point, Oregon was to be open to settlers from both the United States and Great Britain.

John Quincy Adams enjoyed a varied and successful career as a lawyer, scholar, and diplomat until he ran for president in 1824. He won a controversial victory over ANDREW JACKSON in the House of Representatives despite losing in the popular vote and the electoral college. Although Adams continued to articulate a vision of a strong and united nation, his presidency, undermined in part by the nature of his election, was a failure, and he was defeated by Jackson in 1828. Adams was 62 years old when he left the White House in 1829. Rather than retire, he represented his local Massachusetts constituency in Congress from 1830 until his death in 1848. During this period Adams emerged as an articulate and forceful opponent of SLAVERY. He defended the revolting slaves in the *Amistad* case, and his battle to allow the reading of ANTISLAVERY petitions in Congress against a gag rule earned him the title "old man eloquent." Adams died in the House of Representatives on February 23, 1848.

Further reading: Samuel Flagg Bemis, *John Quincy Adams and the Foundations of American Foreign Policy* (New York: Knopf, 1949); James E. Lewis, *John Quincy Adams: Policymaker for the Union* (Wilmington, Del.: SR Books, 2001); Paul C. Nagel, *John Quincy Adams: A Public Life, A Private Life* (New York: Knopf, 1997); William Earl Weeks, *John Quincy Adams and American Global Empire* (Lexington: University Press of Kentucky, 2002).

—Francis D. Cogliano

Adams, Samuel (1722–1803) *Revolutionary War leader*

During the decade from 1765 to 1775, when Boston was at the center of the RESISTANCE MOVEMENT (1764–75) against British rule, Samuel Adams was the town's most important political leader. By 1776 he had gained a transatlantic reputation as a mastermind of the rebellion. Born in Boston on September 27, 1722, Adams was the son of a merchant and brewer. He graduated from Harvard College in 1740 and endeavored, unsuccessfully, to establish himself as a brewer and newspaper publisher.

Between 1756 and 1765 Adams served as a tax collector in Boston. He proved no more successful at collecting taxes than he had at publishing or brewing as the Boston Town Meeting found him to be more than £10,000 in arrears in his collections, partially in sympathy for financially distressed townsmen. Despite, or perhaps because of, his laxness as a tax collector, he was elected to the Massachusetts assembly in 1765. He served as the assembly's clerk until 1780. In this capacity he played a prominent role in coordinating the assembly's opposition to British taxation from 1765 to 1775.

Adams was active in several organizations, including the LOYAL NINE; the North End Caucus; and, most important, the SONS OF LIBERTY. He also served as chair of the Boston Town Meeting. Through his participation in these groups, Adams emerged as the most important popular political leader in Boston prior to the REVOLUTIONARY WAR (1775–83). He was a vocal critic of British taxation and contended that Parliament, along with a few colonial Americans loyal to the king, was seeking to enslave the people of British North America and take away their liberties.

Adams was a very effective political leader, protest organizer, and propagandist, writing newspaper articles that were critical of the British taxation policies. He also organized numerous popular demonstrations and protests. For example, he led the successful movement to demand the removal of British troops from Boston after the BOSTON MASSACRE (March 5, 1770). In 1772 he created the Boston COMMITTEE OF CORRESPONDENCE, which helped to coordinate anti-British resistance throughout Massachusetts and, eventually, across the colonies. He also chaired the extralegal meetings that preceded the BOSTON TEA PARTY (December 16, 1773). In 1774, through the committee of correspondence, he led the call for a continental congress (see CONTINENTAL CONGRESS, FIRST) to coordinate resistance to the COERCIVE ACTS. During the decade between the STAMP ACT (1765) and the outbreak of war at the BATTLES OF LEXINGTON AND CONCORD (April 19, 1775), Adams was at the forefront of the revolutionary movement in Massachusetts and North America. Throughout this time, he sought to balance reasoned principle with emotional crowd politics.

Adams made his greatest contribution to the revolutionary movement prior to the Revolutionary War. Nonetheless, he continued to be important in Massachusetts politics and the revolutionary movement. Between 1774 and 1781 he represented Massachusetts in the Continental Congress. He was an early advocate of the break from Great Britain and was a signer of the DECLARATION OF INDEPENDENCE. He proved to be a stalwart in Congress, serving on numerous committees to help organize the war effort. Back in Massachusetts, he was on the committee that drafted the state's new constitution in 1779 (largely the handiwork of his distant cousin, JOHN ADAMS) and campaigned for the successful ratification of that document.

Although his political influence waned during the postwar period, Adams remained politically active during the 1780s and 1790s. He was elected to the Massachusetts senate and attended the Massachusetts convention that considered the state's ratification of the proposed U.S. CONSTITUTION. Always wary of centralized power, Adams was a moderate ANTI-FEDERALIST. A caucus of Boston ARTISANS, a group that had long been Adams's base of political power, came out strongly in favor of the Constitution. These artisans, as well as an intense campaign within the convention that included the promise of amendments to protect the people's LIBERTY, convinced Adams to give the document his reluctant support. This shift proved instrumental in the convention's decision to endorse the document.

Adams served as lieutenant governor of Massachusetts under JOHN HANCOCK from 1789 to 1793 and as governor from 1793 to 1797. Because of his populist inclinations and suspicion of centralized power, Adams was never really accepted by the FEDERALIST PARTY, which came to dominate Massachusetts politics during the 1790s. In the ELECTION OF 1800 he supported the DEMOCRATIC-REPUBLICAN PARTY candidate, THOMAS JEFFERSON, against his Federalist kinsman, John Adams. Samuel Adams died on October 2, 1803.

See also CONVENTIONS.

Further reading: Pauline Maier, *The Old Revolutionaries: Political Lives in the Age of Samuel Adams* (New York: Knopf, 1980); John C. Miller, *Sam Adams: Pioneer in Propaganda* (Boston: Little, Brown, 1936); Mark Puls, *Samuel Adams: Father of the American Revolution* (New York: Palgrave MacMillan, 2006).

—Francis D. Cogliano

"Adams and Liberty" (1798)

The poem and song called "Adams and Liberty" was written for the fourth anniversary of the Massachusetts Charitable Fire Society by ROBERT TREAT PAINE, JR. It quickly became a hit with the pro-war FEDERALIST PARTY during the QUASI-WAR (1798–1800) and was the most popular political tune of the last years of the 18th century. The song was reprinted throughout the country and even published in GREAT BRITAIN. Like the later "Star Spangled Banner," it could be sung to the English drinking tune "To Anacreon in Heaven."

"Adams and Liberty" is testimony to the brief popularity of President JOHN ADAMS as he confronted the depredations of the French against American shipping:

> Let Fame to the world sound America's voice;
> No intrigues can her sons from the government sever;
> Her pride is her Adams; Her laws are his choice,
> And shall flourish, till Liberty slumbers for ever.

The stanzas also stressed that the United States stood for LIBERTY and freedom in the world, and they emphasized the agrarian and commercial roots of the American ECONOMY:

> In a clime, whose rich vales feed the marts of the
>   world.
> Whose shores are shaken by Europe's commotion
> The trident of Commerce should never be hurled,
> To incense the legitimate powers of the ocean.

The song's anti-French and pro-British bias combined with patriotism so well that it was frequently sung at political meetings and dinners. But it also was sung by common folk, especially SEAMEN and soldiers, during and even after the Quasi-War in taverns and public gatherings.

Africa

The relationship between the people of North America and the people of Africa underwent major transformations in the period of 1754–1815. In the middle of the 18th century the SLAVE TRADE was thriving, and most European Americans viewed sub-Sahara Africa simply as a source for a valuable TRADE in forced labor. By the mid-18th century the slave trade had also transformed much of Africa. Previously, the coastal areas of West Africa had been a political and economic backwater. The area inland was wealthier, healthier, and more advanced, largely because it had come under the influence of the Muslim world, was pivotal in the cross-Saharan trade with the MEDITERRANEAN SEA region, and could sustain the breeding of large domestic ANIMALS. Armed with guns and weapons gained through the slave trade, powerful states emerged near the West African coast that raided territories inland. Europeans had built a series of forts and outposts along the coast to support the slave trade but did not establish control of much territory. The legal termination of the international slave trade by the United States in 1808, as well as by other countries (DENMARK in 1805, GREAT BRITAIN in 1807, The NETHERLANDS in 1814, and FRANCE in 1818, with SPAIN and PORTUGAL limiting the slave trade to south of the equator in 1815 and 1817) altered a centuries-old trade relationship and led to a decline in trade between North America and West Africa. However, because abolishing the international slave trade was relatively recent, the geopolitical situation remained largely unchanged in 1815.

Contact between North America and Africa south of the equator had always been limited. There was some slave trading from the Congo coast, and in the early 18th century an illicit trade had developed between pirates in Madagascar and the British colonies. However, the region had little real interaction with the United States after independence. Portugal exerted considerable influence over much of the coast of southern Africa. The Dutch control of the Cape of Good Hope was finally ended by British conquest in 1806. Arabs also had strong connections to portions of the east African coast. The heaviest concentrations of native population lay well into the interior, ranging from the Ethiopian highlands through modern Uganda into the highlands of modern Zimbabwe. In this region there were several independent states that were well-insulated from much of the rest of the world.

As many AFRICAN AMERICANS gained their freedom as a result of the REVOLUTIONARY WAR (1775–83) and the emancipation movement in the United States, freed and enslaved blacks looked upon Africa with new eyes. Although some African Americans shared European-American false perceptions of Africa as primitive and uncivilized, many others began to perceive Africa as a once-pristine Eden that had been corrupted and spoiled by European slave traders. These African Americans hoped to migrate to Africa, bring Christianity, create colonies peopled by freed slaves, and revamp trade relations with the United States. This COLONIZATION movement spawned the settlement of SIERRA LEONE under British auspices, as well as the creation of Liberia in 1822. Although only a few thousand North American blacks went to Africa, many more developed a closer sense of identity with Africa and asserted an Africanness that can be seen in the BLACK CHURCH MOVEMENT and the creation of a host of African-American institutions during the early republic that proudly bore the words *African, Abyssinian, Ethiopian,* or *Negro* in their names.

There was also change in the relationship with Africa north of the Sahara as the new United States engaged in a series of conflicts with the Barbary states that was not fully resolved until 1815. The British North American colonists had been able to engage in some trade in the Mediterranean, protected by the British navy and the willingness of the British government to pay limited tribute to the Barbary states. Independence left merchant ships from the United States vulnerable to seizure from Morocco, Algiers, Tunis, and Libya. In a series of conflicts with these nations known as the BARBARY WARS, the United States gradually managed to free itself from this burden. In particular, the war with Tripoli, which lasted from 1801 to 1805, and the 1815 attack on Algiers, which ended the Barbary Wars, established the right of U.S. ships to trade unmolested by the North African nations. This experience represented the most prolonged engagement between the U.S. government and any single part of Africa before 1815. The Barbary Wars helped to strengthen the U.S. NAVY and enhanced the developing sense of NATIONALISM in the new nation. They also offered a subtle ANTISLAVERY message because the capture and enslavement of European-American SEAMEN provided an ironic inversion where men of color—the people of the Barbary states—held white men as slaves.

There was little real trade or contact between North America and Egypt, which remained closely wedded to the Ottoman Empire. NAPOLEON BONAPARTE conquered Egypt in 1798, but the British victory at the Battle of the Nile, also in 1798, helped to drive the French out of the Middle East by 1801. In 1805 WILLIAM EATON recruited his polyglot mercenary army to invade Libya in Egypt.

See also SLAVERY.

Further reading: Robert J. Allison, *The Crescent Obscured: The United States and the Muslim World, 1776–1815* (New York: Oxford University Press, 1995); Roland Oliver and Anthony Atmore, *Africa since 1800,* 5th ed. (Cambridge: Cambridge University Press, 2005); James Sidbury, *Becoming African in America: Race and Nation in the Early Black Republic* (New York: Oxford University Press, 2007).

African Americans

African-American life and identity underwent significant changes during the late 18th and early 19th centuries. In 1750, SLAVERY was legal in all British North American colonies, and almost all African-descended people living there were in bondage. The international SLAVE TRADE operated throughout the 1700s: In the 1750s alone, 53,000 Africans per year were transported to the Americas. Before the AMERICAN REVOLUTION, ANTISLAVERY sentiment touched few slaveholding European Americans. By the early 1800s, however, the situation had changed: Every northern state moved to abolish slavery between 1777 and 1804; the international slave trade was banned in the United States beginning in 1808; free black populations grew and prospered, particularly in northern urban locales, such as Boston, Philadelphia, and New York City; and an abolitionist movement took shape, putting issues such as

stopping the domestic slave trade before state and federal politicians (see ABOLITION). At the same time, slavery expanded both geographically and demographically, and slaveholders gained constitutional protections that secured continuing bondage in the South. Even in the more emancipated North, free black communities experienced pervasive racism in the form of discriminatory customs as well as laws restricting movement and access to the vote. In short, African-American history up to 1815 was marked by hope; liberation; disappointment; brutality via continued enslavement; and, perhaps above all, persistent black activism.

Hope came from the ideals of the American Revolution. The focus on LIBERTY and human rights prompted many revolutionary Americans to question the institution of slavery. Pennsylvania QUAKERS had initiated the first colonial attack on bondage in the late 1750s by declaring that all members of the Society of Friends must relinquish slave ownership. The American Revolution brought this religious antislavery sentiment into the mainstream of political and social debate. White colonists opposing the British proclaimed that they were fighting against their own enslavement and began to question all bondage. The Virginian ARTHUR LEE wrote in 1767 that "as freedom is unquestionably the birth-right of all mankind, of Africans as well as Europeans, to keep the former in a State of slavery is a constant violation of that right, and therefore to Justice." Political leaders, religious figures, and others attacked the overseas slave trade as inhumane.

African Americans joined in the call for the end of slavery. The language of liberty used against imperial regulation could be applied to the condition of enslaved African Americans. In 1774 Caesar Sarter, a free African American, wrote an essay published in a Massachusetts newspaper explicitly connecting the plight of slaves to the rhetoric used by revolutionary WHIGS. He wrote "that as *Slavery* is the greatest, and consequently most to be dreaded, of all temporal calamities: so its opposite, *Liberty,* is the greatest temporal good." Addressing himself to the revolutionary leaders, he therefore asked for the liberty of "oppressed Africans" so that "may you with confidence and consistency of conduct, look to Heaven for a blessing on your endeavours to knock the shackles with which your task masters are hampering you, from your own feet." The African-American poet PHILLIS WHEATLEY wrote: "In every human breast God has implanted a Principle, which we call love of freedom; it is impatient of Oppression, and pants for Deliverance" and "the same principle lives in us."

Liberation came to many African Americans in a variety of ways. Tens of thousands of slaves, largely in the southern colonies, ran away during the REVOLUTIONARY WAR (1775–83). In November 1775, Virginia's royal governor, JOHN MURRAY, FOURTH EARL OF DUNMORE, promised slaves freedom if they fled from their masters. Throughout the war, the British continued to attract runaways, recruiting them into the army and offering protection. At the end of the war, thousands of African Americans evacuated with the British army, some to settle in NOVA SCOTIA, others to go the WEST INDIES. Unfortunately, the British commitment to the African Americans was limited. While some achieved freedom, others were abandoned in the United States to be re-enslaved, and still others were forced into slavery in British colonies. Many faced POVERTY and racism after the war. A group that confronted these problems in Nova Scotia later decided to join the British colony in SIERRA LEONE in AFRICA. Despite these problems, most African Americans who fought for "liberty" during the Revolutionary War did so by fighting for King GEORGE III.

While many African Americans sought liberty with the British, others took up arms for the revolutionary cause. One of the earliest martyrs of the RESISTANCE MOVEMENT (1764–75) against imperial regulation was CRISPUS ATTUCKS, half Native American and half African American, who was killed in the BOSTON MASSACRE (March 5, 1770). African Americans fought in the Revolutionary War for the United States. Many sailed on privateers and served in the CONTINENTAL NAVY since they accepted men regardless of race. At the beginning of the war, a few African Americans fought in the army, only to find limitations placed on them by the SECOND CONTINENTAL CONGRESS and state assemblies. As the war continued, however, several states, desperate for recruits of any race, allowed African Americans in their military units. Such men would often be promised freedom in exchange for enlisting.

Liberation for slaves also came from the antislavery ideals that prompted many state legislatures to allow for manumission of slaves by owners and the creation of gradual abolition laws. Hundreds of masters freed thousands of slaves during the late 1770s and 1780s. Virginia, the nation's largest slaveholding state, altered its laws so that masters would no longer need the special permission of the legislature to manumit blacks. Nevertheless, no southern states voted to emancipate slaves, although such legislation was passed in Pennsylvania in 1780, in Connecticut and Rhode Island in 1784, in New York in 1799, and in New Jersey in 1803.

Hope also came from the development of vibrant free black communities. Free black populations nearly quadrupled, growing from roughly 70,000 in 1790 to well over 200,000 by the 1830s. In the South, the presence of free African Americans, mainly in the cities, provided a tantalizing vision of freedom for those who were still enslaved. Equally important, some of these free African Americans obtained property and became leaders of their communities. In northern urban centers, the explosion of black populations proved most significant: Between 1790 and 1820, Philadelphia's African-American population increased by

over 400 percent, New York City's by over 200 percent, and Boston's over 100 percent. Free blacks developed a host of autonomous community institutions in the early national period: churches, associations, INSURANCE societies, libraries, and schools. In Philadelphia, RICHARD ALLEN and ABSALOM JONES formed the Free African Society in 1787 as a black mutual-aid organization. By the early 1790s, Allen and Jones had led an exodus of black parishioners from segregated white churches to establish the African Methodist Episcopal Church and the African Episcopal Church in Philadelphia. In Boston, PRINCE HALL used his Masonic lodge as a community organizing center and activist base. Hall also opened a school for African-American children in his own home after the state assembly delayed starting one. In both cities, free black institutions such as churches, lodges, and debating clubs sponsored the publication of protest pamphlets.

Disappointment came from several sources. During the years of the early republic, southerners soon abandoned any serious discussion of the contradiction between slavery and freedom. Politically and constitutionally, slaveholders received significant new protections to human property during the 1780s and 1790s. While the NORTHWEST ORDINANCE of 1787 prohibited slavery's expansion into the territories north of the Ohio River, another proposed ordinance from 1784 had already failed to limit bondage in the Southwest. This earlier measure would prove significant during THOMAS JEFFERSON's presidency, when the LOUISIANA PURCHASE (1803) opened the sugar plantations of LOUISIANA and other valuable land to migrating slaveholders. By 1810, the Louisiana Territory contained about 35,000 slaves. The U.S. CONSTITUTION enshrined slave property by counting the enslaved population in the apportionment of votes for Congress and the Electoral College (each slave was equivalent to three-fifths of a free person), by guaranteeing masters the return of fugitive slaves, by promising federal support in suppressing rebellions, and by delaying any consideration of a slave trading ban until the congressional session of 1807.

Political and social developments further abetted slavery. Congress in 1790 and 1799 refused to hear abolitionist and free black petitions against the domestic and overseas slave trades. Furthermore, Congress passed fugitive slave legislation in 1793 that made the return of escaped slaves the law of the land. Slaveholders harnessed new technology in the form of the cotton gin at the close of the 18th century to rejuvenate bondage. Moreover, slaveholders in South Carolina and Georgia had already begun articulating publicly that slavery was a positive good. Slavery in 1790 accounted for over 700,000 bondspeople in the United States, and slave territory was confined largely to the Atlantic seaboard. By 1815, three new slave states had entered the union—Kentucky (1792), Tennessee (1796), and Louisiana (1812)—and slavery had spread to the interior of the nation. By 1820, the number of slaves stretched beyond 1.5 million.

Within the South there were some key developments for African Americans. The limited number of imported slaves from Africa—limited by the upheaval of revolution, state law, and federal fiat after 1808—led to the expansion of a separate African-American culture. Crucial to this was the spread of Christianity among slaves, which African Americans molded to their own purposes. White masters hoped the Bible would teach their slaves to be obedient and refrain from challenging earthly authority. Instead, slaves focused on the ideal of Christian equality and identified with the stories of Israel's bondage under Egypt and the assurance of deliverance to the promised land. Christianity proved a recruiting ground for black leaders, and African Americans who became preachers—even those who were slaves—often became the spokespeople for their communities.

Another outgrowth of the decline in the importation of new slaves was a greater balance between male and female African Americans, allowing slaves to form more permanent relationships, have children, and sustain family ties. The ability to form families—even within the context of slavery—provided the foundation for a truly African-American culture. However, while black men and women experienced a greater degree of stability in their relationships, state laws did not recognize slave marriage. Masters retained ultimate power over slaves, at times sexually exploiting their property and more frequently separating family members through sale and migration. In fact, because of the geographical expansion of slavery, many African Americans had the wrenching experience of being forced to move to new locations in the West.

In the North, where slavery was edging toward its gradual abolition in the early 19th century, racial injustice continued. The African Americans who had achieved freedom were not considered equal by most European Americans. A few African Americans became businessmen and ARTISANS, but most were relegated to unskilled labor and to specific poorly paid professions. While the creation of African-American churches represented a major achievement and reflected a new sense of group identity, it also resulted in part from the racial prejudice African Americans encountered in mainstream churches. White Americans resented giving any political voice to African Americans and sought to limit their right to vote. In the early 19th century the African-American community in the North was increasingly subject to mob attacks. In short, racism permeated northern as well as southern society.

The continuance of slavery and racial injustice thus became the defining issue of black life throughout the early republic. Pamphlets from the early 1800s by such writers as William Hamilton of New York City, Russell Parrott and JAMES FORTEN of Philadelphia, and Nathaniel Paul of Albany underscored the discrepancy between liberty (in theory) and racial oppression. Some enslaved people chose outright rebellion as their means of gaining freedom. In 1800 Virginia's Gabriel Prosser planned a revolution outside of Richmond that would have ended bondage and demanded black equality. It was foiled by a massive rainstorm and by informers. Other slave rebellions occurred in 1794 (Southampton, Virginia) and 1811 (near Natchez, Mississippi). These actions were not simply isolated cases but the extreme end of a spectrum of resistance to oppression among enslaved blacks.

See also BANNEKER, BENJAMIN; BLACK CHURCH MOVEMENT; GABRIEL'S REBELLION; HAITI; HEMINGS, SALLY; RACE AND RACIAL CONFLICT; RELIGION; SLAVE TRADE, DOMESTIC.

Further reading: Ira Berlin, *Many Thousands Gone: The First Two Centuries of Slavery in North America* (Cambridge, Mass.: Harvard University Press, 1998); Sylvia Frey, *Water from the Rock: Black Resistance in a Revolutionary Age* (Princeton, N.J.: Princeton University Press, 1991); James Horton and Lois Horton, *In Hope of Liberty: Culture, Community and Protest among Northern Free Blacks, 1700–1860* (New York: Oxford University Press, 1997); Gary B. Nash, *The Forgotten Fifth: African Americans in the Age of Revolution* (Cambridge, Mass.: Harvard University Press, 2006); Richard Newman and Patrick Rael, Philip Lapsanky, eds., *Pamphlets of Protest: An Anthology of Early African American Protest Writing* (New York: Routledge, 2001); Benjamin Quarles, *The Negro in the American Revolution* (1961. Reprint, Chapel Hill: University of North Carolina Press, 1973).

—Richard Newman

African Methodist Episcopal Church   See ALLEN, RICHARD; BLACK CHURCH MOVEMENT; METHODISTS.

agriculture
Between 1754 and 1815, agriculture remained the most important sector of the North American ECONOMY. Although many thinkers, such as THOMAS JEFFERSON, believed that agriculture made North American farmers independent both politically and economically, the nature of agricultural production tied farmers to the Atlantic world. Despite regional differences, therefore, the upheaval of revolution and war spreading across the Atlantic had a direct impact on agriculture in the British colonies and later the United States.

The southern colonies were the most profitable part of the British empire in North America because of their agricultural products. TOBACCO exhausted the soil and often had fallen in price, but it provided income to the Crown and made fortunes for many British merchants. In fact, in the years immediately before the outbreak of the REVOLUTIONARY WAR (1775–83), prices generally rose for tobacco. Because it was a crop that demanded intensive work, tobacco growing was heavily dependent on the labor of slaves. South Carolinians produced RICE and INDIGO and also relied on slave labor. After 1783 there were changes. Following a trend that began before the war, tobacco lost ground as more Chesapeake planters turned to WHEAT and other grains. ELI WHITNEY's 1793 invention of the COTTON gin, which efficiently separated the seeds from cotton, transformed southern agriculture by making it possible to grow short-staple cotton profitably. South Carolina, and then a growing belt of states to its west, Alabama, Mississippi, and Tennessee, produced more and more cotton. In 1791 about 2 million pounds of cotton was grown in the United States; by 1820 the cotton crop had increased to over 127 million pounds. By that time, cotton comprised a third of all exports from the United States. These exports helped to drive the economy's expansion and, since most of the cotton was shipped to GREAT BRITAIN to supply its textile factories during the INDUSTRIAL REVOLUTION, further tied the United States to trans-Atlantic TRADE. The LOUISIANA PURCHASE (1803) added an area of SUGAR production in the lower Mississippi Valley, where the owners of sugar plantations relied on the use of slave labor. Securing the mouth of the Mississippi also encouraged the spread of cotton production west and provided another outlet for the export of cotton from New Orleans.

Colonists north of the Mason-Dixon line were mainly farmers, but they never produced a single cash crop equivalent to tobacco, rice, sugar, or cotton. Instead, northerners produced a variety of foodstuffs based on grains and livestock; FISHING and lumber were also important. Northern farmers exported their produce to the WEST INDIES, Europe, and even the South. They also sought new lands to the west, fueling the great migration across the Appalachian Mountains and the settlement of the Ohio Valley. Starting in the 1790s, and then accelerating after 1803, western farmers sent their produce—often pork and grain—down the Ohio and Mississippi Rivers for export through the port of New Orleans.

Historians have debated when and how farmers became involved in the market and viewed agriculture as a capitalist enterprise. The rural transition to CAPITALISM—centering on the production of agricultural commodities for distant markets—accelerated in the second half of the 18th century and really took off after 1800. We can see this transition in the increased use of cash as a means of exchange, greater specialization in production, and the spread of CONSUMERISM. Traditionally, people in the countryside had relied on barter and informal agreements for the exchange of labor. By 1800 such personal relationships were being replaced by impersonal cash exchange, either noted in account books in dollars and cents, or transacted with the actual use of MONEY—often notes printed by the many new BANKS. Simultaneously, farmers began to focus on specific areas of production. When many eastern farmers could no longer compete with the more productive lands in the West, they turned to specialization, either by centering on fruits and vegetables—which could not be shipped over long distances—or engaging in dairying to supply milk, butter, and cheese. Farmers also became less self-sufficient, relying on the market to purchase many items that might have previously been made at home. Typically, a farmer in the 1790s and early 1800s might sell pork, wheat, butter, leather, or tallow to a storekeeper and purchase textiles, earthenware, rum, sugar, salt, glass, paper, and gin. These tendencies began in the Northeast and then later moved west and south.

War created an upheaval that influenced agricultural production in the North and South, greatly affecting the rural economy. The imperial crisis and the Revolutionary War disrupted exports of the southern cash crops and led to some havoc among food-producing farmers. At times, farmers who grew grain or raised livestock could reap profits as prices rose with the demands of hungry armies. At other times, the ravages of war could destroy crops and devastate farms. Agriculture revived slowly in the 1780s and became fairly robust by 1790. The wars of the FRENCH REVOLUTION (1789–99) in Europe and the West Indies, especially after 1793, tended to further increase the value of agricultural food exports. However, this trend was liable to disruption, especially during the QUASI-WAR (1798–1800) crisis and after the EMBARGO OF 1807. Agricultural production was also hurt by the WAR OF 1812. Some farmers, especially those near the front lines between CANADA and the United States, could profit from supplying the troops of both sides. For others, however, especially as the British tightened a blockade that cut off overseas trade and curtailed interregional shipping, the war created glutted markets in some areas and scarce markets in others. Tobacco, for example, became nearly worthless since it was almost impossible to send it to distant markets.

Although slaves and hired labor worked on some farms, most farmers relied on family labor. As northern states emancipated their slaves, the region—including the area north of the Ohio River—became even more devoted to free labor. Despite the fact that many poor white farmers did not own slaves, southerners simultaneously became more devoted to slavery. European-American women did not usually labor in the fields, although African-American women did. European-American women centered their activities in the barnyard and household, areas in which they were crucial to the productivity and profitability of agricultural enterprise. Often, the special labor of women in the churning of butter, the production of homespun, and, in New England, even the making of brooms, added vital capital to the farm family.

See also COLONIZATION, AFRICAN; LABOR AND LABOR MOVEMENTS; POPULATION TRENDS; RURAL LIFE; WOMEN'S STATUS AND RIGHTS.

Further reading: Christopher Clark, *The Roots of Rural Capitalism: Western Massachusetts, 1780–1860* (Ithaca, N.Y.: Cornell University Press, 1990); John J. McCusker and Russell R. Menard, *The Economy of British America, 1607–1789* (Chapel Hill: University of North Carolina Press, 1985); Douglass C. North, *The Economic Growth of the United States, 1790–1860* (Englewood Cliffs: N.J.: Prentice Hall, 1961).

Alamance, Battle of (May 16, 1771)

In response to RIOTS at the Superior Court in Hillsborough in September 1770, the North Carolina assembly passed the notorious Johnston Act, which turned rebellious farmers into outlaws and provided the governor with the authorization and funds he needed to suppress the farmers with military force. Early in May 1771, Governor WILLIAM TRYON arrived with his MILITIA in the Piedmont region. Officers and "gentlemen volunteers," many of them leading WHIGS who would achieve military honor in the REVOLUTIONARY WAR (1775–83), comprised nearly 10 percent of the army. The troops, only half the number the governor had hoped for, had been difficult to raise since many ordinary North Carolinians sympathized with the backcountry Regulators (see NORTH CAROLINA REGULATION). On May 16, 1771, the governor and his troops met upwards of 2,000 defiant farmers on a field near Alamance Creek, some 20 miles from Hillsborough. After two hours of fighting, in which the Regulators initially had the upper hand, the governor's forces emerged victorious. As many as 20 Regulators were killed in battle, along with about nine militia men. More than 150 men were wounded, many seriously. The next day, the governor ordered an outlawed Regulator who had been captured during the battle executed without trial. Thereafter, the governor led the troops on a destructive rampage through the Piedmont region. In mid-June, six more Regulators were hanged after a hasty trial.

The Battle of Alamance has been hailed as the first battle of the Revolutionary War. Yet Regulators were not fighting to gain independence from GREAT BRITAIN but, rather, to liberate themselves from oppressive local and colonial authorities. The battle and its repressive aftermath decisively ended the collective struggle of free Piedmont inhabitants for independence through social justice. While individual farmers remained defiant well into the Revolutionary War, the Regulation was crushed as an organized movement.

Further reading: Marjoleine Kars, *Breaking Loose Together: The Regulator Rebellion in Pre-Revolutionary North Carolina* (Chapel Hill: University of North Carolina Press, 2002); Wayne E. Lee, *Crowds and Soldiers in Revolutionary North Carolina: The Culture of Violence in Riot and War* (Gainesville: University Press of Florida, 2001).

—Marjoleine Kars

Alaska

The first European to lead an expedition to Alaska was Vitus Bering, a Dane sailing for the Russian Empire. Although Bering died on this expedition, as a result of his explorations in 1741–42, the Russians laid claim to the area. However, Russian settlement was initially sporadic and driven by private individuals in search of furs. Grigory Ivanovich Shelikhov, who headed the largest fur company trading in Alaska, established the first permanent Russian settlement in North America on Kodiak Island in 1784. In 1797, Shelikhov's son-in-law, Nikilay Petrovich Rezanov, consolidated all the fur-trading companies operating in Alaska, and in 1799 he obtained an imperial charter for the Russian American Fur Company, modeled after the British East India Company. Rezanov visited Alaska in 1805–06 and traveled to CALIFORNIA to establish trade contacts with the Spanish. The success of the Russian enterprise, however, was largely due to the management of Aleksandr Andreyevich Baronov, who had been appointed by Shelikhov to take control of Alaskan affairs in 1790. Baronov became the dominant presence in Russian America for almost two decades and established the town of New Archangel at Sitka in 1804. Recognizing his need for supplies, Baronov opened trading relations with GREAT BRITAIN and the United States, even though this action was technically illegal. He also established a base at Fort Ross in California and purchased supplies from the Spanish. During the early 19th century, the company made huge profits, in part by using ships from the United States to bring furs to China. Baronov died in 1819, on his way back to RUSSIA after being forced out of power by company officials.

The Russians treated NATIVE AMERICANS harshly. The early fur traders, following patterns of native dealings established in Siberia, exploited the Aleuts mercilessly. Often fur traders would invade a village, hold the women and children hostage, and compel the men to hunt furs. In the winter of 1763–64 some Aleuts rebelled, destroying four Russian ships and killing as many as 150 Russians. The

Russians responded with brutality, burning 18 villages in 1766; the Aleuts did not oppose the Russians again. As a result of exploitation, DISEASE AND EPIDEMICS, and war, the Aleut population declined from about 20,000 upon contact to 2,000 in 1800. The Tlingit were more hostile to the Russians from the beginning and wiped out some outposts. New Archangel struggled for survival in its first years because settlers could not hunt or fish for fear of Tlingit attack. The Russian church sent missionaries to Alaska in 1794, but they had a limited impact on the natives. The Russian hold on Alaska remained tenuous throughout this period. Their fur trading also had a devastating impact on the ENVIRONMENT, driving some animals to extinction and significantly decreasing the numbers of others.

See also FUR TRADE.

Further reading: Claus-M. Naske and Herman Slotnick, *Alaska: A History of the 49th State* (Norman: University of Oklahoma Press, 1979); S. Frederick Starr, ed., *Russia's American Colony* (Durham, N.C.: Duke University Press, 1987); Alan Taylor, *American Colonies* (New York: Penguin, 2001).

Albany Congress (1754)

The Albany Congress was a meeting of representatives of seven colonies held in Albany, New York, to propose a form of union under the British government that is sometimes held as a precedent for the STAMP ACT CONGRESS (1765), FIRST CONTINENTAL CONGRESS (1774), SECOND CONTINENTAL CONGRESS (1775), and the formation of the United States. The British North American colonies were notoriously independent of one another. Little tied them together in the 18th century other than their connection to GREAT BRITAIN. In 1754, as war loomed with the French, New York lieutenant governor James De Lancey invited representatives from several colonies to meet to discuss their relationship with the all-important IROQUOIS.

In a conflict with FRANCE, the Iroquois, located in what is now upstate New York, held a crucial balance of power. The idea was to come up with a consistent policy shared by all colonies to guarantee that the Iroquois would not be too aggrieved and join the French. Albany was chosen as the location of this meeting because it had been a traditional seat for diplomatic discussions with the Iroquois. Seven colonies sent delegates: New York, New Hampshire, Massachusetts, Connecticut, Rhode Island, Pennsylvania, and Maryland. THEYANONGUIN (Chief Hendrick) presented the Iroquois grievances to the congress, which included the taking of MOHAWK land, too much rum being provided to NATIVE AMERICANS (see ALCOHOL), encroachments by Virginia and Pennsylvania on Iroquois lands in the west, and continued Albany TRADE with the French. The delegates denied all of these grievances and, not surprisingly, did not come to an agreement concerning their relationship with the Iroquois. They did, however, recognize an impending crisis with the French and advocated preparing more defenses on the FRONTIER, the creation of one Indian superintendent, and royal control over the acquisition of Native American land. They also drew up a proposal for an intercolonial union, under the protective umbrella of the British Crown, called the Albany Plan. Following the leadership of men such as BENJAMIN FRANKLIN from Pennsylvania and THOMAS HUTCHINSON from Massachusetts, the delegates suggested that external policy, such as negotiations with Native Americans and issues of defense, be the province of a grand council elected by the colonial assemblies. Under the plan there would also be a president-general appointed by the king.

No colonial assembly ever ratified the Albany plan, and nothing substantial ever came out of it. In fact, during the FRENCH AND INDIAN WAR (1754–63) that followed, the colonies continued to go their own way, often frustrating British efforts to prosecute the war. Some scholars argue that the plan was heavily influenced by the example of the Iroquois Confederation. These scholars therefore trace North American constitutionalism to Native American roots. Most academics question this connection on two grounds. First, they are not convinced that Benjamin Franklin and others were influenced by the Iroquois. Second, many scholars do not believe that the Albany Plan had any impact on the forms of government that came out of the American Revolution.

Further reading: Fred Anderson, *Crucible of War: The Seven Years' War and the Fate of Empire in British North America, 1754–1766* (New York: Vintage, 2000).

alcohol

American colonists drank large amounts of alcohol, in part because they did not have much else to drink. Drinking water was tainted with the stigma of POVERTY, and it could be unhealthy, often carrying refuse and excrement teeming with disease. Those families that had cows reserved the milk to make butter and cheese. In addition, before refrigeration and pasteurization, there was no way to prevent fruit juices from fermenting. Naturally occurring airborne yeast entered any fruit juice and caused fermentation. Coffee was unfamiliar to most colonists until the late 18th century. Tea remained an expensive luxury until tea duties were lowered in 1745. Therefore, when colonists drank, they drank alcohol.

Alcohol was an important part of early modern culture. Colonists drank for religious and secular celebrations, including weddings, births, and funerals. Holidays were commemorated with long rounds of toasts drunk with alcohol. In addition, nearly everyone—including the very young—might use alcohol as MEDICINE, to enhance beauty, and with meals. Men and women of the time believed that alcohol was salubrious. Employers and their workers shared morning toddies and afternoon drinks to cement their relationships. A daily ration of alcohol was the standard practice in the CONTINENTAL ARMY and for SEAMEN aboard both merchant and military vessels. Extra rations were often handed out before battle or after some emergency. MILITIA musters usually ended at TAVERNS and with heavy drinking.

During the colonial period, rum produced from molasses and cider from apples were the forms of alcohol available to most people. For this reason, the British believed the SUGAR ACT (1764) would be an important source of revenue since it taxed imported molasses—a crucial ingredient in producing rum. The Sugar Act also affected the importation of Madeira wine from PORTUGAL—a product that was gaining in popularity in the second half of the 18th century in North America. Wines, however, were favored more by those from the top, rather than the bottom, of society.

In the late 18th century there was a shift in the type of alcohol consumed as whiskey became more popular and more available. European-American settlers who moved west grew corn but needed an efficient way to transport and market their crop. The country's poor roads meant that farmers could not get their corn to market while it was still edible. Western farmers realized that if they distilled their corn into whiskey, they would have a profitable product that would not spoil before it could be sold. This production dropped the price, and levels of consumption increased. In 1791 Secretary of the Treasury ALEXANDER HAMILTON hoped to take advantage of this development for the national government by having Congress pass an excise tax of 25 percent on all production. Efforts to collect this tax from the many independent producers—farmers often had their own stills—led to complaints and the WHISKEY REBELLION (1794). In 1810 Treasury Secretary ALBERT GALLATIN estimated that about 15 million gallons of distilled liquor was produced each year, with about 10 million more imported from overseas (at least when shipping was unfettered by EMBARGOES).

Although beer had been produced in the colonies from the earliest days of settlement, overall production per capita decreased in the 18th century. However, it remained an important product. SAMUEL ADAMS really was a brewer at one point in his life, and many of the Founding Fathers, including GEORGE WASHINGTON and THOMAS JEFFERSON, brewed beer on their own. After independence, beer brewing expanded. In 1810 breweries were so ubiquitous

that Gallatin believed that it was impossible to estimate the total production.

Alcohol was an important TRADE item between European Americans and NATIVE AMERICANS. Unfortunately, many Indians became dependent on alcohol, with devastating effects on their culture. In order to obtain alcohol, Native Americans frequently engaged in overhunting for furs and often made bad bargains with unscrupulous traders. At times Indians would waste an entire season's hunt in an alcoholic binge. Some Native Americans engaged in violent behavior while drunk; others agreed to sell land to European Americans under the influence of alcohol. Many Indian leaders recognized this problem and sought to discourage drinking. A key element of the REVITALIZATION MOVEMENTS of spiritual leaders such as NEOLIN, HANDSOME LAKE, and TENSKWATAWA (the Shawnee Prophet) was to prohibit or limit the drinking of alcohol as Native Americans reasserted their traditional cultures in opposition to European Americans.

AFRICAN AMERICANS had limited access to alcohol under SLAVERY. Some masters would allow slaves to drink during the Christmas holidays; others would not. For the most part, slaves would only have access to alcohol surreptitiously. From the master's point of view, a drunken slave was unproductive and potentially dangerous.

See also TEMPERANCE.

Further reading: W. J. Rorabaugh, *The Alcoholic Republic: An American Tradition* (New York: Oxford University Press, 1979).

Alexander I (1775–1825) *czar of Russia*

Alexander I, czar of RUSSIA from 1801 to 1825, attempted to mediate a peace between GREAT BRITAIN and the United States during the WAR OF 1812 (1812–15). From the time he ascended the throne to 1815, Alexander was preoccupied with NAPOLEON BONAPARTE. Although Alexander had made peace with Napoleon in 1807, he recognized that his participation in the Continental System, excluding TRADE with Great Britain, would be limited and might lead to a break with FRANCE. In fact, Alexander sought better relations with Great Britain. He also recognized that an expanding Baltic trade with the United States, encouraged by Ambassador JOHN QUINCY ADAMS after 1809, was also important to Russia's economy. The deterioration of Anglo-American relations in 1811 and 1812 was thus of concern to Alexander, who asked the British to repeal the ORDERS IN COUNCIL.

In summer 1812 Napoleon invaded Russia, and Alexander signed an alliance with Great Britain and SWEDEN. Faced with this international and military crisis, the czar sought to mediate a peace between the United States and

Great Britain. The British rebuffed these efforts, but the United States responded positively. Adams forwarded the offer to WASHINGTON, D.C., where it arrived in February 1813. President JAMES MADISON accepted the offer and appointed JAMES BAYARD and ALBERT GALLATIN as envoys to join Adams in St. Petersburg. In May 1813 Madison called a special session of the Senate to confirm these appointments, although the Senate refused to confirm Gallatin until he resigned his post as secretary of the treasury. In the meantime, Gallatin and Bayard had headed for Russia, where they arrived on July 21, 1813. By that time the situation had changed. Napoleon's foray into Russia had turned into a disaster during the previous winter, and he was now in retreat. Alexander, heavily subsidized by Great Britain, was in pursuit in Germany, bent on Napoleon's complete defeat. The British remained uninterested in Russian mediation and suggested direct negotiations with the United States in November 1813. This overture led to the meeting at Ghent that culminated in the TREATY OF GHENT, signed on December 24, 1814.

Alexander helped to oversee Napoleon's defeat and became immersed in European diplomacy and Russian politics. He did not pay much attention to the United States for the remainder of his reign. He died on November 25, 1825.

Further reading: Nikolai N. Bolkhovitnov, *The Beginnings of Russian-American Relations, 1775–1815* (Cambridge, Mass.: Harvard University Press, 1975).

Alexander, William (Lord Stirling) (1726–1783)
American military officer
Claimant to a defunct Scottish title, William Alexander was one of the more important divisional commanders in the CONTINENTAL ARMY. He was born into affluence in New York. Before the REVOLUTIONARY WAR (1775–83), Alexander worked as a merchant and married into the prominent Livingston family. He was well educated and exceptionally capable in mathematics and astronomy. In 1756 he traveled to GREAT BRITAIN, staying there until 1761. During this trip he filed suit to claim the title of sixth earl of Stirling as the descendant of the brother of the first earl. Although the House of Lords rejected the claim, for the rest of his life Alexander was known as Lord Stirling.

Alexander was a man of enthusiasms. On a personal level he often ate and drank to excess, and he spent MONEY extravagantly, though he had grand plans for increasing his fortune. After he moved to Basking Ridge, New Jersey, in 1762, he lived like a country gentleman and became involved in a variety of financially unsuccessful schemes. By the eve of the Revolutionary War he had amassed huge debts. Despite his supposed title and aristocratic tastes, in

1775 he declared his support for the revolutionary cause. Since Alexander never did things by half measures, he joined New Jersey's revolutionary committee of safety and became a colonel in the MILITIA. In March 1776 the SECOND CONTINENTAL CONGRESS appointed Alexander a brigadier general.

Alexander had a mixed military career. He was an excellent and brave divisional officer, but somehow things never quite worked out when he acted independently. Typically for him, his great shining moment was during the BATTLE OF LONG ISLAND (August 27–30, 1776), when he had command of the right wing of revolutionary forces and put up a gallant defense. After LORD CORNWALLIS's flanking maneuver, Alexander personally led the rear-guard action as most of his men withdrew to Brooklyn Heights. This act of bravery earned him the admiration of GEORGE WASHINGTON and the British, but it also led to his capture during the battle. Fortunately, he was soon exchanged and participated in much of the campaigning in fall 1776.

Alexander also fought in the Battle of Trenton, and he was promoted to major general in 1777. He served under General JOHN SULLIVAN at the BATTLE OF BRANDYWINE (September 11, 1777) and commanded the reserves at the BATTLE OF GERMANTOWN (October 4, 1777). He was at VALLEY FORGE (1777–78) and, being intensely loyal to Washington, helped to expose the CONWAY CABAL. He commanded the left wing at the BATTLE OF MONMOUTH (June 28, 1778), earning distinction for driving back a flanking attack and for his deployment of artillery. When given an independent command to lead an expedition against Staten Island in January 1780, he was beaten back by the British. In the closing years of the war, Alexander was in charge of the northern department, preparing for an invasion from CANADA that was never launched. A sufferer of gout, he died in Albany on January 15, 1783, while still serving in the Continental army.

Further reading: Paul David Nelson, *William Alexander, Lord Stirling* (Tuscaloosa: University of Alabama Press, 1987).

Alien and Sedition Acts (1798)
The FEDERALIST PARTY passed the Alien and Sedition Acts to suppress political opposition during the QUASI-WAR (1798–1800) with FRANCE. After the French began to seize United States shipping and stumbled into the diplomatic fiasco of the XYZ AFFAIR (1797–98), the threat of war strengthened the hand of the Federalist Party in dealing with the DEMOCRATIC-REPUBLICAN PARTY (Jeffersonians). Not only did the Federalist Party push legislation that expanded the army and navy and increased taxes, they also sought the means to stifle political opposition. The

Alien and Sedition Acts, passed in June and July 1798, were intended to further the party's political agenda. Federalist Party leaders believed that the majority of immigrants, many of whom were from Ireland, were pro-French and pro-Republican. Any restrictions they could place on immigrants, therefore, would aid their cause.

There were three Alien Acts. The first of these, called the Naturalization Act, was passed on June 18 and changed the CITIZENSHIP process for immigrants. Previous legislation in 1795 allowed an immigrant to become a citizen after five years of residence, having declared his intent to do so three years before becoming a citizen. The Naturalization Act increased the residence requirement to 14 years, with a five-year time lag between declaring intent and citizenship. The idea was to restrict immigrant citizenship to limit the impact of these voters at the polls. Oddly, the law actually convinced many immigrants to seek citizenship before the new rules came into effect, thus strengthening the Democratic-Republican vote in the crucial ELECTION OF 1800.

The second measure, called the Alien Friends Act, was passed on June 25, 1798, and empowered the president to deport any alien he deemed a threat to the country. This law was set to expire after two years and was never used by President JOHN ADAMS.

The third part of the legislation was the Alien Enemies Act, passed on July 6, 1798. It declared that any person born in a country at war with the United States, or that invaded the United States, was liable to being "apprehended, restrained, secured, and removed, as enemy aliens." Since the United States never declared war against France, this measure was not used at this time.

Perhaps the most controversial law was the Sedition Act of July 14, 1798, which made it unlawful to combine with others to oppose measures of the government. More significantly, it stated that "if any person shall write, print, utter, or publish . . . Any false, scandalous, and malicious writing or writings against the government of the United States . . . with the intent to defame said government," they could be brought to trial by the federal government and could be assessed up to $2,000 in fines and sentenced to two years in prison. This law has sometimes been held as a violation of civil liberties and contrary to the First Amendment guarantee of freedom of speech and the press. However, it merely put into writing what was common-law practice in England and the United States at the time. It actually protected some rights since it stipulated that "the truth of the matter contained in the publication" could be used as defense in any criminal trial resulting from the law.

The law governing sedition was set to expire at the end of the Adams administration in March 1801, and the government used it to prosecute several Democratic-Republican editors and politicians. At least 14 Democratic-Republican editors were jailed under the law, including BENJAMIN FRANKLIN's grandson BENJAMIN FRANKLIN BACHE, and federal courts convicted Congressman MATTHEW LYON of sedition and sentenced him to four months in prison and a $1,000 fine. Ultimately, the Sedition Act was a political failure since, despite the closing of some significant opposition newspapers, large numbers of printers decided to abandon their nonpartisanship and began to publish more politically inspired newspapers.

Democratic-Republican leaders believed that these laws were unwarranted and outrageous. Vice President THOMAS JEFFERSON and Congressman JAMES MADISON wrote the VIRGINIA AND KENTUCKY RESOLUTIONS (1798) in response to the Alien and Sedition Acts. Once Jefferson was elected president, the two laws that had time limits were not renewed. The Alien Enemies Act was irrelevant as long as the country was not at war. The Republicans repealed the Naturalization Act shortly after Jefferson's election, reinstating the previous rule of the five-year residence period before qualifying for citizenship.

See also BILL OF RIGHTS; IMMIGRATION; POLITICAL PARTIES.

Further reading: Jeffrey L. Pasley, *"The Tyranny of Printers": Newspaper Politics in the Early American Republic* (Charlottesville: University of Virginia Press, 2001); James Morton Smith, *Freedom's Fetters: The Alien and Sedition Laws and American Civil Liberties* (Ithaca, N.Y.: Cornell University Press, 1956).

Allen, Andrew (1740–1825) *Loyalist*

Born into a powerful family in Pennsylvania—his father was WILLIAM ALLEN, chief justice of the colony—Andrew Allen had all the advantages of EDUCATION, social position, and privilege on the eve of the REVOLUTIONARY WAR (1775–83). He graduated from the University of Pennsylvania in 1759, studied law in Pennsylvania and England, and became attorney general of his home province in 1769. As the revolutionary crisis intensified in 1774 and 1775, Allen found himself trying to find a middle way to guarantee justice for the colonies while adhering to his allegiance to the Crown. This type of trimming was not unusual in Pennsylvania, and Allen was prominent and popular enough to be elected to the local committee of safety in 1775 and the provincial assembly in 1776. He went on to serve in the SECOND CONTINENTAL CONGRESS but resigned from that body because he opposed the DECLARATION OF INDEPENDENCE.

Allen's Loyalist sympathies convinced him to join General WILLIAM HOWE in New Jersey in December 1776—a time when the success of the revolutionary cause looked bleak. He moved to New York and then returned to Philadelphia after Howe's conquest of that city in 1777. Because of his prominence in supporting the British, Allen's property in Pennsylvania was seized by the state in spring 1778, and he moved to England before the end of the war. In 1792 he came back to Pennsylvania, where he spent a few years attempting to receive compensation for his lost property. When those efforts failed, he left for England, where he lived the rest of his life. He died in London on March 7, 1825.

See also LOYALIST PROPERTY CONFISCATION.

Further reading: Charles P. Keith, "Andrew Allen," *Pennsylvania Magazine of History and Biography* 10 (1886): 361–365.

Allen, Ethan (1738–1789) *Revolutionary militia officer*

The revolutionary leader Ethan Allen was famous for helping lead the effort to establish the state of Vermont. Born in Connecticut on January 21, 1738 (January 10, 1737, under the Julian calendar), Allen had moved to what is now Vermont by 1769. He quickly became prominent in the movement to attach the area to New Hampshire. At that time the region of the Green Mountains was claimed by both New York and New Hampshire. The colony of New York had the better claim, and the Crown decided in its favor when the case finally came to its attention. But many of the settlers in the area, like Allen, came from New England and opposed the large land grants issued to big landlords in New York. The GREEN MOUNTAIN BOYS, organized in 1770, forcefully opposed efforts by New York authorities to establish law and order in the region. With Allen among their leaders, the Green Mountain Boys compelled New York sheriffs to leave the area and tore down the houses of settlers with deeds from New York. Eventually, New York authorities offered as much as £100 for the capture of Allen, who headed many of the "mobs" and who was also pursuing his own land schemes under New Hampshire claims.

Against this background, news of the BATTLES OF LEXINGTON AND CONCORD (April 19, 1775) arrived. Allen and the Green Mountain Boys saw the rebellion against the British as an opportunity to solidify their position in Vermont. When he received instructions from Connecticut, he led a contingent of Green Mountain Boys and joined BENEDICT ARNOLD in the capture of the British outpost of FORT TICONDEROGA at dawn on May 10, 1775. This action was crucial to the war's opening phases. Artillery from the fort would eventually be taken to Boston and placed on DORCHESTER HEIGHTS, forcing the British to evacuate the city. Moreover, with Ticonderoga in rebel hands, the path was open for revolutionary forces to march into CANADA. In an effort to export the rebellion to the St. Lawrence Valley, two armies moved north. One, under

the command of Benedict Arnold, crossed the Maine wilderness in late fall and the beginning of winter 1775; the other, under General RICHARD MONTGOMERY, headed along Lake Champlain toward MONTREAL. Allen joined Montgomery, who ordered him to reconnoiter near Montreal in September 1775. Allen, thinking that the Canadian city would be an easy target, decided to try to capture it with a small force, but Montreal was not Fort Ticonderoga and, finding himself outnumbered, he was compelled to surrender. Montgomery later captured Montreal. Arnold's depleted force arrived at Quebec in November, and the revolutionaries failed to capture the city in an assault in a snowstorm on December 31. The entire Canadian expedition ended in failure, with many men killed and thousands captured. Ethan Allen remained a prisoner of war for two years, enduring extremely harsh treatment, and was transferred across the ATLANTIC OCEAN and back again before he was finally exchanged in September 1778.

Broken in mind, body, and spirit by his imprisonment and by the news of the death of his son, Allen wrote *A Narrative of Col. Ethan Allen's Captivity* (1779). The book became an important statement of the sacrifices that WHIGS suffered in the revolutionary cause. It also helped to resuscitate Allen's waning reputation and enabled him to identify himself with Vermont's ongoing struggle to establish itself as a state. In 1780 he even opened negotiations with the British to see if they would accept Vermont as a separate province, but these negotiations came to naught.

Allen devoted the rest of his life to his own land investments and Vermont business. Between 1780 and 1784 he wrote a deist tract, *Reason the Only Oracle of God*, published in November 1785. This book brought a great deal of criticism for its attack on organized Christianity. After its publication, Allen retired from public life. He died a few years later on February 12, 1789.

See also LAND RIOTS.

Further reading: Michael A. Bellesiles, *Revolutionary Outlaws: Ethan Allen and the Struggle for Independence on the Early American Frontier* (Charlottesville: University Press of Virginia, 1993); Charles A. Jellison, *Ethan Allen: Frontier Rebel* (Syracuse, N.Y.: Syracuse University Press, 1969).

Allen, Richard (1760–1831) *antislavery activist*

Richard Allen was one of the preeminent leaders of the free African-American community during the early republic. Born a slave in Philadelphia, he grew up in that city and in nearby Delaware. At about age 17, shortly after several members of his family had been sold to cover their master's debts, Allen had a religious experience and began practicing Methodism. He quickly gained a reputation for his piety and ability to preach to others. When he was about 20, Allen's master also became a Methodist. At this time METHODISTS often opposed SLAVERY as a violation of the equality of man before God, and Allen's new master offered him the opportunity to earn his freedom. During the next few years Allen rode the Methodist circuit throughout much of the United States; he supported himself, when not preaching, by hauling wood and making shoes.

By 1786 Allen had stopped his wanderings and centered his ministry on the area around Philadelphia. There he preached to mixed audiences of both whites and blacks, but his preaching attracted more and more AFRICAN AMERICANS, who soon outnumbered whites when he conducted services. This situation led to racial tension as some of the whites insulted the blacks, insisting that they stay in the gallery. Eventually there came a call for a separate African-American congregation, with Allen at its head, in 1794. Other black congregations soon formed throughout the region. In 1816 these black congregations broke from the white-dominated Methodist church entirely, forming the African Methodist Episcopal Church, for which Allen served as the first bishop.

Allen was more than a religious leader. He sought to gain respectability for himself and his people by acquiring property and achieving modest entrepreneurial success. In 1787 he was one of the founders of what was probably the first African-American charity, the Free African Society, which provided several kinds of social assistance and volunteer services. Allen vocally supported the ABOLITION of slavery in all of the United States. He was also one of the organizers of African Americans in Philadelphia during the great YELLOW FEVER epidemic of 1793, when the city was virtually paralyzed by the disease. Believing that African Americans were immune to yellow fever (they are not), Dr. BENJAMIN RUSH appealed to Allen and others to help nurse the sick and bury the dead. Allen and ABSALOM JONES, in the hope that this benevolent role would raise African Americans in the estimation of whites, convinced many Philadelphia blacks to provide assistance during the crisis.

Richard Allen spent his life working for the cause of RELIGION and for his fellow African Americans. He died on March 26, 1831.

Further reading: Gary B. Nash, *Forging Freedom: The Formation of Philadelphia's Black Community, 1720–1840* (Cambridge, Mass.: Harvard University Press, 1988); Richard Newman, *Freedom's Prophet: Bishop Richard Allen, the AME Church, and the Black Founding Fathers* (New York: NYU Press, 2008); Julie Winch, *Philadelphia's Black Elite: Activism, Accommodation, and the Struggle for Autonomy, 1787–1848* (Philadelphia: Temple University Press, 1988).

—Richard Newman

Allen, William (1704–1780) *Loyalist*

One of the leading politicians of colonial and prerevolutionary Pennsylvania, William Allen defended colonial rights against imperial regulation in the 1760s and early 1770s, but refused to support more radical action in 1775 and 1776 and became a Loyalist. Although he was born in Pennsylvania, Allen was trained as a lawyer in England. Upon his return to the colonies, he did not pursue his law career. Instead, he entered his family's lucrative mercantile business and became the richest man in Philadelphia. A Presbyterian, he was a political leader in Pennsylvania, serving in the colony's assembly from 1730 to 1739 and as Pennsylvania's chief justice from 1750 to 1774. Related by marriage to James Hamilton, who was governor from 1748 to 1754 and 1759 to 1763, Allen helped lead the proprietary party (supporters of the Penn family, proprietors of Pennsylvania). He was involved in such civic measures as the College of Pennsylvania and the AMERICAN PHILOSOPHICAL SOCIETY, and he was instrumental in the construction of the state house (later referred to as INDEPENDENCE HALL) in Philadelphia. He also developed the settlement that became known as Allentown.

When the imperial crisis began in 1763, Allen was in England, where he lobbied against the SUGAR ACT and, in 1765, protested the STAMP ACT. But he always believed in compromise. His pamphlet *American Crisis* (1774), which portrayed the RESISTANCE MOVEMENT in negative terms and urged reconciliation between the colonies and GREAT BRITAIN, had little impact. As the revolution in Pennsylvania radicalized, and Allen found himself with little influence on the course of events, he resigned from public life. In 1776 he went to England. He returned to Pennsylvania in 1779 and freed his slaves by the terms of his will. Allen died on September 6, 1780, in Mount Airy, Pennsylvania. His son was the Loyalist ANDREW ALLEN.

Alline, Henry (1748–1784) *clergyman*

Born in Newport, Rhode. Island, Henry Alline became a revivalist minister who moved to Nova Scotia about 1760 as part of the English effort to bring Protestant colonists to the area. After his religious conversion at age 27, Alline began preaching, and he was ordained in 1779 by lay ministers in churches he helped to establish. Alline's career demonstrates that George Whitefield's New Light movement and religious revival transcended the borders that established the United States and had a trans-Atlantic context.

Alline died in Boston on January 28, 1784. Subsequently, *His Life and Journal* (1806), a religious tract called *Two Mites Cast Into the Offering of God for the Benefit of Mankind* (1804), and his *Hymns and Spiritual Songs* (1802) were all published in Boston, attesting to Alline's lasting influence in both Nova Scotia and New England.

See also GREAT AWAKENING, SECOND.

Allston, Washington (1779–1843) *painter*

One of the leading painters of the early republic, Washington Allston was born in South Carolina. After he graduated from Harvard College in 1800, he began painting in the Boston area. However, in 1801 he went to London and studied at the Royal Academy with BENJAMIN WEST. Allston began traveling in Europe in 1804, visiting Paris and Rome. After a brief return to the United States from 1809 to 1811, he went back to England. Many of his paintings had religious themes, and he was heavily influenced by both the Renaissance—he is sometimes referred to as the "American Titian"—and romanticism; he also painted landscapes. Allston was good friends with the English poet Samuel Taylor Coleridge and was a poet himself. Many art critics believe that his best work was done in Europe before he returned to the United States in 1818. He trained several American artists, including Samuel F. B. Morse. From 1818 to his death on July 9, 1843, he resided in and around Boston, Massachusetts.

almanacs

By the mid-18th century, almanacs were a well-established form of published matter in North America throughout the colonies. The most popular almanac, produced by Nathaniel Ames, sold as many as 60,000 copies a year. Although adjusted for local audiences, much of the information in almanacs was basically the same: data on sunrise and sunset, tides, and the weather. Arranged on a calendar year, almanacs also included astrological charts; highlighted holidays, anniversaries, and significant events; and contained a variety of other material and commentary, including the famous aphorisms of "Poor Richard" written by BENJAMIN FRANKLIN during his years as a printer. In addition, almanacs could have poetry, short prose pieces, recipes, cures, anecdotes, and public documents.

Printed on cheap paper and sold inexpensively—as late as 1815 an almanac cost as little as five cents a copy—almanacs were not made to last. In 1783 one commentator explained that "one year passeth and another commeth—so likewise 'tis with almanacs—they are annual productions whose destination and usefulness is temporary, and afterwards are thrown by, and consigned to oblivion." And yet next to the Bible, they were the most frequently read form of published matter. In Pittsburgh between 1786, when the first printing press opened, and 1815, 160 books were printed; 52 of these publications were almanacs. As Nathaniel Ames explained in 1754, the audience for almanacs were the "Poor & Illiterate," and as such he made no pretensions "to direct the Learned." Ames believed that "The Rich and Voluptuous will scorn my Direction, and sneer or rail at any that would reclaim them." Instead, Ames appealed to readers in "solitary Dwellings . . . where the studied Ingenuity of the Learned Writer never comes."

Because of this egalitarian reach, almanacs offer a wonderful window into the ideas and beliefs of common folk. Thus, at the end of the FRENCH AND INDIAN WAR (1754–63), many almanacs were packed with praise for the British military and for GEORGE III. Once the RESISTANCE MOVEMENT (1764–75) began, some almanacs, especially those in New England, began to include comments in opposition to imperial regulations. Nathaniel Ames proclaimed his support for nonimportation in reaction to the STAMP ACT (1765) by advising his readers that "It is better to wear a homespun Coat, than to lose our liberty." Almanacs published outside of New England were less strident in their tone, and those in Virginia contained almost no overtly political commentary. Once the REVOLUTIONARY WAR (1775–83) broke out, almanacs reflected the allegiances of their printers, most of whom sided with the Revolutionaries. But there were some almanacs, like those published by Hugh Gaine, that reflected LOYALIST sympathies. Even almanacs without an overt political agenda revealed their true colors by either highlighting British holidays—like the king's birthday—or a new revolutionary chronology commemorating the BOSTON MASSACRE, the BATTLES OF LEXINGTON AND CONCORD (April 19, 1775), or the FRENCH ALLIANCE.

Almanacs also revealed popular attitudes about less overtly political issues. Often they included illustrations. One crude woodcut from an almanac published in the 1780s mocked LAWYERS by portraying them in the shape of goats—a common iconographical depiction of an agent of the devil—because of the popular belief that lawyers sought ill-gotten gains through manipulation of the law. Further, almanacs demonstrate gender relations of the time. Almanac stories and songs about sexual activity by women before the Revolutionary War were more playful and bawdy, while in the 1790s almanacs depicted female sexuality in negative and harsh terms.

Almanacs underwent a transformation in the 1790s, beginning with the establishment of *The Farmer's Almanack* by Robert B. Thomas. First published in 1792, *The Farmer's Almanack* sought to improve the reader and act as a cultural mediator between the cosmopolitan and local cultures. Thomas included agricultural information that would be helpful to farmers and enable them to increase production. He reduced the astrological information and weather predictions, encouraged EDUCATION, and offered "new, useful, and entertaining matter."

See also BANNEKER, BENJAMIN.

Further reading: David Jaffe, "The Village Enlightenment in New England, 1760–1820," *William and Mary Quarterly* 3rd ser., 97 (1990): 327–346; Clare A. Lyons, *Sex among the Rabble: An Intimate History of Gender and Power in the Age of Revolution, Philadelphia, 1730–1830* (Chapel Hill: University of North Carolina Press, 2006); Allan R. Raymond, "To Reach Men's Minds: Almanacs and the American Revolution, 1760–1777," *New England Quarterly* 51 (1978): 370–395.

American Duties Act   See SUGAR ACT.

American Fur Company

In 1808 JOHN JACOB ASTOR obtained a charter of incorporation from the State of New York to create the American Fur Company to gain control of the FUR TRADE west of the Mississippi. The charter declared that the company would be of "great public utility, by serving to conciliate and secure the good will and affections of the Indian tribes toward the government and people of the United States." The company was capitalized at $1 million, with each share to be sold for $500; its valuation could be doubled in two years. Although Astor was not able to sell all of the shares in the company, he began negotiating with British fur companies in CANADA to relinquish their operations in the territory around the Great Lakes and in the Far West, which belonged to the United States. However, handicapped by the EMBARGO OF 1807 and then the NON-INTERCOURSE ACT (1809), Astor made little headway in the fur trade and in his negotiations with the British. Ultimately, he sought to sidestep these problems and open trade between the Pacific Northwest and China. He therefore created another business—really a partnership—called the Pacific Fur Company and established an outpost, ASTORIA, on the Columbia River. The American Fur Company experienced losses during the WAR OF 1812 (1812–15), but it would become a major force in the fur trade in North America after 1815.

Further reading: John Denis Haeger, *John Jacob Astor: Business and Finance in the Early Republic* (Detroit: Wayne State University Press, 1991).

American Philosophical Society (APS)

The American Philosophical Society, an organization that still exists today, traces its roots to 1743 and BENJAMIN FRANKLIN's Junto, a discussion club he had begun as a young man that expanded its interests to scientific experiments. In 1768 the organization changed its name to the American Philosophical Society, planning to "unite . . . ingenious men" with a view to "promoting Useful Knowledge among the British Plantations of America."

From its beginning, the APS was transatlantic: It had 251 members, 144 Pennsylvanians, 90 from other colonies, and 17 foreigners, including such world-renowned scientists as the Swede Carl Linnaeus and the Frenchmen Antoine Laurent Lavoisier and the marquis de Condorcet. The society consciously modeled itself on the British Royal Society, where papers from throughout the world explaining scientific and practical discoveries and exploring intellectual topics were presented and discussed. The *Transactions of the American Philosophical Society*—first published in 1771 and today the oldest continuously published learned journal in the Western Hemisphere—was modeled on a similar British publication and beautifully printed by WILLIAM BRADFORD of Philadelphia. Copies were sold immediately throughout the colonies and distributed to libraries and universities in Europe.

Despite the political split developing in the colonies that became the AMERICAN REVOLUTION, learned men with different political views—such as Franklin and CHARLES THOMSON ("the Samuel Adams of Philadelphia") as well as LOYALISTS—were admitted to the APS based on merit. Members included the botanist JOHN BARTRAM, College of Pennsylvania president WILLIAM SMITH, former Pennsylvania lieutenant governor James Hamilton, and composer FRANCIS HOPKINSON. Only Governor John Penn, a bitter enemy of Franklin, balked: "I shall never be a patron of a Society that has for its President such a —— as Franklin." Despite Penn, the society soon realized its goal of becoming the principal colonial body disseminating knowledge.

The APS's first major projects supported the local clockmaker and astronomer DAVID RITTENHOUSE. With the society's financial help, he designed the first moving and accurate scale model of the solar system, the orrery still on display at the University of Pennsylvania Museum. Rittenhouse was also one of several colonial Americans who observed the 1769 TRANSIT OF VENUS from different locations. This "event" was the first intercolonial scientific endeavor and one coordinated with similar observations by scientists of many nationalities throughout the world.

The APS was a Pennsylvania-wide as well as a worldwide body. The Juliana Library Company in Lancaster worked closely with the society, encouraging WILLIAM HENRY, manufacturer of the Pennsylvania Rifle, to continue his experiments with steam, resulting in the invention of a system for heating houses and an unsuccessful steamboat. Agricultural experiments by Dr. BODO OTTO in Bethlehem also received society support. The APS's concern with the exploration of the western Illinois country (where society members had interests as land speculators) led to the opening of a public museum where people could examine exotic species of flora and fauna, scientific instruments, and medical curiosities. A canal planned by Thomas Gilpin with the society's support to connect the Delaware River with Chesapeake Bay received endorsement from the Pennsylvania Assembly. It was begun in 1771, before the REVOLUTIONARY WAR (1775–83) intervened and put the society's activities on hold for the duration of the conflict.

Paradoxically, the APS stands as a representative of both British and colonial identity. Modeled on the leading British scientific association, it marked the coming of age of colonials proud of their British connection and anxious to be recognized as equals by their overseas counterparts. It also represented the transatlantic connections of the world of ideas and SCIENCE.

After the Revolutionary War, the American Philosophical Society became, as it remains today, a center that brings together people in the United States engaged in all sorts of "Useful and Scientific" pursuits. Its magnificent library embodies this continuity with the colonial period: It features the journals of MERIWETHER LEWIS and WILLIAM CLARK, photographs of the first atomic bomb, and photographs of Neil Armstrong walking on the moon.

Further reading: Edward C. Carter III, *One Grand Pursuit: A Brief History of the American Philosophical Society's First 250 Years, 1743–1793* (Philadelphia: American Philosophical Society, 1993).

—William Pencak

American Revolution

There are at least three ways of defining the term *American Revolution*. First, and on the most fundamental level, the American Revolution can be described as the movement that led to independence from GREAT BRITAIN. Second, this description can be expanded to include the creation of a new form of republican government. Finally, the American Revolution can also be depicted as a series of political, social, economic, and cultural transformations that altered the American world.

The movement toward independence can be divided into two parts. First is the RESISTANCE MOVEMENT (1764–75) that began in the 1760s in reaction to imperial regulation. After the FRENCH AND INDIAN WAR (1754–63), Great Britain passed a series of regulations intended to rationalize its overseas empire and to raise revenue for the defense of that empire. Colonists objected to these efforts, but their resistance did not lead inevitably to independence. In fact, most colonists believed that they were merely asserting their rights as Englishmen when they opposed imperial regulation. Yet in the process of opposition to such laws as the STAMP ACT (1765), the TOWNSHEND DUTIES (1767), and the TEA ACT (1773), a pattern of conflict, distrust,

and misunderstanding developed that led the colonies and Great Britain to the precipice of war. The conflict that broke out in April 1775, which in turn led to the DECLARATION OF INDEPENDENCE (July 4, 1776), forms another part of this definition of the American Revolution. Without the armed conflict, independence would have been impossible. Only after the defeat of its armies did Great Britain at last acquiesce in the independence of its former North American colonies.

The second definition of the American Revolution picks up the story during the REVOLUTIONARY WAR (1775–83) and carries it through to the writing and ratification of the U.S. CONSTITUTION. During the war, it became obvious to the revolutionary leaders that some form of government must be created to replace the one being overthrown. On the local level, each state wrote or adopted its own constitution. This process was extremely important to the Revolutionaries, since at the time (before 1787) they had only the vaguest notion of a national form of government. What counted were the state constitutions (see CONSTITUTIONS, STATE). Each state experimented with a slightly different form of government in an effort to meet the republican ideal of balanced government that would protect the public welfare. The government of the United States under the ARTICLES OF CONFEDERATION was intended as a limited form of alliance that would bind otherwise independent states to one another. The writing of the U.S. Constitution therefore represented a radical break from the previous form of government. It not only created a truly national government, it also placed tremendous power in the executive and limited democratic input on several levels. The president of the United States became commander in chief of the armed forces, had vast appointive powers, and could veto legislation; his veto could only be overridden by two-thirds of both houses of legislature.

The third definition of the American Revolution is more difficult to date. Many historians now view the entire period running from 1760 to 1830 as the era of the American Revolution. These historians claim that the political transformations and debates that began with the resistance movement and the creation of republican governments continued through the decades of the 1790s and early 1800s as the people of the United States sought to stabilize their republican experiment and formulate a democratic political system. For these historians, the ultimate political end of the revolution came with the rewriting of state constitutions in the 1820s and 1830s that opened up the political process to all adult white men, not just a select few.

Other historians push their definition of the revolution even further to encompass profound social, economic, and cultural change. For these scholars, the colonial world was marked by a social hierarchy cemented by the bonds of deference and paternalism. In such a world, no man was independent; each individual was bound and dependent on others within a social structure that reached to the colonial governor and eventually to the king. The American Revolution overthrew this hierarchical world. The key to this revolution was THOMAS JEFFERSON's phrase: "We hold these truths to be self-evident, that all men are created equal."

The rise of the ideal of equality, however, did not emerge magically overnight. Instead, the triumph of this ideal took decades to become reality. Some men sought to slow or prevent its full implications from taking force. From this perspective, even the Constitution of 1787 was an effort to limit the impact of equality. Likewise, the FEDERALIST PARTY program of the 1790s sought to reinstall a hierarchical ideal in politics. These efforts failed. In Thomas Jefferson's victory in the ELECTION OF 1800, and again in ANDREW JACKSON's victory in 1828, the common man became paramount. The ideal became the independent man—independent from those above and below him and capable of making his own decisions regardless of his economic or social standing. The result was an unleashing of the individual in politics and the ECONOMY, giving rise to an aggressive capitalist and democratic spirit that transformed the political, social, economic, and cultural world.

Finally, more and more historians have come to emphasize the dramatic changes brought about by the Revolution that reached beyond white males and created even more fundamental changes in society. The Revolution offered opportunities for African-American slaves to seize freedom by fighting for the British and the Revolutionaries. It also raised new calls for ABOLITION from AFRICAN AMERICANS and European Americans. The Revolution broadened women's roles, and if it did not change the legal status of women, it at least raised the issue of women's rights and EDUCATION. This social revolution held out the promise for a host of reforms, including calls for public education, the end of imprisonment for debt, and even for new ways to treat criminals.

See also CONSTITUTIONAL CONVENTION; WHIGS; WOMEN'S STATUS AND RIGHTS.

Further reading: Francis D. Cogliano, *Revolutionary America, 1763–1815: A Political History* (London: Routledge, 2000); Paul A. Gilje, *The Making of the American Republic, 1763–1815* (Upper Saddle River, N.J.: Prentice Hall, 2006); Robert Middlekauff, *The Glorious Cause: The American Revolution, 1763–1789* (New York: Oxford University Press, 1982); Gary B. Nash, *The Unknown Revolution: The Unruly Birth of Democracy and the Struggle to Create America* (New York: Viking, 2005); Gordon S. Wood, *The Radicalism of the American Revolution* (New York: Knopf, 1992).

Ames, Fisher (1758–1808) *Massachusetts politician*
Fisher Ames became one of the leading spokesmen for the FEDERALIST PARTY in the 1790s, noted for his wit and biting pen. Ames was born in Massachusetts and entered Harvard when he was only 12 years of age. He started studying law in 1779 and was admitted to the bar in 1781. Although he was an excellent attorney, he never really enjoyed practicing law. However, he loved politics, and the political arena quickly became a showplace for his talents.

Ames was a political conservative. He opposed price fixing during the REVOLUTIONARY WAR (1775–83), decried SHAYS'S REBELLION (1786–87), and supported the U.S. CONSTITUTION of 1787. He feared that the era's democratic impulses would lead to anarchy, and he strove to assert the power of government in support of order. Having gained notoriety in his "Camillus" essays in defense of the Constitution, he was elected to the First Congress, defeating SAMUEL ADAMS. He was reelected three times and served in the House of Representatives until 1797.

During his years in Congress, Ames became one of the leaders of the Federalist Party, supporting ALEXANDER HAMILTON's program and opposing THOMAS JEFFERSON and the DEMOCRATIC-REPUBLICAN PARTY. He also favored the policies of Boston merchants who wanted to maintain strong TRADE connections with GREAT BRITAIN. He was known for his writing and for his speaking ability. One of his speeches in 1794, opposing retaliation against Great Britain for its recent seizures of merchant ships, gained so much notoriety that he was burned in effigy in Charleston, South Carolina. During the debates over the pro-British JAY'S TREATY (1794), which Ames favored, he gave what some scholars call one of the greatest speeches ever uttered in the halls of Congress.

Although he retired from Congress in 1796, returning to his home in Dedham, Massachusetts, Ames still wrote essays attacking Jefferson's party. He believed that the United States should be a Roman-type republic led by a natural elite, individuals like himself. He feared democracy, viewed the FRENCH REVOLUTION (1789–99) as anathema, and saw the followers of Jefferson as Jacobins ready to turn the guillotine upon their opponents. Jefferson's victory in the ELECTION OF 1800 was a hard blow, and in the ensuing years Ames wrote bitterly about the government's policies. Recognizing that regaining national office would be difficult, he encouraged members of the Federalist Party to take control of their state governments.

The Federalist Party lost an important political spokesman when Fisher Ames died on July 4, 1808. His funeral, which included a huge procession in Boston, was not only a testament to his popularity but also a massive demonstration of political support for the Federalist Party.

See also REPUBLICANISM; POLITICAL PARTIES.

Further reading: Winfred E. A. Bernhard, *Fisher Ames, Federalist and Statesman, 1758–1808* (Chapel Hill: University of North Carolina Press, 1965).

Amherst, Jeffrey Amherst, first baron (1717–1797)
British military officer

Jeffrey Amherst was born on January 29, 1717, into a well-connected English family; he joined the British army as an ensign in 1731. Intelligent and hard working, he impressed both Sir John Ligonier and Prince William Augustus, DUKE OF CUMBERLAND. With their patronage and his own diligence, he advanced through the ranks to become a colonel by 1756. Amherst's big opportunity came during the FRENCH AND INDIAN WAR (1754–63) when Ligonier persuaded WILLIAM PITT to place him in command of the assault on LOUISBOURG in 1758. After he captured that fortress in July, Amherst was appointed commander in chief of the British army in North America. In July 1759, with his usual organizational skills, he seized FORT TICONDEROGA, a prize that had eluded the British up until that point. However, he did not push into CANADA that summer since he was unsure of the result of General JAMES WOLFE's campaign at Quebec. The next year, however, Amherst was the architect of the conquest of Canada in a three-pronged invasion, compelling the surrender of MONTREAL and all of New France on September 8, 1760.

Amherst had contempt for British North Americans, but he was able to put aside his personal feelings and work well with colonial officials. He had even greater disdain for NATIVE AMERICANS, and after his conquest of Canada he abandoned the traditional gift giving that had lubricated relations between Indians and European Americans. In part in reaction to this hard-line policy, and in part in reaction against European-American settlers moving west of the Appalachian Mountains, PONTIAC'S WAR broke out late in 1763. Surprised by the Indian attacks, Amherst quickly swung into action and sent troops to the FRONTIER to defeat the Indians. He also encouraged the commander at FORT PITT—who had come up with the idea independently—to provide SMALLPOX-infected blankets to the Indians, explaining that the British needed to "Use Every Stratagem" in their "Power to Reduce them." Displeased with the added expenditures of an unexpected war, and aware of discontent in the army, the British government called Amherst back to England for consultation on the affairs in North America.

The rest of Amherst's life was anticlimactic. Although he received some accolades, eventually including the title first baron Amherst, he never quite got the recognition he thought he deserved. Personally, he had to struggle with a wife who had gone insane. She died in 1765, and Amherst remarried in 1767. Both marriages were childless, and a nephew became his heir, though Amherst also had one illegitimate son who became an army officer. Twice he was offered command in North America during the REVOLUTIONARY WAR (1775–83), but he declined—not out of sympathy for the revolutionaries, but because he did not want to leave England. Instead, he served in a cabinet position as commander in chief. However, he had little input on policy and focused more on administration and the defense of GREAT BRITAIN. He was dismissed with a change in the ministry in 1782 but was reappointed for two years in 1793 after the outbreak of war with FRANCE. He died on August 3, 1797.

Further reading: Fred Anderson, *The Crucible of War: The Seven Years' War and the Fate of the British Empire in North America, 1754–1766* (New York: Knopf, 2000).

Amiens, Peace of (1801–1803)

In autumn 1801, GREAT BRITAIN and FRANCE agreed to make peace, ending a war that had begun in February 1793. Both nations sought a way out of the conflict, which had drained their treasuries and seemed to be locked in a stalemate. The French and British came to an initial agreement on October 1, 1801, in London and then signed a more formal treaty at Amiens, France, on March 25, 1802. Neither power ever fulfilled all of its obligations in the treaty. NAPOLEON BONAPARTE used the peace to consolidate many of his holdings in Europe, while the British did not relinquish all of their overseas colonial conquests and clung to their base in Malta. By early 1803 war again appeared likely, and hostilities resumed on May 18, 1803.

This hiatus in the Anglo-French Wars (1793–1815) had important ramifications for the United States. First, it alleviated the ongoing diplomatic tension between the United States and the belligerent powers over the issue of neutral TRADE and IMPRESSMENT. This development made the early years of President THOMAS JEFFERSON's administration easier, allowing him to pursue his domestic agenda unhindered by major foreign policy concerns and to concentrate naval forces on the BARBARY WARS. Second, it set the stage for the LOUISIANA PURCHASE (1803) since Napoleon Bonaparte used the break in the war to attempt to regain control over the rebellious Saint-Domingue (HAITI). When that effort failed, Napoleon decided that his larger plans for a North American empire would not come to fruition and that he might as well sell LOUISIANA before war broke out again with Great Britain. Third, once war erupted in Europe in 1803, the problems with the belligerent powers intensified, creating diplomatic difficulties that would mark Jefferson's second term and ultimately lead to the WAR OF 1812 (1812–15).

Anderson, Alexander (1775–1872) *engraver*

Alexander Anderson was the leading wood engraver of his age. Born and raised in New York City, Anderson came from an artisan background. During the 1780s and early 1790s, he taught himself to engrave by reading an encyclopedia and watching other engravers through shop windows. He developed his skills further by studying with copperplate engraver Peter Maverick. His intention, however, was not to earn his living as an engraver. Instead, he used his earnings to pay for an education at Columbia College and studied to be a doctor. He began practicing MEDICINE in 1795, but struggled to make ends meet. The YELLOW FEVER epidemic of 1797 in New York was personally devastating to Anderson, wiping out most of his family, including his young wife. Distraught over his loss and his inability to use his medical knowledge to save his loved ones, Anderson abandoned his career as a doctor and devoted the rest of his long life to engraving, creating countless images for newspapers, periodicals, and books. The New York Public Library has scrapbooks of more than 10,000 images made by Anderson that can be examined on the Internet. Alexander Anderson's lifework provides scholars with an unrivaled view of early 19th-century life in the United States.

See also ARTISANS.

Further reading: NYPL Digital Gallery. "America's First Illustrator: Alexander Anderson." Available online. URL: http://digitalgallery.nypl.org/nypldigital/explore/dgexplore.cfm?topic=arts&collection= AmericasFirstIllustr&col_id=221. Accessed November 18, 2008.

André, John (1750–1780) *British military officer, spy*

John André was a British army officer best known for his role in aiding BENEDICT ARNOLD's treason. Born in London to Huguenot parents, André was talented, educated, and sophisticated and spoke French, German, and English fluently. Arriving in the colonies in 1774, he saw firsthand the movement toward the open break with GREAT BRITAIN. In 1775 he was stationed at Quebec, where he was captured by the CONTINENTAL ARMY during its invasion of CANADA. He remained a prisoner of war until late 1776, when he was exchanged. He then saw service in the campaign that led to the capture of Philadelphia in 1777. During the British occupation of Philadelphia in 1777–78, André organized several entertainments for his fellow officers and the local LOYALISTS. He continued these activities in New York after arriving there in 1778 and was particularly noted for his role in theatrical productions, though he was no lightweight fop.

André served on the general staff of General Charles Grey and was involved in several important campaigns between 1778 and 1780. When Grey went back to GREAT BRITAIN, André transferred to General HENRY CLINTON's staff. He quickly became Clinton's most trusted officer, responsible for many of the day-to-day duties of the staff office. Clinton showed further confidence in André by having him run the British army's intelligence in New York. It was in this role that he first made contact with Benedict Arnold and opened negotiations for the surrender of WEST POINT. With Clinton's permission, André traveled through Continental lines for a meeting with Arnold on the night of September 21, 1780. After they met, it was too late for André to return to the British ship in the Hudson that had taken him to the rendezvous. He went into hiding during the day, intending to make his way back to the British lines the next night. During this interlude he took off his uniform and put on civilian clothes (up until this point he had worn an overcoat to hide the uniform). Unfortunately for André, on September 23 he ran into three MILITIAmen near Tarrytown, New York. Once captured, he did not hide his true identity, nor did he provide any information on the people who helped him. He did carry incriminating papers, and when Arnold heard of André's capture, he immediately left West Point and went over to the British.

At his court martial on September 28, André did not defend himself, freely admitting the clandestine nature of his mission. He was quickly sentenced to hang. Clinton desperately sought to exchange André for any prisoner then held by the British. GEORGE WASHINGTON, however, insisted that he would take only one man for Major André—Benedict Arnold. Clinton could not allow that exchange, and André was executed as a spy on October 2, 1780. After the war, citizens of the United States romanticized the dashing Major André in books and plays, contrasting his honesty and loyalty to country to the perfidy of the treasonous Benedict Arnold.

See also SPYING.

Further reading: James Thomas Flexner, *The Traitor and the Spy* (Boston: Little Brown and Co., 1975).

Anglicans

The Anglican Church, also known as the Church of England, was the established church in six British North American colonies: Georgia, South Carolina, North Carolina, Virginia, Maryland, and several counties in New York. During the late colonial era, there were also Anglican congregations in all of the other colonies. The period 1754–1815 saw tremendous upheaval and transformation in the Anglican Church as it had to deal with not only disestablishment but also the independence of the United States and a metamorphosis into the Episcopalian Church of America.

Organization of the colonial church differed in several significant ways from the church in England. First, there was no bishop in North America. Instead, all of the various parishes were under the general authority of the bishop of London. Without a bishop on the colonial side of the ATLANTIC OCEAN, all clergy needed to travel to England for official ordination; moreover, there were no ecclesiastical courts to deal with wayward clergy or parishioners. Second, although the exact church organization varied from colony to colony, generally the laity exerted greater control over the clergy than in England. This development was especially true in Virginia, where the vestry controlled appointments and dictated the salary. Third, EDUCATION of the clergy remained problematic, with most colleges dominated by other denominations. This problem was somewhat alleviated by the establishment of King's College (later Columbia University) in 1754 in New York and, in 1749, the College of Philadelphia (later the University of Pennsylvania), which joined the College of William and Mary as the only Anglican institutions of higher education in the colonies. But the religious orientation of King's College did not go unchallenged, and the Anglicanism of Philadelphia was not that strong. Fourth and finally, until very late in the colonial period, many ministers were born and educated in GREAT BRITAIN.

Regardless of these differences, which were something of a handicap, the Anglican Church grew in the mid-18th century, although not as fast as the population or some evangelical denominations. One hundred new churches were built between 1760 and 1775, and 253 new clergy were added. Although evangelicals dismissed Anglican religiosity, its formalism and emphasis on the sacraments continued to have an appeal. Moreover, the Anglican Church advocated a middle way in its theology between the austerity of strict Calvinism and the simple reliance on good works of Arminianism. The SOCIETY FOR THE PROPAGATION OF THE GOSPEL (SPG), which underwrote the salaries of many ministers, was able to establish a number of churches in New England and the middle colonies and also sent missionaries to meet the religious needs of European Americans on the FRONTIER.

Despite, and in some ways because of, this success the Anglican Church became steeped in controversy in the 1750s, 1760s, and early 1770s over scandals, disputes about salary, and the creation of a North American bishop. In part because it was difficult to find Anglican clergy, some ministers were not of the highest caliber, and a few misbehaved or were inept. The total number of such clergy may not have been high, but in the charged religious atmosphere of the first "Great Awakening" of the period, a few examples trumpeted by evangelicals or individuals discontent with the established church went a long way toward making the Anglican clergy appear corrupt and unfit for the ministry. Simultaneously, there was a great deal of wrangling over pay, especially as many Anglican ministers sought a living commensurate with a social status they believed appropriate to their position. The most famous of such controversies centered on the PARSON'S CAUSE in Virginia, where Anglican ministers successfully sought a royal repeal of a measure limiting their salary, ordinarily paid in TOBACCO, when the price of tobacco increased. More important, there was a clamor over the possible appointment of a bishop for North America. Having a bishop would have aided the Anglican Church tremendously, allowing for ordination in the colonies and providing better oversight of the church. But many people in the colonies saw the creation of a North American bishop as a sign of arbitrary government akin to popery. Moreover, many believed a bishop would be the first step in a Parliament-sanctioned establishment for all the colonies. This action would not only overturn the Congregationalist authority in most of New England, but create a religious establishment where none previously existed—New Jersey, Pennsylvania, Rhode Island, and Delaware. In addition, the rising evangelical numbers in colonies where there was an Anglican establishment also objected. During the RESISTANCE MOVEMENT (1764–75) the anti-bishop crusade became enmeshed in the upheaval against imperial regulation. In the anti-STAMP ACT disturbances, one minister reported that churchmen's windows were broken by crowds shouting, "No bishops! no popery! no kings, lords, and tyrants!"

The REVOLUTIONARY WAR (1775–83) brought the entire Anglican Church in North America into crisis. On one level, the choice of the Anglican clergy should have been simple. The head of their church was the king, ordination demanded an oath to the king, and their liturgy included repeated assertions of loyalty and prayers to the king. Given the intimate relationship between the king and the church, all Anglicans—and certainly all Anglican clergy—should have been LOYALISTS. Following this logic, many clergy became Loyalists, especially in New England and the middle colonies, where Anglicans were a minority and where the church had strong connections to England. In fact, Anglican ministers provided some of the most articulate Loyalist leadership. But the AMERICAN REVOLUTION created a logic of its own: Many of the clergy, especially in Virginia, had more mixed emotions, and some even became ardent supporters of independence. Between 1775 and 1783, of the 318 Anglican clergy in what became the United States, 123 of the Anglican clergy became avowed Loyalists, while 88 supported the Revolution, and 107 strove to be neutral. Given that some Anglican ministers were driven out of their communities and into the arms of the British, these numbers reveal a surprising lack of loyalty to the king despite the strong religious connection between the Crown and the church. Many of the neutral ministers had to close their churches or fudge on the liturgy to continue with their clerical responsibilities.

The Revolution's political ramifications created additional problems for the Anglican Church. Although religious establishments in several New England states lasted into the 19th century, all of the states where the Anglican Church had been officially supported abolished the established church, either in their constitutions or through legislation. In short, during the 1780s the Anglican Church, which now became known as the Episcopal Church, had to adjust to being simply one denomination among many without any state support. Moreover, since the SPG's charter said it could only operate in the British Empire, it withdrew its financial support in the United States. Despite these difficulties, the new Episcopal Church survived, and by 1789 it had about the same number of clergy as the Anglican Church had had in 1775.

Without the king as the head of the church, some sort of new organizational structure also had to be decided upon. In state after state, Episcopalians organized CONVENTIONS with laity and clergy together to decide on liturgy and organization. This new mode of operation reflected the Revolution's republican principles. Connecticut was the first state to seek a bishop and had to go to the Church of Scotland to have SAMUEL SEABURY—who had been as high a Tory as possible during the Revolution—consecrated as a bishop in 1784. In 1787 Parliament passed legislation allowing for the consecration of bishops in the United States without a loyalty oath to the king. In 1785 several state Episcopal conventions led to a national convention, but not every state sent a delegation. Much more important was the 1789 national convention, which settled on a constitution, a set of canons, and a liturgy outlined in a prayer book. This constitution reflected revolutionary values, limiting the power of the hierarchy and divorcing the church organization from Parliament and king. Full integration of every state into this organization would take several more decades, and the Episcopal Church had to operate gingerly so as not to antagonize sensitivities over its onetime connection to the Church of England hierarchy. However, despite what might have been overwhelming difficulties in the Revolutionary War, the church survived and would ultimately expand in the 19th century as an American institution.

See also GREAT AWAKENING, SECOND; RELIGION.

Further reading: Carl Bridenbagh, *Mitre and Sceptre: Transatlantic Faiths, Ideas, Personalities, and Politics, 1689–1775* (New York: Oxford University Press, 1962); Nancy L. Rhoden, *Revolutionary Anglicanism: The Colonial Church of England Clergy during the American Revolution* (New York: New York University Press, 1999).

Anglo-French wars (1754–1815)

GREAT BRITAIN and FRANCE fought a series of five wars between 1754 and 1815 that had a profound impact on North America and the development of the United States. The FRENCH AND INDIAN WAR (1754–63)—known in Europe as the Seven Years' War—was the culmination of a series of earlier wars in which France and Great Britain vied for control of much of North America and for influence on the Indian subcontinent. This conflict also had an impact on Europe as the traditional earlier balance of power shifted, with France, SPAIN, and Austria allying with one another against Great Britain and PRUSSIA. Although the war was something of a stalemate in Europe, the British triumphed overseas, extending their influence in INDIA and gaining control of CANADA, FLORIDA, and the territory between the Mississippi River and the Appalachian Mountains. The new acquisitions in North America created an unprecedented security for the British North American colonists, which convinced Parliament to reform imperial relations. This effort triggered a RESISTANCE MOVEMENT (1764–75) in British North America and contributed to the outbreak of the REVOLUTIONARY WAR (1775–83).

The Revolutionary War offered an opportunity for the French to strike back at the British and seek vengeance for their losses in the previous war. The French provided covert aid to the Revolutionaries in North America until they signed a formal alliance in February 1778. War broke out between France and Great Britain in June 1778. During the war the French successfully isolated the British diplomatically. Great Britain gained no major allies during the war, while France allied itself with Spain and The NETHERLANDS. Much of the rest of the Europe joined the LEAGUE OF ARMED NEUTRALITY to dictate terms of neutral TRADE largely in opposition to British maritime policy. Although the French aided the Revolutionaries in North America, for most of the conflict they were more preoccupied with capturing possessions in the WEST INDIES and preparing an invasion of England (which never took place) than with the North American war. However, in 1781 a combined revolutionary and French land force, along with a French fleet from the West Indies, trapped LORD CORNWALLIS in Chesapeake Bay and forced him to surrender at YORKTOWN (October 19, 1781). Naval reverses in the West Indies and a depleted treasury convinced France to end the war in 1783 with only minor gains for itself and Spain, while also guaranteeing the independence of the United States.

The third war between Great Britain and France broke out on February 1, 1793, after the FRENCH REVOLUTION (1789–99) was well under way. This war continued until the PEACE OF AMIENS, which was agreed to in London on October 1, 1801, and formally signed at Amiens on March 25, 1802. Before this treaty, France and Great Britain fought each other to the point of exhaustion. Britain joined a variety of other nations as an ally, only to see the French defeat these allies on the Continent, often forcing them to become neutral or to join in the war against Great Britain. Thus, France knocked Spain out of the war in 1795, and the Spanish went to war against the British in 1796. The French also conquered The Netherlands and set up a puppet regime in 1795. Prussia agreed to peace with the French in 1795; Austria entered and exited war with France several times.

The war between Great Britain and Revolutionary France had a dramatic effect on the United States. Economically, the war led to great profits for merchants in the United States as exports increased and merchants began a reexport trade taking goods between French and British colonies and their metropolitan centers. This trade increased government revenue through impost duties and tonnage fees, which helped the finances of the national government in the United States. Diplomatically, the United States had to walk a tightrope to sustain its role in neutral trade without alienating either belligerent. This task proved almost impossible as the United States seemed to gyrate first toward war with Great Britain in the crisis that produced JAY'S TREATY (1794) and then into conflict with France in the QUASI-WAR (1798–1800). The Peace of Amiens, however, briefly halted these diplomatic problems. The war in Europe also affected politics in the United States, with the DEMOCRATIC-REPUBLICAN PARTY generally supporting the French and the FEDERALIST PARTY supporting the British.

The resumption of the Anglo-French wars on May 18, 1803, brought an intensified conflict. Again, Great Britain sought allies on the Continent, initially with mixed success as the French continued to defeat the armies it faced in the field. A British coalition with Austria ended after the Battle of Austerlitz (1805), and the one with Prussia ended after the Battle of Jena (1806). Even RUSSIA sought to accommodate NAPOLEON BONAPARTE and the French until 1812, when Napoleon's invasion of Russia failed, and a new coalition formed with Great Britain, Russia, SWEDEN, Prussia, Austria, and other powers all allied against France. A revolt in Spain, aided by a British army under Arthur Wellesley (the duke of Wellington after 1808) also drained French resources. The allied armies marched on Paris in 1814 and forced Napoleon to abdicate.

This war, too, had a big impact on the United States. As the war began, Napoleon Bonaparte decided to raise MONEY by selling the LOUISIANA TERRITORY to the United States—a fortunate turn of events that doubled the size of the new republic. But the war also brought some diplomatic problems. Because his majesty's navy was the only thing that prevented a French invasion of Great Britain, IMPRESSMENT of U.S. sailors increased as the British need for SEAMEN grew. When the war became a stalemate in 1806 and 1807, both the French and British placed restric-

tions on neutral trade that left the United States with few diplomatic alternatives and compelled President THOMAS JEFFERSON to curtail trade to pressure the belligerents to allow the United States free trade. Ultimately, these efforts failed, and the United States entered the WAR OF 1812 (1812–15). Britain's preoccupation with the war in France meant that it had to limit its efforts to subdue the United States for most of that conflict. However, by 1814 the French defeat allowed the British to focus resources on North America.

The fifth war resulted from Napoleon's short-lived effort to regain his empire when he left the island of Elba, seized control of France, and marched into the Low Countries, where he fought a combined British and Prussian army at the Battle of Waterloo (1815). With the British-Prussian victory in that battle, the Anglo-French wars came to a close.

Further reading: Jeremy Black, *Britain as a Military Power, 1688–1815* (London: UCL Press, 1999); John Brewer, *The Sinews of Power: War, Money, and the English State, 1688–1793* (New York: Knopf, 1988); Owen Connelly, *The Wars of the French Revolution and Napoleon, 1792–1815* (London: Routledge, 2006); Charles J. Esdaille, *The French Wars, 1792–1815* (London: Routledge, 2001); Lawrence Stone, ed., *An Imperial State of War, Britain from 1688 to 1815* (London: Routledge, 1994).

animals

Animals played a significant and largely unnoticed role in the development of revolutionary America. Though English colonists brought livestock to eastern North America in the 17th century, the full cultural and environmental ramifications of the arrival of domestic animals were not felt until later. Urban and rural revolutionary families owned an assortment of cattle, chickens, sheep, and hogs. Livestock provided families with a supply of food when crops failed. They were also used to settle debts, sold for profit, or given as dowries. In the Carolinas, wealthy individuals raised cattle on large ranches called "cowpens." By the time of the REVOLUTIONARY WAR (1775–83), there were 70,000 cattle in South Carolina alone. Such market-driven livestock production, however, remained rare outside of the Carolinas. The average Massachusetts family in the 1770s, for instance, owned three cows, one steer, six sheep and goats, and three oxen and horses. Unlike those with cowpens, small families lacked the means and time to clear forests, drain swamps, or enclose fields for pasturage. As a result, they allowed their livestock to forage in nearby orchards and woods. Unsupervised livestock, however, created tension between settlers and NATIVE AMERICANS as they trampled and fed on Indian corn.

The growth in the size and number of herds prompted several environmental changes, some intentional and others unintentional. Unaccustomed to surviving in the wild, cattle and hogs were easy prey for alligators, bears, panthers, wildcats, and wolves. States like Tennessee paid hunters a bounty of three dollars for the scalp of every panther, wildcat, and wolf that they turned in to the authorities. The bounties created additional, unforeseen problems. By culling predators, hunters increased the numbers of squirrels, chipmunks, mice, and rats feasting on crops. Foraging cattle and hogs also compacted the topsoil. Unable to absorb water, the soil washed away into rivers and streams, encouraging periodic flooding. In the Appalachians, livestock devoured river canebrakes, allowing Kentucky bluegrass and other European weeds to flourish.

Wild animals were likewise important. The native fauna of eastern North America was diverse, abundant, and richly varied. European naturalists were awestruck by the quantity and quality of the continent's mammals, birds, and fish. Majestic flocks of the now-extinct passenger pigeon blackened the skies above coastal towns throughout the period. In New England, so many shad and salmon traveled upstream during in the annual fish runs that people could not dip their feet into the rivers without touching a fish. The visible abundance of certain species, however, masked the fact that the FUR TRADE had already decimated the populations of the fur-bearing beaver and otter. Overhunting, too, forced some animals, such as the bison (popularly known as the BUFFALO), to retreat to the West. Nonetheless, many species maintained stable populations during the period, leaving their decline and, in some cases, extinction to a later day. Many animals and birds, including bears, deer, elk, moose, duck, geese, partridges, pheasants, pigeons, quail, and turkeys, remained essential sources of protein. Backcountry farmers hunted smaller animals for their furs. Without access to hard specie, they used beaver, fox, mink, rabbit, raccoon, and opossum skins as a form of backcountry currency, exchanging them for commodities like bullets, coffee, guns, SUGAR, and tools from inland merchants.

Probably the most significant activity involving animals during the revolutionary period was the southern deerskin trade. Though the trade began in the 16th century, it reached its height in the 1760s–70s. Events in Europe persuaded English leather manufacturers to look to the North American South for deerskins. By the mid-18th century, Indian tribes such as the CHOCTAW, CHEROKEE, CREEK, and CHICKASAW had entered the Atlantic ECONOMY, harvesting large numbers of white-tailed deer for merchants in Charleston, Mobile, Pensacola, Savannah, and New Orleans. Indians traded deerskins for guns, ammunition, axes, COTTON, duffel, flannel, knives, metal kettles, and other manufactured goods. The most sought-after item,

however, was rum. Lured by unscrupulous middlemen who diluted their distilled products with water, Indians eagerly procured deerskins to obtain rum. One scholar estimates that by 1770 the Creek had exchanged 80 percent of their skins for ALCOHOL. Unlike durable goods, rum was consumed quickly and remained in constant demand. Whereas merchants annually exported 85,000 deerskins to Europe prior to 1750, during the 1750s and 1760s they shipped 500,000 per year. Along with the pressure on natural habitats produced by the spread of livestock, the deerskin trade decimated deer populations. By 1800, yearly exports had fallen to 100,000 skins. The Choctaw found deer so scarce that they began to hunt west of the Mississippi River. The scarcity of deer convinced some states to restrict the methods and seasons for hunting; South Carolina outlawed night hunting and reduced the number of does and fawns that a hunter could kill.

Changes on the GREAT PLAINS also point to the importance of animals in this period. An enormous grassland, the Great Plains was home to nearly 30 million bison. Plains Indians depended on bison hunting, farming, and gathering for their subsistence. They used bison meat, sinew, fat, and bones to make bedding, belts, shirts, saddlebags, bridles, saddle straps, ropes, cups, spoons, thread, needles, yarn, bow strings, paint, polish, water buckets, lassos, and tents. Popular myth portrays Indians as conscientious conservationists, never wasting any part of their quarry. Yet Indians were also quite capable of influencing animal populations. In some ceremonies Indians used only the bison's choicest parts—tongues, marrow, or fetuses—and left the remainder of the carcass to rot.

The reintroduction of the horse to North America by the 16th-century Spanish would, in time, revolutionize the Indian relationship to the bison. By the 19th century, the Arapaho, Assiniboine, Atsina, Blackfeet, Cheyenne, Comanche, Crow, Kiowa, and Sioux had abandoned farming and gathering to embrace full-time bison hunting. Equestrian hunting was far more efficient than traditional techniques such as running herds over cliffs or cornering them by setting fires. It enabled Indians to kill more bison for distant markets since horses hauled four times as much weight as dogs and pursued herds over longer distances. The combined impact of equestrian hunting, the Atlantic economy, and the competition between livestock, horses, and bison for forage has led some scholars to argue that the bison's decline, often placed in the last quarter of the 19th century, actually began, at least on the southern plains, in the 1790s.

Further reading: Kathryn E. Holland Braund, *Deerskins and Duffels: Creek Indian Trade with Anglo-America, 1685–1815* (Lincoln: University of Nebraska Press, 1993); Donald Edward Davis, *Where There Are Moun-*

tains: An Environmental History of the Southern Appalachians (Athens: University of Georgia Press, 2000); Pekka Hämäläinen, "The First Phase of Destruction: Killing the Southern Plains Buffalo, 1790–1840," *Great Plains Quarterly* 21 (Spring 2001): 101–114; Andrew C. Isenberg, *The Destruction of the Bison* (Cambridge: Cambridge University Press, 2000).

—Anthony E. Carlson

Annapolis Convention (1786)

The Annapolis Convention is notable as the event leading to the CONSTITUTIONAL CONVENTION in Philadelphia in 1787. Delegates from five states, including Delaware, New Jersey, New York, Pennsylvania, and Virginia, met in Annapolis to consider a federal plan for regulating commerce. Because of the lack of attendance, the delegates soon decided to call a new convention to meet the next year with the broad purpose of amending the ARTICLES OF CONFEDERATION.

An earlier conference at Mount Vernon, Virginia, in 1785 had successively resolved a number of disputes concerning the navigation of Chesapeake Bay, thus illustrating the advantages of independent state action. The success of this conference led to Virginia's invitation to the states to meet at Annapolis in 1786, with the purpose of creating a more uniform standard for dealing with interstate commerce. The government under the Articles of Confederation did not have the power to regulate commerce, which often led to difficulties between states. Disputes between Maryland and Virginia over navigation of the Potomac River were the immediate catalyst for the Annapolis Convention. However, discussions were brief and futile as the delegates soon decided that because of such low attendance and the complexities of commerce, there was little they could accomplish. ALEXANDER HAMILTON was key in convincing his colleagues that the issues they were concerned with required revision of other political and economic practices.

After only two days of discussion, the delegates to the Annapolis Convention issued a report, written primarily by Hamilton, requesting the states to select delegates to send to a convention in Philadelphia the next year to revise the Articles. They expressed their opinion that the United States's situation was delicate and critical, requiring the attention of all members of the Confederacy. The delegates stated that the Philadelphia Convention should create "provisions as shall appear to them necessary to render the constitution adequate to the exigencies of the Union." The report was completed on September 11, 1786, and copies were submitted to Congress and to all the state legislatures. The legislatures were asked to send their delegates to Philadelphia in May 1787. This action was technically unconstitutional, but it soon gained the support of the SECOND CONTINENTAL CONGRESS. On the suggestion of the Annapolis Convention, delegates from 12 states met in Philadelphia at the Constitutional Convention, which eventually produced the U.S. CONSTITUTION.

See also CONVENTIONS.

Further reading: Merrill Jensen, *The New Nation: A History of the United States during the Confederation* (New York: Knopf, 1950).

—Crystal Williams

Anti-Federalists

Simply put, Anti-Federalists did not support the U.S. CONSTITUTION. In 1787 most people in the United States probably opposed the Constitution, and among the prominent Anti-Federalists were PATRICK HENRY, JAMES MONROE, and SAMUEL ADAMS. Like the Federalists, Anti-Federalists built their ideas on the republican ideology of the AMERICAN REVOLUTION. Although they were ultimately defeated, their opposition convinced the FEDERALISTS to pass the BILL OF RIGHTS after ratification of the Constitution. Moreover, their belief in the states' supremacy remained an important part of U.S. political theory and was not fully refuted until the Civil War.

There were four main components to the Anti-Federalist position. First, Anti-Federalists objected to the way the Constitution was written. The CONSTITUTIONAL CONVENTION in Philadelphia had been called to revise the ARTICLES OF CONFEDERATION, with the idea of providing the Confederation with the power to raise taxes on its own. Instead, the convention had decided to scrap the Articles for an entirely different form of government. Convention members had also decided to meet behind closed doors, with no reporting of their daily proceedings in the press. This approach smacked of conspiracy and seemed to be a means of hiding the convention's true intentions. These suspicions were enhanced by the ratification procedure, which ignored the amendment process in the Articles of Confederation. Instead, the process relied upon state CONVENTIONS and dictated that the Constitution would be put into place when only nine states had ratified it.

Second, following the best political science of the day, and based in part on the writings of MONTESQUIEU, the Anti-Federalists held that it was impossible for a republic to exist in a large geographic area. They believed that there would be too many interests in a large nation and that with so many of them competing for control, ultimately one interest would seize power and act against the interests of the rest of the society. In such a polity, the public good would no longer be the end of government; rather, government would simply support the concerns of those in power at the expense of others. As could be seen in ancient Greece and Rome, history had demonstrated that large republics inevitably gave way to empires controlled by despots. In other words, as the 18th-century COMMONWEALTHMEN explained, the more power given to the governors—as would inevitably happen in a large republic—the less LIBERTY the people had. In the minds of many Anti-Federalists, the REVOLUTIONARY WAR (1775–1783) had been fought to liberate the people from a too-powerful government that had covered too big a geographic area.

The third complaint about the Constitution was in its specific provisions, which created a powerful government divorced from the common voter. The president was a king-like executive who had broad appointive powers, commanded the army and navy, and was chosen through an electoral college and not by direct vote of the people. Moreover, he could serve in office repeatedly without any limits. The Senate was viewed as an "aristocratic junto" with six-year terms that would make it a veritable House of Lords, dominating government. Like the president, the Senate was not elected by the people but chosen by state assemblies. The popularly elected House of Representatives was little better. Many Anti-Federalists, in an era where annual elections predominated, believed that two-year terms were too long and that the 60,000-person constituency was far too large. The SUPREME COURT, in the eyes of Anti-Federalists, was a refutation of the traditional trial by jury and also too powerful, and they considered the NECESSARY AND PROPER CLAUSE as an open ended invitation for the abuse of power. In short, the Constitution would set up a distant and powerful government that threatened the American republics (the individual states) and would lead to the loss of rights.

To bolster this argument, Anti-Federalists decried the failure to include a Bill of Rights—something which most state constitutions contained. This fourth part of the Anti-Federalist argument was the most potent. Although the Federalists argued that a guarantee of rights was unnecessary, ultimately they had to give in and promised to pass the Bill of Rights if the Constitution was ratified. The Anti-Federalists believed that it was crucial that the fundamental law of the nation stipulate the specific rights to be protected by the government, including freedom of speech, assembly, and religion, as well as assurances of fair judicial procedure. They also pushed for limitations on the extent of the national government and a check on the necessary and proper clause—a provision offered by the Tenth Amendment which guaranteed that "the powers not delegated to the United States by the Constitution, not prohibited by it to the States, are reserved to the States respectively, or to the people."

The Federalists and Anti-Federalists had two different visions of society and government. The Federalists, as the Anti-Federalists charged, had a hierarchical view and believed in a natural aristocracy comprising "the purest and noblest characters" who would be above faction and personal interest. The Anti-Federalists saw things differently. The rich and powerful would always be ambitious and would use government to protect their property rather than the public good. Instead of seeing the natural aristocracy as the repositories of virtue, the Anti-Federalists, as MELANCTON SMITH explained, held that "the substantial yeomanry of the country [common farmers] are more temperate, of better morals and less ambition than the great." Smith called for a government that would include both the rich, whose ambition, if properly checked, could be useful to the republic; and the middling sort, who would be "friendly to liberty and the rights of mankind, which will tend to cherish and cultivate a love of liberty among our citizens."

The ultimate goal of the Anti-Federalists was always the preservation of the republic through the maintenance of state sovereignty and limitations on federal power. Like the Federalists, the Anti-Federalists published pamphlets, the most popular of which was *Letters of a Federal Farmer.* In these publications they articulated their vision of government, attacked the Constitution, and listed the rights that Anti-Federalists felt should be protected. Many Anti-Federalists would eventually become members of the DEMOCRATIC-REPUBLICAN PARTY.

See also STATES' RIGHTS.

Further reading: Saul Cornell, *The Other Founders: Anti-Federalism and the Dissenting Tradition in America, 1788–1828* (Chapel Hill: University of North Carolina Press, 1999); Jackson Turner Main, *The Antifederalists: Critics of the Constitution, 1781–1788* (Chapel Hill: University of North Carolina Press, 1961); Robert Allen Rutland, *The Ordeal of the Constitution: The Antifederalists and the Ratification Struggle of 1787–1788* (Norman: University of Oklahoma Press, 1966); Gordon S. Wood, *The Creation of the American Republic, 1776–1787* (Chapel Hill: University of North Carolina Press, 1969).

antislavery

The antislavery movement became increasingly important during the REVOLUTIONARY WAR (1775–83) and the years of the early republic. THOMAS JEFFERSON represented a moderate stand: He believed that SLAVERY violated religious doctrine and natural law, but it remained perhaps too sensitive an issue (and too economically vital to slave owners) to eradicate altogether. Some Americans, however, began to advocate a means to end slavery, even if it was only piecemeal. Many enslaved AFRICAN AMERICANS seized opportunities to obtain their freedom and advocated ending slavery as quickly as possible.

QUAKERS, led by John Woolman and ANTHONY BENE-ZET, established the first formal antislavery movement in North America during the 1750s. The Society of Friends in Pennsylvania and New Jersey considered slavery a violation of religious principles and therefore created an internal policy: Slaveholders must release their bondsmen or leave the society. Quakers subsequently became leading voices against bondage during the revolutionary era. They also set a precedent for other religious groups. Although every religious sect sanctioned slavery prior to 1770, the METHODISTS, BAPTISTS, and ANGLICANS all began debating their slaveholding practices by the 1780s. In Virginia and Maryland, which contained large slave populations, conscience-stricken masters began manumitting slaves in greater numbers than ever. In 1792 Virginia altered its emancipation policy to accommodate this trend: Masters no longer needed to petition the general assembly to liberate the enslaved. However, neither Methodists nor Baptists in the South adopted Quaker-style prohibitions on slaveholding.

Northern Quakers and their allies established the world's first ABOLITION societies: The Pennsylvania Abolition Society began in 1775, the New York Manumission Society in 1784. These groups petitioned governments to adopt gradual abolition laws, which would slowly end slavery in the United States. Pennsylvania adopted the first gradual-emancipation act in 1780; between 1780 and 1801, several northern states would adopt similar laws. In addition, Vermont banned slavery in its 1777 constitution, and Massachusetts and New Hampshire ended slavery by a judicial decree in the 1780s.

The ideals of the AMERICAN REVOLUTION further encouraged antislavery. As colonists began to protest what they perceived to be Britain's political and economic oppression, they found slavery to be an apt metaphor for their servile condition. Colonial activists began arguing that freedom was the end of just society and all civil governments. In making such arguments about political slavery and human rights, the Revolutionaries prompted widespread consideration of antislavery itself. During the 1760s and 1770s, pamphlets, newspaper essays, and speeches criticized the SLAVE TRADE as inhumane and slavery as unjust. JAMES OTIS questioned slavery in his *Rights of the British Colonies* (1764) by declaring: "Colonists are by the law of nature free born, as indeed all men are, white or black." He wondered, "Can any logical inference in favour of slavery be drawn from a flat nose, a long or short face?" In 1773 BENJAMIN RUSH called slavery "a national crime" that would lead to "a national punishment." THOMAS PAINE, who had just arrived in North America in 1775, began his revolutionary career with an attack on slavery. Southerners including Thomas Jefferson, JAMES MADISON, and GEORGE MASON not only expressed guilt at owning slaves but believed that slavery would gradually disappear once the United States ended the slave trade. Believing slavery an evil, GEORGE WASHINGTON created provisions for the future emancipation of his slaves.

In the new United States, debate persisted over antislavery's place in a country dedicated to freedom. LUTHER MARTIN, who was attorney general of Maryland, believed "that *slavery* is *inconsistent* with the *genius* of *republicanism* and has a tendency to *destroy* those *principles* on which it is *supported,* as it *lessens the sense* of the *equal rights* of *mankind,* and habituates us to *tyranny* and *oppression.*" In 1784 the SECOND CONTINENTAL CONGRESS considered, but did not adopt, an ordinance prohibiting slavery's expansion into future southwestern territories. In 1787 the Second Continental Congress passed a NORTHWEST ORDINANCE prohibiting bondage from being established north of the Ohio River. That same year, delegates to the CONSTITUTIONAL CONVENTION, meeting in Philadelphia to revise the ARTICLES OF CONFEDERATION, debated several clauses relating to slavery and antislavery measures. Ultimately, the convention supported slavery by establishing the THREE-FIFTHS CLAUSE (counting three-fifths of the enslaved population to determine REPRESENTATION in federal elections), guaranteeing of the return of fugitive slaves, and delaying congressional consideration of termination of the overseas slave trade until 1808. (Each state, at least for a while, enacted state statutes to end the slave trade before that date.)

First-generation abolitionists tried to keep antislavery momentum going during the early republic. Hoping to end slavery gradually at the state level, to stop the overseas slave trade at the federal level, and to encourage political leaders to debate emancipation as a national goal, early abolitionists were led by groups in Pennsylvania and New York (although abolition societies appeared in most northern states before 1800 and, for very brief periods, in Maryland and Virginia). These early reformers petitioned Congress on antislavery issues several times between 1790 and 1815, but they never pushed for immediate emancipation nationally. Their most radical proposal was to abolish the slave trade, and perhaps even slavery itself, in the federally controlled District of Columbia. Early abolitionists in Pennsylvania and New York also distinguished themselves by representing kidnapped blacks and occasionally fugitive slaves in courts of law, and they helped liberate hundreds of slaves in negotiations with masters. But the effect was piecemeal; bondage persisted. According to the first federal census of 1790, 700,000 slaves lived in the United States, versus only 63,000 free blacks. Although the number of free blacks grew to 250,000 by 1830, the number of slaves nearly tripled to 2 million. In short, after successes during the revolutionary era, when masters liberated slaves in relatively large numbers and every northern state began the process of abolition, antislavery efforts were stalled by the early 1800s.

Perhaps the most consistent antislavery advocates were free African Americans. The growth of this group came from several sources. During the Revolutionary War, many slaves had taken advantage of bounties, been given offers of freedom from both sides in the conflict, or simply ran away. Manumissions in the North and South freed many others during the war and in the years after the peace, and legal efforts to abolish slavery in the North all but ended the institution in that region by 1830. Although free African Americans were not formally permitted to join early abolitionist organizations, they served as important community contacts and teachers for white reform groups such as the Pennsylvania Abolition Society. Increasingly angered by white abolitionists' racism, however, African-American reformers created a parallel antislavery movement during the early republic. Coming primarily from northern urban centers, a generation of black activists publicized their antislavery views beginning in 1780s and 1790s: RICHARD ALLEN and JAMES FORTEN of Philadelphia, PRINCE HALL of Boston, and PETER WILLIAMS, JR., and William Hamilton of New York City. These men created independent institutions dedicated to community uplift and racial justice. From the pulpit and lectern, black leaders denounced the slave trade, domestic slavery, and racism in areas where gradual abolition laws had already taken effect. Many of these speeches were published as protest pamphlets, and they were a critical part of early efforts to influence the general public to accept African Americans as equal and to establish antislavery policies at both the state and federal levels.

The many pamphlets and speeches prepared by black activists during the early republic formed a distinct brand of antislavery, one that diverged from the conservative, legalistic tactics of early white abolition groups and would become a seminal influence on radical abolitionists emerging after 1830 (such as William Lloyd Garrison). Richard Allen and ABSALOM JONES published the first copyrighted African-American pamphlet in 1794, *A Narrative of the Colored People during the Late Yellow Fever Epidemic.* The pamphlet took Philadelphia's leaders to task for accusing black relief workers of pillaging homes during the city's YELLOW FEVER epidemic of 1793. Allen and Jones noted that black citizens aided white Philadelphians in disproportionate numbers and deserved only commendations. They went on to address the underlying issue: the continuance of slavery. This institution, they claimed, mocked egalitarian creeds and religious principles. Equally important, it denied African Americans the full measure of justice and left them open to the most flagrant abuses imaginable. Remove the stain of slavery, Allen and Jones argued, and African Americans would become valuable citizens in their own right. Before the slave-narrative tradition became a central part of abolitionist activism in the antebellum era, pamphlets such as those published by Allen and Jones were an important means of transmitting African-American antislavery ideas.

See also QUOK WALKER CASE; RACE AND RACIAL CONFLICT.

Further reading: Ira Berlin, *Many Thousands Gone: The First Two Centuries of Slavery in North America* (Cambridge, Mass.: Harvard University Press, 1998); David Brion Davis, *The Problem of Slavery in the Age of Revolution, 1770–1823* (Ithaca, N.Y.: Cornell University Press, 1975); Gary B. Nash, *The Forgotten Fifth: African Americans in the Age of Revolution* (Cambridge, Mass.: Harvard University Press, 2006).

—Richard Newman

Arbuthnot, Marriot (1711–1794) *British admiral*
A British naval officer who had seen combat in several wars, Marriot Arbuthnot became the commander of the North American squadron from 1778 to 1781 during the REVOLUTIONARY WAR (1775–83). At the beginning of the war, Arbuthnot was stationed at Halifax and briefly served as lieutenant governor of NOVA SCOTIA. In January 1778

Royal Navy admiral Marriot Arbuthnot *(National Maritime Museum, Greenwich, London)*

he was promoted to rear admiral, and he took charge of the British ships in North America eight months later. Arbuthnot faced a difficult situation since FRANCE had just entered the war as an ally of the United States and soon sent a fleet to North America; furthermore, he was in his late sixties and lacked initiative.

Arbuthnot cooperated with General HENRY CLINTON in his southern campaign and played an important role in the SIEGE OF CHARLESTON (surrendered May 12, 1780). Thereafter, he ran into difficulties with other British commanders, including Clinton and Admiral GEORGE BRIDGES RODNEY. For most of the rest of 1780, he kept much of his fleet blockading the French at Rhode Island and did not press for any greater action. On March 16, 1781, he fought an indecisive battle with a French fleet off the Virginia capes. Three of his ships were dismasted, but he was able to retreat into the Chesapeake Bay, and the French withdrew to Rhode Island, thus keeping open the supply lines for the British army in Virginia. Arbuthnot retired from active service in April 1781 and returned to GREAT BRITAIN for the remainder of his life. He died in London on January 31, 1794.

architecture

The diverse traditions of architecture in the United States underwent dramatic changes during the late 18th and early 19th centuries. Population grew, cities expanded, and new ideas about public and private life gained currency. During this period architectural fashions shifted, housing standards improved substantially for some people, public buildings diversified and proliferated, and a new type of building designer—the professional architect—gained prominence.

The most readily discernible change in Anglo-American architecture during the period 1754–1815 is that of architectural style. The mid-18th century saw the growing popularity of "Georgian" architecture. First introduced into the North American colonies about 1700 and embraced by the very wealthy, the Georgian style represented the extension of ideas spreading in Europe since the Renaissance. Georgian houses were characterized by a new attention to bilateral symmetry: two windows on either side of an entrance and five windows across the second floor. These houses typically extended two rooms deep with a central hallway; kitchen and work areas were placed in a rear wing. The central hallway, which allowed people to move through the house without intruding into individual rooms, increased personal privacy while also separating work spaces from those for entertainment. The Georgian style of architecture also showcased decorative details borrowed from architectural publications of the period known as "patternbooks." Most popular was the practice of accentuating entrances

with classical ornaments such as pilasters (flat columns applied to a building's surface) or pediments (triangular decorative elements of applied molding). Windows, too, were often topped with pediments and contained many panes of glass in upper- and lower-window sashes. In New England, a good example of Georgian domestic architecture is the Vassal-Craigie-Longfellow house in Cambridge, Massachusetts (1759). Mount Airy in Richmond County, Virginia (1754–64) and the Corbitt-Sharp house, in Odessa, Delaware (1771–72) are also typical examples.

In the decades following the REVOLUTIONARY WAR (1775–83), and lasting well into the 19th century, the Georgian style was replaced by a variant of classical architecture known as "neoclassical" or "Federal." This style of architecture used a refined classical vocabulary that emphasized thinness, verticality, and delicacy. Particularly popular in East Coast seaport towns such as Salem, Massachusetts; Newport, Rhode Island; Annapolis, Maryland; and Charleston, South Carolina, neoclassical buildings retained the Georgian style's emphasis on symmetry but more often rose a full three stories in height with few horizontal breaks in the front facade. Windows of neoclassical houses sported larger and fewer panes of glass, while doorways surrounded by sidelights and fanlights further emphasized the lightness and transparency of the buildings. Surviving examples of neoclassical style buildings include the HARRISON GRAY OTIS House in Boston (1805); the Octagon in WASHINGTON, D.C. (1799–1801); and the Nathaniel Russell House in Charleston, South Carolina (1809).

The changes taking place in domestic architecture from 1754 to 1815 are evident not only in changing architectural fashion but also in the increasing numbers and improving quality of houses for the "middling sort"—primarily yeoman farmers, craftspeople, and prosperous tradespeople. Prior to the mid-18th century, an affluent minority, both rural and urban, lived in substantial houses with a high degree of architectural finish, but the majority of people lived in one- or two-room houses, often with dirt floors, unglazed windows, and wooden chimneys. In the late 18th century and early 19th century, many rural European Americans continued to be housed in flimsy one- or two-room wooden buildings that often measured about 18 by 20 feet. Urban dwellers increasingly resided in multifamily dwellings with only thin partitions dividing one apartment from the next. The very poor, including enslaved AFRICAN AMERICANS, ordinarily lived in spaces used for other purposes, such as garrets or agricultural buildings. Following the Revolutionary War, however, there was a "housing revolution" when domestic structures for the middling sort improved noticeably. Many more people lived in substantial, finely finished houses that adopted some elements of "gentility" or "refinement"—work spaces separated from entertainment spaces by new circulation patterns and increased atten-

This classic Georgian home was built about 1773 in Delaware. *(National Images of North American Living Research and Archival Center, Washington)*

tion to interior finishes, including wooden floors, plastered walls, and paint. In rural New England this late-18th-century "rebuilding" was manifest in large numbers of two-story houses, one-room deep with interior chimneys, and two-story, side-hall houses with two rooms front-to-back. South of New York, the typical house was two-story, with a central passage flanked by single rooms. In German-speaking areas of western Maryland and the Shenandoah Valley, wealthy farmers slowly began to move away from the traditional Germanic three-room asymmetrical house to adopt these fashionable Anglo-American forms.

The "housing revolution" of the postrevolutionary period and the influence of architectural fashion, however, did not directly affect many of the diverse people living in North America. For NATIVE AMERICANS, this was a time of struggle to maintain their traditional livelihoods in the face of war and brutal resettlements. Architectural historians studying Native American building traditions have primarily concentrated on the period of first contact between Europeans and Native Americans, and they have not fully explored the subsequent periods when Native American communities had been profoundly affected by centuries of European colonization. For most Native Americans, housing and sacred architecture constructed during this period reflected the fundamental shift from a migratory to a sedentary way of life and the adaptation of European building forms to traditional lifestyles. Often, however, Native Americans differed among themselves about appropriate housing forms. For instance, prior to their forced relocation, some members of CREEK, CHEROKEE, CHOCTAW, and CHICKASAW communities tried to "Americanize" by building southern-style plantation houses, while others continued living in structures organized around traditional "square grounds" or ceremonial courtyards.

Similarly, the inhabitants of the Spanish Southwest did not experience a "housing revolution" comparable to that of the British colonies. Spanish settlements in FLORIDA, Texas, Arizona, New Mexico, and CALIFORNIA were all outposts of a much larger, southward colonization effort and therefore did not attract the population of their British counterparts. Settlement followed the objectives laid out for town planning in *Law of the Indies,* SPAIN's regulations for colonization in the New World, which specified that new towns be centered on a plaza and bordered by government buildings, churches, and markets, all surrounded by a grid of streets. This intricate city planning was largely unnecessary for Spain's small FRONTIER communities, but towns were laid out as defensive plazas. Chimayo, in northern New Mexico, begun in the mid-17th century, is the best surviving example of a walled town. Most of the buildings constructed by the Spanish in the Southwest were made of adobe bricks or stone, blending Spanish and Native American building traditions. The Spanish goal of converting Native Americans to Catholicism was expressed in the construction of mission churches that ranged from elaborate Spanish baroque structures such as San Xavier del Bac in Tucson, Arizona (1795), to simple pueblo mission churches such as St. Francis of Assisi, Ranchos de Taos, New Mexico (1805–15).

In addition to changing architectural style and some advancement in housing standards, the 1754–1815 period was marked by a proliferation of public buildings that had begun just prior to the Revolutionary War. In New England towns the primary public space during the 17th and early 18th centuries had been the meetinghouse or, in urban seaports, the townhouse. Both of these structures served a wide variety of public functions. Similarly, in the mid-Atlantic region and the South, churches, courthouses, and some market houses accommodated all of a community's public activities. Beginning in the mid-18th century and accelerating through the 19th, civic functions began to split off from these multipurpose buildings, and many towns, small and large, started to support an array of purpose-built public structures: courthouses, market halls, town halls, customs houses, and BANKS. After the Revolutionary War, most of the new states also immediately began construction of buildings to house state governments. Surviving examples of these new state capitols include the Virginia State Capitol, Richmond (1785–89), and the Massachusetts State House, Boston (1795–97).

The most significant public structure was the U.S. Capitol in Washington, D.C. Throughout the 19th century, the Capitol underwent a number of design changes, including the addition of its well-known dome at mid-century, but the core structure was completed by 1828. No fewer than six architects were involved in the Capitol's early design and construction. Particularly influential was the collaboration between President THOMAS JEFFERSON and the architect Benjamin Henry Latrobe, hired by Jefferson in 1803. Jefferson and Latrobe worked closely together to create a neoclassical building with unmistakable symbols of the new nation. Latrobe achieved this synthesis most famously in his design of interior columns capped with indigenous North American plants such as corn and TOBACCO. In 1814 British troops burned the Capitol, leaving just the walls standing. Latrobe was hired to rebuild it in 1815 but resigned in 1817, and President JAMES MONROE hired Bostonian architect CHARLES BULFINCH to complete the structure.

The proliferation of public buildings and their increasing complexity of design highlight the prominence achieved by architects as professional designers during this period. The building process in the 17th and 18th centuries had been dominated by trained craftsmen, both European-American and African-American. In most cases, a master builder or "undertaker" would contract with a client to build a structure for a specific price. The design was normally spelled out in a building contract, with details to be worked out in consultation with the client during construction. In the late 18th century, however, some designers began to assume a new role in the building process. Referring to themselves as "architects" rather than builders, these designers looked to secure control over the entire construction project and began to view their work as a form of art rather than a craft. Architects such as Latrobe, Alexander Parris, Robert Mills, and William Strickland marketed their design services to clients by arguing that they alone had the education and expertise to create fashionable buildings.

The early 19th century brought a new type of architecture to the North American landscape: factory buildings to house the New England textile industry. New England's abundant water power, shipping facilities, and merchant capital made it the most attractive region for mechanized textile production, which began in 1793 with the construction of the Slater Mill in Pawtucket, Rhode Island. The new textile factory had to respond to distinct requirements: housing large pieces of machinery, accommodating the power-transmission system (consisting of waterwheels, belts, pulleys, gears, and shafts), providing adequate natural light, and allowing for open interior spaces. Early mill builders resolved these problems by designing wood-frame, two- to three-story buildings with monitor roofs that admitted light through an extra band of windows set into the roof. Belfries added symbolic importance to mill buildings in addition to providing factory owners with a means of calling workers to the mill. Following the expansion of New England textile production as a result of the EMBARGO OF 1807 and the WAR OF 1812 (1812–15), factory owners built larger buildings—60 feet in length, three to five stories high, made of brick or stone, and incorporating exterior stair towers. These mills, built in Slatersville, Rhode Island (1806–07 and later), and Waltham, Massachusetts (1816), provided the prototype for mill buildings constructed in places such as Lowell, Massachusetts, during the second quarter of the 19th century.

See also CITIES AND URBAN LIFE; INDUSTRIAL REVOLUTION; RURAL LIFE.

Further reading: Edward A. Chappell, "Housing a Nation: The Transformation of Living Standards in Early America," in Cary Carson, Ronald Hoffman and Peter J. Albert, eds., *Of Consuming Interests: The Style of Life in the Eighteenth Century* (Charlottesville: University of Virginia Press, 1994); Lois Craig, *The Federal Presence: Architecture, Politics, and Symbols in United States Government Building* (Cambridge, Mass.: MIT Press, 1976); Dora P. Crouch, Daniel J. Garr, and Axel I. Mundigo, *Spanish City Planning in North America* (Cambridge, Mass.: MIT Press, 1982); Gabrielle M. Lanier and Bernard L. Herman, *Everyday Architecture of the Mid-Atlantic: Looking at Buildings and Landscapes* (Baltimore: The Johns Hopkins University Press, 1997); Peter Nabokov, *Native American Architecture* (New York: Oxford University Press, 1989); William H. Pierson, *American Builders and their Architects, Vol. 1: The Colonial and Neoclassical Styles* (Garden City, N.Y.: Doubleday, 1970); Boyd C. Pratt and Chris Wilson, *The Architecture and Cultural Landscape of North Central New Mexico* (Newport, R.I., 1991); Leland Roth, *A Concise History of American Architecture* (New York: Harper Collins Publishers, 1979).

—Martha J. McNamara

Armand, Charles　See ROUËRIE, CHARLES-ARMAND TUFFIN, MARQUIS DE LA.

Armstrong, John (1717–1795) *colonial militia officer*
Born in Ireland, John Armstrong came from obscure origins, received some EDUCATION, emigrated to North America sometime in the 1740s, and became a surveyor of FRONTIER lands for the Penn family in Pennsylvania. Because of this connection to the Penns, Armstrong emerged as a major landowner and colonial official by the mid-1750s, even serving as a judge in Cumberland County and sitting in the colonial legislature. At the outbreak of the FRENCH AND INDIAN WAR (1754–63), Armstrong accompanied General EDWARD BRADDOCK on his ill-fated expedition to western Pennsylvania. After Braddock's defeat, Armstrong convinced the Pennsylvania legislature to build a series of forts to protect the frontier and, as commander of the Pennsylvania forces west of the Susquehanna, launched a successful attack on the DELAWARE INDIANS' village of Kittitanning in 1756. Armstrong also participated in General JOHN FORBES's campaign to capture Fort Duquesne, and he led Pennsylvania troops in PONTIAC'S WAR (1763–65).

During the 1760s, Armstrong's relationship with the Penns soured, and by 1770 he was no longer in their employ as a surveyor. He remained influential in western Pennsylvania and supported resistance to imperial measures, became a member of the local COMMITTEE OF CORRESPONDENCE in 1774, and led the county MILITIA at the beginning of the REVOLUTIONARY WAR (1775–83). Appointed a brigadier general in the CONTINENTAL ARMY, Armstrong left national service in April 1777 when others were promoted to major general before him. However, he became a brigadier general and later a major general in the Pennsylvania militia and fought without much distinction at the BATTLE OF BRANDYWINE (September 11, 1777) and the BATTLE OF GERMANTOWN (October 4, 1777).

Armstrong was a member of the SECOND CONTINENTAL CONGRESS from February 1779 to August 1780. He remained active in state and local politics. Although something of a radical during the Revolutionary War, encouraging PRICE CONTROLS and harsh treatment of LOYALISTS, he moderated his positions after the war, supported revisions to the democratic Pennsylvania state constitution, and backed ratification of the U.S. CONSTITUTION. He died on March 9, 1795. His son JOHN ARMSTRONG became secretary of war during the WAR OF 1812 (1812–15).

Armstrong, John (1758–1843) *secretary of war*
The son of the MILITIA commander JOHN ARMSTRONG. John Armstrong was secretary of war during the WAR OF 1812 (1812–15). Born in Carlisle, Pennsylvania, Armstrong left Princeton in 1775 to join the CONTINENTAL ARMY and served on the staffs of Generals HORATIO GATES and JOHN FRANCIS MERCER. In March 1783 he was involved in the NEWBURGH CONSPIRACY and, at Gates's suggestion, authored letters that circulated among officers, urging them to meet to discuss their grievances. The episode left Armstrong with a reputation as something of a troublemaker.

After the REVOLUTIONARY WAR (1775–83), Armstrong moved back to Pennsylvania, where he became involved in local politics. In 1789 he married into the wealthy and well-connected Livingston family of New York. He moved to New York, and since the Livingston family supported THOMAS JEFFERSON and Armstrong believed that the FEDERALIST PARTY had not fully recognized his merits, he joined the DEMOCRATIC-REPUBLICAN PARTY. This shift in allegiances paid off when he was chosen to represent New York in the U.S. Senate in 1800.

In 1804 Armstrong resigned from the Senate and became minister to FRANCE. He accomplished little in this role, from 1804 to 1810, as NAPOLEON BONAPARTE dominated continental Europe and had little respect for the United States or its minister. These were years when the United States found itself pressed by GREAT BRITAIN and France as they sought to use TRADE measures against each other. On August 5, 1810, Armstrong received the CADORE LETTER, which implied that France would lift restrictions on American trade, as a result of which he resigned, believing he was ending his ministry on a positive note. Unfortunately, Napoleon had no intention of honoring the letter, and U.S. reaction to it, which was to reinstitute a trade ban on Great Britain, eventually led to the outbreak of the War of 1812.

At the beginning of that conflict, Armstrong was appointed a general and placed in command of the defense of New York City. In January 1813 President JAMES MADISON nominated Armstrong as secretary of war in a political move to placate northern jealousy and garner support for the war. Armstrong instituted a number of important reforms and reorganized the officer corps, but he often clashed with the president over the appointment of generals and the direction of the war effort. He was the scapegoat in 1814 for the failure to defend WASHINGTON, D.C., and resigned from office on September 13, 1814. He then retired to Red Hook, New York, where he spent the remainder of his days, dying on April 1, 1843.

Further reading: Carl E. Skeen, *John Armstrong, Jr., 1758–1843: A Biography* (Syracuse, N.Y.: Syracuse University Press, 1981); J. C. A. Stagg, *Mr. Madison's War: Politics, Diplomacy, and Warfare in the Early American Republic, 1783–1830* (Princeton, N.J.: Princeton University Press, 1983).

—Charles D. Russell

Army, U.S.

The U.S. Army traces its founding to June 14, 1775, when the SECOND CONTINENTAL CONGRESS took responsibility for the troops surrounding Boston and created the CONTINENTAL ARMY. After the British evacuated New York City in 1783, and with most of the Continental army demobilized, General GEORGE WASHINGTON stationed one infantry regiment and one battalion of artillery, totaling 600 men, to protect the military stores at WEST POINT. In summer 1784 Congress released most of these men and authorized the recruitment of a small 700-man regular army under Lieutenant Colonel JOSIAH HARMAR. Despite general opposition to the idea of a standing army, Congress had decided to retain a small national military force to be stationed on the FRONTIER to deal with threats from NATIVE AMERICANS. When the British did not evacuate their forts on U.S. territory, Congress dispatched this small army to Fort Stanwix in New York and Fort McIntosh in Pennsylvania, 30 miles downriver from FORT PITT. By 1785 most of the army had been stationed in a series of forts along the Ohio River. In response to SHAYS'S REBELLION (1786–87), Congress authorized the recruitment of 1,340 men for three years. But after the Massachusetts state MILITIA quelled the rebellion, Congress suspended this effort, dismissed most

of the men already enlisted, and retained two companies stationed at West Point.

The U.S. CONSTITUTION did not immediately alter the situation for the small army, although it shifted responsibility for the military from Congress to the president. Under the command of Harmar, who had been promoted to brigadier general, the army numbered about 800 men. At the urging of President GEORGE WASHINGTON, Congress raised the army's strength to 1,283 men. This force, however, remained inadequate to the task of defending the frontier. Confronted with a multitribal confederation north of the Ohio River, the United States launched two disastrous expeditions, and Indians annihilated a combined army and militia force under Harmar in 1790. Congress authorized the recruitment of more men under ARTHUR ST. CLAIR, but they were routed a year later.

Confronted with these defeats, Congress reacted in 1792 by creating the Legion of the United States, with 5,000 men in the regular army placed under the command of General ANTHONY WAYNE. The legion, a disciplined military force divided into four sub-legions with 1,200 men and combined infantry, cavalry, and artillery all under one command, defeated the Ohio Indians at the BATTLE OF FALLEN TIMBERS on August 20, 1794.

After this victory, however, the political struggle between the FEDERALIST PARTY, which wanted to maintain a larger army, and the DEMOCRATIC-REPUBLICAN PARTY, which accepted the need for a frontier force but wanted to limit its size, led to a series of changes within the army. In 1795 Congress passed legislation to sustain the legion concept, only to replace it by an act in 1796 that reorganized the army into small, almost skeletal units that would occupy isolated outposts along the frontier. The QUASI-WAR (1798–1800) provided an opportunity for the Federalist Party to expand the army. Faced with concerns over a potential French invasion and possible internal rebellion, in 1798 Congress authorized a 12,000-man regular army, ostensibly under Washington. But the old general was reluctant to take the field and, much to the chagrin of President JOHN ADAMS, left the actual command of the army to ALEXANDER HAMILTON. Despite Hamilton's efforts, the army never became an effective force and barely recruited 6.000 men before the crisis with France subsided, and the new army all but disbanded in May 1800.

The ELECTION OF 1800 and the presidency of THOMAS JEFFERSON had an important impact on the army. Jefferson wanted to have a minimal government, although he also accepted that some army units were needed for the frontier. He left the army officially at 5,438 men (although its actual size was closer to 4,000) until March 1802, when the cavalry was eliminated and the army reduced to 3,220 men. Jefferson also pushed for the creation of a military academy at West Point. The army in the 1790s had been highly politicized, and many officer appointments reflected personal connections rather than professional training. Jefferson wanted West Point to be an institution open to the sons of all citizens, an academy that would develop an officer corps based on talent and ability. Despite Jefferson's desire for small government, he requested a 20,000-man voluntary army in the wake of the CHESAPEAKE-LEOPARD AFFAIR (June 22, 1807) and the EMBARGO OF 1807. However, Congress would not approve this expansion and agreed to augment the army by only 2,000 men. Many of these new troops were sent to New Orleans, where, thanks to the incompetence of General JAMES WILKINSON as well as the unhealthy climate, about 1,000 died. The army's condition continued to deteriorate, and by 1810 Congressman NATHANIEL MACON believed that the army had become such an embarrassment that it was "enough to make any man who has the smallest love of country wish to get rid of it."

In 1811 and the first half of 1812, with a deepening international crisis leading up to the WAR OF 1812 (1812–15), Congress gradually expanded the army. Initially it was supposed to grow to 10,000 men, but enlistments only filled half of that number. Then, as war seemed to be more likely, Congress increased enlistment bonuses to complete the recruiting, called for the raising of another 25,000 men for the army, and authorized President JAMES MADISON to enlist 50,000 volunteers and call up 100,000 militia if needed. These measures were inadequate. At the beginning of the war, the army had only about 12,000 men. Despite Jefferson's earlier hopes for West Point, the army's senior officers were mainly political appointees. The army was poorly paid and fed, and it was rife with desertions. Its performance during the war reflected these conditions, beginning with the precipitous surrender of General WILLIAM HULL at DETROIT and the failure to launch sustained and successful invasions of CANADA. The only thing worse than the regular army's performance during the war was the MILITIA's action—or lack of action. However, as time went on, a number of competent army officers emerged, and several units demonstrated increasing professionalism. By early 1815 there were 45,000 men in the U.S. Army.

Further reading: Donald R. Hickey, *The War of 1812: A Forgotten Conflict* (Urbana: University of Illinois Press, 1989); Richard H. Kohn, *Eagle and Sword: The Beginnings of the Military Establishment in America* (New York: Free Press, 1975).

Arnold, Benedict (1741–1801) *Continental military officer, spy*

A man who served brilliantly, if contentiously, as an officer in the CONTINENTAL ARMY during the REVOLUTIONARY WAR (1775–83), Benedict Arnold is best known for betraying the revolutionary cause and joining the British in September 1780. Born on January 14, 1741, to a respectable but not affluent family in Norwich, Connecticut, Arnold apprenticed as a druggist. As a young man he moved to New Haven, Connecticut, set up his own shop; and married Margaret Mansfield, the daughter of a prominent Connecticut official. Arnold expanded his business and became a colonial merchant of some property and standing by the eve of the AMERICAN REVOLUTION. He was an ardent supporter of the resistance to British imperial measures.

When news of the BATTLES OF LEXINGTON AND CONCORD (April 19, 1775) arrived, Arnold, a captain in the MILITIA, volunteered to lead his company to Boston. Once he joined the forces surrounding the British in Boston, Arnold suggested that an attack on FORT TICONDEROGA at Lake Champlain would put much-needed gunpowder and artillery in the hands of the new Continental army, and he headed west with his Connecticut troops. Upon hearing of ETHAN ALLEN's plan to accomplish the same end, he rushed ahead of his men and joined Allen shortly before the attack that brought the poorly defended British outpost into Continental hands. Both Allen and Arnold shared the credit for this victory on May 10, 1775. Arnold then led his own troops on a successful raid to the other side of Lake Champlain at St. John's, CANADA. Returning to Ticonderoga, he quickly became involved in a series of disputes over responsibilities and his expenditures. At the same time, he heard the news of his wife's death on June 19, 1775.

In September 1775 Arnold was made a colonel in the Continental army, given command of 1,000 men, and ordered to invade Canada through the Maine wilderness. During this campaign his leadership and endurance skills came to the fore as he led his men on a nearly impossible expedition. They started on September 19, 1775, and arrived outside Quebec on November 8. By that time a quarter of the men had turned back and the rest were tired, hungry, and sick. In December Arnold was reenforced by troops under General RICHARD MONTGOMERY, who had captured MONTREAL. Together the two men led an ill-fated attack on Quebec during a snowstorm on December 31, 1775. Montgomery was killed in the action, and Arnold severely wounded.

Congress appointed Arnold a brigadier general in January 1776, and he maintained the siege of Quebec after the defeat, until the spring thaw brought British reinforcements, upon which he retreated to Lake Champlain. That summer he entered into a dispute over supplies captured in Canada that were lost or stolen during the retreat. During the fall he organized a small fleet on Lake Champlain to defend against a planned British invasion. On Octo-

Continental army general and British spy Benedict Arnold
(Anne S. K. Brown Military Collection, Brown University Library)

ber 11, 1776, Arnold's fleet met a hastily assembled and larger British force at the BATTLE OF VALCOUR ISLAND. Although the British were ultimately successful in the battle, with Arnold scuttling that part of his fleet that was not destroyed in the fighting, the effort had stalled the British army and compelled the 12,000-man force to return to Canada.

During the winter of 1776–77, Arnold once again became embroiled in controversy when the SECOND CONTINENTAL CONGRESS promoted five junior officers to major general over him. Both GEORGE WASHINGTON, who favored Arnold, and Arnold himself objected. Members of Congress relented and finally promoted Arnold in May 1777, although they did not restore his seniority. Arnold was ready to resign when Washington asked him to join General HORATIO GATES in the defense of New York against the invading British from Canada. Arnold then led a successful column to relieve the SIEGE OF FORT STANWIX (August 2–23, 1777), which was under attack from a combined British and Indian force invading from the Great Lakes. Although Arnold squabbled

with Gates in the fall and did not have direct command, he played an instrumental role at the Battle of Bemis Heights, which led to General JOHN BURGOYNE's surrender at SARATOGA on October 17, 1777. Unfortunately, Arnold was so seriously wounded that it became difficult for him to resume a field command. Washington made him military commandant of Philadelphia after the British evacuated the city the following spring. There, Arnold met and married his second wife, MARGARET (PEGGY) SHIPPEN ARNOLD. In Philadelphia, too, he spent extravagantly, ran into debt, and argued with other officers and local officials.

Sometime in May 1779 Arnold opened communications with the British and supplied information to Major JOHN ANDRÉ, a member of General HENRY CLINTON's staff. His motivation for this treachery is not clear. Perhaps he had become convinced of the hopelessness of the revolutionary cause and believed that he could lead the way to a reconciliation. Had he succeeded he might well have been considered a hero. Perhaps it was the MONEY he had spent in his high life in Philadelphia. Perhaps, too, he was persuaded by the Loyalist sympathies of his wife and her family (see LOYALISTS). Or he may have simply tired of the slights he had suffered and the contentiousness of the Continental army officer corps. Whatever his reasons, by summer 1780 he was ready for a dramatic gesture to change sides. At Arnold's request, Washington gave him the command of WEST POINT. If the British captured this fortress, they could control the Hudson and cut off New England from the rest of the new nation. Before Arnold could turn West Point over to the British, however, Major André (Arnold's main contact with the British) was captured. Upon hearing the news of André's capture, and having met with him a few days before and knowing that his own treachery would certainly soon be found out, Arnold fled to the British lines. His wife, who had probably played an important role in the betrayal scheme, feigned surprise at this action. She returned to Philadelphia but was later allowed to join her husband in New York.

Although Arnold failed to deliver West Point, he issued an appeal to others to join him in switching sides. He also became a British officer and engaged in two notorious raids that only further sullied his reputation in the United States. In December 1780 Clinton sent Arnold to Virginia, where he captured Richmond and destroyed supplies intended for the Continental army. He remained in Virginia until June 1781. His second raid took place in September 1781, only a few miles from where he had grown up in his home state, Connecticut. He burned New London, and troops under his command massacred the defenders of Fort Griswold.

In December 1781 the Arnolds left New York and sailed to England. Although he was paid £6,000 for joining the British and given a pension in England and lands in Canada, Benedict Arnold's act of betrayal became infamous even in England. He asked to serve in the army during the 1790s in the wars against FRANCE, but he was never given an active commission. Benedict Arnold died on June 14, 1801; his wife died three years later.

See also SPYING.

Further reading: James Thomas Flexner, *The Traitor and the Spy* (Boston: Little Brown, 1975); James Kirby Martin, *Benedict Arnold, Revolutionary Hero: An American Warrior Reconsidered* (New York: New York University Press, 1997); William Sterne Randall, *Benedict Arnold: Patriot and Traitor* (New York: Quill, 1990).

Arnold, Margaret (Peggy) Shippen (1760–1804)
Loyalist

The daughter of Edward Shippen, a noted Philadelphia Loyalist, Margaret (Peggy) Shippen became the second wife of BENEDICT ARNOLD on April 8, 1779. Half the age of her husband, Peggy Shippen Arnold had extravagant tastes and is one of the reasons why Benedict Arnold fell into debt while military governor of Philadelphia. Her family's Tory sympathies also antagonized many revolutionaries in Philadelphia, adding to her husband's own political problems. Peggy Shippen Arnold may have also been the conduit for her husband's contact with Major JOHN ANDRÉ. During the British occupation of Philadelphia, Major André socialized with the Shippens and painted a portrait of Peggy. When Benedict Arnold betrayed the CONTINENTAL ARMY and shifted to the British cause, Peggy was in WEST POINT. There she suffered an attack of hysteria that some have come to consider a mere act because they believe that she was a coconspirator in Benedict Arnold's treason. Many of the Continental officers at the time, however, were highly sympathetic to her, and she was eventually allowed to cross enemy lines to join her husband in New York City.

Whatever Peggy's culpability in her husband's betrayal during the revolution, the couple remained devoted to each other. The years after the REVOLUTIONARY WAR (1775–83) were difficult for the Arnolds. Even in British society, Benedict Arnold was never really welcome. The Arnolds had five children and moved to London, then to NOVA SCOTIA, then back to London, all the while struggling financially. Peggy Shippen Arnold died on August 24, 1804, three years after her husband's death.

See also LOYALISTS.

Further reading: James Kirby Martin, *Benedict Arnold, Revolutionary Hero: An American Warrior Reconsidered* (New York: New York University Press, 1997).

art

Two key developments emerged in North American art in the closing years of the colonial period. First, there arose a core of portrait painters, some more skilled than others, who found patronage among the merchants and landed elite. Second, a select group of these individuals began to expand their horizons beyond portraiture. The AMERICAN REVOLUTION would have a profound effect on these developments and the art world of the early United States.

Colonial portrait painters could only succeed if they found a market for their talents. The increased affluence of the colonial elite, and its desire to consume luxury items, provided just such a market. Whether in Virginia or Massachusetts, the colonial political and economic leaders wanted to adorn their homes with paintings of themselves and members of their families. However, no one locality provided enough work to steadily employ an artist. Painters like JOHN SINGLETON COPLEY and RALPH EARL had to travel from community to community in search of new subjects willing to pay for a portrait. The best of the colonial painters decided that they needed to study in Europe. BENJAMIN WEST took the lead in the movement, traveling to Italy and FRANCE and settling in London in 1763. West established himself as one of Britain's premier painters, working in the neoclassical style. His *Death of General Wolfe* transformed the art world not only by depicting a recent historical event but by placing his subjects in contemporary CLOTHING. After the success of this painting, it became the usual practice to commemorate events of the time on canvas. Several North American artists flocked to West's studio to learn from the master, including Copley, Earle, CHARLES WILLSON PEALE, GILBERT STUART, and JOHN TRUMBULL.

The REVOLUTIONARY WAR (1775–83) intruded on these developments. In the upheaval of the war, some artists became LOYALISTS while others supported the cause of independence. West, already well ensconced in cosmopolitan London and under royal patronage, developed his connections further, received a royal stipend, and painted extensively for GEORGE III. Copley had gone to Europe in 1774, was joined in England by his Loyalist family in 1775, and never returned to the United States. Earle also left North America sometime around the beginning of the war, but his politics are more difficult to evaluate. By the 1780s, however, he was back in the United States and was again an itinerant painter. Trumbull was a supporter of independence, served in the CONTINENTAL ARMY as an officer, and was even arrested in London in 1780. Peale, who had left London in 1769, was an ardent Revolutionary, participating in the radical politics of Pennsylvania.

The REPUBLICANISM of the American Revolution created an intellectual problem for many of these artists.

Watson and the Shark, by John Singleton Copley, 1778 *(National Gallery of Art)*

Virtue and self-sacrifice seemed to work at cross-purposes with the self-adulation and luxury represented by a personal portrait. What could be more superfluous than a merchant seeking to immortalize his visage by paying to have his own picture painted? As JOHN ADAMS explained, art had been "enlisted on the side of Despotism and Superstition throughout the ages." A society that valued the artist had vast differences in wealth, with "shoeless beggars and brilliant equipage" next to each other. For many revolutionary Americans, simple republican society with some claim on equality was not the appropriate setting for the artist.

While Loyalists like West and Copley may not have had to worry about this issue, revolutionary WHIGS like Trumbull and Peale did. To gain legitimacy in a republic, they decided not only to continue to paint portraits for MONEY but also to turn their brushes to republican pur-

poses. Trumbull used the historical style developed by West to create a visual chronicle of the American Revolution, painting between 250 and 300 historical scenes of crucial events, such as the signing of the DECLARATION OF INDEPENDENCE and great battles. Peale primarily devoted himself to portraits, but he also created a gallery of revolutionary heroes with portraits of the Founding Fathers and heroes of the Revolutionary War to be viewed in a museum open to the public (for a fee).

Despite their republican aspirations, the revolutionary artists of the period continued to struggle. Trumbull's historical paintings achieved some contemporary success, but his involvement in business and his decline in talent with age limited his financial success. Peale's museum could not sustain an audience, and he ultimately had to develop a more eclectic collection of curiosities to attract visitors.

Further reading: Neil Harris, *The Artist in American Society: The Formative Years, 1790–1860* (New York: George Braziller, 1966); Kenneth Silverman, *A Cultural History of the American Revolution* (New York: T. Y. Crowell, 1976).

Articles of Confederation

Proposed by the SECOND CONTINENTAL CONGRESS in 1777, and finally ratified by all the states in 1781, the Articles of Confederation was the first national constitution. Although many have since written off the Articles of Confederation as a complete failure, at the time it created a viable form of government that reflected the needs and concerns of many Americans. The authors of the Articles saw the threat of too much government as much more ominous than an excess of LIBERTY, and therefore they intentionally sought to limit the powers of the national government. Furthermore, the Articles were successful in that they helped to bring about the Continental victory in the REVOLUTIONARY WAR (1775–83). There were other notable achievements under the Articles, including the NORTHWEST ORDINANCES.

The Second Continental Congress drew up the Articles of Confederation to create a form of government for the colonies of North America then in revolt against GREAT BRITAIN. Having convened in May 1775, Congress had begun to operate as a government, and when war broke out, the body raised an army (see CONTINENTAL ARMY) and established diplomatic contacts. However, its powers were not defined, and as the war continued and independence loomed, many in Congress wanted a more formal central government that could coordinate operations, support the army, and gain allies. Congress organized a committee in June 1776 to create a plan of perpetual union. Chaired by JOHN DICKINSON of Pennsylvania, the committee worked quickly and submitted its draft to Congress within a month. This draft gave the government a great deal of power, with only one serious restriction: It could not impose taxes except in relation to the post office.

As Congress began to debate the committee's proposals, there was immediate disagreement over how strong a central government should be. Some members believed that the union should be only a loosely organized confederation of states. This group—thinking that a strong centralized government would be detrimental to the people's liberty and that power should be kept as close to the populace as possible—feared that a new oppressive government was about to replace the one they had so recently rejected. They held that they were not fighting a war just to exchange one form of tyranny for another. Because of this lingering fear, support for Dickinson's Articles of Confederation was weakened.

The Articles were sent to the states for approval in 1777, but disputes over the lands west of the Appalachian Mountains delayed ratification until 1781. Maryland, which had limited boundaries, refused to take any action until states with large western land claims ceded their western territory to congressional control. When the large states ceded the lands, Maryland finally agreed to ratify. While waiting for ratification, Congress continued to operate as the government of the United States following the provisions of the unratified Articles. Under the Articles, Congress successfully guided the nation through war and passed the NORTHWEST ORDINANCES, which influenced westward settlement for the next century.

The fact that the states were able to organize collectively at all was quite an achievement. The colonies had been founded separately and had developed in very distinct ways; furthermore, there had been disputes among them over territorial claims, as evidenced by the delays in ratification. Nevertheless, the government established by the Articles had considerable powers in FOREIGN AFFAIRS and borrowing MONEY. Article 1 gave the confederacy the title of "The United States of America." Article 4 asserted that all free inhabitants of every state would be entitled to the "privileges and immunities" of every other state; this clause was the basis for national CITIZENSHIP. Article 6 forbade individual states from making treaties or alliances with foreign powers. Article 9 gave Congress sole authority to declare wars, reconcile boundary disputes between the states, manage Indian affairs, and regulate land and naval forces.

While the government had important powers granted to it, there were still many weaknesses in practice. The Articles were more like a treaty among sovereign states than a constitution of a united country. Each state had equal REPRESENTATION in Congress—one vote per state, regardless of population. There was no chief executive officer, and initially government departments were run by committees. The national government could not levy taxes on its own. Instead, it had to request the states to collect taxes and forward their requisitions to the central government, making it difficult to implement laws that required funding. States often acted on their own in military affairs: Despite provisions in the Articles, some states negotiated with foreign countries and some formed their own armies and navies. Currency was another problem: In addition to the national paper bills, states printed their own paper and minted their own coins. The states retained many powers under Article 2, which declared that each state would hold every "power, jurisdiction, and right which is not by this confederation expressly delegated to the United States in congress assembled." Finally, it was almost impossible to change the Articles because amendments required the consent of all 13 states.

During the 1780s some leaders began to argue for a stronger national government. In 1781 Congress dropped the committee system of government and created government departments headed by specific individuals. This reform streamlined government decision making. ROBERT MORRIS, who headed the Finance Ministry, became the de facto head of state. He sought to strengthen the national government further by advocating a 5 percent national impost on all imports. He had hoped that the measure would become law after nine states accepted it; instead the states viewed it as an amendment to the Articles needing unanimous approval. The impost failed when one state, Rhode Island, refused to pass it. Without the impost, and with victory in the war, the nationalist movement fell apart. Efforts to revive the impost in 1785 failed as one state—New York this time—again refused to pass the law. The nationalists had to try a different tactic and eventually called for changes to the Articles, resulting in the CONSTITUTIONAL CONVENTION of 1787. Although the Articles of Confederation were soon replaced by the U.S. CONSTITUTION, they remain important as the first formal system of government in the United States.

See also REPUBLICANISM.

Further reading: Merrill Jensen, *The Articles of Confederation: An Interpretation of the Social-Constitutional History of the American Revolution, 1774–1781* (Madison: University of Wisconsin Press, 1940); Peter S. Onuf, *The Origins of the Federal Republic: Jurisdictional Controversies in the United States* (Philadelphia: University of Pennsylvania Press, 1983); Jack N. Rakove, *The Beginnings of National Politics: An Interpretive History of the Continental Congress* (New York: Knopf, 1979).

—Crystal Williams

artisans

Artisans composed the largest sector of the male working community in colonial and early national cities (most notably Boston, New York, Philadelphia, Baltimore, and Charleston). They learned their trades during an apprenticeship that might last from ages 13 to 21 under the tutelage of a master craftsman (though the period was often shorter). Apprenticeship was a legal contract requiring the apprentice to work for the master for a specified number of years in return for room, board, instruction in the trade, and rudimentary schooling. After completion of an apprenticeship, the trained craftsman advanced to journeyman standing.

Journeymen were skilled wage laborers, many of whom traveled from place to place, looking for work. The amount of time a man would spend as a journeyman depended on talent and fortune. If he were highly skilled and could find capital to buy equipment and rent space, he could open his own store and become a master craftsman, hiring journeymen and apprentices.

Master craftsmen and journeymen were part of the "middling sort" (middle classes) of North American urban society. They ranged from the lower end, most noticeably the shoemakers and tailors, to the upper ranks, such as the goldsmiths, silversmiths, and watchmakers, with the middle tier including butchers, bakers, cabinetmakers. A cabinetmaker could be quite poor, doing rudimentary repair work and making crude furniture—or, if he were one of a city's finest craftsmen, such as New York's DUNCAN PHYFE, he could become quite prominent and employ many journeymen (Phyfe had 100).

From the mid-colonial period on, many artisans achieved "freedom" of the city, a carry over from the English system, which allowed qualified craftsmen to work where they liked and also allowed them to vote—an important factor since voting was normally restricted to property owners. In many colonial elections, artisans made the difference between competing factions. This central role brought them political importance as they were vigorously courted by individuals contending for office. Artisans were crucial to the RESISTANCE MOVEMENT (1764–75) against British imperial regulation. They were at the core of the SONS OF LIBERTY and other extralegal organizations that led the anti-British demonstrations against the hated STAMP ACT (1765), and they protested to limit imports and exports. Artisans made up the heart of the crowd that dumped tea into Boston harbor during the infamous BOSTON TEA PARTY (December 16, 1773).

As war broke out with GREAT BRITAIN, artisans became active in the government of the cities, particularly in New York and Philadelphia. In New York they formed the Committee of Mechanics, which demanded and achieved a share in the city's governance after British control dissolved. While there were artisans who became LOYALISTS, craftsmen usually tended to be radicals, asserting a greater political voice in government. In New York they opposed the merchants and demanded a declaration of independence. Paying close attention to the words of THOMAS PAINE, they also insisted that the new constitution of New York State be ratified by a popular vote of the people. In Philadelphia, after the QUAKER leadership abandoned politics, as did the proprietary faction (those who supported the colony's proprietary family, the Penns), a new group of leaders emerged that included prominent artisans.

During the 1790s, artisans at first aligned themselves with the FEDERALIST PARTY, as advocates of a strong central government. Such a government could enforce tariffs against British imports that threatened to undersell craftsmen's products. However, they were also backers of the FRENCH REVOLUTION (1789–99) and many joined the DEMOCRATIC-REPUBLICAN SOCIETIES. With the rise of the Jeffersonian DEMOCRATIC-REPUBLICAN PARTY, many artisans shifted allegiance, particularly those in the less-wealthy trades, attracted by the party's stance that respected their citizens' right. They were also repelled by Federalist Party tactics that at times attempted to coerce mechanics with threats regarding their employment. These low-paid artisans contributed significantly to the victory of THOMAS JEFFERSON in the ELECTION OF 1800. In the early decades of the 19th century, artisans remained pivotal in elections in the nation's cities, generally favoring the Jeffersonians.

Developments in the ECONOMY had a direct impact on artisans: Expanding TRADE increased the total number of tradesmen, providing greater opportunities for some while limiting opportunities for others. The gap between masters and journeymen grew in several trades as successful masters needed to command more capital and fewer journeymen became masters. These developments were especially marked in major trades such as printing, SHOEMAKING, cabinetmaking, tailoring, and construction (masons and carpenters). Journeymen in these trades began to form trade societies that went beyond the traditional benevolent functions of EDUCATION and welfare for the sick and aged and burials for the deceased. The new societies espoused walkouts as a tactic to compel masters to hire only society members and particularly not to hire semiskilled men who had never completed their apprenticeship. In so doing they were the forerunners of the labor movement in the United States.

See also CITIES AND URBAN LIFE; INDUSTRIAL REVOLUTION; LABOR AND LABOR MOVEMENTS.

Further reading: Howard B. Rock, *Artisans of the New Republic: The Tradesmen of New York City in the Age of Jefferson* (New York: New York University Press, 1979); W. J. Rorabaugh, *The Craft Apprentice: From Franklin to the Machine Age in America* (New York: Oxford University Press, 1986).

—Howard B. Rock

Asbury, Francis (1745–1816) *Methodist bishop*

Francis Asbury was the first bishop of the Methodist Church in the United States. Born on August 20, 1745, near Birmingham, England, Asbury had a religious experience at age 14 and, while serving in an apprenticeship, began to attend prayer meetings, eventually becoming something of a local preacher. During this time he was attracted to the growing Methodist movement, and after he turned 21 he became a full-time preacher, traveling on the Methodist circuit in England. In 1771 he volunteered to go to North America as a missionary.

Asbury was just one of several missionaries sent by the METHODISTS to the North American colonies. In 1772, however, the Methodist founder John Wesley appointed Asbury superintendent of the Methodists in British America. Asbury pursued his own agenda, enforcing his ideas about discipline until June 1773, when Wesley ordered him to surrender his authority to Thomas Rankin. Asbury did not readily do so, and in March 1775 Wesley ordered him to return home. Asbury refused, believing that he needed to be in North America in the upheaval that was then breaking out in the colonies.

During the REVOLUTIONARY WAR (1775–83) the Methodists were often identified as LOYALISTS, and Rankin left for England. When Asbury, who sought to remain neutral, refused to take an oath of allegiance in Maryland, he had to seek refuge in Delaware. Before the end of the war, however, he sided with the independence cause. He also played a prominent role in mediating doctrinal disputes between northern and southern Methodists, emerging from the conflict as virtual head of the Methodists in the United States.

In 1784 Wesley sent the Rev. Thomas Coke to the United States to jointly run the Methodist Church with Asbury, who stalled by insisting that conferences within the United States should make the appointments, rather than Wesley. In December 1784 both Asbury and Coke were appointed joint superintendents by a Baltimore conference. Coke, however, was not as active as Asbury, who started calling himself Bishop Asbury, and the Methodist organization fell largely on Asbury's shoulders.

Asbury's talents were organizational. He traveled incessantly, covering as many as 300,000 miles during his ministry, from one end of the country to the other. Only after 1800, when illness began to seriously weaken him, did he surrender some control of the Methodist organization. He died in Virginia, on his way to a Baltimore conference, on March 31, 1816.

See also RELIGION; RELIGIOUS LIBERTY.

Further reading: Herbert Asbury, *A Methodist Saint: The Life of Bishop Asbury* (New York: Knopf, 1927).

Association, the (Continental Association) (October 20, 1774)

Sometimes called the Continental Association, the agreement known as the Association represented one of the most radical acts of the FIRST CONTINENTAL CONGRESS. Confronted with calls for action against the COERCIVE ACTS (1774), Congress drew up the Association to establish nonimportation (to begin December 1, 1774), nonconsumption (to begin March 1, 1775), and nonexportation (to begin September 10, 1775) as a means of bringing economic pressure on GREAT BRITAIN to repeal its repressive laws. Although some colonists had used similar measures in the controversy over the STAMP ACT (1765) and TOWNSHEND DUTIES (1767), it was a bold and sweeping stand on the part of the colonial opposition leaders. Congress, however, did more than vote on these economic sanctions in the Association; it also empowered local COMMITTEES OF CORRESPONDENCE to become committees of inspection to guarantee compliance with the boycott. These committees were to inspect customhouse papers and publish the names of any violators. For those who ignored the Association, all mercantile connections would be banned. In essence, the Association advocated turning local government over to these committees, thus providing a mechanism to transfer power from the king to the people while still maintaining order.

If the Association advocated economic coercion and provided a political tool for revolution, it also offered a republican vision of society. To sustain the resistance to imperial measures—and to demonstrate the virtue of the people—the Association encouraged "frugality, economy, and industry," while it discountenanced and discouraged "every species of extravagance and dissipation, especially all horse-racing, and all kinds of gaming, cock-fighting, shews, plays, and expensive diversions and entertainments." It even advocated simpler dress during funerals. The Association thus represented a critical step not only toward revolution and breaking ties with Great Britain but also toward a new moral order.

See also REPUBLICANISM.

Further reading: David Ammerman, *In the Common Cause: American Response to the Coercive Acts of 1774* (Charlottesville: University Press of Virginia, 1974).

Astor, John Jacob (1763–1848) businessman

In the early 19th century, John Jacob Astor became the richest man in America through the North American FUR TRADE and real-estate investment. Born in Germany, Astor moved to England as a young man. After the TREATY OF PARIS (1783) he immigrated to the new United States and settled in New York City, where he had an older brother. His early career in the United States is not well documented, though it is known that he quickly became involved in buying and selling—first musical instruments and then furs. In 1785 or 1786 he married Sarah Todd, a woman who would be an able business partner, had influential relatives, and brought him a modest working capital of $300 (about the average yearly earnings of a tradesman). By the 1790s the Astors had parlayed their capital into a small fortune through buying and selling furs and purchasing real estate. In addition, Astor's trading network had begun to reach deep into the interior of the United States.

By 1800 the Astors had amassed about a quarter of a million dollars through investments that ranged from the mundane to the spectacular. On the mundane side, Astor consistently bought real estate in New York City. This was a period of rapid growth for that city, and as New York's population spread uptown, real-estate values sky rocketed. Without ever leaving home, the Astors would have been made fabulously rich this way. But Astor was also a visionary. He began to invest in trading furs directly to China— one voyage alone netted him $50,000 in profit. After the LOUISIANA PURCHASE (1803), Astor decided to set up an outpost, called ASTORIA, directly on the Columbia River and trade furs to countries across the PACIFIC OCEAN. However, his Pacific Fur Company ran into the harsh reality of geopolitics. The outbreak of the WAR OF 1812 (1812– 15) threatened Astor's distant holdings, forcing him to sell Astoria to the British at rock-bottom prices. What he did not sell at the opening of the war was soon seized by the British navy.

Astor may have lost one part of his fortune because of the war. But he gained another by helping to finance the war, when his purchase of government bonds netted him handsome profits. After the war he continued his Far West investments by dominating the fur trade in much of the Missouri Valley. When he retired from the fur-trading business in 1834, his fortune was estimated at $20,000,000. Thereafter, he concentrated on his real-estate ventures and on being a patron of the arts. He died on March 29, 1848.

Further reading: John D. Hager, *John Jacob Astor: Business and Finance in the Early Republic* (Detroit: Wayne State University Press, 1991); Axel Madsen, *John Jacob Astor: America's First Multimillionaire* (New York: Wiley, 2001).

Astoria

With the encouragement of the U.S. government, JOHN JACOB ASTOR sought to gain control of much of the North American FUR TRADE in the years before the WAR OF 1812 (1812–15) by establishing a base called Astoria on the Columbia River in the Pacific Northwest. After a contentious voyage, Astor's ship the *Tonquin* arrived at the Columbia River in March 1811, and under the aegis of the Pacific Fur Trading Company, Astor's partners built Astoria on Point George, about 11 miles from the mouth of the river and on the south bank. The Astorians had a difficult time during the first year, despite some success in trading with the local NATIVE AMERICANS. The *Tonquin* was lost, probably due to an Indian attack to the north, and an overland expedition arrived only after a long arduous journey.

After the War of 1812 broke out, Astoria was in a precarious position as an isolated U.S. outpost. Moreover, many of the Astorians were Canadians. Given this awkward situation, representatives of the Canadian North West Company negotiated a sale of the Pacific Fur Company's assets on the Columbia River, including Astoria. The final arrangements were completed on October 13, 1813, and Astor did not recover Astoria after the war. Although the fort was technically turned over to the United States in 1818, it was run by the Canadian North West Company. The Convention of 1818 between GREAT BRITAIN and the United States set up a joint occupation of the region. A final border agreement for the Pacific Northwest did not take place until 1846.

Further reading: John Denis Haeger, *John Jacob Astor: Business and Finance in the Early Republic* (Detroit: Wayne State University Press, 1991).

Atlantic Ocean

The Atlantic Ocean, the large body of water lying between the Americas and Europe and AFRICA, has had a major impact on the development of American history. Scholars who focus on the interaction between the different parts of the Atlantic basin practice "Atlantic history." This perspective emphasizes transatlantic networks and views the Atlantic as a highway connecting nations and cultures rather than as an obstacle between different parts of the world.

Politically, Atlantic history focuses on the imperial expansion that began with the 15th-century explorations and discoveries of the Portuguese and Spanish, leading to the creation of colonial empires centered in Europe and reaching out across the Atlantic to Africa, North America, and South America. The 18th-century wars between FRANCE and GREAT BRITAIN need to be seen in their Atlantic as well as their North American context, especially the FRENCH AND INDIAN WAR (1754–63), which encompassed a conflict that saw battles fought on all four Atlantic continents and beyond. Likewise, even the REVOLUTIONARY WAR (1775–83) can be viewed as part of the larger competition among European-Atlantic empires wherein France sought to take advantage of the colonial rebellion in the British North American colonies to gain imperial advantage over Great Britain. This idea is reinforced by the fact that much of the fighting between England and France took place in the WEST INDIES once the French entered the war in 1778. Similarly, when the wars of the FRENCH REVOLUTION (1789–99) broke out, the conflict was Atlantic in scope and, despite protestations of neutrality by the United States, had a dramatic impact on the development of POLITICAL PARTIES in the early republic and its economic expansion.

Atlantic history also is important in understanding economic developments. On the eve of the Revolutionary War, most of the British North American colonies were integrated into the transatlantic TRADE network. Not only did the colonies produce such staples as RICE, TOBACCO, INDIGO, fish, WHEAT, lumber, and maritime stores for export to Europe and the West Indies, but colonial Americans were involved in the SLAVE TRADE with Africa and some illicit trade with the Spanish possessions in South America. The Revolutionary War disrupted many of these trade patterns, but they were partially revived in the years after 1783 and expanded greatly during the Anglo-French Wars that began in the 1790s.

Perhaps one of the most important areas of study in Atlantic history is in the migrations of peoples—that is, the effort to understand the interplay between events on one continent with the movement of peoples to another continent. The transatlantic slave trade, which flourished until the outbreak of the Revolutionary War, is one obvious area that has attracted the attention of scholars of Atlantic history. Difficulties in importing slaves from Africa or the West Indies to North America, caused by the presence of British cruisers in the Atlantic, imposed financial strains on the people of the United States. After the war, several states forbade the international slave trade for ideological reasons. (In fact, every state in the United States had prohibited the slave trade by the early 1790s, although Georgia and South Carolina lifted that ban before the federal government outlawed the international slave trade in 1808). There are other important transatlantic connections related to the immigration of thousands of people from Europe to North America, especially among the Germans and British.

The Atlantic Ocean also facilitated the transmission of ideas. During the 1740s and 1750s, evangelical concepts crisscrossed the Atlantic. Preachers such as George Whitefield came from Britain and traveled the length and breadth of British North America, preaching a gospel of personal religious regeneration and spreading what became known as the Great Awakening (see GREAT AWAKENING, SECOND). The essays and sermons of Jonathan Edwards, a leading colonial American divine, were read and discussed in Europe. German pietists of a variety of stripes crossed the Atlantic in the hope of establishing religious communities or of preaching their own special understanding of the gospel. The MORAVIANS were one of the more important of these groups. The ideas of the ENLIGHTENMENT also swept both ways across the Atlantic, as can be seen in the writings of many of the revolutionary generation and the prominence of BENJAMIN FRANKLIN as a symbol of the enlightened man for both the English and the French.

Perhaps more significant was the Atlantic exchange of revolutionary ideals. Once the United States became independent, many people on both sides of the Atlantic began to believe that it was possible to establish a republican government based on the principles of LIBERTY, equality, and fraternity. During the 1790s and through the early 1800s, diverse peoples, stretching from beyond Poland and France to MEXICO, Venezuela, Chile, and Argentina, followed in the Atlantic wake of revolution.

The Atlantic connection was also crucial to the ENVIRONMENT. Many of the developments in this area were long-term, especially concerning flora and fauna, but some of these Atlantic environmental issues can be placed within the 1754–1815 period. The introduction of the horse to the GREAT PLAINS began with the Spanish in New Mexico in the late 17th century, but its full impact was only felt after the mid-18th century with the growth of the Plains Indian culture based on the BUFFALO. Diseases such as SMALLPOX swept through the Atlantic world in the 1770s, spreading from Mexico into the interior of North America and affecting armies on both sides of the Revolutionary War. The revived trade with the West Indies helped to trigger the YELLOW FEVER epidemics of the North American cities in the 1790s and early 1800s.

In short, by focusing on Atlantic history, scholars have studied a variety of political, economic, social, cultural, intellectual, and environmental networks to come to a better understanding of both the interconnectedness of the Atlantic world and the varied effects this connection had on the history of nations bordering the ocean.

See also ANGLO-FRENCH WARS.

Further reading: Bernard Bailyn, *Atlantic History: Concept and Contours*, 2 vols. (Cambridge, Mass.: Harvard University Press, 2005); R. R. Palmer, *The Age of the Democratic Revolution* (Princeton, N.J.: Princeton University Press, 1959, 1964).

Attakullakulla (Little Carpenter) (c. 1710?–1777) *Cherokee peace chief*
Attakullakulla (called Little Carpenter by the British) attempted to maintain CHEROKEE neutrality during the REVOLUTIONARY WAR (1775–83), though he failed in this effort largely because of his son DRAGGING CANOE. Born around 1710, Little Carpenter witnessed the large increase in the number of British colonists in the Carolinas and Georgia during the 18th century. He established ties with the British Indian agent JOHN STUART in an attempt to enforce restrictions against the illegal settlement of colonists on Cherokee lands and stop the violence that plagued the FRONTIER. By 1771 he had negotiated a new westward boundary line with Virginia at the Kentucky River. Four years later, he negotiated another treaty, which ceded 27,000 square miles of Cherokee lands between the Tennessee and Kentucky rivers. These treaties, however, did little to stop land-hungry colonists. Little Carpenter's son

Dragging Canoe opposed his father's conciliatory approach, and when the Revolutionary War broke out, he supported a militant union against the Revolutionaries, uniting several Indian communities (Mingo, SHAWNEE, and DELAWARE) in an alliance with the British. Little Carpenter disagreed with the militant younger chiefs led by his son, fueling a generational and familial dispute within the Cherokee communities. Confronted with this opposition, he eventually agreed to a war, but he wanted to limit attacks to only those European Americans who had settled on lands not yet ceded by the Cherokee.

The Revolutionary War proved disastrous for the Cherokee. By early 1777, cut off from British supplies and suffering from the Revolutionary Americans' reprisals, Little Carpenter sought peace. He died around 1780, with his nation divided and in midst of a devastating war. His son Dragging Canoe, however, continued to fight the new United States until his death in 1792.

Further reading: J. Russell Snapp, *John Stuart and the Struggle for Empire on the Southern Frontier* (Baton Rouge: University of Louisiana State University Press, 1996). Richard White, *The Middle Ground: Indians, Empires, and Republics in the Great Lakes Region, 1650–1815* (Cambridge: Cambridge University Press, 1991).

—Patrick Bottiger

Attucks, Crispus (ca. 1723–1770) *colonial protester*
Born of mixed-race heritage, Crispus Attucks was one of the civilians killed in the BOSTON MASSACRE on March 5, 1770. Since then, he has been held up as an example of a common man who died for the cause of LIBERTY.

Scholars do not know much about Attucks's life before that fateful evening when he was killed. He was probably of African-American and Native American descent, possibly with some European blood. In all likelihood he was born in Mashpee, a Natick Indian community near Framingham, Massachusetts. Despite converting to Christianity in the 17th century, the Indians of this community had been pushed to the economic and social periphery by the European-American settlers. Many of the New England Christian Indians intermarried with the local and relatively small African-American population. They also frequently found themselves in a form of bondage, either as slaves or in long-term indentures. Attucks was some sort of bond servant about 1750, a conclusion based on the discovery of a runaway advertisement with his name and description. Like many New England Indians and mixed-race men of his era, he also probably served on a whaler. By the time of the Boston Massacre, he was described as a sailor.

Unlike the political leaders of the period, Attucks did not leave any written record of his ideas or commitment to the ideal of liberty. Scholars therefore have to surmise from Attucks's actions what brought him to King Street on the night of March 5, 1770. Men like Attucks had many grievances against British imperial policy. For decades they had been liable to IMPRESSMENT and resented this threat to their immediate liberty. Moreover, imperial regulations directly affected their livelihood since work on the waterfront depended on TRADE; laws that limited trade therefore limited employment opportunities. Compounding these difficulties was a postwar recession after the FRENCH AND INDIAN WAR (1754–63). The recession struck Boston particularly hard, leaving many workers unemployed and milling around the docks. Attucks and other waterfront workers also had some more immediate concerns. The presence of British troops in the city made life more difficult for poor Bostonians, since off-duty soldiers competed for jobs along the wharfs and in workshops. During the days leading up to the riot on King Street, soldiers and common people in Boston clashed repeatedly in fights connected to this employment issue. In addition, common folk had great confidence in the power of the mob. Sailors and other waterfront workers had repeatedly rioted against impressment and, starting in the 1760s, joined in demonstrations against the STAMP ACT (1765) and customs regulations. Some of the participation in crowd action was merely rowdyism—the sheer joy of shouting in the street and disturbing the peace. Much of it, however, was connected to the real issues of the imperial crisis and unemployment. Those issues were given a greater significance by the rhetoric of liberty used by the leaders of the RESISTANCE MOVEMENT (1764–75).

On the night of March 5, 1770, a mob confronted a group of British soldiers on King Street. Although a few witnesses denied that Attucks was in the forefront of the crowd, most of the evidence indicates that Attucks was one of the mob's leaders. His huge stature—he was six feet, two inches (which was tall for the 18th century)—and the fact that he was killed by two bullets in the chest support the idea that he was not a bystander. JOHN ADAMS vilified Attucks while defending the soldiers on trial for murder, declaring that it was due to his "mad behavior" that "the dreadful carnage of the night is chiefly ascribed."

Attucks was buried with three other victims of the "massacre" on March 8 in a huge ceremony. Subsequently, he has been honored as a hero of the AMERICAN REVOLUTION. In the 19th and 20th centuries, AFRICAN AMERICANS in particular took pride in his racial identity.

See also RIOTS.

Further reading: Dirk Hoerder, *Crowd Action in Revolutionary Massachusetts, 1765–1780* (New York: Academic Press, 1977); Hiller B. Zobel, *The Boston Massacre* (New York: Zobel, 1970).

Auchmuty, Robert, Jr. (1725–1788) *Loyalist*

A leading Loyalist in Massachusetts, Robert Auchmuty, Jr., was born into a wealthy Boston family and became a lawyer in 1762. Because of his support for the Crown, he was appointed to a number of royal judgeships, including the VICE ADMIRALTY COURT from 1767 to 1776. He was the presiding judge in the case that confiscated JOHN HANCOCK's sloop in the *LIBERTY* RIOT in 1768. Along with his close associate THOMAS HUTCHINSON, he wrote some letters to royal officials suggesting that the Massachusetts charter should be repealed. When BENJAMIN FRANKLIN sent copies of these letters back to Massachusetts in 1773, Auchmuty, Hutchinson, and others were vilified in the press as enemies of the people, more concerned with their own "ambition" than the general welfare.

Auchmuty left Boston in 1776 and was captured at sea by the Revolutionaries. Later exchanged, he went to GREAT BRITAIN, where he became a leader in the Loyalist community. He was officially banished from Massachusetts in 1778, and the new revolutionary state government confiscated his extensive property in 1779. Auchmuty filed a claim for £3,075 for his losses; the British claims commission granted him £1,775, a onetime payment of £600 for lost salary during the war, and a pension of £300 a year.

See also LOYALISTS; LOYALIST PROPERTY CONFISCATION.

Augusta, Georgia, first siege of (September 14–18, 1780)

The first siege of Augusta strengthened British control of Georgia during their southern campaign late in the REVOLUTIONARY WAR (1775–83) when a revolutionary assault failed because of British reinforcements. But it also helped to set up the BATTLE OF KING'S MOUNTAIN (October 7, 1780), which was a major turning point in the war for the United States.

The British occupied Augusta on January 29, 1779. Although British forces subsequently withdrew from the town on February 13, their victories in the area brought many LOYALISTS into arms, and by September 1780 Augusta was a Tory stronghold. With about 400 Loyalist rangers and MILITIA, as well as a few hundred NATIVE AMERICANS and ample stores and trade goods for the Indians, Augusta stood as an important symbol and outpost of British power in the region. Continental colonels Elijah Clarke and James McCall decided to attack Augusta with 450 revolutionary militia, hoping to capture military stores and help win control of the province back from the British.

The initial attack was a success as the revolutionary militia advanced in three columns, surprising some Indians and capturing some of the outposts around Augusta. But the main body of Loyalists rallied and fortified the Mackay

House, a trading post on the outskirts of Augusta. Under the command of Colonel THOMAS BROWN, the Loyalists refused to surrender, even when the Revolutionaries attempted to fire two captured cannon against Brown's forces. (Without trained artillerists, the revolutionary militia had difficulty using the cannon.)

After a four-day siege, about 500 British reinforcements, including regulars and militia, arrived from Ninety-Six, South Carolina. In the meantime, many of the revolutionary militia had drifted away. Some had been forced to join the attack against their will and left at the first opportunity; others had left to visit family. Some, satisfied with the booty already captured, deserted with their packs full of stolen goods. Once the British relief column was in sight, many of the rest of the militia retreated. Clarke attempted to hold his line, though he had little choice but to call off the attack. He lost 60 men killed and wounded. After the battle, the Loyalists, who had only lost a handful of men, executed 13 captured Revolutionaries since they had violated parole and taken up arms after pledging not to do so. Indians and Loyalist militia pursued Clarke and his men, who, along with their families, had to abandon the area. Both sides committed atrocities against one another. It was as a consequence of this pursuit of the revolutionary militia that Colonel PATRICK FERGUSON and his Loyalist followers found themselves deep in the backcountry and attacked by "over-the-hill" frontiersmen at the Battle of King's Mountain, in western South Carolina.

Further reading: Edward J. Cashin, *The King's Ranger: Thomas Brown and the American Revolution on the Southern Frontier* (Athens: University of Georgia Press, 1989); David Lee Russell, *The American Revolution in the Southern Colonies* (Jefferson, N.C.,: McFarland and Co., 2000).

Augusta, second siege of (May 22–June 5, 1781)

By May 1781 the British held only a few outposts in the deep South: Augusta and Savannah, Georgia; and Ninety-Six and Charleston, South Carolina. The Continental general NATHANAEL GREENE—who had headed south after the BATTLE OF GUILFORD COURTHOUSE (March 15, 1781) while the British commander LORD CORNWALLIS marched north to Virginia—sought to regain control of South Carolina and Georgia. He dispatched Lieutenant Colonel HENRY LEE with his cavalry legion to join MILITIA units under General ANDREW PICKENS and Colonel Elijah Clarke to capture Augusta. Defending the town was a force of about 400 Loyalist rangers under Colonel THOMAS BROWN, stationed in three forts—Fort Galphin, Fort Grierson, and Fort Cornwallis.

The Revolutionaries began by capturing the weakest post first. On May 21, Lee ordered the militia to attack

Fort Galphin and then feign a retreat. This plan worked, and revolutionary forces overwhelmed the LOYALISTS who were in pursuit and seized the fort and supplies destined for NATIVE AMERICANS. Without capturing these supplies, the rest of the siege would have never taken place. A few days later, on May 23, the Revolutionaries captured Fort Grierson, defended by only 80 men, by concentrating their fire on the fort. Brown attempted to come to the rescue of his comrades but was beaten back. However, many of the Loyalist defenders, including the commander, Colonel James Grierson, managed to fight their way to Brown at Fort Cornwallis.

The Revolutionaries had a harder time with Fort Cornwallis and its 320 defenders supported by about 200 AFRICAN AMERICANS. Lee and Pickens had their men dig trenches and build a tower for cannon and riflemen. By June 4 the Revolutionaries were in a position to launch an all-out assault on the fort from the tower and trenches. A six-pound cannon on the tower had silenced the Loyalist artillery and could strike at almost any point the inside of the fort. Vastly outnumbered, Brown had tried every ruse he could to destroy the tower and delay the attack. After repeatedly refusing to surrender, he agreed to terms that would protect him and his men. Delays in the negotiations meant that Brown surrendered on June 5, rather than on the king's birthday (June 4). Loyalists would have viewed surrender on the king's birthday as an affront to their monarch.

Lee went to extraordinary lengths to protect Brown, whose life was in danger from vengeful militia. Brown was saved by being sent away under protective custody of a CONTINENTAL ARMY officer. Other Loyalists were not so lucky. Almost as soon as Lee left Augusta after the victory, Colonel Grierson was killed in his own home by vindictive Revolutionaries angered over reported Loyalist atrocities.

Further reading: Edward J. Cashin, *The King's Ranger: Thomas Brown and the American Revolution on the Southern Frontier* (Athens: University of Georgia Press, 1989); David Lee Russell, *The American Revolution in the Southern Colonies* (1943; reprint, Jefferson, N.C.,: McFarland and Co., 2000).

Aupaumut, Hendrick (1757–1830) *Mahican chief*

A Mahican chief sachem from Stockbridge, Massachusetts, Hendrick Aupaumut joined the revolutionary army on June 23, 1775, and was at the siege of Boston (April 19, 1775–March 17, 1776). He continued in the CONTINENTAL ARMY in a special Native American unit and was a lieutenant in the skirmish in 1778 in Westchester County, New York, in which as many as 30 of his fellow STOCKBRIDGE INDIANS were killed. He was subsequently promoted to captain of the Indian company.

After the REVOLUTIONARY WAR (1775–83), Aupaumut fused his Christianity with a REVITALIZATION MOVEMENT—Indian-initiated efforts to reinvigorate Native American cultures—and developed a vision of peaceful coexistence with European Americans. He wanted to adopt many of the cultural traits of the European Americans while simultaneously clinging to his Indian identity. This vision of effectively adapting to European Americans competed with the more antagonistic vision urged by many Native American "prophets" such as TENSKWATAWA. Aupaumut argued for dividing both NATIVE AMERICANS and European Americans into good and bad people regardless of race and used the traditional Mahican role as mediators with the SHAWNEE and others to act as a go-between with European Americans. Aupaumut traveled extensively north of the Ohio River in his efforts to act as a spokesman, or as the Indians put it a "front door," for Native peoples during the 1790s and early 1800s. He visited WASHINGTON, D.C., at least twice; lived in White River, Indiana, from 1808 to 1815; and in 1829 moved to Green Bay, Wisconsin, where he died the following year.

Further reading: Rachel Wheeler, "Hendrick Aupaumut: Christian-Mahican Prophet," *Journal of the Early Republic* 25 (2005): 187–220.

Autosse, Battle of (November 29, 1813)

In wars with NATIVE AMERICANS during the early years of the 19th century, one of the most effective U.S. ARMY strategies was to strike at Indian towns, killing women and children as well as male warriors, and then destroying homes and food supplies. In mid-November 1813, during the CREEK WAR, General John Floyd launched just such a raid against the CREEK town of Autosse, on the banks of the Tallapoosa River in Mississippi Territory, home to the hostile Creek known as RED STICKS. With about 950 Georgia militia and 400 friendly Creek, Floyd surrounded Autosse on the morning of November 29, 1813. The friendly Creek were detached to prevent those inside the town from escaping across the river. However, they did not arrive in time to stop many Red Sticks from escaping to some cliffs on the other side of the river and putting up fierce resistance. On the town side of the river, Floyd used artillery to mow down the remaining Red Sticks. After two hours, the battle was over; 200 Indians were killed and 400 dwellings destroyed, while Floyd lost only 11 killed and 54 wounded. Unable to dislodge the Red Sticks on the other side of the river, Floyd declared himself victorious and returned to his base on the Chattahoochee River.

B

Bache, Benjamin Franklin (1769–1798) *journalist*

The grandson of BENJAMIN FRANKLIN, Benjamin Franklin Bache was a leading journalist who supported THOMAS JEFFERSON and the DEMOCRATIC-REPUBLICAN PARTY in the 1790s. In 1777, his parents, Richard and Sarah allowed him to accompany his famous grandfather to FRANCE; he was educated there and in Switzerland. Young Bache returned with his grandfather to Philadelphia in 1785 and completed his EDUCATION at the College of Pennsylvania in 1787. Franklin launched the young man in the printing business and served as Bache's nominal partner until his death in 1790.

Bache used the skills and inheritance he acquired from Franklin to set up a new newspaper, *The General Advertiser.* It quickly won the favor of Secretary of State Thomas Jefferson for its fine presentation of congressional debates and local and foreign news, as well as its opposition to the FEDERALIST PARTY headed by ALEXANDER HAMILTON. For much of the 1790s, Bache was the chief competitor to JOHN FENNO, whose *Gazette of the United States* presented the Federalist Party line. In 1794 Bache—a staunch supporter of the FRENCH REVOLUTION (1789–99) and friend of numerous refugees in Philadelphia—changed the paper's name to the *Aurora,* since it would "diffuse light, dispel the shades of ignorance, and strengthen the fair fabric of freedom on its surest foundation, publicity and information."

Bache virulently opposed the presidential administrations of GEORGE WASHINGTON and JOHN ADAMS. Upon obtaining a copy of JAY'S TREATY (1794) with GREAT BRITAIN from an ally of Jefferson's, he rapidly printed and distributed it personally from Philadelphia to Boston, ensuring a public outcry against the agreement, which was favorable to Great Britain and seemed to nullify treaties with France.

In 1797 the French reacted to Jay's Treaty by seizing ships, triggering a diplomatic crisis that led to the XYZ AFFAIR (1797–98) and the QUASI-WAR (1798–1800).

Despite the popular war fever, Bache continued to favor the French, even printing a long letter by the French foreign minister CHARLES MAURICE DE TALLEYRAND-PÉRIGORD in his newspaper defending French policy. Efforts to silence Bache—including an indictment for treason—failed. Soon thereafter, Bache was one of 14 people arrested under the Sedition Act, passed in 1798 to squelch criticism of the federal government. From his jail cell, Bache continued to champion freedom of speech. He died while awaiting trial during one of Philadelphia's horrendous YELLOW FEVER epidemics, leaving his wife, Margaret, and four children.

The *Aurora,* with a circulation that had risen from an initial 400 to 1,700 subscribers by the time of Bache's death, was the most prominent Jeffersonian organ in the nation. Margaret married her husband's assistant, WILLIAM DUANE, who continued the newspaper's political tone. Margaret wrote Bache's obituary, calling him "a man inflexible in virtue, unappalled by power or persecution, and who, in dying knew no anxieties but what were excited by his apprehensions for his country—and for his young family."

See also ALIEN AND SEDITION ACTS; JOURNALISM.

Further reading: Richard N. Rosenfeld, *American Aurora: A Democratic Republican Returns* (New York: St. Martin's Press, 1997).

—William Pencak

Backus, Isaac (1724–1806) *Baptist minister*

Isaac Backus was an advocate of RELIGIOUS LIBERTY. Born to an affluent Norwich, Connecticut, family, Backus experienced a religious conversion in 1741 during the first Great Awakening. Inspired by the preaching of James Davenport and George Whitefield, he soon joined a New Light separatist church. At that time, state taxes in Connecticut and Massachusetts still supported the religious establishment of the Congregational Church. During the 1740s and 1750s, Backus began to accept the principle of adult baptism, which helped in elevating the Baptist Church to prominence (see BAPTISTS). In 1756 he became a founding member and then pastor of a Baptist Church in Middleborough, Massachusetts. Backus committed the rest of his life to religious work, serving as the pastor of his Middleborough congregation for the next 50 years. He also traveled thousands of miles each year as an itinerant preacher, seeking converts to the Baptist Church.

Backus's greatest claim to fame was as an advocate of religious liberty who sought an end to the state-established churches in New England. In pursuit of this goal, he petitioned both the state legislatures and the CONTINENTAL CONGRESS for religious liberty. He also supported the independence movement during the REVOLUTIONARY WAR (1775–83) and even attended the 1788 Massachusetts convention for ratification of the U.S. CONSTITUTION. Backus frequently engaged in newspaper and pamphlet controversy in his defense of religious liberty. Although his efforts were not entirely successful in his lifetime, he stands as an important spokesperson for an ideal that was incorporated into the First Amendment of the Constitution.

See also BILL OF RIGHTS; GREAT AWAKENING, SECOND; RELIGION.

Further reading: William G. McLoughlin, *Isaac Backus and the American Pietistic Tradition* (Boston: Little, Brown and Company, 1967).

Bahamas

Controlled by GREAT BRITAIN for most of the period from 1754 to 1815, the Bahama Islands were a minor province in the British Empire. After being dismissed from his command in the FRENCH AND INDIAN WAR (1754–63), WILLIAM SHIRLEY became governor of the Bahamas from 1761 to 1767, since the position was a less significant post and could thus serve as a sinecure for a royal servant who had seen better days and better appointments.

Lying off the southeast coast of FLORIDA, and north of the main body of islands in the WEST INDIES, the Bahamas became a base for SMUGGLING goods to the revolutionaries, and it was the site of several military actions during the REVOLUTIONARY WAR (1775–83). Leading a small flotilla of ships from the CONTINENTAL NAVY, Captain ESEK HOPKINS raided New Providence (Nassau) in the Bahamas on March 4, 1776, capturing several cannon and some munitions. However, he quickly left the island group and headed back to New England. In January 1778 revolutionary privateers also raided New Providence, taking away a large supply of stores. The Spanish, with some assistance from Revolutionaries from the United States, launched a more significant attack on the Bahamas after

securing West FLORIDA and conquered the islands in May 1782. In the final peace treaty, Spain exchanged the Bahamas for East Florida and Minorca. In the last action of the war in the Western Hemisphere, and before news of the peace arrived, the British sent a small force from East Florida and recaptured the Bahamas on April 14, 1783.

After the Revolutionary War, about 5,000 mainly southern LOYALISTS, many with their slaves, settled in the Bahamas hoping to reestablish the lifestyle they had enjoyed on the North American mainland. Planters therefore sought to grow export crops, but with only some success. Efforts at planting COTTON suffered from insect infestations and soil depletion. JOHN MURRAY, FOURTH EARL OF DUNMORE, became governor of the island group from 1786 to 1796 and, despite an assembly packed with exiled Loyalists, wrangled with local politicians over a variety of issues. In 1815 the Bahamas remained a backwater within the British Empire.

Bainbridge, William (1774–1833) *U.S. naval officer*

William Bainbridge was born into an affluent New Jersey family and went to sea at age 15. Within three years he was a ship's officer and quickly became a captain of merchant vessels. He was an excellent and courageous seaman who had an imposing six-foot physique that allowed him to bully mutineers into submission and made him feared—if not respected—by common SEAMEN. During the QUASI-WAR (1798–1800) he obtained a commission in the U.S. NAVY when he was only 23 years old. He soon revealed two interrelated flaws: an inflexibility in command and poor judgment. Both were rooted in his belief in following "rules" that he thought were clear.

On November 19, 1798, Bainbridge surrendered the 14-gun *Retaliation* to two French frigates—the first time a U.S. warship was captured by the French. He had been informed that France had no large vessels in the Caribbean and therefore did not try to escape until the French ships were on top of him. In 1800 he sailed the frigate *George Washington* to the Mediterranean with tribute for Algiers. Unfortunately, he anchored under the guns of the Algerian forts and was surprised when the dey of Algiers insisted that Bainbridge bring Algerian tribute to Constantinople. Having left himself exposed to a devastating bombardment, Bainbridge had to comply.

As embarrassing as these incidents were to the United States—and in both cases Bainbridge was exonerated—his worst mishap occurred during the war with Tripoli (see BARBARY WARS). Early in the war Bainbridge, relying on outdated charts, sailed too close to shore in the frigate *Philadelphia* and became grounded. Unable to free the vessel and surrounded by enemy gunboats, and before he even lost a man, Bainbridge surrendered the ship and its 315 crewmen. Although this capture changed the complexion of the war and led to over two years of imprisonment, even in this case a court-martial decided that Bainbridge was not to blame for the disaster.

Bainbridge spent most of his time between 1805 and the beginning of the WAR OF 1812 (1812–15) on leave from the navy plying the seas as a merchant captain earning MONEY to support his family. When hostilities broke out with GREAT BRITAIN, he was anxious for a command at sea. He replaced ISAAC HULL on the USS *CONSTITUTION* in autumn 1812, after Hull had beaten the HMS *Guerrière*. Since Bainbridge was considered unlucky and a harsh disciplinarian, this change of command was not popular with the crew. He redeemed his reputation, however, in the South ATLANTIC OCEAN on December 29, 1812, by pounding the HMS *Java* into surrender in an intense sea battle where his seamanship and steadfast courage—he was wounded during the battle—came to the fore.

After returning to the United States in February 1813 and enjoying his one moment of fame, Bainbridge remained ashore for the rest of the war. At the end of the conflict he was ordered to command a squadron and punish Algiers for renewed depredations. However, his old luck—or foibles—returned. As Bainbridge deliberately prepared his ships and belatedly recruited crews, STEPHEN DECATUR, with similar orders and a smaller squadron, rushed to put to sea. Decatur defeated the Algerians and ended the conflict before Bainbridge, who was the senior officer, arrived on the scene. Bainbridge continued in the navy for a few more years before retiring. He died in Philadelphia on July 28, 1833.

Further reading: Craig Symonds, "William S. Bainbridge: Bad Luck or Fatal Flaw?," in James C. Bradford, ed., *Command under Sail: Makers of the American Naval Tradition, 1775–1850* (Annapolis: Naval Institute Press, 1985).

Baker, Remember (1737–1775) *Revolutionary militia officer*

A leader of the GREEN MOUNTAIN BOYS, Remember Baker was an early settler of Vermont who was killed during the REVOLUTIONARY WAR (1775–83). Born in Roxbury, Connecticut, Baker served in the provincial army during the FRENCH AND INDIAN WAR (1754–63), fighting near Lake George and Lake Champlain. He moved to the area of present-day Vermont in 1764 at a time when the region was being contested between New York and New Hampshire. Like his cousins ETHAN ALLEN and SETH WARNER, Baker became a land speculator and, as a leader of the Green Mountain Boys, opposed New York's claims. The contro-

versy became so heated in 1772 that New York authorities attacked Baker's house and arrested him. However, the Green Mountain Boys quickly rescued the severely injured Baker and triumphantly brought him back to Bennington. Baker was with Allen during the capture of FORT TICONDEROGA (May 10, 1775) and joined Warner in the attack on CROWN POINT a few days later. However, he was killed by Indians while on a scouting party near St. John's in CANADA on August 12, 1775.

Further reading: Robert E. Shalhope, *Bennington and the Green Mountain Boys: The Emergence of Liberal Democracy in Vermont, 1760–1850* (Baltimore: Johns Hopkins University Press, 1996).

Baldwin, Abraham (1754–1807) *Georgia politician*

A delegate to the CONSTITUTIONAL CONVENTION of 1787, Abraham Baldwin was a major politician from Georgia. He was born in Connecticut in modest circumstances—his father was a blacksmith—and after his EDUCATION at Yale, he served as a chaplain for the CONTINENTAL ARMY during the REVOLUTIONARY WAR (1775–83). Baldwin could have had a promising career as a minister and educator and was even offered a position at Yale after the war, but he decided to practice law instead. In 1783 he was admitted to the bar in Connecticut, and the following year he moved to Georgia, where he continued as a lawyer. He maintained his interest in education in his new state and was a leader in the movement to establish Franklin College, which became the nucleus of University of Georgia.

Baldwin entered Georgia politics almost as soon as he arrived in the state, serving in the SECOND CONTINENTAL CONGRESS and the Georgia assembly during the 1780s. At the Constitutional Convention in 1787, he did not play a very conspicuous part in the debates. However, he did speak up during the crucial discussion over the question of equal REPRESENTATION in the Senate. Originally he opposed the idea, but he shifted his position when he realized how important the issue was to the small states. His willingness to accommodate the small states contributed to the compromise over representation that helped to make the convention a success.

Baldwin continued his public service in the new government created under the U.S. CONSTITUTION by serving in the House of Representatives from 1789 to 1799, and then becoming a member of the Senate from 1799 until his death on March 4, 1807. He was a moderate member of the DEMOCRATIC-REPUBLICAN PARTY who opposed the policies of the FEDERALIST PARTY in the 1790s and supported THOMAS JEFFERSON. He also supported the pro-SLAVERY interests of his adopted state and opposed the reading of ANTISLAVERY petitions in Congress.

Further reading: E. Merton Coulter, *Abraham Baldwin: Patriot, Educator, and Founding Father* (Arlington, Va.: Vandamere Press, 1987).

Ballard, Martha (1735–1812) *diarist, midwife*

Born Martha Moore in Oxford, Massachusetts, Martha Ballard was an obscure midwife who kept a detailed diary of her experiences in Hallowell, Maine, from 1785 to 1812. The historian Laurel Thatcher Ulrich used that diary as the basis for her Pulitzer Prize–winning book *A Midwife's Tale* (1990). Ulrich demonstrates how Martha (who married Ephraim Ballard in 1754) contributed to the economic wellbeing of her family and community by not only overseeing the housework but also supervising the domestic production of cloth and, most important, acting as a midwife at 816 births over 27 years. In the process, Ulrich illuminates daily life on the Maine FRONTIER from 1785 to 1812. Ballard's diary provides insight into medical practices, especially concerning the birth of babies, RELIGION, sexual mores, and the central place of women in the economic and social life of the world of the early republic. More important than political events in her life are the natural rhythms of a life cycle and family development.

See also WOMEN'S STATUS AND RIGHTS.

Further reading: Laurel Thatcher Ulrich, *A Midwife's Tale: The Life of Martha Ballard, Based on Her Diary, 1785–1812* (New York: Knopf, 1990).

Baltimore, Battle of (September 12–14, 1814)

At the Battle of Baltimore, which took place during the WAR OF 1812 (1812–15), the British abandoned their offensive in the Chesapeake Bay region. After the British had burned WASHINGTON, D.C., they turned their attention to the northern Chesapeake Bay and the seaport of Baltimore. Many privateers had sailed from Baltimore and wrecked havoc on British commerce. The people in Baltimore tended to be strong supporters of the war and had expressed hatred of GREAT BRITAIN. On the morning of September 12, 1814, General ROBERT ROSS landed 4,500 troops at North Point, 14 miles from Baltimore. About 3,200 MILITIA led by General John Stricker opposed the British advance. After suffering heavy casualties—including Ross, who was killed by a sharpshooter—the British compelled the militia to retreat. The next day, demoralized by the loss of their commanding officer and confronted by even more U.S. troops dug in just outside of Baltimore, the British halted their assault by land.

At the same time, British admiral Alexander Cochrane's naval approach up the Patapsco River did not succeed. Cochrane had hoped to capture Fort McHenry, defended by 1,000 soldiers, and support the British land attack. He used bomb-and-rocket ships to fire more than 1,500 rounds at the fort on September 13 and 14. This spectacular bombardment did little serious damage, killing only four men and wounding 24. Fire from shore drove back a British attempt to send 1,200 men in barges to force their way up the river to Baltimore. The British withdrew and left the Chesapeake area. As they departed, they liberated more than 2,000 runaway slaves, most of whom subsequently settled in British Maritime CANADA. The inability to capture Baltimore, after their great success in sacking the nation's capital, reflected the difficulty the British had in taking major towns or cities by force. While they might capture territory, the 10,000–15,000 militia in Baltimore provided too stout a defense, despite the British military's superior training and firepower.

The Battle of Baltimore is also noteworthy as the inspiration for FRANCIS SCOTT KEY's poem "The Defense of Fort McHenry." Key had boarded a British ship to negotiate the release of a PRISONER OF WAR. Although he was successful in this effort, the British did not release him until after the bombardment of Fort McHenry. Key thus watched the "rockets' red glare" and the "bombs bursting in air" throughout the night of September 13 and 14. In the morning, despite the tremendous uproar and incredible fireworks, Fort McHenry remained under the tattered U.S. flag. Inspired by this sight, Key penned the words, which he put to the MUSIC of an 18th-century drinking song that became instantly popular. The U.S. Congress made this song, renamed "The Star-Spangled Banner," the national anthem in 1931.

Further reading: Donald R. Hickey, *The War of 1812: A Forgotten Conflict* (Urbana: University of Illinois Press, 1989).

Baltimore riots (June 22–July 28, 1812)

The Baltimore RIOTS began as a protest against the publication of a newspaper that opposed the WAR OF 1812 (1812–15) and spread to a series of disturbances revealing sharp social divisions. In spring 1812, Baltimore was stridently Jeffersonian, with most residents generally supporting the movement toward war with GREAT BRITAIN. However, ALEXANDER CONTEE HANSON published a newspaper called the *Federalist Republican*, which expressed opposition to the war and was a mouthpiece for the FEDERALIST PARTY. On the night of June 22, 1812, a well-organized mob dismantled the *Federalist Republican* office with little interference from city officials and to the approval of most Baltimoreans. Although the disturbance was limited to the destruction of one building, over the next couple of weeks mobs hounded any would-be opponent of the war and members of the Federalist Party. Crowds also attacked several ships loaded with WHEAT intended for the British army in SPAIN (the trade was legal, but considered inappropriate by the Jeffersonian mob). In addition crowds began to attack other targets, revealing ethnic animosity by harassing Irishmen and racial fears by assaulting African Americans who expressed hope that a British invasion would liberate slaves.

Meanwhile, Hanson was not about to be intimidated by the riot of the 22nd. He began printing his paper in Georgetown in the District of Columbia and set up an office to distribute the paper on Charles Street in Baltimore on July 27. A huge crowd surrounded the Charles Street office that evening and began shouting insults and pelting stones. Inside, Hanson had gathered about 30 political friends ready to defend the paper and freedom of the press. The defenders fired shots over the head of the crowd, which only made the mob more bold. The Jeffersonians then charged the building and Hanson's supporters fired at the attackers, killing one and injuring others. After seeing the casualties, the crowd grew angrier. Many now appeared with guns of their own, and some even brought a cannon into view. A small troop of MILITIA arrived but was unwilling to disperse the crowd. Instead, the militia officers negotiated a truce whereby the Federalist Party defenders would surrender to the militia and be escorted to the jail to await legal proceedings.

The next day tempers simmered, and a mob destroyed the *Federalist Republican* office on Charles Street. As night fell, another huge crowd formed outside the jail. The mayor attempted to disperse the crowd, only to be told he was hired by the people of Baltimore and should be leading the crowd instead of trying to stop it. With that he was swept aside as the mob charged into the jail and began to attack the prisoners. In the dark and during the confused melee that followed, a few prisoners escaped, but several were severely beaten. One victim of the mob, REVOLUTIONARY WAR veteran General James Maccuban Lingan, was killed. Hanson and another veteran revolutionary officer, Light Horse Harry (HENRY) LEE, were so severely handled that they never fully recovered from their injuries. The brutality of the assault suggests that more than politics was involved. Most of the mob were ARTISANS and workers—the common folk of Baltimore—who resented the wealth and arrogance of would-be Federalist Party aristocrats from the countryside.

The riots demonstrated how deep political and social divisions had become in the United States on the eve of the War of 1812. Although there was a state investigation of the riot and a few prosecutions of rioters, Baltimore remained a bastion of the Jeffersonian support for the war. The Federalist Party, proclaiming that it was defending the U.S. CONSTITUTION and the ideal of freedom of the press, used the riots to gain some victories in the fall elections in other parts of the country.

Further reading: Paul A. Gilje, *Rioting in America* (Bloomington: Indiana University Press, 1996).

Bank of North America

The Bank of North America was the first real commercial bank in the United States, beginning operations in 1782. The bank first received a charter to operate from the SECOND CONTINENTAL CONGRESS in 1781 and then from the Pennsylvania General Assembly in 1782. Under the direction of wealthy Philadelphians ROBERT MORRIS and THOMAS WILLING, it quickly became an important element in the Philadelphia mercantile community, the Pennsylvania state government, and the national government. The bank began conducting business in 1782 by taking over the operations of the Bank of Pennsylvania, which had been an exclusive tool of the Continental government since 1780. Soon the bank was lending capital to the federal and state governments and beginning to lend MONEY to merchants in Philadelphia. By 1784 it had become a powerful instrument of finance for Philadelphians involved in commerce. Its solid hard-money reserves helped to maintain its financial credibility and the value of its banknotes. Meanwhile, the bank aroused political controversy because rural Pennsylvanians in the assembly viewed it as a corrupt institution that was too closely connected to the state government. Morris himself served in the assembly and debated his rural colleagues in 1785 on the question of the bank's charter. The state revoked its charter, but the bank continued to operate under its federal charter and then won back its state charter in 1787.

The debate over the bank in the 1780s is important because it highlighted differing attitudes on the role of BANKS in the new nation and, in particular, exposed a regional schism surrounding state politics in Pennsylvania. The Bank of North America also served as a model for the BANK OF THE UNITED STATES. It continued to operate as a lender and repository for the Philadelphia mercantile community throughout the years of the early republic until absorbed by another financial institution in 1929.

Further reading: Belden L. Daniels, *Pennsylvania: Birthplace of Banking in America* (Harrisburg: Pennsylvania Banker's Association, 1976); Bray Hammond, *Banks and Politics in America: From the Revolution to the Civil War* (Princeton, N.J.: Princeton University Press, 1957); George David Rappaport, *Stability and Change in Revolutionary Pennsylvania* (University Park: Pennsylvania State University Press, 1996).

—James R. Karmel

Bank of the United States

The controversial Bank of the United States, a commercial institution, provided financial support to the federal government, lent resources for business interests, and helped stabilize the national ECONOMY from 1791 to 1811. The Bank of the United States began operations in 1791 after Congress approved a charter for it to operate for 20 years. The bank—based in Philadelphia with branches in eight major cities around the United States—was one component of the financial plan submitted by Secretary of the Treasury ALEXANDER HAMILTON during President GEORGE WASHINGTON's first term in office. Hamilton modeled his plan on the Bank of England, which had proved to be a stabilizing force for the British economy since the mid-17th century. Hamilton wanted an institution similar to ROBERT MORRIS's BANK OF NORTH AMERICA—only stronger. The bank issued currency, made payments on the national debt abroad, served as a depository for government funds, and lent MONEY to merchants. It also provided a mechanism to raise money for the federal government by selling government bonds. Holders of continental certificates could use these notes to buy shares in the new institution, and new bank stock was offered for sale to private investors. Three-fifths of the bank's capital stock was in the form of government securities, while the government itself owned one-fifth of the original stock.

The bank became a divisive political issue in 1790 as the first two-party system emerged in national politics, pitting the FEDERALIST PARTY against the DEMOCRATIC-REPUBLICAN PARTY (Jeffersonians). The Federalist Party supported the bank by accepting Hamilton's plans and theory that the bank could stabilize and support the national economy. The members of the Federalist Party also argued that it was constitutional, based on the power of Congress to manage national finances, raise government revenue, and create national institutions such as the military. Led by Secretary of the State THOMAS JEFFERSON and Speaker of the House of Representatives JAMES MADISON, the Democratic-Republican Party unsuccessfully opposed the bank's chartering on the basis that the bank was unconstitutional because Congress did not have the explicit power to charter CORPORATIONS. To Jeffersonians, the Bank of the United States represented an abuse of federal power by overriding state legislative authority to charter a bank. Jeffersonians also believed that the bank would give financial speculators and merchants too much influence in the national government, to the detriment of farmers and other producers. The debate over the bank also reflected sectional divisions in Congress, with most of its support coming from New England and mid-Atlantic states, while southerners opposed it.

The bank quickly established itself as an important component of the expanding economy in the early American republic. The bank followed a conservative lending policy to merchants while also lending steadily increasing amounts of money to the federal government. In time, its operations became integrated with government administration. In addition, the branch BANKS served as regulators of the local economies in which they operated, providing credit and exchange facilities for the state-chartered banks that started business in the period from 1791 to 1811. Throughout the bank's 20 years of operation, its managers strictly observed policies that preserved specie, or hard-money reserves, in the bank's vaults rather than extensively lent these resources out to other banks and individuals. An important feature of this policy was the curtailment of banknotes, or paper notes, used by the bank as currency. For example, in 1792 the bank had $976,910 in specie reserves and $1,689,486 in banknotes in circulation. In 1800 the bank had $5,671,949 in specie reserves and $5,469,063 in banknotes in circulation.

Political controversy and an evolving economy affected the bank after the ELECTION OF 1800. Although the Democratic-Republican Party had begun in part to oppose the bank, once Thomas Jefferson became president he followed the advice of Secretary of the Treasury ALBERT GALLATIN and did not move to revoke the bank's charter. The bank kept its special relationship with the national government, even though the government sold its shares in the institution to help pay the national debt. On the local level, growing numbers of state banks intensified pressure on the Bank of the United States to ease its lending policies, and many small farmers and producers around the nation—the core of the Jeffersonian support—never reconciled themselves to the bank's constitutionality or financial necessity. Gallatin—who remained in the treasury after Jefferson stepped down from the presidency—and President Madison supported rechartering the bank in 1810–11. Local bankers and merchants in cities where the bank operated were among its strongest supporters. Their arguments now included the point that the national bank was necessary to regulate the expanding network of state banks around the nation. Opponents of rechartering again tended to be farmers and producers, now acting with considerable strength through state assemblies and congressional delegations. They emphasized STATES' RIGHTS, constitutional issues, and an objection to foreign ownership of the bank's stock (many investors in GREAT BRITAIN and elsewhere in Europe had been purchasing bank shares for over a decade).

The bank lost its charter in early 1811 due to a split Congressional decision to postpone renewal. In the Senate, Vice President GEORGE CLINTON broke a tie by voting against the bank in opposition to President Madison and Secretary Gallatin. Clinton, an old ANTI-FEDERALIST from New York, was characteristic of Jeffersonians who never did accept the bank. After unsuccessfully attempting to secure a charter from the state of Pennsylvania, the bank's trustees liquidated the bank's assets, and it ceased to function by the end of 1811. In 1812 wealthy merchant STEPHEN GIRARD purchased the bank's building in Philadelphia and established his own private bank.

See also DEBT, NATIONAL.

Further reading: Stuart Bruchey, *The Dynamic Economy of a Free People* (Cambridge, Mass.: Harvard University Press, 1990); Bray Hammond, *Banks and Politics in America: From the Revolution to the Civil War* (Princeton, N.J.: Princeton University Press, 1957); John Thom Holdsworth and Davis Dewey, Jr., *The First and Second Banks of the United States* (Washington D.C.: Government Printing Office, 1910).

—James R. Karmel

bankruptcy laws

The issue of bankruptcy became increasingly important during the 1780s and 1790s as the U.S. ECONOMY came to rely more and more on speculative commercial transactions. Traditionally, bankruptcy was seen as a result of moral failure, and it was assumed that a debtor could never escape the debt because he had a moral obligation to fulfill commitments to all creditors. Imprisonment for debt was an instrument of coercion intended to get the debtor and his or her relatives and friends to fulfill those obligations. Bankruptcy entailed a new approach to debt wherein debt became merely a function of economic failure, allowing the debtor to erase an insolvency by simply dedicating all existing assets to creditors pressing a claim. With the financial slate wiped clean, a person could once again enter the world of business without worrying about the old debts. An economic system with bankruptcy laws would thus encourage investment and the development of CAPITALISM.

Before the AMERICAN REVOLUTION, a few colonies had some debtor relief and bankruptcy laws. During the 1780s Pennsylvania and New York passed more significant bankruptcy legislation geared mainly to the commercial interests. However, it was only in the 1790s that there was a national debate on bankruptcy. The U.S. CONSTITUTION gave Congress the power to establish "uniform Laws on the subject of Bankruptcies throughout the United States." All efforts at passing such legislation foundered on the issue of the morality of debt until the Bankruptcy Act of 1800 was passed by a Congress dominated by the FEDERALIST PARTY. The 1800 law stipulated that bankruptcy proceedings were limited to merchants, bankers, brokers, factors, underwriters, and marine insurers and had to be initiated by a creditor who was owed at least $1,000. The creditor petitioned a federal district judge stating that the debtor had committed one or more acts of bankruptcy—absconding, hiding, avoiding arrest, concealing property, conveying property fraudulently, escaping from debtors' jail, or remaining in debtors' jail for more than two months. The judge would then establish a commission that would tally up the person's property and the claimed debts. The debtor would have to undergo at least three examinations in 42 days and make full disclosure of his property. Once this process was completed to the satisfaction of the commissioners and two-thirds of the creditors owed $50 or more, then the debtor was released from any obligation and free to begin his life over again. Obviously the law favored the rich. ROBERT MORRIS was the most spectacular beneficiary of the Bankruptcy Act when his prosecution as a bankrupt freed him from debtors' jail and $3 million owed to creditors.

The Bankruptcy Act did not have much longevity. The DEMOCRATIC-REPUBLICAN PARTY opposed the law and, with the help of members of the Federalist Party who thought the legislation was deficient, repealed the bill in December 1803.

Further reading: Bruce H. Mann, *Republic of Debtors: Bankruptcy in the Age of American Independence* (Cambridge, Mass.: Harvard University Press, 2002).

banks

Following the colonial period of financial dependence on GREAT BRITAIN, American banks began operations in the 1780s and steadily became an important, ubiquitous, and sometimes controversial component of the early U.S. ECONOMY. Previously, banks in colonial North America had existed mainly in the form of merchants' associations, or colonial land offices that issued paper currency or bills of credit to farmers and others in selected colonies such as Pennsylvania, Massachusetts, and Rhode Island. Also, many private individual lenders operated in the absence of real institutionalized banking. Between 1741 and 1773, Parliament passed a series of laws that first restricted and then secured the rights of the colonies to issue paper notes and therefore provide banking facilities for their growing numbers of entrepreneurial farmers, ARTISANS, and merchants. Fear of problems resulting from inordinate land speculation based on the use of paper MONEY issued by colonial governments resulted in two restrictive parliamentary acts in 1741 and 1751. These measures officially banned the issuance of paper money or bills of credit by colonial authorities in New England. In 1764 the CURRENCY ACT banned the use of paper bills of credit as legal tender throughout the colonies, although it allowed for the issuance of paper money that was not used as legal tender. Finally, a 1773 act gave broad clearance to the colonies for the issuance of paper money in the absence of enough gold and silver currency (specie). However, the 1773 act probably came too late to ease the growing revolutionary viewpoint that banking restrictions were similar to other parliamentary actions in that they illegitimately suppressed independent colonial economic pursuits.

The first true bank in the United States began in Philadelphia in 1780 when the financier ROBERT MORRIS and other wealthy Philadelphians organized the Bank of Pennsylvania with private investment to raise revenue to support the CONTINENTAL ARMY. Through their collective efforts, the merchants managed to build credit and supply the army until the end of the war. Between 1780 and 1790, a few commercial banks started operations in Philadelphia, New York, Boston, and Baltimore. The first of these institutions was Morris's BANK OF NORTH AMERICA in Philadelphia, which opened in 1782. Likewise, ALEXANDER HAMILTON organized the Bank of New York in 1784. These early banks existed largely to support the merchant communities of the port cities in which they operated. They lent money, provided other means of credit, sold stock, and issued paper banknotes for use mainly by merchants and others in the urban mercantile communities. At times the banks had greater financial stability than the new state governments since they often had more specie in reserve and held less debt than many of the states. As a result, people relied on bank paper notes more than those issued by the states. In Pennsylvania the new bank aroused the suspicion of rural citizens who viewed it as a scheme by elite Philadelphians to monopolize the state's finances and control the state's political arena via politicians who were also involved in the bank. Significantly, the U.S. CONSTITUTION explicitly banned state governments from issuing paper money but was silent on the subject of banks doing so.

In 1791 Congress chartered the BANK OF THE UNITED STATES to provide revenue, a repository for federal funds, credit, and financial stability to the new nation. President GEORGE WASHINGTON signed the measure into law creating the bank, and it went into operation despite substantial objections. The Bank of the United States provided a regulatory anchor for the growing number of state banks chartered in the same period. From 1791 to 1811, the number of banks in the United States increased from 5 to 117, and their overall capital stock grew from $4,600,000 to $66,290,000. The increase in the number of state banks mirrored the growing national economy, which grew in every respect in those years. Popular demand for capital increased as manufacturing and commerce expanded throughout the nation.

New banks were often designed to support artisans, farmers, and mechanics through loan guarantees or long-term loans. Sometimes the new banks became political entities, designated as either connected to the Jeffersonian DEMOCRATIC-REPUBLICAN PARTY or the FEDER-ALIST PARTY. Regions such as the Ohio River Valley, central Pennsylvania, and rural New England experienced tremendous growth in the financial sector in these years. Typically, the new banks of this period had a substantial popular appeal. Laborers, women, AFRICAN AMERICANS, and NATIVE AMERICANS all became stockholders and customers in the new institutions. In some areas, such as New England, banks developed as money clubs administered by a select few, for their own benefit, or for the benefit of their colleagues and families. The new banks issued millions of dollars in the form of banknotes, which became the standard form of currency used in local marketplaces. State legislatures utilized the new banks in the development of transportation networks by mandating that banks invest in turnpike, bridge, and canal companies in exchange for charters. Political opponents of the Bank of the United States viewed the expanding state banking system as generally favorable because it gave many people more financial opportunities while decreasing the power of the national bank to create and regulate lending policies.

The timing of the demise of the Bank of the United States in 1811 could not have been worse since the WAR OF 1812 (1812–15) put tremendous strain on the national banking system. The failure to recharter the Bank of the United States meant that there was no national banking institution to offer loans to the U.S. government. Moreover, without the Bank of the United States, many of the new banks created after 1811 went unchecked, printing much more money than the specie held in their vaults. This facilitated the purchase of war bonds, which helped the federal government to pay for the war but also created something of a financial balloon. When there was a run on the banks in Baltimore and WASHINGTON, D.C., during the British invasion of the Chesapeake in 1814, vaults quickly emptied and the banks had to suspend payment. This action had a ripple effect, and most banks across the nation had to refuse to redeem notes in specie. Bank notes were therefore discounted at anywhere from 15 to 30 percent. As the war ended, the nation stood at the brink of financial collapse.

President JAMES MADISON and Secretary of the Treasury ALEXANDER J. DALLAS pushed for legislation to establish a new national bank in 1814, but Madison had to veto the charter in January 1815 because the final bill reflected more the needs of bankers than the national government. Only in 1816 was a new national bank—the Second Bank of the United States—chartered by the federal government.

See also CORPORATIONS; INTERNAL IMPROVEMENTS; TRADE.

Further reading: Bray Hammond, *Banks and Politics in America: From the Revolution to the Civil War* (Princeton, N.J.: Princeton University Press, 1957); Naomi Lamoreaux, *Insider Lending: Banks, Personal Connections, and Economic Development in Industrial New England* (New York: Cambridge University Press, 1994); Edwin J. Perkins, *American Public Finance and Financial Services, 1700–1815* (Columbus: Ohio State University Press, 1994); Fritz Redlich, *The Molding of American Banking, Part I: Men and Ideas, 1781–1840* (New York: Johnson Reprint Corp., 1968); Gordon S. Wood, *The Radicalism of the American Revolution* (New York: Knopf, 1992).

—James R. Karmel

Banneker, Benjamin (1731–1806) *mathematician, astronomer, almanac maker*

Born free in 1731 in Baltimore County, Maryland, Benjamin Banneker became one of the most famous AFRICAN AMERICANS of the late 18th and early 19th centuries. He rose from humble roots: Banneker's mother was a freeborn woman of mixed parentage (his own free status flowed from his mother), while his father was a slave taken from African shores. Although he grew up in a rural environment of TOBACCO cultivation and farm labor in which the majority of African Americans were denied not only freedom but EDUCATION, Banneker attended a small country school and displayed early talents in LITERATURE, statistics, and nature observation. As an adult, he became a mathematician, surveyor (he was one of three men to survey the layout of WASHINGTON, D.C., in the 1790s), and astronomer. But he remains best known for his ALMANACS, the first of which dates from 1791, the last from 1797. A calendar of astronomical calculations—as he put it, "the rise in and setting of the sun, the rising, setting and southing place of the moon," the dates of eclipses, and so forth—Banneker's almanac also contained miscellaneous poetry, prose, and other "interesting and entertaining" information.

Beyond its usefulness to farmers and a growing reading public (the almanac circulated in Pennsylvania, Delaware, Maryland, and Virginia), Banneker's publication bolstered early ANTISLAVERY thought and action. Its very production confounded antiblack stereotypes of the late 18th century that served to rationalize the enslavement of people of African descent. In particular, Banneker confronted THOMAS JEFFERSON, who had argued in *Notes on the State of Virginia* (1787) that blacks were inferior mental beings and asserted that African Americans could not master the literary arts or scientific inquiry. In an August 1791 letter to Jefferson, Banneker carefully but also adamantly challenged the Sage of Monticello's racial philosophies. "Now Sir," Banneker argued, "I apprehend you will readily embrace every opportunity to eradicate that train of absurd and false ideas and opinions which so generally prevail with respect to us, and that your sentiments are concurrent with mine, which are that one universal father hath given being to us

all." Jefferson replied to Banneker cordially that he hoped to see further proof of African-American achievement, and he forwarded Banneker's documents to a noted French philosopher and antislavery advocate, the marquis de Condorcet. Jefferson nonetheless remained steadfast in his belief that Banneker was an exception to his racial beliefs. Banneker may have outwitted Jefferson somewhat, however: The exchange between the two writers was published in both pamphlet and periodical form, and subsequent generations of activists and scholars have used it to reexamine Jefferson's racial attitudes as well as black challenges to them. For his part, Banneker did not continue to press Jefferson publicly, nor did he produce any other explicit antislavery literature beyond that found in his almanacs.

Banneker lived his entire life in Baltimore County, passing away on October 9, 1806. Although an enigmatic figure, he remains celebrated in African-American history. In the early 1800s, for example, Baltimore blacks organized the "Banneker Monument Committee" to honor perhaps their most famous son. Modern memorials, scholarships, and schools continue to honor Banneker.

Further reading: Silvio A. Bedini, *The Life of Benjamin Banneker* (New York: Scribner's, 1972).

—Richard Newman

Baptists

The first Baptists were radical Protestants who fled from England to Holland in the early 1600s. This small group took seriously the doctrines of the Reformation, emphasizing an individual's complete reliance on the Bible and the belief that God could only be known through personal experience (hence, they believed in "adult baptism," or baptizing only those who had become true believers). Baptists challenged any connection between earthly authority (the state) and the church, arguing instead for the autonomy of each local congregation. Denying the legitimacy of any authority that ran counter to their beliefs, early Baptists proved a political threat to the established churches, both in England and in colonial North America.

Baptists benefited greatly from the religious fervor surrounding the First Great Awakening (1730s–1740s). Although many Baptist churches divided along the same lines as the Congregationalists and the PRESBYTERIANS, the general upsurge in religiosity and desire for moral orthodoxy made Baptists appealing to many colonists. Following the First Great Awakening, Baptists became a minor yet important presence throughout the colonies. The Great Awakening also spawned a group known as Separate Baptists, who preached the absolute separation of church and state. Separate Baptists were especially strong among small farmers in the western regions of the South. In states like Virginia, they challenged the leadership of the wealthy (usually ANGLICAN) planters in the East. In New England the number of Baptists rose dramatically following the revivals of mid-century.

During the REVOLUTIONARY WAR (1775–83), Baptists capitalized on the backlash against the Anglican Church to gather more adherents. Emphasizing their long tradition of challenging church hierarchies, Baptists appealed to democratic Revolutionaries no longer willing to defer to the established church. The famous Baptist minister JOHN LELAND, a New Englander, moved to Virginia between 1777 and 1791 and encouraged his fellow ministers to bring down the Anglican establishment. In New England, Baptists struggled against efforts to strengthen the Congregational church. ISAAC BACKUS, a prominent minister in Massachusetts and Rhode Island, railed against continued taxation to support Congregationalism in Massachusetts. Joining with the DEMOCRATIC-REPUBLICAN PARTY (Jeffersonians), Baptists in Connecticut, New Hampshire, and Massachusetts were central participants in the battle to disestablish the church.

After the Revolutionary War, the tremendous growth of Baptist churches led to an effort to consolidate and rationalize the denomination. From local associations to state CONVENTIONS and missionary societies, Baptists united around their common cause and shared values. It was not that there was no cooperation before. The Philadelphia Baptist Association was founded in 1707, and it played an important role in establishing Brown University in 1764. The Warren Association in Massachusetts and Rhode Island served as a common space to mediate disagreements among New England Baptists. Yet the efforts to develop denominational institutions in the early decades of the 19th century convinced many Baptists that their leaders were moving away from the central creeds of the early church. These "hard shell" or "primitive" Baptists once again turned to absolute separation between earthly and church authority and reiterated the autonomy of local congregations.

Like many evangelical groups in the late 18th century, the Baptists appealed to a wide audience that included European Americans and AFRICAN AMERICANS. Indeed, the democratic message implicit in the evangelical ideal seemed to attract the poor and disenfranchised. However, as the Baptists became more firmly entrenched in the South during the years of the early republic, they lost some of their egalitarian trappings, and European-American Baptists came to defend the racist doctrine and the institution of SLAVERY that became increasingly important to white southerners.

Although Baptists were a minor presence before the Revolutionary War, they grew tenfold during the three decades following independence. Today Baptists are the largest Protestant denomination in the United States. Since their radical beginnings in the 17th century, Baptists have emphasized individual discipline combined with an absolute commitment to RELIGIOUS LIBERTY.

See also GREAT AWAKENING, SECOND; RELIGION.

Further reading: Christine Leigh Heyrman, *Southern Cross: The Beginnings of the Bible Belt* (New York: Knopf, 1997); Samuel S. Hill, *One Name but Several Faces: Variety in Popular Christian Denominations in Southern History* (Athens: University of Georgia Press, 1996); Rhys Isaac, *The Transformation of Virginia, 1740–1790* (Chapel Hill: University of North Carolina Press, 1982); Anne Devereaux Jordan and J. M. Stifle, *The Baptists* (New York: Hippocrene Books, 1990); William G. McLoughlin, *New England Dissent, 1630–1833: The Baptists and the Separation of Church and State,* 2 vols. (Cambridge, Mass.: Harvard University Press, 1971).

—Johann Neem

Baratarian pirates

Located in the bayeaus and swamps just south of the city of New Orleans, the area called Barataria became the center of illegal activity before the WAR OF 1812 (1812–15). Up until 1804 the region was known mainly as a haven for fishermen who were also petty smugglers. In 1804, when the SLAVE TRADE was outlawed in LOUISIANA, SMUGGLING of slaves offered greater profits and expanded the area's illegal operations. These profits attracted newcomers and so-called privateersmen from the French WEST INDIES who sailed with papers from the Republic of New Granada, which had declared, but not established, independence from SPAIN. Friction between the old-time smugglers and the new arrivals was put aside under the leadership of JEAN LAFITTE, who came to head this illicit activity, which included piracy, in 1810. Close connections with New Orleans merchants and local planters allowed the Baratarians under Lafitte to ignore the law. However, the Baratarians killed a U.S. revenue officer in January 1814 and alienated local support. On July 27, 1814, a federal grand jury indicted Lafitte and his brother Pierre on several accounts of piracy, and on September 16, 1814, the U.S. NAVY attacked and burned the pirates' base on Lake Barataria, seizing half a million dollars' worth of stolen goods and capturing 80 pirates. The Lafittes were not among the prisoners, and they began negotiations with officials from both GREAT BRITAIN and the United States, seeking amnesty in exchange for military service in the upcoming British invasion. Ultimately, Lafitte sided with the United States, and he and the Baratarians fought for ANDREW JACKSON at the BATTLE OF NEW ORLEANS (January 8, 1815). After the war many of the Baratarians returned to piracy, but finding tolerance for their presence diminished in Louisiana, Lafitte and his followers had to relocate to the Texas coast near Galveston.

Further reading: J. H. Ingraham, *The Pirate of the Gulf* (New York: E. P. Dutton, 1970).

Barbary Wars

The navies of several states in North Africa—often referred to as the Barbary pirates—preyed on the shipping interests of the new United States, resulting in several conflicts known collectively as the Barbary Wars. The Barbary States included Morocco, Algeria, Tunis, and Tripolitania (or Tripoli). The rulers of the Barbary States would periodically declare war against one or another European power that had shipping in the MEDITERRANEAN SEA or ATLANTIC OCEAN and send vessels to capture merchant ships to gain treasure and captives who would either be ransomed or sold into SLAVERY. The Barbary States also gained revenue from tributes, or annual payments from European states to protect their nation's shipping from attack. This practice had been going on for centuries. The British navy could have defeated the pirates, but the British government decided it was cheaper to just pay the tribute. Before the REVOLUTIONARY WAR (1775–83) colonial shipping was protected by the British flag.

Independence changed the situation for merchants in the United States. The problems began in 1784 when Moroccans captured a brig with 10 sailors. This crisis, however, was relatively easy to handle. As it turned out, the Moroccan emperor was merely trying to gain the attention of the United States. He had recognized the revolutionary government in 1778 but had not received any acknowledgment. The capture of the ship led to negotiations, brokered by SPAIN, that saw the release of the ship and the sailors, a gift of $10,000 from Congress, and a treaty in 1786 establishing trading relations between the two nations. To the surprise of European nations, the Moroccans did not insist on any annual tribute.

More serious problems developed with Algeria, which was the most powerful of the Barbary States. Encouraged by the British, who hoped to control much of the TRADE of the young United States, the Algerians entered the Atlantic and captured two merchant ships and 21 crew members in 1785. Fortunately for the United States, the Algerians also declared war on PORTUGAL. For most of the next decade the Portuguese blockaded the Straits of Gibraltar, keeping the Algerians penned up in the Mediterranean. JOHN ADAMS and THOMAS JEFFERSON, the leading U.S. diplomats in Europe in the 1780s, hoped to aid the captives. Adams wanted to simply pay the tribute; Jefferson sought

ways to build a coalition of smaller European countries and the United States that would take naval action against the Barbary States. Jefferson's plans came to naught since the United States under the ARTICLES OF CONFEDERATION did not have the wherewithal or will to build a navy. Adams entered negotiations with Tripoli as a precursor to negotiations with the Algerians. However, he quickly discovered that the cost of the tribute was too high. The result was that nothing was done by either diplomat. Meanwhile, U.S. shipping stayed away from the Mediterranean, and the sailors captured in 1785 languished in Algiers as slaves; most of the captives would die before they were finally ransomed 10 years later.

In 1793 the Portuguese, at the urging of the British, made peace with Algiers. Algerian ships swooped into the Atlantic, capturing 11 American ships and more than 100 SEAMEN before Portugal renewed its war with Algiers and closed the Straits of Gibraltar again. These attacks caused a public outcry in the United States, and Congress, now dominated by the FEDERALIST PARTY, created the U.S. NAVY in March 1794 to attack Algiers. It was this legislation that led to the building of super-frigates such as the USS *CONSTELLATION* and the USS *CONSTITUTION*. Simultaneously, diplomats led by JOEL BARLOW, DAVID HUMPHREYS, and Joseph Donaldson negotiated a settlement with Algiers in 1795. The United States agreed to over $600,000 in peace presents and commissions (bribes), and the Algerians promised to stop capturing shipping and release its captives. Because the United States had difficulty in raising the MONEY and delayed payment, the total cost of the treaty grew to around $1 million and included the gift to Algiers of a frigate. This agreement set the pattern for treaties with the other Barbary States: The United States made onetime payments of $107,000 to Tunis and $56,486 to Tripoli. The United States also paid Morocco $20,000 to renew the 1786 treaty. By the end of 1797, shipping from the United States could sail the Mediterranean without fear from attack by the Barbary pirates.

The peace did not last long. War broke out in 1801 when the bashaw (pasha) of Tripoli, YUSUF QARAMANLI, increased his demands for tribute. However, by this time the United States had a navy tested in battle during the QUASI-WAR (1798–1800) and a president—Thomas Jefferson—determined to abandon the tribute system and old world diplomacy. Unfortunately, fighting a war thousands of miles from home turned out to be more difficult than anyone thought. In 1803 Jefferson sent warships to blockade Tripoli. But almost as soon as the navy arrived off the coast of Tripoli, faulty maps and bad judgment led to the grounding of the frigate *Philadelphia* on October 31, 1803. Captain WILLIAM BAINBRIDGE surrendered the stranded ship, handing Qaramanli more than 300 seamen as hostages. To make things worse, the Tripolitans were able to float the *Philadelphia* free from the rocks in a storm a few days later. The U.S. Navy was able to partially atone for this disaster when Lieutenant STEPHEN DECATUR led an expedition into Tripoli Harbor to burn the captured ship a few months later. This attack made Decatur a national hero.

The war, on the other hand dragged out. Because of the weather, the navy could only blockade for a few months a year; most of the rest of the time was spent in Italy. During the summer of 1804 the navy repeatedly bombed Tripoli to little effect. In 1805 the United States sent U.S. army officer WILLIAM EATON to Egypt to convince the bashaw's brother Hamet, who had previously been ousted by Yusuf Qaramanli, to invade Tripoli with a handful of U.S. MARINES and a couple hundred mercenaries and Arab auxiliaries. Somehow this bizarre expedition captured Derne in eastern Libya. In the meantime, a large fleet under Commodore JOHN RODGERS blockaded Tripoli. With supplies cut off from the sea, and an invasion and possible coup in the offing, the bashaw decided to negotiate. He signed an agreement on June 4, 1805, which eliminated future tribute but provided a $60,000 ransom for the officers and crew of the *Philadelphia.* Rodgers then sailed to Tunis, where he compelled that state to sign an agreement without any payment of tribute.

Problems arose again during the WAR OF 1812 (1812–15) when the Algerians captured and ransomed several merchant vessels. As soon as the war was over, the United States sent Commodore Decatur to the Mediterranean. Decatur quickly captured two Algerian ships and compelled the ruler of Algiers to sign a peace releasing the United States from all tribute. Decatur then forced the other Barbary States to make similar treaties. The Barbary States continued to attack some European ships, but after 1830, when the French occupied Algeria, the depredations came to an end.

The Barbary Wars were important in the development of the United States. Not only did they contribute to a growing feeling of NATIONALISM, they also demonstrated, after some false starts, that the United States was willing and able to protect its rights whenever necessary.

See also FOREIGN AFFAIRS; MEDITERRANEAN FUND.

Further reading: Robert J. Allison, *The Crescent Obscured: The United States and the Muslim World, 1776–1815* (New York: Oxford University Press, 1995); William M. Fowler, Jr., *Jack Tars and Commodores: The American Navy, 1783–1815* (Boston: Houghton Mifflin, 1984); Frank Lambert, *The Barbary Wars: American Independence in the Atlantic World* (New York: Hill and Wang, 2005); Glenn Tucker, *Dawn Like Thunder: The Barbary Wars and the Birth of the U.S. Navy* (Indianapolis: Bobbs-Merrill, 1963).

Baring, house of (John and Francis Baring Company, Baring Brothers)

Founded in 1762, John and Francis Baring Company—later Baring Brothers but popularly known as the house of Baring—became one of the leading banking firms in GREAT BRITAIN. Baring Brothers dealt in a variety of commercial enterprises, including foreign exchange and the British national debt. After the REVOLUTIONARY WAR (1775–83), the firm sought connections with bankers and monied men in the United States. Through ROBERT MORRIS, the house of Baring established a financial relationship with WILLIAM BINGHAM and THOMAS WILLING in Philadelphia and Robert and John Oliver in Baltimore. In late December 1795 Alexander Baring, son of the firm's head, arrived in the United States and began investing in land and foreign exchange. He also solidified his connections in Philadelphia by marrying Anne Louisa Bingham, the daughter of William Bingham and ANNE WILLING BINGHAM. His younger brother married Maria Matilda Bingham, another Bingham daughter, a few years later.

Baring Brothers developed a special relationship with the U.S. government. It acted as an agent for the BANK OF THE UNITED STATES for the payment of the national debt in London and The NETHERLANDS, collecting a half-percent commission for the transaction and paying 3–5 percent interest on the MONEY while it was in their hands. The Barings also offered the United States credit when it negotiated "peace payments" with the Barbary States in 1795. The firm facilitated the purchase of military equipment in Britain during the QUASI-WAR (1798–1800) and purchased a large stake in the Bank of the United States. In 1803 Baring Brothers became the official financial agent for the government of the United States and marketed the loan that underwrote the payments to FRANCE for the LOUISIANA PURCHASE (1803). The house of Baring even advanced the United States the money for the loan.

In the early 19th century Baring Brothers continued to expand its business with the United States and included JOHN JACOB ASTOR and STEPHEN GIRARD among its clients. During the difficult years that began with the British ORDERS IN COUNCIL and the French BERLIN DECREE and MILAN DECREE, the house of Baring also worked to aid merchants from the United States when their ships were seized by one power or the other. The WAR OF 1812 (1812–15) left the banking firm in an awkward position because of its relationship to the governments of both the United States and Great Britain. While retaining its close financial ties to the British government, the house of Baring sought ways to maintain the credit of the United States concerning the debt obligations incurred before the war—especially in relationship to the Louisiana Purchase.

See also DEBT, NATIONAL.

Further reading: Ralph Hidy, *The House of Baring in American Trade and Finance: English Merchant Bankers at Work, 1763–1861* (Cambridge, Mass.: Harvard University Press, 1949).

Barlow, Joel (1754–1812) *poet, author, diplomat*
Born in Redding, Connecticut, Joel Barlow had the good fortune to grow into maturity just as the REVOLUTIONARY WAR (1775–83) broke out. An enthusiastic supporter of the cause of independence, he spent part of his summer vacation from Yale University fighting in the BATTLE OF LONG ISLAND (August 27–30, 1776). He graduated from Yale in 1778 and embarked on a variety of careers, including newspaper editor, storekeeper, and military chaplain in the CONTINENTAL ARMY. Barlow kept to this irregular course in the years immediately after the war, but he also gained some notoriety as an author and poet. As one of the CONNECTICUT WITS he coauthored the *Anarchiad,* a series of satirical articles that appeared in newspapers in 1786 and 1787, and an epic American poem called *The Vision of Columbus* in 1787.

Barlow traveled to Europe in 1788 as an agent for land speculators, but he failed in this business effort. He was in Europe during the outbreak of the FRENCH REVOLUTION (1789–99). Between 1790 and 1792, he and his wife were in London, where he became involved in reform politics, befriending THOMAS PAINE and several English radicals. His publications led to his expulsion from GREAT BRITAIN and honorary citizenship in FRANCE. After moving to Paris, he managed to make a fortune in the 1790s. He became the U.S. consul to Algiers in 1795 and negotiated treaties with that country, Tunis, and Tripoli (see BARBARY WARS). In 1805 he returned to the United States, where he retired.

In 1807 Barlow published a revised form of his epic poem, now called *The Columbiad,* which has since been often mocked because of its cumbersome verse. Three years later, THOMAS JEFFERSON persuaded him to serve as the U.S. ambassador to France. In 1812 he traveled to Poland to complete negotiations concerning U.S. TRADE with NAPOLEON BONAPARTE, who was then confronting his devastating defeat in RUSSIA. Unable to meet Napoleon as the French army retreated in the winter of 1812, Barlow died in Poland on December 26, 1812, while on his way back to Paris.

See also LITERATURE.

Further reading: Samuel Bernstein, *Joel Barlow: A Connecticut Yankee in an Age of Revolution* (New York: Rutledge, 1985); James Leslie Woodress, *A Yankee's Odyssey: The Life of Joel Barlow* (New York: Greenwood Press, 1968).

Barlow, Nathan (1775?–1817) *resistance leader*
A poor illiterate squatter and blacksmith, Nathan Barlow became a leader of the WHITE INDIANS resistance to large landowners on the Maine FRONTIER in the first decade of the 19th century. Like many European Americans during the early republic, Barlow was strongly influenced by RELIGION. In January 1801 he had a vision in which Jesus Christ took him to heaven and hell to show him the difference between those who obeyed and those who disobeyed the word of God. He then recounted his mystical experience to anyone who listened and even had it transcribed for publication. His neighbors were impressed by his experience and eagerly supported him when he encouraged opposition to land claims by rich speculators. Barlow led several bands of settlers dressed as Indians—hence the name *White Indians*—in disrupting land surveyors and attacking officials supporting the proprietors' claims. After he led some White Indians in an attack on a local constable in January 1808, he was arrested, tried, and convicted of assault. By the time he finished his sentence of two years in state prison, the White Indian movement had ended. When Barlow died a few years later, he owned no real estate and a minimal amount of property: a cow, a few oxen, eight sheep, a pig, and some tools.

Further reading: Alan Taylor, *Liberty Men and Great Proprietors: The Revolutionary Settlement on the Maine Frontier, 1760–1820* (Chapel Hill: University of North Carolina Press, 1990).

Barney, Joshua (1759–1818) *U.S. naval officer*
Joshua Barney was a naval officer whose career ranged from the REVOLUTIONARY WAR (1775–83) to the WAR OF 1812 (1812–15) and included action in the CONTINENTAL NAVY and French navy, as well as on privateers. Born in Baltimore, Maryland, Barney was an extraordinary seaman and leader who even as a teenager—he assumed his first command at age 15 when the captain aboard his ship died and there was no first mate—managed to successfully negotiate a business venture in Europe and bring his ship safely back to North America. This exploit earned him a berth in the Continental navy in 1775 as a master's mate; he quickly worked his way up to lieutenant. During the Revolutionary War he was captured three times by the British. Twice he was exchanged and once he broke out of prison in England and escaped to FRANCE.

In 1781 the state of Pennsylvania gave Barney command of the *Hyder Alley* and ordered him to escort a fleet of trading vessels to the Delaware Capes. When three British vessels came into sight off the capes, Barney ordered the convoy to disperse and head out to sea. In the action that followed, he outmaneuvered and captured an enemy ship twice the size of his own vessel.

Naval officer Joshua Barney captured in Delaware Bay in 1782 a British warship twice the size of his own vessel. *(Independence National Historical Park)*

After the war, Barney sailed in merchant vessels hoping to make MONEY, but unfortunately success eluded him. In 1794 he was offered the captaincy of one of the six frigates in the U.S. NAVY ordered to be built to fight Algiers in the BARBARY WARS, but in an argument over precedence of rank, Barney declined the commission. In 1796 he entered the navy of the French Republic as a captain and commodore. He fought in several engagements against the British before being discharged in 1802.

Barney's fortunes improved due to a variety of business enterprises after he returned to the United States and settled in Baltimore. He also ran for Congress twice as a member of the DEMOCRATIC-REPUBLICAN PARTY, though he was unsuccessful both times. During the War of 1812 he invested in and commanded privateers. In summer 1814 he took command of a flotilla of GUNBOATS on the Chesapeake Bay, harassing the British until he was forced to abandon his little fleet as the British advanced up the Patuxent River in August. Barney and his contingent of sailors and U.S. MARINES performed bravely, if vainly, in the BATTLE OF BLADENSBURG (August 24, 1814). After the rest of the U.S. forces fled, Barney, who was left sur-

rounded and wounded, had to surrender to the British. He died on December 1, 1818, in Pittsburgh.

Further reading: Louis A. Norton, *Joshua Barney: Hero of the Revolution and 1812* (Annapolis, Md.: Naval Institute Press, 2000).

Barras, Jacques-Melchior Saint-Laurent, comte de
(1721?–1788?) *French naval officer*
A French naval officer, the comte de Barras played an important role in the YORKTOWN campaign of 1781. By the outbreak of the REVOLUTIONARY WAR (1775–81), Barras had become a senior officer in the French navy. He accompanied the COMTE D'ESTAING to North America in 1778, and three years later he became commander of the French squadron in Newport. When the COMTE DE GRASSE set sail for the Chesapeake in August 1781, Barras was ordered to rendezvous with Grasse off the Virginia Capes. Although he initially hesitated to do so, hoping to obtain a more independent command, he sailed for Virginia in late August. In the BATTLE OF CHESAPEAKE CAPES (September 6, 1781) the combined French fleets prevented Admiral THOMAS GRAVES from supporting LORD CORNWALLIS. Moreover, Barras brought with him siege artillery from Newport that pounded the British into surrender at Yorktown.

After the Yorktown campaign, Barras sailed to the WEST INDIES, where he captured the British islands of Monserrat and Nevis. He retired at the end of the war and died sometime before the outbreak of the FRENCH REVOLUTION (1789–99).

Further reading: Jonathan R. Dull, *The French Navy and American Independence: A Study of Arms and Diplomacy, 1774–1787* (Princeton, N.J.: Princeton University Press, 1975).

Barré, Isaac (1726–1802) *British military officer, politician*
A British soldier and politician, Isaac Barré is most remembered for his opposition to the STAMP ACT (1765). Born in Dublin, Ireland, the son of a French refugee, he received his B.A. from Trinity College in 1745. Upon graduation, he opted for military service instead of the law. He served under General JAMES WOLFE, was appointed adjutant general, and was at the FIRST BATTLE OF QUEBEC (September 13, 1759). During the battle, he received a permanent eye injury.

In 1761 Barré entered politics as a member of Parliament with the support of Lord Shelburne (later British prime minister, 1782–83). As one of the few British politicians who knew members of the colonial mercantile class,

Barré kept others in Parliament abreast of colonial opinion. He argued against the Stamp Act and supported efforts for its repeal, believing that Britain would lose the colonies if it taxed them. Known for his powerful speeches, Barré referred to the colonists as "sons of liberty," a phrase that became widely used to describe opponents of the Stamp Act (see SONS OF LIBERTY). Although Barré was critical of many British policies, he still believed in the nation's preeminence and supported the Boston Port Act (1774). However, he did not sanction other coercive policies and believed military action against the colonies was destined to fail.

Barré went on to serve as treasurer of the navy (1782) and paymaster of the forces (1782–83) before his deteriorating eyesight forced his retirement in 1790. He died on July 20, 1802. In an effort to memorialize Barré and his opposition to the Stamp Act, several U.S. towns adopted his namesake: Barre, Massachusetts; Barre, Vermont; and Wilkes-Barre, Pennsylvania (named also for JOHN WILKES).

Further reading: Peter Brown, *The Chathamites: A Study in the Relationship between Personalities and Ideas in the Second Half of the Eighteenth Century* (New York: St. Martin's Press, 1967).

—Lawrence Mastroni

Barren Hill, Battle of (May 20, 1778)

The Battle of Barren Hill in Pennsylvania was a comedy of errors on both the British and revolutionary sides. In mid May 1778, from his encampment at VALLEY FORGE (1777–78), General GEORGE WASHINGTON ordered a reconnaissance in force under the command of the untried MARQUIS DE LAFAYETTE. Washington despatched 2,200 men and five guns—too large to move effectively and too small to fight the British in Philadelphia. If, however, Washington blundered by sending Lafayette and an important part of his CONTINENTAL ARMY into a vulnerable position, the British botched the opportunity to take advantage of the mistake.

Lafayette took his troops to Barren Hill, south of the Schuylkill River about halfway between Philadelphia and Valley Forge. The British reacted quickly as General Sir WILLIAM HOWE hoped to score one more victory before surrendering his command to Sir HENRY CLINTON and returning to England. The British planned to send an overwhelming force to encircle Lafayette. General JAMES GRANT left with 5,000 men on the night of May 19 to take up a position to the north of Lafayette, while General Charles Gray and Howe approached from two different directions from the south. The trap appeared foolproof since Washington's main army was 12 miles away on the other side of the Schuylkill and would be unable to help

Lafayette. Unfortunately for the British, though, Lafayette moved quickly and decisively as soon as he discerned their approach. Before any of the major British columns reached Lafayette, the young French general dispatched skirmishers to slow the British advance, marched the rest of his men on a low-lying road out of the sight of the approaching Grant, whose men were closest to the Continentals, and crossed the Schuylkill. Once across the river, he occupied such a strong defensive position that Grant decided not to risk an assault. Grant also wrongly believed that Washington had advanced and was hoping to trick the British into a bloody encounter.

Frustrated by Lafayette's nimble retreat, the British withdrew to Philadelphia. Much of Lafayette's success in slipping away from the enemy was due in large part to the discipline and training of the Continentals at Valley Forge, which enabled them to march in tight formations and get away before the British could attack.

Barron, James (1769–1851) *U.S. naval officer*

As a naval officer, James Barron is most noted for two unfortunate incidents: In 1807 he was the commanding officer when the USS *Chesapeake* surrendered to the HMS *Leopard,* and in 1820 he killed STEPHEN DECATUR in a duel. Barron was born into a seafaring family in Hampton, Virginia, and as a boy he served aboard a ship in the Virginia navy commanded by his father during the REVOLUTIONARY WAR (1775–83). After the war he continued to pursue a career at sea, first in the Virginia navy and then in the merchant marine. He was commissioned a lieutenant in the U.S. NAVY in 1798, served aboard the USS *UNITED STATES* under JOHN BARRY, and was promoted to captain in 1799. He fought in the BARBARY WARS in the opening years of the 19th century, returning to the United States in 1805.

In 1807 Barron set sail in the USS *Chesapeake* to take command as commodore of the Mediterranean squadron when that ship was intercepted by the British frigate HMS *Leopard* in search of British deserters. As the ranking officer—Captain Charles Gordon actually commanded the *Chesapeake*—much of the disgrace of the surrender fell on Barron's shoulders, even though he was wounded during the brief engagement. The subsequent court-martial acquitted him of cowardice but held that he had not prepared the ship for action at the approach of a foreign warship. Barron was suspended from the navy for five years, during which he was an officer in the French navy. After the suspension was over he returned to the U.S. Navy but was assigned shore duty. Believing that Stephen Decatur was the head of a cabal of naval officers opposing his gaining command of a ship, Barron challenged the popular naval hero to the fateful duel in 1820. Though he was wounded in the encounter, he suffered more from the reaction to the death of his opponent. Despite his seniority, he remained trapped in shore assignments until his death on April 21, 1851.

See also CHESAPEAKE-LEOPARD AFFAIR.

Further reading: Paul Barron Watson, *The Tragic Career of Commodore James Barron, U.S. Navy (1769–1851)* (New York: Coward-McCann, 1942).

Barry, John (1745–1803) *U.S. naval officer*
John Barry was one of the leading naval officers in the REVOLUTIONARY WAR (1775–83) and the early years of the republic. A Roman Catholic born in Ireland, the young sailor settled in Philadelphia at the age of 15. Working his way to becoming a captain on merchant vessels before 1775, he developed strong connections with merchant ROBERT MORRIS. At the outbreak of the war, he eagerly supported independence. Shortly after the founding of the CONTINENTAL NAVY in October 1775, Barry was asked to supervise the outfitting of his old merchant vessel, the *Black Prince*, as the warship USS *Alfred*, though he was not given its command. Instead, he had to wait a few months longer before being named captain of the newly acquired USS *Lexington*. He sailed in that vessel in spring 1776 and had the distinction of captaining the first U.S. warship to capture a British naval vessel, the sloop HMS *Edward*, on April 7, 1776. On returning to Philadelphia, he was given command of a

Naval officer John Barry won the first Revolutionary naval combat victory, on April 6, 1776. *(Naval Historical Center)*

newly built frigate, the USS *Effingham,* but never sailed in her because of difficulties in outfitting the vessel, recruiting a crew, and a British assault on Philadelphia. Against his own judgment, he was ordered to scuttle the *Effingham* to prevent her from falling into the enemy's hands.

During the British occupation of Philadelphia (1777–78), Barry commanded a small squadron on the Delaware to harass and interrupt British supplies, and to transport Continental soldiers across the river. In May 1778 he was ordered to Boston to take command of the USS *Raleigh*. When he set sail in that vessel in August, he quickly ran into a superior British force. Outgunned, he fought tenaciously, finally attempting to scuttle the vessel on a rocky island off the coast of Maine. Barry and most of the crew escaped, but the British managed to salvage the *Raleigh*.

Unable to find another naval ship, Barry took a leave of absence and commanded a privateer on a successful cruise to the WEST INDIES. Upon his return, he was given command of another ship under construction, but the project moved very slowly. In 1780 he accepted command of the USS *Alliance*, one of the few remaining ships in the Continental navy. In the *Alliance*, he crossed the ATLANTIC OCEAN several times, including a voyage in 1782 when he transported the MARQUIS DE LAFAYETTE to FRANCE. He also fought the last naval battle of the war when he engaged and severely damaged the HMS *Sybil*. He was the only active captain in the navy after the war, until Congress sold the *Alliance* in 1785.

After he left the navy, Barry served as a merchant captain again for several years and even made a voyage to China in the new TRADE with the Far East. When the United States decided to build a navy in 1794, Barry again volunteered his services. President GEORGE WASHINGTON appointed Barry the first captain of this reconstituted U.S. NAVY, and he took command of the first frigate built for it, the USS *UNITED STATES*, in 1797. At that time the U.S. government was beginning its involvement in the QUASI-WAR (1798–1800) with France. As senior officer, Barry was named commodore of the naval forces in the West Indies. However, he did not take part in any head-to-head battles with French frigates; that distinction fell to Captain Thomas Truxton in the USS *CONSTELLATION*. In part because of the lack of such a single action victory in the Quasi-War, Barry was criticized as a commanding officer of the fleet. When the United States and France came to an agreement, avoiding all-out war, and with the election of THOMAS JEFFERSON in 1800, the *United States* was laid up at the Washington naval yard, and Barry retired from the navy. He died on September 13, 1803.

Further reading: James C. Bradford, ed., *Command under Sail: Makers of the American Naval Tradition, 1775–1850* (Annapolis, Md.: Naval Institute Press,1985).

Bartlett, Josiah (1729–1795) *physician, New Hampshire politician, governor*

Born on November 21, 1729, in Amesbury, Massachusetts, Josiah Bartlett was an important New Hampshire politician and signer of the DECLARATION OF INDEPENDENCE. Bartlett became a medical doctor in 1750, practicing in the town of Kingston, where he lived with his wife. He held a variety of public offices under the colonial government of New Hampshire, including assemblyman, justice of the peace, and MILITIA colonel.

Bartlett was elected to but did not attend the FIRST CONTINENTAL CONGRESS. However, his support of the resistance to GREAT BRITAIN antagonized the colonial governor, John Wentworth, who dismissed him from his appointed government offices. Bartlett was elected to and attended the SECOND CONTINENTAL CONGRESS, where he supported independence and was the second signer of the Declaration of Independence, after JOHN HANCOCK. During the REVOLUTIONARY WAR (1775–83), he worked as a doctor with the CONTINENTAL ARMY and was at the BATTLE OF BENNINGTON (August 16, 1777). Reelected to Congress in 1778, Bartlett helped draft the ARTICLES OF CONFEDERATION, but he returned home as soon as the Articles were written.

Though Bartlett had no legal training, he was nominated to the New Hampshire Supreme Court in 1782 and subsequently performed his office well. In 1788 he served as the chief justice of the New Hampshire Supreme Court. He also attended New Hampshire's convention to ratify the U.S. CONSTITUTION. In 1790 Bartlett was elected president of New Hampshire; he continued as the state's chief executive after the title was changed to governor but resigned his office in 1794 due to ill health. He died the following year, on May 19, 1795, in Kingston, New Hampshire.

—Michele M. Stephens

Barton, Benjamin Smith (1766–1815) *physician, botanist*

Benjamin Smith Barton, physician, naturalist, and preeminent North American botanist, was a central figure in the early national scientific community. A prolific author and university professor, Barton is known chiefly for *The Elements of Botany* (1803), the first botanical textbook published in the United States. He also lectured to general audiences on all aspects of natural history. At the behest of THOMAS JEFFERSON, who admired his extensive learning, Barton tutored MERIWETHER LEWIS in preparation for the LEWIS AND CLARK EXPEDITION (1803–06).

Barton was born into a scientifically inclined family on February 10, 1766, in Lancaster, Pennsylvania. His father, an Anglican cleric, was a devoted student of botany and mineralogy, and his maternal uncle was the renowned astronomer DAVID RITTENHOUSE. Orphaned by the age of 15, Barton studied MEDICINE in Philadelphia and later at the University of Edinburgh, where he withdrew before receiving a degree. He probably never received a medical degree (other than an honorary M.D. from the University of Kiel in 1796), yet the caliber of his work brought him wide acclaim, and in 1789 he was appointed as professor of natural history and botany at the College of Pennsylvania. When the college became the University of Pennsylvania in 1791, Barton became chair of *materia medica* (medical material; today called pharmacology). Barton's career illustrates the changing nature of the scientific scene in the United States as formal institutions began to lead in the development of the natural sciences. University educated yet not duly credentialed, Barton nonetheless trained the next generation of medical practitioners and academicians.

Barton was elected to the AMERICAN PHILOSOPHICAL SOCIETY in 1789 and served as its vice president from 1802 until his death. He also was editor of the *Philadelphia Medical and Physical Journal,* one of the nation's earliest medical journals. He died on December 19, 1815.

See also SCIENCE.

Further reading: J. Whitfield Bell, "Benjamin Smith Barton, M.D.," *Journal of the History of Medicine* 26 (1971): 197–203; Jeanette E. Graustein, "The Eminent Benjamin Smith Barton," *Pennsylvania Magazine of History and Biography* 81 (1961): 423–438.

—Robyn Davis McMillin

Bartram, John (1699–1777) *botanist*

A Pennsylvania-born QUAKER farmer often described as the "father of American botany," John Bartram developed into colonial America's greatest botanist through self-EDUCATION, keen observation, wide travel, and steady contact with European naturalists. He founded the first botanical garden on the North American mainland, on the west bank of the lower Schuylkill River a few miles south of Philadelphia. Although almost entirely self-schooled, Bartram was by the middle of the century the most renowned European-American man of SCIENCE. As a result, he enjoyed a wide correspondence with European botanists, whom he supplied with coveted specimens of rare indigenous plants.

Bartram's most fruitful correspondence was with the English Quaker merchant Peter Collinson. Though the two men never met, they corresponded for nearly 40 years and exchanged plants, seeds, and natural fauna. Collinson encouraged Bartram to collect every kind of specimen; tutored him in their packing and shipping; and found buyers for his North American seeds, bulbs, plants, and trees. Bartram's clients included some of the most important members of the English landscape-garden movement. As demand grew, he standardized his shipments into a five-guinea box of assorted varieties and sold to professional nurserymen in London. Ultimately, Bartram's specimens traded internationally, and with Collinson acting as distributor, the most important European botanical gardens also received rare North American exotics. During his lifetime the number of North American plants cultivated in Europe more than doubled.

Bartram's son William wrote that his father was "designed for the study and contemplation of Nature, and the culture of philosophy. Although he was bred a farmer, or husbandman . . . he pursued his avocations as a philosopher, being ever attentive to the works and operations of Nature." Indeed, along with his friend BENJAMIN FRANKLIN, Bartram was an original member of the AMERICAN PHILOSOPHICAL SOCIETY. By the time of his death in Philadelphia on September 22, 1777, Bartram had been royal botanist to GEORGE III for more than a decade.

Further reading: John Bartram, *Observations on the Inhabitants, Climate, Soil, Rivers, Productions, Animals, and Other Matters Worthy of Notice* (London: J. Whiston and B. White, 1751); Thomas P. Slaughter, *The Natures of John and William Bartram* (New York: Random House, 1998).

William Bartram *(Library of Congress)*

Bartram, William (1739–1823) *botanist, naturalist*
The son of the famous botanist JOHN BARTRAM, William Bartram became one of North America's leading naturalists, gaining a transatlantic reputation. Born on April 20, 1739, in Kingsessing, Pennsylvania, he floundered in his early life, training as a merchant and trying his hand at farming, although he also had a gift as an artist and as a naturalist. Because of this talent he came under the sponsorship of Dr. John Fothergill in England, who underwrote an expedition to what is now the southeastern United States in 1773–77. Bartram, who was a QUAKER, was charged with collecting seeds and specimens and making drawings of the flora and fauna. The REVOLUTIONARY WAR (1775–83) limited what he could send back to England, but based on this trip Bartram published *Travels through North and South Carolina, Georgia, East and West Florida, the Cherokee Country, the Extensive Territories of the Muscogulges, or Creek Confederacy, and the Country of the Choctaws* (1791). Within the decade, this work would be republished several times on both sides of the ATLANTIC OCEAN and translated into German, Dutch, and French. It became the most important naturalist study of late 18th-century North America, with ample illustrations of plants, birds, and wildlife.

Bartram kept up an extensive correspondence, was elected to several learned societies, and published a number of papers as a naturalist. He turned down a professorship at the University of Pennsylvania in 1786, preferring to live as a bachelor with his brother at his father's famous botanic garden outside Philadelphia. When his brother died, he continued on at the garden and lived in the household of a niece until he died on July 22, 1823.

See also SCIENCE.

Further reading: Thomas P. Slaughter, *The Natures of John and William Bartram* (New York: Random House, 1998).

Bassett, Richard (1745–1815) *Delaware politician*
A member of the CONSTITUTIONAL CONVENTION in Philadelphia in 1787, Richard Bassett was a prominent Delaware politician. He was born in Maryland and grew up to be an affluent lawyer and plantation owner. In 1770 he moved to Delaware, where he became involved in the revolutionary politics during the RESISTANCE MOVEMENT (1764–75). Once the REVOLUTIONARY WAR (1775–83) broke out, Bassett helped to organize the state's MILITIA and troops for the CONTINENTAL ARMY. Starting in 1776, he held a variety of public offices, including membership on the council of safety, the state constitutional convention, and both houses of legislature. He represented Delaware at the ANNAPOLIS CONVENTION (1786) and attended the

Philadelphia Constitutional Convention, although he did not contribute much to its deliberations. However, he supported the U.S. CONSTITUTION and helped engineer Delaware's ratification of the document. For his services he was chosen by the assembly to serve in the U.S. Senate from 1789 to 1793, during which time he became a moderate member of the FEDERALIST PARTY. Bassett supported a strong central government but did not go along with all aspects of ALEXANDER HAMILTON's financial program. He became Delaware's chief justice in 1793 and governor in 1799. He was one of President JOHN ADAMS's midnight appointments as a judge on the U.S. Circuit Court until the DEMOCRATIC-REPUBLICAN PARTY did away with the post in their repeal of the JUDICIARY ACT OF 1801. Besides being politically active, Bassett was a supporter of the METHODISTS. He died in Maryland on August 15, 1815.

See also CONVENTIONS.

Bavarian Illuminati

In the charged political atmosphere of the QUASI-WAR (1798–1800) with FRANCE, a group of New England clergy who supported the FEDERALIST PARTY claimed that a clandestine international society called the Bavarian Illuminati were conspiring to destroy RELIGION and government in the United States. The Bavarian Illuminati had been formed in 1776 as a secret branch of the already secret Freemasons under the leadership of Adam Weishaupt (1748–1830), a professor of canon law in Bavaria, and it supported many of the ideas of the ENLIGHTENMENT, including DEISM. As an organization it spread to other countries in Europe but was suppressed in Bavaria during the 1780s. During the 1790s, however, some European reactionaries blamed the radical actions of the FRENCH REVOLUTION (1789–99) on the Bavarian Illuminati. This conspiracy theory was elaborated in a book published in Edinburgh by scientist John Robinson in 1797. Demonstrating the transatlantic spread of ideas, Robinson's book was subsequently published in New York and read widely in the United States, with notable readers including GEORGE WASHINGTON.

It was the New England Congregational minister JEDIDIAH MORSE who spearheaded the condemnation of the Bavarian Illuminati conspiracy in the United States. In May 1798 he declared that the Bavarian Illuminati were "atheistical" and ranted: "They abjure Christianity—justify suicide—declare death an eternal sleep—advocate sensual pleasures . . . call patriotism or loyalty narrow-minded prejudices, incompatible with universal benevolence—declaim against the baneful influence of accumulated property, . . . decry marriage, and advocate a promiscuous intercourse among the sexes." These ideas were picked up by another Congregationalist minister, TIMOTHY DWIGHT, and others. Dwight asked, "Shall our sons become the disciples of

Voltaire, and the dragoons of Marat; or our daughters the concubines of the Illuminati?"

Since many leaders in the United States were also Freemasons, Morse and the other proponents of the Illuminati conspiracy tried to minimize the connection between the two and instead connected the Bavarian Illuminati to the DEMOCRATIC-REPUBLICAN SOCIETIES. Supporters of the DEMOCRATIC-REPUBLICAN PARTY, however, attacked the conspiracy theory and defended the implied threat to FREEMASONRY. THOMAS JEFFERSON's victory in the ELECTION OF 1800 and the popularity of freemasonry led to the defusing of the conspiracy charges and the end of the Bavarian Illuminati scare.

Further reading: Richard Hofstadter, *The Paranoid Style in American Politics and Other Essays* (New York: John Wiley and Sons, 1964); Joseph W. Phillips, *Jedidiah Morse and New England Congregationalism* (New Brunswick, N.J.: Rutgers University Press, 1983).

Bayard, James (James Asheton Bayard) (1767–1815)
Delaware politician

Representing the state of Delaware in Congress, James Bayard is best remembered as the member of the FEDERALIST PARTY who broke the deadlock of the ELECTION OF 1800, though he also had a long and distinguished career as a politician and statesman. Bayard was born in Philadelphia and educated at Princeton College. He studied law and was admitted to the bar in Delaware and Pennsylvania in 1787. Settling in Wilmington, Delaware, he married Ann Bassett, daughter of RICHARD BASSETT, who was one of the state's leaders of the Federalist Party. Conservative in his politics, Bayard believed that those with a superior EDUCATION, like himself, should be the natural leaders of the country. In 1796 he became Delaware's congressman and an avid supporter of the policies of JOHN ADAMS's presidential administration. He spearheaded the effort in Congress to impeach Senator WILLIAM BLOUNT of Tennessee for plotting with the British to invade Spanish-held LOUISIANA.

In the 1800 election, when the electoral college ended in a tie between THOMAS JEFFERSON and AARON BURR, Bayard was placed in a pivotal situation since he was Delaware's only member of the House of Representatives and could determine the outcome by his actions alone. In an effort to settle the election, he entered into negotiations with several men who claimed to speak for Jefferson. These members of the DEMOCRATIC-REPUBLICAN PARTY assured Bayard that Jefferson would continue to guarantee the public credit, maintain the navy, and not dismiss lower federal officeholders for partisan purposes. Bayard believed that the president had the right to replace major officeholders like members of the cabinet. Once he thought he had these guarantees, he arranged with some other members of the Federalist Party to withhold their votes within their state delegations. This action meant that Delaware did not caste its ballot for any presidential candidate and that the Democratic-Republicans in South Carolina, Maryland, and Vermont could swing their states into Jefferson's column.

Jefferson, who later claimed that there had been no bargain, did not keep the word of his lieutenants. Bayard became a leader in the Federalist Party opposition to Jeffersonian policies in the House and the Senate, which he entered in 1805. He drew closer to the Democratic-Republicans after Jefferson left office, working with ALBERT GALLATIN in the failed effort to recharter the BANK OF THE UNITED STATES. He opposed the WAR OF 1812 (1812–15), but once the conflict began he supported measures to strengthen the nation to prosecute the war. He was one of the peace negotiators sent to Europe in 1814 and participated in the talks leading to the TREATY OF GHENT (1814). He was supposed to join the delegation to negotiate a commercial treaty with GREAT BRITAIN, but he fell ill and returned to the United States. Six days after his arrival in Delaware, he died on August 6, 1815.

Further reading: Morton Borden, *The Federalism of James A. Bayard* (New York: Columbia University, 1955).

Baylor massacre   See TAPPAN MASSACRE.

Beaumarchais, Pierre-Augustin Caron de (1732–1799) *French spy, playwright*

Pierre-Augustin Caron de Beaumarchais was a universal man of the ENLIGHTENMENT who was one of the most famous playwrights of the 18th century and a secret agent who helped supply the CONTINENTAL ARMY during the REVOLUTIONARY WAR (1775–83). As a bourgeois social climber in the French court, he added "de Beaumarchais" to his name after he married a rich widow in his early 20s.

Controversy surrounded almost every move in Beaumarchais's life. He was involved in a complicated financial scheme in the early 1770s that ended in litigation and a judicial ruling against him. To win favor with the French court, he handled secret negotiations for the payment of blackmail to stifle publications hostile to the French Crown in GREAT BRITAIN, The NETHERLANDS, and Germany. Although these efforts met with mixed success, Beaumarchais's contacts in Britain convinced him that the RESISTANCE MOVEMENT (1764–75) and the outbreak of hostilities in North America posed a serious threat to the British Empire and a golden opportunity for FRANCE. In February 1776 he presented the French king with a memo-

randum forcefully arguing that it was in France's interests to support the rebellion in British North America. In part influenced by this report, the French government began to aid the rebellion surreptitiously. In June 1776 Beaumarchais organized a private company under the name Hortalez and Cie, which obtained 1 million livres from the French government, 1 million from SPAIN, and 1 million from investors. Despite difficulties in SMUGGLING weapons out of FRANCE, Hortalez and Cie sent crucial supplies to North America before the formal beginning of the FRENCH ALLIANCE in 1778, and he helped to arm the Continentals who fought at the BATTLES OF TRENTON AND PRINCETON (December 26, 1776, and January 3, 1777) as well as those who compelled General JOHN BURGOYNE's surrender at SARATOGA (October 17, 1777). By the end of the war, Beaumarchais's company had transacted 42 million livres worth of business with the United States.

Questions, however, swirled around these transactions. To this day it remains unclear whether the initial sums provided by France were loans or grants. Moreover, although there was a settlement in 1835 with Beaumarchais's heirs, the United States never fully paid all of its debt to Hortalez and Cie. During the war Beaumarchais worked closely with SILAS DEANE, who became enmeshed in accusations of profiteering and ended in disgrace.

Beaumarchais was a controversial figure for revolutionary Americans and fellow Frenchmen. About the same time that he was engaged in secret dealings and running arms, he was also writing two of the most influential plays in French history. *The Barber of Seville* (1773) and *The Marriage of Figaro* (1778), which were subsequently put into operatic form by Gioacchino Rossini (1792–1868) and Wolfgang Mozart (1756–91), respectively, were so inflammatory that the French government sought to stifle public performances. The plays implicitly criticized the French court and aristocracy and contributed to the explosive atmosphere of the 1780s that erupted into the FRENCH REVOLUTION (1789–99). A republican France, however, did not make Beaumarchais's life more settled. During the gyrations of the French government in the upheaval that followed the fall of the Bastille, Beaumarchais was in and out of favor and at times forced to live in exile. He returned to France in 1796 and died in Paris on May 18, 1799.

Further reading: William D. Howarth, *Beaumarchais and the Theatre* (London: Routledge, 1995); Brian N. Morton and Donald C. Spinelli, *Beaumarchais and the American Revolution* (Lanham, Md.: Lexington Books, 2003).

Beaver Dams, Battle of (June 24, 1813)

During the WAR OF 1812 (1812–15) the United States launched repeated ill-fated invasions across the Niagara

FRONTIER with CANADA. On May 27, 1813, U.S. forces under the command of General HENRY DEARBORN captured FORT GEORGE, across the river from FORT NIAGARA. Dearborn decided to extend his position by attacking the British garrison at Beaver Dams, which comprised about 50 regulars under Lieutenant James Fitzgibbon and 450 Native American allies. The U.S. attackers, commanded by Lieutenant Colonel Charles G. Boerstler, numbered about 700.

Although secrecy was essential to Boerstler's success, when he reached Queenston at about midnight on June 23, his men openly discussed their objective. Laura Secord, the wife of a Canadian militiaman, slipped through the U.S. lines and went to Fitzgibbon with news of Boerstler's plans. Fitzgibbon dispatched his Indian allies to a wooded area just outside Beaver Dams. Since Boerstler marched the next day without proper scouts in front and on his flanks, the Indians caught him by surprise; his men, however, fought them to a standstill. After the Indians gave up the fight, Fitzgibbon appeared with a flag of truce, asking Boerstler to surrender. He convinced the officer, who had been wounded, that there were 1,500 regulars and 700 Indians defending Beaver Dams and that only if Boerstler surrendered could the British guarantee the safety of his men. Boerstler bought the ruse and surrendered 462 men and two artillery pieces.

This little battle had big repercussions. Congress blamed Dearborn for the disaster and for not pressing his earlier advantage hard enough; Secretary of War JOHN ARMSTRONG had to replace the general. Indians began to raid settlements in New York, and eventually the United States abandoned Fort George and pulled back across the Niagara River.

Further reading: Pierre Berton, *Flames across the Border: The Canadian-American Tragedy, 1813–1814* (New York: Little Brown and Company, 1981).

Beckwith, Sir George (1753–1823) *British military officer*

George Beckwith fought as a British officer in the REVOLUTIONARY WAR (1775–83), starting as a lieutenant and rising to the rank of major by the end of the conflict. In 1781 he was given charge of the secret service expenditures in North America. After the war he served in CANADA and became an aide to Guy Carleton (later FIRST BARON DORCHESTER), who gave him several confidential diplomatic missions to the United States. Beckwith visited the United States in 1787 and 1788, meeting important leaders and gathering information. He reported that he found a number of people sympathetic to GREAT BRITAIN and urged that "it will be good policy to hold friendly language" with the United States "and show a disposition to make a treaty of commerce with them."

In September 1789 Beckwith was sent to New York to open informal talks and to lobby against DISCRIMINATION, which threatened to set higher impost duties for Great Britain. Soon after he arrived, he developed a close relationship with ALEXANDER HAMILTON who at one point told him, "I have always preferred a connexion with you, to that of any other country, *we think in English,* and have a similarity of prejudices and of predilections." In 1790 and 1791 Beckwith made a number of other trips from Canada to the United States and even met with GEORGE WASHINGTON. Part of his job was military: He was to see if the troops being organized to fight the NATIVE AMERICANS in the Northwest territories would attack the British forts in the region. He also discussed with Hamilton the U.S. position in the NOOTKA SOUND CONTROVERSY. But in general, his main task was to smooth relations between the two countries as they inched toward an exchange of ministers and more regularized relations.

These activities as part-spy and part-diplomat advanced Beckwith's career, and he was promoted to lieutenant colonel in 1790 and full colonel in 1795. He became the governor of Bermuda in 1797 and was promoted to major general the next year. In 1804 he became governor of St. Vincent, and in 1808 he transferred to Barbados. As commander of British forces in the Leeward Islands, he captured both Martinique and Guadalupe from the French in 1809 and 1810, for which he was knighted. He left the WEST INDIES in 1810 due to ill health and was given the command of British forces in Ireland from 1816 to 1820. He died in London on March 20, 1823.

See also SPYING.

Further reading: Stanley Elkins and Eric McKitrick, *The Age of Federalism* (New York: Oxford University Press, 1993); Frank T. Reuter, *Trials and Triumphs: George Washington's Foreign Policy* (Fort Worth, Tex.: Christian University Press, 1983).

Bedford, Gunning, Jr. (1747–1812) *lawyer, Constitutional Convention delegate*

As a strong advocate for the rights of small states, Gunning Bedford, Jr., served as Delaware's attorney general and represented the state in the SECOND CONTINENTAL CONGRESS and at the CONSTITUTIONAL CONVENTION. Born in Philadelphia, Bedford graduated from the College of New Jersey and then studied law with JOSEPH REED in Philadelphia before moving to Delaware, where he established his law practice. In the 1780s he became Delaware's attorney general and was elected to the state's House of Representatives and as a delegate to the Continental Congress. At the beginning of the Constitutional Convention in 1787, Bedford maintained a conservative position and originally wanted only to amend the ARTICLES OF CONFEDERATION because he opposed any action that threatened the rights of smaller states like Delaware. As a supporter of the New Jersey Plan and protector of the interests of small states, he served on the committee responsible for the Great Compromise over representation. Bedford also believed that a strong bicameral legislature, in which the two houses would keep each other in check, would eliminate the need for a presidential veto, and he argued for a weak executive office. Though these provisions were not adopted, he felt confident that the rights of small states were protected in the new government and signed the U.S. CONSTITUTION in September 1787. He then returned to Delaware to take part in the state's ratification convention that December. He later served as a presidential elector in 1789 and 1793, and President GEORGE WASHINGTON appointed him to a federal district judgeship in September 1789. Bedford held this position until his death on March 30, 1812.

Further reading: Henry C. Conrad, *Gunning Bedford, Junior* (Wilmington: The Historical Society of Delaware, 1900)

—Tash Smith

Belknap, Jeremy (1744–1798) *Congregationalist minister*

Born into an ARTISAN family in Boston, Massachusetts, Jeremy Belknap was educated at Harvard; taught school for a while before earning his master's degree in 1765; and became a Congregationalist minister in Dover, New Hampshire, in 1767. Belknap might have had an obscure career as a provincial clergyman who supported the AMERICAN REVOLUTION had he not run into a dispute with his parishioners over his salary, which had been greatly diminished by the inflation that accompanied the REVOLUTIONARY WAR (1775–83). In 1786 he resigned his Dover pulpit, and the next year he accepted a position as pastor of the Long Lane Church in Boston. This move allowed him to pursue more vigorously a variety of other intellectual interests, especially his passion for history.

Although a Congregationalist minister, Belknap was heavily influenced by the ENLIGHTENMENT in his three-volume *History of New Hampshire* (1784–92), which he had begun in Dover but was able to complete in Boston. He relied on primary sources in this work and approached history in a rational and scientific manner, emphasizing the role of human reason in dictating the course of events. He was a strong nationalist, a supporter of the U.S. CONSTITUTION, and a member of the FEDERALIST PARTY, political positions that are represented in his work.

Concerned with preserving manuscripts and knowledge from the past, Belknap became one of the founders of the Massachusetts Historical Society in 1791. His interests were many and varied. He wrote a number of essays that appeared in MAGAZINES, wrote political commentary, and published a two-volume series of historical essays called *American Biography* (1791–92). He supported several reform initiatives, including ANTISLAVERY, TEMPERANCE, EDUCATION, and efforts to bring Christianity to NATIVE AMERICANS. He was a keen observer, and his writings are a wonderful source on the ENVIRONMENT and on life in the early republic. He died in Boston on June 20, 1798.

Further reading: Russell M. Lawson, *The American Plutarch: Jeremy Belknap and the Historian's Dialogue with the Past* (Westport, Conn.: Praeger, 1998); Louis Leonard Tucker, *Clio's Consort: Jeremy Belknap and the Founding of the Massachusetts Historical Society* (Boston: Northeastern University Press, 1990).

Bellamy, Joseph (1719–1790) *Congregationalist minister*

One of New England's most influential ministers in the 18th century, Joseph Bellamy served for almost 50 years as pastor of the Congregational church in Bethlehem, Connecticut, and became a leader of the NEW DIVINITY movement. Bellamy went to Yale at age 12 and trained as a minister after he graduated under the tutelage of the Congregational minister and theologian Jonathan Edwards. Although he served a rural northwest Connecticut community, his influence spread as a teacher and writer of religious tracts. Inspired by the First Great Awakening in the late 1730s and 1740s, Bellamy strove to avoid the excesses of the more radical evangelicals and the formalism of religious conservatives. A committed Calvinist, he read broadly in the literature of the transatlantic ENLIGHTENMENT during the 1750s and developed a doctrine emphasizing a moral dimension that led him to criticize the increasing commercialization of Anglo-American society. This message found a receptive audience among his rural parishioners and the more than 60 ministers he trained in what amounted to an ad hoc divinity school in Bethlehem.

In the 1770s Bellamy's beliefs were in sympathy with a republican view of the imperial crisis when he portrayed GREAT BRITAIN as a corrupting influence on the North American colonies. He thus became an avid supporter of the AMERICAN REVOLUTION, although his sermons also cautioned against vice and dissipation within the new independent United States. In declining health during the 1780s, he was replaced as regular minister in Bethlehem by one of his students in 1786. He died on March 6, 1790.

See also REPUBLICANISM.

Further reading: Mark Valeri, *Law and Providence in Joseph Bellamy's New England: The Origins of the New Divinity in Revolutionary America* (New York: Oxford University Press, 1994).

Benezet, Anthony (1713–1784) *educator, writer, reformer*

Anthony Benezet was one of the leading Quaker reformers in the 18th century. He was born in Saint-Quentin, FRANCE, into a Huguenot family who later moved to England. In 1731 the Benezets went to Philadelphia where Anthony worked with his brothers as a merchant. Probably sometime after his arrival in Pennsylvania, Benezet joined the QUAKERS. Eschewing the world of business, he became a teacher in 1742 and subsequently devoted the rest of his life to EDUCATION and reform measures. Along with JOHN WOOLMAN he became one of the first European Americans in colonial America to speak out against SLAVERY, writing several pamphlets advocating the ABOLITION of slavery based on the idea that it violated Christianity. As early as 1759, he noted that "nothing can be more inconsistent with the Doctrines and Practice of our meek Lord and Master, nor stained with a deeper Dye or Injustice, Cruelty and Oppression" than the SLAVE TRADE. He helped form an early ANTISLAVERY society and organized a school for AFRICAN AMERICANS in Philadelphia in 1770. He had a transatlantic correspondence with such individuals as the ABBÉ RAYNAL in France and William Wilberforce in England, and he influenced other important reformers such as JOHN WESLEY, BENJAMIN RUSH, and GRANVILLE SHARP.

Benezet became involved in a host of other reform activities as well, including providing assistance to the exiled ACADIANS in the 1750s, defending NATIVE AMERICAN rights, and writing a tract against drinking ALCOHOL. He was also a pacifist, writing in 1766: "War, considered in itself, is the premeditated destruction of human beings, of creatures originally *'formed after the image of God.'*" During the REVOLUTIONARY WAR (1775–83), he strove to remain neutral but maintained good relations with several revolutionary leaders. By the time he died in 1784, Benezet had left a huge legacy of writings and teachings that had a significant impact on both sides of the ATLANTIC OCEAN.

Further reading: George S. Brookes, *Friend Anthony Benezet* (Philadelphia: University of Pennsylvania Press, 1937).

Bennington, Battle of (August 16, 1777)

A few miles west of Bennington, Vermont, approximately 2,000 New England MILITIA under General JOHN STARK defeated about 1,200 Germans, British, LOYALISTS, and Indians under the non-English–speaking German colonel Friedrich Baum. Stark also forced a relief column of approximately 600 German grenadiers to retreat back to General JOHN BURGOYNE's main army. This action not only cost the British close to a thousand men (207 dead and more than 700 captured); it also compelled Burgoyne to continue to rely on his long and vulnerable supply line from CANADA on his thrust into New York State, ultimately contributing to the disaster that led to Burgoyne's surrender at SARATOGA (October 17, 1777). The Revolutionaries lost only about 30–40 killed.

British arrogance and Baum's ineptness and bad luck led to the revolutionary victory. Burgoyne's plan for the raid was too ambitious: He ordered Baum not only to gain horses, cattle, and grains but also to rouse the countryside to the king's banner. As Baum moved against Vermont, he decided to head for Bennington because of a reported cache of supplies there under a militia guard of only a few hundred. Meanwhile, after the British capture of FORT TICONDEROGA in June 1777, New Hampshire had appointed John Stark as its general; the veteran Stark had left the CONTINENTAL ARMY after he had been passed over for promotion. General PHILIP JOHN SCHUYLER, in command of the revolutionary forces opposed to Burgoyne, sent General BENJAMIN LINCOLN to order the New Hampshire men to the Hudson, but Stark insisted on keeping his militia in New England for protection. Lincoln and Schuyler decided not to press the issue, and Stark marched to Bennington. By August 14, as Baum drew near to Bennington, both forces had become aware of each other. Although Baum knew he was outnumbered, he assumed that the militia would withdraw once he began his advance. He did ask for reinforcements but did not press the case for urgency.

It rained all day on August 15, and Baum spread his men out across a mile-and-a-half front in entrenchments west of Bennington and in groups ranging from 50 to a couple of hundred. With his men divided, it would be difficult for the units to act in support of one another. Stark decided to attack on August 16, after it stopped raining, and, taking a risk, he also divided his men. He hoped to pull off a double-enveloping maneuver that would neutralize the discipline of German and British regulars. Colonel Moses Nichols circled around the enemy left to attack a weakly manned position on a hill overlooking the battlefield. Another force under Colonel Samuel Herrick circled around Baum's right to ford the Walloomsac River at the enemy's rear. Stark and the main force attacked the center. Amazingly, this maneuver worked as Nichols overwhelmed the Germans stationed on the high ground. There was fierce fighting on the right, especially in a redoubt held by Loyalists, many of whom were neighbors of the New

General John Stark strategically surrounds an unsuspecting Hessian force and gains a Revolutionary victory at the Battle of Bennington, August 16, 1777. *(National Guard Bureau)*

England militia. The Germans in the middle fought bravely and held the Revolutionaries at bay until Baum was killed. The Revolutionaries then swept the field.

The German relief column under the command of Colonel Heinrich Breymann took too long to march the 25 miles to Baum's assistance, making only eight miles on the 15th in the rain. In late afternoon of the 16th, they were only four miles from the battlefield; by then Baum's force had been annihilated. Fortunately for the Revolutionaries, they too had some reinforcements arrive under SETH WARNER. The militia's discipline had broken down after their victory over Baum: Men were drinking and looting, and many were separated from their units. As Breymann's troops advanced toward Bennington, they were harassed by groups of militia. Stark considered withdrawing but then decided to attack with Warner's men, and a fierce engagement ensued. Although Breymann almost surrendered when his ammunition ran low, at sundown he managed to withdraw most of his men (he lost 20 dead and over 100 as

prisoners), bringing them back to the safety of Burgoyne's army the next day. With his men exhausted from marching and fighting, Stark did not pursue the Germans.

See also HESSIANS.

Further reading: Richard M. Ketchum, *Saratoga: Turning Point of America's Revolutionary War* (New York: Henry Holt and Company, 1997).

Berlin Decree (1806)

NAPOLEON BONAPARTE issued the Berlin Decree in the Prussian capital on November 21, 1806, in answer to the British blockade of FRANCE. Napoleon claimed that by blocking solely commercial ports, GREAT BRITAIN was acting in defiance of international maritime law. The Berlin Decree initiated the Continental System, which declared Britain to be under a blockade. Napoleon sought to wage economic warfare in lieu of having a strong navy to wield against the superior British fleet. Despite this bold prohibition, black markets thrived along Europe's shores. Merchant ships from the United States were quick to capitalize on the illegal TRADE. Both Great Britain and France placed further restrictions on neutral trade with ORDERS IN COUNCIL and the MILAN DECREE.

See also EMBARGO OF 1807.

Further reading: Lawrence S. Kaplan, *Entangling Alliances with None: American Foreign Policy in the Age of Jefferson* (Kent, Ohio: Kent State University Press, 1987).

—Catherine Franklin

Bernard, Sir Francis (1712–1779) *governor of New Jersey and Massachusetts*

Francis Bernard was the governor of Massachusetts throughout most of the turbulent 1760s. He was born in Brightwell, Oxfordshire, England, studied at Christ Church College, Oxford University; and became a lawyer in 1737. He might have lived in obscurity as a country lawyer in Lincolnshire had he not married Amelia Offley, a cousin of Lord Thomas Barrington, who was highly influential at court and served in the British government for most of the time from 1755 to 1778. Politics in GREAT BRITAIN depended heavily on patronage, and Bernard, something of a social climber, soon became a client of Lord Barrington. In 1758 Barrington managed to get Bernard appointed as governor of New Jersey. A talented bureaucrat and a careful politician, Bernard quickly won over the local leaders in that colony and thereby became a successful governor. Barrington and other English officials took note of this success and transferred him to the governorship of Massachusetts, one of the most populous and richest colonies. Unfortunately for Bernard, as he moved from Perth Amboy to Boston in 1760, the British Empire was about to face its greatest challenge.

Interestingly, Bernard recognized that the British-colonial relationship was troubled, and soon after he arrived in Massachusetts, he worked out an elaborate plan to reorganize the North American empire. His advice was not acted upon, but it suggests that independence was not the only possibility available on the eve of the AMERICAN REVOLUTION. Bernard wanted to rewrite the colonial charters to create larger, more coherent colonies, especially in New England, where there were many jurisdictions divided into small entities like Rhode Island and Connecticut. He also wanted to create a North American nobility, which would form an upper house of legislature in each colony and help to stabilize a volatile social situation. He believed that the king in Parliament remained sovereign in the colonies, with the right of taxation, but he also advocated that the colonial assemblies be responsible for most taxes and

that Parliament should be mainly concerned with TRADE regulations.

Instead of acting on these recommendations, the British government began to pass a series of customs duties and laws—the SUGAR ACT (1764), the STAMP ACT (1765), the TOWNSHEND DUTIES (1767)—that made governing Massachusetts all but impossible. The man who had been a successful governor in New Jersey wrestled throughout the 1760s with a tide of events beyond his control. Although sympathetic to many colonial demands, Bernard witnessed outright flounting of customs regulations, the nullification of the Stamp Act through mob action, and the harassment of customs officials. He struggled to keep up with events. The publication in 1769 of a series of letters he had sent home to officials in England complaining of colonial behavior made him extremely unpopular. At the assembly's request, he was recalled to Britain, where he was exonerated, though he did not return to the colonies. He was subsequently made a baronet, becoming Sir Francis Bernard of Needleham, Lincolnshire. He held some other government sinecures, received a pension, and died in relative isolation and retirement on June 16, 1779.

See also RESISTANCE MOVEMENT.

Further reading: Edmund S. and Helen M. Morgan, *The Stamp Act Crisis: Prologue to Revolution* (Chapel Hill: University of North Carolina Press, 1953).

betterment acts

During the 1790s and early 1800s, European-American settlers streamed onto FRONTIER lands, often building homes and farms on property they did not own. These squatters became a potent political force in several states, demanding compensation for their work in developing the land. In 1797 Kentucky passed the first Betterment Act, which compensated settlers for their improvements to property regardless of who owned the title. Other states soon followed this example, including Tennessee, Pennsylvania, Vermont, and Massachusetts (for Maine), extending occupancy rights to squatters and sometimes allowing the squatter to buy the land he occupied for the predeveloped price.

Biddle, James (1783–1848) *U.S. naval officer*

James Biddle was one of the many dynamic naval officers who made a name for himself and the U.S. NAVY in the early 19th century. Biddle was born into a QUAKER family in Philadelphia, attended the University of Pennsylvania, and became a midshipman in 1800, serving aboard the USS *President*. In 1803, during the BARBARY WARS, he was on the USS *Philadelphia* when the Tripolitans cap tured the vessel and imprisoned him and his shipmates for 19 months. After this experience, he served on a gunboat and took a leave of absence in 1807 for a voyage to China. He returned to the navy in 1809, and by the outbreak of the WAR OF 1812 (1812–15), he was a first lieutenant aboard the USS *Wasp*. He participated in that ship's dramatic capture of the British brig HMS *Frolic* and given command of the prize, but before arriving in Charleston, he was in turn taken by a British 74-gun ship. The British paroled him in 1813, and he was given command of the sloop of war USS *Hornet*. Aboard the *Hornet* he successfully fought a rough engagement with a superior British ship, the brig HMS *Penguin* on March 23, 1815, in the South ATLANTIC OCEAN. In the last action of the war, he successfully eluded capture by a British ship of the line in April 1815.

Biddle went on to a distinguished naval career after 1815, sailing to the PACIFIC OCEAN and raising the U.S. flag over Oregon in 1817, searching for pirates in the Caribbean in the 1820s, and negotiating the first treaty between China and the United States in 1846. He died in Philadelphia on October 1, 1848. His brother was the financier Nicholas Biddle.

Further reading: David F. Long, *Sailor-Diplomat: A Biography of Commodore James Biddle, 1783–1848* (Boston: Northeastern University Press, 1983).

Bigot, François (1703–1778) *French government official*

The last intendant (chief civil officer) of New France (CANADA), François Bigot came from an established family in FRANCE with a long history in the civil service. Bigot first went to Canada in 1739, when he was stationed in LOUISBOURG as financial commissary. He remained there until 1745, when an Anglo-American force captured the fortress. He joined a failed expedition to retake Louisbourg the next year, and in 1748 he was stationed at Quebec, where he became intendant. Like other French officials, Bigot used his position to combine public and private operations to make a fortune for himself. When the British captured Canada in 1760 during the FRENCH AND INDIAN WAR (1754–63), the French government blamed local officials like Bigot for losing New France while filling their own pockets. Arrested on his return to France in 1761 and held in the Bastille, Bigot was tried and convicted of corruption. He was ordered to forfeit all of his possessions and was also banished, upon which he moved to Switzerland. Despite the confiscation of a huge quantity of property, Bigot somehow retained enough wealth to live the rest of his life in some comfort. He died in Neuchâtel on January 12, 1778.

Billings, William (1746–1800) *composer*

The leading composer and singing teacher of his generation, William Billings helped to define a distinct North American form of MUSIC. Billings was born into a modest Boston family and apprenticed as a tanner. Although he continued in the tanner trade off and on for the rest of his life, while in his early 20s he began to establish a reputation as a psalm singer and music teacher. By 1769 he had opened his first singing school.

Music underwent an important transformation in the revolutionary era. Church music expanded beyond psalm singing and increasingly included more sacred songs, organ playing, and elaborate choral performances. Initially these changes were introduced based on English practices, but Billings added a particular North American cast to this development. In 1770 he published *The New England Psalm Singer: or American Chorister.* All of this collection, as the book proudly proclaimed, was American and written by Billings. The book contained music and songs for church performances, as well as instructions on how to teach the music. Innovative in its approach and in its New England identity, the book was an instant success.

Over the next couple of decades, Billings taught at singing schools throughout New England. He became an ardent supporter of the AMERICAN REVOLUTION and published another book, *The Singing Master's Assistant, or Key to Practical Music,* in 1778. This work featured many patriotic tunes portraying the revolutionary movement as the work of God. If anything, it was even more popular than the *New England Psalm Singer* and was sometimes called "Billings's Best." Billings continued to write and publish music in the 1780s and 1790s and remained the most popular and renowned composer of sacred music in the United States during his lifetime. Despite this success, he seems to have struggled financially in his later years. After his death in Boston on September 26, 1800, his music declined in popularity as musical tastes shifted in the 19th century.

Further reading: Kenneth Silverman, *The Cultural History of the American Revolution: Painting, Music, Literature, and Theatre in the Colonies and the United States from the Treaty of Paris to the Inauguration of George Washington, 1763–1789* (New York: Columbia University Press, 1976).

Bill of Rights

The Bill of Rights is the collective term given to the first 10 amendments to the U.S. CONSTITUTION. These amendments, which were ratified in December 1791, guarantee such rights as freedom of speech, the press, and RELIGION. Several states had made the inclusion of such amendments a condition of their ratification of the Constitution, arguing that most states had included some sort of declaration protecting the rights of citizens in their own state constitutions.

Although the FEDERALISTS eventually agreed to give the issue consideration, they believed that there were many problems inherent in including an explicit written bill of rights in the Constitution. For one thing, they opposed a statement to protect individual rights because they were concerned that ANTI-FEDERALISTS would use the call for a bill of rights as an excuse to ask for serious changes to the Constitution itself. Federalists also argued that a bill of rights was unnecessary because the federal government could only exert powers that were expressly delegated to it, and thus it did not pose a threat to individual LIBERTY. Moreover, from the Federalist perspective, the greatest threat to a republic came from unchecked popular majorities and not the powers of the government. Giving the people too much liberty might therefore inhibit the government's ability to function. Finally, one of the Federalists' main theoretical concerns was how to decide which rights deserved protecting to the exclusion of all others. In other words, they believed that it was impossible to enumerate all of the rights that needed protection, and the listing of some rights would mean that those rights not mentioned were not protected.

In the end, however, the Federalists capitulated in the interest of appeasing the opposition. In so doing, they hoped to build support for the new government and end talk of calling another CONSTITUTIONAL CONVENTION. Because one of the goals of the Bill of Rights was to squelch resistance to the Constitution, some decisions were influenced by politics as much as principle.

Although JAMES MADISON was among those who thought that a bill of rights was not necessary, he was the one person most responsible for adding them to the Constitution. Madison spearheaded the amendment process in Congress, examining more than 200 proposed amendments and selecting 19 for consideration. After extensive deliberation, Congress accepted most of Madison's suggestions and ratified the first 10 amendments to the Constitution. To deal with the possible exclusion of rights not mentioned, Madison carefully worded what became the Ninth Amendment to state: "The enumeration in the Constitution of certain rights, shall not be construed to deny or disparage others retained by the people." The Bill of Rights also included an assertion of state sovereignty in the Tenth Amendment by stipulating that "the powers not delegated to the United States in the Constitution, nor prohibited by it to the States, are reserved to the States respectively, or to the people." This amendment stood in stark contrast to the NECESSARY AND PROPER CLAUSE in Article 1, Section 8 of the Constitution, which stated that Congress would have the power "To make all Laws which shall be necessary

and proper for carrying into Execution" the other powers of Congress.

The Bill of Rights has had a dramatic impact on the history of the United States. As early as the 1790s, the FEDERALIST PARTY and the DEMOCRATIC-REPUBLICAN PARTY debated issues connected to the Bill of Rights concerning the limiting of the national government's power and the restraint of rights in the ALIEN AND SEDITION ACTS (1798). More recently, it has become the foundation for civil liberties in modern society and is especially important in protecting the rights of minority groups. For example, the First Amendment's protection of free speech allows people to hold opinions that stray from the official or even popular opinion.

One of the more controversial of the first 10 amendments has been the second, which concerns the right to bear arms. At the time the U.S. Constitution was written, some people argue, it was crucial for citizens to be armed to protect against the corrupting power of government; whereas in the 21st century many Americans no longer believe that a well-armed citizenry is good for society at large.

Many of the amendments do not expressly give people rights. Instead, they simply prevent the government from infringing on these rights, a provision embodied in the phrase "Congress shall make no law . . ." The Third Amendment states that soldiers will not be quartered in private homes, while the fourth protects against unreasonable search and seizure. There are also provisions for criminal issues. Speedy trials, trial by jury, and protection from cruel and unusual punishment are guaranteed by the Fifth, Sixth, and Seventh Amendments. The Fifth Amendment also protects individuals against self-incrimination while also stating that no one can be deprived of "life, liberty, or property, without due process of law."

Overall, the effects of the Bill of Rights in practice have been subject to fluctuations in U.S. SUPREME COURT interpretation. The interpretation of these rights has often caused great public controversy. Some scholars attempt to discern the original intentions of the Founding Fathers; others believe that the founders intended the Constitution to be a flexible document and that original meanings are irrelevant. Despite the Federalists' concerns that the national government could do little to protect individual liberties, the Bill of Rights has proved to be a success, protecting U.S. citizens' privileges throughout the nation's history.

See also CONSTITUTION, RATIFICATION OF THE; CONSTITUTIONS, STATE; REPUBLICANISM.

Further reading: Irving Brant, *The Bill of Rights: Its Origin and Meaning* (Indianapolis, Ind.: Bobbs-Merrill, 1965); Leonard Levy, *Constitutional Opinions: Aspects of the Bill of Rights* (New York: Oxford University Press, 1986); Jack

N. Rakove, *Original Meanings: Politics and Ideas in the Making of the Constitution* (New York: Knopf, 1996); Robert A. Rutland, *The Birth of the Bill of Rights, 1776–1791* (Boston, Northeastern University Press, 1983).

Bingham, Anne Willing (1764–1801) *salon hostess*

The daughter of THOMAS WILLING, one of the most affluent men in Philadelphia, Anne Willing Bingham received the best EDUCATION available to rich young women in the late colonial period, enabling her to read, write, and speak in a cultured manner. She undoubtedly also had training in the refinements of MUSIC and ART typical of her class. At age 15 she struck all who met her as beautiful, charming, and accomplished. She certainly captivated her father's business partner, WILLIAM BINGHAM, when he returned to the country from the WEST INDIES in 1780, and by the time she was 16, the two were married. Over the next few years the couple began a family, and as William Bingham worked his way to becoming the richest man in the United States, they traveled in Europe and experienced firsthand the courts in Paris and London. Anne was impressed in particular by the role of women in the political affairs of FRANCE. As she explained to THOMAS JEFFERSON in a letter in 1787, a year after the Binghams had returned to the United States, "The Women in France interfere in the politics of the Country, and often give a decided Turn to the Fate of Empires. Either by the gentle Arts of persuasion, or by the commanding force of superior Attractions and Address, they have obtained that Rank and Consideration in society, which the Sex are intitled to."

During the 1790s Anne Willing Bingham put the lessons she learned in Europe to good use and established the most important salon in the 18th-century European style in Philadelphia, where she became the uncrowned queen of a republican court. Although she and her husband were allied to the FEDERALIST PARTY, members of all political persuasions were invited to her balls and entertainments. A coveted invitation to the huge Bingham mansion was a sign that an individual had arrived in society and politics. Most Philadelphians believed that Anne and her daughters were the most beautiful women in the United States, though some dismissed a Bingham event as mere show and vanity. Anne's charm, hospitality, and wit were accompanied by an intelligence and political acumen worthy of the French women she admired. Even curmudgeonly JOHN ADAMS confessed that he had "something of a political conversation with her" and that she had "more ideas on the subject" than he had imagined "and a correcter judgement."

Anne Willing Bingham's reign of Philadelphia high society came to an end in 1801 when she became ill, went to BERMUDA to convalesce, and died. However, she left an indelible mark in the world. Throughout the 1790s, every-one from GEORGE WASHINGTON to a clerk in the Treasury Department sought out her company and her opinion. Moreover, her image is believed to be the model of the "draped bust LIBERTY" coins minted in the 1790s and early 1800s, and two of her daughters married into the Baring banking family in England (see BARING, HOUSE OF).

Further reading: Robert C. Alberts, *The Golden Voyage: The Life and Times of William Bingham, 1752–1804* (Boston: Houghton Mifflin Company, 1969); Susan Branson, *These Fiery Frenchified Dames: Women and Political Culture in Early National Philadelphia* (Philadelphia: University of Pennsylvania Press, 2001).

Bingham, William (1752–1804) *merchant, Pennsylvania politician*

Perhaps the richest man in the United States when he died in 1804—BENJAMIN RUSH thought he was worth $3 million—William Bingham was a merchant, banker, land speculator, and politician who played a prominent role in the development of the United States during the early republic. Born in Philadelphia, he started life with advantages and was educated at the University of Pennsylvania. He supported the RESISTANCE MOVEMENT, and from 1776 to 1780 he was an agent for the SECOND CONTINENTAL CONGRESS in MARTINIQUE in the WEST INDIES, where he combined public service with private profit for himself and business partners ROBERT MORRIS and THOMAS WILLING. He funneled supplies and equipment to the CONTINENTAL ARMY, owned privateers, and seemed to make a profit on everything that passed his way.

After returning to Philadelphia in 1780, Bingham continued his shrewd business ways and was involved in the creation of the BANK OF NORTH AMERICA. Throughout the 1780s and 1790s, he invested in land, buying huge holdings in Maine and purchasing the area in New York State along the Susquehanna River that became the city of Binghamton, which was named after him. He also speculated in a variety of financial fields, calculating with uncanny success which way the financial markets would go; maintained interests in shipping; and was the first president of the Lancaster-Philadelphia turnpike.

Bingham did not just limit himself to business; as a prominent Philadelphian, he contributed to several philanthropic projects in the city, and he and his wife, ANNE WILLING BINGHAM, maintained an active social life at the highest level. He also entered politics and was elected to the Second Continental Congress, 1786–87. During the 1790s he became a moderate member of the FEDERALIST PARTY, serving in the Pennsylvania Assembly, 1790–95, and in the U.S. Senate, 1795–1801. Bingham formed a close business and personal connection to the Baring banking family (see BARING, HOUSE OF): Two of his daughters married Barings, and he, the Barings, and another partner loaned the United States most of the MONEY for the LOUISIANA PURCHASE. Bingham died on February 7, 1804, while traveling in Europe.

Further reading: Robert C. Alberts, *The Golden Voyage: The Life and Times of William Bingham, 1752–1804* (Boston: Houghton Mifflin Company, 1969).

Bishop, Abraham (1763–1844) *Connecticut politician*
Abraham Bishop was a leading politician of the DEMOCRATIC-REPUBLICAN PARTY in Connecticut. Though educated at Yale College and trained as a lawyer, Bishop spent most of his early adulthood aimlessly. He traveled to Europe in 1787–88, taught school upon his return, and had a failed marriage in the 1790s that ended in divorce. (He married two more times; the second wife died and the third survived him.)

Bishop pursued a radicalism that insisted government should remain close to the people. As a young man he supported the ANTI-FEDERALISTS because he believed that a republic could only exist in a small state and that the U.S. CONSTITUTION was undemocratic. For Bishop the new government set up under the Constitution was "a mere bubble, in which the great body of the people were not interested, and by which a few only are benefitted." Bishop had other radical ideas, including support for female EDUCATION and advocacy for the rights of AFRICAN AMERICANS. He wrote that "the blacks are entitled to freedom, for we did not say all *white* men are free, but *all men* are free."

Although his ideas on race differed from THOMAS JEFFERSON's, Bishop's faith in the common man and his antiaristocratic sentiments brought him into the ranks of the Democratic-Republican Party in the 1790s. In the late 1790s he served as a clerk in a variety of state courts but lost those positions because of his support for Jefferson. His political allegiances paid dividends, however, after the ELECTION OF 1800 when Jefferson first appointed Bishop's father as collector of the port of New Haven and then, when his father died in 1803, appointed Bishop himself (who had been doing most of the work anyway) to the lucrative position. Bishop retained the collectorship until 1829, amassing a great fortune in the meantime.

In the opening decade of the 19th century, Bishop became the epitome of the grassroots politician, organizing public meetings, making grand orations, and publishing pamphlets supporting Jefferson in Connecticut. In this way he managed to generate support for the Democratic-Republican Party even in a conservative state. Members of the FEDERALIST PARTY believed Bishop was "a flaming street orator . . . a blazing meteor of republicanism, and a violent enemy of christianity." Bishop, in turn, claimed that during the 1790s the Federalist Party had attempted to establish an "energetic, aristocratic, monarchic government, which could move without control" and that the New England clergy supporting that government operated from a "clerical delusion." Bishop died one of the richest men in New Haven on April 28, 1844.

Further reading: David Waldstreicher and Stephen R. Grossbart, "Abraham Bishop's Vocation; or the Mediation of Jeffersonian Politics," *Journal of the Early Republic* 18 (1998): 617–657.

black church movement

Triggered by the evangelicalism of the late 18th century, the spirit of freedom that accompanied the AMERICAN REVOLUTION, and a resurgent African identity, AFRICAN AMERICANS not only increasingly turned to Christianity but also organized an ad hoc black church movement by forming congregations that embraced their racial heritage and were distinct from the European-American religious institutions. This movement initially appeared independently in several different urban locations, but the various elements eventually merged and even led to the establishment of African-American denominations. Moreover, especially in its earlier stages, the black church movement was transatlantic in its scope.

The first "African" church in North America began to form in Savannah as a result of the evangelical labors of GEORGE LIELE and DAVID GEORGE during the REVOLUTIONARY WAR (1785–83) when they converted hundreds of African Americans to the Baptist faith during the British occupation of the city, which began in 1778. In 1779 Liele organized the First African Church of Savannah. Liele and George both left the United States with the British at the end of the war. Liele went to JAMAICA, where he organized another racially oriented church, and George went first to NOVA SCOTIA and then to SIERRA LEONE, preaching to members of his own race. Along with other black evangelicals, these men spread the black church movement across the ATLANTIC OCEAN. In the meantime, the leadership of the Savannah BAPTISTS fell to Andrew Bryan (1737–1812), who was ordained a minister in 1788. That same year the First African Baptist Church of Savannah became certified—four years before the city's first white Baptist church. By 1800 the church had about 700 members. During the 1780s African Americans in Williamsburg, Virginia, also organized a Baptist congregation, which received official recognition in 1793 from the state's Baptist association.

By that time the lead in independent "African" churches had shifted north. In 1787 ABSALOM JONES and

RICHARD ALLEN had helped to organize the Free African Society in Philadelphia, a religiously oriented mutual-aid society for blacks. Both men joined the interracial St. George's Methodist Church, but they later left it when they and other African-American members were compelled to sit in a segregated gallery of a new church building in 1792. Jones organized St. Thomas's African Episcopal Church in 1794, and in 1804 he became the first black priest ordained by the Episcopalian Church (see ANGLICANS). Allen remained an adherent to Methodism, forming a black Methodist congregation in 1794 and became the first bishop of the national African Methodist Episcopal Church founded in 1816.

The Black Church movement spread to other cities. As early as 1787, some black METHODISTS in Baltimore were holding meetings separate from their white coreligionists, and in 1793 Baltimore African Americans established the Sharp Street Chapel, which remained unincorporated into the early 19th century. Bishop FRANCIS ASBURY granted African-American Methodists in New York City permission to hold racially separated meetings in 1796. With their own building complete in 1800, the New Yorkers incorporated the African Methodist Episcopal Church (Zion Church) in 1801. In Boston, African-American Baptists organized a church in 1805 and opened their own meeting house in 1806; today the building is a national park. In Wilmington, Delaware, African Americans formed a separate church in 1805 and included in their charter the provision that "none but persons of colour" be allowed to be chosen trustees of the church. Over the next few decades, scores of churches formed by African Americans proudly included the words *African, Abyssinian, Ethiopian,* and *Negro* in their names.

See also RACE AND RACIAL CONFLICT; RELIGION.

Further reading: Dee E. Andrews, *The Methodists and Revolutionary America: The Shaping of an Evangelical Culture* (Princeton, N.J.: Princeton University Press, 2000); Nathan Hatch, *Democratization of American Christianity* (New Haven, Conn.: Yale University Press, 1989); James Sidbury, *Becoming African in America: Race and Nation in the Early Black Republic* (New York: Oxford University Press, 2007).

black guides and pioneers

The British army relied heavily on black guides and pioneers during the REVOLUTIONARY WAR (1775–83). Slaves often knew the local terrain, roads, trails, and streams, and the British used this knowledge to their advantage. For example, at the BATTLE OF SAVANNAH (December 29, 1778), a slave led British troops on a path through a marsh to the rear of the Continental line. The British thus not only defeated but also routed the Revolutionaries defending Savannah.

Black pioneers were runaway slaves who were either assigned to British and LOYALIST regiments or organized into separate units under white officers. The separate units sometimes performed garrison duty on their own, freeing regular troops for field campaigns. Black pioneers also performed a host of auxiliary services such as digging entrenchments, lugging baggage, making and breaking camp, building and repairing bridges, and clearing roads. Casualty rates, especially from DISEASE AND EPIDEMICS, were very high for the black guides and pioneers, and when captured by the revolutionary forces they would be re-enslaved. They were not always well treated by the British, either, but at the end of the war the British evacuated many of the remaining black pioneers despite the provision in the TREATY OF PARIS (1783) that prohibited "carrying away any negroes."

Further reading: Sylvia R. Frey, *Water from the Rock: Black Resistance in a Revolutionary Age* (Princeton, N.J.: Princeton University Press, 1991).

Blackstocks, Battle of (November 20, 1780)

After their defeat at the BATTLE OF KING'S MOUNTAIN (October 7, 1780), the British sought revenge on the revolutionary forces in South Carolina while protecting LOYALIST outposts. When LORD CORNWALLIS heard that General THOMAS SUMTER was heading for Ninety-Six with about 1,000 men, he ordered Colonel BANASTRE TARLETON to intercept him. Rather than confront the regulars under Tarleton, Sumter decided to retreat to the safety of the backcountry. Tarleton set off in pursuit but found it difficult to catch up to Sumter with his infantry and an artillery piece slowing him down. On the afternoon of November 20, Tarleton took an advance guard of dragoons and mounted infantry of about 300 men to see if he could surprise Sumter; the rest of the force was to follow as quickly as possible. That evening Tarlton found Sumter camped at Blackstocks plantation near the Tyger River in a strong defensive position and decided to delay his attack until the next morning, when the rest of his men would arrive. Sumter, however, would not wait for the British reinforcements and launched an assault, which the vastly outnumbered British repulsed. Tarleton, never one to shy away from battle, then ordered a counterattack, which failed to dislodge the Revolutionaries.

Tarleton pulled his men back from the engagement, knowing that he had reinforcements coming, but the South Carolina MILITIA had had enough and continued its retreat that night. Sumter was severely wounded in the battle, and although his force sustained minimal casualties, much of his command quickly disintegrated. Tarleton's losses were much heavier: As many of half his advance force may have been killed or injured. Both sides claimed victory. Tarleton asserted that he had held the field, at least by the next morning; that the Revolutionaries were in retreat; and that he had diverted the attack on Ninety-Six. The Revolutionaries claimed that on the evening of the battle, they had held the field and inflicted greater casualties on the British.

Blackstone, William (1723–1780) *British legal scholar, jurist*

Sir William Blackstone was the author of *Commentaries on the Laws of England* (1765–69), the most influential legal text in the early republican United States. He was born in Cheapside, London, on July 10, 1723, and orphaned before the age of 12. At the age of 15, on the nomination of Sir Robert Walpole, he entered Pembroke College, Oxford University, where his studies focused on the classics. In 1741 he commenced the study of law at the Middle Temple in London, one of several legal academies controlled by the practicing bar. After completing his legal studies, Blackstone was admitted to practice in 1746. His strength and interest lay more in legal EDUCATION, however, and he was nominated for the professorship of civil law at Oxford in 1752. "Civil law" covered the laws of most of the nations of Europe, excluding England. Blackstone was passed over for this appointment, but supporters encouraged him to go to Oxford anyway and lecture on English law. At this time no university in England offered training in English law. Blackstone's lectures were so popular that Oxford established a chair of English law in 1758 and appointed Blackstone its first holder. His success in this position led to the renewal of his law practice, his election to Parliament, and his eventual selection as justice of the Courts of King's Bench and Common Pleas.

Blackstone's fame in the United States rests on his written works. His lectures had been copied by others and circulated, often for sale; to halt this practice, he decided to publish them himself. The first volume, under the title *Commentaries on the Laws of England*, appeared in 1765. Three additional volumes appeared over the next four years, and they were phenomenally successful. Eight editions appeared during Blackstone's lifetime, and the ninth was ready for publication at the time of his death on February 14, 1780. New editions continued to appear with the same frequency for the next 60 years in England, and for even longer in the United States. The reason for their success was their comprehensiveness and readability. Laypeople could pick up the *Commentaries* and gain a basic understanding of English law. While not without error, and while certainly subject to strong criticism (Jeremy Bentham called Blackstone's views on the law "nonsense on stilts"),

the *Commentaries* stood for generations as the standard text on the law.

In the United States, the *Commentaries* had an even greater impact than in England. During the early republican period, very few institutions offered legal training. Most would-be LAWYERS apprenticed themselves to a practicing lawyer for a time. To supplement this experience and gain some knowledge of areas beyond the mentor's field of practice, apprentices needed a textual guide, and that text was Blackstone. The widespread availability of the *Commentaries* led to a democratization of the legal profession in the United States. Anyone with access to the four volumes could hold himself out as a lawyer. This bothered many, including THOMAS JEFFERSON, who worried that a student found in Blackstone "a smattering of everything, and his indolence easily persuades him that if he understands that book he is master of the whole body of the law." At the time, however, the practice was unstoppable, and the lawyer trained on Blackstone quickly became the norm. This circumstance was not without consequence to the development of thinking about legal issues. Blackstone was committed to the preservation of private property, and this commitment forms the major unifying theme of his *Commentaries*. To a great extent, the modern U.S. commitment to private property goes back to Sir William Blackstone and the thousands of early republican lawyers who were trained on the *Commentaries*.

Further reading: Daniel J. Boorstin, *The Mysterious Science of the Law: An Essay on Blackstone's Commentaries* (Cambridge, Mass.: Harvard University Press, 1941).

—Lindsay Robertson

Bladensburg, Battle of (August 24, 1814)

One of the lowest points for the United States during the WAR OF 1812 (1812–15) came with the Battle of Bladensburg and the subsequent burning of WASHINGTON, D.C. British admiral Alexander Cochrane commanded 20 warships, and General ROBERT ROSS had 4,500 soldiers to launch a British attack in the Chesapeake in summer 1814. The British sailed up the Patuxent River and landed troops on August 19. Two day later, outmaneuvered by this land force, the American commander, JOSHUA BARNEY, abandoned a flotilla of boats he had gathered to block the advance of the British navy. He then stationed his 400 SEAMEN to defend the bridge across the Anacostia River near the Washington Navy Yard. The British, however, approached Washington eight miles to the north, near Bladensburg. U.S. general WILLIAM WINDER opposed the British with 6,000 men but had only 500 regulars. Complicating matters, Secretary of State JAMES MONROE arrived on the battlefield and changed the deployment of many of the troops. The MILITIA were unprepared to meet the veterans in the British army, and many ran after only a few volleys. Seeing that his men could not stand up to the British regulars, Winder ordered a withdrawal. The only U.S. officer to gain any credit in the battle was Barney, who arrived with about 400 sailors and U.S. MARINES after the fighting began. His men fought bravely, but in vain. Barney himself was wounded and captured.

The battle lasted about three hours and was over shortly after 4:00 P.M. The British lost 64 killed and 185 wounded; the United States had only 10 or 12 killed, 40 wounded, and about 100 taken prisoners. The U.S. forces lacked training, and the retreat ended in such a rout that the battle became derisively known as the "Blandensburg Races." With no American forces left to defend Washington, the British advanced that night into the nation's capital, torching the public buildings.

See also CHESAPEAKE BAY CAMPAIGN.

Further reading: Charles G. Muller, *The Darkest Day: 1814: The Washington-Baltimore Campaign* (Philadelphia: J. B. Lippincott, 1963); Anthony S. Pitch, *The Burning of Washington: The British Invasion of 1814* (Annapolis, Md.: Naval Institute Press, 1998).

Blair, John (1732–1800) *Supreme Court justice*
John Blair became a jurist in his home state, attended the CONSTITUTIONAL CONVENTION (1787), and served on the U.S. SUPREME COURT. Born into a prominent Virginia family, Blair was educated at the College of William and Mary and studied law at the Middle Temple in London. When he returned to Virginia, he practiced law and then entered the House of Burgesses in 1766. Although not a radical, he supported the RESISTANCE MOVEMENT (1763–75) against imperial regulation and signed the ASSOCIATION in 1774. He attended the state convention that wrote the Virginia constitution in 1776 and became a member of the state's Privy Council. Starting in 1778, Blair began serving in a variety of judicial positions, and in 1782 he participated in a decision asserting the state court's right of judicial review. He attended the Philadelphia Constitutional Convention but did not participate actively in the debates.

Blair generally supported the positions of his friends GEORGE WASHINGTON and JAMES MADISON. Once the new government of the United States was put in place under the U.S. CONSTITUTION, President Washington appointed him an associate justice of the Supreme Court. He served from 1789 until 1796, when he retired. As a justice, Blair generally upheld the division of powers between the legislative and judicial branches and asserted the independence of the courts. He also believed that the federal courts took precedence over state maritime courts, a view he expressed in *Penhallow et al. v. Doane*. After his retirement from the court, Blair lived in Williamsburg until his death in 1800.

Bland, Richard (1710–1776) *Virginia politician*
Richard Bland was an early advocate of popular rights in opposition to Virginia's royal governor and the king. Born at Jordan's Point Plantation in Prince George County, he was educated at the College of William and Mary and a member of the Virginia planter elite. Bland first became a member of the House of Burgesses in 1742 and remained so until 1775. At that time he was elected to Virginia's revolutionary convention and became a delegate to the FIRST CONTINENTAL CONGRESS. He was also elected to the SECOND CONTINENTAL CONGRESS but only attended a few days. Bland was in the forefront in opposition to the imperial regulations of the 1760s and 1770s, being the first to sign the Virginia non-importation agreement in 1769, and served on both the Virginia COMMITTEE OF CORRESPONDENCE set up in 1773 and the Virginia committee of safety organized in 1775. While advocating colonial rights, he hesitated to break entirely from GREAT BRITAIN and the king.

Bland was known for his careful study of Virginia history and respected by his peers for his erudition; THOMAS JEFFERSON referred to him as "the most learned and logical man of those who took prominent lead in public affairs, profound in constitutional lore." As early as 1753 he stood against royal prerogative, opposing the effort by the Virginia governor to gain additional revenue in the Pistole Fee controversy, a debate over the right of the royal governor to charge a fee for sealing land patents. In the early 1760s Bland helped to lead the opposition to the Anglican clergy when they complained about limits on their salaries imposed by the Two Penny Act (which allowed clergy salaries to be paid in MONEY rather than TOBACCO, thus effectively reducing salaries).

While not a fiery speaker, Bland was a powerful writer. Perhaps his most noteworthy work was the pamphlet he published in 1764 concerning the Two Penny controversy, *The Colonel Dismounted*, in which he asserted that colonial Americans enjoyed the benefits of the English constitution and that Virginians as Englishmen "are born free, are only subject to laws made with their own consent, and cannot be deprived of the benefit of these laws without a transgression of them." He also drew a distinction between issues concerning "internal" and "external" affairs that became important in the debates over the STAMP ACT in 1765 and 1766. Bland asserted that the Virginia legislature was responsible for all matters concerning internal affairs—that is, laws within the colony—and that Parliament was responsible for the regulation of the empire and external affairs. In 1766 he pushed some of his ideas about colonial rights further in *An Inquiry into the Rights of the British Colonies*, declaring that as Englishmen colonists had rights that no power could infringe upon.

As the RESISTANCE MOVEMENT (1764–75) moved toward a DECLARATION OF INDEPENDENCE, Bland hesitated to support the break from the king. Ill health and old age limited his political involvement, although before he died in October 1776, Bland came to support a more radical position and even advocated the execution of Virginia's royal governor, JOHN MURRAY, FOURTH EARL OF DUNMORE.

See also PARSON'S CAUSE; REPUBLICANISM.

Further reading: Bernard Bailyn and Jane E. Garrett, eds., *Pamphlets of the American Revolution, 1750–1776* (Cambridge, Mass.: Harvard University Press, 1965).

Bloody Run, Battle of (July 31, 1763)

The Battle of Bloody Run occurred during PONTIAC'S WAR (1763–65) when the British army attempted to attack Pontiac's camp as the NATIVE AMERICAN leader besieged DETROIT. In late July 1763, Captain James Dalyell managed to reach Detroit with 250 British soldiers. In an effort to lift the Indian siege of the outpost, Dalyell led a sortie against Pontiac a few days after his arrival. The Indians were waiting for the British at Parent's Creek, two miles north of the fort. In the fierce fighting, 20 soldiers were killed, including Dalyell, and the British were driven back to Detroit. Since the creek ran red with the blood of the British dead and wounded, the battle was called "Bloody Run." Pontiac did not abandon his effort to capture Detroit until October 30, 1763.

Blount, William (1749–1800) *governor of Tennessee, U.S. senator*

William Blount was the first territorial governor of Tennessee and a U.S. senator who triggered a political controversy in 1797 when he supported a planned pro-British invasion of Spanish North American possessions. Blount was born in North Carolina and worked as a paymaster for that state during the REVOLUTIONARY WAR (1775–83). During the 1780s he became an active politician, serving in both North Carolina's House of Commons (its lower house) and the state senate. On four occasions he was elected Speaker of the state House of Commons. He also represented North Carolina at the CONSTITUTIONAL CONVENTION in 1787, although he did not actively participate in the debates. He signed the U.S. CONSTITUTION at the end of the convention, but his support seemed lukewarm. However, he voted for the Constitution during North Carolina's ratification convention.

An ambitious man, Blount hoped to become a senator from North Carolina. When he was unsuccessful, he sought his fortune by turning west. North Carolina ceded its claims to the trans-Appalachian west in 1789, and in 1790 the U.S. government created a new territory in Tennessee; GEORGE WASHINGTON appointed Blount as governor of this new territory. An able administrator, Blount did well as governor and as superintendent for Indian affairs in the Southern Department. He managed to appease the demands of the FRONTIER settlers, keep the peace with NATIVE AMERICANS, and follow the directives from the national government. Simultaneously, he advanced his own interests in land speculation. This balancing act took a great deal of adroitness. In 1796 he was chosen as president of the Tennessee convention that applied for statehood and was rewarded for his services by being made a U.S. senator from Tennessee.

Blount, however, was always after the main chance. In 1797 he was asked to support a wild scheme wherein a combined force of Native Americans and westerners would invade Spanish LOUISIANA and FLORIDA on behalf of the British government. He agreed to the scheme and even stated in writing that he would head the force himself. Apparently he anticipated a huge land grant and increased political power in a British-governed West. The plan never materialized, and British support was never very strong. However, Blount's letter of support fell into the hands of the newspapers, and copies came to the U.S. secretary of war and secretary of state. Despite the pro-British aspect of the scheme, Blount was an avid Jeffersonian (a supporter of the DEMOCRATIC-REPUBLICAN PARTY). The FEDERALIST PARTY in Congress called for action to be taken against this U.S. senator who was willing to lead an invasion of a foreign country on behalf of another foreign country. The Senate voted 25 to 1 to expel Blount from their chamber, and the House of Representatives clamored to impeach him. This controversy continued for almost two years and led to a debate over whether the Constitution allowed Congress to impeach a senator. Although Blount had briefly been held in custody, ultimately the IMPEACHMENT was dismissed for lack of jurisdiction in 1799.

In spite of the controversy surrounding him, Blount remained popular back in Tennessee. When he returned there in 1798, he was not only elected to the state senate but was chosen as that body's Speaker. Only his death on March 21, 1800, ended his political career.

See also SPAIN.

Further reading: William H. Masterson, *William Blount* (Baton Rouge: Louisiana State University Press, 1954).

Blue Jacket (1740?–1808?) *Shawnee warrior*

Having earlier established a reputation as a warrior, Blue Jacket emerged in the 1790s as the foremost leader of the NATIVE AMERICANS resisting U.S. incursions on territory north of the Ohio River. Blue Jacket was a SHAWNEE who grew up in the region referred to as the Old Northwest. He married twice, once to a European-American captive and a second time to the daughter of a French-Canadian trader and an Indian woman. These marriages provided him with strong family connections to CANADA and European Americans. He probably fought against the Virginians in DUNMORE'S WAR (1774) and for the British in the REVOLUTIONARY WAR (1775–83). In the 1780s, he opposed European-American settlement in Kentucky and the ceding of lands north of the Ohio.

During the 1790s, Blue Jacket became the preeminent Native American leader opposing U.S. expansion in the Northwest. In 1790 he orchestrated a multitribal movement that defeated General JOSIAH HARMAR's invasion of Indian land in Ohio. He also led the forces that beat ARTHUR ST. CLAIR the following year, creating a major crisis for the U.S. government in its efforts to control the territory west of the Appalachians. Blue Jacket helped to organize an Indian congress at the GLAIZE, located in what is now western Ohio, that attracted Native Americans from Canada to west of the Mississippi in late 1792 and early 1793. This meeting endorsed the Shawnee demand for a limit to European-American settlement. After peace negotiations broke down in 1793, Blue Jacket worked to sustain the multitribal alliance to oppose the United States. However, when General ANTHONY WAYNE defeated Blue Jacket's forces at the BATTLE OF FALLEN TIMBERS (August 20, 1794), the Shawnee warrior decided to seek peace. Without the full support of the British, who had failed to protect the Indians after their defeat, Blue Jacket agreed to the TREATY OF GREENVILLE (1795), opening up most of Ohio to U.S. settlement. Blue Jacket remained an important leader of his people, and in the years before his death, he worked to support the developing multitribal confederacy under TECUMSEH.

Further reading: John Sugden, *Blue Jacket: Warrior of the Shawnees* (Lincoln: University of Nebraska Press, 2000).

Blue Licks, Battle of (August 19, 1782)

In a battle at Blue Licks, south of the Ohio River and north of the European-American settlements at Boonesborough and Lexington, Kentucky, NATIVE AMERICANS allied with the British surprised a party of 185 Kentucky MILITIA, killing about a third of the force. This battle and its aftermath demonstrate that on the FRONTIER, the REVOLUTIONARY WAR (1775–83) continued after the British surrender at YORKTOWN (October 19, 1781), and that the final outcome of the war along the Ohio River remained unclear.

The Indians attacked Bryan's Station on August 15, 1782. Unable to take that post, they retreated north, hoping to lure the relief column of Kentucky militia into a trap. The command structure for the 185 Kentuckians was vague, and all decisions were made by council and group discussion. When the militia arrived at Bryan's Station on August 17, they could have waited for more reinforcements, which were a day or so behind them, but the various militia leaders goaded one another into a hot pursuit of the Indians. By August 19 they had reached Blue Licks, where they again held a council. DANIEL BOONE, who led a company of about 45 men, suggested caution and argued that the Indians might be setting a trap. But once again leaders urged each other on with taunts of cowardice, and when one commander jumped on his horse to lead his men across a stream and up a hill, the others, including Boone, decided to follow him. The result of this impetuosity was disaster. As the Kentuckians reached the hill's crest, the Indians opened fire from their hiding places. The militia quickly turned and ran, with each man escaping the best he could. More than 60 were killed and many were wounded as the survivors scrambled back to Bryan's Station.

In the aftermath of the battle, many European Americans headed east over the Appalachian Mountains. Enough Kentuckian fighters remained, however, to launch a devastating raid against Indian towns north of the Ohio in November.

Further reading: John Mack Faragher, *Daniel Boone: The Life and Legend of an American Pioneer* (New York: Holt, 1992).

Bonaparte, Napoleon (Napoleon I) (1769–1821) *emperor of France*

Napoleon Bonaparte is one of the most famous men in history, rising from his birth into an impoverished petty noble family in Corsica to become emperor of the French by 1804 and subsequently conqueror of most of Europe. His invasion of RUSSIA in 1812 ended in failure, and he was forced to abdicate in 1814 and live on the island of Elba in the Mediterranean. He returned to FRANCE in 1815, only to be defeated at the Battle of Waterloo (1815) and forced into exile on St. Helena, an island in the middle of the South ATLANTIC OCEAN. While his actions changed the course of European history, they also had a big impact on the United States.

Shortly after seizing power in France (1799), Napoleon began thinking of extending his empire into the Western Hemisphere. There were two key components to Napoleon's vision. First, he planned to subdue the rebellion in what was once the French colony on the island of Hispaniola, Saint-Domingue (HAITI). Second, he planned to reestablish a French colony on the mainland in the huge territory of LOUISIANA. Haiti had been in rebellion since 1792, and a vicious race war with the ex-slaves there had caused countless French deaths. Napoleon sent his brother-in-law, Victor-Emmanuel Leclerc, and another army to Haiti in 1801. After reconquering Haiti, Leclerc and his army were to be sent to Louisiana, which had been retroceded to France by SPAIN in the TREATY OF SAN ILDEFONSO in 1800. Disease and the opposition of the Haitians destroyed the French army and compelled Napoleon to change his plans. Rather than establishing a French North American empire, he decided to sell the entire Louisiana Territory to the United States in 1803 (see LOUISIANA PURCHASE).

Although Napoleon had signed the PEACE OF AMIENS in 1802, the following year war again broke out against GREAT BRITAIN and her allies. During the next decade Napoleon and his armies set about conquering Europe. With the Continent divided into warring camps, U.S. TRADE, which had thrived during the earlier wars between Revolutionary France and Great Britain, was caught in the middle. The British issued ORDERS IN COUNCIL outlawing trade with countries under the control of Napoleon (most of Europe by 1808), and Napoleon issued the BERLIN DECREE and MILAN DECREE, which prohibited ships from stopping in English ports. Caught in this bind, the government of the United States attempted several measures—the EMBARGO OF 1807, the NON-INTERCOURSE ACT (1809), and MACON'S BILL NO. 2 (1810)—to compel both empires into lifting their restrictions on trade. In 1810 Napoleon suggested that he might repeal the Berlin and Milan Decrees as they pertained to U.S. shipping. President JAMES MADISON decided to stop all trade with Great Britain, precipitating the crisis that brought on the WAR OF 1812 (1812–15).

Although the United States and Napoleonic France fought wars against Great Britain at the same time, the United States never signed a formal alliance with Napoleon. His defeat in 1814, and again in 1815, thus had little direct effect on the Anglo-American war. The ongoing struggle with Napoleon had meant that the North American war remained a side conflict for the British during the years of 1812–14. After Napoleon's first defeat in 1814, however, the British could devote more resources to the war with the United States. His defeat also meant that some of the causes for the war—restrictions on trade and IMPRESSMENT of sailors into the British navy—were removed.

See also FRENCH REVOLUTION.

Further reading: Felix Markham, *Napoleon* (New York: New American Library, 1963).

Boone, Daniel (1734–1820) *frontiersman, militia officer, explorer*

Sometimes hailed as "The First White Man of the West," Daniel Boone was really just one of many European Americans who crossed the Appalachians in the late 18th century. Born into a QUAKER family in Berks County, Pennsylvania, on November 2, 1734, he moved with his parents to North Carolina as a young man. In 1755 he served as a teamster and blacksmith in a North Carolina contingent attached to General EDWARD BRADDOCK's army in its ill-fated march to western Pennsylvania. Boone escaped on a horse after the French and Indians attacked Braddock's forces just south of present-day Pittsburgh. The army experience, however, first introduced Boone to stories about Kentucky.

Boone married a neighbor girl in North Carolina in 1756, shortly after his return from the army. In 1767 he made his first visit to Kentucky, probably in the company of one or two other woodsmen. He returned to Kentucky via the CUMBERLAND GAP with a slightly larger party in 1769, staying there until 1771. As an agent of the Transylvania Company, he headed for Kentucky in March 1775 and set up the community named Boonesborough. Later in the

Daniel Boone hoped to establish the state of Kentucky with his settlement, Boonesborough. *(James Audubon Museum)*

year he returned to North Carolina for his family and to get more settlers.

For over a decade thereafter, Boone worked to build a life in Kentucky. But success did not come easily for him. The REVOLUTIONARY WAR (1775–83) broke out, and there were hostilities with NATIVE AMERICANS. In 1776 Boone famously rescued his daughter and two other girls captured by Indians. In February 1778 he led a party to collect salt and was surprised by a SHAWNEE war party. After Boone was captured, he persuaded the rest of the party to surrender without a fight, an action made all the more controversial when he was subsequently adopted by a Shawnee family. After a few months, Boone escaped and returned to Boonesborough in time to aid in the defense of that outpost against a party of Indians and British (see BOONESBOROUGH, SIEGE OF). Boone thereafter participated in several raids across the Ohio River against the Indians. In 1782 he was a part of the Kentucky force defeated by the Indians at the BATTLE OF BLUE LICKS (August 19), in which he lost his son Israel.

Throughout this period, Boone continued his land speculation. The titles of the Transylvania Company were repudiated by the Virginia legislature, and when he went east with MONEY to secure legal title for his neighbors and himself, he was robbed. He moved several times and claimed many tracts of land, but all of the titles proved invalid. Finally, Boone gave up on Kentucky in 1788, moved to what is now West Virginia, and was elected to the Virginia assembly in 1791. Sometime in 1798 or 1799, when all of his holdings in Kentucky had been clearly lost, he moved to present-day Missouri, which was then in territory belonging to SPAIN. Again he ran into legal problems concerning land titles after the territory was transferred to the United States as part of the LOUISIANA PURCHASE (1803). Congress finally confirmed his title to the Missouri lands in 1814. He died on September 26, 1820, at Femme Osage Creek, Missouri.

Although in many ways Boone's story is unexceptional and demonstrates the troubles confronted by frontiersmen, his life assumed legendary proportions even before he died. John Filson wrote *The Discovery, Settlement, and Present State of Kentucke* (1784), which was supposedly written in Boone's own words (he was nearly illiterate), and identified the frontiersman as the leader of the Kentucky settlement. Other books repeated the tale, and the English poet Lord Byron even devoted seven stanzas to Boone in a poem in 1821. George Caleb Bingham further immortalized Boone in his oil painting *Daniel Boone Escorting Settlers through the Cumberland Gap* (1851–52). The result is that even today Daniel Boone is identified with the westward movement and is known as the first great frontiersman of the United States.

See also the FRONTIER.

Further reading: John Mack Faragher, *Daniel Boone: The Life and Legend of an American Pioneer* (New York: Holt, 1992).

Boonesborough, siege of (September 7–18, 1778)

For 11 days in September 1778, NATIVE AMERICANS and a party of Canadian MILITIA from DETROIT besieged Boonesborough, Kentucky, in an effort to gain control of the trans-Appalachian West during the REVOLUTIONARY WAR (1775–83). The failure to capture the Boonesborough settlement left the FRONTIER in Kentucky a contested ground where bloody warfare between revolutionary forces and pro-British Native Americans and LOYALISTS would persist for years.

Boonesborough was settled in 1775 and named after DANIEL BOONE. As an important outpost in early Kentucky, it was a natural target for Native Americans and the British who sought to control the area. The fact that Daniel Boone was one of the community's leaders also played a role in the British and Indians' decision to try to take the outpost. Earlier in the year, Boone had been captured and adopted by the SHAWNEE leader Blackfish, and apparently he had made promises to assist in gaining Boonesborough's surrender. When the 400 or so Indians and handful of Detroit militia arrived at Boonesborough on September 7, 1778, they immediately called for negotiations with Boone, whose role during the next couple of days remains uncertain as he was only one of several leaders in the fort. Boone and other settler leaders met in the open ground in front of the fort with Blackfish and other chiefs several times to discuss terms of a peace agreement. In these negotiations he may have seriously considered surrender and turning Loyalist, or he could have just been stalling for time in the hope that reinforcements would arrive. Regardless of his intentions, negotiations broke down on September 9. On that day the Boonesborough settlers and Indians had agreed to the Ohio River as a boundary between them, and the Boonesborough leaders may even have been willing to take an oath of loyalty to the king (the exact details of the treaty are lost). But as the Indians stepped forward to embrace the Boonesborough leaders to seal the agreement, something went wrong. Though it is not known exactly what happened, one of the Kentuckians may have feared the Indians were trying to capture them, and a melee broke out. Sharpshooters from both sides opened fire as the Kentuckians broke free from the Indians and ran back to the fort.

Over the next week, the settlers from the stockade and the surrounding Indians exchanged fire. Several times the Native Americans rushed Boonesborough, and they even attacked at night with flaming torches to set fire to the fort. The Indians began a tunnel to undermine the stockade. On the night of September 17, they made an all-out attempt to storm Fort Boonesborough, and although they reached the walls, they could not breach the defenses. On the morning of September 18, the Indians retreated, covering their withdrawal with intermittent gunfire. Only a few of the defenders were killed, although many more were wounded, including Boone, his daughter, and his brother. Daniel Boone estimated that 35 Indians were killed during the siege.

The Native Americans may have failed in taking a well-defended fort, but after the siege they broke into smaller parties and attacked scattered settlements and homesteads, inflicting serious damage on the frontier and killing many European Americans.

Further reading: John Mack Faragher, *Daniel Boone: The Life and Legend of an American Pioneer* (New York: Holt, 1992).

Boston Massacre (March 5, 1770)

The "Boston Massacre" refers to a riot on King Street in Boston on March 5, 1770, in which British soldiers fired on an unruly mob that had been heckling them and throwing snowballs and ice chunks. At the end of the mayhem, five men, including CRISPUS ATTUCKS, lay dead or dying and six others were seriously wounded. The "massacre" was the result of many months of tension between the people of Boston and the soldiers. That tension in part resulted from the opposition to the TOWNSHEND DUTIES (1767), but it was even more the result of the fact that the townspeople viewed the redcoats as threats to their jobs, homes, and families.

The March 5 incident was not the first confrontation between the two groups, as many brawls had erupted on earlier occasions. The problems had begun in 1768, when the commissioners of customs, who were appointed in GREAT BRITAIN but were paid with what they collected in the colonies, requested military protection against crowds opposing imperial regulations. The British government sent about 700 men to protect the customs collectors, and the people of Boston were outraged. At first, most of the troops were unable to find accommodations in town and so set up camp on the town common. Governor FRANCIS BERNARD had planned on housing the troops in local homes, but the city council would not allow it, stating that citizens did not have to provide quarters unless there was no space in local barracks. The council wanted to station the soldiers in a harbor fortification called Castle William, which had plenty of room for the soldiers. However, the governor opposed putting the troops in Castle William because it was too remote for the troops and it would be difficult for them to come to Boston to help quell mobs. Eventually the governor found some empty buildings in the city for the troops.

Once the regulars were stationed in Boston, other problems arose. Many of the soldiers sought part-time work while off duty; since their housing and board were paid for, they could work for lower wages than civilian laborers. Moreover, the men in uniform were competitors with Boston's young men for the attention of local women. At times, too, soldiers would be rowdy and misbehave as they crowded local taverns and drinking establishments. Tension also remained from the FRENCH AND INDIAN WAR (1754–63), when British regulars and local MILITIA eyed each other with suspicion and mutual disrespect. From the point of view of many colonists, the British soldiers were outsiders who were vile and rude and should be kept away from their families. In turn, the British soldiers saw the Boston civilians as country bumpkins who shunned the law and refused to pay taxes.

Given this tension, it took very little to provoke serious confrontations. For several days leading up to March 5, street battles broke out between soldiers and civilians. One of the first episodes occurred a few days before the shooting, when a soldier inquired about a job at a ropewalk and was told he could clean the privy. The soldier decided this offer was an insult—as it undoubtedly was—and a scuffle ensued. Other fights followed. By March 5 passions had reached fever pitch, with gangs of soldiers and civilians cursing and brawling with each other. That evening a soldier of the 29th Regiment was on sentry duty in front of the Customs House when a young man began to shout insults at him. The sentry used the butt of his rifle to rap the boy on the head. The boy screamed and ran for help; someone rang the church bell, and soon a large, unruly crowd had gathered in the street. Now facing an angry mob of around 400 men, the sentry called for assistance, and Captain Thomas Preston of the 29th Regiment responded with six men. The Bostonians threw snowballs and chunks of ice at the soldiers, daring them to fire. The soldiers loaded their guns, but the crowd refused to back down, taunting the soldiers and striking at them with clubs and other weapons. No one will ever know who yelled "Fire," but someone did, and the soldiers shot into the throng. Four men were killed instantly; one other was fatally wounded. THOMAS HUTCHINSON, who had replaced Bernard as governor, took swift action and arrested Captain Preston, the soldiers, and four men who were alleged to have fired shots from inside the Customs House. All troops were immediately removed from Boston.

Three LAWYERS—Sampson Salter Blowers, JOHN ADAMS, and JOSIAH QUINCY—defended the soldiers at their trials, which occurred between October 24 and December 5, 1770. The prosecutors called witnesses to testify to the soldiers' insolent behavior in the period leading up to the massacre and emphasized the troops' hatred for the citizens. However, the talented defense team focused

The Boston Massacre. Engraving by Paul Revere *(Library of Congress)*

their attention on the incidents of that night. None of the soldiers testified on their own behalf. The local press described the crowd as much smaller, comprising around 80 people, and denied that the mob had provoked the soldiers. Nevertheless, these statements were clearly contrary to the facts. Captain Preston and four other men were acquitted, but two of the soldiers were found guilty of manslaughter. However, they were released after being branded on the hand, having claimed the medieval relic of benefit of clergy. (Originally a provision to protect clergy in civil courts, benefit of clergy allowed a person convicted of crimes such as manslaughter to avoid execution by prov-

ing clergy status through reading. By the 18th century this provision had been expanded to include any one who could read.)

Although the Boston Massacre has played a large role in the mythology on the origins of the AMERICAN REVOLU-TION, its immediate impact in the colonies was not great. With the repeal of the Townshend duties in 1770—except for the symbolic tax on tea—the urgency of the resistance to imperial regulation decreased. Moreover, economic conditions, which had been poor in the late 1760s, improved in most colonies at this time. Within Boston the immediate cause of conflict—the presence of the soldiers—was removed, and many leading Bostonians felt relieved that the trial ended without any serious affront to the king and his soldiers. Men like John Adams had come to fear as much the unrestrained mob on King Street as the redcoats who had roamed the city's streets.

More radical leaders, however, sought to capitalize on the episode by labeling it a massacre. PAUL REVERE's engraving of the riot portrayed the soldiers as evil and their shooting intentional and malicious. He also depicted the threatening Boston mob as no more than innocent protestors who posed no threat to the soldiers. Other radicals, led by SAMUEL ADAMS, kept the memory of the massacre alive by commemorating the date with demonstrations every year thereafter. All of this propaganda had an effect, especially once war and independence loomed a few years later, for the Boston Massacre became an important symbol of the Revolution. In the early 21st century there is hardly a U.S. history textbook that does not included Revere's famous print as well as a discussion of how this incident, which was more about local conditions than larger issues, contributed to the defense of LIBERTY and led to the independence of the United States.

See also GOLDEN HILL, BATTLE OF; RESISTANCE MOVEMENT; RIOTS.

Further reading: Dirk Hoerder, *Crowd Action in Revolutionary Massachusetts, 1765–1780* (New York: Academic Press, 1977); Hiller B. Zobel, *The Boston Massacre* (New York: Norton 1970).

Boston Tea Party (December 16, 1773)

The Boston Tea Party set off a chain of events that led eventually to the outbreak of the REVOLUTIONARY WAR (1775–83) and the creation of the United States. The "party" was carried out in reaction to Parliament's TEA ACT (May 10, 1773). At the time, the East India Company, which controlled British affairs in INDIA, was on the verge of bankruptcy. In order to aid the company, the British government granted it a monopoly on all tea exported to the colonies. The East India Company would select a limited group of colonial merchants to sell the tea in North America. From the British perspective, this legislation solved several problems. Previously, most tea sold in the colonies was smuggled from the Dutch since the East India Company tea had to be imported first to GREAT BRITAIN, where a duty would be paid, and then to the colonies, where more taxes (the one remaining Townshend duty) were due. The Tea Act would raise much-needed revenue for the East India Company since the tea could be exported directly to the colonies without paying any customs charges in England. The East India Company would benefit, and the British Empire in India would be secured. Since the tea under the Tea

Act would be cheaper than smuggled tea, colonists would, the British believed, eagerly buy it and pay the Townshend duty, thereby implicitly accepting parliamentary supremacy. The colonists would also gain from the measure since tea would be cheaper and colonial merchants would be the agents of the East India Company.

This seemingly win-win scenario, however, did not work out as the British hoped. The act angered the colonial merchants who would not be East India Company agents and who would no longer be able to profit from SMUGGLING. Many other colonial Americans viewed the law within the context of nearly a decade of resistance to imperial regulation and the ideology of REPUBLICANISM. These individuals believed that the granting of any monopoly—even one that lowered prices—would corrupt the people's virtue and lead to the loss of LIBERTY.

In September 1773 the East India Company planned to ship 500,000 pounds of tea to merchants in Boston, New York, Philadelphia, and Charleston. By this time opposition had grown, and colonial merchants had agreed not to sell the tea. The tea agents in New York, Philadelphia, and Charleston canceled their orders or resigned their positions as tea agents. In these cities, the shipments of tea were either returned to England or put in warehouses. However, in Boston, most of the tea agents were friends or relatives of Governor THOMAS HUTCHINSON, who believed it was important to uphold the supremacy of the law. Opposition in the city was rampant, though; it was led by SAMUEL ADAMS, JOSIAH QUINCY, and JOHN HANCOCK in the form of the COMMITTEES OF CORRESPONDENCE and the SONS OF LIBERTY. When the first East India Company ship reached Boston with its cargo of tea in November 1773, soon followed by two more ships, the radicals quickly convinced their captains to leave without unloading the tea, but Governor Hutchinson would not give them clearance to do so. According to the law, the tea had to be unloaded within 20 days or it would be seized and sold to pay custom duties. The radicals did not want to see this happen either because they felt that this process would still constitute payment of unconstitutional taxes. Further, they feared that if it was unloaded, the majority of the colonists would buy it at the cheap price.

Ultimately, Hutchinson's refusal to allow the tea ships to return to England led to dramatic action. On the night of December 16, 1773, encouraged by several thousand townspeople, about 60 men disguised themselves as MOHAWK Indians and boarded the three ships in Boston Harbor. These "Indians" broke open the chests of tea and threw over £10,000 worth of the East India Company's property into the harbor. It was an effective piece of political theater, inspiring similar actions elsewhere. In the ensuing months, mobs boarded East India Company tea ships in New York and Annapolis, preventing the landing of any tea, and colonists up and down the coast of North America continued to boycott the company's tea. The raid had thus created a crisis between the colonists and Parliament.

British officials condemned the Boston Tea Party as vandalism and passed the COERCIVE ACTS (1774), which curtailed self-government in Massachusetts and closed Boston's port until the colony paid for the tea. These harsh measures generated support and sympathy for the Boston radicals throughout the colonies. Colonists organized committees of correspondence and called for a continental congress, which set up a timetable for nonimportation, nonexportation, and nonconsumption of British goods to protest the repressive Coercive Acts. In the countryside, many colonists began to prepare for war, and British troops again occupied Boston. The stage was set for the events of April 19, 1775, at Lexington Green and Concord Bridge.

See also CONTINENTAL CONGRESS, FIRST; RESISTANCE MOVEMENT; TOWNSHEND DUTIES.

Further reading: Benjamin Woods Labaree, *The Boston Tea Party* (New York: Oxford University Press, 1964); Alfred F. Young, *The Shoemaker and the Tea Party: Memory and the American Revolution* (Boston: Beacon Press, 1999).

—Crystal Williams

Boucher, Jonathan (1738–1804) *Anglican priest, Loyalist*

Compelled to leave the colonies in 1775, Jonathan Boucher was an important Loyalist spokesman who advocated the divine origin of government and established authority. Born on May 12, 1738, Boucher grew up relatively impoverished in Cumberland, England, but managed to obtain some EDUCATION. In 1759 he went to Virginia to tutor gentlemen's sons there. He returned to England in 1762 to take Anglican orders, having been promised a parish in Virginia. As an Anglican priest he became a social climber, using connections with the Chesapeake gentry, including GEORGE WASHINGTON, to obtain a series of posts. He also continued to tutor the children of the wealthy, including John Parke Custis, MARTHA WASHINGTON's son by her previous marriage. Boucher moved to Maryland, was chaplain of the lower house of assembly in Annapolis, and took the desirable rectory of Queen Anne's Parish. He was also granted an honorary master of arts by King's College in New York for his support of a North American episcopacy (he wanted the Anglican church to settle a bishop in the colonies—an unpopular position with many non-ANGLICANS in North America). He married a wealthy woman, bought a plantation on the Potomac, and by 1773 appeared successful and contented.

The imperial controversy, however, prevented his life from proceeding on a peaceful course. As many colonists formed committees of safety and advocated resistance to British imperial measures in 1774 and 1775, Boucher called for compliance with all authority. He had the audacity to announce his intention to preach against resistance to the British, and a group of armed men subsequently refused to allow him to ascend the pulpit. Thereafter, he felt his life was in jeopardy, and he later reported that every time he preached he kept a pair of loaded pistols nearby. Efforts to publish his sermon "On Civil Liberty, Passive Obedience, and Nonresistance" in 1775 were fruitless, since the advocates of resistance controlled the local presses. In this sermon Boucher said that it was God's will that every man should obey the constituted authority. He also argued that the notion of equality was both wrong and dangerous. He wrote: "Man differs from man in everything that can be supposed to lead to supremacy and subjection." Boucher believed that "A musical instrument composed of chords, keys, or pipes all perfectly equal in size and power might as well be expected to produce harmony as a society composed of members all perfectly equal to be productive of order and peace." For such ideas, he was put under surveillance by the committee of safety and burned in effigy by a mob. Consequently, in September 1775 he and his wife sailed for England. Once there, he was provided with another parish and a pension. His property in the colonies was confiscated by Revolutionaries, and he received some compensation from the British government for his loss. In part in response to the FRENCH REVOLUTION (1789–99), Boucher finally published his ideas on the AMERICAN REVOLUTION in 1797 in a book entitled *A View of the Causes and Consequences of the American Revolution*. He died in Surrey on April 27, 1804.

See also LOYALISTS; LOYALIST PROPERTY CONFISCATION.

Further reading: Bernard Bailyn, *The Ideological Origins of the American Revolution* (Cambridge, Mass: Harvard University Press, 1967).

Boudinot, Elias (1740–1821) *lawyer, New Jersey politician*

Elias Boudinot was a prominent New Jersey politician who during the course of his career held many important government positions, including president of the SECOND CONTINENTAL CONGRESS. Born to an affluent Philadelphia family and trained as a lawyer, Boudinot joined the Essex County committee of safety and was elected as a member of the provincial congress in New Jersey in 1775. Although a conservative WHIG, he quickly emerged as an important leader during the REVOLUTIONARY WAR (1775–83).

In June 1777 the Continental Congress appointed him as commissary of PRISONERS OF WAR with the rank of colonel in the CONTINENTAL ARMY. In this role he worked closely with GEORGE WASHINGTON supervising captured British and Hessian soldiers (see HESSIANS) and also reporting on the treatment of Revolutionaries held by the British. He even made an official month long visit to British-occupied New York City in February 1778 to see for himself the atrocious conditions of revolutionary captives on land and in prison ships, and he advanced his own MONEY to assist the prisoners.

In May 1778 Boudinot resigned his post as commissary of prisoners so that he could attend the Continental Congress, to which he had been elected in November 1777. He served in Congress for the remainder of 1778 and again from 1781 to 1782, being elected president in November 1782. A strong nationalist, Boudinot championed the ratification of the U.S. CONSTITUTION in 1787 and 1788 and was elected to the House of Representatives for three terms, beginning in 1789. He supported the policies of the Washington administration but recoiled from the partisan political battles of the 1790s. After leaving Congress, he was appointed director of the U.S. Mint in 1795, retaining that office until he resigned in 1805.

Boudinot wrote several religious books, including a response to THOMAS PAINE's *The Age of Reason* called *The Age of Revelation* (1801). He was involved in many reform activities, advocated for the rights of AFRICAN AMERICANS and NATIVE AMERICANS, and was one of the founders of the American Bible Society in 1816, serving as its first president.

See also CONSTITUTION, RATIFICATION OF THE.

Further reading: George Boyd, *Elias Boudinot: Patriot and Statesman, 1740–1821* (Westwood, Conn.: Greenwood, 1969).

Bowditch, Nathaniel (1773–1838) *mariner, author*

As the author of *The American Practical Navigator*, Nathaniel Bowditch's name has become indelibly linked to the maritime heritage of the United States. Bowditch was born into a modest family in Salem, Massachusetts, and although he began to work in his father's cooper's shop at age 10, through an intensive program of self-EDUCATION he mastered complex mathematics and several foreign languages. Beginning in 1795, he took five ocean voyages as a ship's clerk, then as a supercargo, and finally as a captain, sailing not only to Europe but also to the Far East. On these voyages he discovered about 8,000 errors in the previous standard table for lunar observations. Other than using a chronometer, which was expensive, or relying on dead reckoning, which was making an educated guess,

determining longitude depended on lunar observations with navigational instruments and then looking up the location on published tables. Bowditch used his mathematical expertise and his practical knowledge as a seaman to recalculate the tables for these observations and published his results, first as a correction to the existing tables in 1799 and then in 1802 as his own book, *The New American Practical Navigator*. This book, published in subsequent editions as *The American Practical Navigator*, was more than a list of tables since it contained a host of information to help shipmasters—and anyone planning on a maritime career—including instruction in navigation; data on winds, tides, and currents; a dictionary of sea terms; and a description of rigging. Bowditch also explained many of the business aspects of running a ship, providing models of contracts; ship logs; INSURANCE statistics; methods for exchanging bills; and a list of responsibilities for ship owners, masters, factors, and agents. Almost every oceangoing vessel soon had a copy of Bowditch, and the book went through many editions and was translated into several languages. To this day it remains a standard work in seamanship.

Bowditch was more than a navigator. He was also a scientist who published a number of astronomical papers, was awarded an honorary master's degree from Harvard, and was offered a teaching positions at Harvard and the University of Virginia (he turned down both offers). His status as a transatlantic intellectual was confirmed by membership in several scientific societies: He was elected to the American Academy of Arts and Sciences in 1799, the AMERICAN PHILOSOPHICAL SOCIETY in 1809, and the Royal Societies of London and Edinburgh in 1818. He shifted careers in 1804 to become president of the Essex Fire and Marine Insurance Company, and in 1823 he became the actuary of the Massachusetts Hospital Life Insurance Company—positions in which he could use his mathematical abilities to good effect and personal profit. He died in Boston, Massachusetts, on March 16, 1838.

Bowdoin, James (1726–1790) *scholar, governor of Massachusetts*

James Bowdoin was a politician, scholar, and the second governor of the Commonwealth of Massachusetts. Born into a wealthy Bostonian family, he graduated from Harvard College in 1745 and inherited a large estate upon his father's death two years later. Like many other wealthy merchants, including his friends JOHN HANCOCK and ELBRIDGE GERRY, Bowdoin supported colonial commercial interests against British interference. In 1753 he was elected to the General Court of Massachusetts, and in 1757 he became a member of the colony's council. He held this position until 1774, when General THOMAS GAGE, fearing Bowdoin's revolutionary influence in the government, terminated his council membership. The General Court then elected Bowdoin as a delegate to the FIRST CONTINENTAL CONGRESS, but he declined the position due to poor health.

In 1775 Bowdoin was appointed to the executive council that governed Massachusetts during the REVOLUTIONARY WAR (1775–83), but poor health again forced him to resign two years later. In 1779 he presided over the state convention that created a new constitution for Massachusetts. The first state governor, John Hancock, also appointed Bowdoin to the committee that revised colonial laws for the new independent government. In 1785 Bowdoin was himself elected governor in a close contest that was decided by the state legislature, where wealthy commercial interests prevailed in his favor. As governor, he supported a strong central government in order to regulate and promote commerce. He was reelected by a large majority in 1786; however, his popularity was short-lived. In early 1787 he called up the state MILITIA to suppress SHAYS'S REBELLION (1786–87). Because of his unyielding stance in the tense atmosphere of economic depression, Bowdoin lost the election of 1787 to Hancock. However, his political influence continued as a member of the Massachusetts convention that voted to adopt the U.S. CONSTITUTION in 1788.

In addition to his political involvement, Bowdoin was a renowned scientist. He researched electricity with his friend BENJAMIN FRANKLIN, who presented Bowdoin's papers to the Royal Society of London. In 1780 Bowdoin founded the American Academy of Arts and Sciences, of which he served as president until his death on November 6, 1790. Four years later, Bowdoin College in Brunswick, Maine, was established in honor of his achievements.

Further reading: Frank E. Manuel and Fritzie Manuel, *James Bowdoin and the Patriot Philosophers* (Philadelphia: American Philosophical Society, 2004).

Brackenridge, Hugh Henry (1748–1816) *author, lawyer, politician*

Hugh Henry Brackenridge was an ardent supporter of the AMERICAN REVOLUTION and the author of one of the first novels written in the United States, *Modern Chivalry* (1792–1815). He was born in Scotland but immigrated to Pennsylvania with his family when he was five years old. Although he grew up relatively impoverished, Brackenridge demonstrated an early capacity for learning. A neighboring clergyman taught him the classics, and he began teaching school at age 15 to earn MONEY to further his EDUCATION. Entering Princeton sometime around 1768, he worked his way through college by teaching in a grammar school. At Princeton he became friends with PHILIP

FRENEAU and JAMES MADISON, sharing with them a love for LITERATURE and politics. In 1771 Brackenridge and Freneau coauthored a commencement poem called *The Rising Glory of America* (published in 1772), which was an early statement of American national feeling. He took a master's degree in divinity in 1774. During the REVOLUTIONARY WAR (1775–83) he served as a chaplain in the army and wrote several patriotic pieces extolling revolutionary valor.

Brackenridge's career took a new turn in 1778 when he left the ministry to set up a literary magazine (see MAGAZINES). His expectations, despite his own and Freneau's contributions, were met with failure, and the *United States Magazine* ceased publication after only a year. He then studied law in Annapolis with SAMUEL CHASE and was admitted to the bar in 1780. With legal, literary, and educational credentials, Brackenridge decided to seek his fortune on the FRONTIER and moved to the newly settled community of Pittsburgh. There he found several outlets for his energy, being elected to the Pennsylvania state legislature, starting a newspaper (the *Pittsburgh Gazette*) in 1786, opening a bookstore, helping to found the Pittsburgh Academy, and practicing law. Politics remained his true passion throughout the 1780s.

Brackenridge was typical of many leaders in the revolutionary generation. While a strong advocate of independence and republican values, he believed that the mass of people should rely on the judgment of an educated elite. This natural aristocracy, like Brackenridge, did not have to be born into its social position. Rather, leadership was to be an outgrowth of education and talent—just the path taken by men like Brackenridge.

However, much to Brackenridge's chagrin, the voters did not necessarily agree with him. In 1787 he supported the new document that his friend Madison and the others at the Philadelphia CONSTITUTIONAL CONVENTION had written, a position that reflected his long-standing NATIONALISM. Most of the people in western Pennsylvania, on the other hand, feared a strong central government and opposed the new U.S. CONSTITUTION. As a result, Brackenridge was defeated by an Irish immigrant for a seat at the state's convention to ratify the Constitution which was done despite western opposition. This failure left him both bitter and unpopular, and he withdrew from politics to restore his declining law practice.

In 1794, Brackenridge attempted to regain popularity by engaging in an awkward balancing act during the WHISKEY REBELLION. He sought to join and guide the rebellion while also trying to mediate a settlement with the federal government. The result was that he narrowly escaped being charged with treason, which did not add to his popularity in western Pennsylvania. Nevertheless, he became the region's leader of the DEMOCRATIC-REPUBLI-

CAN PARTY in the late 1790s and was rewarded for his party loyalty by being appointed to the Pennsylvania Supreme Court in 1799.

Among Brackenridge's writings, two stand out as reflecting his odd mixture of democratic and elitist politics. In *Incidents of the Insurrection in Western Pennsylvania in 1794* (1795), he tells the story of the Whiskey Rebellion from his perspective, emphasizing how he had only appeared to lead some aspect of the rebellion to minimize violence and defuse the situation. He strove to portray himself as both a popular leader and a supporter of the government. Brackenridge offered a more powerful social criticism in *Modern Chivalry,* a book that he first published in 1792 and to which he added several sections in subsequent printings until 1815. Patterning the book after Miguel de Cervantes' *Don Quixote,* his central character, Captain John Farrago, travels the countryside with an ignorant sidekick, an Irishman named Teague O'Regan. Like Brackenridge, Farrago is a natural aristocrat who is not recognized for his talents, and the people are shown to be easily misled. To demonstrate this popular ignorance, Teague is offered a variety of positions during their journeys, including congressman, minister, philosopher, Indian chief, and husband to a rich widow. When the captain finally allows Teague to take a position for which his ignorance should have disqualified him, excise officer on the eve of the Whiskey Rebellion, the Irishman gets his just desserts by being tarred and feathered.

Although he satirized the new democratic society of the early republic, Brackenridge also expressed faith that the United States could be saved when the public was educated and could make more intelligent decisions. He died in Carlisle, Pennsylvania, on June 25, 1816.

Further reading: Hugh Henry Brackenridge, *Incidents of the Insurrection,* edited by Daniel Marder (New Haven, Conn.: College and University Press, 1972); Brackenridge, *Modern Chivalry,* edited by Lewis Leary (New Haven, Conn.: College and University Press, 1965); Daniel Marder, *Hugh Henry Brackenridge* (New York: Twayne, 1967).

Braddock, Edward (1695–1755) *British general*

Edward Braddock was a British general most noted for his military defeat in the North American wilderness a few miles from Fort Duquesne (modern Pittsburgh) on July 9, 1755. Born into a military family in Perthshire, Scotland, Braddock served much of his career as an officer in the elite Coldstream Guards. He fought in several European campaigns, and at the beginning of the FRENCH AND INDIAN WAR (1754–63) he was appointed commander in chief of all British forces in North America, with orders to drive the French from the forks of the Ohio River and capture CANADA. However, he was given only two short-handed British regiments to accomplish this feat, and once he arrived in North America in February 1755, he was immediately bogged down by the lack of intercolonial cooperation. Regardless of these difficulties, he reinforced his regiments with colonial recruits to about 1,400 regulars and added about 700 provincial troops from several colonies. The young Virginian colonel GEORGE WASHINGTON, who became one of his aides, greatly admired Braddock's military bearing and professionalism. Braddock had hoped to add NATIVE AMERICAN auxiliaries to his force but had difficulty getting Indians to join him.

On June 10, 1755, Braddock set out from Fort Cumberland, Maryland, and began building a road so that his long train of equipment and artillery could be brought across the mountains for the attack on Fort Duquesne. He soon realized that he was moving too slowly, and on June 16 he divided his men, advancing with half the troops while the other half slogged their way through forests with the heavier baggage. On July 9, Braddock was within 10 miles of his objective when his advance guard ran into about 800 French and Indians. While the French attacked the front, the Indians, who numbered about 600, fanned out along the flanks of the British column. The British advance guard retreated pell-mell into the main body, creating confusion among the ranks. With many raw troops, the soldiers did not always respond to the orders of their officers, many of whom were killed in the early stages of the battle. The confused fighting lasted three hours before the British managed to withdraw, losing about half their men in casualties. Officers suffered the most: 63 out of 89 officers were either killed or wounded. Braddock was shot and carried with the army as it retreated back down the road to the half of the army with the heavier baggage 60 miles away. He died on July 17, and his body was buried on the road that the British army now used to continue its retreat so that the tramping feet and wagon wheels would hide it from marauding Indians.

Braddock's defeat has often been viewed as a result of British arrogance and inability to adapt to the North American way of fighting. However, it was more a result of the disorganized and petty nature of colonial American politics than any inadequacies on the part of the British. Later in the French and Indian War, British discipline and initiative would bring some great victories, including success at Fort Duquesne, which resulted more from an organized advance across the wilderness than battlefield heroics.

Further reading: Fred Anderson, *Crucible of War: The Seven Years' War and the Fate of Empire in British North America, 1754–1766* (New York: Knopf, 2000); Paul E. Kopperman, *Braddock at the Monongahela* (Pittsburgh: University of Pittsburgh Press, 1977).

Bradford, William (1722–1791) *printer*

Known as the "Patriot Printer of 1776," William Bradford was one of the leading printers during the colonial period and a strong advocate of the RESISTANCE MOVEMENT (1764–75) against British imperial regulation. He came from a family of printers—his grandfather, William Bradford (1663–1752), was the official printer for the colony of New York—and in 1742 he set up his own shop in competition with BENJAMIN FRANKLIN. That same year, he began publishing the *Weekly Advertiser, or Pennsylvania Journal,* a newspaper that he or a member of his family kept publishing, except for some gaps during the REVOLUTIONARY WAR (1775–83), until 1793. Bradford also attempted to set up some of North America's first MAGAZINES, but he was less successful in this effort.

In 1765 Bradford opposed the STAMP ACT (1765), denouncing the law the day it was to go into effect with a skull and crossbones printed on his newspaper. Bradford was active in the committees set up to organize resistance to GREAT BRITAIN, and on the July 27, 1774, issue of his newspaper he began publishing a masthead with the now-famous logo featuring a divided snake and the motto "Unite or Die." Once the war broke out, despite being in his 50s, Bradford joined the CONTINENTAL ARMY as an officer and fought in several battles. He was wounded at Princeton but continued in the army until the British evacuation of Philadelphia in 1778. He also served throughout most of the war in a variety of civilian positions in support of the rebellion. Though he suffered physically and financially in the Revolutionary War, he remained a committed WHIG. Following the war, he returned to publishing in partnership with his son Thomas. He died in Philadelphia on September 25, 1791.

See also JOURNALISM.

Branagan, Thomas (1774–1843) *abolitionist*

An Irish Catholic by birth, Thomas Branagan lost his mother at a young age and ran away to the sea when he was only 13, sailing on a slaver in 1790 and later becoming an overseer on a plantation on Antigua. He returned to Ireland after his father died but found himself unwelcomed by his relatives since he had become a METHODIST. In 1798 Branagan headed for Philadelphia, where he immediately began to think about ways to abolish SLAVERY. He published his first ANTISLAVERY tract, arguing for the end of the SLAVE TRADE and gradual ABOLITION, in 1804. He contended that these actions would further the salvation of European Americans, enhance black dignity, and protect the integrity of the family. In 1805 he began to revise his ideas and came to think that European Americans and AFRICAN AMERICANS could not live together. Believing that many of Philadelphia's African Americans were "starv-ing with hunger and destitute of employ," Branagan also feared the intermingling of races. He therefore advocated the creation of a colony in LOUISIANA reserved for freed slaves. An ardent evangelical, Branagan continued to publish essays on RELIGION, reform, and abolition, although he never became a member of PENNSYLVANIA ABOLITION SOCIETY or the American Colonization Society.

Further reading: Gary B. Nash, *Forging Freedom: The Formation of Philadelphia's Black Community, 1720–1840* (Cambridge, Mass.: Harvard University Press, 1988); Beverly Tomek, "'From motives of generosity as well as self-preservation': Thomas Branagan, Colonization, and the Gradual Emancipation Movement," *American Nineteenth-Century History* 6 (June 2005): 121–147.

Brandywine, Battle of (September 11, 1777)

During the REVOLUTIONARY WAR (1775–83) armies under General GEORGE WASHINGTON and General SIR WILLIAM HOWE clashed on Brandywine Creek, southeastern Pennsylvania, in September 1777. This Revolutionary defeat helped open the way for the British conquest of Philadelphia.

In early June 1777, with two humiliating setbacks for the king's forces at the BATTLES OF TRENTON AND PRINCETON (December 26, 1776, and January 3, 1777) suffered the previous winter, Howe began a series of maneuvers designed to lure the CONTINENTAL ARMY out of its winter quarters at MORRISTOWN, New Jersey, and to confuse Washington as to the British general's ultimate goal. By the end of June, however, Howe was back in New York with little to show for his efforts. Then, on July 23, he and his army—complete with baggage, artillery, horses, and provisions for a month—disappeared into the ATLANTIC OCEAN aboard vessels in the fleet of his brother, LORD HOWE. The army landed at Head of Elk, Maryland, intending to march on Philadelphia, which was almost 50 miles away. To prevent the British advance, Washington placed his army along the eastern shore of the Brandywine, a creek of uneven depth that had several fords, or shallow areas, where crossing was possible.

Howe divided his army into two divisions under LORD CORNWALLIS and General WILHELM VON KNYPHAUSEN. His plan was to keep Washington preoccupied with a frontal assault from Knyphausen's division, while Cornwallis marched north to a ford to outflank the Revolutionaries. Hearing first that Howe was on the west bank, Washington ordered General JOHN SULLIVAN's division to cross over the stream and attack. But soon a second dispatch from Sullivan arrived refuting that information, and Washington retracted his orders. In the meantime Howe, Cornwallis, and two-thirds of their forces had crossed Brandywine Creek and approached the right of the Continental line. By withdrawing Sullivan's men from their advance, Washington had unwittingly spared almost certain annihilation of that division and maintained the integrity of his position. When word arrived that the British were on his right, he sent the three divisions to the Birmingham (Quaker) Meeting House to meet them. Washington initially remained at the center with General NATHANAEL GREENE's division, while General ANTHONY WAYNE's forces were to stand on the left against Knyphausen at Chadd's Ford.

The battle opened late in the afternoon near the Meeting House, with Knyphausen beginning a bombardment of Wayne's position shortly thereafter. The terrain was uneven and the Revolutionaries were badly situated, with Sullivan's division separated from the other two. While attempting to close the gap, the British and their Hessian mercenaries (see HESSIANS) bore down on the Revolutionaries with bayonets drawn, and the unnerved troops began to scatter. The outnumbered remnants of the three divisions rallied bravely but fell back into the ranks of Greene's division, which had moved north to assist them. The reorganized line held for a time but could not withstand the enemy's steady advance. Greene began a slow, fighting retreat, and when the sun finally set, he withdrew his entire division; the British, exhausted by the action and with night falling, did not follow. Wayne's forces were also no match for Knyphausen, and they too withdrew with the rest of the Continental army toward Chester. Howe was the victor, and he marched into Philadelphia on September 26, 1777. But he had failed to deliver a crushing blow to Washington at Brandywine.

Further reading: Robert Middlekauf, *The Glorious Cause: The American Revolution, 1763–1789* (New York: Oxford University Press, 1982).

—Rita M. Broyles

Brant, Joseph (Thayendanegea) (1743–1807)
Mohawk chief

Born in Ohio, Joseph Brant helped lead the MOHAWK and many other IROQUOIS people through the difficult period from the start of the REVOLUTIONARY WAR (1775–83) until his death in 1807. His sister, MOLLY BRANT, was the common-law wife of WILLIAM JOHNSON, the British agent for the Mohawk, and this relationship gave Joseph Brant his first opportunity for advancement. Johnson sent the young Brant to Reverend ELEAZOR WHEELOCK's school in Lebanon, Connecticut, for an English-style EDUCATION. There he learned to read, write, and speak English as well as other lessons about European-American society. He left the school's stern discipline after less than two years.

Mohawk warrior and ardent Loyalist Joseph Brant continually sought unity among the Six Nations of the Iroquois. *(Fenimore Art Museum, Cooperstown, New York)*

During the closing days of the FRENCH AND INDIAN WAR (1754–63), Brant accompanied some Iroquois war parties against the French. William Johnson's patronage and Brant's friendship with GUY JOHNSON, William's nephew, kept Brant close to the center of power in the Mohawk world. Soon his own abilities as a speaker and a leader brought him to the attention of his people. In the early days of the Revolutionary War, he sailed to England, where he was presented to King GEORGE III, was well received by English society, and committed himself to fighting with the British in hopes of maintaining Iroquois land and sovereignty.

Brant returned to North America in 1776 to find the colonists in full rebellion against the king, but after personally witnessing British power and might, he thought they stood little chance of winning. Meanwhile, his friend Guy Johnson inherited the late William Johnson's post as the Crown agent to the Iroquois. When the war started, Johnson fled the Mohawk Valley. Joseph Brant's loyalty fell to the British, and he worked to get his fellow Mohawk to side with the Crown.

Brant organized a company of Iroquois warriors and LOYALISTS to fight for the British. In 1777 the company traveled with Colonel BARRY ST. LEGER's column as they marched through western New York on their way to meet with General JOHN BURGOYNE on the Hudson River. Brant led the force that ambushed General Nicholas Herkimer's relief column attempting to reach the besieged Fort Stanwix at the BATTLE OF ORISKANY (August 6, 1777). The siege, however, fell apart after the British received news of the approach of BENEDICT ARNOLD and another relief force. St. Leger withdrew to CANADA, leaving Burgoyne isolated and contributing to his surrender at SARATOGA (October 17, 1777).

At that point, Brant and his men cut loose from the main army to attack settlements and farms along the FRONTIER. He gained a reputation as a clever but bloody commander responsible for the deaths of many innocent civilians. The Revolutionaries responded with equally ferocious raids on any Native American villages they could find, whether the inhabitants sympathized with the British or not. General JOHN SULLIVAN led troops from the CONTINENTAL ARMY through Iroquois territory in 1779 and broke the back of the Six Nations' ability to make war.

The war split the Iroquois into those who favored the United States and those who supported GREAT BRITAIN. When the conflict ended in 1783, the United States controlled most of the Iroquois land. Brant moved to Grand River in Canada, where the British purchased land for a new home for the Iroquois. He spent the last years of his life struggling to reunite the Iroquois people under his leadership in Canada. He died in Ontario on November 24, 1807.

See also FORT STANWIX, SIEGE OF.

Further reading: Barbara Graymont, *The Iroquois in the American Revolution* (Syracuse, N.Y.: Syracuse University Press, 1972); Isabel Thompson Kelsay, *Joseph Brant, 1743–1807: A Man of Two Worlds* (Syracuse: Syracuse University Press, 1984); Alan Taylor, *The Divided Ground: Indians, Settlers, and the Northern Borderland of the American Revolution* (New York: Knopf, 2006).

—George Milne

Brant, Molly (Mary Brant, Konwatsi'tsiaienni, Degonwadenti) (ca. 1736–1796) *tribal leader*

Molly Brant is most noted for the powerful influence she exercised among the Iroquois throughout the REVOLUTIONARY WAR (1775–83). As a MOHAWK clan mother, Brant wielded considerable authority among her people. During the war she became a valuable asset to the British, working on their behalf as a Loyalist spy and as an emissary of her people. Molly and her younger brother JOSEPH BRANT are often credited for keeping the majority of the IROQUOIS loyal to the British.

Brant, whose Mohawk name was Konwatsi'tsiaienni, spent the majority of her childhood at Canajoharie, a Mohawk village in what is now upstate New York. Her birth father, Peter Tehowaghwengaraghkwin, died in 1742 shortly after Brant's mother Margaret gave birth to Joseph. In 1753 Margaret remarried for the second time (her second husband Lykas died in battle against the CATAWBA in 1750) to Brant Canagaraduncka, a Mohawk of considerable influence. Molly and Joseph took their stepfather's first name as their surname.

In 1759, at the age of 23, Molly Brant accepted the position of housekeeper in the home of Sir WILLIAM JOHNSON, the British superintendent of Indian affairs and her stepfather's friend. Though she was 20 years his junior, by the time Brant arrived at Johnson's manor home, the two were already romantically involved, and she gave birth to the first of their nine children only a month later. The couple lived together until Johnson's death in 1774, but they never officially married. Able to move freely in both Johnson's European-American world and among her own people, Brant rose to prominence.

After Johnson's death, Brant and her children returned to Canajoharie, where she opened a store with the MONEY Johnson had left her. Once the Revolutionary War broke out, Brant provided food, ammunition, and shelter to LOYALISTS and the British. She also relayed information on Revolutionary troop locations back to the British. At a council meeting at ONONDAGA in 1777, Brant gave an impassioned speech, successfully urging the Iroquois chiefs to remain loyal to GREAT BRITAIN. She spent the majority of the war traveling between FORT NIAGARA, her home in Canajoharie, and Fort Haldimand on Carleton Island.

Following the defeat of the British, Brant moved to Cataraqui, near Kingston, Ontario, CANADA. The end of the war marked the end of her political influence among her people. In recognition of her many services, the British government built a mansion for her and granted her an annual pension of £100. Molly Brant died in Cataraqui on April 16, 1796, at the probable age of 60.

See also NATIVE AMERICANS; SPYING.

Further reading: James Taylor Carson, "Molly Brant: From Clan Mother to Loyalist Chief," in *Sifter: Native American Women's Lives*, edited by Theda Perdue (New York: Oxford University Press, 2001); Earle Thomas, *The Three Faces of Molly Brant* (Kingston, Ontario: Quarry Press, 1996).

—Emily R. Wardrop

Braxton, Carter (1735–1797) *Virginia politician*
A conservative revolutionary, Carter Braxton was a signer of the DECLARATION OF INDEPENDENCE and a leading Virginia politician during the revolutionary era. Born into the Virginia elite, Braxton was educated at the College of William and Mary and spent from 1757 to 1760 in England after his first wife died. He married Elizabeth Corbin in 1761 and in the same year entered the Virginia House of Burgesses. He also supported the RESISTANCE MOVEMENT (1764–75) against British imperial measures.

In July 1775 Braxton became a member of the Virginia committee of safety, and he was appointed to the SECOND CONTINENTAL CONGRESS early in 1776. He initially opposed the idea of independence but was eventually persuaded to sign the Declaration of Independence. He also advocated an extremely conservative form of government for Virginia, with a monarch-like governor who would continue "in authority during his good behavior," a council for life, and a lower house elected every three years. Braxton feared the "tumult and riot incident to a simple democracy."

During the REVOLUTIONARY WAR (1775–83), Braxton invested in PRIVATEERING and commercial ventures, but he was not very successful. Other investments also did not turn out well, and in 1786 he had to leave his inherited estate for more modest accommodations in Richmond. After the war, although he served in the assembly for a number of years and in other state offices, he did not play a conspicuous role either on the local or national scene. He died on October 10, 1797.

Further reading: Alonzo Thomas Dill, *Carter Braxton, Virginia Signer: A Conservative in Revolt* (Lanham, Md.: University Press of America, 1983).

Brearly, David (David Brearley) (1745–1790) *lawyer*
Born in Spring Grove, New Jersey, on June 11, 1745, David Brearly attended the College of New Jersey (later Princeton University) and became a lawyer before the outbreak of the REVOLUTIONARY WAR (1775–83). An active WHIG, he joined the CONTINENTAL ARMY as a lieutenant colonel from 1776 to 1779 and subsequently was a colonel in the MILITIA. He also attended the New Jersey constitutional convention and was appointed the state's chief justice in 1779. In that position he issued an important ruling in 1780 that helped to establish the precedent of judicial review of laws passed by a legislature. Brearly attended the CONSTITUTIONAL CONVENTION (1787) as a delegate from New Jersey; he was an advocate of the rights of the small states and did not want REPRESENTATION to be based on population.

However, he supported the final document that came out of Philadelphia and presided over the New Jersey ratification convention. A Mason and a member of the Order of the Cincinnati, he was appointed a federal district judge in 1789. He died a few months later, on August 16, 1790.

See also CINCINNATI, ORDER OF THE; FREEMASONRY.

Breckinridge, John (1760–1806) *Kentucky politician; U.S. senator, attorney general*
Born in Staunton, Virginia, John Breckinridge grew up on the Virginia FRONTIER and later became a leading member of the DEMOCRATIC-REPUBLICAN PARTY in Kentucky. He studied for two years at the College of William and Mary, served in the MILITIA during the REVOLUTIONARY WAR (1775–83), and was admitted to the Virginia bar in 1785. In 1793 he gave up a promising political career in Virginia and moved to Kentucky. In his new home near Lexington, he quickly developed a lucrative practice litigating land disputes and also became active in politics, joining the local Democratic-Republican Society (see DEMOCRATIC-REPUBLICAN SOCIETIES), unsuccessfully running for the U.S. Senate in 1794, and being appointed state attorney general in 1795.

Breckinridge was an advocate of the rights of frontier settlers and even flirted with some movements to create an independent nation in the West. However, he became a strong supporter of THOMAS JEFFERSON, and after resigning as attorney general in 1797, he entered the Kentucky legislature in 1798 and served as Speaker of the state house in 1799–1800. In 1798 Breckinridge introduced Jefferson's Kentucky Resolutions to the state legislature, slightly amending two of the resolutions and guiding them to passage. From 1801 to 1805 he served as a U.S. senator from Kentucky. He resigned when Jefferson appointed him attorney general and died while still in Jefferson's cabinet on December 14, 1806.

Briar's Creek, Battle of (March 3, 1779)
The Battle of Briar's Creek marked a major defeat for Revolutionary forces in the South during the REVOLUTIONARY WAR (1775–83). After the BATTLE OF SAVANNAH (December 29, 1778), the British sought to expand their control of Georgia and occupied Augusta on January 29, 1779. Though they hoped they could rally a large number of backcountry LOYALISTS to the king's cause in the area, they had only limited success in recruiting Loyalist units around Augusta. Meanwhile, the Revolutionaries began to amass a large force across the Savannah River in South Carolina. Significantly outnumbered,

the British in Augusta withdrew toward Savannah on February 14; Continental general John Ashe, with some soldiers and about 1,500 MILITIA, followed the British, halting his men at Briar's Creek to repair a bridge and make camp. Their location effectively cut the British off from the backcountry and offered what Ashe thought was a good defensive position, with Briar's Creek to the south and west and the Savannah River to the east. Swampland made any advance across Briar's Creek or along the river virtually impossible.

British general AUGUSTINE PREVOST—on the recommendation of Archibald Campbell, who had commanded the troops in Augusta—decided to strike back at the Revolutionaries. The British were based at Ebenezer, 15 miles south of Briar's Creek. With much fanfare, Prevost sent about 500 men back up the road to within three miles of Ashe's forward positions as a diversion. Simultaneously, he had his younger brother, Lieutenant Colonel Mark Prevost, take a combined force of 900 regulars and Loyalists on a 50-mile circuitous march to the rear of Ashe's men. It remains unclear whether Ashe's patrols detected this movement, but Ashe did little to prepare for an attack from the north.

On the afternoon of March 3, a rider came screaming into the Continental camp declaring that a British column was eight miles away. The British were actually closer than that: Fifteen minutes later, as the revolutionaries scrambled to form lines, Prevost's troops appeared and began to deploy 150 yards from Ashe's men. The Revolutionaries fired a few volleys but remained disorganized, and as they maneuvered for position they opened a gap in their lines. The British charged this weak point with fixed bayonets and effectively swept the militia away. Seventy Georgia Continentals held their ground, only to be totally engulfed and compelled to surrender. Many of the men who fled had to swim across the river for safety.

The battle was a disaster for the Revolutionary cause. Ashe lost between 150 and 200 drowned or killed and more than 220 captured. The British had only five killed and 11 wounded. In addition, the British seized a hoard of abandoned weapons and equipment. Most of the Revolutionaries who ran that day deserted and went to their homes, never to fight again. However, since the Revolutionaries under the overall command of General BENJAMIN LINCOLN continued to build up their numbers on the other side of the Savannah River, the British had to withdraw to Savannah and await reinforcements before they could extend their campaign into South Carolina.

Further reading: David K. Wilson, *The Southern Strategy: Britain's Conquest of South Carolina and Georgia, 1775–1780* (Columbia: University of South Carolina Press, 2005).

Brissot de Warville, Jacques-Pierre (1754–1793)
French journalist and politician

One of a number of French journalists who attacked the old regime in the years before the FRENCH REVOLUTION (1789–99), Jacques-Pierre Brissot de Warville was briefly thrown in the Bastille in 1784 for criticizing the queen. Born Jacques-Pierre Brissot (he assumed the "de Warville" tag later in life) and trained as a lawyer, he was inspired by the ENLIGHTENMENT and advocated reform of society, believing that crime was the result of POVERTY, ignorance, and oppression. Holding to the ideal of free thought, Brissot de Warville argued for religious toleration and opposed anti-Semitism. An advocate of racial equality, he was a founder of the Société des Amis des Noirs and called not only for the ABOLITION of the SLAVE TRADE but of SLAVERY as well.

During the 1780s Brissot de Warville became increasingly interested in the United States. In 1788 he traveled to North America, supposedly to investigate the opportunities for investing in the U.S. debt, but he also had other goals. As he explained, he was "[i]ndignant at the despotism under which France was groaning in 1788" and wanted "to ascertain the means with which to accomplish a similar revolution" in FRANCE. He was also prepared, however, to settle in the United States if there was no hope for a revolution in his own country. Armed with a letter of introduction from the MARQUIS DE LAFAYETTE, Brissot de Warville met GEORGE WASHINGTON and a host of other leading men in the United States. In 1789 he was elected to membership in the AMERICAN PHILOSOPHICAL SOCIETY. Enthralled with what he saw of the young republic, Brissot de Warville was ready to settle in Pennsylvania when he heard the news of the French Revolution.

Brissot de Warville returned to France in 1789 hoping to use the new U.S. CONSTITUTION as a "perfect model" for his countrymen to follow. Having written two previous books on the United States, Brissot de Warville published a third based on his visit to demonstrate the success of REPUBLICANISM in North America. As he explained, he wanted "to study men who had just acquired their LIBERTY." He also became involved in French politics and published a newspaper called *Le Patriot français*. Eventually Brissot de Warville emerged as a leader of the Girondins, a radical group of revolutionaries. However, his party found itself in disfavor in 1793, and the Jacobins guillotined Brissot de Warville on October 31, 1793.

Further reading: Frederick A. De Luna, "The Dean Street Style of the French Revolution: J.-P Brissot, Jeune Philosophe," *French Historical Studies* 17 (Spring 1991): 159–190.

Brock, Sir Isaac (1769–1812) *British general*

Sir Isaac Brock was a British major general responsible for the defense of Upper CANADA during the early part of the WAR OF 1812 (1812–15). Brock was born in Guernsey on October 6, 1769, and entered the British army as an ensign in 1785. He advanced in the military through purchase of positions as well as through his talent, serving in the WEST INDIES and in several European campaigns during the French Revolutionary and Napoleonic Wars (1793–1815), before being sent to Canada in 1803 as a regimental commander. Promoted to major general in 1811, he became lieutenant governor of Upper Canada in October that same year and commanded the British army there at the opening of the War of 1812. After U.S. general WILLIAM HULL's abortive invasion into Upper Canada at the beginning of the war, Brock decided to attack DETROIT even though he had far less men than Hull. In a major defeat for the United States, Hull lost his nerve when he was surrounded by Brock's soldiers and Native American allies, and on August 16, 1812, Hull surrendered Detroit and more than 2,000 soldiers. In recognition of this victory, Brock was knighted, and his success helped to convince many wavering Canadian settlers to join the British cause.

On October 13, 1812, while opposing an invasion on the Niagara River frontier, Brock was rallying his troops when he was shot and killed at the BATTLE OF QUEENSTOWN HEIGHTS. Although their commander died on the battlefield, the British-Canadian forces won the day and captured another 1,000 prisoners. For his actions at Detroit and at Queenstown Heights, Brock is considered a national hero in Canada.

Broom, Jacob (1752–1810) *Delaware politician*

Jacob Broom was one of the five delegates from the state of Delaware to the 1787 CONSTITUTIONAL CONVENTION in Philadelphia. Born in Wilmington, he worked as a surveyor, manufacturer, and civic leader in the region and began his political career as a burgess of Wilmington in 1776. In 1776 and 1777 he surveyed lands under orders from General GEORGE WASHINGTON. Broom served in many Delaware political offices in the 1780s, including as assemblyman from 1784 to 1788 and as justice of the peace in 1785.

Broom supported a stronger central government and attended the ANNAPOLIS CONVENTION in 1786. At the Constitutional Convention the following year, he was disappointed that the delegates did not create an even more conservative central government; he thought that the president should serve until he was voted out for bad conduct, and believed that senators should have nine-year terms. Additionally, Broom hoped that the new national capital would be in his hometown of Wilmington, although he recognized how important compromise was to the success of the convention. In mid-July the convention threatened to end in a deadlock. A majority of delegates had just voted for a bicameral legislature, which benefited small states. In response, delegates from populous states called for a recess and a measure to set a later meeting date. On July 16, 1787, Broom spoke against adjournment, stating that it would be fatal to stop without a document to send to the states. After his speech, enough votes changed to agree to reconvene the next day.

Between 1788 and 1803 Broom continued his public service in Wilmington. He built the first known cotton mill in Delaware in 1795, and on April 25, 1810, he died a wealthy respected citizen.

Further reading: M. E. Bradford, *A Worthy Company: Brief Lives of the Framers of the United States Constitution* (Marlborough, N.H.: Plymouth Rock Foundation, Inc., 1982); John A. Munroe, *History of Delaware* (Newark: University of Delaware Press, 1979).

—Charles D. Russell

Brown, Charles Brockden (1771–1810) *author*

Charles Brockden Brown is known as the first author in the United States who attempted to live by his pen alone. Born into a relatively affluent Philadelphia family, he was well educated and trained for a law career in the late 1780s. He gave up law in 1793 to turn his attention to writing. Living mainly in New York City in the late 1790s, he published six novels between 1798 and 1801. He also edited a short-lived magazine called *The Monthly Magazine and American Review* (1799–1800). In 1800 he returned to Philadelphia and became a merchant, in partnership with his brothers. After some success, their business fell on hard times, and Brown became a small trader for the remainder of his life, occasionally writing some essays and editing the *Literary Magazine and American Register* (1803–07) and the *American Register or General Repository of History, Politics, and Science* (1807–11).

Brown's novels reflected the influence of the romantic movement in the United States at this time and deal with both the supernatural and with the psychology of his characters. They often revolve around issues of how and why people do evil in this world. Perhaps his most noted work is *Weiland* (1798), which centers on the mysterious death of one member of a family; occult RELIGION; and the practice of ventriloquism, a subject considered akin to the supernatural in the 1790s. Although his work is often characterized as gothic, Brown set his stories within a North American context and offered some interesting views of the world of the new republic. *Weiland* takes place in Philadelphia and its surrounding countryside. His books *Ormond* (1799) and *Arthur Merwyn* (published in two parts in 1799 and 1800) provided graphic descriptions of the horror of the YELLOW FEVER epidemics that struck Philadelphia and other cities during the 1790s. Not only did he depict the physical devastation of the epidemics, he also explored the mental anguish and psychic costs of the disease. He placed another of his works, *Edgar Huntly* (1799) on the FRONTIER with Native American hostility as a background for his plot.

Brown has been criticized for the similarity of his novels, his debt to the English writer Charles Godwin, and his sometimes difficult and ponderous prose. More recently, however, several scholars have viewed Brown's achievement as central to the development of culture in the United States. In particular, scholars have looked at both his fiction and nonfiction to emphasize their role in the "reading revolution" of the early republic and the effort in his work to probe "the limits of individualism."

See also LITERATURE; MAGAZINES.

Further reading: Cathy Davidson, *Revolution and the Word: The Rise of the Novel in America* (New York: Oxford University Press, 1986); Steven Watts, *The Romance of Real Life: Charles Brockden Brown and the Origins of American Culture* (Baltimore: Johns Hopkins University Press, 1994).

Brown, Thomas (1750–1825) *Loyalist*

Born into a respectable family in Whitby, England, Thomas Brown determined to settle FRONTIER Georgia by sponsoring a large number of indentured servants and colonists to emigrate from GREAT BRITAIN. This enterprise may have cost him as much as £3,000, which he had obtained from his father as his patrimony. Unfortunately for Brown, his timing was poor since he moved to Georgia in 1774 in the midst of fighting with the CREEK and on the eve of the REVOLUTIONARY WAR (1775–83). However, he quickly ingratiated himself to the royal governor and began to build his plantation in the backcountry.

Once the Revolutionary War broke out, Brown tried to remain neutral, but when he refused to agree to the ASSOCIATION on August 2, 1775, a crowd dragged him from his house, cut off his hair, beat him, and gave him a partial coat of tar and feathers. Brown escaped a few days later and became an ardent Loyalist. In 1776 he began to organize Loyalist supporters in the Georgia and South Carolina backcountry and build alliances with NATIVE AMERICANS; despite having almost no experience with Indians, he quickly developed cordial relations with the Creek. He also became the leader of a Loyalist military organization called the King's Rangers, based sometimes in FLORIDA and sometimes in Georgia and South Carolina. The King's Rangers participated in a nasty internecine war with their WHIG counterparts in which looting and executing prisoners was commonplace.

In 1779 Brown became superintendent of the Creek and CHEROKEE for the king. By the end of the war, many Revolutionaries viewed him as a bloodthirsty killer—a reputation that would be perpetuated by the early histories of the Revolution written in the United States. Brown denied these charges, although the nature of the warfare in the South was such that both sides committed atrocities. After the war he moved first to Florida and later to the BAHAMAS and St. Vincent. Always resilient, Brown maintained and built his fortune despite a variety of economic and legal difficulties.

See also LOYALISTS.

Further reading: Edward J. Cashin, *The King's Rangers: Thomas Brown and the American Revolution on the Southern Frontier* (Athens: University of Georgia Press, 1989).

Bryan, George (1731–1791) *Pennsylvania politician*

Arriving from Ireland in 1752, George Bryan became a merchant in Philadelphia and was an active politician in Pennsylvania from the 1760s until his death. During the 1760s, he supported the Penn family and their proprietary party in opposition to BENJAMIN FRANKLIN and JOSEPH GALLOWAY who wanted to make Pennsylvania a royal colony. He also attended the STAMP ACT CONGRESS in 1765. Throughout the rest of the 1760s and into the 1770s, Bryan held a variety of local government positions. He became more prominent in politics during the REVOLUTIONARY WAR (1775–83) and was a supporter of Pennsylvania's radical constitution and its unicameral legislature. Bryan was elected to the state's executive council in 1776, chosen as its vice president, and briefly acted as the council's president in 1778. He was elected to the assembly in 1779 and was made a judge of the state supreme court in 1780. He advocated an active prosecution of LOYALISTS and believed in making government as simple and democratic as possible. He supported the ABOLITION of SLAVERY and has been credited with sponsoring Pennsylvania's gradual abolition law in 1780. He attacked any effort to strengthen the national government, including the creation of the BANK OF NORTH AMERICA. A member of the ANTI-FEDERALISTS in 1787 and 1788, he participated in the Harrisburg convention of September 1788 that called for the amendment of the newly ratified U.S. CONSTITUTION, and he unsuccessfully opposed any changes to the Pennsylvania constitution. He died on January 27, 1791.

buffalo (bison)

Buffalo, as the bison is commonly called, once roamed the North American continent ranging as far north as northern CANADA, as far south as MEXICO, and stretching across the present-day United States from the ATLANTIC OCEAN to the PACIFIC OCEAN. The only large land mammal to escape the massive extinction of mega fauna during the Pleistocene epoch nearly 11,000 years ago, buffalo became a major source of food for many NATIVE AMERICANS.

Early Indian groups hunted the buffalo on foot using spears or drove herds over cliffs called "buffalo jumps." As the Indians were always quick to adopt new technologies, the bow and arrow soon replaced the spear as the preferred hunting weapon, and after TRADE began with Europeans, the gun replaced the bow and arrow. But neither the bow and arrow nor the gun had as much impact on the Indian's buffalo hunting strategies as the horse. The first Spanish horses arrived in the New World in 1519, but it took nearly 250 years for the species to spread across the continent. By 1750 several Native American groups had developed elaborate cultures on the GREAT PLAINS based on the use of the horse and the hunting of buffalo. These groups became more diffuse politically, and as they became less dependent on AGRICULTURE, they also became more male-centered.

Horses not only encouraged some semisedentary groups to become exclusively nomadic buffalo hunters, but their arrival and diffusion complicated life for the North American buffalo. Between the mid-18th and late 19th centuries, the buffalo almost died out. Overhunting by both Indians and European Americans, made easier by the proliferation of horses and guns, caused a severe drop in the buffalo population. Coupled with the competition from horses for forage and a series of droughts, the buffalo herds that once roamed the North American continent, dwindled to just a few dozen. Today, thanks to protection and conservation, their numbers are on the rise again.

See also ANIMALS.

Further reading: Andrew C. Isenberg, *The Destruction of the Bison, An Environmental History, 1750–1920* (Cambridge: Cambridge University Press, 2000); Shephard Krech III, *The Ecological Indian, Myth and History* (New York: Norton, 2000).

—Emily R. Wardrop

Buffon, Georges-Louis Leclerc, comte de (1707–1788) *French naturalist*

The French naturalist and writer Georges-Louis Leclerc, comte de Buffon, was best known for his magisterial work on natural history, the 36-volume *Histoire naturelle, générale et particulière* (1749–88). Written in a vivid style, the *Histoire* was the first modern attempt to deal systematically with the whole of nature. Buffon concerned himself with anthropology, natural history, and geology and wrote on the earth, humankind, minerals, ANIMALS, and birds. One of the most popular works of the century, the *Histoire* was translated into various languages and widely read throughout Europe and North America.

In volume 5, published in 1766, Buffon unfavorably compared North American mammals to those of Europe in order to elaborate his theory of New World degeneracy. He hypothesized that the climate of the North American continent, being (he imagined) both cooler and more humid, led to degeneration of the flora and fauna, and he argued explicitly that the animals, vegetation, and even human beings of North America were weaker, less diverse, and smaller both in size and number.

THOMAS JEFFERSON forcefully criticized this conjecture, challenging it while in Paris as the U.S. minister to FRANCE. Jefferson arranged for examples of North American mammals—including the skin, skeleton, and antlers of a moose—to be shipped to Buffon in the hope that physical proof would convince him of his error. More significantly, while in France, Jefferson published his one book, *Notes on the State of Virginia* (1787), as a rebuttal to Buffon's theory of natural decay. Composed ostensibly in reply to inquiries made by the French legation seeking statistical information on the new nation, Jefferson presented extensive data favorably comparing the sizes and varieties of North American quadrupeds to those of Europe. Shifting between description and passionate argumentation, Jefferson organized the *Notes* as a way to refute and discredit what he considered the false and damaging premises behind Buffon's views.

Further reading: Otis E. Fellows and Stephen F. Milliken, *Buffon* (New York: Twayne Publishers, 1972); Jacques Rogers, *Buffon: A Life in Natural History*, translated by Sarah Lucille Bonnefoi (Ithaca, N.Y.: Cornell University Press, 1997).

—Robyn Davis McMillin

Bulfinch, Charles (1763–1844) *architect*

Charles Bulfinch brought the architectural style of neoclassicism to postrevolutionary New England. Born into a wealthy Boston family, Bulfinch graduated from Harvard College in 1783. After college, like other elite young gentlemen of his time, he embarked on a tour of Europe. There he was impressed with a newly popular style of ARCHITECTURE that took its inspiration from the classical world of ancient Greece and Rome. Returning to Boston in 1787, Bulfinch married a well-to-do woman, Hannah Apthorp, and began to design buildings as an intellectual and civic-minded pursuit. By the early 1790s he had provided plans for a number of Massachusetts meetinghouses and for the Connecticut State Capitol in Hartford, as well as houses for wealthy family friends.

In 1793–94, Bulfinch's construction of the Tontine Crescent, an elegant and expensive row of Boston townhouses, became a financial disaster and forced him to turn to architecture as a means of support rather than as a gentlemanly pursuit. His most important commission, the Massachusetts State House in Boston, quickly followed in 1795–97. Despite the popularity of his designs, the practice of architecture could not provide Bulfinch with any financial security. To supplement his income, he became chairman of Boston's Board of Selectmen and the town's superintendent of police.

For almost 20 years, Bulfinch's service as both an architect and administrator enabled him to transform Boston's architecture through construction of almost two dozen public buildings and approximately 30 houses. During this time, he also designed public buildings and prominent residences in other towns throughout Massachusetts. On a tour of Boston in 1817, President JAMES MONROE was delighted with Bulfinch's work and offered him a position as architect of the U.S. Capitol, succeeding Benjamin Henry Latrobe. Bulfinch accepted and moved to WASHINGTON, D.C., in 1818 to oversee construction of the building, which had been only partially completed and also partly burned by the British during the WAR OF 1812. While in Washington, he also designed the federal penitentiary and a Unitarian church before returning in 1830 to Boston, where he died on April 15, 1844.

Further reading: Harold Kirker, *The Architecture of Charles Bulfinch* (Cambridge, Mass.: Harvard University Press, 1969); Harold Kirker and James Kirker, *Bulfinch's Boston, 1787–1817* (New York: Oxford University Press, 1964).

—Martha J. McNamara

Bull, William (1710–1791) *Loyalist*

William Bull was a South Carolina leader during the colonial period and a Loyalist during the REVOLUTIONARY WAR (1775–83). Although he studied MEDICINE, he concentrated most of his efforts on his plantation, where he owned almost 300 slaves; he also worked as an amateur scientist and devoted much of his life to public service. He served both in the South Carolina House of Commons and on the colonial council before becoming lieutenant governor in 1759. As lieutenant governor, he was acting governor at least five times for a total of eight years and had to deal with the CHEROKEE WAR (1759–61) and the SOUTH CAROLINA REGULATION, as well as various phases of the RESISTANCE MOVEMENT (1764–75). Like many LOYALISTS, he felt trapped by circumstances in 1774 and 1775. As a result, he sought to avoid confrontation and attempted to prevent the colony's legislature from appointing delegates to the SECOND CONTINENTAL CONGRESS. Although popular within his own colony, Bull finished his last term as acting governor in 1775. He left South Carolina in 1777 but returned in 1781 in an ill-fated effort to help establish British civil government. Bull left South Carolina for good in 1782 when the British army withdrew at the end of the war. Although he received permission to return to the state in 1787, he died in exile in London.

Further reading: Kinloch Bull, Jr. *The Oligarchs in Colonial and Revolutionary Charleston: Lieutenant Governor William Bull II and His Family* (Columbia: University of South Carolina Press, 1991).

Bull's Ferry, Battle of (July 21, 1780)

The Battle of Bull's Ferry was one of many small engagements fought in the no-man's-land surrounding British-occupied New York. LOYALISTS held a blockhouse at Bull's Ferry, New Jersey, about four miles north of Hoboken, and used it as a base for woodcutting and foraging. GEORGE WASHINGTON ordered General ANTHONY WAYNE to capture the outpost, which was manned by only about 70 men. Wayne had many more men, but probably not the 2,000 estimated by British general HENRY CLINTON. The Continentals first attempted to bombard the blockhouse with an artillery piece. After firing some 50 shells to little effect, Wayne's men charged the entrenched Loyalists, but they were driven back and gave up the attack. The Continentals lost 15 killed and about 50 wounded; the Loyalists sustained 21 casualties. In their newspapers, the British trumpeted the failure of a much superior force to dislodge a handful of Loyalists, and Major JOHN ANDRÉ even wrote a poem mocking Wayne's efforts.

Bunker Hill, Battle of (June 17, 1775)

The Battle of Bunker Hill is often considered the first major battle of the REVOLUTIONARY WAR (1775–83). After the BATTLES OF LEXINGTON AND CONCORD (April 19, 1775), the British army in Boston found itself besieged by an ad hoc army of New England MILITIA that filled the surrounding countryside. Recognizing the need to occupy the nearby high ground outside Charlestown—Bunker Hill and Breed's Hill—to secure Boston Harbor, the British planned to move in mid-June. Report of the British plan reached the Revolutionary commanding officer, General ARTEMAS WARD, who hesitantly decided to strike before the British made their move. Both Bunker Hill and Breed's Hill stood on Charlestown Peninsula, which was connected to the mainland by a narrow neck. Any Revolutionary forces on the peninsula could be subject to cannon fire on three sides from the British navy in the harbor. Likewise, an attack

Despite the British victory at the Battle of Bunker Hill, Revolutionary militia performed well against the most powerful military force in the world. *(U.S. Army Center of Military History)*

focused on the neck could cut the Revolutionaries off from reinforcements or retreat. Ward ordered Colonel WILLIAM PRESCOTT to fortify Bunker Hill on the night of June 16. Once the force of about 1,000 Revolutionaries reached the Charlestown Peninsula, however, General ISRAEL PUTNAM and Colonel Richard Gridley, chief engineer of the colonial army, decided that Prescott should fortify the lower Breed's Hill, which was closer to Boston. Putnam remained at Bunker Hill and began to entrench there. By morning, to the surprise of the British, Prescott had built a redoubt on Breed's Hill, and the entire Charlestown Peninsula was in the hands of the Revolutionaries.

The British reacted quickly. Warships soon began a bombardment, and more than 2,000 regulars prepared to dislodge the Revolutionaries. Rather than placing his men behind Prescott's position, General WILLIAM HOWE, who had command of the attack, opted for a frontal assault. There are several possible explanations for this tactic. Con-

ventional military wisdom suggested that it was best not to place your men between two lines of the enemy. Had the British attacked Breed's Hill from the rear, their own rear would have been subject to enemy fire. Second, the British believed that the Revolutionaries were untrained and unprepared to face professional soldiers. British officers argued that if they were to be successful in putting down a rebellion, they had to demonstrate the absolute superiority of their soldiers in battle. Finally, and connected to the second point, the British seriously underestimated their opponents.

The result was a near disaster for the British. Three times the British regulars marched up the hill. Twice they were forced to retreat by a withering fire. On the third assault, the British overwhelmed Prescott's men, who were almost out of ammunition. The Revolutionaries fell back in partial disorder. The British, however, had become so disorganized themselves that they had difficulty following up their victory. The remaining Revolutionaries retreated from the peninsula.

The British had won a tactical victory; they held onto the contested ground. But they also suffered devastating casualties, sustaining 226 dead and 828 wounded, while the revolutionaries lost 140 killed and 271 wounded.

Bunker Hill, as the battle was called, quickly became an important symbol of Revolutionary fortitude. Untrained soldiers had stood against the best-trained army in the world. While the British had finally driven Prescott's men from the hill, Revolutionaries considered the battle a triumph and used the phrase "Bunker Hill" as a rallying cry during the war. The British also took note of the action. Henceforth, they paid more attention to their battle tactics and did not assume their opponent would run at the sight of redcoats and glistening bayonets. General Howe would also be much more cautious in his subsequent campaigns in 1776 and 1777.

Further reading: Richard M. Ketchun, *Decisive Day: The Battle for Bunker Hill* (New York: H. Holt, 1999); Robert Middlekauf, *The Glorious Cause: The American Revolution, 1763–1789* (New York: Oxford University Press, 1982).

Burgoyne, John (1722–1794) *British general*
General John Burgoyne is most noted for his surrender at SARATOGA (October 17, 1777). Born into a military family in England, Burgoyne used his friendship with a schoolboy friend, James Stanley-Smith, Lord Strange, to advance his career. However, he alienated the powerful Stanley family by eloping with his friend's sister, Lady Charlotte Stanley, in 1743. Without patronage, and having accumulated gambling and other debts, Burgoyne sold his commission as a junior captain in 1745 and commenced a nine-year self-imposed exile on the European continent, where he and his wife traveled in FRANCE and Italy. There Burgoyne used some of his time profitably by learning French and studying European military innovations, especially the use of light dragoons and light infantry.

Reconciled with his father-in-law, the powerful Lord Derby, in 1756, Burgoyne returned to England and reentered the army, quickly advancing through the ranks via purchase and promotion. He was elected to the House of Commons in 1761 and kept his seat in Parliament for most of the remainder of his life. He also wrote on subjects connected to the army and advocated treating soldiers like human beings who could think for themselves. This approach would gain him the nickname "Gentleman Johnny" from his men when he obtained his independent command during the REVOLUTIONARY WAR (1775–83).

Burgoyne was one of three generals sent to Boston in spring 1775 to help advise General THOMAS GAGE (the other two were HENRY CLINTON and WILLIAM HOWE). By the time they arrived, battles had been fought in LEXINGTON AND CONCORD (April 19, 1775) and the war had begun. Burgoyne saw a little action during the engagement at the BATTLE OF BUNKER HILL (June 17, 1775). In spring 1777 he was appointed commander in chief of the army in CANADA that was to invade New York and sever New England from the rest of the colonies. His aim was to join with Colonel BARRY ST. LEGER approaching Albany from the Great Lakes and to connect with William Howe's forces centered on New York City. Burgoyne's army of about 10,000 troops began their long thrust into the wilderness of New York in June 1777. His forces included some of the best regiments in the army, as well as 3,000 Hessian mercenaries (see HESSIANS). He also had about 400 Indian allies at his disposal. Although the NATIVE AMERICANS proved of limited use during the campaign, their depredations managed to antagonize many FRONTIER settlers.

Burgoyne's task should have been daunting. He had to take his army through 200 miles of rough territory, often

General John Burgoyne was a leader of considerable merit; however, defeat at the Battle of Bennington caused his strategic planning and position to deteriorate rapidly. Painting by Sir Joshua Reynolds *(Frick Collection)*

constructing roads as he went along. That he was able to capture several outposts, including FORT TICONDEROGA, and almost reach Albany is testimony to his leadership and the quality of the men under his command. However, the distance was too great and the delays too many for him to gain the ultimate prize. St. Leger was driven back from Fort Oswego, and a raiding party to Vermont was beaten at the BATTLE OF BENNINGTON (August 16, 1777). Moreover, the plan of the larger campaign had never been fully agreed upon. Howe decided to focus most of his attention on capturing the revolutionary capital of Philadelphia. Henry Clinton in New York City believed he did not have enough men to force his way up the Hudson, although late in the campaign Clinton tried to come to Burgoyne's assistance. The result was that the early fall found Burgoyne deep in enemy territory with a long line of supplies. His army had shrunk to about 5,000 through losses in battle and detachments to protect his line of communications. Canadians and Indians had also deserted. He was confronted with a combined Continental and MILITIA army over twice the size of his own forces. The core of the CONTINENTAL ARMY had taken up defensive positions on Bemis Heights, commanding the path south along the Hudson. When efforts to dislodge this army failed on September 18, Burgoyne should have pressed the attack within another day or two. Delay caused his own supplies to dwindle further and allowed even more Revolutionaries to gather against him. On October 7, 1777, the Revolutionaries beat back a reconnaissance in force in the Battle of Freeman Farm, compelling Burgoyne to retreat to Saratoga, where he waited to see if Clinton's relief column would arrive. Revolutionary troops cut off his retreat, however, leaving him little choice but to surrender his army on October 17, 1777, under whatever terms he could obtain.

According to the surrender agreement, the army was to be sent back to GREAT BRITAIN under the promise that it would not fight in North America again. These generous terms were not accepted by General GEORGE WASHINGTON and the SECOND CONTINENTAL CONGRESS, and Burgoyne's army—known after the surrender as the "Convention Army," named for the convention, or surrender, agreement—was held captive throughout the war. Burgoyne, however, was allowed to sail back to Britain in spring 1778. There he quickly became embroiled in controversy as he sought exoneration for his defeat. The government did not support him in this effort, and he joined the parliamentary opposition. He was also an accomplished playwright. He died on August 3, 1792, and was buried at Westminster Abbey in London.

Although something of a flamboyant person who had four children by a mistress late in life, Burgoyne was a popular officer with his men. Contrary to the account that appears in some histories, he did not slow the army down with personal baggage and wine; marching through 200 miles of northern New York was a logistical nightmare that would have slowed any army. His failure can be blamed on circumstances as much as anything else.

Further reading: Richard J. Hargrove, *General John Burgoyne* (Newark: University of Delaware Press, 1983); Max M. Mintz, *The Generals of Saratoga: John Burgoyne and Horatio Gates* (New Haven, Conn.: Yale University Press, 1990).

Burke, Aedanus (1743–1802) *South Carolina jurist, politician*

Born in Galway, Ireland, Aedanus Burke was educated in FRANCE and visited the WEST INDIES before immigrating to the American colonies. He settled in South Carolina, where he began practicing law. During the REVOLUTIONARY WAR (1776–83) he served as a minor officer in both the CONTINENTAL ARMY and the MILITIA. He found his main calling when he was appointed a judge in 1778, although the South Carolina courts were closed from 1780 to 1783. After the war he advocated a policy of leniency toward LOYALISTS in a state that had seen bitter internecine partisan warfare. He served several terms in the state legislature during the 1780s and opposed the ratification of the U.S. CONSTITUTION because he disliked the fact that the executive could be reelected.

As a member of the first U.S. Congress, Burke followed his own peculiar path. Although he sought to limit the power of the government by opposing the excise tax and BANK OF THE UNITED STATES, he supported the assumption of state debts and the full funding of the national debt as fair and appropriate public policy. After serving one term in Congress, Burke returned to South Carolina and resumed his judicial duties. During the 1780s he had helped to draw and revise the state legal code. In 1799 he became chancellor of South Carolina's court of equity. He died on March 30, 1802.

See also CONSTITUTION, RATIFICATION OF THE; DEBT, NATIONAL.

Burke, Edmund (1729–1797) *British author, politician*

Edmund Burke was a British politician who supported the North American colonists in their opposition to British imperial measures in the 1760s and 1770s but later criticized the FRENCH REVOLUTION (1789–99). He was born in Ireland, attended Trinity College in Dublin, and trained as a lawyer. Giving up his legal practice sometime in the 1750s, Burke set out to become a man of letters. He wrote several pamphlets and established a magazine called the *Annual Register* in 1758. Although his career took a variety of turns after 1760, he continued to be involved with the publication of the *Annual Register* into the 1780s. In 1765 he became the private secretary of CHARLES WENTWORTH, MARQUIS OF ROCKINGHAM. That same year, Rockingham became First Lord of the Treasury (the chief minister in the British government), and consequently Burke entered the realm of politics and was given a seat in Parliament. Although the district he would represent changed a few times, he remained a member of Parliament (MP) for most of the rest of his life. He also became something of a spokesman for the Rockingham Whigs, using his gifts as an orator and his command of the facts to quickly become a prominent MP.

Rockingham's administration lasted only until July 1766, a turn of events that placed Burke among the opposition as GREAT BRITAIN headed for a crisis with its North American colonies in the 1770s. In 1774 and 1775 he argued for a pragmatic position in the controversy. Rockingham's government had taken a similar line during his brief time in power: The Rockinghams had repealed the STAMP ACT (1765) as an unwise measure but passed the DECLARATORY ACT (1766), asserting the right of Parliament to legislate for the colonies in all cases whatsoever. In the 1770s, Burke did not contest that Parliament was sovereign and had the right to tax the colonies. He only believed that it was foolish and impolitic to push the point. He thought that the colonies were a great source of wealth for Great Britain through TRADE, even if no taxes were levied there. He wanted Parliament to repeal the TEA ACT (1773) and opposed the passage of the COERCIVE ACTS (1774). When colonial Americans heard of these positions, they viewed Burke as a hero, a statesman, and a defender of their rights. But he was less a defender of colonial rights and more a pragmatic politician who wanted to preserve the empire.

Burke also took a pro-American stand once hostilities broke out. He advocated an acceptance of the Continental Congress (see CONTINENTAL CONGRESS, FIRST; CONTINENTAL CONGRESS, SECOND) as a representative body for the colonies and held that only an American legislature should raise taxes in North America. His ideas were rejected by the majority in Parliament, and by the time Rockingham regained political power in 1782, it was too late for anything but independence for the United States. Burke held a minor office briefly in the 1780s, but the Rockingham control did not last.

During the 1780s, Burke is best known for his role in Parliament's investigation into the affairs of the British administration of INDIA. But he gained his greatest fame in Great Britain after 1790 for his opposition to the French Revolution. In that year he published *Reflections on the Revolution in France,* which has been held up ever since as the epitome of the conservative approach to govern-

ment and society. Burke argued that tradition and inherited institutions are the true bulwark of politics and society. Overthrowing the past, from this perspective, was innately bad. In 1790 the French Revolution, which had not even taken some of its most radical steps, threatened to overturn all that was good in the hope of replacing it with some unknown new future. For Burke this was anathema. He published his study at a time when many in Great Britain still had hope that the French Revolution would bring about a truly enlightened government; THOMAS PAINE wrote *The Rights of Man* (1791) in opposition to Burke's *Reflections.* When the French Revolution entered its radical phase, as mass executions followed more mass executions and as the French took their king to the guillotine in 1793, many Englishman began to think that Burke was right. Burke retired from Parliament in 1794 and died three years later, on July 9, 1797.

Further reading: George W. Fasel, *Edmund Burke* (Boston: Twayne, 1983).

Burke, Thomas (ca. 1747–1783) *North Carolina jurist, politician*
Born in Galway, Ireland, to a prominent family, Thomas Burke immigrated to Virginia in 1764 and entered North Carolina politics soon after he arrived in that colony in 1771. He was licensed as a lawyer and became a judge but gained prominence in the North Carolina provincial congresses of 1775 and 1776, where he was an early advocate of independence and supported a radically democratic state constitution. North Carolina sent Burke to the SECOND CONTINENTAL CONGRESS in December 1776.

As a delegate to Congress, Burke often followed his own agenda based on his ideas concerning the rights of his state. He thus opposed the ARTICLES OF CONFEDERATION as threatening to the states' independence but supported an impost as a means of revenue for the national government. Perhaps his most noted iconoclastic action was his walking out of a debate over a reply to a report by GEORGE WASHINGTON in 1778. By leaving the session he prevented a quorum and stifled further action by the Congress. Burke refused to return, even when ordered to do so by the president of Congress. The Congress censured him for this affront, but Burke refused to accept their censure, saying that Congress did not have that power, which he believed resided in his state's constituents.

Burke remained in the Congress until 1781, when he was elected governor of North Carolina. Faced with a war emergency, he asserted his authority as executive and was so successful in organizing the state's defense that LOYALISTS raided Hillsboro to capture him on September 12, 1781. Even in captivity, Burke followed his own path and violated the conditions of his relatively lenient treatment to escape from the British lines. He did not seek reelection as governor in 1782 and retired to his home where he died on December 2, 1783.

Further reading: Jennings B. Sanders, "Thomas Burke in the Continental Congress," *North Carolina Historical Review* 9 (1932): 22–37.

Burnt Corn, Battle of (July 27, 1813)

On July 27, 1813, a party of U.S. soldiers riding out from Fort Mims, Alabama, attacked CREEK warriors at Burnt Corn Creek, in southern Alabama, touching off the Battle of Burnt Corn. This battle is considered to be the first official fight in the CREEK WAR (1813–14), though other, smaller-scale skirmishes had occurred in the previous weeks. There were approximately 180 U.S. soldiers led by Colonel James Caller and Captain Dixon Bailey, who fought roughly 80 Red Stick warriors (see RED STICKS), commanded by the Creek leader Peter McQueen.

The skirmish occurred as McQueen and his party of warriors returned from Pensacola, FLORIDA, where they had received small amounts of munitions from the Spanish, and possibly the British, stationed in the area. The U.S. troops, who had heard of this mission, set out to intercept the Indians, who were ambushed as they were bedding down for the night alongside Burnt Corn Creek. After the initial attack, Creek warriors fled into the forest and watched as the soldiers looted and destroyed supplies. The Indians used this lack of discipline to regroup and attack. Because Caller's troops retreated, the Creek captured the battlefield, thus "winning" the battle. Two soldiers perished and probably 10 warriors died in the fighting.

See also NATIVE AMERICANS.

Burr, Aaron (1756–1836) *U.S. vice president*

Aaron Burr was an officer in the CONTINENTAL ARMY and an important politician who was almost elected president. Overly ambitious, he killed ALEXANDER HAMILTON in a duel and became involved in conspiracies to establish an independent nation in the West.

Burr was born on February 6, 1756, in Newark, New Jersey, the son of Aaron Burr, second president of the College of New Jersey (now Princeton University) and Esther Edwards. His mother was the daughter of the famous religious leader Jonathan Edwards. When Burr was three, his parents died, and he was raised by an uncle, Timothy Edwards. At age 13 he enrolled at the College of New Jersey, graduating with distinction in 1772. In 1774 he began to study law, but the REVOLUTIONARY WAR (1775–83) erupted. Burr immediately joined the Continental army

and served as a captain under BENEDICT ARNOLD in the BATTLE OF QUEBEC (1775–76). Because he displayed great valor and leadership during the failed campaign, he was promoted to major and appointed to GEORGE WASHINGTON's staff. However, he and Washington did not get along with each other, so Burr transferred to the staff of General ISRAEL PUTNAM, Washington's second in command. During the British attack on New York City, he helped to rescue trapped soldiers at Brooklyn Heights, and in recognition of this act the SECOND CONTINENTAL CONGRESS promoted him to lieutenant colonel. However, after the BATTLE OF MONMOUTH (June 28, 1778) in New Jersey, Burr suffered increasing bouts of illness. Given his poor health and his belief that his assignment held no promise of advancement, he resigned his commission in March 1779.

Burr resumed his legal studies in 1780 and soon began his political career. In 1782 he was admitted to the New York bar and married Theodosia Prevost, a woman 10 years older than he. (She would die in 1794 due to poor health). The next year the couple moved to New York City, where they had one child. Burr rose to prominence as a lawyer

Aaron Burr *(Library of Congress)*

and competed with Alexander Hamilton for the city's best legal cases. He was elected to the state assembly in 1784, and in 1789 he was appointed attorney general of New York by Governor GEORGE CLINTON. He served one term in the U.S. Senate (1791–97), during which he became a die-hard member of the DEMOCRATIC-REPUBLICAN PARTY. As such, he ran in the ELECTION OF 1796 as THOMAS JEF-FERSON's vice president. The campaign was unsuccessful, but Burr used his rising recognition to build a following in New York. Known as the Burrites, this group of Demo-cratic-Republicans helped win New York in 1800, which allowed Burr to be Jefferson's running mate in the presi-dential ELECTION OF 1800. At that time electors did not cast separate votes for the president and vice president but instead cast two votes for two separate candidates. Who-ever won the most votes won the presidency; whoever had the second most votes became the vice president. Jefferson and Burr received equal numbers of votes. Burr did not concede the election to Jefferson, and the decision was left to the House of Representatives. Each state delegation had only one vote, and it took 36 ballots before the election was decided in Jefferson's favor. No one knows exactly what changed the vote, but Burr, and others, believed that Ham-ilton influenced some members of the FEDERALIST PARTY in Congress to allow Jefferson to win.

Burr served only one term as vice president because of an ideological and personal rift between him and Jefferson. George Clinton was selected to replace Burr as the vice presidential candidate in 1804, and Burr subsequently lost a bid for the New York governorship to the Jeffersonian candidate. During this election Hamilton published letters denouncing Burr, who angrily sought a retraction, which Hamilton refused to do. This argument culminated in the famous Burr-Hamilton duel at Weehawken, New Jersey, on July 11, 1804. Burr mortally wounded Hamilton, who died the next day. The outpouring of grief and anger—many northerners saw him as a murderer—forced Burr to flee to Philadelphia and the southern states to avoid warrants for his arrest.

During this flight, Burr sought support for a scheme to create a new North American empire—although whether this empire would be based in New Orleans and the LOUI-SIANA Territory or involved the seizure of Spanish lands beyond the Mississippi remains unclear. Burr's allies included the wealthy Harman Blennerhassett as well as General JAMES WILKINSON, the ranking U.S. general who was secretly in the pay of the Spanish government. Burr may also have discussed the plot with ANDREW JACKSON and other western leaders. In autumn 1806 he established a cache of weapons on Blennerhassett Island in the Ohio River and gathered about 60 men to sail down the Ohio River to the Mississippi. By this time word of the plot had reached Jefferson, and Wilkinson got cold feet and

betrayed Burr. Ohio MILITIA raided Blennerhassett Island just after Burr's expedition had left. Burr joined his small army on the Ohio River, and he managed to get them as far as an outpost north of Natchez, Mississippi, in early Febru-ary 1808 before the army stopped them. He abandoned his followers and escaped, but was arrested just north of the border with Spanish FLORIDA a month later. He sub-sequently stood trial for treason, but, much to Jefferson's chagrin, he was acquitted.

Burr spent the years 1808–12 in Europe attempting to interest the European powers in his plan, with no success. In 1812 he returned to New York, where he practiced law. In 1833 he married Elizabeth Brown Jumel, a rich widow, but after he managed to squander her MONEY, she filed for divorce. Burr died on September 19, 1836, as the divorce was being finalized.

Further reading: Thomas J. Fleming, *Duel: Alexander Hamilton, Aaron Burr, and the Future of America* (New York: Basic Books, 1999); Nancy Isenberg, *Fallen Founder: The Life of Aaron Burr* (New York: Viking, 2007); Roger G. Kennedy, *Burr, Hamilton, and Jefferson: A Study in Char-acter* (New York: Oxford University Press, 2000); Arnold A. Rogow, *A Fatal Friendship: Alexander Hamilton and Aaron Burr* (New York: Hill and Wang, 1998).

—Michael L. Cox

Burroughs, Stephen (1765–1840) *confidence man*
Perhaps the most notorious criminal and confidence man in the early republic, Stephen Burroughs was born in New Hampshire. Even as a young boy, he admitted that his "thirst for amusement was insatiable" and proudly pro-claimed that he was considered "the worst boy in town." After a short stint in the CONTINENTAL ARMY, which he reported that he "suddenly left," Burroughs returned to his father's house. He then obtained some schooling and attended Dartmouth College, which he departed two years later after a disagreement with the administration. Follow-ing a few years of attempting to make his way legitimately in the world, Burroughs pretended to be a preacher and began his career as a confidence man. During most of the 1780s and 1790s, he engaged in a variety of scams and crimes, including theft and counterfeiting. He also acted the rogue, seducing schoolgirls and assuming a variety of identities. His reputation became so widespread that crimes he did not commit were often ascribed to him, and other criminals sometimes gave his name when captured. Hav-ing spent some time in jail, Burroughs left New England and, by the opening decade of the 19th century, Burroughs settled in CANADA, where he continued counterfeiting bank bills and sending them to the United States. In 1798 Burroughs published *Memoirs of Stephen Burroughs*, in

which he tried to portray some of his illicit deeds in as positive manner as possible. This book was reprinted in various forms about 20 times, including an edition in 1988.

See also CRIME; MONEY.

Further reading: Stephen Burroughs, *Memoir of Stephen Burroughs*, edited by Philip F. Gura (Boston: Northeastern University Press, 1988); Daniel E. Williams, "In Defense of Self: Author and Authority in the *Memoirs of Stephen Burroughs*," *Early American Literature* 25 (1990): 96–122.

Bute, John Stuart, earl of (1713–1792) *chief minister to King George III*

John Stuart, third earl of Bute, was the tutor of GEORGE III before the latter became king and was the monarch's chief minister briefly between 1762 and 1763. Bute taught the young George languages and the usual kingly skills—riding, fencing, and etiquette—from 1755 to 1760, and also spent a great deal of time with him studying European and British history, especially concerning the British constitution. The first two Georges of the House of Hanover had been little more than German princes who had been elevated to the Crown of GREAT BRITAIN. George III, who was only 22 when he ascended the throne in 1760, was thoroughly British. Bute and Prince George had read the works of Viscount Bolingbroke, which held that the British constitution was best protected by a patriot king who would not only reign but also govern. When George became king, he decided to put these ideas into practice. He did not intend to become an absolute monarch, but as king he did believe that it was his constitutional right to select his chief advisers. This approach began a period of political instability in the British government that led to seven changes in administration in 10 years. It also led to inconsistencies in policy that had a devastating effect on British and colonial relations.

One of those seven administrations was organized under Bute, the king's teacher, friend, and adviser. Bute advised the king in a variety of official and unofficial capacities, forcing first WILLIAM PITT and then THOMAS PELHAM-HOLLES, DUKE OF NEWCASTLE, out of the government. He was appointed First Lord of the Treasury (the king's chief minister, subsequently prime minister) on May 26, 1762. His most significant achievement was to end the Seven Years' War (known as the FRENCH AND INDIAN WAR in colonial America). However, his political maneuvers, his influence over the king, and the terms of the peace were extremely unpopular. Moreover, there were false rumors that Bute was having an affair with the king's mother. As a result, it became very difficult for him to govern, and he was compelled to resign on April 8, 1763. Many politicians continued to fear that Bute was still active behind the

scenes, and he was forced to withdraw completely from the king's household in 1765.

During Bute's administration, only one crucial decision was made concerning colonial affairs: to maintain an army in North America after the French and Indian War. But that decision contributed to the imperial crisis, providing a rationale for taxation and thus creating an irritant to colonials who detested British soldiers living in their midst. Bute also became an important symbol of the unpopularity of the British government in colonial North America. During the STAMP ACT (1765) demonstrations, for example, some crowds marched through the streets with a boot as a mocking symbol of the man who was believed to be an evil influence on the king.

After 1765, Bute had little impact on British and imperial politics. Rumors persisted concerning his secret influence, however, contributing to a distrust of British politics on both sides of the ATLANTIC OCEAN. He died in London on March 10, 1792.

See also RESISTANCE MOVEMENT.

Further reading: James Lee McKelvey, *George III and Lord Bute: The Leicester House Years* (Durham, N.C.: Duke University Press, 1973).

Butler, John   See BUTLER'S RANGERS.

Butler, Pierce (1744–1822) *South Carolina politician*

The third son of a prominent Irish family, Pierce Butler went from being a British army officer to fighting as colonial Revolutionary in a very short time. His parents purchased for him a commission in the British army when he was only 11, and three years later he went to North America, where he served during the FRENCH AND INDIAN WAR (1754–63). In 1771 he married a South Carolina heiress, and two years later he sold his commission—he was a major by this time—to settle down to life as a South Carolina planter. During the REVOLUTIONARY WAR (1775–83) he sided with the WHIGS but worked more in staff positions for the Colony of South Carolina than in any direct military capacity. He was elected to the state assembly in 1776 and, with some interruptions, remained in the legislature until 1799. In 1787 he represented South Carolina at the CONSTITUTIONAL CONVENTION, worked to defend SLAVERY, and saw the U.S. CONSTITUTION as reasonable compromise that was good for the nation.

An unconventional politician, Butler initially supported the program of ALEXANDER HAMILTON and the emerging FEDERALIST PARTY, but by the mid-1790s he had moved closer to the DEMOCRATIC-REPUBLICAN PARTY because he was pro-French and opposed JAY'S TREATY (1794). He was chosen to represent South Carolina in the Senate in 1789, was reelected once, and resigned in 1796. However, he returned to the Senate to finish a term vacated by a death in 1802; he resigned again in 1804.

Butler spent the last years of his life in Philadelphia as an absentee plantation owner. At his death on February 15, 1822, he was worth over $1 million, owned about 1,000 slaves, and had property interests in several states, including South Carolina, Georgia, Tennessee, and Pennsylvania.

Further reading: Terry W. Lipscomb, ed., *The Letters of Pierce Butler, 1790–1794: Nation Building and Enterprise in the New American Republic* (Columbia: University of South Carolina Press, 2007).

Butler's Rangers

Organized by Lieutenant Colonel John Butler, originally a farmer from the Mohawk Valley in New York, Butler's Rangers was a military unit of LOYALISTS formed in September 1777. During the summer that year, Butler had joined Colonel BARRY ST. LEGER's campaign and demonstrated his effectiveness in working with the IROQUOIS. As a result, GUY CARLETON, (later, FIRST BARON DORCHES-TER,) authorized Butler to recruit a force of Loyalists who could fight with NATIVE AMERICANS and raid settlements supporting the Revolution. Based in FORT NIAGARA, Butler's Rangers participated in a number of engagements, including the so-called WYOMING MASSACRE (July 3–4, 1778), the CHERRY VALLEY MASSACRE (November 11, 1778), and the unsuccessful defense of Iroquois territory at the BATTLE OF NEWTOWN (August 29, 1779). By the end of the war some companies of the unit had been dispatched to DETROIT and had fought alongside Indians against the Kentuckians at the BATTLE OF BLUE LICKS (August 19, 1782). His son Walter Butler served as an officer in Butler's Rangers. After the TREATY OF PARIS (1783) Butler's Rangers was disbanded, and most of the men settled in CANADA, where Butler became a local office holder and Indian agent. Within the United States, Butler's Rangers were associated with the ravages of FRONTIER warfare, and the European Americans in the unit were compared to savages. Canadians, however, looked on Butler's Rangers as FRONTIER heroes and viewed the unit's successes with pride.

Further reading: Howard Swiggett, *War Out of Niagara: Walter Butler and the Tory Rangers* (New York: Columbia University Press, 1933).

C

Cadore Letter (1810)

The Cadore Letter was one of the major causes of an increasing hostility between the United States and GREAT BRITAIN, leading to the WAR OF 1812 (1812–15). The letter derives its name from its author, Jean-Baptiste Nompere de Champagny, duke of Cadore, who was the French minister to the United States at the time. It was sent to JOHN ARMSTRONG, then U.S. ambassador to FRANCE on orders from NAPOLEON BONAPARTE, who was seeking to extract maximum advantage from the United States's position of neutral commerce, and to distract Great Britain from its war with FRANCE. The letter indicated that Napoleon would repeal the BERLIN DECREE and MILAN DECREE, which put limits on neutral shipping, if the United States would reimpose a policy of nonintercourse with Great Britain. Even though the Cadore Letter was a nonofficial piece of correspondence, and as such came with no guarantee that France would stop attacking ships from the United States, President JAMES MADISON jumped at the chance to reactivate his policy of nonintercourse in order to restore his standing in the DEMOCRATIC-REPUBLICAN PARTY. Agreeing to Napoleon's terms, in a desperate attempt to ease pressure on U.S. TRADE, Madison reinstated nonintercourse with Great Britain in November 1810.

By December 1810, as the French continually harassed U.S. shipping, it was apparent that France was not living up to the promises of the Cadore Letter and that Napoleon deceived the United States in order to put economic pressure on the British. Had the letter turned out to be an actual precursor of change in French policy, Madison would not have seemed to be such a dupe in the eyes of his opponents in the FEDERALIST PARTY, who used the Cadore Letter to decry Madison's presidency. Madison responded by presenting the letter as an example of European corruption. He also used the incident and the failure of nonintercourse with Great Britain to shift U.S. foreign policy to a war footing, which would lead to the outbreak of conflict in the War of 1812.

See also FOREIGN AFFAIRS.

Further reading: Clifford L. Egan, *Neither Peace Nor War: Franco-American Relations, 1803–12* (Baton Rouge: Louisiana State University Press, 1983); J. C. A. Stagg, *Mr. Madison's War: Politics, Diplomacy, and Warfare in the Early Republic, 1783–1830* (Princeton, N.J.: Princeton University Press, 1983).

—Charles E. Russell

Calabee, Battle of (January 27, 1814)

The Battle of Calabee was a part of the larger CREEK WAR of 1813–14. On January 27, 1814, General John Floyd's volunteer MILITIA clashed with Red Stick warriors from the CREEK nation at Calabee Swamp in present-day Alabama. Floyd's troops consisted of 1,300 European Americans from the Carolinas and Georgia and 400 "friendly" Creek who opposed the hostile RED STICKS. Many of the Red Sticks, who may have numbered 1,800 men, were poorly armed and did not have guns. The battle began before sunrise, when the Red Sticks attacked Floyd's camp. Although the assault surprised Floyd's men, his troops rallied and held off the warriors in fierce combat, which included the use of artillery by the European Americans. The militia counterattacked with fixed bayonets and drove the Indians from the battlefield. At least 79 Red Sticks were killed; Floyd lost 17 militia and five Creek. The apparent victory was short-lived, however. Floyd, concerned with taking care of his wounded, departed the next day for Fort Mitchell, and the Red Sticks regained control of the swamp.

Further reading: Frank Lawrence Owsley Jr., *Struggle for the Gulf Borderlands: The Creek War and the Battle of*

New Orleans, 1812–1815 (Gainesville: University Press of Florida, 1981).

—Emily R. Wardrop

Calhoun, John C. (1782–1850) *South Carolina politician*

Although most of his extensive public career took place after 1815, John Caldwell Calhoun first rose to prominence as an ardent supporter of the WAR OF 1812 (1812–15). Calhoun was born on March 18, 1782, in the South Carolina backcountry to a modestly prosperous family. He was educated at Yale and attended TAPPING REEVE's law school in Litchfield, Connecticut. With a limited inheritance, a good marriage, and his law career, Calhoun attained some wealth. He was elected to Congress in 1810, and as an ardent member of the DEMOCRATIC-REPUBLICAN PARTY, he became a WAR HAWK calling for military action against GREAT BRITAIN. As he explained, with any other course of action, "the independence of the nation is lost." Although at times critical of the prosecution of the war, Calhoun worked in Congress to provide as much support for it as possible.

By the time of the TREATY OF GHENT (1814), Calhoun had become a strong nationalist (see NATIONALISM). However, during the 1820s he reversed that position and ultimately became a spokesman for STATES' RIGHTS and a defender of the institution of SLAVERY. Calhoun remained on center stage in U.S. politics for more than 40 years, serving as a congressman and a senator and holding a variety of public offices, including secretary of war, secretary of state, and vice president for both JOHN QUINCY ADAMS and ANDREW JACKSON. He was again serving as a U.S. senator when he died in WASHINGTON, D.C., on March 31, 1850.

Further reading: Margaret L. Coit, *John C. Calhoun: American Portrait* (Columbia: University of South Carolina Press, 1991); John Niven, *John C. Calhoun and the Price of Union: A Biography* (Baton Rouge: Louisiana State University Press, 1988); Merrill D. Peterson, *The Great Triumvirate: Webster, Clay, and Calhoun* (New York: Oxford University Press, 1987).

California

In the 1760s, concerned that the English or the Russians might claim California, the Spanish government decided to colonize the region. Instrumental in this effort was José de Galvéz, who as inspector general of New Spain (MEXICO) organized the first Californian settlements. Galvéz sent an expedition to Alta California, as the Spanish called the area, in 1769, establishing a precarious foothold and presidio at San Diego. The Spanish also explored up the California coast nearly to San Francisco Bay. Over the next few years, Franciscan fathers built a series of missions and the Spanish founded three other presidios: Monterey (1770), San Francisco (1776), and Santa Barbara (1782). Never more than a backwater FRONTIER of the Spanish-American empire, the Hispanic population of California had reached about 3,200 by 1821.

California's early years were difficult for the colony, which remained dependent on supplies from Mexico. From 1774 to 1776, the Spanish sent out several reconnaissance parties to expand California's boundaries and explore the possibility of land communication with Sonora in Mexico and the settlement at Santa Fe in New Mexico. Communication with New Mexico across what is now the state of Arizona appeared unfeasible. An overland trail was discovered to Sonora, but it required maintaining an outpost at the juncture of the Colorado and Gila rivers. When the Yuma Indians destroyed that outpost in 1781, California again became almost entirely dependent on communication by sea. Spanish explorers also traveled in the PACIFIC OCEAN as far north as ALASKA, establishing SPAIN's claim to the area of the current northwest United States and coastal British Columbia.

By the early 1780s, California was becoming more self-sufficient with expanding cattle herds and developing AGRICULTURE. In recognition of the growing importance of Alta California, the Spanish Crown ordered the provincial seat of government to be moved from Baja California to Monterey in 1776. The Franciscan missions contributed to this success; they converted thousands of NATIVE AMERICANS to Christianity and used Indians for labor on the missions. As many as 23,000 California Indians lived in the missions by 1821, but runaways and high mortality constantly put a strain on the missions' native populations. Conditions for all California Indians deteriorated over the course of Spanish colonization, with the region's diverse native population declining from about 300,000 to 200,000 between 1769 and 1821.

Although never overly successful, Spanish California helped to forge the Hispanic culture of the Southwest that was sustained by Mexico until the region was conquered by the United States in the Mexican War (1846–48). Contact with the United States before 1815 was minimal; by that date a few vessels from the United States had reached the Californian shore as merchants began to TRADE in the Pacific.

Further reading: Steven W. Hackel, *Children of Coyote, Missionaries of St. Francis: Indian-Spanish Relations in Colonial California, 1769–1850* (Chapel Hill: University of North Carolina Press, 2005); David J. Weber, *The Spanish Frontier in North America* (New Haven, Conn.: Yale University Press, 1992).

Callender, James T. (1758–1803) *journalist*
With a modest EDUCATION and a scathing pen, James Thomas Callender was responsible for bringing the sexual indiscretions of both ALEXANDER HAMILTON and THOMAS JEFFERSON to public view in the United States. Scottish by birth, Callender left GREAT BRITAIN in 1793 after having written a critique of the British government called *Political Progress of Britain* (1792); he was one of many radicals compelled to leave the country during the 1790s and early 1800s. Once in the United States, he became a journalist, reporting on the debates in Congress and writing essays supporting the DEMOCRATIC-REPUBLICAN PARTY and attacking members of the FEDERALIST PARTY. In 1797, perhaps with the connivance of Jefferson, Callender published an account of Hamilton's sordid affair with Maria Reynolds. Throughout the late 1790s and in the ELECTION OF 1800 he published political attacks on the Federalist Party and received financial support from Jefferson and other leading Democratic-Republicans.

In June 1798, threatened with prosecution under the Sedition Law and possible deportation under the Alien Acts (see ALIEN AND SEDITION ACTS), Callender fled Philadelphia and went to Richmond, Virginia. There he seems to have had a change of heart and decided that he would not mind being prosecuted under the Sedition Act as a political martyr and thereby bolster Jefferson's chances for being elected president. He wrote numerous newspaper articles against the Federalist Party and also published *The Prospect Before Us,* lambasting President JOHN ADAMS and his administration as corrupt. Arrested in May 1800, he was convicted the next month of violating the Sedition Act in a federal court presided over by SAMUEL CHASE, fined $200, and sent to jail for nine months. Once Jefferson became president, he pardoned Callender and even—after some delays—remitted his fine. But the president's refusal to appoint him postmaster of Richmond, a position that would have provided financial stability, turned Callender away from Jefferson.

Over the next several years, Callender became embroiled in a series of political controversies with moderate Democratic-Republicans and found himself personally attacked by JAMES DUANE and other editors who were close to Jefferson. Knowing from personal experience that Jefferson could have easily halted these attacks, Callender lashed out at the president. On September 1, 1802, he wrote, "It is well known that the man, *whom it delighteth the people to honor,* keeps, and for many years has kept as his concubine, one of his own slaves. Her name is Sally." He went on to say incorrectly that SALLY HEMINGS had a son named Tom whose "features are said to bear a striking resemblance to those of the president himself."

Callender continued to engage in political controversy after this attack on Jefferson. With a long history of heavy drinking, he was found drowned in the James River on July 17, 1803, after having been seen in a drunken stupor.

Further reading: Michael Durey, *"With the Hammer of Truth:" James Thomson Callender and America's Early National Heroes* (Charlottesville: University Press of Virginia, 1990).

Camden, Battle of (August 15, 1780)
Three months after capturing Charleston (May 12, 1780), with virtually the entire CONTINENTAL ARMY in the South, British forces under LORD CORNWALLIS overwhelmed Revolutionary troops at Camden, South Carolina, and brought about the fall of HORATIO GATES, the hero of SARATOGA (October 17, 1777). After the surrender of Charleston, Congress had appointed Gates as head of the Southern Department. Unfortunately for the Revolutionary cause, his tenure was riddled with poor decisions. Upon assuming his command, Gates immediately targeted the British supply base at Camden, which was vital to their intended campaign to subjugate the Carolinas and Virginia. His subordinates, who were familiar with the region, suggested a circuitous route to Camden through rich farming country, where anti-British sentiment was high and the troops would easily find sustenance. Unwilling to march an extra 50 miles, Gates ignored the advice and plotted a direct route through a barren, pro-British area that was permeated with sandy plains, swamps, and dense forests.

Although Gates promised issues of rum and rations en route, none were forthcoming, and the soldiers were forced to subsist mainly on peaches, green apples, and green corn as they marched in the heat and humidity of a Carolina summer. As reinforcements slowly joined Gates's army, its strength in numbers grew, but the men were sick and debilitated. In Charleston, word reached Cornwallis of Gates's advance, and he set off for Camden, ordering additional troops into the area so that ultimately about 2,200 men were at his command. Gates, on the other hand, was ignorant as to the size of his army, believing he had over twice the number of available troops than the slightly more than 3,000 men who were actually fit for duty.

Gates continued to undermine his own operations. Planning a night march to surprise the enemy, he placed dragoons at the front of the line, despite protests from his officers that the enemy would be able to hear the horses' hooves from a great distance. Presumably trying to fortify the sick and hungry army for the battle ahead, rations of beef, cornmeal, and molasses were procured and given to the men prior to breaking camp. The meal had severe gastrointestinal consequences, however, and throughout the march, soldiers continually broke ranks in order to relieve themselves, which only weakened them further. Around

2:30 A.M., British cavalry ran into Gates's dragoons, and after a flurry of gunfire and saber fighting in the dark, the Continental cavalry retreated to its line of infantry, upon which both armies halted further action until daylight.

With the knowledge that Cornwallis was personally commanding the British forces and that the two armies were fairly even in size, Gates would have been wise to retreat to a stronger defensive position. As an ex-British officer, he must have known that, even with fewer men, the superior training and experience of the British gave them the advantage over the raw MILITIA units that constituted much of his army. Vacillating over his course of action, Gates asked his officers for their opinions. None suggested a withdrawal, but one emphatically stated that it was too late to do anything but fight. Gates agreed and ordered the officers to their various commands straddling the Charlotte road. Stands of pine trees on either side of the route offered cover for sniper fire, and swamps on both sides of the trees protected against flanking movements. Gates positioned himself and his staff at the remote distance of 600 yards to the rear of the line. Following European military convention, the British placed their strongest unit on the right of their line. Gates, also a traditionalist, deployed his troops in similar fashion, which meant his inexperienced militia units would be on the left, facing the best of the enemy forces.

The British began their advance in the early morning hours, and Gates's artillery opened fire as they approached. British artillery responded, and as their troops were moving from columns into the line of battle, one of the Revolutionary officers reported to Gates that he could attack them before they completed their deployment. Gates gave him the order to do so, which was apparently the last command he gave at Camden. Receiving their instructions, the militia on the left of the line advanced clumsily. Many of these men had never been in battle and had little or no training with the bayonets they had been issued. Cornwallis noticed their hesitation and ordered a bayonet charge. Seeing the steady advance of the British regulars with their deadly steel implements and hearing their blood-curdling shouts, the raw troops ran for their lives. When more than 2,000 of these fleeing men came storming through the reserve units behind the main line of battle, Gates, mounted on an excellent horse and believing the cause was lost, left the field in full gallop. He maintained the frantic pace until he reached the safety of Charlotte, 60 miles away. Meanwhile, the experienced troops at the right of the Revolutionary line, though badly outnumbered, managed to push the enemy back with repeated bayonet charges. When the British dragoons finally joined the fray, the Revolutionaries gave up the fight and escaped into the woods and swamps, ending the battle. Total British casualties in killed, wounded, and missing comprised about 15 percent of the number engaged. Estimates of Revolutionary losses reach as high as

one-third of Gates's army, a devastating blow following the losses at Charleston. Gates, who claimed he went to Charlotte to rally the survivors of the battle, was exonerated for his conduct, but he never held a command again.

Further reading: Robert Leckie, *George Washington's War: The Saga of the American Revolution* (New York: HarperCollins, 1993); Henry Lumpkin, *From Savannah to Yorktown: The American Revolution in the South* (New York: University of South Carolina Press, 1981).

—Rita M. Broyles

Cameron, Alexander (1720?–1781) *British government official*

Alexander Cameron was a British Indian agent who was important as a liaison between the CHEROKEE and the British government. Cameron moved from his native Scotland to South Carolina in the 1730s. He served with the British during the FRENCH AND INDIAN WAR (1754–63), and in 1764 he was appointed commissary to the Cherokee town of Chota. He married a Cherokee woman, fathering several children and exerting a strong voice in Cherokee affairs. In early 1776 European-American settlers in Tennessee blamed him for an outbreak of FRONTIER warfare, although Cameron claimed he was attempting to mediate a peace. However, he supported the British government during the REVOLUTIONARY WAR (1775–83) and was appointed superintendent for the Southwest in August 1779. In that position he sought to ally the Cherokee, CHOCTAW, and CREEK with GREAT BRITAIN against the United States. He died in Savannah, Georgia, in December 1781.

Campbell, George W. (1769–1848) *U.S. senator, secretary of the treasury*

George W. Campbell was born in Scotland and moved to North Carolina with his family in 1772. He graduated from Princeton after only one year in 1794, studied law, and moved to Tennessee, where he quickly became one of the state's leading attorneys. In 1803 he entered the House of Representatives as a member of the DEMOCRATIC-REPUBLICAN PARTY and became an active supporter of the administration of THOMAS JEFFERSON. After three terms he declined reelection and returned to Tennessee, where he briefly served on the state supreme court. On October 8, 1811, he became a U.S. senator, filling a vacancy caused by a resignation. In the Senate he quickly became an outspoken proponent for war against GREAT BRITAIN, and during the WAR OF 1812 (1812–15) he was one of the most important supporters of the administration of JAMES MADISON.

In 1814, after failing to recruit a better-qualified candidate, Madison appointed Campbell as secretary of the treasury. As one contemporary put it, Campbell "was entirely out of place in the Treasury" and as a result he struggled as the nation stood on the brink of bankruptcy. In his final report to the Congress in September 1814, Campbell concluded that the nation faced a more than $11 million shortfall that could only be made up with more taxes and by offering even higher interest rates on treasury notes. The next month, claiming ill health, he resigned from the cabinet. He was subsequently reelected to the Senate, where he served until 1818, when he was appointed as minister to RUSSIA. After two years in St. Petersburg, Campbell returned to the United States. His only other public service was on the French claims commission in 1831. He died in Nashville on February 17, 1848.

camp followers

Civilian men and women who accompanied armies in the 18th century, camp followers provided various skills and services to the military establishment. The military and civilian components of the community that gathered around the army recognized their need for one another and that their mutual survival was vital for success. In the REVOLUTIONARY WAR (1775–83), the CONTINENTAL ARMY patterned much of its camp follower employment and organization after the long-established model of its enemy, the British. The army regulated the living and working arrangements, and under the articles governing them, camp followers could not be asked to perform military duty but were bound in every other way to maintain the peace and order of the command structure.

Although a common assumption has been that camp followers were predominantly female prostitutes, the number of such women was actually small. Female camp followers were generally family members of the officers and soldiers, who were either refugees needing the army's protection or women simply wanting to be near their loved ones and to tend to their needs. Countless wives and daughters worked as laundresses, cooks, seamstresses, and nurses during the war. However, the majority of nonmilitary personnel attached to the army were men. Many were sutlers, the name given to merchants and traders who were licensed to sell goods to the troops. A variety of employees, such as laborers, artificers, wagoners, cooks, and launderers, provided much-needed services to the army and freed soldiers from these noncombatant duties. Some of the staff members in the quartermaster and commissary departments were civilians working under contract. African-American camp followers of both sexes, slave and free, performed domestic and labor-intensive tasks.

For those with a choice to do so, motives for following the army were undoubtedly as varied as the people themselves: contracts or financial arrangements with the military, devotion to family members, the need for protection, belief in the political cause, or the hope of personal freedom. Camp followers received various forms of rationing or compensation, but most also experienced equal portions of deprivation and suffering during the war. Sutlers and contract laborers did not get rich from their bargains with the military, and they frequently lost provisions and tools. African-American slaves did not necessarily obtain freedom by their service to either the British or the Continental army. Women and children often lost their husbands and fathers in battle, and everyone was susceptible to the DISEASE AND EPIDEMICS that spread through the camps. Though camp followers provided vital services to the army establishment and thus figured largely in the success of military ventures, when peace came and the troops disbanded, the civilian support services faded into oblivion, their contribution to the war effort generally overlooked.

Further reading: Holly A. Mayer, *Belonging to the Army: Camp Followers and Community during the American Revolution* (Columbia: University of South Carolina Press, 1996).

—Rita M. Broyles

camp meetings

Toward the close of the 18th century and the beginning of the 19th century, evangelical Christians developed the camp meeting as a means of generating enthusiasm for RELIGION and gaining converts to their particular brand of Christianity. The camp meeting built upon the outdoor preaching of revivalists such as George Whitefield, which began in the 1740s, but it often lasted for days and included much more audience participation. Camp meeting organizers encouraged testimonials by individuals struck by the power of God without respect to age, gender, or even race. Participants would sometimes clap their hands, stand and shout, twist and contort their bodies in all sorts of directions, speak in tongues, and even bark like dogs. Special sections were set aside for those whose souls were ready to be transformed.

Camp meetings were controversial. In the United States, METHODISTS such as Bishop FRANCIS ASBURY believed that camp meetings were "the Battle ax and weapon of war" that would "break down walls of wickedness, part hell, superstition, false doctrines." In England camp meetings were deplored by Methodists, who saw the disorder and popular activism of camp meetings as threatening. Conservatives in the United States also decried camp meetings because of what they saw as shallow enthusiasm, the mixing of different types of people, a perceived sexual licentiousness, and "the air of a cell in Bedlam" that seemed to dominate the proceedings.

Whatever the objections, the camp meeting worked for many evangelicals and had a special appeal to the rural population of much of the United States as a way of gathering souls together by the thousands and gaining new converts to a Christianity that emphasized personal conversion and a democratic nonceremonial church that reflected the ideals of equality.

See also CANE RIDGE, KENTUCKY; DOW, LORENZO; GREAT AWAKENING, SECOND.

Further reading: Nathan O. Hatch, *The Democratization of American Christianity* (New Haven, Conn.: Yale University Press, 1989).

Canada

Sixteenth-century French explorers derived the name *Canada* from the Huron-IROQUOIS word *kanata*, meaning a village or settlement. In the 17th century the name became synonymous with New France, which eventually included not only the St. Lawrence River colony but also Acadia on the Atlantic coast. Throughout the colony's existence the FUR TRADE provided a solid economic basis. Skillful and energetic French voyageurs, or fur traders, used their good relations with the Algonquian and Huron Indians to penetrate far into the interior of the continent. Political authority resided with a royal governor who exercised military and diplomatic power, an intendant (administrative official) responsible for internal affairs, and an appointed council. This highly centralized and authoritarian colonial government, combined with a semifeudal landholding system, was partly responsible for a much slower rate of growth than that of the English colonies to the south. By the mid-18th century, New France had a population of only 70,000, compared with more than 1 million in the British colonies.

The French and their Indian allies relentlessly expanded the fur trade to the west, engaging in competition with the English and their Iroquois allies for land and strategic advantage. In 1754 fighting erupted in the Ohio River Valley, signaling the beginning of the FRENCH AND INDIAN WAR (1754–63). This North American contest was part of a series of wars and a worldwide Anglo-French conflict that had begun in 1689. After struggling in the early stages of the French and Indian War, the British conquered Canada. Under the terms of the TREATY OF PARIS (1763), FRANCE gave up its possessions east of the Mississippi to the British.

This victory relieved the British-American colonists of the constant threat of attacks by the French and their Indian allies and lessened their dependence on British troops for protection. The British gained control of the Canadian fur trade and thousands of new subjects with an alien language, culture, and RELIGION. The Quebec colony was first governed under a royal proclamation—often referred to as the PROCLAMATION OF 1763—that provided for a governor and a legislative assembly. However, being CATHOLICS, the French colonists, or habitants, were not permitted to vote or sit in the assembly. In addition to creating the colony of Quebec, the proclamation forbade the inhabitants of the 13 colonies from moving into the territory between the Appalachians and the Mississippi River. This action greatly angered the American colonists who wanted access to the western lands for land speculation and also resented British protection of NATIVE AMERICANS.

After 1763, the population of Quebec remained overwhelmingly French, attracting only a few hundred English and Scottish traders who took control of the fur trade. The British military rulers were sympathetic to the habitants; however, they failed to adequately understand the dynamics of French-Canadian society and chose to ally themselves with the French colonial elite of seigneurs (landlords) and churchmen. In 1774, at the urging of Governor GUY CARLETON, later FIRST BARON DORCHESTER, the colony was reorganized under the QUEBEC ACT. This measure allowed Catholics to hold office and provided for a governor and council, but no assembly. There were also protections for the French language, the Catholic religion, and French civil law. Despite some admirable features, the Quebec Act upset the delicate balance of colonial politics. The new regime alienated the habitants by granting new powers to the Catholic Church and the seigneurs. The residents of the other British colonies viewed the Quebec Act with undisguised hostility. The British had resurrected a much-feared enemy that British-American colonists thought had been vanquished a decade earlier.

In 1775 the SECOND CONTINENTAL CONGRESS, having failed to enlist the support of the French Canadians in their dispute with the British, decided to invade Canada. The invasion force led by RICHARD MONTGOMERY and BENEDICT ARNOLD captured MONTREAL and laid siege to Quebec. Poor training and lack of organization, combined with a harsh winter and the death of Montgomery, doomed the invasion. After the unsuccessful siege of Quebec City, the revolutionaries retreated. The failed invasion of Canada guaranteed a British presence on the continent, and Quebec became a staging ground for the British military during the REVOLUTIONARY WAR (1775–83).

At the end of the Revolutionary War, about 100,000 LOYALISTS, many having fought for the British, left the United States. Half of these exiles went to Quebec and NOVA SCOTIA. Although they were in many respects a diverse group, Loyalist refugees shared a belief that their liberties were more secure within the British Empire than in an independent United States. While the refugees were profoundly American, many coming from families that had been in the colonies for several generations, they had strong negative feelings about the new United States. The number of refugees was large in relation to the relatively small population of "old settlers," in Quebec and Nova Scotia, and they were destined to exert a powerful influence on the development of British Canada.

The Loyalist IMMIGRATION had its greatest initial impact in Nova Scotia, where 32,000 refugees, including several thousand AFRICAN AMERICANS who had fled to the British to gain freedom from SLAVERY, joined a population of New England Yankees, Acadian French (see ACADIANS), and Maliseet and Micmac Indians. A new Loyalist colony, New Brunswick, was carved out of Nova Scotia in 1784 to accommodate the expanding population.

In Quebec the problem of absorbing the Loyalists was more complicated. The initial influx of Loyalists amounted to only a few thousand, but following the war "late loyalists" swelled that number. These immigrants moved more for economic than political reasons. The British offered cheap land virtually free from taxes in an effort to lure more settlers to the region north of Lakes Ontario and Erie. British officials envisioned the "late loyalists" as supporters of the king who had somehow not been able to leave the United States at the end of the war. Many, however, were individuals of ambiguous allegiances who, much like their cousins in the United States, were eager to capitalize on whatever opportunities the FRONTIER offered. These settlers found it difficult to live under the Quebec Act. As Protestants, they objected to the influence of the Roman Catholic church. Being Anglo-Americans, many of whom were inspired by the REPUBLICANISM of the AMERICAN REVOLUTION, they expected to have the traditional "rights of Englishmen," including the right to own land and participate in representative government. The concerns of the "late loyalists" put the British in a difficult position as they could not easily renege on the concessions granted to the French by the Quebec Act. The solution was the Constitution Act (1791), which created two new colonies out of Quebec. In Lower Canada (present-day Quebec), the new act retained protections for the French language, law, and religion and added a legislative assembly. The British hoped that in such a system the French population would be gradually assimilated. Upper Canada (present-day Ontario) was given a conventional British-style colonial government that attempted as far as was practical to apply the principles of the British constitution. Similar governments developed in Nova Scotia and New Brunswick. In each case British policy was aimed at avoiding a repetition of the American Revolution.

During the FRENCH REVOLUTION (1789–99) British North America, like the United States, was at the mercy of international events beyond its control. Canada first suffered and then profited from the wartime ECONOMY. The French Revolutionary and Napoleonic Wars (1793–1815)

created tension between Canada and the United States. The ongoing rivalry in the fur trade furthered animosities. The TREATY OF PARIS (1783) and JAY'S TREATY (1794) should have effectively removed Canadian fur trappers and traders from U.S. territory. However, the Canadians continued to trade furs in the area surrounding the Great Lakes. The Canadians believed they had a right to do so since the United States had not paid reparations for LOYALIST PROPERTY CONFISCATION during the Revolutionary War. Canadians also had better relations with Native Americans based on decades of interaction and the fact that they posed less of a threat to Indians than settlers from the United States scrambling for new lands. The people of the new western states, recognizing the close connections between Indians and Canadians, blamed the Canadians for keeping the Indians stirred up and supplying them with arms. Western politicians known as WAR HAWKS believed that conquering Canada would eliminate the Indian problem and give U.S. speculators access to huge amounts of new land. In 1812 the United States declared war on GREAT BRITAIN. Canadians viewed the WAR OF 1812 (1812–15) as little more than an excuse for an invasion by aggressors from the United States.

The military conflict was inconclusive, and in the absence of a winner, both sides claimed victory. The Canadians had driven back repeated invasion attempts, and the BATTLE OF QUEENSTON HEIGHTS (October 13, 1812) became part of Canada's founding tradition. The United States was equally pleased that it had frustrated British invasion attempts, and the BATTLE OF NEW ORLEANS (January 8, 1815) provided a sense of national unity and pride. In the TREATY OF GHENT (1814), both sides agreed to return to prewar conditions. The treaty did not settle any outstanding boundary issues, but it set up a dialogue to clarify the Canada-U.S. border that would continue until the 1840s.

After 1814, relations between Great Britain, its North American colonies, and the United States remained strained for a time. However, starting in the 1820s, improving economic and political cooperation marked the beginnings of a strong and stable Anglo-American relationship.

See also QUEBEC, BATTLE OF; QUEBEC, FIRST BATTLE OF; QUEBEC, SECOND BATTLE OF.

Further reading: W. J. Eccles, *France in America* (New York: Harper & Row, 1972); Desmond Morton, *A Short History of Canada* (Toronto: McClelland & Stewart, 1995); Francis Parkman, *France and England in North America,* 9 vols. (Boston: Little, Brown, 1865–92): Alan Taylor, *The Divided Ground: Indians, Settlers, and the Northern Borderland of the American Revolution* (New York: Knopf, 2006).

—Robert Lively

Cane Ridge, Kentucky

In August 1801, between 10,000 and 20,000 people attended a CAMP MEETING revival at Cane Ridge, Kentucky. Historians have often cited the Cane Ridge camp meeting as the beginning of the SECOND GREAT AWAKENING, but the gathering at Cane Ridge reflected more an extreme statement of an ongoing trend than the beginning of a new movement. There had been other camp meetings with thousands of participants before Cane Ridge, and similar gatherings would continue for decades. However, Cane Ridge was an important event that was ecumenical in nature, with ministers from several denominations preaching to the assembled masses. As with other camp meetings, conservatives complained about the emotional outbursts that sounded more like pandemonium than a religious service. Evangelicals—PRESBYTERIANS, METHODISTS, BAPTISTS, and more—saw the hand of God in the shouts and contortions of the masses and bragged that 3,000 individuals opened their hearts to Christ that August in Cane Ridge. As one young convert explained: "Some of the people were singing, others praying, some crying for mercy in the most piteous accents, while others were shouting most vociferously." But this chaos was successful since the convert saw in one instance "at least five hundred swept down in a moment, as if a battery of a thousand guns had been opened upon them, and then immediately followed shrieks and shouts that rent the very heavens."

Further reading: Stephen Aron, *How the West Was Lost: The Transformation of Kentucky from Daniel Boone to Henry Clay* (Baltimore: Johns Hopkins University Press, 1996).

Canning, George (1770–1827) *British government official*

Although born into a prominent Irish family, because his father was disinherited and his mother came from an undistinguished family, George Canning started life in straitened circumstances. Despite these dubious beginnings, when Canning was eight years old, his extended family intervened in his upbringing—by then his father was dead and his mother had become an actress—and saw to it that he was educated at Eton and Oxford, where he excelled. Trained as a lawyer, Canning abandoned his early reformist principles and befriended William Pitt, the Younger. Pitt secured Canning a seat in the House of Commons and a job as an undersecretary of FOREIGN AFFAIRS in 1796. He left that position in 1799 and held a variety of government offices thereafter. He also married Joan Scott, a woman with her own fortune, in 1800.

Canning served as foreign secretary from 1807 to 1809, a crucial period in GREAT BRITAIN's war against FRANCE and for its relations with the United States. He countered NAPOLEON BONAPARTE's Continental System with ORDERS IN COUNCIL, which made neutral TRADE almost impossible to sustain. He did little to settle the *CHESAPEAKE-LEOPARD* AFFAIR and believed that the "wisest, safest, and most manful policy" in response to the EMBARGO OF 1807 was to do "absolutely nothing." When Canning sent David Erskine to be minister to the United States, he issued instructions that limited Erskine's ability to negotiate a settlement. After Erskine came to a provisional accord with the United States in the ERSKINE AGREEMENT, Canning repudiated the negotiations and recalled the minister from WASHINGTON, D.C. These actions reflected Canning's sense that Great Britain had to act from a position of strength in its death struggle with Napoleonic France. He was also responsible for having the British navy bombard Copenhagen and destroying the Danish fleet.

Canning was forced from the foreign secretary's office by the internal politics of the Tory Party. He did not hold any major offices thereafter until 1814. He became foreign secretary again from 1822 to 1827 and briefly served as prime minister before he died on August 8, 1827.

Further reading: Peter Dixon, *George Canning: Politician and Statesman* (New York: Mason/Charter, 1976).

Cannon, James (1740–1782) *radical writer*

One of the leading radicals in the AMERICAN REVOLUTION in Pennsylvania, James Cannon was born in Edinburgh, Scotland. He was educated at both the University of Edinburgh and the College of Philadelphia (later the University of Pennsylvania) and graduated from the latter institution in 1767. In 1773 Cannon became a professor of mathematics at the College of Philadelphia. In the upheaval in Pennsylvania that accompanied the Revolution, he became a spokesmen for the more democratic faction, participating in meetings and opposing conservatives. Perhaps the second most important radical writer in Pennsylvania behind THOMAS PAINE, Cannon wrote the influential "Cassandra" letters advocating independence. In these essays he proclaimed that GREAT BRITAIN could not come up with "*any plan* of *constitutional dependence* which will not leave the future enjoyment of our liberties to *hope, hazard,* and *uncertainty.*" As a member of the state constitutional convention in 1776, Cannon quickly emerged as one of the primary authors of Pennsylvania's democratic state constitution. He was secretary to the extremist Committee of Privates in Philadelphia; sat on the Pennsylvania council of safety from July 14, 1776, to December 4, 1777; and became a justice of the peace. He died in Philadelphia on January 28, 1782.

capitalism

The development of capitalism in North America had a profound and dialectical relationship with the AMERICAN REVOLUTION. It was profound because without the trumpeting of equality that became the hallmark of the American Revolution, it would have been more difficult for a market ECONOMY—an essential characteristic of capitalism—to emerge in the United States. It was dialectical because the colonial American behavior that can be labeled as *capitalistic* helped to trigger the American Revolution, and in turn, the American Revolution created a political and social structure that accelerated the further development of capitalism.

There are many definitions of *capitalism*. For the purpose of understanding its relationship to the American Revolution, capitalism is defined here as an economic system where prices and wages are ordinarily set by the impersonal mechanisms of the market rather than personal or community-oriented concerns. Crucial to an understanding of capitalism is a particular mindset that is focused on profit and where the end goal becomes the accumulation of more capital. Capitalists place a premium on investment for profit and emphasize those values that came to be identified with the 19th-century middle class: hard work, personal discipline, and delayed gratification.

Throughout the colonial period there were some individuals who behaved in a capitalist manner. However, the vast majority of the population lived on farms and remained wedded to a precapitalist order where the goal was economic competence—that is, a farmer and his wife sought to earn enough to sustain a family and pass on a small legacy to their children. These families lived in a world with a limited cash economy, where most economic interactions were based on personal face-to-face relationships and where communal needs predominated over larger impersonal market forces. By the mid-18th century, though, more and more colonial Americans were being driven by profit and beginning to engage in TRADE and so they sought to sell their produce to the highest bidder. These practices sometimes violated community sensibilities and made many colonial Americans fear that their society was becoming corrupt, with men seeking their own benefit rather than guarding the public good. The American Revolution, and the REPUBLICANISM that accompanied it, became a way for these individuals to reassert more traditional values and reject the commercialism and capitalism that seemed to be sweeping their society.

Rather than halting or even reversing these economic changes, however, the Revolution accelerated the development of capitalism. Although the REVOLUTIONARY WAR (1775–83) created havoc as armies and MILITIA destroyed farms and seized goods, most of the time farmers could make MONEY by selling to the military—the British and the French paid in specie, which was preferable to the CONTINENTAL ARMY's script. Merchants, ARTISANS, and others could also profit by selling supplies and making goods. In other words, although some people lost property as a result of the war, others gained property, and the drive for profit that had bothered many during the 1750s and 1760s became even more widespread in the 1770s and 1780s. This shift did not go uncontested. Members of the SECOND CONTINENTAL CONGRESS debated the propriety of individuals seeking profit while serving the Revolution, and many common people clamored for PRICE CONTROLS to combat the skyrocketing cost of food.

Accelerating these changes was the rise of the ideal of equality that accompanied the Revolution. For many people in the United States in the 1780s, 1790s, and early 1800s, *equality* meant that each person should have the same access to the marketplace and a maximum profit from their investment in goods and services. For these individuals, privilege of place no longer mattered. It became possible for a wheelwright and shopkeeper like WILLIAM COOPER to take advantage of land previously owned by LOYALISTS and turn it into a huge profit as he sold plots to aspiring farmers around Lake Otsego in New York State. In the scrambling postwar economy, fortunes were won and lost with amazing fluidity. This was a mobile population that turned its back on distinctions. As one correspondent wrote to JAMES MADISON from Kentucky, the new settlers in the region made "a very different mass from one which is composed of men born and raised on the same spot. . . . They see none about them to whom or to whose families they have been accustomed to think themselves inferior" and because they were "ambitious themselves . . . they suppose all others to be equally so, and that all have self interest in view more than the public good." Even in long-settled regions, there was a change as new people moved in and old inhabitants moved out. With some exaggeration—but with more than a germ of truth—WASHINGTON IRVING depicted this transformation in the Hudson River hamlet inhabited by Rip Van Winkle. Irving described the fictional village before the Revolution as being marked by an "accustomed phlegm and drowsy tranquility," whereas after the war the town had "a busy, bustling, disputatious tone about it."

Thus, the most important change that marked the rise of capitalism in the period after the Revolutionary War was a mindset—a way of thinking that encouraged the pursuit of profit and personal gain. As one tradesman explained to his brother in a purposeful slip of the pen, he was seeking "to obtain consequence," not just "competence." That shift from competence to consequence could best be obtained by embracing the new middle-class values of hard work, personal discipline, and delayed gratification.

It took more than the rise of equality to lead to the growth of capitalism in the early republic. The new United States also provided a set of conditions that encouraged capital investment. Besides the creation of a stable national government, which provided an environment suitable for long-term investment, several other key developments accelerated capitalist enterprise. These included a flexible currency, banking, CORPORATIONS, transportation systems, industrial development, and CONSUMERISM.

During the Revolutionary War, both the Second Continental Congress and the state governments used fiat currency—money printed by the government that could be used for taxes—as a means of paying for the conflict. Unfortunately, these currencies were highly inflationary and did not provide a stable means of exchange. After the war had ended, several states continued with their own currencies, with mixed success. Under the U.S. CONSTITUTION the states were prohibited from coining money, and the states' money supply was gradually retired during the 1790s. In its place there emerged a new, more stable, yet flexible, currency. This money supply was essential to the growth of a capitalist economy because it provided an impersonal medium of exchange necessary for market transactions. Although the federal government began minting some specie coins during the 1790s, this form of government-produced money was not that central to the money supply during the early republic. However, the national government's financial plan under ALEXANDER HAMILTON created a capital market for government bonds that underwrote much of the period's expansive capital supply.

Central to this development was the emergence of BANKS. Preeminent in this form of capital formation was the BANK OF THE UNITED STATES (BUS), chartered by the federal government in 1791. The BUS brought in investment, largely in the form of government securities originally issued during the Revolutionary War, and issued bank notes; by 1800 the BUS had more than $5 million in notes in circulation. Equally important in terms of capitalist development, the BUS exerted a stabilizing influence over the many state banks that were chartered during this period. Only a few of these institutions had appeared before the BUS, but by 1811 there were 117 banks with capitalization of over $66 million. Each of these banks printed notes that were used as money and provided a medium of exchange. Other financial institutions, such as INSURANCE companies, also printed notes. All told, the result was a tremendous expansion of capital that could be invested and used as a medium of exchange to facilitate economic growth and the development of capitalism.

Most of the banks used acts of incorporation issued by states—or, in the case of the BUS, issued by the federal government—as the basis of their organization. Neither the bank nor the corporation was a new institution. However, both became democratized in the United States and thus emerged as egalitarian tools for investment. Corporations had traditionally been special rights and privileges granted to groups of individuals to pursue some government-sanctioned activity for the public good. After the Revolutionary War, more and more individuals sought this privilege, and it became increasingly difficult to limit incorporation to only a few people in society. For example, if the merchants controlled the Bank of New York and thereby had access to borrowing cash, then the mechanics (ARTISANS) wanted their own bank to provide cash for their investments. Corporations soon became financial vehicles with a legal identity to pool resources for any group of investors, whether they wanted to establish a bank or an insurance company or to engage in another type of enterprise.

Transportation facilities became an important form of economic activity funded through corporations. Although the federal government underwrote the building of postal and military roads, many other roads needed private investment. During the late 18th and the beginning of the 19th century, corporations funded thousands of miles of private turnpikes and began building canals. This transportation revolution would continue after 1815 with a canal boom in the 1820s and 1830s and a railroad boom in the 1840s and 1850s. Such an increasingly integrated transportation system allowed producers to send goods cheaply to distant markets and brought more and more farmers, artisans, and others into a capitalist economic system.

The INDUSTRIAL REVOLUTION—which was just beginning in the period—was encouraged by the developing transportation system, and some industries moved into factories before 1815. But industrialization also included increased levels of work done by women and families in the home, changing the nature of artisanal production. Taken together, these three systems of production led to a growth in manufacturing. By 1815 the United States was producing $200 million worth of manufactured goods.

Someone had to buy these goods, and an important component of the rise of capitalism was also the rise in consumerism. This development did not simply mean that individuals would have the ability to buy items more cheaply; it also meant there was an increased demand for consumer goods that could be mass-produced and delivered to the market. Thus, inexpensive textiles allowed an individual to purchase a bolt of cloth—or a finished set of CLOTHING—for less money than it would take to produce the item at home. The price differential represented a significant saving, but not all of that saving would be retained since the individual might then decide to purchase two pieces of clothing instead of one. This demand, in turn, led to an increase in production, which would drive down the price further and might convince an individual to purchase three pieces of clothing, or the savings on the one purchase could be used for another item—perhaps one that was previously considered totally superfluous. Consumerism thus encouraged the manufacturer's production, but it also created an incentive for consumer production since the consumer might seek out new ways of earning cash to enter the capitalist marketplace more frequently. In short, consumerism fed into a capitalist system and furthered economic development.

By 1815 the new capitalist system was not fully in place, but the basic outlines of an economic system based on the investment of capital had been created.

Further reading: Paul A. Gilje, *The Making of the American Republic, 1763–1815* (Upper Saddle River, N.J.: Prentice Hall, 2005); James A. Henretta, *The Origins of American Capitalism: Collected Essays* (Boston: Northeastern University Press, 1991); Allan Kulikoff, *The Agrarian Origins of American Capitalism* (Charlottesville: University of Press of Virginia, 1992).

Carey, Mathew (1760–1839) *publisher*

Mathew Carey became one of Philadelphia's leading publishers in the 1790s and was a noted proponent of protective TARIFFS in the early 19th century. Born and raised in Dublin, Ireland, Carey did not receive much schooling as a child, even though his parents were relatively well-off. However, he read extensively, and as a child he decided to become a printer and bookseller. His father disapproved of this choice of a profession, but Carey persisted and apprenticed as a printer. A Roman Catholic, he became interested in defending his RELIGION in Ireland, and he published an anonymous pamphlet on the issue in 1779. When a reward was offered for the author's identity—the pamphlet was condemned in Parliament—Carey's family sent him to Paris. There he met the MARQUIS DE LAFAYETTE and BENJAMIN FRANKLIN and even worked in a printing office set up by Franklin.

After a year in exile, Carey returned to Ireland. He worked for others in a newspaper office until 1783, when his father underwrote the publication of his own newspaper, the *Volunteer's Journal.* This paper trumpeted the cause of Irish NATIONALISM and created a great stir. After some articles led to a demonstration, in which the young Carey took an active part, the British arrested him. When he was released after a short period, and when further legal action loomed, he headed for North America. Disguised as a woman, he departed GREAT BRITAIN on September 7, 1784.

When he arrived in Philadelphia, Carey did not have much money; however, he quickly obtained the patronage of Lafayette. In January 1785 he was able to begin printing another newspaper, the *Pennsylvania Herald.* Newspa-

pers in this era generally were strongly political, and Carey quickly aligned himself with those who wanted a weaker central government. He also published the debates in the Pennsylvania state assembly, a new practice. In October 1786 he abandoned the newspaper business and began publishing the *Columbian Magazine.* He left this project to begin the *American Magazine* in 1787, and during the 1790s his printing business grew. He also authored an important book that described the conditions of the YELLOW FEVER epidemic of 1793 and played a vital role in dealing with the health crisis created by that epidemic.

An avid member of the DEMOCRATIC-REPUBLICAN PARTY (Jeffersonians), Carey became embroiled in several political controversies, most notably with the FEDERALIST PARTY spokesman WILLIAM COBBETT. During the 1790s he did business worth over $300,000 and kept as many as 150 men working in his printing shop. He may have begun his career as an ARTISAN, but by 1800 he had evolved into an entrepreneur specializing in the publishing and marketing of books. In 1802 he was elected a director of the Bank of Pennsylvania, and in 1810 he was one of the few Democratic-Republicans to advocate rechartering the BANK OF THE UNITED STATES.

After the WAR OF 1812 (1812–15), Carey became a noted spokesmen for protective tariffs to encourage the development of manufacturing. Throughout his career he retained an interest in the Irish cause, forming a Hibernian Society in the 1790s and defending Irish Catholics in print. He died in Philadelphia on September 16, 1839.

See also JOURNALISM; MAGAZINES.

Further reading: Earl L. Bradsher, *Mathew Carey, Editor, Author, and Publisher: A Study in American Literary Development* (New York: AMS Press, 1966); Rosalind Remer, *Printers and Men of Capital: Philadelphia Book Publishers in the Early Republic* (Philadelphia: University of Pennsylvania Press, 1996).

Carleton, Guy   See DORCHESTER, GUY CARLETON, FIRST BARON.

Carlisle, Abraham   See TREASON TRIAL OF ABRAHAM CARLISLE AND JOHN ROBERTS.

Carlisle Commission

After the surrender of General JOHN BURGOYNE at SARATOGA (October 17, 1777), the British government feared an expanded war that would include FRANCE and SPAIN. In early 1778, despite the initial opposition of King GEORGE III, LORD NORTH's ministry put together a peace commission under Frederick Howard, fifth earl of Carlisle, and empowered it to promise a repeal of all parliamentary legislation that had triggered the imperial crisis and place relations between the rebellious North American colonies and GREAT BRITAIN on a pre-1763 basis. This offer was too little too late.

In addition to Carlisle, the commission included William Eden, first baron Auckland, and George Johnstone, a British navy officer who was also a member of Parliament. All three men were sympathetic to the Revolutionaries and left Britain on April 16, 1778. By the time they reached Philadelphia on June 6, however, their mission had become hopeless: Nothing but full independence would placate the Revolutionaries, who had signed a formal alliance with France. Moreover, with the British army about to evacuate Philadelphia and French assistance on its way, many Revolutionaries believed that they were on the cusp of winning the war. Soon after Carlisle arrived, the SECOND CONTINENTAL CONGRESS informed him that the only points it would negotiate were British withdrawal and recognition of independence. When Johnstone's foolish effort to bribe ROBERT MORRIS, JOSEPH REED, and Francis Dana became public in August, Congress ordered that all further communication with the commission was at an end. Johnstone resigned from the commission and headed for England. Carlisle and Eden stayed in New York through the fall, trying to appeal to the public and hoping for some movement on the part of the Revolutionaries. In the end, there was little for the commission to do, and on November 27, 1778, Carlisle and Eden left for Britain empty-handed.

Carroll, Charles (1723–1783) *businessman, lawyer, Maryland politician*

Known as Charles Carroll the Barrister to distinguish him from the other members of his Catholic family with the same name, Charles Carroll was a leading planter, lawyer, iron manufacturer, and businessman in Maryland. One of the richest men in the colony and owner of the estate named Mount Clare, which today is a museum just north of Baltimore, Carroll was active in colonial politics, sitting in the assembly from 1756 to 1761 and maintaining cordial relations with all of the leading men in the colony thereafter. He served in the Maryland convention in 1774 that became the colony's ad hoc government in Maryland; was a member of the state's council of safety in 1775 and 1776; and probably authored the state's declaration of independence issued on July 3, 1776. Nonetheless, Carroll was a moderate Revolutionary. He participated in writing Maryland's conservative state constitution, which retained a powerful senate that was relatively immune from the influence of the electorate. He sat in that senate from 1777

to his death. He was also a delegate to the SECOND CONTINENTAL CONGRESS in 1776–77. He died on March 23, 1783, at Mount Clare.

Carroll, Daniel (1730–1796) *businessman, Maryland politician*

Daniel Carroll belonged to the famous Catholic Carroll family in Maryland; he was a cousin of CHARLES CARROLL OF CARROLLTON and the older brother of JOHN CARROLL, who became the first Catholic bishop in the United States. Educated in St. Omer's College in French Flanders, Daniel Carroll became a successful planter and merchant, and at his death he owned almost 8,000 acres in Maryland and 32 slaves. As a Catholic he was disenfranchised until the AMERICAN REVOLUTION. Under the Maryland constitution of 1776, he was selected as a member of the state's executive council in 1777, and in 1781 he became a state senator. Also in 1781 he was chosen as a delegate to the SECOND CONTINENTAL CONGRESS, where, as a part of the Maryland delegation, he refused to sign the ARTICLES OF CONFEDERATION until the larger states agreed to cede most of their claims to western lands to the national government. During the 1780s he speculated in confiscated Loyalist land and invested in a canal on the Potomac River. An advocate of a stronger central government, he attended the 1787 CONSTITUTIONAL CONVENTION in Philadelphia and worked for the ratification of the U.S. CONSTITUTION in Maryland. He was elected to Congress in 1789 and took an active role in the passage of the BILL OF RIGHTS, especially concerning the First Amendment's separation of church and state. Despite, or perhaps because of, his personal interests, President GEORGE WASHINGTON appointed Carroll to the commission planning the national capital on the Potomac River. He died on July 15, 1796.

Carroll, John (1735–1815) *first Catholic bishop in the United States*

A member of the prominent Carroll family in Maryland, John Carroll became the most important Catholic in the United States during his lifetime. He was educated at St. Omer's College in French Flanders, but rather than becoming a planter-businessman like his brother DANIEL CARROLL or cousins CHARLES CARROLL OF CARROLLTON and CHARLES CARROLL the Barrister, John Carroll became a Jesuit priest in 1769. He remained a priest after the papal dissolution of the Jesuit order in 1773 and returned to Maryland in 1774.

Like most of his family, Carroll supported the RESISTANCE MOVEMENT against GREAT BRITAIN and even joined a delegation to CANADA in 1776 to try to convince the French-speaking inhabitants to join the Revolutionary cause. This effort was largely unsuccessful, especially in the face of the failure of the Revolutionary invasion of Canada that same year. Later Carroll became an outspoken defender of the rights of CATHOLICS in the new nation. In 1789 he authored an essay in which he proclaimed that Catholics supported, along with other citizens, a government "from whose influence America anticipates all the blessings of justice, peace, plenty, good order and civil and religious liberty."

In 1789 Carroll became the first Catholic bishop in the United States. Over the next 25 years he oversaw a dramatic expansion of Catholicism in the United States despite Protestant prejudice. He also helped to establish three colleges, including the institution that became Georgetown University. He died in Baltimore on December 3, 1815.

See also CATHOLICS; RELIGIOUS LIBERTY.

Further reading: Annabelle M. Melville, *John Carroll of Baltimore: Founder of the American Catholic Hierarchy* (New York: Charles Scribner's Sons, 1956).

Carroll of Carrollton, Charles (1737–1832)
businessman, Revolutionary leader, U.S. senator
A member of a leading Catholic family in Maryland, Charles Carroll of Carrollton—he added "of Carrollton" to distinguish himself from his father, Charles Carroll of Annapolis, and other relatives with the same name— became an important Revolutionary leader and signed the DECLARATION OF INDEPENDENCE. After leaving home at age 10, like many affluent Maryland CATHOLICS, Carroll was educated at St. Omer's College in French Flanders. He remained abroad until February 1765 after further EDUCATION in Paris and London.

As a Catholic, Carroll was debarred from voting and holding civil office in colonial Maryland despite his wealth. However, he entered local politics in 1773 when he wrote the "First Citizen" essays in opposition to the effort by DANIEL DULANY to increase fees charged by public officials. Carroll joined with other Maryland politicians to organize a "popular party," which swept the colonial elections in 1773. Opposition to imperial regulation in 1774 offered Carroll an opportunity to get more directly involved in politics when he became a member of Maryland's second provincial convention, and he was an early advocate of independence. In March 1776 the SECOND CONTINENTAL CONGRESS sent Carroll—along with his cousin JOHN CARROLL and BENJAMIN FRANKLIN—to CANADA to stir up support for the Revolutionary cause. Although this effort was not successful, after Carroll's return he was chosen as a delegate to the Second Continental Congress, where he and others signed the Declaration of Independence on August 2.

Carroll may have supported independence, but he was no democrat. In Maryland he helped to write the conservative state constitution that would guarantee his class continued political dominance. Once the new government was in place, however, he sought to make it popular by shifting the tax burden from a poll tax to a tax on land and slaves. He also supported a law that allowed paper currency to be used to pay prewar debts. These positions antagonized his father, but Carroll believed that it was better to steer with the popular current than against it if one hoped to guide the ship of state. He remained active in politics until 1800, serving in the Second Continental Congress in 1776 and in 1777–78. He also became a Maryland state senator and sat in the U.S. Senate from 1789 to 1792. He declined attending the CONSTITUTIONAL CONVENTION but supported the U.S. CONSTITUTION as the best way to restrain the "excesses of an uncontrolled Democracy." During the 1790s he sided with the FEDERALIST PARTY, and he opposed the election of THOMAS JEFFERSON as president in 1800.

Carroll was also a successful planter and businessman. Not only did he own more than 300 slaves and tens of thousands of acres in Maryland, Pennsylvania, and New York, he also had interests in IRON MANUFACTURING, BANKS, foreign stocks, turnpikes, and canals. Toward the end of his life he even invested in railroads. Carroll was the last of the signers of the Declaration of Independence to die, and at his death on November 14, 1832, he was worth an estimated $1.5 million.

Further reading: Thomas O'Brien Hanley, *Charles Carroll of Carrollton: The Making of a Revolutionary* (Washington, D.C.: Catholic University of America Press, 1970); Thomas O'Brien Hanley, *Revolutionary Statesman: Charles Carroll and the War* (Chicago: Loyola University Press, 1983).

Carter, Landon (1710–1778) *Virginia planter, politician, diarist*
Born into one of the leading families of Virginia, Landon Carter was a successful planter and member of the ruling elite. Carter both inherited and married into wealth; three marriages provided him with massive dowries and seven children who lived to adulthood. He served in several county offices, including as a local justice of the peace and on the parish vestry. He was elected to the House of Burgesses from 1752 to 1768; he failed to be reelected in 1768 because, as he put it, he did not "familiarize" himself "among the People." While in the House of Burgesses he was a leader in defending that body in the PARSON'S CAUSE. He also was in the forefront of the opposition to the STAMP ACT (1765) and other imperial measures. A

prolific author, he wrote at least four major pamphlets and 50 newspaper essays on a variety of political issues. He was also interested in SCIENCE and was elected to the AMERICAN PHILOSOPHICAL SOCIETY in 1769.

Carter's greatest legacy is a massive diary in which he reflected on his own life and anxieties and offered a wonderful insight into the inner world of the Virginia gentry. In the diary, Carter appears as a man of the ENLIGHTENMENT and reveals how he sought distinction through public service and the pursuit of knowledge. He also believed in the need for constitutional government. His opposition to British imperial policies came from his belief that GREAT BRITAIN had violated the British constitution by taxing the colonists without their consent. Diary entries in the years leading up to the DECLARATION OF INDEPENDENCE (1776) reflected his concerns with rebellion both at home—several of his slaves ran away as a result of the proclamation of Governor Dunmore (see DUNMORE, JOHN MURRAY, FOURTH EARL OF) and within the nation. However, although Carter hesitated to take the leap toward independence, he reconciled himself to this action before he died on December 22, 1778. At his death he owned more than 50,000 acres and probably as many as 500 slaves.

Further reading: Jack P. Greene, *Landon Carter: An Inquiry into the Personal Values and Social Imperatives of the Eighteenth-Century Gentry* (Charlottesville: University Press of Virginia, 1965); Rhys Isaac, *Landon Carter's Uneasy Kingdom: Revolution and Rebellion on a Virginia Plantation* (New York: Oxford University Press, 2004).

Carter, Robert, III (1728–1804) *Virginia planter, politician*

The grandson of Virginia governor Robert "King" Carter and nephew of LANDON CARTER, Robert Carter III was born into one of the most powerful and wealthy families in the colony. In his early 20s, he went to London to study law, although he never attended classes at Inner Temple or stood for the bar exam. He returned to Virginia, where he entered politics, losing consecutive elections for a seat in the House of Burgesses. Faced with this humiliation, Carter moved to Maryland. In Baltimore, he married Frances Tasker, daughter of one of the most prominent families in the colony. In 1758 he returned to political life in Virginia, taking a seat on the governor's council. When the REVOLUTIONARY WAR (1775–83) broke out, he was a reluctant WHIG. Although he did not care for Virginia's royal governor, Lord Dunmore (see DUNMORE, JOHN MURRAY, FOURTH EARL OF) he disliked the uproar that accompanied the rebellion.

Carter's spiritual life set him at odds with the Virginia elite, who were mostly ANGLICANS or deists. He had great sympathy for dissenting sects such as the METHODISTS, BAPTISTS, and PRESBYTERIANS. In 1778 he became a Baptist and lent his considerable resources to furthering evangelicals in Virginia. However, by the 1790s he had become disillusioned with the denomination's increasingly conservative stance on SLAVERY. Always something of a mystic, Carter embraced the Swedenborgian faith after he left the Baptists. His most notable action, however, was the emancipation of his more than 450 slaves in the 1790s. In 1791, inspired by the evangelical idea that all men stood equally before God, and fired by the democratic ideals of the FRENCH REVOLUTION (1789–99), he drew up his "Deed of Gift," a document that called for the gradual emancipation of his slaves. The process began in 1792 and was finished by 1797. Increasingly ostracized by the Virginia gentry for his radical views, Carter moved back to Maryland where he lived until his death on March 10, 1804.

See also ABOLITION.

Further reading: Andrew Levy, *The First Emancipator: The Forgotten Story of Robert Carter, the Founding Father Who Freed His Slaves* (New York: Random House, 2005); Louis Morton, *Robert Carter of Nomini Hall: A Virginia Tobacco Planter of the Eighteenth Century* (Charlottesville: University Press of Virginia, 1945).

—David C. Beyreis

Cass, Lewis (1782–1866) *governor of Michigan Territory, secretary of war, U.S. senator*

Born and raised in New Hampshire, Lewis Cass moved to Ohio around 1800 and became a lawyer. Because he was an ardent supporter of the DEMOCRATIC-REPUBLICAN PARTY, President THOMAS JEFFERSON appointed him a federal marshal in 1806. A colonel in command of an Ohio regiment during the opening phases of the WAR OF 1812 (1812–15), Cass participated in several battles in the Great Lakes region before being appointed governor of Michigan Territory in 1813—a crucial position during the war since the territory stood on the front lines and contained large numbers of hostile or potentially hostile NATIVE AMERICANS. Cass excelled in this delicate position, defusing potential conflicts with Indians, gaining land cessions, and remaining governor until 1831, when President ANDREW JACKSON appointed him secretary of war. Cass subsequently also served as ambassador to FRANCE and was later elected to the U.S. Senate as a conservative member of the Democratic Party. He was the Democratic nominee for president in 1844 and served as President James Buchanan's secretary of state, resigning on the eve of the Civil War because he was a strong nationalist and opposed Buchanan's conciliatory approach to the South. He died on June 17, 1866.

Castlereagh, Robert Stewart, second viscount (Lord Castlereagh) (1769–1822)

Robert Stewart, second viscount Castlereagh—generally known as Lord Castlereagh—was born into a leading Irish noble family and rose to prominence in the 1790s in both Irish and English political circles by allying himself to William Pitt the Younger (son of WILLIAM PITT the Elder) and the Tory Party. Castlereagh supported the Irish union with GREAT BRITAIN in 1800. During the first decade of the 19th century, he continued to play an important role in parliamentary politics whether his party was in or out of power. He became secretary of war in 1807 and was appointed to direct the British foreign office on February 28, 1812.

Although in both the war department and the foreign office Castlereagh's main preoccupation was with the war in FRANCE, he also exerted a great deal of influence on relations with the United States. Because the EMBARGO OF 1807 removed the United States as a competitor in TRADE and stopped supplies flowing to France, Castlereagh declared that "I look upon the embargo as operating at present more forcibly in our favor than any measure of hostility we could call forth were war actually declared." However, by 1812, as the crisis that led to the WAR OF 1812 (1812–15) accelerated, he shifted his position and admitted that U.S. trade restrictions had hurt British manufacturers. On June 16, 1812, Castlereagh announced that the ORDERS IN COUNCIL would be lifted in a vain and belated effort to avoid war. However, at the same time he refused to consider changing British policy concerning IMPRESSMENT. When the British government declined Czar ALEXANDER I's offer of Russian mediation to end the war with the United States, Castlereagh's proposal to open direct peace negotiations in November 1813 led to the TREATY OF GHENT (1814). He remained in office and led the Tory Party in Parliament after the end of the Napoleonic Wars, but the turbulent nature of British politics took its toll on him, and he committed suicide on August 22, 1822.

Further reading: C. J. Bartlett, *Castlereagh* (New York Scribner, 1966).

Catawba

The Catawba were a Native American tribe comprising an amalgamation of many Carolina and Piedmont indigenous peoples displaced or decimated by European contact. They were also one of the few native groups to support the AMERICAN REVOLUTION. By the mid-18th century the Catawba realized that violent resistance to the British-American colonists was futile. During the FRENCH AND INDIAN WAR (1754–83), the tribe joined the British against the French, and they fought with the colonists against the

CHEROKEE when the CHEROKEE WAR (1759–1761) broke out. Their contribution to the war effort was so important that at the end of the French and Indian War, the colonial government of South Carolina granted them a reservation, a part of which they leased out to European Americans.

By the time of the REVOLUTIONARY WAR (1775–83), Catawba numbers had fallen so low that only a handful of warriors could be mustered in support of the Revolutionary cause. Even so, the tribe provided crucial assistance. On June 28, 1776, they took part in the defense of Charleston, South Carolina, at the Battle of Sullivan's Island. Thereafter, they served as scouts for Colonel Andrew Williamson and General Griffith Rutherford. Perhaps their most important contribution, however, was their service as scouts under General NATHANAEL GREENE during the campaign of 1781 and at the BATTLE OF GUILFORD COURTHOUSE (March 15, 1781). After the war, the Catawba continued to maintain peaceful relations with their European-American neighbors and clung to their native culture as they became surrounded by non-native people.

See also NATIVE AMERICANS.

Further reading: Douglas Summers Brown, *The Catawba Indians, the People of the River* (Columbia: University of South Carolina Press, 1966); James H. Merrell, *The Indians' New World: The Catawbas and Their Neighbors from European Contact through the Era of Removal* (Chapel Hill: University of North Carolina Press, 1989).

—Michele M. Stephens

Catholics

Before the REVOLUTIONARY WAR (1775–83) the British colonies in North America were overwhelmingly Protestant. In 1780 there were only 56 Catholic churches in the United States—mostly in Maryland and Pennsylvania—compared to nearly 2,900 congregations representing various Protestant denominations. Prior to the war, many colonial Americans—steeped in British political and religious tradition—associated Catholicism with the tyranny, oppression, corruption, and savagery they ascribed to their French and Native American enemies. Anti-Catholic feeling was especially strong in Congregationalist-dominated New England, where the pope was ritually burned each year on November 5 (POPE DAY). During the RESISTANCE MOVEMENT, many colonial Americans, especially in New England, came to believe that GEORGE III and his ministers were engaged in a new "popish plot" to subvert their liberties. Some WHIGS claimed that a campaign to establish an Anglican bishopric in the colonies, combined with the QUEBEC ACT (1774), was evidence that the Crown was giving precedence to Catholics at the same time that it was curtailing the rights of Protestants. In consequence, there was an upsurge in anti-Catholic feeling in British America on the eve of independence. Anti-Catholicism, while not a major cause of the AMERICAN REVOLUTION, contributed to the worsening relationship between the Crown and its colonies.

The War of Independence undermined this anti-Catholicism. North American Catholics supported the rebels in proportions comparable to their Protestant neighbors. Perhaps the most famous Catholic among the Revolutionaries was CHARLES CARROLL OF CARROLLTON, Maryland. Hailing from one of the wealthiest families in North America, Carroll was a fervent supporter of the Revolution and served in a variety of positions at the state and local level during and after the war. Carroll was the only Catholic to sign the DECLARATION OF INDEPENDENCE. After the war his cousin, JOHN CARROLL, became the first Catholic bishop in the United States.

Of greater importance than the contributions of the small number of American Catholics like the Carrolls were those of the French. In 1778 the new United States found itself allied with the traditional Anglo-American Catholic enemy—FRANCE. The FRENCH ALLIANCE undermined old assumptions and undercut the colonial anti-Catholic tradition.

The recognition that Catholics contributed materially to independence, combined with the libertarian ideology of the Revolution, resulted in greater RELIGIOUS LIBERTY for Catholics. In their constitutions many of the states repealed or weakened the legal restrictions previously placed on Catholics. Even Massachusetts, where anti-Catholicism was strongest before independence, guaranteed religious and political freedom to Catholics under its 1780 constitution. With the adoption of the BILL OF RIGHTS in 1791, freedom of religion was guaranteed at the national level.

During the early republic, tens of thousands of Catholics immigrated to the new United States. Most came from Ireland and other parts of the British Empire, while some of these were political radicals who had fled from political repression in GREAT BRITAIN in the wake of the FRENCH REVOLUTION (1789–99). The small number of Catholic radicals and the much larger number of nonpolitical Catholic immigrants, usually of humble origin, were attracted by economic opportunity and religious freedom in the young nation. They established Catholic institutions—schools, churches, and voluntary societies—throughout the United States, but especially in the cities and towns. Boston, New York, Philadelphia, Baltimore, and Charleston all had significant Catholic populations by 1800.

Politically, the growing Catholic population tended to identify with the DEMOCRATIC-REPUBLICAN PARTY (Jeffersonians). During the war scare of 1798, the FEDERALIST PARTY–dominated Congress adopted the ALIEN AND SEDITION ACTS (1798), intended, in part, to stifle internal dissent and to limit the political rights of immigrants. Although not specifically anti-Catholic, the acts adversely affected Catholics, who were an important immigrant group. Nonetheless, the acts were short-lived and did little to stem Catholic IMMIGRATION, which continued to grow until the outbreak of the WAR OF 1812 (1812–15). The LOUISIANA PURCHASE (1803) resulted in a further expansion of the Catholic population with its addition of tens of thousands of French, Spanish, Metí, and Native American Catholics to the new nation.

In 1776 Catholics were a tiny minority with limited rights found in small pockets around the rebellious colonies. By 1815 the United States had a large, diverse, and growing Catholic population enjoying full civil and political rights. Although the United States would remain predominantly Protestant throughout the 19th century, and anti-Catholic feeling would continue to be an occasional feature of national life, Catholics were among those who gained significant political and religious liberty as a result of the American Revolution.

See also RELIGION.

Further reading: Francis D. Cogliano, *No King, No Popery: Anti-Catholicism in Revolutionary New England* (Westport, Conn.: Greenwood Press, 1996); John Tracy Ellis, *Catholicism in Colonial America* (Baltimore: Helicon, 1965); Martin Griffin, *Catholics in the American Revolution*, 3 vols. (Philadelphia: Loyola University Press, 1909–11); Charles Metzger, *Catholicism and the American Revolution* (Chicago: Chicago University Press, 1962).

—Francis D. Cogliano

Charleston, siege of (April 1–May 12, 1780)

In spring 1780, British forces under Sir HENRY CLINTON laid siege to Charleston, South Carolina, one of North America's largest port cities; its capture was vital to the British southern strategy. Already in control of Savannah and eastern Georgia, Clinton envisioned moving northward and conquering the Carolinas and Virginia, gathering support from the presumably large populations of LOYALISTS in those areas. The British might then have a better chance to crush the rebellion in the northern colonies.

Charleston was a strategic target because it boasted a good harbor and lay at the confluence of two navigable rivers, the Ashley and the Cooper. These attributes also made the peninsular city vulnerable to attack from the water on three sides and along the narrow strip of ground, called the Neck, that connected it to the mainland. With troops and ships at his disposal, Clinton made none of the mistakes that had doomed the CHARLESTON EXPEDITION OF 1776. Yet despite having the advantages of troop strength and position, the British commander moved surprisingly slowly in the deployment of his men. Though the British landed below Charleston on February 10, 1780, it was not until March 29 that Clinton had guns in place on the peninsula. The delay should have facilitated the city's evacuation before all avenues of escape were closed, but instead the inhabitants worked at strengthening their untenable defenses. Adding to the tragedy of the situation, General BENJAMIN LINCOLN, who commanded the 5,000 Continentals, ships in the harbor, and the considerable supply of military stores in Charleston, vacillated between the conflicting advice of his officers to abandon the city and the entreaties of the citizens and local leaders to stay and fight.

Lincoln remained undecided as to his course of action even as the British dug in along the Neck. Then, on April 11, eight British frigates easily passed the guns at Fort Moultrie to take command of the harbor and cut off Charleston by sea. A few days later, British troops under Colonel BANASTRE TARLETON surprised Revolutionaries north of the city in the BATTLE OF MONCK'S CORNER (April 14, 1780), severing Lincoln's line of communications. Reinforcements under Lord Rawdon (see HASTINGS, FRANCIS RAWDON, FIRST MARQUIS OF) and LORD CORNWALLIS arrived that stretched British control from the Edisto Inlet, west of the Ashley River, to the Ashley; from the Ashley to the Cooper River; and from the Cooper to the ATLANTIC OCEAN.

On April 21, acknowledging that the situation was hopeless, Lincoln naively proposed terms of capitulation that included an unmolested withdrawal of his troops from the city with full honors to any destination they chose. Clinton refused. Minor skirmishes took place as the British continued their advance until finally, on May 8, with opponents within shouting distance of one another, Clinton demanded the city's surrender. In a final act of frustration, the Revolutionaries instigated further hostilities that brought on a frightful bombardment of the town. The citizens then insisted that Lincoln surrender. On May 12 the CONTINENTAL ARMY marched out of Charleston and laid down its weapons. The MILITIA were allowed to return to their homes under parole and with the promise not to take up arms against the British unless they were exchanged in absentia for PRISONERS OF WAR held by the Revolutionaries. Clinton's masterful siege of Charleston cost the United States a valuable port, but had Lincoln been an authoritative commander, he would not have also lost virtually the whole southern army.

Further reading: John Buchanan, *The Road to Guilford Courthouse: The American Revolution in the Carolinas* (New York: Wiley, 1997); Robert Leckie, *George Washington's War: The Saga of the American Revolution* (New York: HarperCollins, 1993); Henry Lumpkin, *From Savannah to Yorktown: The American Revolution in the South* (Columbia: University of South Carolina Press, 1981).

—Rita M. Broyles

Charleston expedition of 1776

The Charleston expedition of 1776 was a misconceived disaster for the British in the South during the early phases of the REVOLUTIONARY WAR (1775–83). Encouraged by several royal governors from southern colonies, the British government ordered General HENRY CLINTON to rendezvous with a force from Ireland under the command of LORD CORNWALLIS and a fleet under Sir Peter Parker off Cape Fear, North Carolina. Clinton was to then join with the LOYALISTS in the region and secure the southern colonies. The orders were vague, contradictory, and well beyond the abilities of the approximately 3,000 soldiers given to Clinton. By the time he made his way south—he was ordered to make haste and to stop in several ports along the way—Loyalist forces suffered several defeats, including the devastating rout at the BATTLE OF MOORE'S CREEK BRIDGE (February 27, 1776). Moreover, Parker and Cornwallis were delayed in leaving Ireland and had a long and difficult crossing of the ATLANTIC OCEAN. Clinton left Boston on January 10, 1776, and it was not until mid-April that the Irish troops began arriving. The entire British force was not together until the end of May. Recognizing the difficulties he confronted, Clinton wanted to move on the Chesapeake, but Parker persuaded him to attack Charleston instead.

In the meantime, the Revolutionary forces had been busy preparing defenses around Charleston, especially on Sullivan Island, guarding the entrance to the harbor. In early June, however, the fortifications were not complete, and General CHARLES LEE, whom the SECOND CONTINENTAL CONGRESS had sent to take command of the CONTINENTAL ARMY in the South, thought that the position was vulnerable, and if it were overrun the defenders would have no avenue of retreat. Colonel WILLIAM MOULTRIE determined otherwise and believed that the British would not be able to dislodge him.

Once Clinton arrived off Charleston in June, British ill luck and a series of blunders saved Moultrie from the fate Lee had predicted. Clinton landed his army on Long Island, just north of Sullivan's Island, only to discover that the channel between the two was pockmarked with deep holes in the seafloor, making crossing difficult; the passage was too deep to ford in some places and too shallow to cross in boats in others. Clinton might have still launched an attack had Lee not redeployed the troops opposing the British into a stronger defensive position. When the battle began, Clinton would be unable to get his troops across the channel in the face of enemy fire.

On June 28 Parker began a naval bombardment on Moultrie and sent three vessels up the channel past the fortifications, but all three missed the deepwater channel and ran aground. Had they managed to get behind the fort, where the defensive works were incomplete, they could have pulverized Moultrie. Instead, Parker had to engage the strongest point in the revolutionary defenses. He still might have succeeded had he brought his ships closer to the island and fired at point-blank range, but instead he kept his ships more distant, and his fleet got the worst of the engagement. By nightfall, two of the three grounded ships managed to free themselves and get back to sea—the third had to be burned—and the entire fleet had to pull back out of range of Moultrie's guns. About a dozen defenders and just under 100 British were killed in the fighting. Over the next couple of weeks Clinton withdrew from Long Island and then sailed to join General WILLIAM HOWE in his attack on New York.

Further reading: David K. Wilson, *The Southern Strategy: Britain's Conquest of South Carolina and Georgia, 1775–1780* (Columbia: University of South Carolina Press, 2005).

Charlotte, Battle of (September 26, 1780)

After the victory at the BATTLE OF CAMDEN (August 16, 1780), LORD CORNWALLIS ignored his instructions from General HENRY CLINTON and decided to move into North Carolina in preparation for an invasion of Virginia. The only Revolutionary forces he had to deal with were relatively small groups of MILITIA and a handful of regulars from the CONTINENTAL ARMY: About 100 men under Colonel William Davie occupied Charlotte in an effort to slow down the progress of Cornwallis's army. Twenty dismounted dragoons under Davie took cover behind a stone fence and opened up a withering fire as the advance party from Colonel BANASTRE TARLETON's mounted legion approached. Much to Cornwallis's frustration, the legion was unable to drive the dragoons off, and it took some light infantry to push the dragoons and other militia in the area back. The legion then pursued the Revolutionaries, inflicting more casualties. Approximately 30 of Davie's men and 15 British were killed in the fighting. Although the battle was small, it reflected the difficulties that the British confronted in the South. Shortly after the engagement at Charlotte, Cornwallis learned of the defeat of PATRICK FERGUSON's LOYALISTS at the BATTLE OF KING'S MOUNTAIN (October 7, 1780) and decided to call off his winter campaign in North Carolina.

Charlottesville raid (June 4, 1781)

During his summer campaign in Virginia in 1781, LORD CORNWALLIS's troops swept through the state almost unopposed. Upon learning that Governor THOMAS JEFFERSON and the Virginia legislature were meeting in Charlottesville, Cornwallis ordered Colonel BANASTRE TARLETON to capture Jefferson and disrupt the legislature. Tarleton and about 250 mounted dragoons left Cornwallis's camp before dawn on June 3 and rode 60 miles to surprise the Virginians. However, Captain John Jouett of the Virginia MILITIA spotted the British column that evening and set off to warn Jefferson. Even though Tarleton's men were in the saddle most of the night, Jouett arrived in Charlottesville first and spread word of the raiders. Jefferson and his family left Monticello barely 10 minutes before Tarleton's men arrived. A few legislators were captured by the British, and significant amounts of weapons and supplies were captured and destroyed. Tarleton was able to return to the main body of British troops unmolested. Although Jefferson had eluded the British, and his term of office technically ended on June 2, he suffered the ignomiy of having been chased from his mountaintop home by the British and was accused of leaving the state government in disarray. This event hurt Jefferson's reputation and sullied his wartime record as governor.

Chase, Samuel (1741–1811) *Supreme Court justice*

A controversial figure, Samuel Chase was a signer of the DECLARATION OF INDEPENDENCE and was tried for impeachment as a U.S. SUPREME COURT justice by the Senate. Born in Maryland, Chase trained as a lawyer and was admitted to the bar in 1761. He served in the Maryland assembly from 1764 to 1784, quickly establishing his credentials as an opponent to the royal governor and as a leader of the RESISTANCE MOVEMENT (1764–75) against imperial regulation.

Oddly for a man who would later declare that expanding suffrage would lead to a mobocracy, Chase took an active role in the Maryland anti-STAMP ACT mobs, served on a variety of Revolutionary committees, and was a leading radical as the REVOLUTIONARY WAR (1775–83) broke out. He attended both the FIRST CONTINENTAL CONGRESS and the SECOND CONTINENTAL CONGRESS, orchestrated Maryland's support for the Declaration of Independence, and rode 150 miles in two days to Philadelphia in time to vote for that document in 1776. In 1777 and 1778 he was an important member of Congress and supported GEORGE WASHINGTON as commander in chief of the CONTINENTAL ARMY without reservation. Toward the end of 1778, however, Chase became embroiled in a controversy concerning his efforts to speculate in flour based on knowledge he had gained as a government official. Accused of corruption, he was compelled to withdraw from public life. When he was again chosen as a delegate to Congress two years later, he was not as active as he had been. Like many of his generation, he sought new opportunities in the independent United States, only to find his speculations and business enterprises ending in failure. He declared bankruptcy in 1789.

Samuel Chase. Reproduction of a painting by Charles Willson Peale *(Library of Congress)*

At the same time Chase again entered politics, opposing the U.S. CONSTITUTION written in 1787 and voting against it at Maryland's ratifying convention. He became a Maryland judge in 1788 and chief justice of the Maryland general court in 1791. Although he had been rabidly anti-British, sometime in the 1790s he became more conservative. As a result, his old friend George Washington nominated him to the U.S. Supreme Court in January 1796. Quickly ratified by the Senate, Chase played a prominent role in the court prior to the rise of JOHN MARSHALL, and he wrote several significant opinions, which helped to assert national treaties over state laws, defined ex post facto laws, articulated procedures for amendments to the Constitution, and clarified the relationship between federal and the common law.

At times, Chase behaved high-handedly. When he delivered a charge to a Baltimore grand jury that attacked the DEMOCRATIC-REPUBLICAN PARTY and the expansion of the right to vote in 1803, President THOMAS JEFFERSON encouraged supporters to impeach Chase. This effort was part of a general Jeffersonian assault on a judiciary dominated by the FEDERALIST PARTY. Had the Senate managed to remove Chase, many scholars believe that the Jeffersonians would have next acted against Chief Justice John Marshall. However, the case against Chase, presented in the Senate in 1804, was not particularly strong. Although he had uttered intemperate remarks and behaved so badly

in the trial of John Fries for his role in a tax rebellion that President JOHN ADAMS had pardoned the convicted Fries (who had been sentenced to death in Chase's court), none of the eight counts levied against him could stand up to an able legal defense and careful scrutiny. In short, they did not amount to high crimes and misdemeanors.

Chase remained on the court for the rest of his life, but ill health limited his attendance. He died on June 19, 1811.

See also FRIES'S REBELLION.

Further reading: Richard E. Ellis, *The Jeffersonian Crisis: Courts and Politics in the Young Republic* (New York: Oxford University Press, 1971); William H. Rehnquist, *Grand Inquests: The Historic Impeachments of Justice Samuel Chase and President Andrew Johnson* (New York: Morrow, 1992).

Chastellux, François-Jean de Beauvoir, marquis de
(1734–1788) *French military officer, writer*
François-Jean de Beauvoir, marquis de Chastellux, entered the French army as a second lieutenant when he was only 13 and was a colonel by the time he was 21. He fought in several campaigns in Europe during the Seven Years' War (the FRENCH AND INDIAN WAR in North America). During the REVOLUTIONARY WAR (1775–83) Chastellux was a major general serving under the COMTE DE ROCHAMBEAU with the French army in North America. Because of his ability to speak English fluently, he acted as a crucial liaison between the staffs of the French army and CONTINENTAL ARMY, a position of vital importance. He also participated in the campaign that led to the surrender of LORD CORNWALLIS at YORKTOWN on October 19, 1781.

Besides his military career, Chastellux was also a literary figure. In 1772 he published a book on philosophy and was afterward elected to the French Academy. After returning to FRANCE in 1783, he wrote *Travels in North America in the Years 1780, 1781, and 1782* (1786; published in English, 1787), which not only covered his experiences as a military officer but also offered vivid descriptions of life in the United States during the closing years of the Revolutionary War. In this popular work he described GEORGE WASHINGTON as "Brave without temerity, laborious without ambition, generous without prodigality, noble without pride, virtuous without severity." The marquis de Chastellux died in Paris on October 24, 1788.

Châteauguay, Battle of (October 26, 1813)
During the WAR OF 1812 (1812–15), after the campaign along the Niagara fizzled in 1813, U.S. forces invaded CANADA along the northern New York border from two directions. Overall command fell to General JAMES WILKINSON,

who advanced up the St. Lawrence; a second force, under General WADE HAMPTON, marched up the Lake Champlain corridor. Although 1,400 New York MILITIA refused to cross the Canadian border, claiming they were a defensive force, Hampton continued up the Châteauguay River with 4,000 inexperienced regulars. On October 25 Hampton's army reached a log barrier defended by 1,700 Canadians and a few NATIVE AMERICANS. Hampton sent a large flanking force across the river. These men, after getting lost in the swampy forest typical of that part of the country, were stopped the next morning by a smaller body of Canadians. Hampton decided to attack the barricade head-on and fought an indecisive two-hour battle. The Canadians used bugles and Indian war whoops to convince U.S. forces that they were facing a large army. After losing about 50 dead and 200 wounded, Hampton withdrew his soldiers. He returned to the United States, claiming that many of his men were sick and that he lacked supplies. Hampton, who distrusted Wilkinson and believed that he had not been fully supported by the War Department, resigned his command in disgust.

Further reading: Pierre Berton, *Flames across the Border: The Canadian-American Tragedy, 1813–1814* (New York: Little Brown and Company, 1981).

Chauncey, Isaac (1782–1840) *U.S. naval officer*

A cautious naval officer, Isaac Chauncey served in the BARBARY WARS and the WAR OF 1812 (1812–15). Born in Black Rock, Connecticut, Chauncey went to sea as a young man, and by the age of 19 he had been given command of his first vessel. When the U.S. NAVY expanded because of a threatened war with FRANCE (the QUASI-WAR, 1798–1800), Chauncey was commissioned a lieutenant to serve on the frigate USS *President*, which was then being built in New York, and subsequently took one cruise on that vessel to the WEST INDIES before peace was reestablished. He remained in the navy after the DEMOCRATIC-REPUBLICAN PARTY (Jeffersonians) reduced the size of the peacetime force; fought against Tripoli in 1804–05, distinguishing himself in that conflict; and was promoted to captain in 1806. While taking a leave of absence from the navy, he made a merchant cruise to the Far East for JOHN JACOB ASTOR. When he returned, he went on active duty and was given charge of the navy yard in New York.

At the beginning of the War of 1812, Chauncey was sent to the Great Lakes to build a navy. An excellent and experienced administrator, he did well at this task, centering himself in Sackets Harbor on Lake Ontario. Although he had several opportunities during the war, he was too cautious to risk his fleet in battle with the British. The result was that the war on Lake Ontario ended in a stalemate, with neither side gaining an advantage.

Chauncey served in 1815 and 1816 in the MEDITERRANEAN SEA against Algiers as captain of one of the United States's largest ships. From 1816 to 1818 he commanded the Mediterranean fleet. Thereafter he remained in the U.S. Navy in administrative positions. He died on January 27, 1840.

Further reading: William M. Fowler, Jr., *Jack Tars and Commodores: The American Navy, 1783–1815* (Boston: Houghton Mifflin, 1984).

Chauncy, Charles (1705–1787) *Congregationalist minister*

Ordained as a Congregationalist minister in New England and known for his rationalist opposition to the First Great Awakening, Charles Chauncy's development of universalist ideas helped to weaken the primacy of Calvinism in New England and anticipated UNITARIANISM, while his opposition to the introduction of an ANGLICAN bishop helped lead to his later role as a prominent supporter of the AMERICAN REVOLUTION. Harvard-educated, Chauncy became first the assistant (1727–69) and then the minister (1769–87) of Boston's First or Old Brick Church. Having emphasized the importance of reason over emotion during his opposition to the First Great Awakening of the 1740s, by the 1760s Chauncy had developed universalist ideas, believing that due to God's essential benevolence, all mankind was eventually destined for happiness after a period of redemptive suffering for the degenerate. He also emphasized the importance of works in conjunction with faith as part of the process of redemption. Due to the controversial nature of these claims, he long delayed announcing his ideas directly, eventually publishing *The Mystery Hid from Ages and Generations* anonymously in 1784.

Chauncy opposed the introduction of an Anglican bishop in the 1760s, printing several pamphlets, notably *A Complete View of Episcopacy* (1771), in opposition to the arguments of Thomas Bradbury Chandler. He advocated resistance to the British in *A Letter to a Friend, Giving a Concise, but Just, Representation of the Hardships and Sufferings the Town of Boston is Exposed To* (1774), arguing that the British blockade of Boston would develop from an attack on economic to political liberties. His support for the REVOLUTIONARY WAR (1775–83) was so well-known that he was forced to leave Boston when it was occupied by the British. He died in Boston on February 10, 1787.

Further reading: Charles H. Lippy, *Seasonable Revolutionary: The Mind of Charles Chauncy* (Chicago: Nelson-Hall, 1981).

—Alison K. Stanley

cheese, mammoth

In 1801 women in Cheshire, Massachusetts, made a huge cheese to commemorate the election of THOMAS JEFFERSON to the presidency. The cheese measured four feet in diameter, was 18 inches tall, and weighed 1,200 pounds. Cheshire, located in the Berkshire Hills of western Massachusetts, was overwhelmingly BAPTIST and Jeffersonian in a state that was dominated by the FEDERALIST PARTY and still had Congregationalism established as the official state church. Members of the Federalist Party labeled the gift as the "Mammoth Cheese"—mammoth since at this time CHARLES WILLSON PEALE was digging up the bones of a MAMMOTH in a scientific project sponsored by Jefferson. The Federalist Party press ridiculed the "mummery of the *Cheshire* simpletons," joked that the cheese was "made out of *asses'* milk," and even suggested that the rotting inside portion of the cheese—an inevitable development given its size—was a metaphor for the inner corruption of Jefferson and his administration.

The ridicule, however, did not take, and Democratic-Republicans seized on the mammoth cheese label as symbolic of the success of agrarian hard work and virtue. Two citizens of Cheshire escorted the cheese to WASHINGTON, D.C.—one was the Baptist minister JOHN LELAND—and presented it to Jefferson on January 1, 1802, with the inscription "THE GREATEST CHEESE IN AMERICA—FOR THE GREATEST MAN IN AMERICA." Leland read a message from the people of Cheshire declaring: "The supreme Ruler of the Universe . . . has raised up a Jefferson for this critical day to defend Republicanism and baffle all the arts of Aristocracy." Jefferson responded by stating that he viewed the gift as a "mark of esteem from freeborn farmers, employed personally in the useful labors of life." (The fact that the cheese had been made by women did not appear relevant to Jefferson in the male-dominated political world of the early republic.)

The mammoth cheese thus came to represent a number of different threads in the Jeffersonian creed. It reflected the fruits of Jefferson's "chosen people of God"—farmers. It symbolized his alliance with evangelicals in pursuit of RELIGIOUS LIBERTY—Jefferson released his response to the DANBURY BAPTIST ASSOCIATION ADDRESS TO THOMAS JEFFERSON calling for "building a wall of separation between Church & State" on the same day he received the mammoth cheese. And it epitomized the new political culture of the early republic, where common people expressed themselves in public demonstrations and where the meaning of those expressions was debated in print.

See also ELECTION OF 1800; REPUBLICANISM.

Further reading: Jeffrey L. Pasley, "The Cheese and the Words: Popular Political Culture in the Early American Republic," in *Beyond the Founders: New Approaches to the*

Political History of the Early American Republic, edited by Jeffrey L. Pasley, Andrew W. Robertson, and David Waldstreiche (Chapel Hill: University of North Carolina Press, 2004), 31–56.

Cherokee

In the second half of the 18th century, the Cherokee were the most powerful Native American nation in the South. They played a crucial role in the REVOLUTIONARY WAR (1775–83) and in the CREEK WAR (1813–14). They also adopted many technological and governmental practices from their European-American neighbors, becoming the only NATIVE AMERICANS to create their own writing system.

After ejecting the CREEK from what is now northern Georgia, the Cherokee controlled the mountains west of the Carolinas and southern Virginia. During the FRENCH AND INDIAN WAR (1754–63), they initially sided with the British. However, tensions between the colonists and the Indians mounted during the conflict. These tensions burst into full-scale war in 1759 after a party of Cherokee returning from fighting the French were ambushed by Virginians. The subsequent CHEROKEE WAR (1759–61) took a heavy toll. Colonial and British armies destroyed several Cherokee towns and burned acres of crop land. The Cherokee had to cede land to the colonies after hostilities had ceased.

Another round of concessions took place immediately before the Revolutionary War. In the TREATY OF SYCAMORE SHOALS (1775), several Cherokee leaders sold eastern and central Kentucky to the Transylvania Land Company. DRAGGING CANOE led a faction opposed to the land sale. He and his followers slipped into the rugged terrain in the Chickamauga Valley and conducted a bloody guerrilla war for nearly two decades against the European Americans trying to settle in the region.

The Revolutionary War devastated the Cherokee, many of whom sided with the British soon after the war began. This action merely provoked the states of North Carolina, South Carolina, Georgia, and Virginia into sending large MILITIA expeditions into Cherokee territory. With attacks coming from several directions, the Indians soon asked for peace, and the Treaties of DeWitt's Corner and Long Island (both signed in 1777) surrendered more lands in the Carolinas. But the war would not end so quickly for the Cherokee: The Chickamaugan band under Dragging Canoe fought on, dividing the nation into two factions, an accommodationist party and a pro-British war party. The pro-war faction expanded after the British victory at the BATTLE OF SAVANNAH (December 29, 1778) and an influx of TRADE goods from GREAT BRITAIN. Revolutionary forces launched additional invasions into

Cherokee territory in 1779, 1780, and 1781, destroying towns, burning fields, and wreaking havoc.

By the end of the war, half the Cherokee towns lay in ashes; great stretches of territory had been lost; the tribe was divided; SMALLPOX had killed hundreds, if not thousands; and the Indians' traditional cultural framework emphasizing harmony was disrupted. Yet they still faced more demands to sell their lands. The Treaty of Hopewell (November 28, 1785) promised to keep settlers off the remaining Cherokee hunting grounds. In 1791 President GEORGE WASHINGTON assured the Cherokee that if they ceded their land in eastern Tennessee, the United States would not ask for any more territory. These promises spurred the Cherokee to learn to read and write. They were sure that if they could understand the documents and treaties without the help of interpreters, they could ward off swindlers. But promises and treaties did not keep the U.S. ARMY from demanding that it be allowed to build a road through Cherokee lands, to be used only for military purposes. The Cherokee leaders correctly feared that the road would bring settlers and, with them, more demands for land sales.

The Chickamaugans continued to resist the United States and aided the MIAMI in their wars of the early 1790s. After the BATTLE OF FALLEN TIMBERS (August 20, 1794), the Chickamaugans answered the invitation of the governor of Spanish LOUISIANA to move west of the Mississippi River to act as a buffer against the land-hungry settlers from the United States already sneaking into Spanish territory.

Out of this turmoil arose a reborn Cherokee Nation in the East whose leaders decided that only by adopting European-American ways could the Cherokee survive. Early in the first decade of the 19th century, the U.S. government opened trading posts in Cherokee lands with the idea of interesting the Cherokee people in farming and other modern practices. The Cherokee readily adopted the technologies that the trading posts brought. They had already formed the "Light Horse" (1799) as a police force for the tribe, and soon farms, ranches, and frame houses dotted the countryside. Some Cherokee even used slaves to work the new plantations.

The SHAWNEE leader TECUMSEH tried to enlist the Cherokee in his confederation of tribes, but his pleas fell on deaf ears. When the WAR OF 1812 (1812–14) broke out, the Cherokee cast their lot with the United States and assisted General ANDREW JACKSON against the Creek. More than 500 mounted Cherokee warriors fought at the BATTLE OF HORSESHOE BEND (March 27, 1814), and the tribe aided in tracking down the RED STICKS (Creek) who escaped into Spanish FLORIDA.

The service the Cherokee provided the United States did not prevent Jackson from demanding their lands at the negotiations at Fort Jackson in 1814, nor did their adoption of European-American styles of farming and government help them. As ever-increasing swarms of European-American settlers ate up land faster and faster, the Cherokee gave in to Jackson's demands in 1817, and two years later they surrendered all their lands in eastern Georgia. These cessions set the stage for the final removal of the Cherokee from their homes in the East.

Further reading: Thomas M. Hatley, *The Dividing Paths: Cherokee and South Carolinians through the Era of Revolution* (New York: Oxford University Press, 1995); William G. McLoughlin, *Cherokee Renaissance in the New Republic* (Princeton, N.J.: Princeton University Press, 1986).

—George Milne

Cherokee War (1759–1761)

After beginning the FRENCH AND INDIAN WAR (1754–63) as allies of GREAT BRITAIN, the CHEROKEE fought British Americans from 1759 to 1761 in a conflict triggered by Carolinian desire for Cherokee land and FRONTIER distrust of all NATIVE AMERICANS. The Cherokee reluctantly sent about 300 warriors to Pennsylvania to join British general JOHN FORBES's expedition against Fort Duquesne. Poorly treated and not respected by Forbes, the Cherokee left his army disenchanted with the British. On their return to their own lands in autumn 1758, at least 30 Cherokee were killed by Virginian frontiersman who hated all Indians, whether they were allies or enemies. Several Cherokee reacted to this violence by attacking some settlers in the Carolinas following traditional Native American practices of retaliatory killing as a way to "cover" the dead. In reaction to the raids, Governor William Henry Lyttelton of South Carolina invaded Cherokee lands in autumn 1759 despite a Cherokee delegation that had arrived in Charleston apologizing for the violence and seeking peace. As he marched off to the backcountry in September, Lyttelton took 22 Cherokee headmen as hostages. Although this incursion successfully destroyed several Cherokee towns, ultimately Lyttelton and his 1,200 fighting men did not accomplish very much. Illness, compounded by a SMALLPOX outbreak in late December, led to massive desertions and then a retreat. When he arrived at Charleston, Lyttelton declared victory, even though negotiations with the Cherokee had led to no settlement. The hostages were placed in Fort Prince George.

In early 1760 the situation in South Carolina deteriorated. Smallpox followed the army to Charleston, and at least 4,000 people were infected in the city. In February Cherokee warriors killed an officer outside of Fort Prince George. Retaliating, the soldiers murdered all 22 Cherokee hostages. This action led to extensive Cherokee raids on the frontier, creating panic and an exodus from the backcountry. Colonel Archibald Montgomery marched into Cherokee territory with 1,200 newly arrived regulars, 300 South Carolina Rangers, and some allied Indians, hoping to reach the 200 troops stationed at Fort Loudoun deep in the interior. Montgomery's column destroyed some villages but was ambushed near Etchoe, losing about 20 killed and 70 wounded. Like Lyttelton the year before, Montgomery claimed victory and retreated from the frontier. On August 7, 1760, the garrison at Fort Loudoun surrendered with the promise that they would be allowed to travel safely to the nearest British outpost. Two days later, however, a group of Cherokee attacked the withdrawing garrison, killing 32 and taking the rest as captives.

By 1761, the destruction of crops and villages having taken its toll, many of the Cherokee were ready for peace. However, the British were determined to punish them on yet another expedition. Major JAMES GRANT led 2,800 regulars, MILITIA, rangers, and Indian allies on a 33-day incursion that destroyed 15 towns and 1,000 acres of corn. He met limited resistance but did fight a battle at Cowee on June 10, 1761, with 10 men killed and 50 wounded. More successful than his predecessors, Grant, too, eventually turned around before getting to the furthest Cherokee towns. But his invasion led to a treaty with ATTAKUL-LAKULLA and other chiefs that established peace and arranged for an exchange of prisoners.

Both the British Americans and Native Americans suffered dramatically as a result of this conflict, but ultimately the Cherokee, despite intense resistance, ceded land and suffered greater losses.

Further reading: Thomas M. Hatley, *The Dividing Paths: Cherokees and South Carolinians through the Era of Revolution* (New York: Oxford University Press, 1995); Ian K. Steele, *Warpaths: Invasions of North America* (New York: Oxford University Press, 1994).

Cherry Valley Massacre (November 11, 1778)
In an effort to create panic in the frontier and regain control of the Mohawk Valley, Loyalist captain Walter Butler led an attack on the fort and settlement at Cherry Valley, New York, in November 1778, during the REVOLUTIONARY WAR (1775–83). Butler commanded a force of more than 300 Indians, 150 rangers, and 50 regular British troops. He was also accompanied by a number of MOHAWK and SENECA leaders, including JOSEPH BRANT. The staff at Fort Stanwix alerted Ichabod Alden, the local commander at Cherry Valley, that scouts had identified a large Loyalist force on its way to his area. Alden, relying on his own forward patrols, did not believe that such a large contingent could be approaching. In the meantime, Butler's men seized a party of Alden's scouts and learned of Cherry Valley's minimal defenses. Alden's

men also revealed the identity of the civilian residence outside of the fort where many CONTINENTAL ARMY officers were quartered. The raiders attacked that building first, killing Alden and several other officers. Despite this initial success, Butler was unable to capture the fort. The Indians attacked anyone outside the gates of the fort, killing nearly 50 soldiers and civilians, and the raiders took 71 captives, many of whom were women and children. Butler released more than half of the captives before he left Cherry Valley and began the 300-mile trek to FORT NIAGARA.

The battle was a tactical success for Butler but a public relations fiasco for the British. Even though both sides had committed similar atrocities before, the Revolutionaries seized on this episode to argue that LOYALISTS and NATIVE AMERICANS were responsible for all kinds of outrages on the FRONTIER. These reports even made it to GREAT BRITAIN, leading to expressions of public opposition toward the employment of Indians in waging war against the United States.

Further reading: Colin Calloway, *The American Revolution in Indian Country: Crisis and Diversity in Native American Communities* (Cambridge: Cambridge University Press, 1995).

Chesapeake Bay campaign (1813–1814)
Beginning in February 1813, and continuing for the rest of the WAR OF 1812 (1812–15), the British maintained a naval force in the Chesapeake Bay region that blockaded U.S. shipping and could raid the coastal areas with relative impunity. The British also engaged in larger land and sea operations that led to major battles and the burning of WASHINGTON, D.C.

When the British moved into the Chesapeake in 1813, they quickly gained complete dominance on the water. They seized a number of islands, including Tangier Island, which they held until the end of the war. Hundreds of escaped slaves joined the British during the campaign and thereby obtained their freedom. In April Admiral SIR GEORGE COCKBURN swept through the upper Chesapeake, blockaded Baltimore, raided towns and villages in the area, captured stores of flour and supplies, and destroyed an iron foundry. The only setback the British had was in their ill-conceived assault on CRANEY ISLAND (June 22, 1813) outside of Norfolk. A few days later, however, they were able to occupy Hampton and carry on raids along the James River. For the rest of the year, they kept up the pressure, capturing scores of vessels heading in and out of the bay.

With the defeat of NAPOLEON BONAPARTE in 1814, the British sent both naval and land reinforcements to the Chesapeake. During the first half of the year, they continued their destructive small-scale raiding and probed U.S.

defenses. Captain JOSHUA BARNEY organized a small flotilla of GUNBOATS in May that provided some resistance to the British, but by the end of June, he found himself pushed up the Patuxent River with little room to maneuver or to attack the enemy. During the summer the British determined to strike at the U.S. capital, and in August they made their move, forcing Barney to abandon his flotilla on the Patuxent and defeating a poorly organized U.S. ARMY at the BATTLE OF BLADENSBURG (August 24, 1814). They then marched into Washington and burned the nation's public buildings. After this success, the British decided to attack Baltimore. However, that city's defenses and MILITIA were more formidable than they had expected, and they were beaten back in the BATTLE OF BALTIMORE (September 12–14, 1814) with heavy losses, including the death of General ROBERT ROSS. Despite this setback and the withdrawal of some ships and men for the attack on New Orleans, the British did not leave the Chesapeake until the end of war.

Further reading: Christopher T. George, *Terror on the Chesapeake: The War of 1812 on the Bay* (Shippensburg, Pa.: White Maine Books, 2000); Charles G. Muller, *The Darkest Day: 1814: The Washington-Baltimore Campaign* (Philadelphia: J. B. Lippincott, 1963).

Chesapeake Capes, Battle of (September 5, 1781)

Although there were few sea battles that involved entire fleets during the REVOLUTIONARY WAR (1775–83), the Battle of Chesapeake Capes, off the coast of Virginia between a French squadron under Admiral COMTE DE GRASSE and a British squadron under Admiral THOMAS GRAVES, determined the outcome at YORKTOWN and helped guarantee the independence of the United States. The fighting itself was a draw, but Graves's decision to return to New York to refit doomed LORD CORNWALLIS to surrender his army at Yorktown on October 19, 1781.

The stage was set for the battle when Grasse agreed on July 28, 1781, to sail from the Caribbean to North American waters. Word of this decision reached Generals COMTE DE ROCHAMBEAU and GEORGE WASHINGTON in New York State on August 14. After some hesitation, Washington agreed to abandon his planned attack on New York City and shift the French and Continental armies to the Chesapeake to rendevous with Grasse. In the meantime, Admiral COMTE DE BARRAS was ordered to bring supplies and French troops from Newport, Rhode Island, to the Chesapeake. Anticipating Grasse's move, Admiral SAMUEL HOOD sailed for the Chesapeake from his station in the WEST INDIES, arriving on August 25, before the French fleet. Finding no French ships in the Chesapeake, Hood continued on to New York to join forces with Graves.

Grasse made it to the Chesapeake on August 30, and on the same day, with Hood sailing outside New York harbor ready for action, the British received news that Barras had sailed from Newport on August 25. The British realized that if the two French squadrons were to unite, the French would have overwhelming numbers. On August 31 Graves left New York to join Hood, hoping to either intercept Barras on his way south or engage Grasse before Barras got to the Chesapeake.

With Graves in command as the senior officer, the British arrived off the Virginia Capes on September 5. Grasse immediately ordered his ships to sea to meet the British threat. Graves had 18 ships of the line (with 64 or more guns), Grasse had 24, but Graves had the advantage of the wind with his ships already at sea. Had he attacked the French immediately as they left the Chesapeake, and before they could organize a line, he might have fared better. Graves, however, intended on following the conventional battle plan of engaging the enemy ship against ship, rather than concentrating his forces and disabling one part of the French fleet before attacking the rest. The result was that although the French got underway shortly after noon, the two fleets spent until five o'clock maneuvering for position before commencing the actual fighting. The battle was intense for a little over an hour and a half when the growing darkness compelled both sides to disengage.

During the following days, the two fleets stayed within sight of each other as they drifted south off the coast of North Carolina in something of a stalemate. The British had been so badly mauled—eventually they had to sink one ship because it had been severely damaged—that even though they maintained an advantage with the wind, they had to delay another attack until repairs could be completed on several ships. The French hoped for a change in the wind so that they could attack the British. On the evening of September 8, Grasse decided that he had gone too far south and that if the British headed for the Chesapeake and got there before him, Yorktown could be relieved and cooperation with the land forces would be rendered impossible. On September 9 the British lost contact with the enemy, although they knew the French had headed north. Belatedly, Graves ordered his fleet back to the Chesapeake, but by the time they returned on September 12, the French were already there and had been joined by Barras. With the odds greatly against him, Graves decided to head for New York, hoping for reinforcements and looking to refit his fleet. With that decision, and without fully pressing the action, he sealed the fate of Cornwallis and his army at Yorktown.

Further reading: Jonathan R. Dull, *The French Navy and American Independence: A Study of Arms and Diplomacy* (Princeton, N.J.: Princeton University Press, 1975).

Chesapeake-Leopard affair (June 22, 1807)

On June 22, 1807, the HMS *Leopard* attacked the USS *Chesapeake* just outside the Chesapeake Bay, forcefully removing four men whom the British claimed were deserters. This confrontation led to a major diplomatic crisis and contributed to the growing animosity between the United States and GREAT BRITAIN that finally broke out into the WAR OF 1812 (1812–15).

The British had some legitimate concerns in manning their navy during their long struggle with FRANCE. They relied on their naval supremacy to prevent an invasion of Great Britain and to check the expansionist aims of the French, but they needed hundreds of thousands of SEAMEN to do so. At the same time, U.S. shipping expanded rapidly as a neutral power while France and Great Britain were at war. Although many people in the United States went to sea in this era, merchants also recruited British and other foreign seamen. The British claimed that during this period as many as 10,000 men deserted the poor pay, harsh conditions, and dangers of the Royal Navy to sail under the U.S. flag.

Aware of these problems, the senior British officer on the North American station in 1807 ordered his captains to remove any deserters that they knew were aboard U.S. warships. At the time, a squadron of British ships was stationed in Chesapeake Bay, hoping to capture two French vessels that had sought safety in the neutral U.S. port of Norfolk. Officers from this squadron visited Norfolk and actually met British deserters in the streets, discovering that they were now in the U.S. NAVY. This knowledge compelled the British to act when the USS *Chesapeake* put to sea; not to intercept the frigate would have been a violation of a direct order. The HMS *Leopard* was dispatched to search the *Chesapeake* as soon as it entered international waters. Unprepared for battle and with a new, untrained crew aboard, the *Chesapeake* did not clear for action, a standard naval practice whenever a foreign warship approached. The British captain demanded to be allowed to search the frigate for deserters, but Commodore JAMES BARRON refused. Detecting the British intent, he ordered his men to quietly clear for action, but it was too little too late, as the British were at close range and opened fire. In the confusion aboard the *Chesapeake*, many of the cannons could not even be readied for fire. After one shot to save face, Barron surrendered to the British, who found four deserters aboard the vessel.

A tremendous public outcry arose against this attack. War was threatened, but President THOMAS JEFFERSON instead instituted the EMBARGO OF 1807, with devastating effects for the U.S. ECONOMY. The British issued an apology for the attack, but U.S. diplomats insisted on tying a discussion of the incident to the larger issues of IMPRESSMENT and neutral TRADE, two areas on which the British were not prepared to make many concessions. The result was increased tension between the two nations, which helped to lead to the War of 1812.

Often lost in the discussion of the diplomatic haggling over the attack on the *Chesapeake* was the fate of the four deserters. Three turned out to be U.S. citizens who had either been impressed or had volunteered for duty in the British navy. One of these died while being held by the British; the two others were turned over to the United States after the opening of hostilities in the War of 1812. The fourth was clearly a British subject, and he was hanged for desertion.

See also FOREIGN AFFAIRS; FREE TRADE AND SAILORS' RIGHTS.

Further reading: Spencer C. Tucker and Frank T. Reuter, *Injured Honor: The Chesapeake-Leopard Affair, June 22, 1807* (Annapolis, Md.: Naval Institute Press, 1996).

Cheves, Langdon (1776–1857) *South Carolina politician, Speaker of the House of Representatives*

Langdon Cheves was one of the most prominent WAR HAWKS to support the WAR OF 1812 (1812–15). Born in Rocky River, South Carolina, he had some formal EDUCATION before serving an apprenticeship as a clerk in Charleston and studying law. Admitted to the bar in 1797, Cheves entered local politics in the early 1800s and gained a seat in Congress in 1810. An ardent member of the DEMOCRATIC-REPUBLICAN PARTY, he supported the movement to go to war with GREAT BRITAIN and pushed for an expansion of the U.S. NAVY. During the War of 1812 he became a leader in the House of Representatives, chairing the Ways and Means Committee. When HENRY CLAY left Congress to go to Europe to participate in the peace negotiations, Cheves became Speaker of the House. In 1815 Cheves left WASHINGTON, D.C., to practice law in South Carolina. In the wake of the panic of 1819, he agreed to serve as the president of the Second Bank of the United States. An able administrator, Cheves helped to bring order to the bank; he stepped down as president in 1823. Subsequently, he was a commissioner of claims under the provisions of the TREATY OF GHENT (1814) and practiced law in Philadelphia until 1829, when he moved back to South Carolina. He died in Columbia on June 26, 1857.

Chickasaw

The Chickasaw were an important southeastern Native American tribe who were British allies since the 1720s. Chickasaw share a dialect of Muskogean with the kindred CHOCTAW, who were French allies and with whom the Chickasaw fought frequently. In the mid-18th century, the main Chickasaw villages were located near present-day Tupelo, Mississippi, although some bands ranged as far as South Carolina and Pennsylvania. The Chickasaw occupied hunting lands between the Mississippi and Tennessee rivers until their forced removal in 1837.

The Chickasaw maintained their allegiance to the British during the REVOLUTIONARY WAR (1775–83). The Indian agent JOHN STUART, sent by General THOMAS GAGE, met with the tribe in 1775 to secure their goodwill. He shipped them 3,000 pounds of shot and powder and raised a force of 500 warriors for a 1776 campaign against settlements in Virginia and the Carolinas. At Chickasaw Bluffs, the site of present-day Memphis, Tennessee, the Chickasaw established positions in an effort to control the Mississippi River. GEORGE ROGERS CLARK established Fort Jefferson upriver in what is now Kentucky, from which he launched raids against SHAWNEE villages in the Ohio Valley. The Chickasaw unsuccessfully assaulted the fort in late spring 1781. On May 2, 1782, they attacked a convoy of ammunition and supplies bound for the Spanish in St. Louis.

A pro-Revolutionary faction of the Chickasaw sought peace with the Spanish in late 1782, and a delegation led by Piomingo made a treaty with the United States on November 5, 1783. The treaty called for the expulsion of Loyalist refugees from the Chickasaw Nation in return for assurances that European-American settlers would be kept out of Chickasaw country. Although the United States sought and obtained cessions of territory throughout the early 19th century, the Chickasaw remained U.S. allies and fought against the RED STICKS in the CREEK WAR (1813–14).

See also NATIVE AMERICANS.

Further reading: James R. Atkinson, *Splendid Land, Splendid People: The Chickasaw Indians to Removal* (Tuscaloosa: University of Alabama Press, 2004).

—Stephen A. Martin

Chief Hendrick   See THEYANONGUIN.

China trade

After 1784, U.S. and Chinese merchants carried on a lucrative TRADE in products such as silk, tea, porcelain, silver, and ginseng. Colonials had traded with China through the British East India Company, but the newly independent United States began to trade with China directly in 1784 when the ship *Empress of China* embarked on a long journey from New York City to Canton. The ship returned to New York in 1785 loaded with teas, silks, and porcelain from which its investors made a healthy 30 percent profit. U.S. trade with China took place through the exclusive organization called the Co-Hong, or Hong, merchants.

The Co-Hong had a corporate monopoly granted by the Qing dynasty to conduct trading operations with all foreigners. The Hong merchants also coordinated and managed various trading factories in Canton; these served as warehouses, offices, treasuries, and residences for foreign traders in Canton, including those from the United States.

U.S. neutrality with regard to the European wars allowed the nation's ships free trading opportunities in China, without fear that merchant ships would be captured. By the 1790s, trade between China and the United States focused mainly on silver, silks, and tea. U.S. merchants carried millions of dollars' worth of silver bullion obtained in South America to China in exchange for tea and silks. In Canton, U.S. merchants competed for the Co-Hong's trade with merchants from various Western nations.

By far, the largest rival to United States trade with China was the British East India Company. The company dominated trade with China and was less dependent on silver than other Western traders. The East India Company relied more on its own trade proceeds to purchase Chinese teas and silks, thereby reducing its burden to provide the Hong merchants with silver. This put the other traders at a considerable disadvantage due to the expense of purchasing and transporting silver for trade in Canton.

Further reading: Yu-Kwei Cheng, *Foreign Trade and Industrial Development of China* (Washington, D.C.: University Press of Washington, D.C., 1956); Weng Eang Chong, *The Hong Merchants of Canton: Chinese Merchants in Sino-Western Trade* (Surrey, England: Biddles Limited, 1997).

Chippewa, Battle of (July 5, 1814)

In summer 1814, General Jacob Brown launched an invasion of CANADA across the Niagara River. After capturing the weakly defended FORT ERIE, he marched his 3,500-man army north along the Niagara. Opposing him was General Phineas Riall with about 2,000 British regulars, Canadian MILITIA, and NATIVE AMERICANS. Riall had formed a defensive line along the Chippewa River, with the Niagara River on one side and a dense wood on the other. After some skirmishing on July 4, Brown withdrew to a defensive position behind Street's Creek, leaving a mile separating the two armies. On July 5 Brown sent Brigadier General Peter B. Porter with a force of militia and SENECA into the woods on his left to sweep away snipers harassing his soldiers. Unfortunately for Porter, he was surprised when he ran into a strong body of Canadians and Native Americans who compelled him to retreat.

In the meantime, Riall had determined to attack Brown and began to advance onto the plain late that afternoon. Riall believed that the gray coats worn by WINFIELD

SCOTT's brigade meant that the center was held by militia who would retreat before British regulars. Scott, for his part, was not expecting a battle that day and was preparing to drill his troops. However, at the urging of Brown, he quickly formed his men into a concave line, withstood musket and artillery fire, beat off the assault, and drove the British from the field with a furious counterattack. The British lost about 200 dead and 360 wounded or captured; Brown lost around 60 dead and 270 wounded. Nonetheless, since the British had pulled up the planks on the only bridge over the Chippewa, and Riall held onto strong defensive positions behind the stream, Brown could not immediately follow up on his success.

Although the impact of this battle on the final outcome of the WAR OF 1812 (1812–15) was minimal, the victory had an important effect on the moral of the U.S. ARMY since regulars stood up to and beat British troops. In commemoration of the Battle of Chippewa, WEST POINT cadets wear gray dress uniforms.

Further reading: Pierre Berton, *Flames across the Border: The Canadian-American Tragedy, 1813–1814* (Boston: Little, Brown, and Company, 1981).

Chisholm v. Georgia (1793)

Considered the most important U.S. SUPREME COURT decision prior to the era of JOHN MARSHALL, *Chisholm v. Georgia* established the precedent that an individual from one state could sue another state without that state's permission in the federal courts. So many people objected to this assault on state sovereignty that the ELEVENTH AMENDMENT to the U.S. CONSTITUTION was passed to prevent similar suits.

The case originated in unpaid expenses incurred by the state of Georgia in 1777 during the REVOLUTIONARY WAR (1775–83). Two commissary agents for Georgia purchased supplies and equipment from Robert Farquhar of Charleston, South Carolina, for $169,613.33. However, although the state of Georgia claimed to have forwarded the MONEY to the agents, they never paid the debt. Farquhar died in 1784, leaving it to his executors, one of whom was Alexander Chisholm (also spelled Chisolme), to try to collect the money. After Farquhar's daughter and heir married Peter Trezevant in 1789, and after the ratification of the U.S. CONSTITUTION, those efforts intensified. The state legislature investigated the claim and decided that it was not liable since it had authorized the payment to the commissaries who were either dead or insolvent. In 1791 the case was taken to the U.S. District Court and decided in favor of the state of Georgia.

Chisholm, as the executor, appealed to the Supreme Court, which first heard the case in August 1792. Since Georgia did not send an attorney to represent the state, the case was postponed until February 1793. Again, Georgia did not send any legal representation, so the case was decided in favor of the plaintiff, although Justice JAMES IREDELL dissented (he had sat on the original circuit court decision). Georgia stalled on payment, leading to more legal wrangling, but in 1794 the state settled. Instead of paying the $500,000 requested in the suit (the original amount plus interest and damages), Georgia agreed to pay approximately $30,000 in state certificates. Trezevant redeemed about $8,000 in certificates to cover legal and other expenses and held on to around $22,000. Subsequent legislative action in Georgia made such state certificates almost worthless so that when Trezevant attempted to redeem them in 1838, negotiations dragged out until 1845, when Georgia at last agreed to pay $22,222.22.

Further reading: Doyle Mathis, "*Chisholm v. Georgia:* Background and Settlement," *Journal of American History* 54 (1967): 19–29.

Choctaw

The Choctaw are NATIVE AMERICANS who once lived in what became the state of Mississippi until they were forced to move west into Indian Territory in the 1820s and 1830s. Expert diplomats, they thrived by playing the French, British, and Spanish against each other. Once the expansion of the United States cut the Choctaw off from outside help, however, they soon fell prey to European-American demands for their lands.

Before the FRENCH AND INDIAN WAR (1754–63), the Choctaw dealt primarily with French traders along the Mississippi River. When the war broke out, the British strangled the flow of French goods by controlling the shipping lanes to New Orleans, and by the end of the conflict the Choctaw had drifted into the British camp. They found that the Anglo-American merchants trekking over the mountains to the east paid handsomely for the deerskins the Indians harvested in the forests. The Choctaw maintained contact with the Spanish through New Orleans, which the French king gave to SPAIN after the war.

When the REVOLUTIONARY WAR (1775–83) broke out, many Choctaw sided with GREAT BRITAIN. However, in 1779 Spain entered the fighting against Britain, and some Choctaw began to doubt whether the British could win; therefore they started to make friendly approaches to Spain and the United States. The British surrendered FLORIDA to Spain at the TREATY OF PARIS (1783), and the Choctaw managed to keep the United States and Spain bidding for their support during the years just after the war.

Though Spanish Florida and LOUISIANA were very sparsely settled, European Americans were now crossing the Appalachian Mountains and soon appeared in the lands to the north of the Choctaw. At the turn of the 18th century, the United States built a military road through Choctaw land, which brought in more European-American immigrants from the East. The U.S. government also opened trading posts in the region to encourage the Choctaw to take up farming and ranching. Many Choctaw adapted to the new ways, some even using slaves to raise COTTON on their plantations. Most were not that rich but began farming while still hunting for deer to obtain hides to trade. They also maintained their diplomatic contacts with Spain to keep the United States from becoming too influential over Choctaw policy.

The U.S. government's trading posts led to many Choctaw falling into debt buying goods at the stores, and in 1804 and 1805, they signed away some of their land in the Mississippi Territory to satisfy those debts. This agreement cut down on hunting grounds, and small parties of Choctaw began to cross into Louisiana to find game. During the WAR OF 1812 (1812–15), many Choctaw fought for the United States during the CREEK WAR (1813–14), though their loyalty did not keep European Americans from demanding more land. Even though the Choctaw instituted a regular government and farmed like European Americans, the U.S. government wanted them to sell all their land and move west. During the 1830s the Choctaw migrated to Oklahoma.

Further reading: James Taylor Carson, *Searching for the Bright Path: The Mississippi Choctaw from Prehistory to Removal* (Lincoln: University of Nebraska Press, 1999).
—George Milne

Church, Benjamin (1734–1778) *Loyalist spy*

Doctor Benjamin Church was a LOYALIST who passed secret information to the British before and during the REVOLUTIONARY WAR (1775–83). Born in Newport, Rhode Island, he graduated from Harvard College in 1754 and studied MEDICINE in London before setting up his practice in Boston. He became involved in the city's Revolutionary politics, working his way into the councils of the RESISTANCE MOVEMENT. He served on the Boston COMMITTEE OF CORRESPONDENCE, and in 1774 he was selected as a delegate to the Massachusetts Provisional Congress. Although some Revolutionaries, such as PAUL REVERE, were suspicious, the Revolutionary leadership was unaware of Church's duplicity. Suspicions probably should have been raised in late April 1775 when Church, supposedly going to Boston to pick up medicines, was captured (he said) and taken before the British general THOMAS GAGE. At this meeting Church gave Gage information about business being discussed by the Massachusetts Provisional Congress and almost a full month's notice of the plans to fortify Bunker Hill.

Events overtook the spy in September 1775 when General NATHANAEL GREENE intercepted a coded letter from Church. The doctor claimed it was a letter to his brother, but when it was deciphered it was clear that he was providing military intelligence to the British. In October 1775 a council of war found Church guilty of communicating with the enemy; he was jailed at Cambridge, Massachusetts, and then sent to Norwich, Connecticut. Claiming ill health, Church later petitioned for a reprieve, and although it took several months, he was paroled to Boston. In 1778 he left Boston in poor health for the WEST INDIES, but his ship disappeared at sea.

Further reading: Allen French, *General Gage's Informers* (Ann Arbor: University of Michigan Press, 1935).
—J. Brett Adams

Cincinnati, Order of the (Society of the Cincinnati, Order of Cincinnati)

In April 1783, as the REVOLUTIONARY WAR (1775–83) was winding down, a group of CONTINENTAL ARMY officers led by General HENRY KNOX established the Order of the Cincinnati. Based on their experience in the war and recognizing the special bond they had developed as a result of their sacrifices, these men wanted to create a society that would help them to sustain their ties. The order took its name from the Roman general Luis Quintius Cincinnatus, who had left his plow to defend the Roman republic, declined a crown after his victories, and returned to his life of agrarian simplicity.

While clinging to a pose of humility, the officers were ambitious and anticipated that their organization would exert political influence in the new republic. They also planned on using the Order of the Cincinnati to lobby for overdue back pay. To add both visibility and additional honor, Knox persuaded GEORGE WASHINGTON to head the order. The Cincinnati, however, made one mistake: They limited membership to officers and their firstborn sons.

The public outcry was tremendous. As an exclusive military club and an inherited privilege, the Order of Cincinnati was "full of danger to the rights of man" and seemed a violation of the ideals of REPUBLICANISM. As Knox explained to Washington, the organization was accused of being "created by a foreign influence, in order to change our form of government." SAMUEL ADAMS proclaimed that the Cincinnati represented "as rapid a Stride towards hereditary Military Nobility as was ever made in so short a Time." The Order's eagle and blue ribbon, instead of being a political asset, became a political liability. One Massachusetts candidate promised to withdraw from the order in an effort to get elected. The Rhode Island legislature went so far as to disenfranchise any one who was a member. Amid this outcry, Washington resigned his leadership role, but the society survived, relegated to being one of many interest groups in the democratic politics of the new United States. Today it continues to exist as a historical and educational organization called Society of the Cincinnati.

Further reading: Minor Myers, *Liberty Without Anarchy: A History of the Society of the Cincinnati* (Charlottesville: University of Press of Virginia, 1983). Society of the Cincinnati Web site: URL: http://www.societyofthecincinnati.

cities and urban life

North American cities underwent a dramatic expansion in the years between 1754 and 1815. At the beginning of the period there were perhaps half a dozen locations with 5,000 or more people; by 1820, there were 35; two cities, New York and Philadelphia, grew from a population of around 20,000 to more than 100,000. Although most people in the Unites States still lived in rural settings, cities had become vital in politics, the ECONOMY, and society.

Much of the RESISTANCE MOVEMENT (1764–75) took place in cities. Boston was the most prominent hub of activity, leading the way in the agitation against the STAMP ACT (1765), customs regulation, and the TEA ACT (1773). One reason cities were so important in the opposition to imperial regulation was the TRADE that was funneled through their warehouses, though the fact that large numbers of people congregated in cities was also a major factor. Along the wharves of every port there were SEAMEN and dockworkers with plenty of grievances against GREAT BRITAIN and eager to join a crowd. Large numbers of ARTISANS also populated the cities, and they became increasingly articulate and schooled in the ideology of REPUBLICANISM. Many merchants and LAWYERS also resided in cities, providing further leadership for the resistance movement. In short, it was in the cities that each level of society met in enough of a concentration to provide an explosive mix that resulted in the AMERICAN REVOLUTION.

Most North American cities suffered during the REVOLUTIONARY WAR (1775–83); Boston, Newport, New York, Philadelphia, and Charleston were each occupied by the British army at some time, creating tremendous upheaval. When the British arrived, some people fled, buildings were commandeered, churches were turned into stables, and LOYALISTS moved to the cities for asylum. When the British later evacuated, the Loyalists either left with their protectors or remained behind to be harassed by the Revolutionaries. More people moved in to replace the exiles, and the cities began to rebuild. Of the five major colonial cities, only Newport failed to recover rapidly, though its decline

was due more to the competition from upstart Providence than to the effects of the war.

Cities became the locus of a contentious political scene in the early national era. The same artisans who had been so important to the resistance movement and revolution now viewed themselves as the bulwarks of society and rightful heirs to republican CITIZENSHIP. Initially the FEDERALIST PARTY used ties of patronage and the promise of commercial prosperity to attract the city voter. By the mid-1790s, however, mechanics, as artisans called themselves, asserted an equality that seemed more in concert with the ideals of the DEMOCRATIC-REPUBLICAN PARTY. This shift in allegiance contributed to the victory of THOMAS JEFFERSON in the ELECTION OF 1800. Artisans believed that as producers and craftsmen—men who lived by the work they did—they had a special role within the republic. No longer was the ideal to be a gentleman who did not labor with his hands; now the muscular arm holding a tool and proclaiming "With Hammer and Hand, All Arts Flourish and Stand" became a symbol of the republic.

Concentrated in cities, mechanics and merchants helped to keep commerce moving. If cities had been central to the colonial economy, they became even more crucial to the economy of the new republic. While rural areas produced an agricultural surplus that could be exported overseas, it was the dock facilities, artisanal production, and banking services that kept goods moving. When FRANCE and Great Britain went to war in 1793, creating greater economic opportunity for the United States, cities became even more important.

City life, however, was not easy. Because it was difficult and expensive to develop the land on the edge of urban areas, builders relied on multifamily dwellings. Crowding became typical of these urban spaces, with high-cost housing and great disparities between rich and poor. Streets were unpaved and often filthy. The most efficient garbage collection system were the hogs that roamed the streets. There were no sewers; people used privies in their backyards. Drinking water was not easy to come by since everyone depended on a handful of wells or water carted from the countryside. DISEASE AND EPIDEMICS spread rapidly: Before and during the Revolutionary War, SMALLPOX was the biggest fear, while in the 1790s and early 1800s there were repeated outbreaks of YELLOW FEVER that struck several cities. The affluent headed for the safety of the country during such epidemics. Those who remained behind, usually the poor, died by the hundreds and even thousands.

Although by 1800 many cities required building with brick, there were still many wooden structures that burned all too easily in a fire. With the city depending only on volunteer fire companies, it was not unusual for entire blocks to burn down in one conflagration. Police departments did not exist, either. The main deterrent to CRIME was the night watch and a constable or two who were more concerned with gaining a reward than crime prevention. Prostitutes plied their trade all too openly, and public drunkenness and raucous behavior violated the sensibilities of many. Disorderly mobs could form at any moment in a tavern brawl or over some supposed affront. In case of popular disorder or RIOTS, the mayor or some other municipal officer would try to step into the breach and use his personal connection with some in the crowd—the cities were still small enough that the official might know someone—to avert too much violence.

If there was a nasty quality to urban life in this period, there were also many positive features as well. The same streets that could be so repulsive could also be the source of entertainment; urban dwellers seemed to relish the city's hustle and bustle. On special occasions crowds numbering into the thousands gathered in celebration or to watch a parade march by. Booths and small shops sold food and other items, and TAVERNS and THEATERS added to the city's enjoyments, offering a level of entertainment impossible to match in the countryside. Printing presses rolled out newspapers, books, and pamphlets, providing an exciting intellectual life. Communal activity was also easier in the city, where there were greater varieties of groups. Although it might be difficult to sustain a larger sense of community, it was easier to develop more personal networks along job, ethnic, or religious lines. Free AFRICAN AMERICANS, for example, flocked to cities to interact with others of their own race. Like the African Americans, other groups created their own institutions, including schools and churches. Neighborhoods began to emerge that developed a particular character all their own.

Finally, although there was a great deal of POVERTY in cities, there was also economic opportunity. African Americans sought to gain personal independence by moving to urban areas. Not every job was open to them, but many became storekeepers, ran oyster bars, or cut hair. Large numbers of African-American men found work on the waterfront or signed on as sailors. European Americans, too, came to the city in the hope of new careers. A building boom meant jobs for many laborers and skilled artisans, and the expansion of overseas commerce provided further skilled employment as shipbuilders, sailmakers, blockmakers, and coopers. For those further up the economic scale, starting as a clerk could be the first step to becoming a merchant and owning one of the fancy multistory brick houses that dominated the most prominent streets. While women had less opportunity, the city offered a more independent existence than the countryside since it was possible for a woman to find employment as a seamstress or in the service industry.

Cities in the Revolutionary and early national period were vibrant and expanding. Despite war and upheaval, or perhaps because of war and upheaval, they remained the epicenter of much of American life.

See also IMMIGRATION; POPULAR CULTURE; POPULATION TRENDS.

Further reading: Carl Bridenbaugh, *Cities in Revolt: Urban Life in America, 1743–1776* (New York: Knopf, 1955); Paul A. Gilje, *The Road to Mobocracy: Popular Disorder in New York City, 1763–1834* (Chapel Hill: University of North Carolina Press, 1987); Gary B. Nash, *The Urban Crucible: Social Change, Political Consciousness, and the Origins of the American Revolution* (Cambridge, Mass.: Harvard University Press, 1979); Alfred F. Young, *Liberty Tree: Ordinary People and the American Revolution* (New York: New York University Press, 2006).

citizenship

The concept of citizenship underwent a fundamental transformation during the Revolutionary era from a relatively restricted notion centered on the educated and politically active to a more inclusive idea that encompassed all who owed allegiance to the United States. Simultaneously, there was a shift from viewing everyone as subjects of a king to seeing each individual as a citizen of the nation. In some ways these changes resulted from ongoing trends in the Anglo-American world; in other, more fundamental ways they were an outgrowth of the AMERICAN REVOLUTION and rise of the ideal of equality.

Prior to the 18th century the key element of national identity in the Anglo-American world centered on being a subject of the king. The notion of citizenship, which had antecedents in both the ancient and medieval world, implied civic responsibility and participation in the regular political process. All Englishmen and Anglo-American colonists were subjects and only a limited number of adult males—the aristocracy, large landowners, and a few others—were citizens who were directly involved in the political process and voted. In the beginning of the 18th century, in part as a result of the Glorious Revolution of 1688, which asserted parliamentary supremacy over the Crown, and in part as a reflection of the ENLIGHTENMENT's emphasis on nature and reason, Anglo-American ideas on citizenship were in flux and some thinkers—especially the radical WHIGS—began to push for an even wider definition of citizenship. In North America the situation was less clear than it was in GREAT BRITAIN. On the one hand, few aristocrats and members of the upper gentry settled in the British colonies, which theoretically should have limited the number of politically active individuals. On the other, the electorate expanded because it was relatively easy to gain enough property to obtain the franchise. Moreover, many colonial American leaders read the radical Whig ideas and came to see them as apt descriptions of the ideal English constitution. These factors brought more adult European Americans into the political process and potential inclusion as citizens.

If increasing numbers of people came to view themselves as citizens during the colonial period in British North America, many more remained excluded. Immigrants other than from GREAT BRITAIN posed some problems since they technically owed their allegiance to a foreign power. In 1740 Parliament passed the Plantation Act, which allowed all non-Catholic aliens to become English subjects if they paid a small fee, resided in a colony for seven years, received the sacraments at a Protestant church, swore allegiance to the king, and declared that they were Christians. (Special provisions were made for JEWS as non-Christians and QUAKERS who would not swear oaths). Naturalized foreigners, if they met the other qualifications for voting, could participate in the colony's civil affairs and thus take on the trappings of citizenship. Whether British, foreign, or colonial-born, however, such privileges were not extended to minors, women, and those without property. Although the British government claimed that NATIVE AMERICANS living within the boundaries of the North American colonies were subjects of the king, most Indians were excluded from any notion of civic responsibility to the colonies or the king. Similarly, since almost all AFRICAN AMERICANS were slaves before 1775, they, too, were subjects but would in no way be considered citizens.

The RESISTANCE MOVEMENT (1764–75) and the REVOLUTIONARY WAR (1775–83) threw the whole issue of national identity and citizenship into a state of turmoil. In many ways the opposition to imperial regulation hinged on the status of colonial Americans as citizens and subjects. If all colonial Americans were merely subjects, then they had best heed the laws of Parliament; if, on the other hand, they were citizens, then they had the right to participate in the decision-making process that governed them. Confusing the issue further, during the 1760s and 1770s the SONS OF LIBERTY, COMMITTEES OF CORRESPONDENCE, and other ad hoc Revolutionary organizations increasingly turned to the populace at large—whether they voted or not—to collect in crowds and express themselves politically. Although the committees might bring the people into the political process under the heading of "inhabitants," ultimately this action awakened a civic consciousness among larger numbers of people—many of whom were propertyless males, but some of whom were women, minors, and African Americans. Whether the leadership of the Revolution liked it or not, more and more people came to think of themselves as *citizens*, with the rights that went with that word.

Independence complicated the situation even more. First, there was the fundamental division between those who wished to remain loyal subjects to the king and those who supported the Revolution. From the point of view of the LOYALISTS, Revolutionaries were traitors whose actions had negated their civic rights. The Whig position was more awkward. The Revolutionaries compelled compliance with their cause by insisting on oaths of allegiance and punished those who would not comply by driving them from their homes and seizing their property. However, the Revolutionaries struggled for a rationale for this behavior since they were the ones who had shattered the existing bonds of society. The SECOND CONTINENTAL CONGRESS clarified its position on the transition from royal government on June 24, 1776, as it was about to declare independence from Great Britain, by resolving "That all persons residing within the United Colonies, and deriving protection from the laws of the same, owe allegiance to the said law." In other words, by remaining within the bounds of the rebellious colonies—about to become states—each individual owed allegiance to that colony/state and not the king. From this perspective, allegiance and citizenship were created upon the formation of the states. In 1805 the U.S. SUPREME COURT reiterated this position in *McIlvaine v. Coxe* by stating "that those residing at the time of the revolution in the territory separating itself from the parent country, are subject to the new government, and become members of the new community, on the ground either of tacit consent evidenced by their abiding in such territory; or on the principle that every individual is bound by the majority." Only in the 1830s did the Court back off from this position and allow that allegiance might have been undecided until the TREATY OF PARIS (1783).

Second, throughout the war, into the 1780s, and even beyond, it remained unclear whether citizenship would be rooted in the individual state or in the national government. One measure of this confusion can be seen in the fact that states set up the initial procedures for naturalization. Pennsylvania, New York, North Carolina, and Vermont spelled out the method whereby an immigrant became a citizen in their constitutions. Maryland, Virginia, South Carolina, and Georgia relied on legislation to articulate naturalization procedures. The result was a hodgepodge of laws that set varied residency requirements. In Pennsylvania an immigrant had to wait only one year before he became a "free denizen," while in neighboring Maryland the immigrant needed to be a resident for seven years before he had the same rights as a "natural born subject of this state." (As these provisions indicate with their reference to "free denizens" and "subjects of this state," the language of citizenship had not become fully developed during the 1770s and 1780s.)

To make the situation even more confusing, neither the ARTICLES OF CONFEDERATION nor the U.S. CONSTITUTION defined citizenship. Both documents, however, included some mention of citizenship. The Articles stipulated that "the free inhabitants of these states (paupers, vagabonds, and fugitives from justice excepted) shall be entitled to all privileges and immunities of free citizens in the several states," and the Constitution included a similar provision by asserting, "The Citizens of each State shall be entitled to all Privileges and Immunities of Citizens in the Several States." The Constitution did have other provisions concerning citizenship, including preventing anyone not born in the United States from becoming president and indicating the number of years an immigrant had to be a citizen before he could be elected to the Senate or the House of Representatives. The issue of defining citizenship remained unclear until the Fourteenth Amendment, passed after the Civil War.

On both the state and national level, however, Revolutionaries furthered the idea of citizenship by guaranteeing the rights of individuals with written declarations. Several state constitutions had their own BILL OF RIGHTS protecting a host of liberties and thereby infusing even those who did not vote with a belief that they as citizens were protected by government. Central to this development was freedom of the press, which, as the Virginia Declaration of Rights in 1776 made clear, was "one of the greatest bulwarks of liberty," and which ensured an informed citizenry. Although the FEDERALISTS initially opposed a Bill of Rights for the government under the Constitution, they agreed to the first 10 amendments as a price for getting the document ratified (see CONSTITUTION, RATIFICATION OF). These declarations on the state and national level increased public awareness about the rights of citizens as they applied to nearly everyone in society.

During the 1790s and into the 1800s, citizenship became a partisan issue. The FEDERALIST PARTY and the DEMOCRATIC-REPUBLICAN PARTY approached citizenship differently, especially when it came to laws concerning naturalization. Leaders in the Federalist Party tended to follow British thinking concerning nationality—and hence citizenship. They held that national origin was at the core of citizenship and pushed for laws that made it more difficult for immigrants to become citizens. The Democratic-Republicans saw nationality and citizenship as more a function of allegiance and residence. The first naturalization law passed by Congress in 1790 was relatively lenient, allowing an immigrant to become a citizen after two years of residence. In 1795 Congress extended the waiting period to five years, and in 1798, during the height of the crisis over the QUASI-WAR (1798–1800) with FRANCE, the Federalist Party pushed the immigrant's wait until 14 years—an action that fit their ideological approach to citizenship and also suited their political interests since the Federalist Party believed that most immigrant citizens voted for the Democratic-Republicans. After THOMAS JEFFERSON became president, a Democratic-Repub-

lican–dominated Congress in 1802 reduced the waiting period back to five years.

Besides the laws concerning IMMIGRATION, there were other political debates that centered on citizenship. Several members of the embryonic Federalist Party challenged the election of Swiss-born ALBERT GALLATIN to the Senate in 1793, claiming he had never completed the naturalization process in any one state and therefore did not meet the nine-year citizenship rule to qualify for the Senate. Gallatin had arrived in the United States in 1780 and had thereafter moved from state to state until 1785, when he settled in Pennsylvania. In the meantime, he began but did not complete the process of becoming a citizen of Virginia. Gallatin responded by declaring: "Every man who took an active part in the American Revolution, was a citizen according to the great laws of nature and reason" regardless of the letter of the laws passed regarding naturalization. Claiming to be "one of the people," he argued he was a citizen and should not be kept from his seat in the Senate. In part reflecting the partisanship that was beginning to permeate the national government, and in part reflecting the ambiguous and conflicting notions of citizenship, the Senate refused to seat Gallatin.

The Federalist Party also raised questions about citizenship during the debates over the LOUISIANA PURCHASE (1803). By this time the Federalist Party was in the minority and struggling to maintain its presence in national politics. The Louisiana Purchase Treaty provided that all of the current inhabitants—hitherto Spanish subjects or French citizens—would have full citizenship within the United States. This stipulation violated the naturalization law and, to the Federalist Party leaders, seemed to go beyond the constitutional treaty-making power. From their point of view, if the national government had the right to arbitrarily add citizens from foreign nations, then it could simply pass legislation conferring citizenship on anyone and everyone it wanted and thereby overwhelm political opponents and further weaken the voice of regions like New England where the Federalist Party remained strong. The Federalist Party may have had a valid argument, but it had little impact on the treaty's final ratification.

By the early 1800s the idea of citizenship, despite being contested politically, was becoming intimately attached to nationality. The FRENCH REVOLUTION (1789–99) contributed to this development by seizing upon the term *citizen* as a new label that asserted the equality of mankind. This practice leaped across the ATLANTIC OCEAN and was embraced by the Democratic-Republican Party in the 1790s. Even women were included in this new identity as "citizeness." Although members of the Federalist Party detested the notion that all inhabitants were "citizens," the term became more and more prominent as the nation moved away from a discussion of "free denizens" and "subjects of this state" to a rhetoric that centered on the rights and obligations of citizenship.

Although members of the Federalist Party rejected the French revolutionary rhetoric, they took a dramatic step to extend the definition of citizenship with legislation in 1796 to protect SEAMEN born in the United States from IMPRESSMENT into the British navy. These documents—called PROTECTIONS—were certificates issued by magistrates in any U.S. court that provided the name of the sailor, his place of birth, and a description. They became official when signed by the sailor, a magistrate, and a witness. Whether intentional or not, Congress had extended its protective umbrella to some of the poorest men in the country and infused them with the identity of citizens. This extension of citizenship became contested ground in FOREIGN AFFAIRS. The State Department emerged as an active agent in protecting U.S. citizens abroad—mainly poor sailors—not only against impressment by Great Britain but also from seizure by the Barbary States. Under the Jeffersonians the national government also defended naturalized citizens when the British insisted that nativity should dictate nationality.

Citizenship expanded with the extension of suffrage to more European Americans. Vermont provided for universal white manhood suffrage in 1777, and Kentucky did the same when it became a state in 1792. Over the next couple of decades, as voting rights were extended in state after state, the idea of citizenship spread—even to the few African Americans who could vote.

But the idea of citizenship during the early republic was not limited to those who participated in the political process. Without a king, the notion of being a "subject" dissolved, and in its place rose a sense of being a citizen, regardless of gender and sometimes even regardless of race. Although republican motherhood may have been fully developed only among the upper echelons of society in the United States, the idea that women were the special repositories of virtue responsible for training the next generation of republican citizens meant that women had a civic role that allowed them to claim citizenship. Indeed, this identity reached downward in society to anyone who had any rights and independence. When a young servant girl in New York was asked where her mistress was, she responded that she had no mistress—only slaves had mistresses—and that she was a female citizen.

Although most African Americans remained excluded from any notion of citizenship—despite their bizarre inclusion in calculating REPRESENTATION in the Constitution under the THREE-FIFTHS CLAUSE—some free blacks did vote and asserted their rights as citizens. It was even possible for some African Americans to sue for their freedom based on the Declaration of Rights in the Massachusetts constitution of 1780. Possibilities of citizenship for African Americans, however, remained limited, and several states, especially but not exclusively in the South, denied rights to both free and slave African Americans.

Throughout the early republic, despite the dramatic changes in the understanding of citizenship, Native Americans were not considered citizens of the United States, with a few exceptions in the areas settled the longest by European Americans. All Indians did not become citizens until the Native American Citizenship Act of 1924.

Further reading: Richard D. Brown, *The Strength of a People: The Idea of an Informed Citizenry in America, 1650–1870* (Chapel Hill: University of North Carolina Press, 1996); James H. Kettner, *The Development of American Citizenship, 1608–1870* (Chapel Hill: University of North Carolina Press, 1978).

Claiborne, Ferdinand Leigh (1772–1815) *American military officer*

Ferdinand Leigh Claiborne was born in Sussex County, Virginia, on March 9, 1772. He entered the U.S. ARMY in 1793 as an infantry ensign, was promoted to lieutenant in 1794, and became captain in 1799. He left the army in 1802, and in that same year he married Magdalene Hutchins, the daughter of a British army colonel.

Claiborne was named brigadier general of the Mississippi MILITIA on February 5, 1811. When tensions with the CREEK faction called RED STICKS arose, he recruited a regiment of Mississippi volunteers and was put in command of forts on the Alabama and Tombigbee rivers. Many people blamed Claiborne for the FORT MIMS MASSACRE (August 30, 1813), saying he had not acted aggressively enough, even though he had been ordered to take a defensive posture. He redeemed himself at the BATTLE OF THE HOLY GROUND (December 23, 1813) when he destroyed a town belonging to the Red Sticks.

Claiborne was elected to the Mississippi legislative council, taking office on February 4, 1815, and presided over the legislature's deliberations. He died in Natchez, Mississippi, on March 22, 1815.

Further reading: Karl Davis, "'Remember Fort Mims': Reinterpreting the Origins of the Creek War," *Journal of the Early Republic* 22 (2002): 611–636.

—Stephen A. Martin

Claiborne, William C. C. (1775–1817) *jurist, congressman, first governor of Louisiana*

William Charles Cole Claiborne was born in Sussex County, Virginia, and studied at the College of William and Mary before moving to New York City at age 15. After working as assistant to John Beckley, clerk of the House of Representatives, in New York and Philadelphia, he studied law in Virginia and then settled in Tennessee in 1794. Governor JOHN SEVIER appointed him to the newly created Tennessee Supreme Court in 1796. A supporter of THOMAS JEFFERSON, Claiborne resigned from the court in 1797 to run for Congress. After he had served two terms in the House of Representatives, Jefferson appointed him territorial governor of Mississippi in 1801.

Claiborne became governor of the Orleans Territory from its organization in 1804 until it entered the union as the state of LOUISIANA in 1812, when he was elected the state's first governor. In Louisiana Claiborne worked well with the French-speaking population and had a mixed relationship with General JAMES WILKINSON, especially during the conspiracy led by AARON BURR, when Wilkinson asserted military control over New Orleans. Following orders from President JAMES MADISON, Claiborne annexed Baton Rouge and several parishes of West FLORIDA to Louisiana in 1810. He also brutally suppressed the DESLONDES REVOLT of African-American slaves in early 1811. During the WAR OF 1812 (1812–15) he had some disagreements with General ANDREW JACKSON, who placed Louisiana under martial law in late 1814 before the BATTLE OF NEW ORLEANS (January 7, 1815). Stepping down as governor in 1816, Claiborne was named to the Senate in 1817, but he died on November 23, 1817, before he could take his seat in WASHINGTON, D.C.

Further reading: Joseph T. Hatfield, *William Claiborne: Jeffersonian Centurion in the American Southwest* (Lafayette: University of Southwestern Louisiana, 1976).
—Stephen A. Martin

Clark, Abraham (1726–1794) *New Jersey politician*

A signer of the DECLARATION OF INDEPENDENCE, Abraham Clark was a supporter of radical democratic ideas during the Revolutionary era. Before the AMERICAN REVOLUTION Clark was a man of modest affluence. He owned a farm in Elizabethtown, New Jersey, and earned some of his income as a surveyor. During the 1760s and 1770s he held local public offices, including sheriff of Essex County. In 1774 he became a member of the New Jersey committee of safety, and he was elected to the provincial legislature in 1775. In June 1776 New Jersey's Revolutionary government sent Clark, an advocate of independence, to the SECOND CONTINENTAL CONGRESS. He remained a congressman for much of the REVOLUTIONARY WAR (1775–83) and also served a term in the late 1780s. However, he was not always an active participant in congressional deliberations, taking pride in his lack of speech making and often absenting himself because of obligations in New Jersey.

In Congress, Clark advocated civilian control of the military; at one point he questioned General GEORGE WASHINGTON's judgment, stating, "Tho I believe him honest, I think him fallible." He also opposed the centralizing policies of ROBERT MORRIS and supported STATES' RIGHTS. Clark viewed the national government only as a useful instrument for protecting New Jersey interests. He attended the ANNAPOLIS CONVENTION (1786) but declined to go to the CONSTITUTIONAL CONVENTION (1787) in Philadelphia. He was a lukewarm supporter of the U.S. CONSTITUTION but accepted the document after there was a promise of a BILL OF RIGHTS. He participated in a contested election to the House of Representatives in 1789 and was denied his seat. However, he was elected to Congress in 1791 and quickly became allied with JAMES MADISON and the nascent DEMOCRATIC-REPUBLICAN PARTY before his death on September 15, 1794.

Clark outlined his political ideas in an anonymously published pamphlet called *The True Policy of New Jersey* (1786). This essay supported the passage of paper-MONEY laws that would help poor farmers and ARTISANS. It also articulated a radical democratic vision of society consistent with his other positions. Clark declared that it was the farmers and mechanics who alone had changed New Jersey "from a howling wilderness to pleasant fields, gardens, towns, and cities." He disparaged LAWYERS, merchants, and speculators, while declaring that moneyed individuals who were not "under the necessity of getting bread by industry" lived "by the labour of the honest farmer and mechanic." From this perspective, ultimately it was "the common people" on whom the safety of "rights and liberties" depended.

Further reading: Ruth Bogin, *Abraham Clark and the Quest for Equality in the Revolutionary Era, 1774–1794* (Rutherford, N.J.: Fairleigh Dickinson University Press, 1982).

Clark, George Rogers (1752–1818) *frontier militia officer*

George Rogers Clark was born in Virginia on November 19, 1752, the son of second-generation Scottish immigrant planters. One of his younger brothers was WILLIAM CLARK of the LEWIS AND CLARK EXPEDITION (1803–06). At age 20 Clark journeyed to Pittsburgh, Pennsylvania; traveled by boat down the Ohio River; and claimed land near modern-day Wheeling, West Virginia. He had hardly begun his life as a farmer when DUNMORE'S WAR (1774) broke out. During that conflict, Clark joined the Kentucky settlers in defending their homes against Indian raids.

When the REVOLUTIONARY WAR (1775–83) began, Clark was sent by a group of settlers who wanted inde-

George Rogers Clark led a successful surprise attack on British lieutenant governor Henry Hamilton at Vincennes in 1779. *(Filson Historical Society, Louisville, Kentucky)*

pendence to acquire gunpowder from Virginia governor PATRICK HENRY; he spent many months transporting the gunpowder to the FRONTIER. In 1777 NATIVE AMERICANS of the Ohio tribes, primarily SHAWNEE, MIAMI, and Wyandot, rejected the Revolutionary claim to Kentucky and, with British backing, attacked the settlers in an effort to drive them away. Clark, now a major of the MILITIA and in charge of defending the settlements, decided on the seemingly outrageous scheme of cutting the Indian supply lines by capturing two British forts at the towns of Kaskaskia, on the Mississippi River in present-day Illinois, and VINCENNES, on the Wabash River on the present-day Indiana-Illinois border. The plan would require a small force to travel more than 400 miles through wilderness with few supplies. However, Clark convinced Governor Henry that the element of surprise would make up for the difficulties. His plan was approved, and he was promoted to lieutenant colonel.

In June 1778 Clark led 175 men down the Ohio River from Pittsburgh to the mouth of the Tennessee River. To travel the rest of the way by boat would have allowed their enemies to discover them easily, so the small army marched across country for 125 miles, reaching Kaskaskia in six days and easily taking the unsuspecting fort. Upon learning that Fort Sackville in Vincennes was undefended, Clark sent Captain Leonard Helm to occupy the outpost. The seizure of Fort Sackville was short-lived, however, as HENRY HAMILTON, known as "Hair Buyer"—for purchasing scalps taken by Indians—recaptured the fort for the British using Canadian militia and Native Americans. Clark led an army of 170 men through the cold and wet of winter and across a broad, flooded plain around the Wabash River to Vincennes. By the time they arrived on February 23, 1779, the men were exhausted, low on ammunition—and outnumbered by the British defenders. Clark decided to convince the British that the Revolutionaries had the larger force by flying a number of FLAGS and beginning siege operations, while keeping his main body out of sight. To further intimidate the British, he executed some Native Americans in plain sight of the fort. Believing he was surrounded and had few options, Hamilton surrendered on February 25, 1779.

Clark's seizure of the two forts helped to neutralize the British forces in the West but did not represent a resounding victory. He was unable to extend his campaign and capture his main objective—DETROIT. Although most textbooks assert that these victories also allowed the United States to claim the Northwest after the war, and that Clark earned the nickname "conqueror of the Northwest" for his efforts, the war in the region continued after 1779. Decisive Native American victories at the BATTLE OF SANDUSKY (June 4–5, 1782) and the BATTLE OF BLUE LICKS (August 19, 1782) convinced many Indians that by 1783 they were winning the war in the Ohio Valley. Moreover, the conflict in the Ohio River Valley did not end with the TREATY OF PARIS (1783) and continued almost unabated until the BATTLE OF FALLEN TIMBERS (August 20, 1794).

Whatever fame Clark may have earned during the Revolutionary War, his life thereafter was marked by failure. He had borrowed substantial amounts of MONEY from traders to finance his war efforts; but the records authorizing the Virginia government to repay him were destroyed during the war, and repayments authorized by the United States in the 1780s were never made. To evade his creditors, Clark signed his property over to his relatives and, living on a small tract of land, became a loner and an alcoholic. He had a stroke in 1812 that partially paralyzed him, and he died of a second stroke on February 13, 1818.

Further reading: Patrick Griffin, *American Leviathan: Empire, Nation, and Revolutionary Frontier* (New York: Hill & Wang, 2007); Landon Y. Jones, *William Clark and the Shaping of the West* (New York: Hill and Wang, 2004); George Macgregor Waller, *The American Revolution in the West* (Chicago: Nelson-Hall, 1976).

—Michael L. Cox

Clark, William (1770–1838) *U.S. military officer, explorer*

An influential figure in the early republic, William Clark helped to explore and describe the North American West with his partner MERIWETHER LEWIS during the LEWIS AND CLARK EXPEDITION (1803–06). He then became closely involved with the management of western lands and their inhabitants in the decades of settlement that followed.

Born on August 1, 1770, Clark was from a prominent Virginia family whose members included his older brother, GEORGE ROGERS CLARK. In 1784 he moved with his family to Kentucky, where his parents established an estate called Mulberry Hill. With a minimal formal EDUCATION, he learned how to survey land, manage slave labor, and explore the natural world. He also developed his skills in drawing and cartography. His direct and pragmatic mindset later served him well in his years as an explorer and FRONTIER settler and administrator.

Clark began his military career early, and he may have joined his brother as an Indian fighter at age 16. By 1789 he was serving in a volunteer MILITIA under Colonel John Hardin in his fight against NATIVE AMERICANS near the White River. Clark's military experience continued throughout the early 1790s, and in March 1792 he was commissioned a lieutenant of infantry in the Legion of the United States (see ARMY, U.S.). Besides seeing action in several battles, including the BATTLE OF FALLEN TIMBERS (August 20, 1794), he was given military assignments to negotiate with Native Americans. Clark acted as a representative to the CHICKASAW near Memphis, trading rifles and ammunition in exchange for allegiance to the United States against SPAIN. He met Meriwether Lewis in 1794 during the campaigns against the Native Americans in Ohio.

In 1796 Clark resigned his commission and returned to Louisville, where he tried to salvage the fortune of his brother George Rogers Clark, who was deeply in debt. On June 19, 1803, Meriwether Lewis wrote, inviting him to join in the transcontinental expedition proposed by President THOMAS JEFFERSON to explore the Far West and (it was hoped) discover an all-water route to the PACIFIC OCEAN. As a man who had lived on and explored the frontier for most of his life, Clark was drawn to the planned expedition and brought with him the practical experience and resourcefulness necessary for such a dangerous trip. Beginning in May 1804, for more than two years the LEWIS AND CLARK EXPEDITION traveled up the Missouri River, across the Rocky Mountains, down the Columbia River to the Pacific Ocean, and back again to St. Louis. During the return trip, Clark separated from Lewis for a while to navigate part of the Yellowstone River. Throughout the epic journey, he took responsibility for many of the practical tasks necessary to survival, drew the maps, measured mile-age with remarkable accuracy, and described the new western landscape through his diaries and drawings.

In 1807 Clark resigned from the army and became brigadier general of the militia for the LOUISIANA Territory he had just explored. In 1808 he married Julia Hancock, a young woman from his native Virginia. Living in St. Louis, Clark became superintendent for Indian affairs in the Upper Louisiana (later called Missouri) Territory; his old friend Meriwether Lewis was governor of the territory. In the first years after their triumphant return, both men were preoccupied with establishing order in the administration of the West. Clark fared better financially than his friend Lewis and often acted as his de facto caretaker as Lewis's mental state became more volatile.

After Lewis's death in 1809, Clark declined the president's offer to make him Lewis's successor but eventually accepted a later opportunity to be governor in 1813. During the WAR OF 1812 (1812–15), Clark's organized the defense of St. Louis but met with limited success when he led an expedition to Prairie du Chien on the Upper Mississippi, as his forces were attacked there and downriver at Rock Island. After the war ended, Clark, remained active as a businessman trading on the frontier and as a government official negotiating treaties with Indians.

He gained the respect of many Native Americans and was known as the "Red-Headed Chief." If he could be sympathetic to Indians, he remained an imperious slave owner, for many years refusing to free York, the African-American slave who had traveled with him on the Lewis and Clark Expedition (though York was eventually freed through persistent badgering of his master). While historians now contend that Clark's actions as an explorer, administrator, and businessman compromised the future vitality of western Indian tribes, he continued to act for what he considered to be their best interests. He left an ambiguous legacy of conquest and conciliation, which was not unusual for Indian agents during the early 19th century. William Clark died in St. Louis on September 1, 1838.

See also LOUISIANA PURCHASE.

Further reading: John Bakeless, *Lewis and Clark: Partners in Discovery* (New York: William Morrow, 1947); Thomas P. Slaughter, *Exploring Lewis and Clark: Reflections on Men and Wilderness* (New York: Random House, 2003); Reuben Gold Thwaites, ed., *Original Journals of the Lewis and Clark Expedition* (1904–05; reprint, New York: Arno Press, 1969).

—Eleanor H. McConnell

classicism

Classicism, the following of ancient Greek and Roman models, greatly influenced the political discourse of the

18th century on both sides of the ATLANTIC OCEAN. Next to Christianity, classicism was the predominant intellectual pursuit in the colonies and served as the basis for university EDUCATION, professional practice, and acceptance in the ranks of cultured society. Alongside the political philosophy of JOHN LOCKE and MONTESQUIEU, classicism helped shape the ideological origins of the AMERICAN REVOLUTION.

Though distanced from the Greek and Roman world by nearly 2,000 years, educated gentlemen commonly referenced ancient LITERATURE to lend strength to their discussion of virtue and theories of government. By 1750 the pattern for such discussion was well established during a period in which the COMMONWEALTHMEN wrote extensively on the dangers of political vice and the slippery slope leading to tyrannical rule; in the process, these writers commonly referred to the fall of the Roman republic and the rise of imperial power as their primary case study.

As tensions between the colonists and GREAT BRITAIN intensified, the ideological architects of the American Revolution readily identified with the WHIGS' application of classical models in their own critique of British ministerial control. The British opposition theorists signaled a warning that corruption and private interest posed an immediate threat to LIBERTY even under the best of constitutional arrangements, and after 1763 the colonists perceived British taxation and TRADE policies as the fulfillment of a conspiratorial prophecy and an invasive attempt on the part of parliament to subvert the people's liberty, both at home and abroad.

Through their Greek and Latin education, the revolutionary leaders had direct access to the classical literary canon, which they believed contained the best source for understanding the dynamics of republican government and the accompanying dangers of corruption, mob rule, and tyranny. Some historians have described this ideological impulse as REPUBLICANISM; more than a manifestation of John Locke's liberal self-interest, the American Revolution represented a quest for political virtue and civic self-sacrifice, informed by axiomatic principles in the classical world that provided the necessary tools to construct and maintain a modern utopian republic.

For the Founding Fathers, the character and quality of the citizenry served as liberty's ultimate defense. In contrast to what they perceived as the corrupting influences evident in the British political system, typified by self-interest, self-aggrandizement, and luxury, the colonists set their aspirations on the rustic "Country Party" values of thrift, industry, and simplicity. In their writings they denounced Julius Caesar and glorified such Roman heroes as Cato the Younger and Cicero, statesmen who had used their oratorical skill and sacrificed their lives in the face of tyranny. JOHN ADAMS, the most persistent advocate for a tripartate

system of government, expounded on Cicero's description of the failure of ancient republics to preserve a balance of powers. THOMAS JEFFERSON looked to the writings of Virgil to inform his vision for the new republic—a pastoral, agrarian order anchored by a virtuous citizenry.

Although classicism was significant in the 18th century, historians have debated the extent to which Greek and Roman ideology shaped the origin and course of the American Revolution. Other intellectual currents, including Christianity and the ENLIGHTENMENT tradition, were also necessary components of change. Whether classicism provided only a common rhetorical resource or constituted the substance of the Revolutionary ideological impulse, the models and anti-models from antiquity legitimized the break with Britain and provided the necessary intellectual foundation to inspire faith in the success of the Revolutionary enterprise.

Further reading: Bernard Bailyn, *The Ideological Origins of the American Revolution* (Cambridge, Mass.: Harvard University Press, 1967); Carl J. Richard, *The Founders and the Classics: Greece, Rome, and the American Enlightenment* (Cambridge. Mass.: Harvard University Press, 1994); Caroline Winterer, *The Culture of Classicism; Ancient Greece and Rome in American Intellectual Life, 1780–1910* (Baltimore: Johns Hopkins University Press, 2002); Gordon S. Wood, *The Creation of the American Republic, 1776–1787* (Chapel Hill: University of North Carolina Press, 1969).

—Daniel Moy

Clay, Henry (1777–1852) *U.S. senator, Speaker of the House of Representatives*

Born in Hanover County, Virginia, Henry Clay moved to Kentucky as a young lawyer and became one of the most prominent politicians of the first half of the 19th century. Clay had a limited formal EDUCATION, but at age 15, through the influence of his stepfather, he became the secretary to the prominent lawyer GEORGE WYTHE in the state chancery office in Richmond. Wythe recognized Clay's intelligence and abilities and taught him law and history. Clay completed his legal training with Robert Brooke, Virginia's attorney general, and was admitted to the bar in 1797. He then moved to Kentucky and set up practice in Lexington, where his skills as a speaker and lawyer quickly earned him a reputation as a first-rate attorney. He married Lucretia Hart in 1799 and began to develop his own peculiar brand of politics as a member of the DEMOCRATIC-REPUBLICAN PARTY with strong ties to the Hart family's banking and commercial interests.

As a rising political star, Clay was elected to the state lower house in 1803 and became a U.S. senator in November 1806, even though he had not reached the constitutionally required age of 30. He served as AARON BURR's defense attorney, winning an acquittal before Justice JOHN MARSHALL when Burr was indicted for planning an expedition into Spanish territory west of the Mississippi. Clay headed back to the Kentucky legislature in 1807—he was only serving out a vacated unexpired term in the Senate—and became Speaker of the state house in 1808. Returned to the Senate in 1810, he decided that he preferred to sit in the House of Representatives and was elected to Congress in August 1810. The young "Harry of the West" was immediately elected Speaker of the House by a group of aggressive Democratic-Republicans called the WAR HAWKS, who urged a bellicose stand against GREAT BRITAIN. As Speaker, Clay revamped the way the House of Representatives operated and centralized control in his own hands, making the Speaker the second most powerful position in the government behind the president. Clay and the war hawks helped drive the United States into the WAR OF 1812 (1812–15).

Clay remained Speaker of the House for most of the rest of the decade. His only break in service came when President JAMES MADISON appointed him to the commission to negotiate the TREATY OF GHENT (1814). Although this agreement did not settle any of the outstanding differences between Great Britain and the United States, just by reinstating the borders and conditions to the situation before the war was considered a triumph by most people in the United States. Clay also participated in the negotiations that led to the CONVENTION OF 1815 with Great Britain, which established reciprocal TRADE status between the two countries.

After Clay came back to the United States, he resumed the speakership and led a movement to strengthen the national government, pushing for chartering the Second Bank of the United States, protective TARIFFS, and INTERNAL IMPROVEMENTS. He also advocated recognition of the rebellious colonies of SPAIN as independent nations and helped to put together the Missouri Compromise (1820) regulating SLAVERY in the western territories. Clay retired from Congress in 1821 to recover from financial losses suffered during the Panic of 1819, but in 1823 he returned to office and became Speaker again. In the presidential election of 1824, he had the fourth most electoral votes behind ANDREW JACKSON, JOHN QUINCY ADAMS, and WILLIAM CRAWFORD. Clay supported Adams when the election fell to the House of Representatives in an agreement that the Jacksonians proclaimed a corrupt bargain, particularly as Adams appointed Clay secretary of state.

Although Clay retired briefly from politics after Jackson's election in 1828, Kentucky again sent him to the Senate in 1831. He formed the foundation for first the National Republican Party and then the Whig Party. Throughout the 1830s and 1840s he remained at the center of national politics and ably defended the Whig Party. Clay ran for president unsuccessfully in 1832 and again in 1844, and though he retired from the Senate from 1842 to 1849, he was again elected to another term, beginning in March 1849. The following year he was one of the masterminds of the Compromise of 1850. He died in Washington, D.C., on June 29, 1852.

Further reading: Robert V. Remini, *Henry Clay: Statesman for the Union* (New York: Norton, 1991); Kimberly C. Shankman, *Compromise and the Constitution: The Political Thought of Henry Clay* (Lantham, Md.: Lexington Books, 1999).

Clinton, DeWitt (1769–1828) *New York politician*

DeWitt Clinton held many offices—U.S. senator, mayor of New York City, governor of the state of New York—but his most significant achievement was ensuring the construction of the Erie Canal. Scion of an important political family—his uncle was long-time New York governor GEORGE CLINTON—and trained as a lawyer, Clinton already wielded considerable political influence by the time he was 20. Like his uncle, he opposed the U.S. CONSTITUTION and allied himself with the DEMOCRATIC-REPUBLICAN PARTY (Jeffersonians) in the 1790s. In 1797 Clinton was elected to the New York State assembly, and in 1801 he was appointed to the crucial Council of Appointments, the agency that doled out most of the state jobs. Previously the council had accepted a governor's nominations without question. Clinton engineered something of a coup by challenging this practice. With a Jeffersonian state assembly to support him, he virtually took over the patronage that had been in the control of JOHN JAY, FEDERALIST PARTY governor from 1795 to 1801. With this success behind him, he was quickly selected to fill a vacancy in the U.S. Senate in 1802, but in 1803 he resigned that office to become mayor of New York City. From Clinton's perspective, this position, which he held for most of the time until 1815, was more prestigious, had a greater income, and kept him close to the politics of his home state.

Clinton was an active mayor, overseeing charities, pushing school reform, and supervising the daily workings and expansion of what was quickly becoming the nation's largest city. While mayor he also served as a state senator (1806–11) and as lieutenant governor (1811–13). But in the ELECTION OF 1812 he allowed himself to be nominated by the Federalist Party, which had previously opposed him politically, as their candidate for president. He lost that contest to JAMES MADISON and also lost some credibility with many of his followers. By 1815 he was compelled to abandon all of his political offices. He then turned his energies to a new project, the building of the Erie Canal.

Clinton had been appointed a canal commissioner in 1810, but only after 1815 did he really push the project. As the state began to survey the area between Albany and Buffalo for construction, Clinton found his popularity was back on the rise. In 1817 he was elected the state's governor, and as such he became wholly identified with what some derisively called "Clinton's Ditch." The building of the canal was one of the greatest engineering feats of the era, but before it could be completed, Clinton ran into some more political problems. After a new state constitution broadened the franchise, he lost his bid for reelection in 1822 to Martin Van Buren's Democratic Party. However, Van Buren's supporters overplayed their hand when, as an additional affront to Clinton, they removed him from his role as a canal commissioner. This insult elicited the sympathy of many New Yorkers, who elected Clinton their governor again in 1824, and he therefore presided over the opening of his 362-mile canal in 1825. The building of the Eric Canal guaranteed the future growth of both the state and city of New York. Clinton died on February 11, 1828, while still governor.

Further reading: Evan Cornog, *The Birth of Empire: DeWitt Clinton and the American Experience, 1769–1828* (New York: Oxford University Press, 1998); Craig Hanyan, *DeWitt Clinton and the Rise of the People's Men* (Montreal: McGill-Queens University Press, 1996); Craig Hanyan, *DeWitt Clinton: Years of Molding, 1769–1807* (New York: Garland, 1988).

George Clinton *(Library of Congress)*

Clinton, George (1739–1812) *governor of New York, vice president of the United States*

Known as the father of New York State, George Clinton served as governor seven terms, and then as vice president of the United States for two terms. Clinton came from middling origins and grew up in Ulster County, New York. He served briefly on a privateer during the FRENCH AND INDIAN WAR (1754–63) and was a junior officer in a British expedition against FORT FRONTENAC on Lake Ontario in that conflict. After the war he became a lawyer and was elected to the provincial assembly in 1768.

Clinton was an ambitious social and political climber. He gained a reputation as a defender of LIBERTY by speaking out on behalf of ALEXANDER MCDOUGALL in 1770 and strengthened his political position by marrying into a locally prominent family. During the intensification of the imperial crisis in 1774 and 1775, he emerged as an important spokesman for the resistance to GREAT BRITAIN and was selected to be a member of the state's COMMITTEE OF CORRESPONDENCE. In December 1775 he was elected to the SECOND CONTINENTAL CONGRESS. He voted for independence in 1776 but did not sign the DECLARATION OF INDEPENDENCE since he was busy with the defense of New York. (Having had some military experience in the French and Indian War, he had been appointed a brigadier general in the state's MILITIA.) In 1776 and 1777 he organized the defenses of the HUDSON HIGHLANDS CAMPAIGN and recruited men into the militia and CONTINENTAL ARMY. He inspired confidence in his men and within the state, and as a result Congress appointed him a brigadier general in the Continental army in 1777. Because of his popularity, and much to the displeasure of the aristocratic leadership in New York, he was elected as governor in the same year.

Few men have confronted more desperate times than Clinton when he was inaugurated as governor of New York in July 1777. The British occupied New York City, Long Island, and the lower reaches of the Hudson River Valley. A powerful army under General JOHN BURGOYNE was working its way south from CANADA, and a force of British soldiers and Indians threatened the state from the Great Lakes. The GREEN MOUNTAIN BOYS of Vermont were declaring themselves an independent state, even though their territory technically belonged to New York, and much of the population under the control of the state government was neutral at best, if not outright loyal to King

GEORGE III. In short, there was not much left of New York State to govern. In summer 1777 Clinton set out to prevent British troops from moving up the Hudson to join with Burgoyne's forces heading south from Canada. However, he was outmanned and outgunned, and the best he could do was slow the enemy down. He lost the forts guarding the Hudson Highlands, and the British were able to burn Kingston. Despite these defeats, he had delayed the invasion long enough to leave Burgoyne isolated at SARATOGA, and the British general was forced to surrender on October 17, 1777. With the failure of their thrust from the Great Lakes at Fort Stanwix, and Burgoyne's surrender, the British were compelled to withdraw to New York City. New York State survived its most perilous moment.

As wartime governor, Clinton followed a policy of rigorous prosecution of LOYALISTS, confiscating their property to pay for the war and to relieve the state from an excessive tax burden. He also sought to regulate the ECONOMY and limit inflation. The popularity of these measures not only secured the state for the Revolutionary cause, it also led to Clinton's repeated reelection. During the 1780s his policies put the state on such a sound financial base that he did not see the need for a stronger central government. He therefore opposed the U.S. CONSTITUTION of 1787, writing ANTI-FEDERALIST tracts and working to defeat its ratification. Despite his control of patronage as a political weapon, his political star began to fade as the FEDERALIST PARTY gained in ascendancy in the 1790s. He declined a reelection bid in 1795, believing defeat likely, but after the victory of the Jeffersonian DEMOCRATIC-REPUBLICAN PARTY in 1800, he came out of retirement and was elected governor again in 1801.

In 1804 the Democratic-Republicans selected Clinton as THOMAS JEFFERSON's running mate, replacing the tarnished AARON BURR. The now aged and somewhat feeble Clinton became vice president, and though he considered a presidential bid in 1808, he instead became JAMES MADISON's running mate. Although he did not like Madison, Clinton remained vice president until his death on April 20, 1812.

See also ELECTION OF 1808.

Further reading: John P. Kaminski, *George Clinton: Yeoman of the New Republic* (Madison, Wis.: Madison House, 1993).

Clinton, Sir Henry (1730–1795) *British general*

Sir Henry Clinton was a British General during the REVOLUTIONARY WAR (1775–83), serving as commander in chief of the British army in North America from 1778 to 1782. Although Clinton was born in England, he spent much of his youth in New York, where his father was the

royal governor. When he returned to England in 1749, he used his aristocratic connections to join the army. During the FRENCH AND INDIAN WAR (1754–1763) he served with gallantry and distinction in Germany. He was promoted to the rank of major general in 1772 and elected to Parliament that same year.

Clinton was one of the three generals (along with WILLIAM HOWE and JOHN BURGOYNE) sent to Boston in 1775 to advise General THOMAS GAGE after the BATTLES OF LEXINGTON AND CONCORD (April 19, 1775). Before the BATTLE OF BUNKER HILL (June 17, 1775), Clinton recommended a flanking maneuver to get behind the Revolutionary lines to cut off retreat and to minimize casualties. Gage ignored the advice and opted for a frontal assault, carrying the hill with tremendous losses. When Howe replaced Gage, Clinton became his second in command. Clinton advocated action to destroy the enemy's army, while Howe was more concerned with conquering territory. However, it was Clinton who drew up the plan at the BATTLE OF LONG ISLAND (August 27–30, 1776) that led to a resounding victory and almost entrapped GEORGE WASHINGTON's army.

Howe ignored Clinton's advice for similar enveloping maneuvers in the subsequent campaign that drove Washington out of New York and across New Jersey. Clinton also opposed Howe's decision to take Philadelphia in 1777, arguing that he should move up the Hudson River and join with Burgoyne advancing south from CANADA. Left with a relatively small detachment as Howe embarked on his Philadelphia campaign, Clinton struck up the Hudson in autumn 1777, recognizing the desperate situation that was developing for Burgoyne. He seized the forts that guarded the Hudson Highlands and captured and burned Kingston in the HUDSON HIGHLANDS CAMPAIGN. On the day that Burgoyne surrendered at SARATOGA, October 17, 1777, British ships had reached to within 45 miles of Albany. With the loss of Burgoyne's army, Clinton had to withdraw to New York City. Howe resigned his command of the British armies in North America in February 1778, and Clinton became commander in chief.

After Saratoga, FRANCE entered the war, and much of the British focus centered on the WEST INDIES, leaving Clinton with limited resources. In June 1778 he abandoned Philadelphia, which Howe had captured the previous year. On the way to New York, he fought the inconclusive BATTLE OF MONMOUTH (June 28, 1778) in New Jersey. At the end of 1778 he also launched an attack on Georgia and began to develop a strategy for the war in the South. In 1780 he pursued this strategy and achieved his greatest victory by capturing Charleston (May 12, 1780) and 5,000 Revolutionary troops in the SIEGE OF CHARLESTON.

If Clinton demonstrated flashes of military brilliance, he had significant flaws that had an important impact on the Revolutionary War: He had difficulty getting along with others, including his superiors and those below him; he never had strong political connections in GREAT BRITAIN; and although he had many suggestions when second in command, they were rarely followed because Howe disliked him. Indeed, Clinton was generally disliked by both his officers and the men under his command. He also had trouble with LORD CORNWALLIS, who was his subordinate. Clinton had encouraged a slow and careful campaign in the South that would build upon a Loyalist base, but Cornwallis abandoned this policy in 1781, cutting his army loose to eventually invade Virginia. That campaign ended in failure when Cornwallis surrendered at YORKTOWN (October 19, 1781).

Clinton's greatest flaw may have been his propensity to become more cautious when he was completely in charge. He could have ordered Cornwallis to withdraw from Yorktown before the French fleet arrived, but he hesitated and did not take direct command of the situation. The result was that Clinton, not Cornwallis, was blamed for the defeat at Yorktown. Cornwallis, who had better political connections, returned to Britain first, and by the time Clinton arrived there in 1782, he found himself with almost no support. He retired from active duty, but he came back into favor in the 1790s and briefly served as governor of Gibraltar in 1794. He died in London on December 23, 1795.

Further reading: George Athan Billias, ed., *George Washington's Opponents: British Generals and Admirals in the American Revolution* (New York: William Morrow, 1969).

clocks

The manufacturing of clocks underwent a significant change during the early republic, reflecting the combination of innovation, CONSUMERISM, and the market that ultimately had a significant impact on how European Americans in the United States measured work and viewed time. For most of the 18th century, only the rich owned clocks, and they were more a symbol of wealth than a practical instrument. Most common folk measured time and work in terms of the part of the day—forenoon, noon, and afternoon—rather than by the hour. Clocks were produced by skilled ARTISANS who could make only about 25 clock movements a year at a cost of at least $25 an instrument. Around 1802 clockmaker Eli Terry in Connecticut developed a more efficient production method using water-powered machinery and wooden parts. In 1806 Terry signed a contract to deliver 4,000 clocks to a distributor who hired itinerant salespeople to vend the clocks throughout the countryside. Within the next decade and a half, there was a dramatic increase in the number of clocks owned as farmers and middling people across the Northeast purchased the timepieces. With more clocks available, work increasingly came to be measured by the hour, and a new more precise understanding of time emerged.

Further reading: David Jaffe, "Peddlers for Progress and the Transformation of the Rural North, 1760–1860," *Journal of American History* 78 (1991): 511–535.

clothing

Clothing offers insight into the daily lives and values of a society. Both BENJAMIN FRANKLIN and THOMAS JEFFERSON were fully conscious of how the language of clothing transmitted crucial messages. Franklin was shrewd enough to adapt his clothing to the circumstances to be sure that he sent the right message. When he was earning his living as a printer, he "took care not only to be in Reality Industrious & frugal, but to avoid all Appearances of the Contrary. I drest plainly." In GREAT BRITAIN and FRANCE in the 1750s and 1760s, when he had hopes of joining the intelligentsia, he made sure he was attired in the highest fashion. He explained that for his audience with the French king in 1767, he hired a tailor and wig maker who "transformed" him "into a Frenchman." But for his visit to France as a representative of the United States during the REVOLUTIONARY WAR (1775–83) he donned a simple dark suit, fur cap, and no wig. The contrast with the other diplomats was intentional: During the age of the ENLIGHTENMENT, Franklin hoped to cast himself as a true disciple of nature and reason. Jefferson, too, used clothes to send political messages. While ambassador to France in the 1780s, he was fully capable of wearing appropriate court attire. However, when he became president, he sought to counter the trappings of monarchy he believed the FEDERALIST PARTY had sought by greeting visitors in yarn stockings and slippers and established a "a raw and rude court" compared to the administrations of GEORGE WASHINGTON and JOHN ADAMS.

Further understanding of the cultural significance of clothing can be gleaned through an examination of apparel in the 1754–1815 period. For this purpose clothing can be divided into four general areas: formal wear for men and women; work clothes donned for everyday use and worn by common folk; slave clothes; and Native American garments. These areas were not entirely distinct and often had an impact on each other.

Around 1800 the nature of formal clothing for European Americans underwent a significant change. Previously, despite some shifts in fashion, formal wear followed similar patterns. Both men and women's dress was brightly colored with elaborate prints. Women wore cone-shaped bodices with wide skirts that were lined with hoops, and stays were used to mold the upper body. The result was a distorted view of the female form, which appeared almost like a small vee plunging to the waist, with the body enlarged from the waist down. Men's clothes had a similar, but less extreme, effect. Suits were in three pieces, with a waistcoat, breeches, and a long jacket that earlier in the period widened at the hips. Such outfits entailed the use of a great deal of cloth and denoted a higher social status.

During the second half of the 18th century there was a trend toward slimming the figure for both men and women. But starting in the 1790s and into the early 1800s, a revolution in fashion matched the political revolutions in North America and France. For women, neoclassical styles predominated with a raising of the waistline to just under the breast and a new looser style that followed the body's natural outlines. Material was less multicolored, with gentle prints and light shades, including plain white. Many women did away with stays entirely, which, given sometimes sheer clothing, had startling effects. In 1804, after attending several balls in WASHINGTON, D.C., one commentator noted that there was one woman who wore "dresses so transparent and tight that you can see her skin through them, no chemise at all." This style did not flatter all women's figures. The same observer went on to describe the wife of the British ambassador, declaring that she was "very fat and covers only with fine lace two objects which could fill a fourth of a bushel!"

Men's clothing, too, changed. Men abandoned knee breeches and long-tailed broad coats, as well as the tricornered hat. Instead they wore pants and shorter jackets with somber collars, denoting a more egalitarian orientation. As clothing historian Linda Baumgarten explains, "Plain suits were appropriate for businessman whose clothing had to communicate trustworthiness, stability, and competence through personal achievement in an emerging capitalist society."

In a trend that has continued in democratic societies, this change, especially in men's clothing, reflected an effort to copy the style of clothes used by working men. Laborers and sailors had long worn pants as a more effective attire while working to protect the legs, and shorter jackets—sailors wore them only down to the waist—allowed greater flexibility while working. Those who did wear breeches often had them made out of leather, a strong, pliable material that allowed better ease of movement. Although by the early 19th century fewer and fewer laborers used leather breeches, they became fashionable among the elite for riding and then for use in general—until pants came to dominate fashion completely.

Working women could not afford as much cloth for their skirts and dresses, but for much of the 18th century they modeled their clothing after that of the rich. Women had two basic forms of clothing. Short gowns were worn with a shift draping over the top of the waist. This outfit paralleled the styles of the affluent, with fuller skirts earlier in the period and a higher waist and more of a hanging look by 1800. Bed gowns were single-piece dresses that could have a variety of different types of collars and sleeves and were worn for sleeping and everyday work. These gowns had a straight-line cut, opened in the front, fit loosely, and lacked a waist seam. As such, they could have something of the appearance of the formal gowns popular around 1800. Common folk might at most own two or three outfits for working and perhaps one better suit of clothes for worship or special occasions.

Slaves had little choice in their clothing. On the most fundamental level, slave clothing was similar to that worn by European-American workers, only of even coarser cloth with less variation. Adult male slaves would ordinarily get a pair of shoes, stockings, breeches, a jacket or waistcoat, and a couple of shirts. Women also received shoes and stockings, but they would be given a petticoat or dress and two shifts. The material for this clothing would be coarse wool or linen—or some combination—called linsey-woolsy. The whole kit would consist of about 10 yards of cloth per year and, despite the cheapness of the cloth, was usually imported from England. The actual sewing of the cloth would probably be done in North America, usually by slaves, who often had even less clothing than the minimum described here.

Although the basic outfit of slaves reflected European-American styles, AFRICAN AMERICANS might add a more traditional African touch such as distinctive head wraps. Slave clothing reflected low status in a society dominated by whites. The nature of the clothing was so standard that a runaway advertisement often provided only a general description—for example, "such a crop Negroes usually wear" or "the common dress of field slaves."

NATIVE AMERICANS across North America wore a wide range of clothing as could be expected from diverse and numerous cultures spread across a continent. Indians east of the Mississippi, with many variations, wore clothing that was an amalgamation from both Native and European-American culture. Indians were quick to substitute traditional textiles made in Europe for animal skins. Frequently men would use white linen or calico shirts worn hanging below their hips without buttons. Rather than breeches, they had breechcloths with flaps in the front and back. They might also have leather leggings and have moccasins on their feet. Beadwork and silver brooches were donned for display. Women's clothing was similar but would include a petticoat that would run down to the knee.

Many frontiersmen adopted some elements of Native American dress since it was well suited to life in the woods. Hunting shirts and leather leggings, in particular, were used extensively and even became part of the uniform of some units during the Revolutionary War.

See also CLOTH PRODUCTION.

Further reading: Linda Baumgarten, *What Clothes Reveal: The Language of Clothing in Colonial and Federal America* (New Haven, Conn.: Yale University Press, 2002); Jack Larkin, *The Reshaping of Everyday Life, 1790–1830* (New York: Harper & Row, 1988); Philip D. Morgan, *Slave Counterpoint: Black Culture in the Eighteenth-Century Chesapeake and Lowcountry* (Chapel Hill: University of North Carolina Press, 1998).

cloth production

Within the British North American colonies there were five different sources of cloth production: silk, hemp, flax, wool, and COTTON; however, despite several experiments, silk never became a major source of cloth. Flax and hemp, both the products of agricultural fibers, were important crops. Hemp was used to make rope and canvas and therefore was central in supplying the shipping industry, which expanded throughout the 18th century and became crucial to the ECONOMY of the early republic. Flax was used in the production of linen. While flax was never a major area of cloth production in any one region, many farms produced some flax for linen to be used at home and sold in local markets. Both Pennsylvania and Connecticut, however, exported large amounts of flax seed for the Irish linen industry during the colonial period.

Many farms also produced wool during the colonial period. Sheep were useful for fertilizer and as a source of meat, and wool was a by-product of keeping a limited number of sheep on a farm; they would be sheared once or twice a year. However, the quality of the wool was not high, and it was not until after 1790, when some farmers began to concentrate on sheep breeding—especially following the introduction of MERINO SHEEP—that more extensive wool supplies appeared.

Before the 1790s, in South Carolina and elsewhere in the South, planters and farmers grew some cotton, most of which was used locally to produce cloth. The invention of the cotton gin in 1793 increased the production of cotton for an export market and made possible the beginnings of cloth manufacturing in New England and the middle states.

Growing or raising the raw material was only the first step in the complicated process of cloth production. The next step was to transform the raw material into a fiber. Flax and hemp were handled in similar ways: The plant had to be broken and then hackled—straightening the fiber and separating the long from the short strands in preparation for spinning. Most of this work was physically demanding and utilized specialized tools. Some farmers did this preparation themselves; others hired specialists who owned machines. After the REVOLUTIONARY WAR (1775–83), flax became a less important crop, and linen production declined in the United States. Hemp, however, remained

important. The area around Lexington, Kentucky, began to specialize in hemp and the manufacturing of rope and canvas. Almost every seaboard and river port had a ropewalk to supply local shipping needs. Wool, too, needed to have the fibers aligned before spinning, either through carding from shorter and finer fibers or by combing from longer and coarser fibers. Initially, carding and combing were part of the household work of women on the farm, but during the 1790s and early 1800s the number of water-driven carding mills expanded, allowing an increase in the amount of wool yarn available.

Once the fibers were created, they had to be spun into yarn, which then needed to be turned into cloth. Spinning yarn, performed by women on spinning wheels, was an important component of household work on most farms. There were different types of spinning wheels for different fibers, with larger frames used to spin wool yarn and smaller frames for linen. Although it entailed some training and skill, spinning could be done in between other types of housework, and it was interrupted easily, thus fitting the work patterns of many farm women. Spun yarn was used both for home consumption and for a market. Indeed, many women would spin to earn MONEY to supplement the overall income of the family unit and to purchase consumer items. With the introduction of spinning jennies and machine spinning in textile factories in the 1790s, home spinning declined. By the 1830s factory yarns had become so ubiquitous and cheap that the spinning wheel became a relic of the past.

Yarn could be turned into cloth through either knitting or weaving. Women did most knitting in the home, though there was some frame knitting performed with machinery run by men to produce stockings more quickly and cheaply than hand knitting. Weaving also involved larger machinery and more skill. Traditionally, weaving was a male-dominated craft in Europe, and the practice was brought to North America. During the 18th century in New England, however, women took over much of the weaving, which was done largely for home use or the local market. Elsewhere, such as in Pennsylvania, weaving remained the work of men who were both rural ARTISANS and farmers.

The final stage in making cloth was fulling—bleaching, cleansing, stretching, brushing, dyeing, and shrinking the cloth to make it the appropriate color and consistency. Seldom was this done in the home, as the process was highly skilled and usually conducted in fulling mills by men trained in the trade. Fullers would also rework used cloth, a task that became especially important during the Revolutionary War when textile imports almost ceased and the demands of the CONTINENTAL ARMY for blankets and uniforms was high.

Until the early 19th century, overall textile production remained limited in North America. In the late 18th century the average Pennsylvania farm household needed 42 yards of textiles a year just for CLOTHING; this figure does not include the textiles used for bedding, curtains, tablecloths, sacks, wagon covers, and other farm uses. With the average farm producing wool that could make only three yards of cloth a year, and with most weavers working only part-time, local production could not meet demand. Importation of cloth and involvement in the wider Atlantic world of TRADE therefore remained crucial. However, domestic and imported cloth did not compete with each other in the market; instead, they were complementary. Production of yarn or cloth in the home often provided the additional capital needed to buy imported fabric. Although most of the finest cloth was imported, some North American weavers were capable of producing high-quality work. Homespun, moreover, was not so much a label for cloth made at home as it was a general term to describe all coarse and cheaper fabric.

Around 1800 the textile industry began to change. With the expansion of factory-produced yarn, weavers could increase output more easily. Thus, rural master weavers who might have woven around 600–700 yards of cloth a year in the 1790s began to hire journeymen to work their looms and double or even triple their output to 1,800 yards annually 10 years later. In cities such as Philadelphia, the transformation was more profound because an influx of British immigrant weavers, displaced by industrialization in GREAT BRITAIN, provided a labor force that allowed for the growth of hand loom weaving on a small scale and in factories. Most of this new and growing textile production relied on cotton shipped from the South, but production of other fabrics also increased. In 1810 there was one Philadelphia establishment with eight looms that could make 17,000 yards of canvas a year. The textile industry in New England moved along a different path. With the increase of spinning factories after the success of the mill established in 1793 in Pawtucket, Rhode Island, by SAMUEL SLATER, manufacturers developed an extensive outworker system using women weavers in their homes in the countryside. In 1814 the Boston Associates built the first fully integrated textile production factory, including weaving and fulling, in Waltham, Massachusetts, which became the model of the larger Lowell Mills built in the 1820s.

See also CONSUMERISM; INDUSTRIAL REVOLUTION; WOMEN'S STATUS AND RIGHTS.

Further reading: Adrienne D. Hood, *The Weaver's Craft: Cloth, Commerce, and Industry in Early Pennsylvania* (Philadelphia: University of Pennsylvania Press, 2003); Barbara M. Tucker, *Samuel Slater and the Origins of the American Textile Industry, 1790–1860* (Ithaca, N.Y.: Cornell University Press, 1984): Laurel Thatcher Ulrich, *The*

Age of Homespun: Objects and Stories in the Creation of an American Myth (New York: Knopf, 2001).

Clouds, Battle of the   See WARREN OR WHITEHORSE TAVERN, BATTLE OF.

Clymer, George (1739–1813) *Pennsylvania businessman, politician*

On the eve of the REVOLUTIONARY WAR (1775–83), George Clymer was one of the richest men in Philadelphia as well as one of the earliest advocates of independence. Born in Whiteville, Pennsylvania he had been orphaned at the age of one, was brought up by an uncle, and inherited a mercantile business. Clymer supported the RESISTANCE MOVEMENT against British imperial measures in the 1770s, often serving on various organizing committees. From July 1775 to August 1776 the SECOND CONTINENTAL CONGRESS appointed him one of two "joint treasurers of the United Colonies," and in July 1776 he became a member of the Congress, serving from July 1776 to September 1777 and again from November 1780 to November 1782. Although he had not taken part in the deliberations leading to the DECLARATION OF INDEPENDENCE, he signed the document.

Even as he occupied himself with making MONEY through his business as a merchant, trading through SINT EUSTATIUS, Clymer was active in politics and in directing financial affairs on both the national and local level. He opposed the radically democratic 1776 state constitution of Pennsylvania but served in the state assembly. During the 1780s he was a conservative in politics, supporting revisions of the Pennsylvania constitution, opposing paper money schemes, and advocating banking interests. He also speculated in western lands before his retirement from business.

An advocate of a strong central government, Clymer attended the CONSTITUTIONAL CONVENTION in 1787 and helped guide the ratification process in Pennsylvania. In his one term in the House of Representatives (1789–91), he supported the ALEXANDER HAMILTON's fiscal program and advocated locating the capital in Philadelphia. In 1791 President GEORGE WASHINGTON appointed him to supervise the collection of revenues in Pennsylvania. Unfortunately for Clymer, the unpopularity of the EXCISE TAX and his own prejudice against westerners created problems, and after the WHISKEY REBELLION (1794) broke out, he resigned from the position. His wealth enabled him to dedicate most of the rest of his life to pursuing other interests beyond politics and business, including serving as a trustee of the University of Pennsylvania. In 1803 he became the first president of the Philadelphia Bank, and he also served as president of the Pennsylvania Academy of Fine Arts. He died on January 24, 1813.

Cobbett, William (1763–1835) *journalist*

The son of an English innkeeper and farmer, William Cobbett rose from plebeian origins and a limited EDUCATION to become an influential transatlantic journalist and political agitator. Born in Farnhan, Surrey, England, Cobbett enlisted in the British army at age 21 and was posted to CANADA. He returned to England in 1791 and brought charges against his superior officers for corruption and injustices against the common soldier. Fearing retaliatory charges from his former officers, he fled to FRANCE at the height of the FRENCH REVOLUTION (1789–99). Following a six-month stay in France, he sailed to North America, began a career in Philadelphia teaching English to French immigrants, and became deeply engaged in the intense debates over whether the United States would support the revolutionary cause in France, as the DEMOCRATIC-REPUBLICAN PARTY proposed, or remain neutral, as the FEDERALIST PARTY desired. Cobbett not only supported the Federalist Party's pro-British rhetoric in his writings, he also intentionally aggravated his Democratic-Republican Party opponents by placing portraits of aristocrats and royalty in his bookshop windows.

During Cobbett's literary career in the United States from 1792 to 1800, he wrote 12 volumes of political commentary criticizing democracy under the pen name "Peter Porcupine." In 1800 he returned to England after being sued by BENJAMIN RUSH for libel. There he continued his political writings, and in 1802 he began a weekly paper called the *Political Register* in which he condemned governmental abuses. He was imprisoned for libel in 1810–12, and after learning that the British government was about to arrest him for sedition, he fled to New York in 1817 and subsequently rented a farm on Long Island. He carried on writing for the *Political Register,* and in 1819 he returned to England with the exhumed bones of THOMAS PAINE. Although less influential than earlier in his career, he resumed his work as a journalist and political reformer, and in 1832 he was elected to Parliament. Cobbett died of influenza on June 18, 1835.

Further reading: Ian Dyck, *William Cobbett and Rural Popular Culture* (New York: Cambridge University Press, 1992); Leonora Nattrass, *William Cobbett: The Politics of Style* (New York: Cambridge University Press, 1995); David A. Wilson, *Paine and Cobbett: The Transatlantic Connection* (Kingston, Ontario: McGill-Queen's University Press, 1988).

—William R. Smith

Cockburn, Sir George (1772–1853) *British naval officer*

One of the leading figures in the British navy in the first half of the 19th century, Sir George Cockburn began his naval career in 1786. He rose through the ranks quickly, experiencing single-ship battles, fleet action, and extensive cooperation with land forces in the French Revolutionary and Napoleonic Wars. By the outbreak of the WAR OF 1812 (1812–15), Cockburn was a rear admiral. In April 1813 he swept into the Chesapeake Bay, raiding towns along the shore with near impunity and capturing huge stores of supplies while giving refuge and freedom to runaway slaves. He sustained this campaign throughout the spring and even briefly occupied Hampton, Virginia. In 1814 he was part of the fleet that accompanied the British army's incursion into the Chesapeake region under General ROBERT ROSS. His skill and experience in leading landing parties and raiding coastal regions was crucial to the British success in the CHESAPEAKE BAY CAMPAIGN (1813–1814). Cockburn encouraged Ross to attack WASHINGTON, D.C., and was with Ross when the latter was killed at the BATTLE OF BALTIMORE (September 12–14, 1814).

Cockburn continued to rise in the British navy after 1815, eventually leading to his promotion to admiral of the fleet. He also oversaw crucial reforms in the modernization of the British navy. He died on August 19, 1853.

Further reading: Christopher T. George, *Terror on the Chesapeake: The War of 1812 on the Bay* (Shippensburg, Pa.: White Maine Books, 2000).

Coercive Acts (Intolerable Acts) (1774)

After the BOSTON TEA PARTY (December 16, 1773), the British government under LORD NORTH decided that the colonists needed to be forced to recognize parliamentary SOVEREIGNTY. To compel colonial compliance with imperial regulation, Parliament passed a series of laws called the COERCIVE ACTS—sometimes referred to as the Intolerable Acts—in spring 1774. The first measure passed was the Boston Port Bill (March 31, 1774), which closed the port of Boston until its inhabitants had paid the British East India Company for the tea that had been destroyed. This regulation effectively ended most business in Boston, and since that left inhabitants without jobs or the ability to import food by sea, they were threatened with starvation. It also elicited the sympathy of many other colonists for the people of Boston. If the king could close down the port of Boston to compel submission, he could do the same to any other community that might oppose him.

Believing that "the democratic part of government" had gotten out of hand in the colonies, Lord North also passed the Massachusetts Government Act (May 20, 1774). This law altered the charter of Massachusetts and provided for greater royal control and less popular participation. Previously the Massachusetts General Court (the lower house of assembly) had appointed members of the council. Now they were to be appointed by the king. The royal governor was given the power to appoint many of the colony's judges and most civil officials. The long arm of the Crown was to reach into every community, as the law provided that there could be only one town meeting a year to elect local officials. Any additional meetings needed the governor's permission and had to follow a preapproved agenda. Juries also were to be chosen by a royal official, the sheriff, rather than the freeholders. The alteration of the colony's charter concerned many colonists because it meant that no written charter was inviolate and that Parliament could alter the colony's government at will. The provision limiting town meetings brought the conflict into the countryside as well. Many farmers who had considered the debate over the TEA ACT (1773) or the TOWNSHEND DUTIES (1767) to be far from their daily world now came to see how their lives would be changed by an inability to sustain local control in politics.

The two remaining Coercive Acts were also viewed as steps toward tyranny. The Administration of Justice Act (May 20, 1774) was passed by Parliament to solve a real problem—the inability of colonial courts to convict violators of imperial regulations. This law allowed the Crown to move the location of a trial to a different colony or to England if officials believed that it was impossible to prosecute a person in his own community with a local jury. While appearing as a logical solution to an ongoing problem for the British government, it struck colonial Americans as unfair and unjust to have such trials moved; it also would cost the defendant much more MONEY. The fourth measure was a Quartering Act (June 2, 1774) that would have the colonies pay for the support of troops assigned to enforce these laws.

A fifth law was lumped together with the four coercive acts as also being intolerable. On June 22, 1774, Parliament passed the QUEBEC ACT to deal with a complex situation in CANADA, which had been conquered by the British in the FRENCH AND INDIAN WAR (1754–63). Most Canadians spoke French and were Roman CATHOLICS. The British sought to incorporate these people into their empire in as fair a manner as possible. Thus, the Quebec Act tolerated the Roman Catholic faith, accepted provisions of the French legal code, and allowed the land-tenure system that had been in place to continue. It also created a major increase in territory for Canada, including all of the lands between the Mississippi River and the Appalachians. Many colonial Americans found this law distressing because it seemed to favor the French in Canada at the expense of the English in the colonies. Most Anglo-Americans at this time viewed Catholics as agents of the devil; toleration of Catholics was therefore unacceptable. Similarly, colonial

Americans had been eager participants in the French and Indian War and had expected to be rewarded with western lands. The PROCLAMATION OF 1763 had been a temporary measure to prevent settlers from crossing the Appalachians. Now the Quebec Act made that measure permanent, which seemed an infringement of colonial American rights. NATIVE AMERICANS living in the area, on the other hand, liked this provision for protecting their homelands from a European-American invasion.

In reaction to the Coercive Acts, colonists formed COMMITTEES OF CORRESPONDENCE up and down the coast to pass resolutions against these measures. The committees also organized relief efforts to aid Boston and joined in a nonimportation movement to compel the British to rescind the laws. The colonies went on to organize the FIRST CONTINENTAL CONGRESS (1774) to discuss further action. MINUTEMEN in Massachusetts and elsewhere began to collect arms and drill. The stage was set for more direct conflict which would come on April 19, 1775, at the BATTLES OF LEXINGTON AND CONCORD.

See also RESISTANCE MOVEMENT.

Further reading: Ray Raphael, *The First American Revolution: Before Lexington and Concord* (New York: New Press, 2002).

Coker, Daniel (1780–1846) *abolitionist minister*

Daniel Coker was a preacher, educator, and ANTISLAVERY writer who helped found the African Methodist Episcopal Church. The son of an African father and a white mother, he was born Isaac Wright in Maryland but later took the name of his white half brother and obtained a rudimentary EDUCATION by accompanying his brother to school as his valet. In time he joined the Methodist Church and met Bishop FRANCIS ASBURY, who made him a deacon around 1800. Coker also taught in the school established for free blacks in Baltimore. There he joined Sharp Street Church, which had an uneasy relationship with the mostly white METHODISTS. He published an antislavery tract, "A Dialogue Between a Virginian and an African Minister," in 1810 and founded a group in Baltimore that became the African Methodist Bethel Society in 1815. RICHARD ALLEN, leader of the black Methodists in Philadelphia, was then also forming a church, and he, Coker, and representatives of three other black Methodist congregations organized the African Methodist Episcopal Church in April 1816. Coker was elected bishop but declined, allowing Allen to take the position. In 1818 Coker was found guilty of an unknown charge and expelled from the church, but he was reinstated in 1819. The following year, he and a small group of AFRICAN AMERICANS moved to Freetown, SIERRA LEONE, in AFRICA, where he died in 1846.

Further reading: James T. Campbell, *Songs of Zion: The African Methodist Episcopal Church in the United States and South Africa* (New York: Oxford University Press, 1995); Carol V. R. George, *Segregated Sabbaths: Richard Allen and the Rise of Independent Black Churches, 1760–1840* (New York: Oxford University Press, 1973).

—Stephen A. Martin

Colden, Cadwallader (1688–1776) *government official, scientist*

Born in Ireland to Scottish parents, Cadwallader Colden graduated from the University of Edinburgh and studied MEDICINE in London. He moved to Philadelphia in 1710 but eventually settled in New York when Governor Robert Hunter promised him a government position. In 1720 Colden became surveyor general of New York and a member of the colony's council (he remained on the council for the rest of his life). He was not only an active participant in colonial politics but also an avid scientist with wide-ranging interests. As senior councilor, Colden took over the administration of the colony in 1760 when Lieutenant Governor James De Lancey died; he subsequently became lieutenant governor himself. Since New York's royal governors often absented themselves from the colony, Colden administered the colony for several years: He was the de facto governor in 1760–61, 1763–65, 1769–70, and 1774–75.

Colden alienated much of the colony's elite by opposing their control of the legal system and attempting to limit their political influence. Simultaneously, his defense of the royal prerogative made him unpopular with the common people. During the opposition to the STAMP ACT (1765), mobs paraded through the streets with effigies of Colden, the pope, and Charles Edward Stuart (the young Pretender) thus combining the image of the lieutenant governor with traditional Anglo-American symbols of tyranny and oppression to highlight popular resistance to the Stamp Act. The crowd also threatened Colden's life; he had to seek the safety of a Royal Navy ship and only reluctantly agreed not to enforce the Stamp Act. Colden also played a major role in the prosecution of ALEXANDER MCDOUGALL when McDougall opposed the colony's funding of the QUARTERING ACT (1765), and he was in charge when the COERCIVE ACTS (1774) were passed and during the disintegration of royal government after the BATTLES OF LEXINGTON AND CONCORD (April 19, 1775). He died on his estate in Flushing on September 20, 1776, shortly before the British recaptured New York City.

Further reading: Alfred R. Hoerman, *Cadwallader Colden: A Figure of the American Enlightenment* (Westport, Conn.: Greenwood Press, 2002).

colonization, African

Although the national organization called the American Colonization Society would not be formed until 1816, the idea of African colonization had emerged decades earlier in tandem with the challenge to SLAVERY posed by the AMERICAN REVOLUTION. With the possibilities of freedom offered to some AFRICAN AMERICANS by the Revolution, both they and European Americans became concerned about the future of free blacks in North American society. African Americans who linked their identities to AFRICA were becoming more assertive but also filled with apprehension about the racial prejudice and inequality they confronted in a white-dominated society. Many European Americans seemed willing to end slavery but could not imagine a multiracial society. Both groups found the answer to these concerns in the policy of colonization—the "return" of free African Americans to Africa or the establishment of a black state somewhere other than in the European-American settled part of the United States. From this perspective, African colonization had the added benefit of bringing "civilization" (as defined by European-American standards) and Christianity to otherwise "barbarian" lands.

Almost as soon as a significant free black community emerged in North America, some African Americans began to discuss the possibility of returning to Africa, whether they had been born overseas or within North America. In 1773 a group of free blacks in New England petitioned for help to move to "some part of the coast of Africa." Black Masons in Boston drew up a petition in 1787 asking for aid to emigrate to their "native country." The petition declared that they or their "ancestors" had been "brought from Africa and put into slavery in this country," but now that they were free they found themselves in a "disagreeable and disadvantageous position." By moving to Africa they would be in a "warm climate" that was "more natural and agreeable" to them. Once in Africa they would form a "civil society" with a "political constitution" and a Christian base that would be good for them and their "brethren"—the natives who had remained.

Interest in a colony of free blacks emerged in GREAT BRITAIN at about the same time. In 1787, instigated by GRANVILLE SHARP, reformers established a "province of freedom" in SIERRA LEONE for the growing number of poor free blacks in the London area—many of whom were refugees from the REVOLUTIONARY WAR (1775–83). Although this effort ended in failure, in 1791 Parliament charted the Sierra Leone Company, which recruited about 1,000 black LOYALISTS in NOVA SCOTIA to move to West Africa in 1792. Despite some difficulties with British authorities and local native rulers, these "Nova Scotians," along with others from the WEST INDIES and elsewhere, became the nucleus of a successful colony. The Sierra Leone colony continued to attract the interests of many African-American leaders in the

United States in the early 19th century. Captain PAUL CUFFE made several voyages to the colony and planned on settling there himself before he died. However, by the 1820s, just as many European Americans in the United States formalized plans for their own African state as a haven for free blacks—Liberia—most African-American leaders abandoned colonization, believing that they needed to create a better life for themselves and their people in North America.

Within North America, most European-American advocates of African colonization did so largely because they wanted to remove African Americans from their society and create a racially pure nation. As early as 1773, THOMAS JEFFERSON advocated colonization for blacks. Jefferson believed that it would be impossible to create a multiracial society after granting slaves their freedom. In his *Notes on the State of Virginia* (1787) he wrote that "deep rooted prejudices entertained by the whites, ten thousand recollections, by the blacks, of injuries they have sustained" when combined with "new Provocations" and "real distinctions which nature had made" would "produce convulsions which will probably never end but in the extermination of the one race or the other." The best way to avoid this race war would be to establish "an asylum to which we can, by degrees, send the whole of that population from among us." He believed that such a colony under the "patronage and protection" of the United States would allow blacks to become "a separate free and independent people, in some country and climate friendly to human life and happiness." In 1811 Jefferson reiterated these points when he wrote that colonization was "the most desirable measure which could be adopted for gradually drawing off" of African Americans from North America and that "nothing is more to be wished than that the United States should themselves undertake to make such an establishment on the coast of Africa."

As a precursor to the creation of the American Colonization Society in 1816, several local organizations formed to advocate colonization. For example, the Society of Inquiry Respecting Missions, founded in 1810, favored African colonization. But these colonization efforts were not directed solely at Africa. As early as 1800, the Virginia legislature had urged Governor JAMES MONROE to contact the national government to discuss purchasing land in the West for free blacks. In 1815 the Kentucky Colonization Society petitioned Congress asking that some land in the West "be laid off as an asylum for all those negroes and mulattoes who have been, and those who may hereafter be, emancipated within the United States; and that such donations, allowances, and encouragements, and assistance be afforded them as may be necessary for carrying them thither and settling them therein." Colonization would remain an important part of the ANTISLAVERY movement throughout the antebellum era, especially among European

Americans, and would re-emerge among African Americans in the back to Africa movement of the 20th century.

Further reading: Simon Schama, *Rough Crossing: Britain, the Slaves and the American Revolution* (London: BBC Books, 2006); James Sidbury, *Becoming African in America: Race and Nation in the Early Black Republic* (New York: Oxford University Press, 2007).

Combahee Ferry, Battle of (August 27, 1782)

During the last phases of the REVOLUTIONARY WAR (1775–83) in the South, the British were confined to holding Charleston, South Carolina, an outpost from which they would send out foraging expeditions to obtain supplies. In late August 500 British soldiers moved up the Combahee River with 18 boats of various sizes. Continental general Mordecai Gist sent Colonel JOHN LAURENS with several hundred men to intercept the British and placed a howitzer 12 miles below the ferry to cut off any British retreat. Unfortunately for Laurens, the British detected the Revolutionary soldiers' approach and ambushed the advance guard from some tall grass at Cheraw Point. They then pursued the retreating Continentals and reformed a line in some woods, where the thick forest cover prevented a cavalry counterattack. Laurens and one other soldier were killed in the fighting; 19 were wounded. The British also captured the howitzer set up to stop their return to Charleston. Although this British victory was little more than a skirmish and had no impact on the outcome of the war, the battle is noteworthy for the death of Laurens, who was from a leading South Carolina family and a close friend of ALEXANDER HAMILTON and GEORGE WASHINGTON.

committee(s) of correspondence

Similar to the SONS OF LIBERTY, committees of correspondence developed between 1772 and 1775 to exchange information between colonies and communities and to organize resistance to British imperial measures. There were two types of committees of correspondence, intercolonial and local. The intercolonial committees were established by colonial assemblies. The local committees, however, were more important. As the conflict with GREAT BRITAIN intensified after the passage of the COERCIVE ACTS (1774), the local committees expanded their roles. When government began to break down in the wake of the BATTLES OF LEXINGTON AND CONCORD (April 19, 1775), the committee system became more elaborate and started to assume administrative duties. Often the committees of correspondence then adopted new names (such as "committee of safety"), and they became a central driving force behind the AMERICAN REVOLUTION.

Although tensions between the colonies and Great Britain were reduced after the repeal of the TOWNSHEND DUTIES in 1770, many colonial Americans believed that they needed to be on guard against other encroachments on their LIBERTY. Upon receiving news of the GASPÉE AFFAIR (1772), the Virginia House of Burgesses decided to establish a committee of correspondence to keep in contact with other colonial assemblies. Within a year, every colony but Pennsylvania had established a similar committee.

The local committees—developed at different times and in different places—acted as direct representatives of the people. Boston and smaller Massachusetts towns took the lead in organizing these committees. When the British government moved to make judges' salaries independent of the legislature, SAMUEL ADAMS was outraged. He convinced the Boston town meeting to call for the legislature to meet, and when the governor refused to gratify this request, Adams thought that it was time to create an organization to help guard the liberty of the people. In November 1772 he asked for a committee of correspondence to be formed "to state the Rights of the Colonists . . . as Men, as Christians, and as Subjects; to communicate and publish the same to the several Towns in this Province and the World as the sense of this Town, with the Enfringements and Violations thereof that have been, or from time to time may be made." He also wanted the committee to request that each town freely communicate "their Sentiments on this Subject." While not every community responded, half of the towns and districts in Massachusetts had set up committees of correspondence by April 1773.

Sam Adams could not have timed his organizational efforts better. In May 1773 Parliament passed the TEA ACT, and the committees of correspondence were abuzz with discussions of this new presumed attack on liberty. The Boston committee of correspondence organized the protest that culminated in the BOSTON TEA PARTY (December 16, 1773), and then guided the reaction to the Coercive Acts (1774), calling for nonimportation. Outside Boston, the New England committees of correspondence joined in this movement, while more committees started to appear elsewhere. As colonial Americans came to understand the full implications of the Coercive Acts, support for Boston grew. Committees began to organize the local MILITIA as New England prepared for armed conflict. By the time hostilities broke out, long organizational experience that had begun with the Sons of Liberty in 1765, and had accelerated with committees of correspondence in the 1770s, prepared men from a wide spectrum of society to assume the new responsibilities of self-government. During the REVOLUTIONARY WAR (1775–83) this experience would give the committeemen an edge over the LOYALISTS in gaining control over local communities.

See also RESISTANCE MOVEMENT.

Further reading: Richard D. Brown, *Revolutionary Politics in Massachusetts: The Boston Committee of Correspondence and the Towns, 1772–1774* (Cambridge, Mass.: Harvard University Press, 1970); Edward Countryman, *A People in Revolution: The American Revolution and Political Society in New York, 1760–1790* (Baltimore: Johns Hopkins University Press 1981).

Common Sense (1776)

In January 1776 THOMAS PAINE published *Common Sense,* a radical pamphlet that urged that British North Americans declare independence from GREAT BRITAIN. This work had a tremendous impact, selling more than 100,000 copies within the year and convincing many of the need to break free from King GEORGE III. Although hostilities had begun in April 1775, and even after George III asserted that the colonies were in a state of open rebellion in August 1775, many Revolutionary Americans were unable to take the imaginative leap and sever their British ties. Paine's pamphlet, however, paved the way for the DECLARATION OF INDEPENDENCE in July 1776.

Paine used plain language, references to the Bible, and logic from ENLIGHTENMENT writers to present his argument, which relied on simple and direct assertions. For example, in his introduction, Paine declared that "the cause of America is in great measure the cause of mankind" and thereby claimed a larger meaning for the conflict. He struck a similar note with brilliant imagery by declaring that "the sun never shined on a cause of greater worth." He continued this line of thought with the statement "Tis not the affair of a city, a country, a province, or a kingdom, but of a continent" and by proclaiming that all posterity had a stake in its outcome. With phrases like these, Paine swept away opposition and pressed the idea that right then and there, in the winter of 1776, was the time to strike for independence and create the United States.

Paine understood that the Bible was the one book that most Anglo-Americans were familiar with, and he used it with skill and determination. He did not just attack King George III—he attacked the very idea of monarchy and cited the Bible as proof of this position: "Monarchy is ranked in the scriptures as one of the sins of the Jews." Paine then went on to cite chapter and verse about how the Jewish insistence on having a king had led to the downfall of ancient Israel, quoting long sections of Samuel to highlight God's displeasure with the idea of having a king. He then concluded in his straightforward prose: "These portions of scripture are direct and positive. They admit no equivocal construction. That the Almighty hath entered here his protest against monarchical government is true, or the scripture is false."

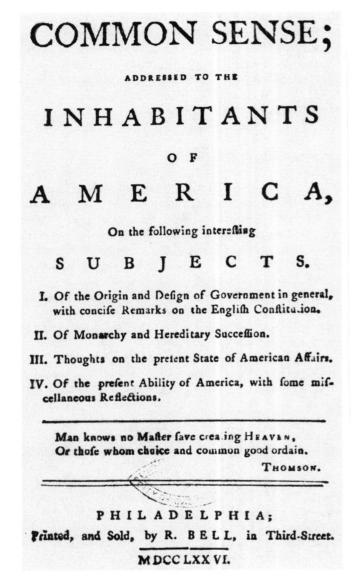

one." In short, "government, like dress, is the badge of lost innocence." From this perspective "the palaces of kings are built on the ruins of the bowers of paradise."

Combining forthright language with biblical references and Enlightenment ideas, Paine leveled a devastating attack on the English constitution, the king of England, and even hereditary aristocracy. Until the publication of his pamphlet, most colonial Americans revered the British constitution, believed that the king was ultimately good, and clung to notions of hierarchy. *Common Sense* therefore marked a radical break from the past. Paine had little respect for the balance of powers that supposedly lay at the core of the English constitution. He posited that if the king could not be trusted and had to have his power balanced, what good was he in the first place? Moreover, the king held the greatest weight in the balance, tipping the scale in his favor through the use of patronage and pensions. The British had great faith in their supposedly balanced constitution, but this confidence "arises as much or more from national pride as reason." From Paine's perspective, "the fate of Charles the First," who was executed in 1649 by the English people for abusing power, "hath made kings more subtle—not more just." Ultimately, it was the constitution of the people and not the constitution of the government that was the source of LIBERTY.

Paine derided the king, writing that "there is something exceedingly ridiculous in the composition of a monarchy." He argued that the king lived so removed from the people that it was impossible for him to truly know those he governed, yet he was daily expected to make decisions as if he understood what the world was like for common people. The origins of the British monarch also could not bear close scrutiny. The kings of England claimed their descent from William the Conqueror. Paine wrote that this lineage was not "a very honorable one" since William was nothing more than "a French bastard landing with an armed banditti," who established himself king "against the consent of the natives." Such a claim to the throne "is in plain terms a very paltry rascally original—It certainly hath no divinity in it."

Paine continued this logic by attacking all hereditary succession, including an aristocracy. He believed that it was possible for a man to rise and show distinction in this world, and that it was just and right for him to be honored. But the fact that one person could stand out does not guarantee that his children and his children's children would also share the same qualities. By using hereditary succession, then, a society guaranteed that at some point power would fall into the hands of an incompetent, or an imbecile, or someone even worse.

Paine argued not only for independence but also for a national republic. He called for a national single-house legislature with a weak executive chosen by the Congress. He also expressed tremendous confidence in the new nation to

If Paine used RELIGION, he relied on the ideas of the Enlightenment even more. The influence of the Enlightenment, which centered on a belief in the relationship between nature and reason, can be seen in the repeated references to "natural principles." Paine also simplified the ideas of JOHN LOCKE by putting complex thoughts on the origin of government into prose almost everyone could understand: "Society is produced by our wants, and government by our wickedness." Thus, humans were seen as social individuals who must rely on government for some protection. Paine wrote that "society in every state is a blessing, but government is but a necessary evil; in its worse state an intolerable

wage a successful war against Great Britain and to create a government that would protect the rights of every citizen, including freedom of religion, and thus meet the true objectives of government. His would be an almost invisible republic since he believed "that the more simple any thing is, the less liable it is to be disordered."

As compelling as these ideas appeared at the time, many revolutionary leaders opposed them. Men like JOHN ADAMS, who also advocated independence, thought that Paine's radicalism went too far. Regardless of Adams's opinion, Paine's pamphlet had a tremendous impact and significantly affected the course of history.

See also REPUBLICANISM.

Further reading: Eric Foner, *Tom Paine and Revolutionary America* (New York: Oxford University Press, 1976).

commonwealthmen

During the 18th century a group of thinkers and writers developed a critique of the British government, which was dominated by the Whig political party. This group, which historians call the commonwealthmen, saw themselves as the real or true WHIGS—advocates of the tradition of limited government inherited from the English civil wars of the 1640s and the Glorious Revolution of 1688–89. While the commonwealthmen were only a minority in GREAT BRITAIN and never wielded any political power, their writings had a profound influence in North America and were the source of many of the ideas held by the leaders of the RESISTANCE MOVEMENT (1764–75) against imperial regulation. The ideology of REPUBLICANISM grew out of the commonwealthmen tradition.

Although commonwealthmen traced their roots to 17th-century thinkers such as James Harrington, JOHN LOCKE, and even Thomas Hobbes, scholars argue that they emerged as an identifiable group shortly after the overthrow of James II in 1688. They wanted to push reform even further than had occurred with the agreement between Parliament and the new monarchs, William and Mary. Commonwealthmen warned against the consolidation of power in the hands of the ministry, argued for full religious toleration, and wanted to reform Parliament to make it a truly representative body. A leading figure of this movement was Robert Molesworth, whose *Account of Denmark* (1694) outlined how a free state could fall into absolutism, especially through the combination of religious and political tyranny.

One of the most influential works for British Americans was *Cato's Letters* (1723) by John Trenchard and Thomas Gordon, who offered a critique of the government of Sir Robert Walpole, the Whig Party, and the Bank of England. Trenchard and Gordon highlighted the inverse relationship between the power of government and the liberty of the people. From this perspective, "Whatever is good for the People, is bad for the Governors; and whatever is good for the Governors is pernicious for the People." They expressed tremendous faith in the will of the people: "It is certain that the whole People . . . are the best Judges whether things go ill or well with the Publick." The humblest individual could be trusted to understand the basic facts concerning liberty since "every Cobbler can judge as well as a Statesmen, whether he can sit peaceably in his Stall; whether he is paid for his Work; whether the Market, where he buys his Victuals, will be provided; and whether a Dragoon or a Parish Officer comes to him for his Taxes. . . ." Therefore, it was up to the people to protect their liberty and, through the constitution—which in England was unwritten—to ensure the limits on power. "Power is like Fire; it warms, scorches, or destroys, according as it is watched, provoked, or increased."

Commonwealthmen continued to make their views known throughout the 18th century. They believed in a balanced constitution and held that British citizens were entitled to be ruled by laws of their own choosing. They even extended this principle to all of mankind. As a corollary to this ideal, they argued for freedom of thought in RELIGION and in politics. They wanted to spread the benefit of EDUCATION to include the poor as well as the middle classes. While commonwealthmen seldom pushed for a radical overhaul of the social structure, their ideas questioned privilege and encouraged equality. In the mid-18th century they took up the cause of Ireland, and much of the British support for colonial rights in the 1760s and 1770s could trace itself to commonwealth ideas. This last point is hardly surprising since many Revolutionary leaders had read extensively in the true Whig tradition and incorporated commonwealth ideas into their rationale for resisting imperial regulation.

Further reading: Bernard Bailyn, *The Ideological Origins of the American Revolution* (Cambridge, Mass.: Harvard University Press, 1967); Caroline Robbins, *The Eighteenth-Century Commonwealthman: Studies in the Transmission, Development and Circumstance of English Liberal Thought from the Restoration of Charles II until the War with the Thirteen Colonies* (Cambridge, Mass.: Harvard University Press, 1959).

Confederation Congress   See CONTINENTAL CONGRESS, SECOND.

Conjocta Creek, Battle of (August 3, 1814)

After U.S. forces were driven back at the BATTLE OF LUNDY'S LANE (July 25, 1814), British general SIR GORDON DRUMMOND planned to attack FORT ERIE. He ordered

Colonel John Tucker and 380 men across the Niagara River to occupy a position on the exposed right flank of the fort. A regular army regiment of 240 men under Major Lodowick Morgan, however, interceded, having taken up a defensive position behind Conjocta Creek. They leveled a withering fire on the British advance, and after a two-hour battle that began at dawn, Tucker withdrew with 12 men killed, 17 wounded, and five missing. Morgan lost only two men killed and eight wounded.

Connecticut Farms, Battle of (June 7, 1780)

Believing that the CONTINENTAL ARMY was on the verge of collapse, General WILHELM VON KNYPHAUSEN launched a major sortie into New Jersey. Knyphausen, in command of British forces in New York while General SIR HENRY CLINTON was in South Carolina, also hoped to rally the support of LOYALISTS in the wake of Clinton's capture of Charleston on May 12, 1780, known as the SIEGE OF CHARLESTON. Landing near Elizabethtown, Knyphausen advanced to Connecticut Farms (modern day Union, New Jersey) with 5,000 soldiers, intending to attack the Revolutionaries at MORRISTOWN. He met with resistance from some Continental troops and local MILITIA and, realizing that his plan would not succeed, withdrew on the night of June 8 to Elizabethtown, where he dug in and built a pontoon bridge to Staten Island. The British burned about 30 homes in Connecticut Farms and killed at least one civilian before leaving the town. The Revolutionaries lost about 15 killed and 40 wounded in the fighting around Connecticut Farms; British casualties have been estimated at around 100.

Further reading: Harry M. Ward, *General William Maxwell and the New Jersey Continentals* (Westport, Conn.: Greenwood Press, 1997).

Connecticut Wits

Sometimes referred to as the Hartford Wits, the Connecticut Wits were a group of writers who as young men expressed great enthusiasm for REPUBLICANISM and the AMERICAN REVOLUTION in the 1770s and early 1780s. Feeling betrayed by the democratic and egalitarian currents of the age, they generally became conservative by the late 1780s and identified with the FEDERALIST PARTY in the 1790s and early 1800s. Most notable of this group were TIMOTHY DWIGHT, John Trumbull (cousin of the painter JOHN TRUMBULL), DAVID HUMPHREYS, NOAH WEBSTER, and Lemuel Hopkins. JOEL BARLOW is also often counted as a Connecticut Wit in his early years, but he never underwent the conservative conversion and retained a commitment to revolution and the ideals of equality. Most of the wits were from Connecticut and had attended Yale.

Even before the REVOLUTIONARY WAR (1775–83), the Wits expected great things of their culture. John Trumbull in 1771 wrote that "America hath a fair prospect in a few centuries of ruling both in art and arms." Hoping to be in the vanguard of this movement, the Wits became disillusioned, especially in the wake of SHAYS'S REBELLION (1786–87). Several of the Wits had a hand in a long poem, "The Anarchiad," first published in the *New Haven Gazette* in 1786 and 1787, criticizing the rebellion. They accused the farmers of seeking luxury and corrupting the republic. The poem declared:

> Here shall my best and brightest empire rise.
> Wild riot reign, and discord greet the skies.
> Awake my chosen sons, in folly brave.
> Stab independence! Dance o'er Freedom's grave.

However betrayed they may have felt by overreaching farmers and "Each leather-apron'd dunce," the Wits still had hope for the United States. In his "Greenfield Hill" (1801), Timothy Dwight extolled the virtues of rural Connecticut, "where Freedom walks erect, . . . And mild Simplicity o'er manners reigns." In this vision the farmer becomes a repository of virtue, and

> The harmony of life more sweetly blend;
> Hence labour brightens every rural scene;
> Hence cheerful plenty lives along the green.

See also LITERATURE.

Further reading: Edwin H. Cady, ed., *Literature of the Early Republic,* 2nd ed. (New York: Holt, Rinehart and Winston, 1969); Henry F. May, *The Enlightenment in America* (New York: Oxford University Press, 1976); Robert E. Shalhope, *The Roots of Democracy: American Thought and Culture, 1760–1800* (Boston: Twayne, 1990).

conspiracy labor trials

During the first decade of the 19th century, employers tried to weaken labor organizations by initiating several trials to prosecute journeymen workers for conspiracy in restraint of TRADE. Prosecutors argued that associations of workers were illegal when they attempted to control wages or dictate conditions in the workplace. These cases represent key developments in labor as masters, who were once merely ARTISANS who owned their own shop, became employers seeking to maximize profits.

The first, and most important, of these cases occurred in Philadelphia in 1806. Encouraged by master shoemakers, the prosecutors claimed that a group of journeymen shoemakers (also known as cordwainers) "did combine, conspire, confederate, and unlawfully agree together" to "increase and augment the prices and rates usually paid"; refused to work or lodge with other journeymen who were paid a lesser wage; threatened and intimidated those other workers and their employers; and "unlawfully *perniciously,* and deceitfully" designed and intended "to form and unite themselves into a club and combination." The case represented a culmination of developments that began in the early 1790s when the journeymen first organized an association—a labor union—in response to masters who were expanding production and driving wages down. Masters had shifted operations from "bespoke" work, which was done for a specific customer, to "shop" work, where shoes were made for general sale in the shop, and then to "order" work in which the master contracted for many pairs of shoes to be sold at a market in another city. In the process masters, who now made thousands of dollars a year, distanced themselves economically from shoemakers, who were lucky to earn a few hundred dollars a year.

The defense attorneys, including Caesar Rodney, pursued a four-pronged strategy. First, they argued a point of law by asserting that application of English common law, which was the basis of the prosecution's charge of conspiracy, was inappropriate. The American Revolution, contended the defense, had liberated colonial Americans from English tyranny, and that included the anachronistic precedents decided in feudal courts. Since Pennsylvania did not have a conspiracy statute, the defendants had violated no law. To convict, Rodney asserted, would mean reversing the outcome of the Revolution.

Second, they contested the facts of the case. The shoemakers had not restrained trade in any meaningful way. All they had done was decide for whom and with whom they would work. In other words, by refusing to work for an employer who hired scabs either during or after a strike, the defendants had merely exercised their rights as independent laborers. Nor, the Lawyers claimed, did the shoemakers coerce anyone to join them.

Third, the lawyers relied on the U.S. Constitution by claiming that the workers had a right to establish an association under the First Amendment's "right of the people to assemble." Rodney facetiously pointed out that shoemakers had as much right to form an organization as people who joined a dance society, students organizing a college club, or the masters getting together to lobby the city government to prosecute the journeymen.

Finally, the defense asserted a sense of social justice embedded in the egalitarian ideals of the Revolution. Rodney decried the greediness of the masters who were unsatisfied "with the rapid rate at which they were at present amassing wealth" and wished "to make their fortunes by a single turn of the wheel." He was afraid that if the masters could dictate the terms of employment now, they might someday even determine where the journeymen could live and what they could eat.

These arguments resonated with many Philadelphians, even if they had little impact in the courtroom. William Duane, the radical Jeffersonian newspaper editor, wrote in the *Aurora* that "the case of the shoemakers is only another proof of the tendency of *lazy luxury* to enslave the men of industry who acquire their bread by labor." Judge Moses Levy, who like Duane and Rodney was a member of the Democratic-Republican Party, saw things differently. If one branch of the Democratic-Republicans in the early 19th century remained concerned with the plight of the common man, another branch, represented in this instance by Levy, took the Jeffersonian emphasis on the importance of the individual and applied it to free-market economics. Levy told the jury before its deliberations, "The usual means by which the prices of work are regulated, are the demand of the article and the excellence of the fabric." Applying the ideas of Adam Smith, Levy proclaimed that "where the work is well done, and the demand is considerable, the prices will necessarily be high. Where the work is ill done, and the demand is inconsiderable, they will unquestionably be low." The effort by the journeymen shoemakers to set wages interfered with these laws of economics by instituting "an artificial regulation" and fixing an "arbitrary price, governed by a standard, controuled by no impartial person, but dependant on the will of the few who are interested." This approach was "the unnatural way of raising the price of goods and work," was counter to the public good, and constituted a conspiracy. Armed with this charge, the jury convicted the shoemakers.

The 1806 Philadelphia conspiracy case became a precedent for other antilabor prosecutions in the early republic and throughout the 19th century. When New York shoemakers went on strike in 1809, the masters pushed for a conspiracy trial. In this case the journeymen sought not only to dictate wages and control which journeymen the masters could hire, but also to limit the number of apprentices in each master's shop. Many masters had begun to use apprenticeship not as a means to train young men to become journeymen but as a source of cheap labor; the men would only be half-trained and would never become as skilled as the journeymen. The defense in the New York case reiterated many of the same arguments Rodney and the other defense attorneys had used in Philadelphia, with a similar lack of success. The journeymen were convicted and the control of the masters of their own shops vindicated.

Further reading: John Rogers Commons, ed., *A Documentary History of Industrial Society*, vols. 3–4 (Cleveland: The A.H. Clark Company, 1910–11).

Constellation, USS

The USS *Constellation* was the first frigate commissioned by the U.S. NAVY as part of the fleet of six frigates ordered in 1794 and built following the design of JOSHUA HUMPHREYS. Launched on September 27, 1797, just in time for service in the QUASI-WAR (1798–1800) with FRANCE, the *Constellation* quickly earned fame in the WEST INDIES in two ship-on-ship actions. Under Captain Thomas Truxton, the 38-gun *Constellation* defeated the French 40-gun *L'Insurgente* on February 9, 1799, in a battle that lasted an hour and a half. The *Constellation*'s broadsides were accurate and devastating; the French lost 29 killed and 41 wounded, while Truxton had only one killed and three wounded. Almost a year later, on February 1, 1800, the *Constellation* took on a bigger foe and fought a battle with the 54-gun *La Vengeance*. After a four-hour contest in the dark, the French ship veered off. The *Constellation*'s masts and rigging were so damaged that Truxton could not pursue. Both sides claimed victory, although the French had higher casualties—about 100 killed and wounded to the *Constellation*'s 18 killed and 21 wounded. Truxton remained convinced that had the French not used the night to escape, he would have captured *La Vengeance*.

The *Constellation* remained in active service until 1853. The ship was stationed in the MEDITERRANEAN SEA during the BARBARY WARS, taking part in several actions, including the bombardment of Tripoli. However, during the WAR OF 1812 (1812–15) the *Constellation* was blockaded in Norfolk, unable to get to sea. In the 20th century the frigate *Constellation* in Baltimore harbor had been identified as the ship launched in 1797. However, during the 1990s historical evidence indicated that the Baltimore tourist attraction was really a newer ship launched in 1854, a year after the older vessel had been broken up.

Further reading: William M. Fowler, Jr., *Jack Tars and Commodores: The American Navy, 1783–1815* (Boston: Houghton Mifflin, 1984).

Constitution, ratification of the

The ratification of the U.S. CONSTITUTION was a near thing. Modern assumptions about the need for a strong government and more than 200 years of history testifying to the success of the U.S. government under the Constitution have obscured this fact. In all likelihood, had there been a referendum on the Constitution, it would have been rejected. The authors of the Constitution understood the precariousness of their position and therefore created a ratification procedure intended to sidestep the amendment provisions of the ARTICLES OF CONFEDERATION, which mandated a unanimous decision by the states for amendment. The Constitution declared that the new form of government would be put into place once nine states had ratified and thus eliminated the unanimous requirement, which had stalled efforts to strengthen the Articles—for instance, it prevented the SECOND CONTINENTAL CONGRESS from having the power to tax. Moreover, since the members of the CONSTITUTIONAL CONVENTION feared that the state legislatures would hesitate to endorse a form of government that weakened the power of the states, the Constitution placed ratification in the hands of special state CONVENTIONS. The FEDERALISTS planned to move as quickly as possible and engineered ratification within a year of the Philadelphia Convention's adjournment.

The first wave of ratification was largely by those states that had the most to gain by the creation of a stronger union. Many people in the smaller states believed that they needed the protection of the federal government and that they would have a significant voice in national affairs within the Senate and the electoral college. Delaware became the first state in the new union when it ratified the Constitution on December 7, 1787, with a vote of 30-0. New Jersey, which carried a heavy debt and had little revenue of its own, voted for ratification on December 18, 1787, with a 39-0 vote. Georgia, which at the time was a small state with borders exposed to the Spanish in FLORIDA, powerful groups of NATIVE AMERICANS occupying the backcountry, and a large and potentially rebellious slave population, also ratified unanimously (26-0) on January 2, 1788. The final small state to join in early ratification was Connecticut, where there was some opposition to the Constitution from farmers and rural communities. But most merchants, LAWYERS, and clergy supported ratification, and on January 9, 1788, the Connecticut convention voted 128-40 for the Constitution.

The Constitution was a more contentious issue in the larger states. Pennsylvania Federalists managed to gain a speedy ratification before the opposition could really get organized. They pushed through the state assembly a call for a ratifying convention on September 28, 1787—the same day Congress submitted the Constitution to the states. A quick election brought a Federalist majority to the state convention and ratification on December 12, 1787—just five days after Delaware. However, the ANTI-FEDERALISTS did not go down without a fight. The division in the state reflected the divisions that had emerged over the Pennsylvania state constitution, with the "constitutionalists" backing the democratic state constitution and opposing the U.S. Constitution and the "republicans"—who wanted to alter the state constitution and make it more conservative—becoming Federalists. Although the Federalists won in the convention voting, 46-23, after the state convention the Pennsylvania Anti-Federalists met in Carlisle, Pennsylvania, and issued a manifesto that aptly summarized their objections to the Constitution and helped to provide an outline of the Anti-Federalist cause. They attacked the Constitution for creating too much power in government at the expense of the people's LIBERTY and demanded a BILL OF RIGHTS with guarantees similar to those written into the Pennsylvania constitution.

If, by the end of January, the Federalists had built up a certain momentum toward ratification, the real test of their political skills was still before them. Without Massachusetts, New York, and Virginia there could be no United States—and beyond these big three, South Carolina, Maryland, New Hampshire, North Carolina, and Rhode Island had still not ratified. In all of these states the acceptance of the Constitution was problematical at best.

Maryland and South Carolina ratified the Constitution in early spring. Some of the most important leaders in Maryland opposed the Constitution, including two signers of the DECLARATION OF INDEPENDENCE, SAMUEL CHASE and WILLIAM PACA; and two members of the Constitutional Convention who had left before deliberations were complete and who refused to sign the document, LUTHER MARTIN and JOHN FRANCIS MERCER. However, few Anti-Federalists attended the state convention, which voted 63-11 to endorse the new government on April 26, 1788. South Carolina was divided between up-country farmers who opposed the Constitution as undemocratic and low-country planters and merchants who supported it. The legislature voted 76-75 to call the state convention, which ended up with a disproportionate number of low-country representatives and met in Charleston, where the Federalists were strongest. With many planters viewing the Constitution as protecting SLAVERY, South Carolina voted 149–73 in favor of the document on May 23, 1788.

By the time Maryland and South Carolina had acted, Massachusetts—the first of the final big three states—had ratified despite an Anti-Federalist majority at the state convention. The Federalists were explicit about the economic benefits of belonging to a stronger union and argued that under the Constitution, New England could capture the carrying TRADE of the South from the British. Such appeals to economic interests fueled the fears of many of the Anti-Federalists who decried the "lawyers, and men of learning, and moneyed men" who expected "to be managers of this Constitution, and get all the power and money into their own hands" so that they could "swallow up" the "little folks, like the great Leviathan . . . just as the whale swallowed up Jonah." Despite such rhetoric, ratification ultimately turned on the question of a BILL OF RIGHTS, and after winning over such Anti-Federalist leaders as JOHN HANCOCK and SAMUEL ADAMS with promises of amendments, Massachusetts ratified with the slim margin of 187-168 on February 16, 1788.

The ninth state to ratify—and thus put the new government into effect—was New Hampshire. Its convention

first met in February and voted 70-30 against ratification. Rather than calling it quits, however, the Federalists managed to get an adjournment until June. Many of the delegates had been instructed to vote no to the Constitution, and the Federalists hoped the extra time would bring a release from these obligations. A few months of an intensive Federalist newspaper campaign (see FEDERALIST PAPERS), along with the fact that eight other states had ratified, worked wonders. On June 21, 1788, the New Hampshire convention voted 57-47 in favor of the Constitution.

After New Hampshire's action, the new Constitution had become a reality—yet its viability remained in doubt as long as New York and Virginia were undecided. In both states a Bill of Rights became the main sticking point. An almost evenly divided convention met in Virginia on June 2, 1788. If the Federalists could boast the support of GEORGE WASHINGTON and JAMES MADISON, the Anti-Federalists were led by PATRICK HENRY, RICHARD HENRY LEE, GEORGE MASON, and BENJAMIN HARRISON. Henry headed the attack by declaring that the Constitution created a "consolidated government" that took power away from the states and gave it to a central government. A final bitter compromise emerged. The Federalists successfully achieved ratification, avoiding a demand for a list of amendments submitted by Henry, but they also had to promise to instruct Virginia's congressional delegation to do everything it could to adopt the proposed Bill of Rights and amendments. The final vote was a close 89-79 on June 26, 1788.

The New York convention began on June 17 with the most powerful politician in the state, Governor GEORGE CLINTON, set against the Constitution, backed by a clear majority of the 64 delegates, 46 of whom were allied to Clinton. Facing an uphill battle, the Federalists did everything they could to obtain ratification, stalling for time as they awaited news from New Hampshire and Virginia. The Federalists twisted arms, made promises, and threatened to have New York City secede from the state to join the union. The Anti-Federalists decried the Constitution as a threat to the state's integrity and a vehicle for the rich and well-born to rule, and they lambasted the document for its failure to include a bill of rights. After news of ratification by New Hampshire and Virginia, some of the Anti-Federalists realized that New York had to join the union. Therefore leaders including MELANCTON SMITH reluctantly changed sides and voted for ratification, which passed by a 30-27 vote on July 26, 1788. The convention also voted unanimously to call for a second convention to reconsider the document, strengthen the states' power, and include a Bill of Rights.

In less than a year, 11 states had approved the system of federal government set out by the Constitution. Two states, however, hesitated to ratify it. The North Carolina convention, which met from July 21 to August 4, 1788, decided "to neither to ratify nor reject the Constitution proposed for the government of the United States," insisting on amendments before taking any definitive action. But once the new government went into operation, the people of North Carolina changed their minds. A new convention met and, on November 21, 1789, ratified the document and reiterated the call for a declaration of rights with a 194-77 vote. Rhode Island was more obstinate. In a vote by towns in March 1788, Rhode Islanders rejected even holding a state convention, 28-2. In 1790, when Congress threatened to treat the state as foreign territory and cut off direct trade, a new movement to ratify emerged. A convention met in March 1790, adopted a set of proposed amendments, and adjourned. The convention reconvened and, despite a strong Anti-Federalist presence, on May 29, 1790, voted 34-32 to accept the Constitution.

See also CONSTITUTIONAL PROCESSIONS.

Further reading: Linda Grant Depauw, *The Eleventh Pillar: New York State and the Federal Constitution* (Ithaca, N.Y.: Cornell University Press, 1966); Michael Allen Gillespie and Michael Lienesch, *Ratifying the Constitution* (Lawrence: University of Kansas Press, 1989); Owen S. Ireland, *Religion, Ethnicity, and Politics: Ratifying the Constitution in Pennsylvania* (University Park: Pennsylvania State University Press, 1996); Jackson Turner Main, *The Anti-Federalists: Critics of the Constitution, 1781–1788* (Chapel Hill: University of North Carolina Press, 1961); Robert Rutland, *The Ordeal of the Constitution: The Antifederalists and the Ratification Struggle of 1787–1788* (Norman: University of Oklahoma Press, 1965).

Constitution, U.S.

With some amendments, the U.S. Constitution created the fundamental law of the government of the United States from 1787 to the present. It established two houses of legislature, a powerful executive, a Supreme Court, and a process for ratification and amendment.

The Constitution opens with a preamble declaring that the document has been written in the name of the "people of the United States" and that the purpose of the document is "to form a more perfect union." Article 1 outlines the government's legislative branch. Section 1 describes the bicameral makeup of the legislature and the powers with which Congress is vested. Section 2 concerns the House of Representatives, stipulating that members are to be elected every two years and that REPRESENTATION is based on population, which is to be set by a census every 10 years. To determine representation, the government will add to the number of free individuals three-fifths of the total number of "all other persons" (slaves; see THREE-FIFTHS CLAUSE). (The Thirteenth Amendment [1865] freed slaves in the

United States, and the Fourteenth Amendment defined CITIZENSHIP to include AFRICAN AMERICANS.) Members of the House of Representatives must be at least 25 years old and citizens for seven years. The House chooses its own Speaker and has sole responsibility for impeachment.

Section 3 deals with the Senate. Each state has two senators serving six-year terms on a rotating basis so that no more than one-third of the Senate comes up for election every two years. State legislators choose the senators (this provision was changed by the Seventeenth Amendment [1913]). Senators must be at least 30 years old, citizens for nine years, and residents of the states that elected them. The vice president is to be president of the Senate, but the Senate elects all other officers of that body. The Senate has the power try impeachments; conviction will lead to removal from office.

Sections 4–6 elaborate on procedures concerning both houses, allowing the states to set conditions for the election of the legislative branch and requiring annual meetings. Both houses of the legislative branch have control over their own proceedings, and members are paid for their service. They are also immune from most arrests and prevented from holding other civil offices.

Section 7 gives the House of Representatives exclusive power to originate revenue measures, but the Senate can offer amendments. This section also allows the legislative branch to override presidential vetoes with a two-thirds majority.

Sections 8 and 9 outline Congress's broad powers to legislate on a host of issues, including declaring war and raising taxes. To ensure that it can extend these powers, the Constitution declares that Congress can "make all laws which shall be necessary and proper for carrying into execution" the legislation. Section 9 begins by prohibiting Congress from outlawing the international SLAVE TRADE, though this is stated without using the word *slave*.

Article 2 is about the executive, who is to be called "President of the United States." An electoral college comprising individuals selected by the states—with each state having a total number of electors equal to the number of senators plus the number of members of the House of Representatives from the state—selects the president every four years. The person with the greatest number of votes in the electoral college becomes president, and (in a clause later changed) the person with the second-greatest number of votes becomes vice president, who is to assume the presidency in the event of death or if for some reason the president cannot fulfill his duties as chief executive. If no one receives a majority, then the election goes to the House of Representatives, which votes for the president by state delegations. Only those who are natural-born citizens, or citizens at the time of the adoption of the Constitution; at least 35 years old; and residents of the United States for

14 years can become president. (The TWELFTH AMENDMENT [1804] altered electoral procedure to have separate elections for the president and vice president, and the Twenty-second Amendment [passed 1947; ratified 1951] set a two-term limit on the president.) The president has broad powers and is commander in chief of the armed forces. He can make treaties with the advice and consent of the Senate and appoint officers of the government as determined by future legislation. The president can veto laws passed by Congress—subject to a two-thirds majority override—and can be removed from office by IMPEACHMENT only for "treason, bribery, or other high crimes and misdemeanors."

Article 3 establishes a SUPREME COURT and empowers Congress to create other inferior federal courts. Judges, as stipulated in Article 3, Section 2, are appointed by the president with the advice and consent of the Senate and hold office "during good behavior"; they are thus exempt from specific terms or executive removal. Federal judges can only be forced from office through the impeachment process. The Constitution did not, and still does not, give the Supreme Court the power to decide on the constitutionality of laws, although at the time it was written, some people believed that such a power was implied in the Constitution, and the Supreme Court assumed that duty in 1803. The Constitution gives the Supreme Court jurisdiction over cases that derive from the Constitution, federal laws, and treaties made by the United States. The Court also has jurisdiction over maritime law and cases involving states and individuals from different states. Article 3 defines *treason* as levying war against the United States or supporting the nation's enemies.

Article 4 outlines additional powers of the federal government as they relate to the states. These measures stipulate that the laws in one state must be respected by the other states. This provision includes a fugitive-slave clause—using the phrase "person held to service or labor" instead of the word *slave*—ensuring the return of escaped slaves from one state to another. Article 4 also empowers the federal government to admit new states, guarantees a republican form of government in each state, and pledges states to protect each other in the event of invasion.

Article 5 sets up the means whereby the Constitution can be amended. This provision makes it difficult to change the Constitution but falls short of the unanimous-state requirement for amendment under the ARTICLES OF CONFEDERATION. Amendments need to be proposed by two-thirds of both houses of legislature and then ratified by either three-fourths of the state legislatures or, if Congress so deems, three-fourths of specially called state CONVENTIONS. A new federal convention to consider amendments need the approval of two-thirds of the state legislatures.

Article 6 is relatively short but includes three important provisions. First, it pledges the new government to honor all contracts and debts of the previous government and thus asserts a commitment to deal with the national debt (see DEBT, NATIONAL). Second, it proclaims that all laws and treaties of the national government are the supreme law of the land, asserting the supremacy of the national government over the state governments. Finally, Article 6 binds all government officers to an oath of office in support of the Constitution but refuses to include a religious test as a qualification for office. This provision helped to establish the separation of church and state even before the BILL OF RIGHTS.

Article 7 sets up the procedure by which state conventions ratify the Constitution and, sidestepping the amendment requirement in the Articles of Confederation, established the new government once nine states had ratified.

Although subsequently amended 27 times, the basic outlines of the U.S. Constitution remain the same as it appeared in 1787.

See also ANTI-FEDERALISTS; CONSTITUTION, RATIFICATION OF THE; CONSTITUTIONAL CONVENTION; FEDERALISTS; FUGITIVE SLAVE LAW; NECESSARY AND PROPER CLAUSE; STATES' RIGHTS.

Constitution, USS

The USS *Constitution* was one of six frigates authorized by Congress in 1794 to become the core of the young U.S. NAVY in order to meet threats from Algiers and possibly the British and French. Designed by JOSHUA HUMPHREYS, these vessels were super frigates, larger than most vessels of that class, and just as fast. Each was built in a different part of the United States. The *Constitution* was built in Boston and launched on October 21, 1797, just in time for the U.S. conflict with FRANCE in the QUASI-WAR (1798–1800). Although the *Constitution* cruised the waters of the Caribbean, protecting U.S. commerce from 1798 to 1801, it was not involved in any sea battles. The frigate was laid up in Boston in 1802 during President THOMAS JEFFERSON's initial efforts to cut back on naval expenditures. However, in 1803 Jefferson sent the ship to the MEDITERRANEAN SEA to join the campaign against Tripoli (1801–05). As a part of that effort, the *Constitution* and other naval vessels bombarded that city. The final peace treaty with Tripoli was signed on the deck of the *Constitution* in June 1805.

The *Constitution* earned its reputation during the WAR OF 1812 (1812–15). Soon after the war began, the men who served on the frigate demonstrated their fortitude—and their ship's sailing qualities—when a squadron of five British ships pursued the *Constitution* for three days, starting on July 17, 1812. With all vessels becalmed off the coast of New Jersey, the men of the *Constitution* first towed their vessel in rowboats, then kedged it—repeatedly towing an anchor away from the vessel, dropping it, and pulling the ship to the anchor's location—to keep just ahead of their pursuers. When a wisp of wind finally appeared, the speedy *Constitution* managed to get clean away.

Over the next six months, the *Constitution* would engage in two battles of almost equal opponents and emerge victorious. On August 19, 1812, the ship met and defeated the HMS *Guerriere* about 600 miles east of Boston. In this short and brutal fight, the *Constitution*'s superior qualities came to the fore: Her thick oak sides seemed to repel the shot of the British vessel, and because of this apparent impregnability, her men began to call her "Old Ironsides." The *Guerriere* was pulverized into surrender, losing 79 men to the *Constitution*'s 12. The British vessel was so badly damaged that it had to be sunk.

On December 29, 1812, the *Constitution* fought the HMS *Java* off the coast of Brazil. The battle lasted more than two hours, and both ships suffered damage, but by the time the *Java* surrendered, she was a wreck and had lost her captain and about 150 men; the *Constitution* sustained 34 casualties, and the *Java,* too, had to be scuttled. For most of the rest of the war, the *Constitution* remained blockaded in Boston. However, in December 1814, she managed to slip out of port. On February 20, 1815, unaware of the TREATY OF GHENT (1814), the *Constitution* ran across two smaller British warships, HMS *Cyane* and HMS *Levant.* She fought and captured both, but only managed to return to the United States with the *Cyane* as the *Levant* had been recaptured by a British squadron.

After the War of 1812, "Old Ironsides" served for several decades as a U.S. warship. After 1855 she was converted to a training ship and was later used as a barracks. Today, the *Constitution* can be visited at the Charlestown Navy Yard in Boston, still part of the U.S. Navy and a proud representative of her national heritage.

Further reading: William M. Fowler, Jr., *Jack Tars and Commodores: The American Navy, 1783–1815* (Boston: Houghton Mifflin, 1984).

Constitutional Convention (1787)

In May 1787 the Constitutional Convention convened in Philadelphia with the purpose of revising the ARTICLES OF CONFEDERATION. The delegates decided to go beyond the scope of their original charge and create a new form of government, embodied in the U.S. CONSTITUTION.

The convention met at the recommendation of the ANNAPOLIS CONVENTION (1786), which had gathered to discuss commerce on the Chesapeake Bay. Unable to make any progress after three days, the delegates at Annapolis called for a new convention to assemble in Philadelphia in summer 1787 "to devise such further provisions as shall appear to them necessary to render the constitution of the Federal Government adequate to the exigencies of the Union." In February Congress belatedly agreed to the convention but insisted that it confine itself to suggesting needed revisions. Nationalists had a different idea. Frustrated by the inability of the U.S. government to raise taxes under the Articles of Confederation without the unanimous assent of all the states, and believing that the states were too susceptible to the fickle will of the people, the nationalists seized on this opportunity to form a more powerful central government.

In May, delegates representing 12 states began assembling in Philadelphia (Rhode Island was never involved in the convention), eventually numbering 55; there were usually only around 30–40 delegates in attendance on any given day. The majority of the delegates had come to believe that the United States needed a more powerful central government dominated by, as JAMES MADISON explained, "the purest and noblest characters"—a natural aristocracy—who would be able to "protect the public interest." Most of the delegates had some experience on the national stage in the FIRST CONTINENTAL CONGRESS, SECOND CONTINENTAL CONGRESS, or the CONTINENTAL ARMY. As a whole they were a young and ambitious group of men: The average age of the delegates was 42. There were a few elder statesmen such as BENJAMIN FRANKLIN and GEORGE WASHINGTON, but their own experience during the REVOLUTIONARY WAR (1775–83) made them just as committed to the nationalist cause as their younger counterparts. Washington was the unanimous choice for president of the convention, and his prestige increased the chances of the country accepting its outcome. A few of the other prominent active members were GOUVERNEUR MORRIS of Pennsylvania, RUFUS KING and ELBRIDGE GERRY of Massachusetts, and ALEXANDER HAMILTON from New York. Hamilton, in particular, was intent on promoting a nationalist vision. Perhaps the most influential delegate was Madison, who would eventually be known as the "Father of the Constitution," since he drew up the Virginia Plan, which would become the blueprint for the Constitution. In addition, Madison's meticulous notes remain our main source for the convention's daily proceedings. There were also a number of important statesmen who were absent, including JOHN ADAMS, who was in England; THOMAS JEFFERSON, who was serving as minister to FRANCE; and PATRICK HENRY, who had declined to participate since he supported state sovereignty and was suspicious of the proceedings.

Much of the work and compromising took place in the informal gatherings, of which we have little record. The meetings were held in INDEPENDENCE HALL in complete secrecy, although this had been a point of spirited debate. The majority of the delegates supported the closed-door sessions, believing that daily reports of the debates would lead to grandstanding and prevent open discussion. Not allowing the public access to the deliberations would also limit the opportunity for the opposition to organize and develop their arguments.

Crucial to the entire enterprise was the question of how much power the state governments should have as opposed to the national government. In a concession to state sovereignty, and following the pattern of voting in the Continental Congress under the Articles of Confederation, each state was given one vote. Ultimately, however, the delegates hoped to strengthen the national government and limit the power of the states. In particular, they believed that in order to operate efficiently, the central government had to have powers, especially to tax, to coin MONEY, to regulate matters between the states, and to deal with FOREIGN AFFAIRS.

The proponents of a strong national government seized the initiative when EDMUND RANDOLPH introduced the Virginia Plan on May 29. Based on Madison's careful study of political theory and natural law, the Virginia Plan provided for a bicameral legislature, with the lower house elected by the people and the upper house elected by the lower house. There was also to be a judiciary and an executive (a president named by Congress), with a committee formed from these two groups that would have a veto on legislation. REPRESENTATION was to be based on the number of free inhabitants in a state. The national government would have an independent source of revenue and control over printing money, and it would guarantee contracts between individuals in different states. The committee of the whole discussed the Virginia Plan and made some significant alterations: State legislatures, instead of the lower house, were to choose the upper house (the Senate), and the executive alone was to have veto power. They also allowed for ratification of the new Constitution by state CONVENTIONS.

Some delegates feared that this arrangement would weaken the states and allow the larger ones to dominate the smaller ones. These men devised an alternative plan called the New Jersey Plan—sometimes called the Paterson Plan, after its main author, WILLIAM PATERSON. The New Jersey plan was merely a revision of the Articles of Confederation that would keep representation based on the states but would give Congress the powers to regulate commerce and to tax. The debate over the two plans threatened to disrupt the whole convention. In early July delegates worked out the so-called Great Compromise, which created two houses of legislature, with the upper house representing the states and the lower house representing the population within the states. The Senate was to have a greater say in foreign affairs and the lower house would have the exclusive power to originate money bills.

In August another intense debate erupted concerning SLAVERY. Most delegates from the northern states believed that slavery was evil and that at a minimum, the Constitution should abolish the SLAVE TRADE. They also objected to the idea that slaves should be counted in the population for representation. Southerners such as CHARLES PINCKNEY vehemently defended slavery as having existed in all great civilizations. Other southerners argued that slaves produced wealth and therefore would increase the taxes paid and strengthen the national government. A compromise of sorts was worked out. The word *slave* was not to appear in the Constitution, and the federal government was given the authority to abolish the slave trade in 20 years. Representation was to be based on the number of free inhabitants and "three-fifths of all other Persons"—a provision called the THREE-FIFTHS CLAUSE. Moreover, the federal government was empowered to pass fugitive slave legislation and given extensive authority in putting down rebellions, either by disgruntled citizens—as had occurred in SHAYS'S REBELLION (1786–87)—or by slaves.

Only 41 of the 55 original delegates were still present when the document was finished on September 17, 1787, and three of these refused to sign. The Constitution was then sent to the states for ratification. Ignoring the amendment process set up by the Articles of Confederation—which insisted on the unanimous approval of all state governments—special ratifying conventions, rather than the state legislatures, were called. Only nine states had to approve the document before it would take effect; other states could then approve it and join the union when they were ready. While ANTI-FEDERALISTS objected to the Constitution because it appeared to give the national government too much power and limit the participation of the people, the FEDERALISTS supported the document, arguing that it rested on the sovereignty of the people and represented a republican form of government.

See also CONSTITUTION, RATIFICATION OF THE; REPUBLICANISM.

Further reading: Catherine Drinker Bowen, *Miracle at Philadelphia: The Story of the Constitutional Convention, May to September, 1787* (Boston: Little, Brown, 1966); Paul Finkelman, *Slavery and the Founders: Race and Liberty in the Age of Jefferson* (Armonk, N.Y.: M. E. Sharpe, 1996); Gordon S. Wood, *The Creation of the American Republic, 1776–1787* (Chapel Hill: University of North Carolina Press, 1969).

constitutional processions

Beginning with a celebration by sailors and ship carpenters in Philadelphia on December 12, 1787, several urban communities held constitutional processions to commemorate the ratification of the U.S. CONSTITUTION. This first procession featured a horse-drawn, scaled-down model ship with sailors pretending to take soundings, shouting, "Three and twenty fathom—foul bottom" (23 ANTI-FEDERALISTS had voted against the Constitution at the Pennsylvania state ratification convention that day) and "Six and forty fathom—sound bottom, safe anchorage" (46 FEDERALISTS had voted for the Constitution).

Other cities had more elaborate parades that incorporated not only a model ship but also participants from a wide array of social backgrounds and occupations. Boston held its procession in the snow on February 8, 1788, after the state had ratified the Constitution. Its model ship was christened the *Federal Constitution,* and the celebration featured 4,000–5,000 tradesmen. On May 1, 1788, the people of Baltimore organized a constitutional procession with the ship *Federalist* and an elaborate order of march dividing the participants by trade. On May 27, 1788, there was a procession in Charleston, South Carolina, centered on a ship also called the *Federalist.*

The largest processions were held in Philadelphia (for a second time) and New York. Philadelphia Federalists decided to use the Fourth of July to restate their support of the Constitution and marshal the city's ARTISANS and workers in a public spectacle that would outdo everything that had been done previously. As many as 17,000 may have joined the procession—every trade in the city was represented in the parade. As one song (supposedly written by BENJAMIN FRANKLIN) proclaimed, "Ye merry Mechanics, come join in song, And let the brisk chorus go bounding along; Though some may be poor, and some rich there be, Yet all are contended, and happy, and free." The Philadelphia ship, dubbed the *Union,* was supposedly an actual barge captured by JOHN PAUL JONES. The parade in that city included floats that combined the skills of the artisans with the cause of a stronger federal government. Many floats contained workmen demonstrating their skills actually making products during the parade, and the banner of the Society for the Promotion of Manufactures declared, "May the Union Government Protect the Manufactures of America."

New Yorkers delayed their procession, hoping to wait until after their state had ratified the Constitution. But as July wore on and the debates at the state constitutional convention continued, the New York Federalists decided that a demonstration of mass support might help convince recalcitrant Anti-Federalists to accept the new government. On July 24, 1788, the New Yorkers held a massive procession that followed the pattern set by the other cities. Their model ship—named the *Hamilton* after the state's leading Federalist, ALEXANDER HAMILTON—not only had a crew of 30 sailors and marines but also carried enough cannon to fire a 13-gun salute. During the procession the *Hamilton*

was part of a poignant street theater when it took on a pilot to guide the ship from the "old Constitution" to the "new Constitution" in front of the building that housed the SECOND CONTINENTAL CONGRESS. Like the earlier processions, artisans played a prominent part, demonstrating their crafts on floats and marching under banners that combined the interests of their trade with the creation of a stronger national government. The banner of the pewterers—which is currently owned by the New-York Historical Society—included a painting of several tradesman at work making pewter pots, tableware, and mugs under a sign reading "The Federal Plan Most Solid & Secure, Americans Their Freedom Will Ensure, All Arts Shall Flourish in Columbia's Land, and All Her Sons Join as One Social Band." At the end of the parade the participants were served a huge feast in a pavilion designed by PIERRE-CHARLES L'ENFANT.

Despite the public display of support for the Constitution in these processions, many people in the United States—indeed, many workers in the cities where the processions took place—opposed the creation of a stronger national government and saw it as a threat to LIBERTY.

Further reading: Whitfield J. Bell, Jr., "The Federal Procession of 1788," *New-York Historical Society Quarterly* 46 (1962): 5–39; Paul A. Gilje, "The Common People and the Constitution: Popular Culture in New York City in the Late Eighteenth Century," in *New York in the Age of the Constitution, 1775–1800,* edited by Paul A. Gilje and William Pencak (Rutherford, N.J.: Associated University Presses, 1992), 48–73; Carl Van Doren, *The Great Rehearsal: The Story of the Making and Ratifying of the Constitution of the United States* (New York: Viking Press, 1948).

constitutions, state

American Revolutionary leaders in 1776 were excited about the opportunity of creating government from, in JOHN LOCKE's phrase, tabula rasa (a clean slate). JOHN ADAMS wrote of "how few of the human race have ever enjoyed an opportunity of making an election of government . . . for themselves and for their children." JOHN JAY agreed, declaring that the Revolutionaries were "the first people whom heaven has favoured with an opportunity of deliberating upon, and choosing the forms of government under which they should live." The government that so occupied the Revolutionary leaders, however, was not the federal organization under ARTICLES OF CONFEDERATION, and certainly not that of the U.S. CONSTITUTION, which would be written over a decade later. Instead, these men abandoned the SECOND CONTINENTAL CONGRESS in order to write the original state constitutions. In the process, they experimented with a variety of forms of government in an effort to find the best balance and the safest means to guarantee a republic. These new forms of government ranged from the extremely democratic frame of government, best represented by the constitution of the state of Pennsylvania, to the more conservative balanced constitution, such as that written in the state of Massachusetts.

Pennsylvanians wrote their state constitution at the height of Revolutionary fervor in 1776. Believing that the king had sought to destroy the people's LIBERTY, Pennsylvania's radical Revolutionaries created a government with a weakened executive. In fact, there was no single individual left to govern the state, only an executive council to carry out the directives of the popular assembly. Similarly, Pennsylvanians did not see any need for two houses of legislature. They were the only colony that had a single legislative body, and the idea of an upper house was still attached to the belief that, like the House of Lords, it represented the aristocracy. Such distinctions were of no use to the Pennsylvania radicals: The one-house legislature was always to have open-door sessions, allowing the people to see their representatives in action, and all laws were to be published and placed in prominent locations for the people to read and discuss. There was a broad franchise that included almost all male taxpayers and their adult sons as well as annual elections, and no law became permanent unless passed by two successive sessions. Judges were elected, and there was a guarantee of rotation of office. The constitution also created a council of censors, which was to meet every seven years and review all legislation. Only Georgia and Vermont—which was not even recognized as a separate entity by the other states—followed this radical model.

Many states, however, expressed similar concerns about limiting the government's power and protecting the people's liberty. Most state legislatures had two houses, which were viewed as a "double representation" of the people and a check on each other. Several states sought to restrain the executive. New Yorkers, who confronted a military crisis during the REVOLUTIONARY WAR (1775–83), created a strong executive elected for a three-year term, but they also sought to restrain the governor by not giving him an exclusive veto and control over appointments. Instead, they created a council of revision, comprising the governor and several judges, to review legislation; and a council of appointment, comprising the governor and four state senators, to name people to state offices. The Virginia constitution, largely authored by THOMAS JEFFERSON, also had a single executive, but he was to be elected annually by the two houses of legislature and had to rely on advice from an eight-member council of state, also selected by both houses of legislature. Virginia, Pennsylvania, Maryland, Delaware, North Carolina, and Massachusetts all included a bill of rights as a guarantee of certain inalienable rights that each member of society retained regardless of the government's

power. Having lived through a crisis that was blamed on a usurpation of rights, these states wanted to ensure that the people's liberty would be protected from government abuse of power.

The Massachusetts constitution of 1780 was the most conservative state constitution and served as a model for later revisions by the states—Pennsylvania changed its constitution in 1790—and the U.S. Constitution. Much of this document flowed from the pen of John Adams. It included a strong executive, who could make appointments and veto laws. The governor could be given so much power because, unlike the king, who had no direct connection to the people, the governor was a representative of the people and depended on them for his election. The Massachusetts constitution also included two houses of legislature. There were high property qualifications to be a candidate for governor; likewise, property qualifications for the upper house, as a means of distinction, were higher than for the lower house. The suffrage for white men was narrower than in any other state.

Massachusetts was also instrumental in the development of using a convention to write a constitution. Before 1780, states struggled over what representative body should write constitutions. Some states relied on their assemblies or Revolutionary governing bodies to draw up their fundamental law, but critics began to argue that a legislature that could write a constitution could also change it at will. There needed to be some extraordinary representation of the people that convened only to write fundamental law. CONVENTIONS were just such a representation of the people, but they had traditionally lacked a sense of legitimacy. When states like Pennsylvania used a convention to write their constitutions, the exigencies of war confused the issue and blurred the boundary between creating fundamental law and writing legislation. In Massachusetts, and in New Hampshire, there was an open debate concerning how to go about writing a constitution, leading to the conclusion that a convention was the best and most legitimate way to make fundamental law. Revisions would depend on a similar body that could be called into being under special circumstances.

The writing of state constitutions entailed an important period of political experimentation that had as its legacy the creation of the U.S. Constitution at the Philadelphia CONSTITUTIONAL CONVENTION of 1787.

See also REPUBLICANISM.

Further reading: Marc W. Kruman, *Between Authority and Liberty: State Constitution Making in Revolutionary America* (Chapel Hill: University of North Carolina Press, 1997); Gordon S. Wood, *The Creation of the American Republic, 1776–1787* (Chapel Hill: University of North Carolina Press, 1969).

consumerism

Sometime in the mid-18th century, British North Americans became increasingly interested in consumer goods. This development had profound implications for the way people lived and for the colonial relationship with GREAT BRITAIN. Purchasing more goods transformed consumers' material lives. At the highest level, colonial Americans sought to copy the lifestyles of the British aristocracy, building houses in the Georgian style and filling their homes with fine imported furniture; paneling their walls with English wood; and surrounding themselves with fine drapery, china, silver, and pewter. The elite even sought to adorn themselves in suits tailored in England. GEORGE WASHINGTON ordered much of his CLOTHING from England even though he complained to his purchasing agent that the workmanship was inferior and the style out of date.

It should not be surprising that the elite copied the British aristocracy. However, in the second half of the 18th century, the concern with consumer goods spread downward in society as even middling ARTISANS and farmers sought the lineaments of refinement. In his autobiography, BENJAMIN FRANKLIN offers the reader a glimpse into the mechanism of this creeping consumerism even before 1750. As a tradesman, Franklin saw nothing wrong with eating his meals with a pewter spoon and an earthen bowl, even though his success as a printer meant he could afford better tableware. His wife DEBORAH READ FRANKLIN, perhaps knowing her husband better than he was willing to admit, thought differently and served him his meal in a china bowl with a silver spoon one day. She made no excuse for this change other than "she thought *her* husband deserv'd a silver spoon and China bowl as well as any of her neighbors."

Purchasing imported goods had an impact on the relationship between the colonies and Great Britain. First, the colonies became increasing important to the British ECONOMY in the 18th century, and by the 1760s North America was the most important market for British manufactured goods. However, buying so many things came at a price and an ever-increasing personal debt. After his marriage to Martha Custis (MARTHA WASHINGTON), George Washington went on a spending spree with the wealth his bride had brought him. Within a few years he was lamenting this extravagance and wrote that his purchases had "swallowed up" his fortune and brought him into debt. Although the ability to borrow is one measure of wealth—no one wanted to lend MONEY to someone who did not have property as collateral—the expansion of debt for consumer goods was so rapid in the 1760s as to become frightening. Between 1760 and 1772 the personal debt of colonial Americans doubled from £2 million to £4 million. This debt had a psychological cost, as Washington's comment suggests. Many colonial Americans began to question themselves and wonder if they were too interested in pursuing wealth to obtain luxury.

Consumerism thus contributed to the origins of the AMERICAN REVOLUTION. The anxiety over consumerism, debt, and luxury augmented a sense of unease that challenged traditional notions of a corporate society and underpinned colonial reaction to the imperial regulation of the 1760s and 1770s. One author in a Connecticut paper commented in 1765 that the efforts of "every single Person to imitate the person next above him" in gaining possessions spread in "the most ridiculous Mimickry, the Fashions of London . . . to the poorest, meanest Town in Connecticut." Franklin, speaking to the House of Commons in 1765, declared that the goods colonial Americans imported were largely "superfluities," which were purchased and consumed, because "they are mere articles of fashion in a respected country." As such they were unnecessary, and in any conflict they would become "detested and rejected." During the RESISTANCE MOVEMENT (1764–75), protestors against imperial regulation organized nonimportation pledges and boycotts, in part to put economic pressure on British merchants but also in part to demonstrate that virtuous colonial Americans did not need Franklin's "superfluities" and could produce other items that were more necessary or convenient for themselves.

The REVOLUTIONARY WAR (1775–83) tested that virtue and self-sufficiency. Throughout the war there was a dearth of consumer goods that made life more difficult for most people, whether WHIGS or LOYALISTS. Once the war was over, however, a renewed flood of British goods into the United States again set people scrambling to purchase consumer goods from Great Britain and other European countries. Consumerism regained the momentum it had developed before the war and spread wider and wider in society. FRONTIER regions participated in this consumerism, and as early as 1792, 20 different stores were started in Lexington, Kentucky. Interest in purchasing goods encouraged greater participation in a market economy. Even for families actively engaged in producing homespun cloth—that is, cloth made at home—much of that homespun would be sold for cash, which would then be used to purchase other goods. A rural New England family might have its daughter spin woolen shirting while simultaneously buying "fabric for gowns" and "fashionable hats, purple satin lined with straw."

Both NATIVE AMERICANS and AFRICAN AMERICANS participated in the world of consumer goods. Indians eagerly traded furs and skins for blankets, cloth, and metal tools and implements. Even Native Americans who explicitly rejected European-American culture might be attired in clothing obtained through TRADE: Pictures of TECUMSEH show him sporting a military jacket with epaulets; and HANDSOME LAKE, despite a plumed headdress and body piercings, donned a European-style overcoat and a blanket made from European textiles. Slaves and free blacks sought consumer goods whenever they could obtain them. One Kentucky slave bought tea, shoes, buckles, velvet, and thread from a store with a small amount of cash and a variety of trade goods. Elizabeth Sandwith Drinker of Philadelphia complained of the extravagant dress of her African-American servants, describing a female servant as decked out "in white muslin dizen'd with white ribbon from head to foot, yellow morocco shoes and white bows."

But it was among the European Americans that consumerism had its greatest impact, leading to a tremendous variety of items available in the marketplace. For example, in Baltimore in 1806 a consumer could purchase coffee from the East and West Indies and the Isle of Reunion in the Indian Ocean. Also available were six kinds of tea from China, eight varieties of sugar, and a wide range of spices from around the world. By the early 19th century, consumer items such as textiles and shoes were being produced in greater quantities within the United States. In addition, in one of the key characteristics of modern consumerism, the introduction of new products also created demands and changed the way people lived. Before 1800 the broom was not a mass-produced item as most people made their own or relied on local Indians to produce them. Brooms, however, because of different standards in housekeeping, were not used frequently and were not considered an essential item for the average household. In 1797 Levi Dickinson, a farmer in Hadley, Massachusetts, started to grow broom corn. At first his neighbors mocked him, but soon many began to join him as Dickinson and his family used the slack winter months to fashion hundreds of brooms. With large numbers of brooms coming on the market, and with more common people seeking the gentility that a cleanly swept floor seemed to represent, a new standard for household order emerged, which included daily floor sweeping and expanded the demand for brooms. In 1810 New England produced 70,000 brooms annually.

By 1815 consumerism had permeated the European-American population of the United States. In preparation for a tax on luxury goods, federal government assessors went from house to house evaluating the consumer products each family owned, excluding beds, kitchenware, family portraits, and homemade items. The assessors found a plethora of luxury goods, including clothes presses, dining and tea tables, coffee urns and teapots, chandeliers, fancy porcelain, prints, pianofortes, and a host of other items not necessary for daily living but which added comfort and refinement to most homes. Of the approximately 800,000 households in the country, less than a third owned luxury items of less than $200 and were exempt from the tax. About half of the households held property with luxury goods valued between $200 and $600, while more than 100,000 had more than $600 in possessions. In short, the vast middle of society had become active consumers and participants in the market economy.

Further reading: T. H. Breen, *The Marketplace of Revolution: How Consumer Politics Shaped American Independence* (New York: Oxford University Press, 2004); Richard L. Bushman, *The Refinement of America: Persons, Houses, Cities* (New York: Knopf, 1992); Cary Carson, Ronald Hoffman and Peter J. Albert, eds., *Of Consuming Interests: The Style of Life in the Eighteenth Century* (Charlottesville: University Press of Virginia, 1994); Paul A. Gilje, *The Making of the American Republic, 1763–1815* (Upper Saddle River, N.J.: Prentice Hall, 2005).

Continental army

After the bloodshed at the Battles of Lexington and Concord (April 19, 1775) and the formation of a New England army, the Second Continental Congress in Philadelphia began planning for a national force to deal with the growing hostility between Great Britain and the North American colonies. Because the New England defenders viewed their military struggle as one ultimately involving the protection of all the colonies against British aggression, they asked Congress to take responsibility to support and finance their troops around Boston. This action would emphasize that the conflict was not merely regional and would broaden the base for the military.

On June 14, 1775, Congress took financial responsibility for the existing New England troops, and authorized 10 companies of expert riflemen—though within a month this number had swelled to 13—from other regions. The riflemen were the first troops raised specifically for the Continental army, with six companies from Pennsylvania and two each from Maryland and Virginia. Each was allotted one captain, three lieutenants, four sergeants, four corporals, one drummer or horn player, and 68 privates. The term of enlistment was for one year. Delegates from the respective colonies turned over recruitment responsibilities to county committees, with commanders of the new units generally drawn from the local gentry. Congress also approved an enlistment form and appointed a committee to draw up regulations for governing the new army.

On the next day, June 15, 1775, the Continental Congress unanimously named George Washington commander in chief of all the forces raised in opposition to the British. Thereafter, Congress authorized various staff positions to assist Washington with administration of the army. Since some of the conflict with Great Britain centered around the presence of regular British forces in the colonies, Congress and Washington had to be careful in their use of the Continental troops so as not to undermine

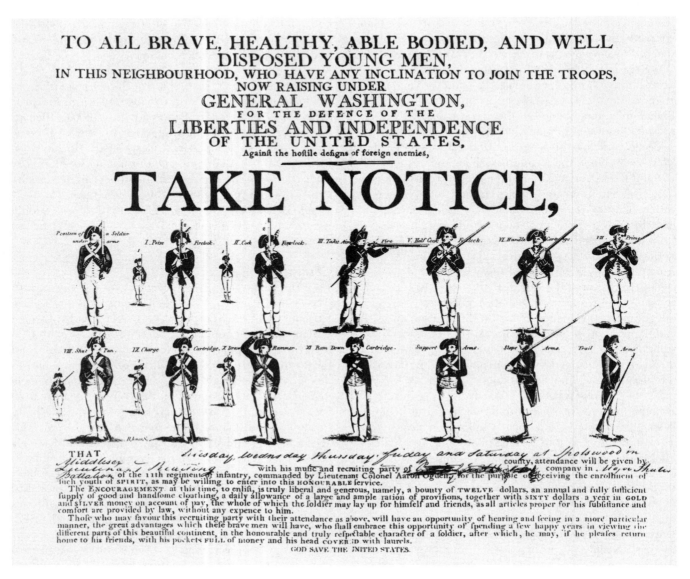

Recruiting poster for the Continental army *(Dover Publications)*

belief in the adequacy of the local MILITIA and create anxiety over a standing army. To ease those fears, Congress carefully stressed the defensive nature of its actions; the relatively small numbers of Continental troops to be raised and the short terms of enlistment were meant to bolster that position.

As the conflict widened and more companies were authorized, the army became a truly national institution. Washington, however, wanted to increase its professional standards in the belief that militia units, which were increasingly called upon to reinforce the Continental troops, could not meet the British regulars on equal terms. Too often in the heat of battle, the militia would run at the sight of the redcoats and shining bayonets. Washington

wanted an army more like the British regulars and pressed Congress to lengthen enlistments so that he could retain experienced men. In autumn 1776, Congress agreed to three-year terms and allowed cash bonuses and postwar land grants as recruitment incentives. With longer enlistments and better incentives, more men from the margins of society entered the Continental army. By the end of the war, the typical soldier was not an embattled farmer who owned property, because such men had too much to lose from long enlistments; instead, the typical soldier was poor, often young, and often a recent immigrant who owned little or no property.

The Continental army lost many battles in the early part of the war, often due to lack of resources and poor judgment within the officer corps. The arrival of Baron Frederick von Steuben and his Prussian military expertise at the Valley Forge encampment in winter 1777–78, however, brought discipline to the army. The drills and regulations Steuben initiated gave uniformity to battlefield maneuvers, and their newfound precision instilled confidence in the men. The Continental army that marched out of winter quarters in June 1778 was a much more professional force. They still lost some battles, but they were more capable of standing up to the British and Hessian regulars (see Hessians). The Continental soldiers also suffered from poor and often delayed pay, pitiful provisions, and inadequate medical treatment, leading to several mutinies. However, Washington managed to keep the army together and avoided large battles in the northern theater for the rest of the war. The arms training and professionalism of the army paid off at Yorktown, where Lord Cornwallis surrendered on October 19, 1781.

The final peace in 1783 rekindled concerns over a standing army. Not until June 1784 did Congress create a peacetime military establishment that was acceptable to all political factions, a small regular army led by Continental veterans and ordered by Steuben's regulations and drill manual.

See also Army, U.S.; Continental army, mutinies of the; Continental army pensions.

Further reading: E. Wayne Carp, *To Starve the Army at Pleasure: Continental Army Administration and American Political Culture, 1775–1783* (Chapel Hill: University of North Carolina Press, 1984); Charles Royster, *The Revolutionary People at War: The Continental Army and the American Character, 1775–1783* (Chapel Hill: University of North Carolina Press, 1979); Robert K. Wright, Jr., *The Continental Army* (Washington, D.C.: Center for Military History, U.S. Army, 1989).

—Rita M. Broyles

Continental army, mutinies of the

There were four major mutinies in the Continental army during the Revolutionary War (1775–83). The men who joined these mutinies had serious grievances: They were poorly supplied and owed back pay. On December 25, 1779, two regiments from Connecticut that had assembled on the parade ground at Morristown, New Jersey, refused to obey their officers and threatened violent action. Officers called on a veteran Pennsylvania brigade to arrest the ringleaders and force the rest of the men back to duty.

Two other mutinies occurred a year later. At Morristown on December 31, 1780, men from Pennsylvania rebelled, having been unpaid for almost a year; many of them were poorly clothed and fed. They also complained that their enlistments had run out and that new recruits were paid large bounties. Perhaps stimulated by additional rum to celebrate the New Year, they decided to take matters into their own hands, and when officers attempted to restrain them, they were roughly handled. The next day, under the command of a committee of sergeants, the Pennsylvania soldiers marched toward Philadelphia with baggage and artillery. The mutineers got as far as Trenton before they were intercepted by loyal troops from New England. The authorities then negotiated with the Pennsylvanians, allowing those who claimed their three-year enlistment was up to go home, and promising pay and supplies for the remainder.

In the meantime, New Jersey troops revolted at Ringwood, New Jersey, on January 20. This time there was to be no compromising. General George Washington declared that "unless this dangerous spirit can be suppressed by force there is an end to all subordination in the Army, and indeed to the Army itself." New England soldiers were ordered to surround the New Jersey men, who were then mustered without their arms. Twelve mutineers were selected as a firing squad and were compelled to shoot two of their leaders. This action quelled any further mutiny.

The final mutiny took place in June 1783, just as the army was about to be demobilized. Some recruits from Lancaster, Pennsylvania, marched on Philadelphia, where they were joined by other soldiers who demanded their pay. The disgruntled troops surrounded Independence Hall and briefly held Congress members hostage, but no serious harm was threatened, and the representatives left the building unmolested. Before loyal soldiers could arrive, the mutinous crowd dispersed. Angered by this affront to its dignity, Congress left Philadelphia and reconvened at Princeton.

Further reading: E. Wayne Carp, *To Starve the Army at Pleasure: Continental Army Administration and American Political Culture, 1775–1783* (Chapel Hill: University of North Carolina Press, 1984); Lawrence Delbert Cress, *Citizens in Arms: the Army and Militia in American Society to the War of 1812* (Chapel Hill: University of North Carolina Press, 1982); Charles Royster, *The Revolutionary People at War: The Continental Army and the American Character, 1775–1783* (Chapel Hill: University of North Carolina Press, 1979).

Continental army pensions

The issue of pensions for the Continental army's veterans of the Revolutionary War (1775–83) emerged soon after the conflict began. On August 26. 1776, the Second Continental Congress passed a national pension act, offering compensation of up to half pay to soldiers injured during the war. Two years later, Congress made this law retroactive to the beginning of the war on April 19, 1775, and in 1782 soldiers who were sick or wounded were offered five dollars a month for life if they were unfit for duty and accepted a discharge. During the 1780s Congress relied on the states to determine eligibility and to pay the pensions, with the money spent to be deducted from what the states owed the federal government. This policy led to a hodgepodge pension system. In 1790, after the creation of the new government under the U.S. CONSTITUTION, Congress decided to take over the pension payments, and by March 1792 they had drawn up a list of 1,358 noncommissioned officers and 1,472 enlisted men, all designated as disabled veterans who would be given pensions not to exceed five dollars a month. The pension law was altered a number of times thereafter in an effort to provide more efficient distribution and to avoid illicit claims. By 1806 procedures had been ironed out, and the government established that pensions would be paid only to those who had been injured during their military service, and following the provisions of an 1803 statute, the secretary of war was given supervision of the pensions.

If Congress was relatively eager to aid injured war veterans, it was more hesitant about awarding pensions to the officers of the Continental Army. At VALLEY FORGE during the winter of 1777–78, the army faced a crisis when large numbers of officers resigned. To maintain an experienced an officer corps, several officers proposed a pension of half-pay for life. Despite General GEORGE WASHINGTON's support of this proposal, Congress stalled. In August 1779, however, the legislature recommended to the states that they provide a pension to officers of half-pay for life. Several states, including Virginia and Pennsylvania, agreed to some pension for officers, but in October 1780, in the wake of the betrayal of BENEDICT ARNOLD, Congress finally agreed to the half-pay pension, albeit with the right to provide some future form of substitute compensation. Many in Congress and the public at large believed that pensions seemed unrepublican, with officers placing their own interests ahead of the public interest, and reflected the type of corruption typical of monarchies, where pensioners could be counted on to support a strong government that could threaten the people's LIBERTY. Officers, on the other hand, saw pensions as a recognition of their sacrifice and as a financial cushion that could help ease the transition to civilian life.

By October 1782, however, officers had come to recognize the unpopularity of pensions, and they petitioned Congress to commute the life provision to full pay for a limited term of years. A committee chaired by ALEXANDER HAMILTON agreed to this proposal but set the term at five years. With the war almost over and the army about to disband, both the common soldiers—who wanted back pay—and the officers—who wanted their pensions—were restless and threatening action against the civil authorities. Nationalists in Congress used this potentially explosive situation to push for an impost and a strengthening of the federal government. Army officers, in turn, circulated two inflammatory pamphlets and called a meeting at Newburgh, New York. General Washington did not want the military to impose its will on the civil government, so he attended the meeting and defused the so-called NEWBURGH CONSPIRACY. In 1783 Congress passed the commutation bill providing pensions for officers for five years, which launched a huge public debate that lasted into early 1784. The pension bill remained in place despite the public outcry, and officers were given a lump-sum payment in certificates bearing 6 percent interest.

While the national government agreed to provide pensions for the officers of the Continental army, the common soldier received little for his service. When and if the enlisted men received pay at the end of the war, it was often in the form of promissory notes or grants of lands on the FRONTIER. Most regular soldiers sold these scraps of paper for pennies on the dollar. The national government avoided a more comprehensive measure until 1818, when the Limited Service Pension Act provided $8 a month to soldiers and $20 a month to officers, if they had served nine months in the Continental army or the MILITIA and were in "reduced circumstances." In 1832 a new law established pensions for all veterans of the Revolutionary War.

Further reading: John Resch, *Suffering Soldiers: Revolutionary War Veterans, Moral Sentiment, and Political Culture in the Early Republic* (Amherst: University of Massachusetts Press, 1999); Charles Royster, *The Revolutionary People at War: The Continental Army and the American Character, 1775–1783* (Chapel Hill: University of North Carolina Press, 1979); Emily J. Teipe, *America's First Veterans and the Revolutionary War Pensions* (Lewiston, N.Y.: Edwin Mellon Press, 2002).

Continental Association   See ASSOCIATION, THE.

Continental Congress, First (1774)

From September 5 to October 26, 1774, the First Continental Congress met in Philadelphia, where delegates passed three important resolutions: endorsing the SUFFOLK RESOLVES (1774), approving an economic boycott against GREAT BRITAIN, and adopting a petition to the king detailing colonial rights and grievances. As an extralegal body, the Continental Congress depended on obtaining and retaining the support of colonial assemblies and the public; therefore, Congressional delegates placed a premium on cooperation and compromise among the colonies. The First Continental Congress thus set the tone for future resistance to British rule and for the practice of politics in the United States.

Massachusetts called the meeting in Philadelphia to formulate a response to the COERCIVE ACTS (1774) then being imposed upon the colony. Massachusetts's WHIGS sought advice and direction from the other colonies about how far they should go in resisting the Massachusetts Government Act, the Boston Port Act, and the new royal governor, THOMAS GAGE. Of the original thirteen colonies, only Georgia did not send a delegation to Philadelphia.

Among the 56 delegates were men destined to lead the AMERICAN REVOLUTION and the new nation. Cousins JOHN ADAMS and SAMUEL ADAMS represented Massachusetts, while ROGER SHERMAN served for Connecticut. Virginia sent RICHARD HENRY LEE and GEORGE WASHINGTON; JOHN JAY, the future Chief Justice of the U.S. SUPREME COURT, represented New York; and JOHN DICKINSON and JOSEPH GALLOWAY represented Pennsylvania. Not all delegates favored radical solutions—men like Galloway searched for a moderate resolution to the crisis. Radical delegates did not dominate the proceedings, but the Continental Congress succeeded because delegates were able forge a consensus that would help sustain unity among the colonies.

In its first public act on September 17, 1774, the Congress unanimously endorsed the Suffolk Resolves, which declared the Coercive Acts unconstitutional and recommended economic sanctions against Great Britain as the best course of action. Thus, Congress accepted resistance but strove to avoid direct confrontation with the British troops stationed in Massachusetts. It issued a warning to Great Britain that other colonies supported Massachusetts's actions and also provided direction for Massachusetts's resistance. Yet, by only approving defensive measures and rejecting proposals for more forceful action, Congress cautioned Massachusetts that not every deed would meet with unanimous approval. For the time being, resistance would remain within guidelines proposed by the Suffolk Resolves. This first resolution established two important precedents: First, by accepting congressional direction, Massachusetts effectively encouraged Congress to assert similar authority over all colonies. Second, by emphasizing unanimity, delegates made consensus more important than armed resistance.

The Continental Congress's second accomplishment was to approve an economic boycott of Great Britain, Ireland, and the WEST INDIES. On September 22 the delegates unanimously passed a resolution recommending the temporary suspension of imports from Great Britain pending a firm decision by Congress. Just five days later,

on September 27, the delegates unanimously agreed to a resolution to stop importation of British and Irish goods after December 1. They further resolved to stop exports to Britain, Ireland, and the West Indies after September 10, 1775. Thus, Congress endorsed the resumption of commercial resistance first tried during the STAMP ACT (1765) crisis. No one seriously questioned this path except Galloway. For the most part, the key issue was more a question of the boycott's scope than whether to impose one at all. For example, Virginia delegates had been instructed to approve a boycott, but not one beginning before August 1775, and South Carolina wanted its staple crops—RICE and INDIGO—exempted.

Finally, on October 20 Congress formed the Continental ASSOCIATION to execute the "non-importation, non-consumption, and non-exportation agreement." Congress instructed that new local committees of safety be elected to oversee implementation and enforcement. It sanctioned extralegal committees and sought to direct and regulate their activities while allowing for local initiative and flexibility to fit each community's needs. Like earlier such agreements, there was a moral dimension to the Association born out of the ideology of REPUBLICANISM. The Association encouraged "frugality, economy, and industry"; promoted "agriculture, arts and the manufactures of this country"; and discouraged "every species of extravagance and dissipation, especially all horse-racing, and all kinds of gaming, cock-fighting, exhibitions of shews [shows], plays, and other expensive diversions and entertainments." So great was the concern with asserting virtue and simplicity that the Association even dictated what to do to commemorate "the death of any relation or friend" by declaring "none of us, or any of our families, will go into any further mourning-dress, than a black crape or ribbon on the arm or hat, for gentlemen, and a black ribbon and necklace for ladies, and we will discontinue the giving of gloves and scarves at funerals."

Third, Congress debated and approved a declaration of rights and grievances. During these debates, delegates considered the North American colonies' position within the British Empire and the proper interpretation of the unwritten British constitution. Galloway, who would become a LOYALIST, proposed a new imperial constitution. His plan of union would have created an intercolonial legislature responsible for "regulating and administering all the general police and affairs of the colonies" and during war to grant "aid to the crown." While the British Parliament would still have the power to enact laws for the colonies, all laws would have to be approved by both Parliament and the intercolonial assembly. Galloway's plan represented the most conciliatory proposal considered by Congress. Delegates effectively rejected it on September 28 on a procedural motion. New York delegates Jay and JAMES DUANE proved more effective advocates of a moderate approach to the crisis than Galloway. Duane and Jay had the support of moderates from the middle colonies of New York, Pennsylvania, and Maryland.

Eight of the 10 resolutions considered for the declaration of rights passed unanimously, but not without debate. The debate focused on whether the colonies should base their grievances on the law of nature or the British constitution. Delegates favored the latter over the former justification. The other main issue was how much authority and power colonies should concede to Parliament. The delegates rejected a resolution defiantly asserting that colonial assemblies had the exclusive power of legislation in cases of taxation and internal policy subject only to approval by the Crown; this was replaced by more conciliatory and ambiguous language. Congress agreed that colonial assemblies should assent to bona fide acts of Parliament concerning the regulation of external commerce for the general good of the British Empire. Taxation for the purpose of raising revenue was only acceptable if the colonial assemblies consented. The declaration of rights broke no new ground and was consistent with the constitutional arguments that had been made in the colonies for the past decade. In one conciliatory act, Congress decided against including complaints about parliamentary acts before 1763 among its grievances.

The actions of the First Continental Congress further exacerbated rather than ameliorated relations between Great Britain and its colonies. It endorsed the autonomy of colonial legislatures and a very limited legislative role for Parliament over the colonies and firmly accepted the proposition that conciliation had to be initiated by Great Britain. Most important, the First Continental Congress made future intercolonial cooperation and unified resistance possible.

Further reading: Merrill Jensen, *The Articles of Confederation: An Interpretation of the Social-Constitutional History of the American Revolution, 1774–1781* (Madison: University of Wisconsin Press, 1940); Jack N. Rakove, *The Beginnings of National Politics: An Interpretative History of the Continental Congress* (New York: Knopf, 1979).

—Terri Halperin

Continental Congress, Second (Confederation Congress) (1775–1789)

The Second Continental Congress, also called the Confederation Congress, convened on May 10, 1775, and, except for a few recesses, met until the U.S. CONSTITUTION took effect in 1789. This body issued the DECLARATION OF INDEPENDENCE (1776), prosecuted the REVOLUTIONARY WAR (1775–83), and governed the new nation.

There was significant continuity between the First and Second Continental Congresses. Fifty of the 65 delegates who attended the initial session of the Second Continental Congress had also served in the FIRST CONTINENTAL CONGRESS (1774). When the meeting was called, it seemed that this Congress would face many of the same issues as the first one had, but by the time delegates arrived in Philadelphia, circumstances had changed significantly. The Congress convened three weeks after the BATTLES OF LEXINGTON AND CONCORD (April 19, 1775) and only a little more than a month before the BATTLE OF BUNKER HILL (June 17, 1775).

While the Continental Congress continued to give advice and direction to the colonies, particularly Massachusetts, about the course of resistance, it began to transform itself from a purely deliberative body into one that assumed executive responsibilities as well. In mid-June 1775, Congress created the CONTINENTAL ARMY and appointed GEORGE WASHINGTON as commanding general. Thus, it established the first national institution, an entity that it would now have to supply, finance, and regulate. To begin to fulfill these obligations, Congress issued its first bills of credit to finance the expanding war that same month. Funding the war by printing MONEY and issuing loan certificates to maintain the army became the body's major preoccupations. However good the delegates' intentions, Congress struggled throughout its existence since it had no power to compel the states to contribute either to troop quotas or to revenue to conduct the war.

Although many great men served in the Second Continental Congress, it was plagued by poor attendance even as early as December 1775. Some of the most noted members included Virginia's George Washington, PATRICK HENRY, EDMUND PENDLETON, PEYTON RANDOLPH, THOMAS JEFFERSON, and JAMES MADISON; Massachusetts's JOHN ADAMS, SAMUEL ADAMS, and JOHN HANCOCK; and Pennsylvania's BENJAMIN FRANKLIN. Concerns about political events at home and their own livelihoods and families, however, made many delegates reluctant to spend months in Philadelphia or wherever Congress was meeting. Despite a rule adopted in November 1775 that no member could be absent without congressional permission, and several entreaties from Congress to the states to maintain their representation, absenteeism plagued the institution. The problem became particularly acute in the 1780s after the adoption of the ARTICLES OF CONFEDERATION, which stipulated that two delegates be present for a state to be able to record its vote. Consequently, because the Articles also required that nine states agree on many issues, Congress often found it difficult to conduct business. Expertise, continuity, and stability were hard to achieve.

The exigencies of war encouraged the necessary unity among the states but also allowed delegates to delay addressing particularly prickly issues, whether substantive or organizational. Like the First Continental Congress, delegates voted by state and not individually. The president of Congress carried out many ceremonial and administrative duties but could not act without being directed to do so by Congress. Thus, leadership was collective and variable rather than individual and institutionalized. Between 1774 and 1781, Congress experimented with several administrative arrangements to try to overcome the problems of a large workload and rampant absenteeism. At first, members relied on ad hoc committees, each intended to tackle a crisis or issue as it was raised, but by autumn 1775 Congress had begun to name permanent standing committees for specific purposes. Starting in September 1775, the Secret Committee was responsible for importing munitions and procuring supplies for the army. The Committee on Secret Correspondence, formed in November 1775, conducted all diplomatic communications. In January 1776 Congress organized the Marine Committee to oversee naval operations, but it took until June 1776 to finalize a Board of War to manage the conduct of the war. In February 1776 Congress established a treasury committee, which, along with a Committee on Accounts, was responsible for finances. Committees would propose actions that would be accepted or rejected by the whole Congress and could not make decisions without such approval. Congress relied on provincial officials, military personnel, or its own delegates to implement any resolutions adopted. Thus, New Jersey delegates were charged with transporting gunpowder to Dobbs Ferry, New York, and JAMES WILSON of Pennsylvania was instructed to report on how much "Duck, Russian sheeting [etc.] . . . could be procured . . ." in Philadelphia. Many delegates felt overburdened by the workload and Congress's inefficiency.

This growing frustration culminated in December 1776, when ROBERT MORRIS of Pennsylvania complained that Congress should be relieved of the more mundane tasks and utilize the expertise of others outside the institution. The outcome was the creation of executive boards composed of delegates, who would retain the ultimate control and authority, and nondelegates, who could provide the necessary expertise. From autumn 1777 through late 1779, Congress created four boards: the Board of War, the Board of Admiralty, the Board of Treasury, and the Committee of Foreign Affairs. Ultimately, members never fully trusted these quasi-independent organizations and could not resolve how much authority to delegate to them. The line between making policy and simple execution of congressional directives was difficult to delineate, and Congress never found a comfortable position vis-à-vis the boards.

As can be seen from some of the responsibilities of the committees and boards, the Continental Congress controlled FOREIGN AFFAIRS since it provided a vehicle through which other nations could interact with the new United States. The body thus dealt with diplomatic correspondence and appointed representatives and ambassadors to foreign nations. The most important mission was to FRANCE, which signed mercantile and military treaties with the United States in 1778. Congressional agents also negotiated foreign loans and dealt with a wide array of business on the international front.

In late 1780, encouraged by nationalists who wanted a stronger central government, Congress abandoned the board system and began to establish civil executive departments with one administrator in command who was accountable to and elected by Congress. Members created four departments: war, marine affairs, treasury, and foreign affairs. Robert Morris served as the superintendent of finance and became something of a prime minister for the United States because his control over finances meant he often set the agenda for the nation. Morris became so identified with the national government that he even issued notes in his own name—popularly called "Morris Notes"—to sustain the Revolution when government finances were on the verge of collapse. Because of the problems with raising revenue, Morris pushed for an independent source of income from an impost for the United States. Since the states had decided that such a measure was an amendment to the Articles of Confederation, all states had to consent to the impost. When Rhode Island refused to ratify the impost in 1782, the nationalist program was dealt a severe blow. The department system, although an improvement over the more cumbersome boards, never functioned smoothly since even if the departments relieved delegates of the day-to-day operations, they did not significantly reduce their workload because Congress insisted on retaining final control.

Organizational issues were not the only ones that vexed the Continental Congress during its 15-year existence. During and after the war, the body moved a number of times. When British troops came too close to Philadelphia in autumn 1776, Congress retreated to Baltimore. In 1777 the British occupied Philadelphia, forcing delegates to meet in York, Pennsylvania. Even the Continental army caused problems: After mutinous soldiers surrounded INDEPENDENCE HALL in 1783, the delegates left Philadelphia for good, first reconvening in Princeton, then moving to Annapolis and Trenton before settling in New York City.

After the TREATY OF PARIS (1783), the underlying reason for unity among the states disappeared. The Continental Congress was ill-equipped to resolve some difficult issues, especially regarding repaying Revolutionary War debts, securing an independent source of revenue, regulating western lands, resolving disputes between states, and finding a permanent national capital. Despite these weaknesses, Congress did provide national leadership during the War of Independence and created the first national government. Perhaps its most singular achievement after the war was the passage of the NORTHWEST ORDINANCES in 1785 and 1787.

The Confederation Congress contributed to its own demise in that its members belatedly approved the CONSTITUTIONAL CONVENTION in Philadelphia in 1787 to revise the Articles of Confederation. Although Congress did not positively endorse the resulting Constitution, which abandoned the Articles, it did send the Constitution to the states for ratification. The Second Continental Congress continued to meet until the First Federal Congress convened in 1789.

Further reading: Calvin Jillson and Rick K. Wilson, *Congressional Dynamics: Structure, Coordination, and Choice in the First American Congress, 1774–1789* (Stanford, Calif.: Stanford University Press, 1994); Peter Onuf, *The Origins of the Federal Republic: Jurisdictional Controversies in the United States, 1775–1787* (Philadelphia: University of Pennsylvania Press, 1983); Jack N. Rakove, *The Beginnings of National Politics: An Interpretative History of the Continental Congress* (New York: Knopf, 1979).

—Terri Halperin

Continental navy

Soon after the outbreak of hostilities between GREAT BRITAIN and her colonies in 1775, the SECOND CONTINENTAL CONGRESS began discussing the creation of a navy, but it was not until October 13, 1775, that it officially approved the formation of the Continental navy. On November 28, 1775, the Continental Congress adopted the "Rules and Regulations of the Navy of the United States," drafted by JOHN ADAMS, who based the document on the regulations of the British navy for discipline and punishment. However, the Continental navy's rules were less severe in punishment than the British rules.

At first, the navy came under the supervision of the naval committee, but a marine committee composed of one person from each colony replaced the naval committee in January 1776. The marine committee was too unwieldy for efficient administration, and in November 1776 the Navy Board for the Middle Department, composed of three men, superseded it. In April 1777 Congress authorized a second naval board, based in Boston, for the eastern department. As the war continued, these organizations also appeared inefficient, and Congress established the five-member Board of Admiralty in October 1779 to oversee the navy. This organization, too, ran into problems, and in accordance with other administrative reforms by Congress, the navy was placed under a single executive, the secretary of marine, in 1781. However, no one would accept this

position, and it fell by default to the minister of finance, ROBERT MORRIS. By the time Morris left the government in 1784, the navy had all but ceased to exist.

The administrative instability of the Continental navy reflected the numerous problems that confronted it. In many ways it was impractical for the Continental Congress to even try to organize a navy since nothing it could do would seriously challenge the hundreds of ships in the British navy. Moreover, Revolutionary efforts at sea took on a variety of forms, ranging from GEORGE WASHINGTON's ad hoc commissioning of ships to attack British supply lines in 1775; the creation of 11 state navies (only Delaware and New Jersey did not form their own navies); and, most important, the extensive PRIVATEERING that occurred during the war. Taken altogether, these efforts were a drain on financial and manpower resources that could have gone to the Continental navy. The navy administration compounded their difficulties by often relying on patronage for appointments. The most senior captain of the navy in 1775 was ESEK HOPKINS, brother and business partner of navy board member STEPHEN HOPKINS.

The Continental navy had a mixed record during the REVOLUTIONARY WAR (1775–83). Its first major expedition was led by Esek Hopkins, who ignored his orders and raided New Providence in the BAHAMAS instead of clearing Chesapeake Bay of the British and cruising along the southern coast to relieve the area of British naval raids. After Hopkins sailed to New England and avoided a battle with a British warship, he was severely criticized and eventually forced to leave the navy. The officers in the navy seemed to be constantly arguing over rank and seniority (as did officers in the CONTINENTAL ARMY) to the point where it adversely affected naval operations. However, a few captains stood out for their daring exploits and captures of British shipping. JOHN PAUL JONES was the most famous of these, especially after his victory aboard the *Bon Homme Richard* over the HMS *Serapis* on September 23, 1779. But Jones, like most other officers in the Continental navy, was often embroiled in controversy, and many of the men aboard his ships detested their autocratic captain.

Typical of the Continental navy's difficulties was the fate of its ambitious building program for 13 frigates, authorized on December 13, 1775. Because of poor planning and difficulties in getting building materials, construction of the ships was delayed. Only seven of the frigates got to sea, and by 1781 all seven had been captured by the British; the six uncompleted vessels had to be destroyed in their shipyards to prevent their seizure by the British. By the end of the war, about 60 vessels of various sizes had been commissioned into the Continental navy, which had captured about 200 British merchant and naval vessels. By comparison, there were at least 2,000 privateers commissioned that had captured about 2,200 British vessels.

In 1783 there were only a few ships left in the Continental navy. All but the USS *Alliance* were sold as soon as hostilities had ceased. Some members of Congress wanted to keep the *Alliance* to fend off pirates and possibly deal with the Barbary states, but without any MONEY to support a navy, Congress had to accept the inevitable and sold the ship for $26,000 on August 1, 1785 ending the history of the Continental navy.

See also BARBARY WARS; NAVY, U.S.

Further reading: Gardner W. Allen, *A Naval History of the American Revolution,* 2 vols. (Boston: Houghton Mifflin Company, 1913); Nathan Miller, *The U.S. Navy: A History,* 3rd ed. (Annapolis, Md.: Naval Institute Press, 1997).

Contrecoeur, Claude-Pierre Pécaudy de (1705–1775) *French military officer*

An officer in the French *troupes de la marine* (troops of the marine), Claude-Pierre Pécaudy de Contrecoeur was born in MONTREAL. He had experience working with NATIVE AMERICANS and had traveled throughout the Great Lakes and Ohio River Valley in the 1740s and early 1750s. Contrecoeur commanded FORT NIAGARA in 1752. When the MARQUIS DE DUQUESNE ordered Contrecoeur to occupy the Ohio River Valley, Contrecoeur compelled a small force under Ensign Edward Ward to evacuate the forks of the Ohio. Contrecoeur then built Fort Duquesne on the strategic location. After Colonel GEORGE WASHINGTON stumbled into a French patrol at the BATTLE OF JUMONVILLE GLEN (May 28, 1754), in which Washington's Indian allies massacred Ensign Joseph Coulon Jumonville and others, Contrecoeur ordered an attack on Washington at FORT NECESSITY. These actions began the FRENCH AND INDIAN WAR (1754–63).

Contrecoeur retired from the French military in 1759 and remained in CANADA after the British took over. He retained his extensive property and exerted some influence with the British colonial administration. Shortly before his death in 1775, he also became a member of the colonial legislative council.

Further reading: Fred Anderson, *The Crucible of War: The Seven Years' War and the Fate of the British Empire in North America, 1754–1766* (New York: Knopf, 2000).

Convention of 1800 (Treaty of Mortefontaine)

In early 1800, hoping to bring an end to the QUASI-WAR (1798–1800) with FRANCE, President JOHN ADAMS sent three peace commissioners—OLIVER ELLSWORTH, WILLIAM RICHARDSON DAVIE, and WILLIAM VANS MURRAY—to Paris to negotiate a settlement. The commissioners found that conditions had changed in France and that with the rise of NAPOLEON BONAPARTE, a settlement was possible. After several delays and months of negotiations, the two countries agreed to the Convention of 1800, which is sometimes referred to as the Treaty of Mortefontaine.

The agreement had four main provisions. First and foremost, it established "a firm, inviolable, and universal peace, and a true and sincere Friendship between the French Republic, and the United States of America," ending more than two years of naval warfare between the two countries. Second, the treaty declared that since the United States and France could not agree on the status and meaning of the treaties of 1778, which had created a military alliance and close commercial relations, both countries consented to delay a final resolution on the interpretation of these treaties until "a convenient time" for further negotiations; the Convention stipulated that until "that convenient time," the treaties "shall have no operation." Third, since France and the United States could also not agree on indemnities for the hundreds of merchant ships seized and condemned by France before and during the Quasi-War, the issue of compensation for the ship owners would also be left open for future negotiations at "a convenient time." More immediately, however, France and the United States agreed to return any ships that had been captured and not yet condemned. Finally, the Convention clarified commercial relations between the two countries, providing most-favored-nation trading status for their merchant vessels, defining war contraband narrowly, and asserting the ideal that "free ships shall give a freedom to goods."

The Convention of 1800 was not a diplomatic triumph since all it did was end the war and did not address the seizure of millions of dollars worth of U.S. shipping. Recognizing this problem, in February 1801 a Senate dominated by the FEDERALIST PARTY initially refused to ratify the treaty without a proviso, insisting that the issue of indemnity could be put off for only eight years. Napoleon refused to accept this change, and the result was that a final version of the treaty dropped any call for indemnity and any provision to reconsider the military alliance. Content to swap the demand for indemnity for ending the FRENCH ALLIANCE, a newly elected Senate controlled by the DEMOCRATIC-REPUBLICAN PARTY ratified the treaty in December 1801.

Convention of 1815

After the TREATY OF GHENT (1814) was signed, JOHN QUINCY ADAMS, HENRY CLAY, and ALBERT GALLATIN traveled to London to negotiate a commercial agreement between GREAT BRITAIN and the United States. The result was "A Convention to Regulate the Commerce between the Territories of The United States and of His Britannick

Majesty" on July 3, 1815. This agreement was a crucial step in regularizing the relationship between the two countries as they emerged from the WAR OF 1812 (1812–15). The treaty declared "a reciprocal liberty of Commerce" between the United States and Great Britain (and British possessions in Europe) and thereby went beyond the most-favored-nation status for both powers that had existed under JAY'S TREATY (1794). The second article stipulated: "No higher or other duties or charges shall be imposed in any of the Ports of the United States on British Vessels, than those payable in the same ports by Vessels of the United States; nor in the ports of any of His Britannick Majesty Territories in Europe on the Vessels of the United States than shall be payable in the same ports on British Vessels." However, this right did not extend to Britain's non-European possessions. Ships from the United States could TRADE with the British East Indies, including INDIA and Australia, on a most-favored-nation status, but not partake in the local carrying trade. Any U.S. ship involved in the East India trade, or in the CHINA TRADE, could stop at the Cape of Good Hope, St. Helena in the ATLANTIC OCEAN, or any other British possession "for refreshment but not for commerce." After the British government decided to exile NAPOLEON BONAPARTE to St. Helena, it added a codicil which banned all non-East India Company ships from visiting the island. Both nations were permitted to set up consulates in each other's territory. The Convention specifically excluded British territory in North America and the WEST INDIES. The agreement was to last four years but was extended another 10 years by the Convention of 1818.

Further reading: Frank A. Updyke, *The Diplomacy of the War of 1812* (Baltimore: Johns Hopkins Press, 1915).

conventions
Conventions became important instruments for expressing the will of the people during the AMERICAN REVOLUTION. Ultimately, Revolutionary Americans came to view conventions as special REPRESENTATIONS of the people, providing suitable bodies to write constitutions and fundamental law.

Before the revolutionary era, Anglo-Americans had experience with conventions, which were meetings of people who came together in an ad hoc assembly to deliberate on important ecclesiastical, political, or social matters. Throughout the medieval period in England, a convention was a forum for a meeting outside the established institutions of the Crown. But by the 15th century, representation of the different components of society—nobles, clergy, and the people—tended to be more directly identified with Parliament. Conventions were therefore seen as less representative of the political nation than Parliament. This dis-

tinction became more important in the political upheaval of the 17th century, even though it was the Lords and Commons as a convention that was responsible for the transfer of power from James II to William and Mary. As Parliament became more important and gained SOVEREIGNTY in the Anglo-American world, conventions came to be seen as outside the normal channels of government and legally deficient. Moreover, conventions were tainted since they resembled the people-out-of-doors and were affiliated with mobs and popular disorder.

The RESISTANCE MOVEMENT (1764–75) began to change the popular attitude toward conventions in British North America. Colonial Americans had to organize committees and hold public meetings—forms of conventions—to coordinate resistance, and once the imperial crisis intensified in 1774 and 1775, Revolutionaries rallied around colony-wide congresses and conventions since a colonial governor could call and dismiss assemblies at will. In colony after colony, leaders of the resistance movement met to pass resolutions and recommendations outside of the normal channels and removed from the governor's control. In short, whether labeled a congress or convention, these assemblages took over the reins of government and added new meaning to the idea of the convention as a special representation of the people.

As the Revolutionaries groped toward independence, two other crucial developments helped to alter popular understanding of the importance of conventions. First, on May 15, 1776, the SECOND CONTINENTAL CONGRESS authorized the colonies—now considered states—to draw up their own constitutions. Leaders in each state had to decide not only the form of government but also how that constitution would be written. Second, the Revolutionaries drew a distinction between statutory and fundamental law. Statutory laws were the regulations that guided daily behavior within society. Fundamental laws were the rules of governance—that is, fundamental law establishing the process by which statutory law would be written. Statutory law defined crimes and penalties for punishment. Fundamental law determined how many houses of legislature there would be, what kind of executive would govern, and what form the judicial system would take.

The Revolutionaries quickly discerned that these two developments made for problems. If a sitting legislature wrote both fundamental law and statutory law, then the distinction between the two became blurred. Worse, if a legislature established the conditions under which its members served, then what was to stop a legislature from changing the rules and increasing their terms of office, extending them for life and even making them hereditary? A body that had the ability to create could also alter. Revolutionaries had come to distrust the power of government and viewed the legislature not simply as a reflection of the will of the people but as a separate entity that had the potential of having a different interest from the people. What was needed was an extraneous body meeting for the special purpose of writing fundamental law—a constitution—that would then dissolve and could only be called into existence following procedures set up in the constitution.

Conventions, with their long history of being a special representation of the people, fit these needs precisely. Pennsylvanians recognized the special qualities of a convention to write fundamental law in 1776. They even put into their constitution a process whereby a convention could be called to amend the constitution. But the overall process of writing constitutions varied from state to state, with some states relying on conventions, some on congresses, and some on the legislature. Moreover, there remained some blending of fundamental and statutory law even in Pennsylvania, where the convention, facing the exigencies of war, passed legislation to define treason and to organize Revolutionary tribunals on a local basis. Ideas about conventions as the proper agent to create government gained clarity by 1780 in Massachusetts and New Hemphshire, where constituents refused to ratify constitutions until conventions were used as special representations of the people to draw up the documents and articulate fundamental law. Following these precedents the convention became the accepted means of defining fundamental law in constitutions.

That precedent had profound implications for the writing and ratification of the U.S. CONSTITUTION. It was the ANNAPOLIS CONVENTION of 1786—a special assemblage to discuss interstate commerce and trade—that issued the call for the CONSTITUTIONAL CONVENTION, which was held in Philadelphia in 1787. The Constitutional Convention, in turn, put aside its supposed purpose of revising the ARTICLES OF CONFEDERATION and formulated a whole new system of government. The Constitution also sidestepped the amendment process in the Articles of Confederation and the state legislatures and relied on state conventions to ratify the document. On the one hand, these actions were technically illegal and represented a coup d'etat since the Articles of Confederation had clear provisions for amendments. On the other hand, the idea that a convention was a special representation of the people provided a rationale for the radical procedures taken by the Founding Fathers. Since the people were sovereign, so the FEDERALISTS could argue, then the Constitutional Convention and the state ratifying conventions were all legitimate expressions of their will.

Conventions remained important in the United States after 1787: States used conventions to rewrite their constitutions, private and religious organizations in the 1790s and early 1800s used conventions to assemble members and express their collective will, and politicians used conventions to explain positions and assert principles. Members of the FEDERALIST PARTY organized the HARTFORD CONVENTION to express opposition to the WAR OF 1812 (1812–15). Eventually, but not until 1828, POLITICAL PARTIES also held conventions to select candidates running for office.

See also REPUBLICANISM.

Further reading: Marc W. Kruman, *Between Authority and Liberty: State Constitution Making in Revolutionary America* (Chapel Hill: University of North Carolina Press, 1997); Gordon S. Wood, *The Creation of the American Republic, 1776–1787* (Chapel Hill: University of North Carolina Press, 1998).

Conway, Henry Seymour (1721–1795) *British government official, military officer*

Henry Seymour Conway was a professional British soldier and politician noted for his Whig principles and opposition to imperial taxation in the British North American colonies. Educated at Eton, he entered the army in 1737 and first became a member of Parliament in 1741. Although he married and had a daughter, there were (and continued to be) suggestions that his close personal relationship with his cousin Horace Walpole was also a sexual one. Nonetheless, Conway worked his way up to a senior position in the army and became a member of the MARQUIS OF ROCKINGHAM's administration in 1765–66. As secretary of state for the Southern Department, he played a central role in the repeal of the STAMP ACT (1765); he remained in the cabinet, but not in the secretary of state position, until 1770.

Throughout the 1760s and 1770s, Conway opposed other measures to tax the colonies and was against the use of military force in North America. He had no combat role during the REVOLUTIONARY WAR (1775–83), although he was the absentee governor of the Isle of Jersey, which was attacked by the French. In 1782 he proposed the motion that led to the fall of LORD NORTH's administration and joined the new Rockingham-Shelburne administration as commander in chief—a position he held only until December 1783. He failed to be elected to Parliament in 1784 and thereafter retired from an active role in politics.

Conway Cabal

An ill-defined political and military intrigue that peaked and fizzled out in the winter of 1777–78, the Conway Cabal aimed at removing GEORGE WASHINGTON as commander in chief of the CONTINENTAL ARMY and replacing him with HORATIO GATES. The so-called conspiracy is named for the group's most tenacious and vocal member, Brigadier General Thomas Conway. The movement drew support from two sources: within the SECOND CONTINENTAL

CONGRESS, where detractors such as SAMUEL ADAMS were especially distrustful of a standing army and feared Washington might use his popularity with the people to become a military dictator; and within the army itself, where a few of Washington's officers—among them Generals Conway and Gates, who had trained and served as professional soldiers in foreign armies—viewed their native-born commander as an incompetent amateur. After the crucial victory at SARATOGA (October 17, 1777), credited to Gates, the conspirators believed they had a suitable replacement.

Washington was soon aware of the maneuvering against him. In the afterglow of Saratoga, Gates became increasingly insubordinate, bypassing Washington and making his reports directly to Congress. Conway, a boastful self-enthusiast who lacked Washington's support for promotion, began badgering Congress for advancement and denigrating his commander's military leadership. Congress responded by aligning both Conway and Gates against Washington. Conway was promoted to inspector general, a position independent of the commander in chief and answerable to Gates as chairman of the Board of War. Infuriated, Washington treated Conway coldly but with the proper respect. Conway was nevertheless incensed, and his letters to Washington thereafter were insolent and duplicitous.

The crumbling of the cabal was already underway, however. Through indiscreet gossip and revelations from private correspondence, Washington had learned of a letter Conway had written to Gates disparaging the abilities of Washington and his aides. When he confronted Conway with the report, Conway tried to explain his meaning, but his condescending attitude only made matters worse. Gates, though merely the recipient of the damning communiqué, mired himself in the mess by foolishly accusing one of Washington's trusted aides of secretly copying the letter. His reputation was then further damaged when reports began filtering in from participants at Saratoga that BENEDICT ARNOLD, and not Gates, had been largely responsible for the victory. As exposure of the intrigue grew, most of the plotters shrank from sight, but Conway continued his attacks until John Cadwalader, a general of the Pennsylvania MILITIA, shot Conway through the mouth in a duel. Only the thought of impending death prompted Conway to apologize for his disparaging remarks, though he recovered from his wound and went to France; he died in Ireland in 1800.

Further reading: Robert Leckie, *George Washington's War: The Saga of the American Revolution* (New York: Harper-Collins, 1993); Page Smith, *A New Age Now Begins: A People's History of the American Revolution, Vol. 2.* (New York: Penguin Books, 1989).

—Rita M. Broyles

Conyngham, Gustavus (1744?–1819) *Continental naval officer*

Gustavus Conyngham was born in Ireland and moved to British North America in 1763. In Philadelphia his family was connected to a mercantile house, and he apprenticed as a seaman. He quickly worked his way up to become a captain of a merchant ship. In 1775 he sailed to The NETHERLANDS to pick up military supplies but was unable to do so because of British opposition. In Europe, Conyngham found employment as a captain in the CONTINENTAL NAVY with a commission from the representatives of the United States in FRANCE—BENJAMIN FRANKLIN, SILAS DEANE, and ARTHUR LEE. On May 1, 1777, Conyngham sailed from Dunkirk—the British would dub him the "Dunkirk Pirate"—and quickly captured two prizes. However, when he returned to Dunkirk, the French seized his prizes, took his commission, and arrested him since France and GREAT BRITAIN were not yet at war. Conyngham was soon released and given a new commission by Franklin, and by the end of July he was cruising British waters in a new vessel, a cutter called the *Revenge*. He wreaked havoc on British shipping, ranging from water close to the British Isles to the WEST INDIES, and captured or sank at least 60 British

Captain Gustavus Conyngham attacked British shipping for 22 months beginning in 1777, capturing or sinking a record 60 British ships. *(Naval Historical Center)*

vessels. However, this voyage was not without controversy, as Conyngham commanded a polyglot and cutthroat crew that compelled him to make some questionable seizures. One of the reasons he sailed to the Caribbean was that these actions created problems for him in SPAIN, which he had used as a base of operations.

Arriving in Philadelphia in February 1779, Conyngham began another cruise in April—this time as a privateer—but he was captured by the British and sent to Mill Prison in England. On his third attempt, Conyngham escaped confinement and went to France, where he briefly joined JOHN PAUL JONES on the USS *Alliance*. He left Jones early in 1780 and headed back to Philadelphia, where he took command of another privateer, the *Experiment*. But this voyage also ended in capture by the British, who held him as a prisoner until June 1781 when he escaped from Mill Prison again. After the war, Conyngham became a merchant and sought compensation for his service to the United States. In this effort he was unsuccessful since his original commission had been seized by the French and Congress decided not to honor his second commission because they decided it was temporary. Conyngham died on March 27, 1819, and was buried in Philadelphia.

Further reading: E. Gordon Bowen-Hassell, Dennis M. Conrad, and Mark L. Hayes, *Sea Raiders of the American Revolution: The Continental Navy in European Waters* (Washington, D.C.: Naval Historical Center, 2003).

Cooche's Bridge, Battle of (September 3, 1777)

The only significant battle in Delaware during the REVOLUTIONARY WAR (1775–83) was a bloody skirmish at Cooche's Bridge as General WILLIAM HOWE's army marched on Philadelphia from Head of Elk, Maryland. GEORGE WASHINGTON sent General William Maxwell to slow the British advance. Maxwell's men opened fire on the British about 9:00 A.M., but they were quickly swept from the field by British and German light infantry. Despite several attempts to assume a new line and delay the British further, this running fight by Maxwell's Continentals quickly turned into a rout as the Revolutionaries precipitously retreated. Maxwell's men did not stop running until they reached Washington's main force near Brandywine Creek (see BRANDYWINE, BATTLE OF). Casualty figures vary: Maxwell lost between 20 and 40 dead; the British claimed only three dead and 20 wounded.

Cook's Mills, Battle of (October 19, 1814)

Although the Battle of Cook's Mills did not have a crucial influence on the WAR OF 1812 (1812–15), it was the last military engagement in CANADA between regular forces.

On October 12, 1814, Major General GEORGE IZARD's right division was united with Major General Jacob Brown's left division near Niagara Falls. The two military leaders disagreed over how to engage Lieutenant General GORDON DRUMMOND's British forces, safely ensconced behind the Chippewa River. Brown preferred a quick assault, while Izard favored enticing Drummond out of his redoubt. Disagreement over tactics resulted in Brown's departure with his division for Sackets Harbor.

After artillery on October 15 failed to drive Drummond from his fortification, Izard devised another strategy. He had heard that British grain was kept at Cook's Mills at Lyon's Creek, an artery of the Chippewa River. He also knew that Drummond was having difficulty feeding his troops. Therefore, on October 17 he deployed Daniel Bissel's brigade of four infantry battalions (approximately 900 men) to either destroy or seize the grain with the hope of drawing out Drummond. Drummond, however, had learned of the advance of U.S. forces and sent his deputy quartermaster, Colonel Christopher Myers, to investigate. The British and U.S. forces met and battled at Lyon's Creek on October 19. U.S. losses numbered 12 soldiers dead and 55 wounded; the British suffered one fatality and 55 wounded. While the United States was victorious in destroying the grain and driving back the enemy, they never forced Drummond from his stronghold. Izard made one final and unsuccessful attempt to draw out Drummond on October 21.

Further reading: Richard V. Barbuto, *Niagara 1814: America Invades Canada* (Lawrence: The University Press of Kansas, 2000).

—Lawrence Mastroni

Cooper, Thomas (1759–1839) *scientist, lawyer, political writer, educator*

Born in London, Thomas Cooper attended University College at Oxford but did not graduate because of his refusal to sign the required Articles of Faith, the beginning of a lifelong tendency toward unorthodox thinking. He became a barrister in 1787, was vice president of the Manchester Literary and Philosophical Society, and was also a founding member of the Manchester Constitutional Society. Acting on behalf of the latter organization, Cooper spoke before the Jacobin Society in Paris in 1792, an action that prompted a rebuke from EDMUND BURKE in Parliament.

Disheartened by the slow pace of reform in England, Cooper immigrated to the United States in 1794 and, along with JOSEPH PRIESTLEY, his friend and scientific colleague, settled in Northumberland, Pennsylvania. After struggling as a farmer, he practiced law and also wrote controversial political essays that opposed the ALIEN AND SEDITION ACTS. The FEDERALIST PARTY condemned his writings, and Cooper was convicted of libel against President JOHN ADAMS in 1800. He served six months in prison, but his political fortunes soon changed. After the ELECTION OF 1800 he became a land commissioner and was appointed a district judge in Pennsylvania in 1804.

In addition to the law, Cooper worked as a scientist and had a long career in teaching and administration in colleges and universities, teaching chemistry at Carlisle College, the University of Pennsylvania, and South Carolina College. He published on chemistry, law, metaphysics, economics, and politics. After Priestley's death in 1804, Cooper added appendices to the scientist's works. In 1820 he was elected president of South Carolina College, although his tenure was marked by controversy over his religious views. On the other hand, his support of STATES' RIGHTS, nullification, and SLAVERY—a reversal of his prior views—won favor from the South Carolina people. He died on May 11, 1839, and was buried in Columbia, South Carolina.

See also LAWYERS; RELIGION; SCIENCE.

Further reading: S. L. Newman, "Thomas Cooper, 1759–1839: The Political Odyssey of a Bourgeois Ideologue," *Journal of Southern Studies* 24 (1985): 295–305.

—Lawrence Mastroni

Cooper, William (1754–1809) *New York businessman, judge, congressman*

From modest beginnings in Pennsylvania, William Cooper became an entrepreneur, land speculator, and founder of Cooperstown, New York. In the process he amassed a fortune before he overextended himself in lands in upstate New York. Poorly educated, Cooper trained as a wheelwright but had grander visions. He was only 19 when he married Elizabeth Fenimore and settled in Burlington, New Jersey, where his wife's affluent family lived. During the 1770s and 1780s Cooper became a storekeeper and businessman and embarked on an ambitious plan of self-improvement. Affable and always looking for the next deal, he set his sights on a huge parcel of land near Lake Otsego in New York State. With the help of a talented lawyer, ALEXANDER HAMILTON, he turned a questionable land purchase of LOYALIST property into a successful settlement at Cooperstown. Cooper recognized that the key to successful land speculation was to resell the land as quickly as possible to the stream of migrants that poured out of New England in the 1790s and early 1800s. He offered easy credit—sometimes not even requiring any MONEY down—and lax mortgage payment terms. However, at times he played a little too fast and loose with surveys and land titles, a policy that would eventually entangle him and his heirs in legal complications. Cooper explained his method of settle-

ment in his *Guide to the Wilderness* (1810), published a year after his death.

Although his humble origins, rough manners, and positive relationship with most of the settlers of Cooperstown might suggest that Cooper should have joined the DEMOCRATIC-REPUBLICAN PARTY, he was an ardent partisan of the FEDERALIST PARTY, viewing himself as a self-made patriarch of the community. He was elected to Congress from 1795 to 1797 and 1799 to 1801 and served as the local judge in his community. He included among his friends Hamilton, JOHN JAY, and PHILIP SCHUYLER. THOMAS JEFFERSON, who was no Cooper fan, referred to him as the "Bashaw of Otsego." The opening decade of the 19th century, however, saw much of his influence wane in politics, and he found himself overreaching economically by trying to replicate his early success in the St. Lawrence River Valley. The impact of this overextension, however, did not become fully evident until after his death and was a problem for his heirs, one of whom was his son, the novelist James Fenimore Cooper, who would draw a sympathetic portrait of his father in the character of Judge Marmaduke Temple as a paterfamilias of an ungrateful community in *The Pioneers*.

See also LAWYERS; LOYALIST PROPERTY CONFISCATION.

Further reading: Alan Taylor, *William Cooper's Town: Power and Persuasion on the Frontier of the Early American Republic* (New York: Knopf, 1995).

Copley, John Singleton (1738–1815) *painter*

John Singleton Copley was one of North America's most noted portrait artists, but he left the country of his birth in 1774, never to return. Copley was born in Boston and probably gained his artistic training from his stepfather, Peter Pelham. By the 1760s he had become a well-known portrait painter in Boston and supported himself with an ample income from his painting. In 1769 he married Susannah Farnham Clarke, whose father was a merchant, and he built a house on Beacon Hill (site of the present state capital building). In 1771 and 1772 he traveled to New York and Philadelphia, painting the portraits of many leading citizens there. Although he was not politically active, his family members were largely LOYALISTS.

Friends had long encouraged Copley to take a trip to Europe for artistic studies, and he left for England in 1774, influenced by the political climate in Boston. To further his artistic credentials, he toured the Continent in 1774 and 1775, visiting FRANCE and Italy. When he returned to England, he found his wife and her family had left Boston as Loyalist refugees in 1775, and they remained in GREAT BRITAIN for the rest of his life. Although he was a successful painter, working on portraits and historical scenes, Copley struggled to maintain his household as he grew older. He painted portraits of members of the British royal family as well as many noted Revolutionary Americans, including JOHN ADAMS and JOHN QUINCY ADAMS when they stayed in England. He died on September 9, 1815, in London.

See also ART.

Further reading: Neil Harris, *The Artist in American Society: The Formative Years, 1790–1860* (New York: George Braziller, 1966); Kenneth Silverman, *A Cultural History of the American Revolution* (New York: Columbia University Press, 1976).

Copus massacre (September 15, 1812)
Animosity between European Americans and NATIVE AMERICANS was high in Ohio in the early days of the WAR OF 1812 (1812–15). Military officials wanted some peaceful DELAWARE removed from their village near the home of James Copus in northern Ohio and asked Copus to persuade the Delaware to temporarily abandon their homes. As the Delaware were being escorted away by some soldiers, others soldiers looted the Delaware homes and then burned the village. Angered by this action, several Delaware escaped and sought revenge. On September 12, 1812, they killed five people at the home of Frederick Zimmer. On September 15, 1812, as many as 45 Indians struck at Copus's home, which nine soldiers had been detached to protect. Seven were attacked that morning as they carelessly bathed in a nearby stream; one escaped with his life and warned Copus. The three soldiers and members of the Copus family fought the war party off, although Copus, his young daughter and one soldier were wounded.

Corbin, Margaret "Molly" Cochran (1751–1800)
camp follower, soldier
Born in Chambersburg, Pennsylvania, Margaret Cochran was orphaned at an early age and married John Corbin when she was 21 years old. Her husband enlisted in the CONTINENTAL ARMY after the outbreak of the REVOLUTIONARY WAR (1775–83) and Margaret Corbin, like many women married to poor soldiers, became a CAMP FOLLOWER. As such, she had an official position on the rolls of her husband's regiment, and her duties were cooking, cleaning and mending clothes, and nursing the sick.

After her husband was killed during the battle for FORT WASHINGTON (November 16, 1776), Margaret Corbin took his place "manning" an artillery piece in action against the HESSIANS. As frequently happens in such instances of unusual battlefield behavior, legend has embellished the action. As a result, several sources indicate that Corbin actually aimed the cannon for the artillery crew and did so with such accuracy that she drew special fire from the Hessian artillery. Whether true or not, she was severely wounded in the battle and was paroled back to the Continental lines, along with other critically wounded Revolutionaries captured at Fort Washington.

On July 6, 1779, the SECOND CONTINENTAL CONGRESS voted to give Margaret Corbin a half-pay pension for life in recognition of her service. She also remained on the military rolls for the remainder of the war and lived most of the rest of her life as a partial invalid at WEST POINT. She died in Highland Falls, New York, on January 16, 1800.

Further reading: Holly A Mayer, *Belonging to the Army: Camp Followers and Community during the American Revolution* (Columbia: University of South Carolina Press, 1996).

Cornplanter (Gyantwaka, John Abeel) (1732?–1836)
Seneca chief
The SENECA chief Cornplanter sought to guide the IROQUOIS Confederacy through the upheaval that accompanied U.S. independence from GREAT BRITAIN. He was born in Genesee River Valley to a Dutch father named John Abeel and an Iroquois mother; his brother was HANDSOME LAKE. The record of Cornplanter's early life remains unclear. Some documents place him on the French side during the FRENCH AND INDIAN WAR (1754–63), and he was alleged to have taken part in the ambush of General EDWARD BRADDOCK's column in 1755. During the REVOLUTIONARY WAR (1775–83), Cornplanter fought for the British, defended his homeland against the invasion led by General JOHN SULLIVAN in 1779, and became a major Iroquois war chief.

After the war, Cornplanter believed that NATIVE AMERICANS had been betrayed by the British and decided to work with the United States. The Revolutionary War had devastated the Iroquois and split the Indian confederation into pro-British and anti-British factions. The Iroquois were also divided by the international border that ran between the settlement on the Grand River in CANADA and those living in New York State.

Cornplanter persuaded the Iroquois to accept the terms of the Treaty of Fort Stanwix of 1784. This agreement gave the state of New York title to much of the old hunting grounds that were already filling up with European-American settlers from the coast. Several more treaties followed during the next decade, further whittling down the Iroquois lands. Cornplanter argued each time that to surrender to the territorial demands of the United States was the only way to save the lives of the people; the United States was too strong and would destroy them if they resisted. In 1791 President GEORGE WASHINGTON sent Cornplanter on a peace mission to the tribes of the Ohio Territory, but he

Seneca chief and warrior Cornplanter joined Loyalists to fight against Revolutionary forces. After the war, he negotiated many treaties with the new nation and offered his services in the War of 1812. *(New York Historical Society)*

failed to convince the Native Americans in the area to yield to U.S. government demands. He did, however, manage to keep the Six Nations out of the confederation of Native Americans that met with a disastrous defeat at the BATTLE OF FALLEN TIMBERS on August 20, 1794.

Cornplanter's unremitting accommodation to European-American demands cost him the respect of many of his own people. One of his most vocal opponents was the Seneca chief RED JACKET, who wanted to hold onto as much land as possible in defiance of the United States. In 1802 Cornplanter visited THOMAS JEFFERSON in WASHINGTON, D.C. He supported the United States in the WAR OF 1812 (1812–15) and offered to fight the British even though he was about 80 years old. His son led a band of warriors against the British in the Niagara region. Cornplanter died peacefully on February 18, 1836, on a farm given him by Pennsylvania.

Further reading: Anthony F. C. Wallace, *The Death and Rebirth of the Seneca* (New York: Knopf, 1969).

—George Milne

Cornstalk (Hokoleskwa) (1720?–1777) *Shawnee chief*

Though Cornstalk commanded a group of SHAWNEE at the BATTLE OF POINT PLEASANT (October 10, 1774) during DUNMORE'S WAR (1774), he is best remembered for spending his remaining years advocating accommodation with European Americans. This approach was especially challenging as other Shawnee chiefs, such as BLUE JACKET, remained militant and hostile to European-American settlers.

Cornstalk reacted strongly to the Shawnee defeat at the Battle of Point Pleasant and the terms of the earlier TREATY OF FORT STANWIX (1768), finding support among the neutrality-minded Shawnee from the Mequashake and Kispokos bands. The loss of traditional hunting grounds in Kentucky to the European Americans convinced him that further resistance was futile. Fearing another destructive war, he represented neutralist Shawnee factions at several treaty councils, while also informing colonial and Revolutionary American agents of the hostile intentions of other Indian communities, specifically the Piqua band of the Shawnee. His neutralist stance, however, became more difficult to sustain after the outbreak of the REVOLUTIONARY WAR (1775–83) led to further violence. While Cornstalk negotiated with the Revolutionaries at Point Pleasant in 1777, Matthew Arbuckle, the Revolutionary commander at nearby Fort Randolph, imprisoned him without cause. Soldiers within the fort then killed Cornstalk, his son and two other hostages in retaliation for the unrelated murder of a soldier. The unprovoked assassination of the peaceful Cornstalk, along with several subsequent killings, convinced many neutral SENECA, Shawnee, and DELAWARE to support the British.

Further reading: Gregory Evans Dowd, *A Spirited Resistance: The North American Struggle for Unity, 1745–1815* (Baltimore: Johns Hopkins University Press, 1992).

—Patrick Bottiger

Cornwallis, Charles, Lord (1738–1805) *British military officer*

With all the advantages of wealth and aristocratic birth, Charles Cornwallis, first marquis Cornwallis, expected only great military triumphs. While he did experience many successes, he is best known in the United States as the British general who surrendered at YORKTOWN on October 19, 1781, ending the last major military campaign of the REVOLUTIONARY WAR (1775–83). Lord Cornwallis rose quickly in the British army because of his personal and political connections and his individual valor. Educated at Eton, instructed in military science by a Prussian officer, he also attended the Turin military academy. He was 17 when he obtained his first commission in 1758. He fought in several engagements in the German campaign of the Seven Years' War (1756–63; known as the FRENCH AND INDIAN WAR in North America, 1754–63), was promoted to lieutenant colonel by 1761, and in 1766 became a colonel of his own regiment. His noble birth led to several offices within the king's household during the 1760s. In 1760 he was elected to the House of Commons, but he entered the House of Lords two years later when his father died and he inherited his title (second earl Cornwallis).

When the Revolutionary War broke out, Cornwallis was stationed in Ireland with his regiment. He volunteered for service in North America and was promoted to major general. His first exposure to battle in the war was not particularly noteworthy. He was sent to North Carolina to link up with General HENRY CLINTON, did little there, and took part in the misguided CHARLESTON EXPEDITION of 1776. However, he also participated with distinction in the BATTLE OF LONG ISLAND (August 27–30, 1776) and in the ensuing campaign that forced GEORGE WASHINGTON to flee across New Jersey. He was about to return to England to visit his ill wife when Washington struck at Trenton on December 26, 1776. Cornwallis took command of the advance troops but allowed Washington to slip away from Trenton, march around the British flank, and attack Princeton (January 3, 1777). He participated in General WILLIAM HOWE's campaign against Philadelphia and led the force that outflanked the CONTINENTAL ARMY at the BATTLE OF BRANDYWINE (September 11, 1777). Cornwallis also played an instrumental role in the British victory at the BATTLE OF GERMANTOWN (October 4, 1777) and in driving Continental forces from DELAWARE RIVER FORTS that controlled the entrance to Philadelphia. The following year, he became second in command behind Clinton and fought in the BATTLE OF MONMOUTH (June 28, 1778).

Clinton and Cornwallis had initially been friends, having known each other for years and served together in the German campaign during the Seven Years' War, but by 1778 their relationship had become estranged. Clinton was not the warmest of individuals and was never popular with officers and men. Cornwallis, on the other hand, was extremely well liked by officers and the rank and file. Moreover, almost from the day Clinton replaced Howe, Cornwallis vied for an independent command and sought to be made commander in chief—something his connections in England had promised him if and when Clinton stepped down.

This personal animosity and misunderstanding between the two generals increased in 1780 and contributed to the British disaster in 1781. Clinton and Cornwallis invaded the southern states in 1780, taking the city of Charleston on May 12, 1780—a victory that was largely due to Clinton's strategy in the SIEGE OF CHARLESTON. Clinton wanted to

move slowly in South Carolina, expanding areas of control, supporting LOYALISTS, and consolidating the British position. But when he left for New York, placing Cornwallis in command of the southern campaign, the earl saw things differently. The Revolutionaries sent an army under General HORATIO GATES south to challenge British control, and Cornwallis met this force at the BATTLE OF CAMDEN (August 16, 1780). In this battle, Britain's superior troops and their general's tactical abilities provided a smashing victory. Cornwallis became emboldened, believing that he had secured his base in South Carolina. However, he had been letting his men loot at will, often alienating the local population. This practice continued as he headed to North Carolina. He also seemed to ignore the depredations of several MILITIA units that harassed Tories and threatened his communications. Nor did he fully support those Loyalists who had taken up arms to fight for the king.

Disaster struck when a large Loyalist force was wiped out at the BATTLE OF KING'S MOUNTAIN (October 7, 1780) in the South Carolina backcountry. Cornwallis, faced with the appearance of another army of Continentals under General NATHANAEL GREENE, withdrew to South

British general Charles Cornwallis, an honorable and proud officer, led a brilliant attack against Continental soldiers at Brandywine and countered General Washington's move toward Germantown in October 1777. *(National Portrait Gallery, London)*

Carolina, dispatching Colonel BANASTRE TARLETON to deal with General DANIEL MORGAN, who commanded one contingent of the Revolutionary army. Unfortunately for Cornwallis, Morgan decisively beat Tarleton at the BATTLE OF COWPENS on January 17, 1781. Angered by this action, and wishing to cripple the Revolutionaries the way he had at Camden, Cornwallis set off after Morgan with his whole army. Morgan joined Greene, and the Revolutionaries eluded the British as the two forces shadowed each through the North Carolina countryside. Cornwallis finally caught up with Greene and Morgan and beat them at the BATTLE OF GUILFORD COURTHOUSE on March 15, 1781, though it was a costly victory for the British. Cornwallis decided to reconnect with his supply lines and headed for the coast at Wilmington. Once there, he made another important strategic decision, and rather than returning to South Carolina to firm up his base, he headed for the Chesapeake, where other British forces had been active.

Initially, the British could do whatever they wanted in Virginia, capturing Richmond, and with an army now augmented to almost 8,500, Cornwallis appeared triumphant. But if the British dominated the battlefield, the larger strategic situation began to deteriorate as Cornwallis and Clinton disagreed over a course of action and both generals vacillated. Clinton wanted reinforcements to ward off a supposed threat to New York; Cornwallis started to send some men, and then reversed his decision. Asked to establish a base that would provide protection for a British fleet, he chose Yorktown, then changed his mind, then changed it again. Once at Yorktown, with the full summer heat affecting his men, he did not rigorously entrench his position. Finally, by the end of August he began to realize his desperate situation, but by then it was too late. The French beat back a British relief fleet in the BATTLE OF CHESAPEAKE CAPES (September 5, 1781), and a huge army of French and Continental soldiers marched in from the North, surrounding Yorktown and laying siege to Cornwallis's position. Outmanned, outgunned, and running out of supplies, Cornwallis surrendered at Yorktown on October 19, 1781.

Oddly, Cornwallis was not really blamed for this defeat as his political connections were too strong. Instead, Clinton, who was commander in chief, but who had little influence on Cornwallis's southern campaign in 1780 and 1781, was blamed. Cornwallis later had a brilliant career as governor general of INDIA and lord lieutenant of Ireland. He died in India on October 5, 1805, and was buried in Ghazipur, in a spot overlooking the Ganges River.

Further reading: George Athan Billias, *George Washington's Opponents: British Generals and Admirals in the American Revolution* (New York: William Morrow, 1969); Franklin and Mary Wickwire, *Cornwallis: The American Adventure* (Boston: Houghton Mifflin, 1970).

corporations

Between 1789 and 1815, state legislatures chartered many new business corporations in banking, construction, INSURANCE, and manufacturing. During the colonial period, the British government had granted corporate charters (detailed contracts between corporations and government institutions) to various organizations such as colleges, towns, and fire associations. These corporations enjoyed special and privileged licenses—to govern or educate, for example. Though they were usually reserved for aristocrats or others with political connections, they also served to maintain organizations devoted to public service. The British government granted only six corporate charters for business purposes in North America during the entire colonial era.

After independence, state governments redefined the meaning of the corporation to focus on building the ECONOMY of the early republic. Consequently, state governments granted more than 300 corporate charters between 1789 and 1800, and 1,800 business charters between 1800 and 1817. New York alone granted 220 charters to business corporations between 1800 and 1810. An important ideological shift characterized the new approach to incorporation. People in the United States now looked at corporations as entities responsible to the democratic legislatures that granted them charters. Given this new public accountability, states permitted the establishment of corporations designed to support the public interest, which in the early republic was tied to economic development. Therefore, state legislatures often looked favorably upon corporate proposals to build roads or bridges, or to open new BANKS and insurance companies.

The new business corporations retained certain rights from the states that chartered them. These usually included powers to raise capital by various means, monopolistic control of a certain TRADE, and limited liability for stockholders. In addition, the new corporate charters became vehicles by which the states could regulate business enterprise. Consequently, states often restricted the new companies by defining boards of directors, qualifying limited liability, establishing maximum interest rates in the case of banks, specifying dividend amounts, and setting prices in the case of utilities. The concept of limited liability sometimes became a flashpoint in debate over new charters, as public officials expressed reservations over allowing stockholders to be removed from debts incurred by the companies they owned. State legislatures sometimes connected new corporations to each other via investment mandates. For example, the corporate charters of many early republic banks in Pennsylvania required them to invest in companies carrying out specific INTERNAL IMPROVEMENTS.

The development of corporations as vehicles to conduct business and invest capital continued after 1815. The U.S. SUPREME COURT's decision in *Dartmouth College v. Woodward* (1819) helped to protect charters of incorporation against state interference by asserting that a corporation's property rights were sacred and could not be subsequently altered by a state. In the 1820s and 1830s, the number of business corporations continued to increase as trade networks and business enterprise expanded around the country.

Further reading: Morton J. Horwitz, *The Transformation of American Law, 1780–1860* (Cambridge, Mass.: Harvard University Press, 1977); George David Rappaport, *Stability and Change in Revolutionary Pennsylvania* (University Park: Pennsylvania University Press 1996); Gordon S. Wood, *The Radicalism of the American Revolution* (New York: Knopf, 1991).

—James R. Karmel

corporatism

In the 18th century, many people in colonial America and GREAT BRITAIN believed that society consisted of a single giant interest. This ideal, which historians call corporatism, may not have fully reflected reality, but its proponents held that both society and politics were a single body, or corpus. Within this theoretical framework, there was no room for interest-group politics because anyone not working for the single interest was held to be working against it. There was also no such thing as "loyal opposition." Whether one was rich or poor, whatever your race or gender, all was subsumed to the ideal of the greater interest.

The cement that held this corporate—single-bodied—society together was paternalism and deference. Paternalism was the belief that those who were on top of the social and political scale—the king, lords, governors, and gentry—would protect the interests of society and take care of those below them, as a father does for a child. Within the body of society, the elite were to be the head; the people were the arms and the legs. Common folk, therefore, would defer to the judgment of their betters, assuming that the elite knew best for everyone concerned. This concept is crucial for understanding how people in the 18th century perceived the world. Faith in the king and a hierarchy was permeated with the ideal of corporatism. If an individual no longer believed that the king protected the welfare of the people, then the whole fabric of society as it was then known would unravel.

On one level, the colonial Americans who revolted from King GEORGE III began to loose their faith in corporatism. THOMAS PAINE attacked the whole notion of monarchy in *COMMON SENSE* and naturally included an assault on hierarchy as well. When THOMAS JEFFERSON wrote the DECLARATION OF INDEPENDENCE, which accused the king of no longer protecting the interest of the colonies, he began with an assertion of the antithesis of hierarchy by stating that "all men are created equal."

American Revolutionary leaders did not readily abandon the ideal of corporatism, despite the words in *Common Sense* and the Declaration of Independence. As they struggled to create new government in the states, which would eventually result in the U.S. CONSTITUTION, they wrestled with the ideal of corporatism. REPUBLICANISM as an ideology of the Revolutionary era was dependent on the ideal of corporatism. As republicanism gave way to the rise of a new democratic United States that emphasized equality, corporatism lost much of its hold, and it became possible to see a greater good emerge out of competing political, economic, and social ideas.

Further reading: Gordon S. Wood, *The Radicalism of the American Revolution* (New York: Knopf, 1992).

Correa da Serra, José Francisco (1750–1823)
botanist

A close friend of THOMAS JEFFERSON and a preeminent botanist, José Francisco Correa da Serra was part of the transatlantic scientific community and served as the Portuguese minister plenipotentiary to the United States from 1816 until 1820. Educated in Rome, where he took holy orders, Correa da Serra began his diplomatic career in 1797, when he became the secretary to the Portuguese ambassador in GREAT BRITAIN. While in England, he became a member of the Royal Society and a close associate of the scientist Sir Joseph Banks. He resided in Paris from 1802 until he moved in 1813 to the United States, where he taught botany at the University of Pennsylvania and wrote on the nature of North American soil, especially in Kentucky. Correa da Serra traveled throughout the United States as a philosopher and botanist, but it was not until 1816 that he received his diplomatic appointment as the minister plenipotentiary from PORTUGAL. In 1820 he left this post and returned to Portugal in ill health. He was elected to the Constitutional Cortes in Lisbon in 1822 and died the following year.

Further reading: Richard Beale Davis, "The Abbé Correa in America, 1812–1820: The Contributions of the Diplomat and Natural Philosopher to the Foundations of our National Life," *Transactions of the American Philosophical Society* 45, no. 2 (1955), 87–197; Douglas L. Wheeler, ed., *Historical Dictionary of Portugal*, 2nd ed. (Lanham, Md.: Scarecrow Press, 2002).

—Michele M. Stephens

Coshocton

Though Coshocton (an Indian word meaning "union of waters") was initially a settlement of refugee DELAWARE and SHAWNEE Indians, it played an increasingly important role in North American imperial politics during the REVOLUTIONARY WAR (1775–83). Located at the confluence of the Walhonding and Tuscarawas rivers in present-day Ohio, Coshocton, with nearly 2,000 inhabitants, served as the center for several satellite communities of NATIVE AMERICANS. The political decisions at Coshocton often influenced the actions of other nearby Delaware and Shawnee settlements, making its inhabitants potential military allies for both GREAT BRITAIN and the United States during the War for Independence. Though Delaware chiefs GEORGE WHITE EYES and JOHN KILLBUCK, JR., and Shawnee leaders CORNSTALK and Nimwha espoused neutrality in the face of war, peace remained elusive. Civil strife erupted in 1779 between the people of Coshocton and other Ohio Valley Indians who supported the British. White Eyes had developed a close relationship with the U.S. government, which enraged several nativist and pro-British Indian communities. A crisis within Coshocton also developed when a pro-British leader, Captain Pipe, openly challenged Killbuck's neutralist stance. Pipe's access to British goods, as well as growing FRONTIER violence, made his rhetoric attractive, while Killbuck's promises went unfulfilled, largely a result of the U.S. government's failure to deliver promised supplies. Several families left Coshocton to follow Captain Pipe, further undermining Killbuck's power. By 1781 the Coshocton Delaware and Shawnee had reversed their neutralist policies, replaced Killbuck, and sided with Britain. One year later, the MIAMI, Wabash, and Peoria Indians had done the same, effectively making the area north of the Ohio River pro-British.

Further reading: Richard White, *The Middle Ground: Indians, Empires, and Republics in the Great Lakes Region, 1650–1815* (New York: Cambridge University Press, 1991).

—Patrick Bottiger

Cosway, Maria Lousia Catherine Cecilia Hadfield
(1759–1838) *educator*
Born to a wealthy family in Florence, Italy, Maria Lousia Catherine Cecilia Hadfield displayed an aptitude for ART and MUSIC. Educated in various convents, she was competent in five languages, deeply religious, and one of the youngest artists to be admitted to the Academy of Fine Arts at Florence. With the death of her father in 1778, Maria contemplated taking vows and entering a convent; instead, her mother persuaded her to journey to London, where she met her future husband, Richard Cosway (1742–1821). Beautiful, eloquent, and graceful, Maria captivated London society, though she longed for the simplicity and tranquility of Florence. Richard and Maria shared a love of art and,

after they were married, ran one of the most popular salons in London. Even though Richard prevented Maria from painting professionally, she continued to paint landscapes, portraits of friends, and religious imagery.

In summer 1786 Maria Cosway met the U.S. diplomat THOMAS JEFFERSON in Paris and immediately detected a kindred spirit. Although the exact details of her relationship with Jefferson remain unknown, the two intellectuals grew very close and may have had an affair. Jefferson wrote his famous "head and heart" letter to Cosway in which he set up a dialogue, where the head was "allotted the field of science" and the heart the field of morals. Up until Jefferson's death in July 1826, the two corresponded on a variety of subjects.

In 1803 Cosway realized an old dream when she became a teacher for girls at a school in Lyon, France. Her teaching was interrupted when she was summoned home to care for her dying husband. After Richard's death in 1821, she opened the College Della Grazie in Italy. Living out the rest of her life managing the college, Maria Cosway died on January 5, 1838, after receiving one last communion and dictating directions for the school's future.

Further reading: Helen Duprey Bullock, *My Head and My Heart* (New York: G.P. Putnam's Sons, 1945).

cotton
Cotton had a profound impact on the history of the United States as its cultivation moved from the agricultural sidelines during the colonial period to become the most important staple of the southern United States in the antebellum period, dominating the regional and even the national ECONOMY. This great transformation occurred during the years of the early republic for several reasons: introduction of the appropriate seeds for conditions in the southern United States, effective machinery to process the cotton, an entrepreneurial outlook that sought to grow marketable crops, demand for the product, and a slave labor system.

Throughout the 18th century, British North Americans and the Spanish and French settlers in FLORIDA and LOUISIANA grew cotton. Although some of this cotton was exported, most of it was used for domestic CLOTH PRODUCTION. During the REVOLUTIONARY WAR (1775–83) cotton cultivation expanded since the conflict had disrupted the exportation of marketable crops such as RICE and INDIGO and made imported cloth difficult to obtain. Indeed, for European Americans domestic cotton production became a symbol of patriotism for the Revolutionary cause while simultaneously utilizing land and labor that might have otherwise been idle. However, amid the upheaval of war, masters could not press their African-American slaves too hard for fear of driving them to join the British. Instead, many allowed slaves to grow crops, like cotton, for their own use or for sale in local markets. Ironically, the very crop that epitomized the brutal institutionalization of SLAVERY during the antebellum era represented an assertion of independence from the planters' authority during the Revolutionary War.

At the end of the war, planters in Georgia and South Carolina sought to rebuild their world, which had been torn apart by the British invasion and a bitter internecine conflict. Many lowland planters sought to revitalize rice production through the development of tidal irrigation, while other planters searched for new crops. In 1786–87 several planters in the South Carolina and Georgia sea islands began to experiment with cotton seeds sent to them by LOYALISTS in the BAHAMAS. These strains of cotton were superior to the black-seeded cotton generally grown before the war and quickly spread throughout the ATLANTIC OCEAN coastal region of the Deep South. Annual exports in sea-island cotton from South Carolina alone rose from less than 10,000 pounds in the year from October 1, 1789, to September 30, 1790, to more than 8 million pounds in the year from October 1, 1800, to September 30, 1801.

The long-staple sea-island cotton, however, did not thrive in the uplands of South Carolina and Georgia, a region that underwent a tremendous increase in settlement by European Americans in the last decades of the 18th century. These newcomers wanted to live like the planters of the coastal region and sought marketable crops in TOBACCO and grains. The short-staple cotton that could be grown in the upcountry had seeds that were difficult to separate from the cotton fibers, and therefore it was not particularly profitable. Several individuals began to experiment with designing machines to separate the seeds, including ELI WHITNEY, who invented his cotton gin in 1793. Although Whitney was never able to defend his patent on the gin successfully, copies and modifications of the machine spread throughout the South, allowing an expansion of cotton cultivation. By 1800 the United States was exporting just under 20 million pounds of cotton and by 1810 over 90 million pounds.

GREAT BRITAIN was the largest market for this cotton as its manufacturers increased production of cloth with the INDUSTRIAL REVOLUTION. During the early 1770s, the British imported about 7 million tons of cotton, but the development of textile machinery and factories led to an increase in imports to over 23 million tons in 1787 and about 56 million tons in 1800. This demand was more than the previous sources for cotton—the WEST INDIES, Brazil, the East Indies, and the Middle East—could provide.

These developments had profound implications for the United States. During the Revolutionary War, many European Americans had come to look at slavery as a dying institution. Several leading Revolutionaries believed that without continued importation of slaves from AFRICA, slavery would simply fade away because it was unprofitable. However, the expansion of the "cotton kingdom"—which spread from the upcountry of Georgia and South Carolina across the Mississippi Territory and even north into Tennessee—dictated a different course for the nation. Cotton could have been grown on small plots by independent farmers. Instead, its production increasingly depended on slave labor organized in work gangs to insure greater control and allow less independence for the slave than the task system of the Low Country (the task system set a certain level of work for a slave to do each day). The greatest profits could be had by those who used enslaved labor, and soon the economies of scale, combined with the ambitions of cotton growers in newly settled regions and the desire to emulate the lifestyle of lowland planters, made for an economic system where slavery became entrenched as the "peculiar" institution.

Cotton also had an impact on the northern United States. As northern businessmen started to build their own textile factories in the 1790s and early 1800s, they, too, came to rely on the South's cotton. Perhaps more important was the U.S. economy's dependence on cotton. The shipping industry, controlled by merchants in northern ports, relied heavily on its ability to take southern cotton across the Atlantic. Likewise, the nascent INSURANCE industry and a growing number of financial institutions relied on the profits that cotton generated. ARTISANS in seaports and common SEAMEN all gained employment because of the rise of the export sector. Eventually, even European-American small-scale farmers owed a part of their income to their ability to produce a surplus to help feed the slaves busy growing cotton.

Further reading: Joyce E. Chaplin, *Anxious Pursuit: Agricultural Innovation and Modernity in the Lower South, 1730–1815* (Chapel Hill: University of North Carolina Press, 1993); Lewis Cecil Gray, *History of Agriculture in the Southern United States to 1860,* Vol. 2 (Washington, D.C.: Carnegie Institution of Washington, 1933).

Cowan's Ford, Battle of (February 1, 1781)

After the BATTLE OF COWPENS (January 17, 1781) during the REVOLUTIONARY WAR (1775–83), British general LORD CORNWALLIS headed into North Carolina in pursuit of Continental general NATHANAEL GREENE. Greene feared a confrontation with the superior British force and led Cornwallis on a chase across the state. Hoping to slow down the pursuit, he ordered local MILITIA to do everything they could to delay the British. General William L. Davidson therefore stationed about 300 militia at Cowan's Ford on the Catawba River to oppose the advancing enemy.

When Cornwallis reached the ford on the morning of February 1, he ordered his men to cross the swollen stream led by a LOYALIST from the area. Although the British struggled in the high water, and Cornwallis's own horse was struck with a bullet, they managed to get across the Catawba and drive the militia from the field before reinforcements could arrive. Davidson was killed soon after the battle began, and his militia was dispersed.

Cowboys and Skinners

Cowboys and Skinners were the names given to the marauders who terrorized the no-man's-land between the British and Revolutionary lines in Westchester County, New York. The names were used during the REVOLUTIONARY WAR (1775–83) and were later made famous by James Fenimore Cooper in his novel *The Spy* (1821). Although used generically, both Cowboys and Skinners referred to specific units. The Cowboys were known as De Lancey's Cowboys, also called the Westchester Refugees, a unit of about 500 volunteer LOYALISTS who were organized by JAMES DE LANCEY and stationed at King's Bridge. Labelled Cowboys for taking so many cattle, they kept the road to King's Bridge open so that supplies could be delivered to the British army while they raided behind enemy lines in foraging parties. The Skinners were the Cowboys' Revolutionary counterparts. Their name may have two possible derivations. First, the Skinners have been associated with a New Jersey regiment under General Courtlandt Skinner. Second, the unit reportedly skinned their victims of their purses and valuables. In half-mocking tones, Cooper described the depredations of both groups by declaring that "neither stopped to ask the politics of horse or cow which they drove into captivity; nor, when they wrung the neck of a rooster did they trouble their heads to ascertain whether they were crowing for congress or King George."

As losers in the war, De Lancey's Cowboys suffered the most in reputation. Although some men in the Westchester Refugees committed excesses and crimes, for the most part the unit maintained discipline despite their involvement in irregular warfare. In reality, units from all the forces in the region—the British, HESSIANS, Loyalists, regular Continentals, Revolutionary MILITIA, and the French—at times took advantage of the lack of law and order in the no-man's-land between the lines. Moreover, criminal elements without allegiance to either side were also active and willing to blame their thievery on Cowboys, Skinners, or both.

Further reading: Catherine S. Crary, "Guerrilla Activities of James De Lancey's Cowboys in Westchester County: Conventional Warfare or Self-Interested Freebooting?" in Robert A. East and Jacob Judd, eds., *The Loyalist Americans: A Focus on Greater New York* (Tarrytown: Sleepy Hollow Restorations, 1975), 14–24.

Cowpens, Battle of (January 17, 1781)

Fought in northwestern South Carolina, this late battle in the REVOLUTIONARY WAR (1775–83) was a significant victory for the United States. The British were making substantial gains in the southern colonies, where they hoped to expand their control and eventually move north and crush the rebellion. The CONTINENTAL ARMY desperately needed a successful battle to turn the tide against the British and secure the loyalty of the southerners. Recently promoted by General GEORGE WASHINGTON, General NATHANAEL GREENE commanded the entire southern campaign. The British, brilliantly led by LORD CORNWALLIS, controlled most of South Carolina in December 1780. Attempting to flank the enemy, Greene divided his army, sending General DANIEL MORGAN west toward a grazing area called the Cowpens, while he occupied a post near Cheraw, South Carolina, to rally the local MILITIA and to keep an eye on Cornwallis.

In response to this move, Cornwallis dispatched Colonel BANASTRE TARLETON to pursue Morgan. Tarleton was a tactician experienced in defeating forces larger than his own, and his ego often bolstered his military confidence. In this instance, Tarleton's troops outnumbered the Revolutionaries, while Morgan faced swollen rivers ahead and eager British regulars from behind. Instead of fording difficult waters, he decided to lead Tarleton to the Cowpens, forcing a battle. The Cowpens was a large, rolling pasture in the midst of forest and underbrush. Morgan took full advantage of the terrain, placing his troops behind the soft embankments and out of Tarleton's sight. To further fortify his troops, he deployed a line of marksmen at the clearing's entrance. Tarleton confidently charged the line ahead, and the commotion of early battle kept the colonel from detecting the bulk of the Continental army, which remained hidden. On Morgan's command, the first line of troops retreated, luring the British further into battle. A second line, composed of militia, then faced the onrushing British, firing a few volleys and also falling back. Sensing victory, Tarleton brashly pressed on against Morgan's men—and fell into the trap. Morgan had left his better-trained Continentals in the rear, forming a third line. The British had by this time become convinced of victory and rushed forward in disarray, hoping to capture and loot the enemy. Instead they were met by a disciplined line of Continental soldiers, who soundly routed them. Tarleton escaped capture, but he lost most of his force: 112 British were killed and 702 were captured. Morgan, on the other hand, lost 12 killed and 60 wounded.

The Battle of Cowpens, January 17, 1781, was a major tactical victory for the Revolutionaries. *(U.S. Army Center of Military History)*

The Battle of Cowpens is often portrayed as a turning point in the war, because after the battle Cornwallis abandoned his previous strategy and set off in pursuit of Morgan and Greene. That decision eventually led him to Virginia and his surrender at YORKTOWN on October 19, 1781. This narrative ignores the ordeal faced by both sides during the campaigning in 1781. The victory at Cowpens did bolster support for the Revolutionaries in the South, but there remained many LOYALISTS in the region, and the internecine fighting between Loyalist and Revolutionary militias remained bitter and intense in the South throughout the rest of the year and beyond. Moreover, the British may have faced a reverse at Cowpens, but Cornwallis still commanded a powerful army, which Greene sought to avoid in battle. When Cornwallis entered Virginia later in 1781, he swept all opposition before him. It took the arrival of a French fleet from the WEST INDIES and the combined might of Revolutionary and French armies marching from the North to secure the victory at Yorktown.

Further reading: Lawrence E. Babits, *A Devil of a Whipping: The Battle of Cowpens* (Chapel Hill: University of North Carolina Press, 1998); Kenneth Roberts, *The Battle of Cowpens: The Great Morale-Builder* (Garden City, N.Y.: Doubleday, 1958).

Coxe, Tench (1755–1824) *Pennsylvania businessman, politician*

Tench Coxe is best known as an advocate for a strong central government in the 1780s and 1790s and as a supporter for the development of manufacturing in the United States. Coxe came from an affluent Philadelphia family, attended the College of Philadelphia (later the University of Pennsylvania), and was trained in the law. However, he entered his father's counting house instead of practicing law, becoming a full partner in his father's business in 1776. During the early years of the REVOLUTIONARY WAR (1775–83), Coxe was arrested for his support of King GEORGE III but was later paroled. This experience convinced him to side with the cause of independence, and he seems to have repaired his fortunes by the end of the Revolutionary War. By the mid-1780s he had become a nationalist, advocating a more powerful central government and attending the ANNAPOLIS CONVENTION in 1786 that issued the call for the CONSTITUTIONAL CONVENTION of 1787 in Philadelphia.

Coxe was a strong FEDERALIST, writing a pamphlet entitled *An Examination of the Constitution of the United States* (1788) to support the U.S. CONSTITUTION. Once the new government was ratified and put into place, his talents were recognized by ALEXANDER HAMILTON, and he was appointed assistant secretary of the treasury. In this position he had an important hand in guiding national fiscal policy and contributed significantly to Hamilton's "Report on the Subject of Manufactures" submitted to Congress on December 5, 1791. Coxe was involved in various efforts to start factories in the United States, including the SOCIETY FOR ESTABLISHING USEFUL MANUFACTURES, and he encouraged the development of COTTON in the South. In the belief that the safest way for the United States to become fiscally independent was to have a complete ECONOMY, he wanted cities and factories to develop the production of goods and to provide markets. Coxe also was one of the leaders of the PENNSYLVANIA ABOLITION SOCIETY, serving as its secretary for many years. However, despite his support for ABOLITION, he held that AFRICAN AMERICANS were inferior and published *Considerations Respecting the Helots of the United States* (1820), in which he described blacks as "uncivilized or wild men, without our moral sense" and not "capable of genuine modern civilization."

Coxe had a strange political career. In 1792 he became commissioner of the revenue, a post he held until 1797, when a conflict with Secretary of the Treasury OLIVER WOLCOTT, JR., led to his dismissal because Wolcott believed that Coxe was too sure of himself and had been insubordinate. Coxe then left the FEDERALIST PARTY and became a member of the DEMOCRATIC-REPUBLICAN PARTY. During the ELECTION OF 1800, he published a letter he had received from JOHN ADAMS in 1792 that politically embarrassed the president. In 1803 THOMAS JEFFERSON appointed Coxe purveyor of public supplies, a position he held until 1812. Throughout his career, he was involved in land speculation, and he bought land in Pennsylvania with coal deposits, hoping that this investment would pay when manufacturing expanded. While he did not reap the rewards of this foresight, his descendants did profit from the investments. He died on July 17, 1824, in Philadelphia.

Further reading: Jacob E. Cooke, *Tench Coxe and the Early Republic* (Chapel Hill: University of North Carolina Press, 1978).

Craney Island, Battle of (June 22, 1813)

During the WAR OF 1812 (1812–15), the British determined to attack Norfolk to capture or destroy the USS *Constellation* during their CHESAPEAKE BAY CAMPAIGN (1813–14). Fourteen GUNBOATS, supported by the *Constellation*, blocked the passage from Hampton Roads to the Elizabeth River and Norfolk. The British decided that they would begin their assault by taking Craney Island, which lay on the west side of the river's mouth and was defended by less than 700 men. This attack was poorly conceived as the British navy could not get close enough to bombard the island, so a direct assault was decided upon. On June 22 approximately 2,000 British soldiers landed a few miles northwest of the island. Their advance came to a halt when they reached a creek that was too deep to ford, and withering fire from artillery on the island forced them to retreat. An uncoordinated amphibious assault by 1,300 men in 50 barges was also broken up as many of the British boats became grounded 300 yards from the island. When the men began to go over the side to wade ashore, they found themselves in thick slimy mud, making it impossible to proceed. Cannon fire from the island and U.S. flotilla compelled a withdrawal. The British lost 88 killed and wounded and 62 missing; U.S. losses were negligible. This battle was the only serious check to British operations in the Chesapeake Bay in 1813 and saved Norfolk from being sacked.

Further reading: Christopher T. George, *Terror on the Chesapeake: The War of 1812 on the Bay* (Shippensburg, Pa.: White Maine Books, 2000).

Crawford, William (1732–1782) *frontiersman, military officer*

A Virginian, surveyor, land speculator, and close friend of GEORGE WASHINGTON, William Crawford was a resident of Frederick County at the beginning of the FRENCH AND INDIAN WAR (1754–63) and was an ensign in the Virginia MILITIA during the fateful expedition of General EDWARD BRADDOCK in 1755. He served as a captain under Washington during General JOHN FORBES's more successful advance through western Pennsylvania in 1758. In 1765 Crawford settled in Youghiogheny River Valley in what is now southwestern Pennsylvania, but which both Virginia and Pennsylvania then claimed. In 1770 Washington visited Crawford and the two, along with a few others, sailed down the Ohio River to the Kanawha River. Crawford was a local justice of the peace and adviser to Washington on land investments in the West. He also participated in attacks against NATIVE AMERICANS during DUNMORE'S WAR (1774).

During the REVOLUTIONARY WAR (1775–83) Crawford joined the CONTINENTAL ARMY as a lieutenant colonel, and he was with Washington during the campaign of 1776–77. He then moved to FORT PITT, closer to his home and an area where his knowledge of Indians and the FRONTIER could be put to use. In 1782 Crawford took command of about 500 troops and invaded the Ohio country. In two days of fighting at the BATTLE OF SANDUSKY (June 4–5, 1782), the Revolutionaries lost about 50 men and decided to pull back, but Crawford and one other man were separated from the main body and captured. The Native Americans were enraged by several massacres by European-American frontiersmen and decided to torture and kill Crawford. They stripped Crawford, cut off his ears, shoved burning sticks into his skin, scalped him while he was still alive, and then put hot ashes and coals on the bare part of his head. Reports of this brutal execution further exacerbated tensions on the frontier just as the Revolutionary War was coming to a close.

See also SCALPING.

Further reading: Patrick Griffin, *American Leviathan: Empire, Nation, and Revolutionary Frontier* (New York: Hill & Wang, 2007).

Crawford, William Harris (1772–1834) *secretary of the treasury, secretary of war*

Although a Virginian by birth, William Harris Crawford moved to Georgia as a young boy with his family and became the preeminent politician of the Peachtree State in the early 19th century. Though he grew up in the Georgia backcountry, Crawford was reasonably well educated and began practicing law in 1799. His reputation for clear thinking and articulate arguing won him many clients, and he was elected to the state legislature in 1803. In the factional politics of the DEMOCRATIC-REPUBLICAN PARTY of Georgia, he aligned himself with the Jeffersonian James Jackson and fought at least two duels—in one of which he killed his opponent—to defend his political reputation. In 1807 he was chosen as a U.S. senator and quickly rose to national prominence. Although he had argued against the EMBARGO OF 1807, he opposed its repeal because he believed that the United States had committed to the policy and that the only alternative was war. Crawford also led the fight to recharter the BANK OF THE UNITED STATES in 1811; in that same year he was elected president pro tempore of the Senate.

Having turned down the position of secretary of war during the WAR OF 1812 (1812–15), Crawford became minister to FRANCE in 1813—a delicate task considering that both France and the United States were fighting wars against GREAT BRITAIN without being allies. When he returned to the United States in June 1815, he became secretary of war and then, in November 1816, secretary of

the treasury. Despite having strong congressional support to run for president, Crawford backed JAMES MONROE, who kept Crawford in the treasury for eight more years. He was again one of the favorites leading into the election of 1824, but he was incapacitated by a stroke and came in third behind ANDREW JACKSON and JOHN QUINCY ADAMS. He never fully recovered from the stroke and returned to Georgia, where he served as a state judge for the remainder of his life. He died in Crawford, Georgia, on September 15, 1834.

Further reading: Chase C. Mooney, *William Crawford, 1772–1834* (Lexington: University of Kentucky Press, 1985).

Creek

The Creek Nation was a Native American tribe residing in what is today Georgia and Alabama. They were divided into two groups: The Upper Creek, who lived further from the European Americans; and the Lower Creek, who, living closer to the English settlements, more readily adopted European-American ideas and practices. In the years before the FRENCH AND INDIAN WAR (1754–63), the Creek raided their neighbors to capture prisoners to sell at the slave markets in Charleston. During the war itself, they stayed neutral, though many Creek leaders favored the French. They felt little pressure from either the French or the English colonies until after 1763, when Georgia experienced an explosion of its nonnative population. Although affected by disease and warfare, they sustained themselves before the REVOLUTIONARY WAR (1775–83) by playing off the rivalries between GREAT BRITAIN, FRANCE, and SPAIN. After 1783 they continued this delicate diplomatic dance with the United States added to the mix.

Although the Creek had only limited involvement in the Revolutionary War, independence for the United States marked an important watershed in their history. ALEXANDER MCGILLIVRAY, who had a Creek mother and a Scottish father, became an important figure in tribal politics and led a pro-British faction that did some damage to the Revolutionaries. JOHN STUART, a capable agent for the Crown, also convinced some of the Creek to support the British cause. After the war, the Creek started to drive away European Americans who had illegally settled on Creek lands; the Spanish in FLORIDA helped them in their efforts. However, once the United States established an effective central government, the state of Georgia could draw on the resources of the entire nation to fight the Creek. The federal government opened trading posts to encourage the tribe to adopt European-American style farming and culture, which succeeded with the Lower Creek but not with the Upper Creek. A national council replaced the old system of clan government about 1800.

The situation became more tense in the first decade of the 19th century, when the United States built a road through Creek territory, to which many of the tribe objected. When government agents said it was to be used by the army, the Creek responded by saying that it would also bring European Americans into the region, a prediction that proved to be correct. Settlers streamed into Georgia and the Mississippi Territory, demanding more land, and several times the Creek ceded parts of their hunting grounds. By the time the great SHAWNEE leader TECUMSEH visited the Creek in October 1811, many were ready to listen to him. Tecumseh called for a confederation of native peoples to stand against the United States, but the Lower Creek wanted to avoid conflict. In part, their position reflected the fact that much of the Lower Creek leadership were of mixed European-American and Native American ancestry and had adopted much of the European-American culture, though the accommodationists also believed that confronting the United States would bring certain defeat and even more cessions of land. The Upper Creek, however, wanted to assert traditional Creek culture and eagerly responded to the nativist message. This anti-U.S. group came to be known as the RED STICKS.

This division soon broke out into a civil war between the two Creek factions and then into a conflict with the United States known as the CREEK WAR (1813–14). In turn, the Creek War became part of the larger WAR OF 1812 (1812–15). The TREATY OF FORT JACKSON (1814) ended the Creek War and forced cessations of land from both the Upper Creek and the Lower Creek, even though the latter had fought for the United States. ANDREW JACKSON said this cession was to cut the Creek off from the Gulf of Mexico to prevent the Spanish or British from helping them in the future. Within a few decades, however, almost all the Creek lands had been seized, and the United States began to move all the Creek west of the Mississippi, a removal to which they finally agreed in the 1830s.

See also NATIVE AMERICANS.

Further reading: Andrew K. Frank, *Creeks and Southerners: Biculturalism on the Early American Frontier* (Lincoln: University of Nebraska Press, 2005); Michael Green, *The Politics of Indian Removal: Creek Government and Society in Crisis* (Lincoln: University of Nebraska Press, 1982); Steven C. Hahn, *The Invention of the Creek Nation, 1670–1776* (Lincoln: University of Nebraska Press, 2004).

Creek War (1813–1814)

During the WAR OF 1812 (1812–15), a split developed within the CREEK Nation. Most of the Lower Creek sought to accommodate themselves with the United States, while the Upper Creek, known at this time as the RED STICKS, wanted to rid their country of European Americans. The Red Sticks were heavily influenced by TECUMSEH's "nativist" movement and sought to reassert older elements of their traditional culture. By 1813 a civil war had erupted among the Creek as WILLIAM MCINTOSH (the son of a Creek mother and a LOYALIST father) led a quasi-police force against the Red Sticks. The war expanded to include the United States after the BATTLE OF BURNT CORN (July 27, 1813), when about 180 soldiers riding out from Fort Mims, Alabama, attacked the Creek Indian village of Burnt Corn. After defeating the outnumbered Creek warriors, the soldiers began looting and destroying Indian property. Seeing the soldiers preoccupied, the Indians counterattacked and drove the soldiers off. In retaliation for this attack, 800 Red Sticks under Peter McQueen and WILLIAM WEATHERFORD (Chief Red Eagle) attacked and killed nearly 500 European Americans and métis (mixed-blood) Creek in the FORT MIMS MASSACRE (August 30, 1813).

This action led to the mobilization of troops and MILITIA from the United States against the Upper Creek. Three armies invaded Creek territory. From the north came ANDREW JACKSON with Tennessee volunteers and Indian allies, including some Lower Creek; from the west came an army under FERDINAND LEIGH CLAIBORNE, while Georgia militia under General John Floyd approached from the east. By October, Jackson had set up a base at Fort Strother on the Coosa River. Because there was an Upper Creek village only 10 miles away, he ordered General John Coffee to attack the town, and Coffee sent a small detachment ahead to draw the Creek warriors into the open. In the BATTLE OF TALLUSHATCHEE, (November 3, 1813), when the Red Sticks attacked the detachment, the rest of Coffee's 1,000 man army opened up a murderous fire, killing a reported 186 warriors and capturing 84 women and children; Coffee lost five dead and 40 wounded. A few days later Jackson received a call for help from the Lower Creek village of Talladega, which was being besieged by Red Sticks. Jackson marched to their aid with 2,000 men and drove the Upper Creek off in the BATTLE OF TALLADEGA (November 9, 1813). However, because of supply problems, and with the enlistments of many of his men about to expire, Jackson could not follow up this victory.

In the meantime, other forces from the United States entered the conflict. A column of additional Tennessee militia arrived in Creek territory under Major General John Cocke and destroyed the town of Hillabee on November 18, 1813, in what became known as the HILLABEE MASSACRE. This attack, which had not been coordinated with Jackson, occurred while the general was negotiating for a peace. Although the battle was a result of a breakdown in communications, it convinced many of the Red Sticks that Jackson could not be trusted. About a month later, 950 Georgia militia and 400 friendly Creek under General Floyd struck at the town of Autosse, killing more than 200 NATIVE AMERICANS and destroying 400 dwellings; Floyd lost only 11 killed and 54 wounded. However, many Red Sticks managed to escape across a river despite Floyd's effort to cut them off.

In December Claiborne fought the BATTLE OF THE HOLY GROUND (December 23, 1813) at the village of Ecunchatee. The Indian prophet Josiah Francis had assured his followers that any enemy approaching the community would be destroyed by the Great Spirit. This protection did not work for the Creek when Claiborne attacked. Fortunately for the Red Sticks, Weatherford had been less trusting and had removed most of the women and children from the town and prepared some defenses. Weatherford and a small cohort of followers therefore delayed Floyd's onslaught while the rest of the warriors escaped. A month later, on January 27, 1814, the Red Sticks surprised Floyd in the BATTLE OF CALABEE. Floyd's 1,300 troops from the Carolinas and Georgia, plus 400 "friendly" Creek, fought the attackers off in a fierce struggle, but after the battle Floyd, who had supply problems, withdrew from the area. At least 79 Red Sticks were killed; Floyd lost 17 militia and five Creek.

The BATTLE OF HORSESHOE BEND (March 27, 1814) ended the Creek War. With about 2,600 troops and 500 CHEROKEE and 100 Lower Creek, Jackson attacked the Red Stick village of Tohopeka. After sending mounted troops and Native American allies across the river to cut off possible Red Stick retreat, Jackson began the battle with a two-hour artillery bombardment. He then ordered a bayonet charge on the barricaded Indian defenses and overwhelmed the Red Sticks. Having promised no quarter to the Indians if they opposed him, Jackson's men may have killed 800 warriors—many in the act of surrendering or trying to escape—while 350 women and children were captured. Jackson lost about 55 killed and 155 wounded. Although the battle ended the Upper Creek resistance, some Red Sticks went to FLORIDA and fought alongside the SEMINOLE in later wars.

At the TREATY OF FORT JACKSON, which marked the official end of the Creek War, Jackson insisted that the Creek give the United States 23 million acres in present-day Alabama and western Georgia. This cession included land from both the Upper Creek—the Red Sticks—and the Lower Creek, who had been Jackson's allies. The Creek were also forbidden to have contact with either the British or the Spanish and agreed to allow the United States "to establish military posts, roads, and free navigation of waters" in Creek territory.

Further reading: Michael D. Green, *The Politics of Indian Removal: Creek Government and Society in Crisis* (Lincoln: University of Nebraska Press, 1982); Benjamin W. Griffith, Jr., *McIntosh and Weatherford, Creek Indian Leaders* (Tuscaloosa: University of Alabama Press, 1988); Joel W. Martin, *Sacred Revolt: The Muskogees' Struggle for a New World* (Boston: Beacon Press, 1991); Frank Lawrence Owsley, Jr., *Struggle for the Gulf Borderlands: The Creek War and the Battle of New Orleans, 1812–1815* (Gainesville: University Press of Florida, 1981).

Creole

The term *Creole* initially meant a person of European descent who was born in the Spanish colonies of the Americas. In particular, *Creole* implies that since the individual was indigenous to the region, even if his or her parents came from elsewhere, the Creole did not need to adjust to the colonial climate or culture. Within the Spanish context, the difference between a Creole and someone from Europe also reflected a status gap, with the person born in SPAIN having a distinct advantage. Despite the importance of Creoles in maintaining the power of the Spanish-American empire, the choicest positions in imperial administration were usually reserved for Europeans.

Because the word *Creole* can also be used to describe a person whose parents or ancestors came from a different part of the world, it has been extended to a variety of uses in the WEST INDIES and North America. For example, scholars also use it to describe slaves of African descent who were born in the Americas and would have had no immediate knowledge of AFRICA, the process of enslavement, or the enforced passage of Africans to the New World. They would ordinarily be born into SLAVERY and remain slaves their entire lives. Creole slaves were not necessarily docile, but they were less likely to challenge the institution of slavery than those who had had some experience with freedom. Creole slaves, too, would be better seasoned to the climate of the region of their birth and would have developed a hybrid African and American culture.

The French in LOUISIANA adopted the use of the word *Creole* to describe the descendants of French and Spanish settlers in the area who retained a special speech pattern and culture that distinguished them from the Cajun settlers (see ACADIANS) who arrived in the second half of the 18th and early 19th centuries. Simultaneously, in Louisiana the word also came to be used to identify the offspring of interracial sexual liaisons between Creoles and African Louisianians.

More recently, a few scholars have begun to apply the term to the settlers of European descent who were born in British North America, but this use of the word is not widespread.

Cresap, Michael (1742–1775) *frontiersman militia officer*

Despite evidence to the contrary, Captain Michael Cresap's name will forever be linked with the massacre of Mingo chief JOHN LOGAN's family at Yellow Creek in Ohio. In his *Notes on the State of Virginia*, THOMAS JEFFERSON vilified Cresap and his actions during the campaign known as DUNMORE'S WAR (1774), calling Cresap "a man infamous for the many murders he had committed on those much injured people [the Indians]." In 1789 Jefferson received a letter that cleared Cresap of any wrongdoing and actually placed him at a different location on the day of the Yellow Creek Massacre. Yet Jefferson failed to amend his earlier categorization of Cresap, forever linking his name with infamy.

Cresap was born on April 17, 1742, near the present-day town of Havre-de-Grace, Maryland. As a frontiersman, he traded with NATIVE AMERICANS and was involved in land speculation. In 1774 he traveled to the Ohio Territory for the purpose of clearing some lands he had recently acquired. Rumors of recent Indian attacks had whipped many of the European-American settlers in the area into a frenzy, and the murders of Chief Logan's family at Yellow Creek only exacerbated the already tense situation, culminating in a war. During the fighting, better known as Dunmore's War, Cresap led a group of volunteer soldiers in the defense of Redstone Old Fort. Once the hostilities subsided, he returned to his family in Maryland.

In 1775 Cresap accepted a commission from the state of Maryland. On July 18, 1775, he and his volunteers marched from Frederick, Maryland, to join GEORGE WASHINGTON outside of Boston. He and his men made the trek in 22 days, but the grueling pace took its toll on Cresap, who was suffering from a preexisting illness. Giving up his commission after only two months and setting out for his home in Maryland, he died during his journey, on October 18, 1775, in New York City.

Further reading: John J. Jacob, *A Biographical Sketch of the Life of the Late Captain Michael Cresap* (New York: Arno Press, 1971); Anthony F. C. Wallace, *Jefferson and the Indians: The Tragic Fate of the First Americans* (Cambridge, Mass.: Harvard University Press, 1999).

—Emily R. Wardrop

Crèvecoeur, J. Hector St. John de (Michael-Guillaume-Jean de Crèvecoeur) (1735–1813) *essayist*

When J. Hector St. John de Crèvecoeur asked, "What is an American?" in 1782, he could not have imagined how many times he would be quoted, cited, and misunderstood. Crèvecoeur had no intention of defining a U.S. national character. Instead, he was concerned with the special beneficial characteristics of *British* North America, and while he painted a generally positive picture, he included negative images when he described the horrors of SLAVERY and the depredations of FRONTIER warfare. Whatever Crèvecoeur's intentions, scholars in the 20th century seized upon his question for their own purposes because it seemed to go to the heart of a national character pleasing to those with a European background and tracing it to a time when the United States had just achieved its independence. From this perspective, Crèvecoeur was reassuring: The American "is either an European, or the descendant of an European" who is a mixture of ethnic groups. More important, though, "*He* is an American, who, leaving behind him all ancient prejudices and manners, receives new ones from the new mode of life he has embraced, the new government he obeys, and the new rank he holds." In short, "The American is a new man, who acts upon new principles; he must therefore entertain new ideas and form new opinions." For scholars and politicians who wanted to emphasize the European origins of the United States and claim an exceptional history without the relics of the past, Crèvecoeur and his book, *Letters from an American Farmer* (1782), seemed tailor-made.

There was more to this Frenchman-turned-American than met the eye. Born to an impoverished aristocratic family in Normandy, FRANCE, Crèvecoeur was well educated and became a junior officer in the French army in 1755. Stationed in New France (CANADA) during the FRENCH AND INDIAN WAR (1754–63), he fought against the British and colonial Americans, taking part in the assault on Fort William Henry in 1757, and was wounded in the BATTLE OF QUEBEC on the Plains of Abraham (September 13, 1759). Shortly after the battle, he surrendered his commission and, with the MONEY he was paid, set sail for New York, where he arrived in December 1759. During the next decade he traveled throughout the colonies, from NOVA SCOTIA to Virginia, as a salesman and surveyor. He even joined one expedition to the West, visiting the Mississippi and the Great Lakes region. In 1765 he became a naturalized subject of GREAT BRITAIN and a resident of New York. He settled down in 1769, marrying Mehetable Tippet, member of a prominent Westchester family in New York. Although in his writings Crèvecoeur took on the persona of a farmer in Pennsylvania, the farm he now settled, called Pine Hill, was in Orange County, New York. He and his wife enjoyed seven years of peace, having three children and achieving some prosperity.

The REVOLUTIONARY WAR (1775–83) shattered this life. While his *Letters from an American Farmer* sounds like a paean to the new American identity, Crèvecoeur was really describing an ideal world in colonial America under a beneficent King GEORGE III. This position was only suggested in the last chapter of *Letters*, where he described how war intruded on the peace of the American farmer. A second work, not discovered until 1923, revealed his LOYALIST sympathies more explicitly. Many editions of the *Letters* are now published with the addition of this second work, called *Sketches of Eighteenth-Century America.*

In 1778, fearful of persecution as a Tory, concerned with the possibility of an Indian raid, and determined to protect his children's inheritance in France, Crèvecoeur left his farm and family to travel to British-occupied New York to seek passage to France. There, however, the British arrested him under the suspicion that he was a rebel. Imprisonment brought illness and something of a mental breakdown. Friends managed to get Crèvecoeur released, and after much travail he arrived in France in 1781. He did not return to New York until 1783, but this time he arrived as a diplomat—the French consul for that city. His appointment was in part due to the fame he had achieved by publication of the *Letters* the previous year. By then his wife had died, and his children had been sent to Boston. He remained in New York, reunited with his children, until 1790. During that time he was busy facilitating Franco-American commerce, was active in SCIENCE (mainly horticulture) and LITERATURE, and was elected to the AMERICAN PHILOSOPHICAL SOCIETY. He returned to France in 1790, retired from the diplomatic service and lived in relative obscurity until his death on November 12, 1813.

More than anything, Crèvecoeur's written work was a product of the ENLIGHTENMENT; he dedicated *Letters* to ABBÉ RAYNAL (1711–96), one of France's leading intellectuals. His main purpose was to argue that North America was a land where nature and reason existed side by side. Portraying himself as a humble farmer, Crèvecoeur asserted a moral superiority to the ancient relics of Europe. He proclaimed that "here [in North America] Nature opens her broad lap to receive the perpetual accession of newcomers" and that we "might contemplate the very beginnings and outlines of human society." From this perspective, the farmer was the happiest of men, "possessing freedom of action, freedom of thought" and lived in harmony with nature. This pleasant vision, which has attracted so much attention by scholars as representative of the new American, was also the vision that Crèvecoeur believed was wrecked by the revolution that created the new nation.

See also CORPORATISM; REPUBLICANISM.

Further reading: Gay Wilson Allen, *St. John de Crèvecoeur: The Life and American Farmer* (New York: Viking, 1987); J. Hector St. John de Crèvecoeur, *Letters from an American Farmer and Sketches of Eighteenth-Century America,* edited by Albert E. Stone (New York: Penguin, 1981).

crime

Three general areas of crime were important during the period of 1754–1815. First, moral crimes violated social sensibilities concerning appropriate individual behavior. These crimes included bastardy, fornication, rape, drunkenness, contempt for authority, and vagrancy. Second, crimes against property centered on stealing or swindling personal and public property. Counterfeiting became an important form of property crime during the early republic with the proliferation of BANKS printing their own notes with separate designs, making it too easy to fabricate paper MONEY. Third, violent crime entailed attacks on individuals, including assault and murder.

All three types of crime continued to some degree throughout the late colonial and early national era. However, there were important differences in the nature of crime depending on region, and some changes took place over time. The South was more persistently violent than the North: South Carolina had a personal-violence rate that remained around 55 percent of all prosecuted crimes, with a property-crime rate that hovered about 30 percent during the period. In Massachusetts, crimes concerning morality made up almost 51 percent of the prosecuted case before the REVOLUTIONARY WAR (1775–83) but dwindled to about 7 percent during the period from 1790 to 1830. In the same state, crimes against people and property combined reached only 28 percent of prosecutions from 1760 to 1774, while between 1790 to 1830, prosecutions against property crimes alone were about 41 percent. The contrast between South Carolina and Massachusetts reflects extremes between the South and New England. Crime statistics in mid-Atlantic states fits between these extremes, but the pattern of crime was closer to the South than New England. Pennsylvania, for example, persistently experienced more personal and property crime than Massachusetts and had a level of prosecution for moral crimes of less than 10 percent throughout the 18th century. New York's experience was similar to Pennsylvania, with a rise in personal and property crimes in the second half of the 18th century and into the early 19th century.

Several reasons explain the different levels of crime rates. The Massachusetts figures reflect not so much a change in behavior as they do a change in definition of crime from being a sin to being an act that threatened property or persons. South Carolina, Pennsylvania, and New York had moved their definitions of crime away from sin much earlier than had Massachusetts. In South Carolina, in part because of the legacy of SLAVERY and in part because of the number of SCOTS-IRISH on the FRONTIER, there developed a culture of violence that would cast a long shadow across much of the South's history. On South Carolina's disorderly frontier, an outbreak of lawlessness of all types—attacks on persons, violations of property rights, and immorality—led to the development of the SOUTH CAROLINA REGULATION in the late 1760s. This vigilante movement fought crime with a lawlessness of its own. Pennsylvania became increasingly polyglot as the main depot for IMMIGRATION in the 18th century, and this diverse and often impoverished population added to the property emphasis in its crime rate. New York had been marked by diversity from its inception, and as New York City expanded during the early republic, urbanization seemed to create a new kind of society conducive to crime. In 1811 Charles Christian, a police magistrate, wrote that "the obvious inequalities of fortune" and the baser passions led to "the insatiable appetite for animal gratification . . . in weak and depraved minds" whose inevitable "wretchedness" created "a heterogeneous mass" that committed crimes and somehow had to be controlled.

Beyond the overall trends evident in long-term crime rates, the Revolutionary War itself led to a breakdown of order that increased criminal activity. Wherever government was weak or absent, people seized the opportunity to plunder, rape, maim, and kill. In particular, areas between zones of control, whether it be the no-man's land in New Jersey or New York between the CONTINENTAL ARMY and the British army, or through large sections of the South after the British invasion of 1780, individuals and groups committed criminal acts. Sometimes these looters, pillagers, and killers were in the bands of MILITIA organized by WHIGS and sometimes by LOYALISTS; often they were just acting independently. Only the conclusion of the war brought an end to this marauding in the settled regions, although criminals and gangs would remain active along the frontier during the early republic and throughout the 19th century.

See also BURROUGHS, STEPHEN; RIOTS; PROSTITUTION; SMUGGLING.

Further reading: Douglas Greenberg, *Crime and Law Enforcement in the Colony of New York, 1691–1776* (Ithaca, N.Y.: Cornell University Press, 1974); Michael Stephen Hindus, *Prison and Plantation: Crime, Justice, and Authority in Massachusetts and South Carolina, 1767–1878* (Chapel Hill: University of North Carolina Press, 1980); Jack D. Marietta and G. S. Rowe, *Troubled Experiment: Crime and Justice in Pennsylvania, 1682–1800* (Philadelphia: University of Pennsylvania Press, 2006); William Edward Nelson, *Americanization of the Common Law: The Impact of Legal Change on Massachusetts Society, 1760–1830* (Cambridge, Mass.: Harvard University Press, 1975); Harry M. Ward, *Between the Lines: Banditti of the American Revolution* (Westport, Conn.: Praeger, 2002).

critical period

Many scholars have traditionally referred to the 1780s as the critical period as a rationale for the creation of the U.S. CONSTITUTION. According to this interpretation, the ARTICLES OF CONFEDERATION had created a weak and ineffective national government that needed to be replaced by the Constitution's more powerful central government. This argument claims that there was too much state power, an ineffectual national legislature, and no strong executive under the Articles of Confederation. In addition, the United States was not respected by foreign powers, had to face unrest in the West from NATIVE AMERICANS and its own European-American settlers, and confronted serious economic difficulties. Although there is an element of truth to each of these charges, they overstate the case and obscure the real history of the 1780s.

First, it must be remembered that the REVOLUTIONARY WAR (1775–83) had been fought against an extremely strong and controlling government, and nearly all Revolutionaries believed that the more power government had, the less LIBERTY was retained by the people. The one thing the Revolutionaries wanted to guarantee in the 1770s was that there would not be another usurpation of power by a centralizing government's strong executive. The Articles of Confederation therefore purposefully avoided any king-like governor as executive and were written to tie the rebellious colonies together, gain allies, and win a war. In all three areas the government of the United States under the Articles was successful. Once the war was over, however, the central government could simply disappear, as far as most people in the country were concerned. Moreover, most people believed that the individual states were supposed to be sovereign. States therefore had the power to raise revenue from import duties, although not from products that originated within other states. The more responsible state governments even began to pay off their revolutionary war debt and assume their share of the national debt (see DEBT, NATIONAL).

Of course, such an inchoate form of national government had difficulty gaining respect from foreign powers. None of the major European countries took the United States seriously: GREAT BRITAIN refused to open its WEST INDIES colonies to TRADE and retained forts on U.S. territory, SPAIN laid claim to a vast area east of the Mississippi River and enticed people on the FRONTIER to swear allegiance to the Spanish king, and even FRANCE seemed little concerned with its wartime ally. Moreover, starting in 1785, Algiers and other Barbary States began to attack U.S. commerce on the seas. While all of these problems surfaced in the 1780s, writing and ratifying the Constitution did not change the diplomatic situation. Great Britain maintained its posts on the frontier until 1795 and only surrendered them when given an advantageous trade deal. The British did not officially open the West Indies to trade until the 1830s, although beginning in the 1780s U.S. merchants illegally traded with British possessions in the region. Spain began to make concessions in 1796, more from its own weakness than in reaction to U.S. strength. If anything, problems with the French intensified in the 1790s and early 1800s, while difficulties with the Barbary States would last until 1815.

During the 1780s and into the 1790s, the U.S. government had to deal with a number of rebellions, including SHAYS'S REBELLION (1786–87), an uprising of discontented farmers in western Massachusetts that was put down by state force; and the WHISKEY REBELLION (1794), a violent response by Pennsylvania farmers to the federal government's imposition of an excise tax on whiskey. The government also had problems with squatters and speculators in the West in the 1780s, but those problems persisted under the U.S. Constitution. Similarly, NATIVE AMERICANS remained a powerful threat to European-American settlement west of the Appalachians, both before and after the Constitution was written and ratified. If anything, under the Articles of Confederation, the United States took an important step in solving its western problems with the passage of the NORTHWEST ORDINANCES of 1785 and 1787. These laws established a mechanism for integrating new territories into the union as states and thereby alleviated one of the largest potential difficulties confronting the nation—how to treat its own new settlements.

There was economic upheaval in the 1780s. This development, however, was the natural outcome of a post-war economy, which can fall into a depression in the immediate years after a major conflict. By the mid-1780s the economy was recovering. Cities like New York, which had been left devastated by the war, had rebuilt and expanded. Most farmers, except those in states with oppressive taxes—as in Massachusetts—seemed to be recovering. As GEORGE WASHINGTON exclaimed in 1786, "The people at large . . . are more industrious than they were before the war. Economy begins, partly from necessity and partly from choice and habit, to prevail. . . . Houses are rebuilt, fields enclosed, stocks of cattle which were destroyed are replaced, and many a desolated territory assumes again the cheerful appearance of cultivation."

In short, problems existed during the 1780s, but they were not limited to that decade, and they were not as severe as has been traditionally portrayed. How, then, can we explain the urgency with which the Founding Fathers framed the U.S. Constitution? The answer is that the real critical period lay in the minds of the framers, who came to believe that they needed a national government to encourage economic development and protect the interests of the elite. As Washington explained, overly independent state governments were a recipe for "anarchie [and] Confusion" that would lead to the rise of a demagogue who would usurp the people's liberty. Washington desired "a Government of respectability under which life—liberty and prop-

erty" would be protected. JAMES MADISON complained of the multiplicity and mutability of the state laws, referring to a "luxuriancy of legislation" where statutes would be "repealed or superceded, before trial can have been made of their merits; and even before a knowledge of them can have reached the remoter districts."

The crisis, then, was a lack of stability in government, which only a strong central authority somewhat removed from the transitory wishes of the people could provide. Madison and the other FEDERALISTS sought to end this critical period by creating a constitution that would "extract from the mass of the Society the purest and noblest characters" who would protect the public interest.

See also REPUBLICANISM.

Further reading: Merrill Jensen, *The New Nation: A History of the United States during the Confederation, 1781–1789* (New York: Knopf, 1950); Gordon S. Wood, *The Creation of the American Republic, 1776–1787* (Chapel Hill: University of North Carolina Press, 1998).

Croghan, George (1720–1782) *Irish-American interpreter, trader*

George Croghan was an important intermediary with NATIVE AMERICANS as well as a trader and land speculator on the FRONTIER during the decades leading up to the REVOLUTIONARY WAR (1776–83). In 1741 Croghan emigrated from Dublin to Pennsylvania, where he set up an Indian trading post near Carlisle. He quickly learned DELAWARE and IROQUOIS and mastered the intricacies of Indian diplomacy and ceremony. From Carlisle, he expanded his interests into the Ohio country. In 1752 the French, fearing Croghan's presence would inspire other British traders to follow, launched an attack that destroyed his outpost at Pickawillany on the Great Miami River. By 1754 his trade network was in shambles, but Sir WILLIAM JOHNSON rewarded his Indian expertise by making him deputy superintendent of Indian affairs.

During the FRENCH AND INDIAN WAR (1754–63), Croghan served with JOHN FORBES in the expedition against Fort Duquesne and with Henry Bouquet at DETROIT. In 1764 he traveled to England to press colonial claims for further western expansion. He also played a key role in negotiations with numerous tribes following the war and traveled to the Illinois country to meet with Pontiac. In 1765 he helped facilitate a treaty with the SHAWNEE, Delaware, and SENECA at Detroit. He was also present at the signing of the TREATY OF FORT STANWIX in 1768.

Croghan speculated heavily in western lands, and in 1763 he was party to a fraudulent cession that nearly bankrupted him. He later received a grant of 250,000 acres in New York and nearly secured 200,000 more near

Pittsburgh, but he never gained a clear title to this land. Croghan organized land companies with colonial notables including SIR WILLIAM JOHNSON, BENJAMIN FRANKLIN, and WILLIAM FRANKLIN. He was also a member of the abortive Grand Ohio Company, which sought to establish the independent state of Vandalia south of the Ohio River. During the REVOLUTIONARY WAR (1775–83), critics charged that Croghan had LOYALIST sympathies. Although cleared of treason charges in 1778, he never profited from his land speculation and became financially solvent. He died on August 31, 1782.

Further reading: Nicholas B. Wainwright, *George Croghan: Wilderness Diplomat* (Chapel Hill: University of North Carolina Press, 1959).

—David C. Beyreis

Crowninshield, Benjamin W. (1772–1851) *secretary of the navy, congressman*

A member of a prominent merchant family in Salem, Massachusetts, Benjamin William Crowninshield went to sea at a young age and probably served as a captain before joining the family's business. During the WAR OF 1812 (1812–15), Crowninshield made a fortune investing in PRIVATEERING. Although up until 1814 he had a political career limited to serving in the Massachusetts lower house and senate, he and his family ardently supported the DEMOCRATIC-REPUBLICAN PARTY. In December 1814 President JAMES MADISON asked him to become secretary of the navy. After some hesitation, Crowninshield accepted the position though the war was effectively over by the time he took over the department in early 1815. He served into JAMES MONROE's administration, finally leaving office in September 1818. During that time, he oversaw the naval action with Algiers and presided over a modest expansion of the navy that included a new administrative system. After resigning from office, he served four terms in the House of Representatives and expanded his business interests to include banking. He died on February 3, 1851.

Crown Point

In 1734 the French built a fort at Crown Point, New York, located about 30 miles north of the southern tip of Lake Champlain on a peninsula that juts out into the lake. This outpost, which the French named Fort St. Frederic, became a major objective in the wars between the French and British in the mid-18th century, but it was superseded somewhat in 1755 by FORT TICONDEROGA, which was constructed 12 miles to the south. The French abandoned and blew up Fort St. Frederic on July 31, 1759, after the British captured Fort Ticonderoga. The British then rebuilt

and extended the fort prior to their invasion of CANADA, but with the TREATY OF PARIS (1763) and the end of the French presence in North America, the fort's strategic value declined. A fire and explosion in 1773 destroyed much of Crown Point. Revolutionaries seized it on May 11, 1775, the day after their capture of Fort Ticonderoga, but the British retook the fort during General JOHN BURGOYNE's invasion of 1777 and held it for the rest of the REVOLUTIONARY WAR (1775–83). The fort was abandoned thereafter. The location became a state park in the early 20th century, and the fort has been reconstructed for visitors.

Crysler's Farm, Battle of (November 11, 1813)

During the WAR OF 1812 (1812–15), the Battle of Crysler's Farm saw British-Canadian forces beat back an invasion by the United States. After the failure to follow up initial successes on the Niagara FRONTIER in the spring and summer of 1813, the United States attempted to capture MONTREAL by advancing from two directions: General WADE HAMPTON moved along the Lake Champlain corridor with 4,000 men, while General JAMES WILKINSON marched up the St. Lawrence with 8,000 men. Neither U.S. force was successful, even though they vastly outnumbered their enemy.

Wilkinson did not leave Sackets Harbor, New York, until October 17, which was late in the season for any campaign on the northern New York–Canadian border. He moved his army in open boats, and near Crysler's Farm the army disembarked on the Canadian shore to allow the boats to maneuver through some rapids. As they advanced, they were met by about 1,200 British and Canadian soldiers under Lieutenant Colonel Joseph Morrison. Though the U.S. troops numbered some 4,000, most of them were poorly trained, sick, and cold, and they attacked Morrison's men in a series of uncoordinated assaults. In almost three hours of intense fighting, the U.S. forces proved no match for their more disciplined enemy, and after losing 400 killed, wounded, and captured, Wilkinson withdrew. Although the battle was a triumph for CANADA, Morrison lost a sixth of his men.

Wilkinson, who was ill and did not command during the battle, decided to go into winter quarters, especially since he heard that the British had checked Hampton's invasion at the BATTLE OF CHÂTEAUGUAY (October 26, 1813). Hampton and Wilkinson, who did not get along, blamed each other for the campaign's failure. Wilkinson was recalled in March 1814 and brought before a court-martial. Although he won an acquittal, he was not given another command.

Further reading: Pierre Berton, *Flames Across the Border: The Canadian-American Tragedy, 1813–1814* (New York: Little Brown and Company, 1981).

Cuba

In the 18th century Cuba, the largest island in the Caribbean, was important for its plantations and its strategic position astride the shipping lanes to the rest of SPAIN's empire in the Americas. A captain-general, who answered directly to the Spanish king, ruled Cuba and other Spanish possessions in the WEST INDIES, as well as FLORIDA and LOUISIANA. Spanish treasure ships from the viceroyalties first came to the capital city and principal port of Havana before sailing on to Europe under convoy. A ring of fortresses guarded Havana Bay, and the city was protected by walls whose construction began in 1663. English privateers had sacked the city twice before the walls were built, once in 1585 and again in 1660.

A British invasion force under Lord Albermarle captured the capital in the 1762 SIEGE OF HAVANA and occupied the city for 10 months. During that time, the island's ECONOMY flourished as merchants were able to TRADE freely with British colonies. The free trade meant an end to restrictions on the importation of African slaves, with perhaps as many as 10,000 brought to Cuba during the occupation. Free trade and the influx of captive laborers led to a massive expansion of sugar plantations. The British left Cuba only after receiving Florida in the TREATY OF PARIS (1763), which followed the FRENCH AND INDIAN WAR (1754–63).

Cuba was used as a base for intelligence and diplomatic missions prior to direct Spanish involvement in the REVOLUTIONARY WAR (1775–83). After the declaration of war against GREAT BRITAIN in 1779, the Spanish used Cuba as a base for attacks on Florida, which Spain subsequently regained as a result of the war.

The FRENCH REVOLUTION (1789–99) and the Napoleonic Wars took a heavy toll on Cuba, which was called upon to send its troops to garrison Louisiana and Florida. Troops from MEXICO were mobilized to replace those from Cuba, although local militias became the primary defensive forces on the island. This put Cuban leaders in a position to survive the upheaval that accompanied the French replacement of the Spanish king between 1808 and 1814.

Further reading: Allan J. Kuethe, *Cuba, 1753–1815: Crown, Military, and Society* (Knoxville: University of Tennessee Press, 1986).

—Stephen A. Martin

Cuffe, Paul (1759–1817) *African-American activist, mariner*

A famed African-American ship captain and activist, Paul Cuffe was born free in colonial Massachusetts; his father was a freed slave and his mother a Wampanoag Indian. Cuffe became perhaps best known as an advocate of voluntary black emigration to AFRICA, and he earned a distinction as one of the earliest black petitioners in revolutionary America. In 1780 he and six other men sent a memorial to the Massachusetts legislature complaining about being taxed without their consent. The petition, largely Cuffe's work, stated: "We are not allowed the privilege of free men of the state, having no vote or influence on those that tax us." For the remainder of his life, Cuffe would be animated by this sense of injustice.

Cuffe was a transatlantic figure who had a remarkable range of contacts in North American, British, and African locales. He was a compatriot of black activists in the United States, including JAMES FORTEN of Philadelphia and PETER WILLIAMS of New York, and he worked with European-American members of the PENNSYLVANIA ABOLITION SOCIETY, gathering information on slave-trading activities in U.S. ports and discussing voluntary emigration schemes to Africa. Cuffe also had strong connections with the QUAKERS, a group known for its ANTISLAVERY position, and he joined the Westport Monthly Meeting of Friends in 1808. He befriended British reformers such as Thomas Clarkson and William Wilberforce, working with them to establish the SIERRA LEONE settlement on the coast of West Africa.

Like many free AFRICAN AMERICANS during the Revolutionary era and the years of the early republic, Cuffe seized the opportunities offered by life as a sailor. He went to sea while in his teens, serving on a whaling vessel sailing in the Gulf of Mexico, and took other voyages up to the start of the REVOLUTIONARY WAR (1775–83). In 1776 the British captured Cuffe and put him in prison for several months. After farming for a few years and studying navigation, he returned to the sea in the early 1780s. Cuffe constructed his own boat, as he put it, "from keel to gunwale," only to have it captured by pirates, but a subsequent venture with a new craft brought him a generous profit. By the 1790s, Cuffe had a 25-ton vessel called the *Sunfish* and then a 42-ton ship, the *Mary*. With 10 African-American crew members, he caught several whales. By 1795 he had built an even bigger boat and set sail for Norfolk, Virginia, where he not only delivered cargo but viewed southern SLAVERY for the first time. Cuffe observed that "the white inhabitants were struck with apprehension of the injurious effects on the minds of their slaves" on seeing a black captain, and he managed to escape unharmed after a violent confrontation. He settled in Westport, New York, and continued to sail the Atlantic coast while becoming the owner of several more ships of various sizes, not to mention land and houses.

Cuffe undertook several trips to Sierra Leone. In 1811 his all-black crew delivered cargo and surveyed the colony; he stayed for three months and vowed to return for an extended period of time, perhaps even to settle.

He returned later in 1811–12 and then again in 1815. He died on September 9, 1817, in the United States, just as debates over the American Colonization Society (ACS) were prompting many black activists (including some friends and early advocates of Cuffe's back-to-Africa call) to organize against repatriation plans. Although the ACS grew rapidly in the decade after Cuffe's death, the majority of the black population opposed colonization schemes, voluntary or otherwise. Still, generations of black reformers remembered Cuffe as both a legendary ship captain and entrepreneur, not to mention a fierce advocate of African-American identity.

See also COLONIZATION, AFRICAN.

Further reading: Sidney Kaplan, *The Black Presence in the Era of the American Revolution* (Washington, D.C.: New York Graphic Society Ltd., 1973); Lamont Thomas, *Rise to Be a People: A Biography of Paul Cuffe* (Urbana: University of Illinois Press, 1986).

—Richard Newman

Cumberland, Prince William Augustus, duke of
(1721–1765) *British prince, military officer*
Prince William Augustus, duke of Cumberland, was the second surviving and favorite son of King George II. Although not in the direct line of succession, which went through his older brother Prince Frederick and Frederick's son (who became King GEORGE III), Cumberland was showered with honors and was the leading military figure of the day, becoming a major general and fighting on the Continent against the French in the 1740s. He assumed command of the forces sent against the Jacobite Rebellion in 1745–46, winning the decisive Battle of Culloden (April 16, 1746), which made him a national hero. However, because of his brutal military suppression of even hints of Jacobitism in Scotland, he was called "Butcher" by his political opponents.

When the FRENCH AND INDIAN WAR (1754–63) broke out, Cumberland exerted a great deal of influence over military policy. On his advice, the British government sent General EDWARD BRADDOCK and 1,400 regulars to North America to capture Fort Duquesne. After that failure, Cumberland arranged for the appointment of JOHN CAMPBELL, FOURTH EARL OF LOUDOUN, as supreme commander in North America. Loudoun's inability to capture LOUISBOURG and the disaster of the FORT WILLIAM HENRY "MASSACRE" contributed to Cumberland's political downfall, but his real problems occurred on the Continent. In April 1757 the king sent Cumberland to Germany to support PRUSSIA. However, when military defeat at the hands of a French army threatened the Electorate of Hanover, the king instructed Cumberland to arrange a separate peace for Hanover, guaranteeing the electorate's territorial integrity and neutrality. The king subsequently rescinded that instruction, but by then Cumberland had concluded a peace for Hanover with the French. Blamed for this abandonment of the Prussian alliance—the king nullified the peace treaty—Cumberland returned to England in disgrace and resigned his command of the army. However, he retained some political influence, especially after his nephew became king. Cumberland was largely responsible for the MARQUIS OF ROCKINGHAM becoming chief minister in 1765, and he was generally sympathetic to the North American colonies during the STAMP ACT (1765) controversy. He died on October 31, 1765.

Further reading: Fred Anderson, *Crucible of War: The Seven Years' War and the Fate of Empire in British North America, 1754–1766* (New York: Vintage, 2000).

Cumberland Gap
The Cumberland Gap is a pass in the Appalachian Mountains that sits near the modern borders of Virginia, Kentucky, and Tennessee. Reputedly discovered in 1750 by Dr. Thomas Walker, a Virginia physician and explorer, the Cumberland Gap had been used for centuries by NATIVE AMERICANS as an avenue by which groups could move east and west through the mountains. Several European-American hunters passed through the Cumberland Gap during the 1760s and 1770s, including DANIEL BOONE. Beginning in 1775, European Americans began to stream through the gap as a convenient route to lands in Kentucky. The other major way to go to Kentucky was down the Ohio River, which brought the migrants closer to hostile Native Americans and left them more vulnerable to attack while floating on the river's open waters. The National Park Service estimates that between 1775 and 1810, about 300,000 people moved through the gap. Now the site of a national park, Cumberland Gap is most associated with Daniel Boone's migration to Kentucky, especially since there is an iconographic painting of Daniel Boone leading a party through the mountains by George Caleb Bingham.

Currency Act (1764)
Concerned with the issuance of paper MONEY in the colonies, Parliament passed the Currency Act in April 1764 to prevent the colonies from printing more. In 1751 a similar measure had been passed that was limited to only the New England colonies, but the 1764 measure was to include all of North America. The British enacted the law because colonial currency had been highly inflationary, and as a result, a note issued by a colony was not equal to a note of the same denomination in GREAT BRITAIN. Colonists

used their own notes to pay off debts to British merchants, thereby cheating their creditors of their full due. The simplest way to avoid this problem was to prevent the colonies from printing money.

From the colonists' point of view, the law was unjust. Because colonial debt increased rapidly in the years around mid-century, there was a constant drain of hard specie—that is, colonial Americans sent whatever gold and silver coin they had to Great Britain to pay their debts. It was therefore difficult to make transactions of any kind since there was so little hard currency available. Notes printed by colonies, even inflationary notes, thus had an important use in the colonial ECONOMY. To further complicate the situation, the currency restriction was passed at about the same time as new parliamentary taxation—the SUGAR ACT (1764) and the STAMP ACT (1765)—which increased the demand for more hard currency. While the Currency Act was not the focal point of the resistance to imperial measures that occurred in the 1760s and 1770s, it contributed to the overall sense of grievance that many colonial Americans developed at this time.

See also RESISTANCE MOVEMENT.

Cushing, William (1732–1810) *Supreme Court justice*

William Cushing was a noted jurist from Massachusetts who served as an associate justice on the U.S. SUPREME COURT from 1789 to 1810. Born in Scituate, Massachusetts, Cushing graduated from Harvard College and in 1755 was admitted to the bar in Boston. In 1772 he became an associate justice on Massachusetts's Superior Court of Judicature. During this time his actions, including his support for judicial independence from British officials, drew him closer to the Revolutionary cause as he associated with noted leaders such as JOHN ADAMS and JAMES BOWDOIN. He was a delegate to Massachusetts's constitutional convention in 1779 and was appointed chief justice of the state's Supreme Judicial Court the following year. As chief justice, Cushing's work was disrupted by SHAYS'S REBELLION (1786–87); he would eventually preside over the treason trials of several of the rebellion's leaders in 1787.

Convinced of the nation's need for a strong federal government, Cushing supported the ratification of the U.S. CONSTITUTION and served as vice president at Massachusetts's ratification convention. In 1789 GEORGE WASHINGTON appointed him to the Supreme Court, though his overall contribution to the court was limited. He was an associate justice for over two decades, but he delivered only 19 opinions because poor health prevented him from traveling his appointed circuit. However, Cushing's opinion in *CHISHOLM V. GEORGIA* (1793), which allowed a South Car-

olina citizen to sue the state of Georgia in federal court, led to the ELEVENTH AMENDMENT, which prevented similar lawsuits in the future. In 1796 Washington nominated him as chief justice of the Supreme Court, but Cushing stepped down after one week due to health concerns. Unable to retire because of financial restraints, he remained on the court until his death on September 13, 1810.

Further reading: Fred L. Israel, ed., *The Justices of the United States Supreme Court: Their Lives and Major Opinions* (New York: Chelsea House, 1995).

—Tash Smith

Cutler, Manasseh (1742–1823) *educator, legislator, minister, physician, scientist*

A man of varied interests and exceptional talents, Manasseh Cutler was born in Connecticut; graduated from Yale College in 1765; and worked as a teacher, merchant, and lawyer before being ordained a Congregational minister in 1771. During the REVOLUTIONARY WAR (1775–83), he served as a chaplain to soldiers defending Boston in 1776 and later accompanied troops campaigning against the British. After his military service, Cutler trained in MEDICINE and worked as a physician to supplement his minister's salary. He also began running a prominent boarding school.

Cutler's role in westward expansion began in 1786, when he helped found the OHIO COMPANY OF ASSOCIATES, a group organized to purchase and settle land near the Ohio River. He played a critical part in negotiating the company's land deal with Congress and in drafting and securing passage of the NORTHWEST ORDINANCE of 1787. In 1788 he helped lead the first group of settlers into the Ohio region and participated in the founding of Marietta, the territory's first European-American settlement. In 1800 he entered the Massachusetts legislature as a member of the FEDERALIST PARTY. In that same year he was elected to Congress for the first of two terms.

Cutler was also an accomplished scientist whose interests ranged from meteorology and astronomy to botany and nautical navigation. A member of the American Academy of Arts and Sciences, his botanical studies provided the first scientific categorization and analysis of New England plant life. Cutler died in Hamilton, Massachusetts, on July 28, 1823, at the age of 81.

See also SCIENCE.

Further reading: Robert Elliot Brown, *Manasseh Cutler and the Settlement of Ohio* (Marietta, Ohio: Marietta College Press, 1938).

—Chris Davis

D

Dale, Richard (1756–1826) *U.S. naval officer*

Richard Dale was born to a shipwright in Norfolk, Virginia; grew up near the waterfront in Portsmouth; and went to sea when he was 12 years old. By 1775 he was commanding vessels sailing to the WEST INDIES. When the REVOLUTIONARY WAR (1775–83) broke out, Dale became a lieutenant in the Virginia state navy. However, after he was captured, he agreed to sign on as a mate in a LOYALIST vessel. When that ship was taken by the *Lexington,* he switched sides again and became a midshipman in the CONTINENTAL NAVY in July 1776. After the British captured the *Lexington* in September 1777, Dale was sent to Mill Prison in England. He was successful on his second attempt to escape and traveled to FRANCE in time to serve as a lieutenant under JOHN PAUL JONES aboard the *Bon Homme Richard* in 1779. He remained in the navy for most of the rest of the war and commanded the *Queen of France* for several months in 1782.

After the war, Dale became a merchant captain and made several voyages to China before being named a captain in the newly established U.S. NAVY in 1794. Because the war scare with Algiers ended in 1795, he was not assigned to any ship and therefore returned to the merchant marine. Dale was given command of a converted merchant ship during the QUASI-WAR (1798–1800) but saw little action. After becoming engaged in a squabble over seniority, he left the navy, returning when the controversy was settled in his favor. In May 1801 he was given command of the squadron sent against Tripoli during the BARBARY WARS. His fleet accomplished little in the two years of his command, occasionally appearing off the Libyan coast and setting up an ineffectual blockade. After being replaced as part of a regular rotation and returning to the United States, Dale retired from the navy and settled in Philadelphia, where he died on February 28, 1826.

Further reading: William M. Fowler, Jr., *Jack Tars and Commodores: The American Navy, 1783–1815* (Boston: Houghton Mifflin, 1984).

Naval officer Richard Dale. Painting by John Ford *(U.S. Naval Academy Museum)*

Dallas, Alexander James (1759–1817) *secretary of the treasury*

Alexander James Dallas was born in Kingston, JAMAICA, on June 21, 1759, and moved to the United States in 1783. He and his wife made Philadelphia their home and became U.S. citizens on June 17, 1783. During the 1780s, Dallas practiced law in Philadelphia, and from 1791 to 1801, he served as secretary of the Commonwealth of Pennsylvania. He was also a founder of a Democratic-Republican Society (see DEMOCRATIC-REPUBLICAN SOCIETIES) in 1793, which placed him in formal opposition to the FEDERALIST PARTY. During the 1790s, he spoke out against JAY'S TREATY (1794) and supported THOMAS JEFFERSON's campaign for president in 1796. His backing of Jefferson during the ELECTION OF 1800 earned him an appointment to the office of U.S. attorney for the eastern district of Pennsylvania, where he served from 1801 to 1814.

On October 6, 1814, President JAMES MADISON appointed Dallas secretary of the treasury. With the treasury in a shambles because of the WAR OF 1812 (1812–15), Dallas had inherited a major challenge. In response to the nation's dwindling finances, he proposed the heaviest taxes that had ever been levied by the national government. He also advocated reinstituting the national banking system since the charter for first BANK OF THE UNITED STATES had expired in 1811. The political battle over the Dallas's financial plan lasted two years, but it was finally passed on April 3, 1816.

Dallas resigned as treasury secretary on October 21, 1816, and returned to Philadelphia to continue his law practice. He died soon after, on January 16, 1817, of complications relating to a recurring stomach illness.

Further reading: J. C. A. Stagg, *Mr. Madison's War: Politics, Diplomacy, and Warfare in the Early American Republic* (Princeton, N.J.: Princeton University Press, 1983); Raymond Walters, *Alexander James Dallas: Lawyer, Politician, Financier, 1759–1817* (Philadelphia: University of Pennsylvania Press, 1943).

—Charles D. Russell

Danbury Baptist Association Address to Thomas Jefferson (October 7, 1801)

Although THOMAS JEFFERSON was not particularly popular among the Congregationalist establishment in New England, his position on RELIGIOUS LIBERTY and general espousal of democratic principles attracted a number of religious minorities in the region, including the BAPTISTS. On October 7, 1801, several months after Jefferson had been inaugurated as president, the Danbury Baptist Association in Connecticut sent him a congratulatory letter in which they proclaimed that their "sentiments are uniformly on the side of religious liberty—that religion is at all times and places a matter of between God and individuals." While acknowledging that Connecticut law provided some religious privileges, they believed that under the cur-

rent state legislation they "enjoy favors granted, and not as inalienable rights." Realizing that the president could not intervene directly to change state law, they hoped that "the sentiments of our beloved president" would "like the radiant beams of the sun, shine and prevail though all the states and all the world, till hierarchy and tyranny be destroyed from the earth."

On January 1, 1802, Jefferson seized the opportunity provided by the Danbury Address to make a sweeping statement of principle concerning religious freedom that has had a tremendous and controversial impact in the United States. Jefferson's response has been used to interpret the BILL OF RIGHTS guaranteeing the freedom of RELIGION and was cited by SUPREME COURT justice Hugo Black in 1947 in the majority opinion in *Everson v. Board of Education* upholding the use of public funds for school buses for children attending Catholic schools. In particular, Jefferson declared that by supporting the First Amendment, the people of the United States were "building a wall of separation between Church & State." The exact meaning of the "wall of separation" metaphor has been debated in political, legal, and historical circles for decades. Some commentators have argued that Jefferson intended a complete separation between the government and religious establishments; others have suggested that he only intended a partial separation and that the government would not favor one religion over another. Following the second interpretation, government-sponsored religious expression would be perfectly acceptable as long as there was no one established religion. Although the debate may never be settled, in all likelihood Jefferson was seeking to strip government support for religion in order to encourage the people of the United States to approach the subject from the perspective of the ENLIGHTENMENT and develop a rational moral philosophy similar to his own ideas on Christianity, which lay somewhere between DEISM and UNITARIANISM.

Further reading: James H. Hutson, "Thomas Jefferson's Letter to the Danbury Baptists: A Controversy Rejoined," *William and Mary Quarterly* 3rd ser., 56 (1999): 775–790; Johann Neem, "Beyond the Wall: Reinterpreting Jefferson's Danbury Address," *Journal of the Early Republic* 27 (2007): 139–153.

Danbury Raid (April 23–28, 1777)

During the REVOLUTIONARY WAR (1775–83), in spring 1777, the British sent 2,000 men to destroy supplies at Danbury, Connecticut. The raid was under the command of General WILLIAM TRYON, who was the last royal governor of New York. The British departed from New York City on April 23, 1777, and after being delayed by headwinds for two days, they landed on the Connecticut shore just east of Norwalk on April 25 and marched almost unopposed to Danbury, 23 miles inland. They arrived in Danbury on April 26, drove 150 Continentals out of the town, and destroyed vast quantities of supplies, including 1,600 tents, 5,000 pairs of shoes, 4,000–5,000 barrels of meat and flour, and 2,000 bushels of WHEAT. They also burned 19 houses. On April 27 the British withdrew along a different route than the one they had come by, catching the gathering Connecticut MILITIA and Continentals off balance. General BENEDICT ARNOLD, along with Generals Gold Selleck Silliman and David Wooster, sought to stop the British from reaching the coast. Near Ridgefield, Wooster's troops attacked the British rearguard and captured a few prisoners, but he was mortally wounded. In the meantime, Arnold's and Silliman's forces blocked the British front but were driven back after about three hours of fighting; Arnold had a horse shot out from under him. The Revolutionaries reformed along one road, while the British marched around them and camped on Compo Hill, not too far from Long Island Sound. On the morning of April 28, the British struck first, driving the Revolutionaries back. This action prevented any further attack and allowed the British to embark without much molestation. During the raid the Revolutionaries lost about 100 killed and wounded; General WILLIAM HOWE reported that he had lost 60 killed and wounded. The SECOND CONTINENTAL CONGRESS recognized Arnold's heroism by giving him his long-delayed promotion to major general despite the failure to inflict serious damage on the British. General GEORGE WASHINGTON also ordered that in the future all major caches of supplies were to be stored more than a day's march from the coast.

dance

Dance was an important part of the social and cultural expression of all components of North American society in the period of 1754–1815. Among European Americans, dance allowed for interaction between men and women, reflected social status, and could even be a form of competition. For AFRICAN AMERICANS dance not only provided some amusement in an otherwise oppressive racial and slave system but was also a way to bond together in opposition to the dominant European-American culture of their masters. NATIVE AMERICANS used dance in a variety of ways, including in celebrations, religious rituals, and preparations for war.

European Americans danced in several different settings. The elite in colonial and revolutionary America held balls in private homes or in buildings built especially for the purpose of dancing assemblies. During the 1780s and 1790s, however, the elite also used more public spaces such as exclusive TAVERNS like Fraunces Tavern in New York or the City Tavern in Alexandria, Virginia. Further down in society, dances were held in taverns, barns, or sometimes in the open air.

Society leaders seized on dancing as a vehicle to demonstrate their status through costume, manners, and grace in the mastery of the complicated steps and movements of 18th- and early 19th-century dances. Balls were usually opened with the most socially prominent individual leading off a minuet, and it was assumed that every young gentleman and lady would know how to dance. GEORGE WASHINGTON was known as a particularly elegant dancer. Poor dancers were often mocked. In the second half of the 18th century dancing schools, which taught not only dance steps but also social graces, became more common. Common folk used dances as a means of entertainment, and young men often competed to demonstrate their mastery of dancing. Dances were also an important means for young women and men to meet and interact with one another in a public setting.

European Americans practiced a variety of dances. The most popular dance for the upper echelons of society was the minuet, which had been developed in the 17th-century French court and entailed four steps in six beats as the dance partners moved symmetrically across the entire dance floor in set patterns that had an almost endless variation. Included in the minuet was a series of promenades, bows, and curtsies typical of formal occasions. More egalitarian were the so-called English country dances, which were popular with common folk but could also be danced at the gentry's balls. There were thousands of different movements in country dance: At least 2,800 patterns for country dances between 1730 and 1810 have been identified in manuscript and published sources for North America. The basic form of the country dance had two lines, one male and one female, with the lead pair going through the figures for the dance and then moving down the line to the last place so that the second couple could take the lead. This progression was repeated until the original lead pair were back in the place that they began.

The French also developed a country dance—the cotillion—which had a profound impact on North America beginning in the 1790s. In the cotillion the dancers formed a square with four couples, who then engaged in a series of "changes" such as forming circles, hand turns, crossing hands, allemande turns, as well as many other maneuvers. Although introduced as early as the 1770s, the cotillion became popular in the 1790s and early 1800s and even entered elite ball rooms. However, in the 1790s the dance had political implications, with those supporting the FEDERALIST PARTY rejecting its egalitarian and French flavor, while supporters of the DEMOCRATIC-REPUBLICAN PARTY embraced the dance. Eventually the cotillion became Americanized, with the dance moves shouted out by a "caller"; it became known as square dancing.

Watching dancing was a popular form of entertainment. The hornpipe or jig was a display dance intended for an audience. This dance usually had a 2/4 meter and was free-form, with the dancer demonstrating his or her athleticism and creativity in a variety of different steps and movements. Young men might break into a competitive exhibition of a hornpipe at a ball or dance, but generally this form of dancing lacked the elegance of more formal occasions. Sailors also enjoyed the hornpipe and would dance jigs aboard ships for entertainment or while ashore. Hornpipes were also performed in THEATERS, sometimes in sailor costume. One of the most famous professional dancers was John Durang (1768–1822), who drew a self-portrait of himself on the Philadelphia stage wearing a sailor outfit. By the early 19th century, dancing girls had also begun to appear in the more plebeian theaters.

There was a great deal of interchange between African Americans and European Americans in both MUSIC and dance. The hornpipe/jig might have originated in Europe, but as danced in North America it often acquired African-American characteristics. One English visitor before the REVOLUTIONARY WAR (1775–83) described the Virginia jig as lacking "any method or regularity" and was "a practice originally borrowed . . . from the Negroes." African Americans were also employed as musicians at balls and dances held by European Americans. In the early 19th century, free blacks in New York City earned MONEY in the local markets by doing a jig or "shake down" on a board about five feet by six feet and kept time with the noise from their heels—an early version of a tap dance—and by having other blacks "beating their hands on the sides of their legs."

Although there are frequent references to slave dances in the period, little information exists about the exact nature of the steps used. African-American music emphasized rhythm and percussion, and the main instruments were the banjo; fiddle; drums; or simply, as with the free black dancers of New York, the slapping of hands on the sides and clapping. One famous painting of slaves dancing shows men and women bobbing to the music of a banjo, with one man facing two women with handkerchiefs waving in their hands and who in turn are followed by two other men. An overseer in the 1770s described slaves dancing "pair in Pair in their own way, hollowing, shrieking, and making intolerable noise." Intolerable or not, masters would occasionally join in these dances. African Americans also mimicked the more formal dances of the European Americans, as much in the spirit of satire and subtle form of resistance as anything else. Slaves and free blacks would often congregate in the countryside, sometimes numbering as many as 200 for all-night dances. Such gatherings, however, were not welcomed by white masters. In all likelihood, African-American dancing was an amalgamation of styles inherited from several different regions in AFRICA combined with some European-American practices. It fostered a sense of community and African-American identity.

Almost all Native American groups danced, but the meaning and form of their dancing was very different from European-American or African-American practices. Moreover, given the number of different native groups spread across the North American continent, Indian dances varied greatly. In general, Native American dance was a community event that included singing, storytelling, gift exchange, either feasting or fasting, public speaking, and spiritual meaning. Dances were a means of exchanging information, conducting diplomacy, expressing religious beliefs, solidifying tribal identity, and recreation. The IROQUOIS, for instance, would often dance during treaty negotiations and welcomed the participation of European Americans such as SIR WILLIAM JOHNSON. Similarly, when MERIWETHER LEWIS and WILLIAM CLARK traveled to the Far West, they witnessed dances performed by the NATIVE AMERICANS they visited. Most Indian dances involved movement around a fire in a large circle, with the steps following a rhythm dictated by drums or song.

Further reading: Cary Carson, Ronald Hoffman, and Peter J. Albert, eds. *Of Consuming Interests: The Style of Life in the Eighteenth Century* (Charlottesville: University Press of Virginia, 1994); Kate Van Winkle Keller and Charles Cyril Hendrickson, *George Washington: A Biography in Social Dance* (Sandy Hook, Ct.: The Hendrickson Group, 1988); Philip D. Morgan, *Slave Counterpoint: Black Culture in the Eighteenth-Century Chesapeake and Lowcountry* (Chapel Hill: University of North Carolina Press, 1998).

Dane, Nathan (1752–1835) *Massachusetts politician*

A chief architect of the NORTHWEST ORDINANCE of 1787, Nathan Dane was a legal expert who represented Massachusetts in the SECOND CONTINENTAL CONGRESS. Born in Ipswich, Massachusetts, on December 29, 1752, Dane graduated from Harvard College and was admitted to the bar in 1782. He served briefly in the local MILITIA during the siege of Boston in 1775–76, was elected to the Massachusetts House of Representatives in 1782, and became a delegate to the Continental Congress in 1785. While many other congressmen traveled to Philadelphia in 1787 for the CONSTITUTIONAL CONVENTION (1787), Dane remained in New York and was instrumental in the drafting of the Northwest Ordinance. The ordinance addressed the problems of governing the Northwest Territory while also protecting the rights of U.S. citizens as they moved west. Dane supported the extension of civil liberties and civil rights for those living within the new territory, and he introduced the provision that banned SLAVERY and involuntary servitude north of the Ohio River. When the government adopted the U.S. CONSTITUTION, Dane returned to Massachusetts in 1790 and served in the state's senate. Increasing deafness and the inability to participate in debates forced him out of government in 1798. During the WAR OF 1812 (1812–15), he participated in the HARTFORD CONVENTION (1814), which many members of the DEMOCRATIC-REPUBLICAN PARTY considered to be a FEDERALIST PARTY plot to break up the union. Dane spent most of his later years involved in legal studies, which included publishing his revision of Massachusetts law in 1814 and an influential nine-volume legal text, *General Abridgement and Digest of American Laws,* in the 1820s. He died in Beverly, Massachusetts, on February 15, 1835.

Further reading: Andrew J. Johnson, *The Life and Constitutional Thought of Nathan Dane* (New York: Garland, 1987)

—Tash Smith

Dartmoor prison (HM Prison Dartmoor)

Dartmoor prison, located in southwest England near Plymouth, was the compound used by the British in the WAR OF 1812 (1812–15) to hold as many as 6,000 captured SEAMEN and privateersmen from the United States. These PRISONERS OF WAR hated Dartmoor's desolate location on a barren moor. While many suffered illness and malnourishment, others set up trades and stores within its walls to service their fellow prisoners. Confined in a world unto themselves, the prisoners even established schools to teach navigation, dancing, and boxing. The most famous section of the compound was Prison Number 4. In 1814 the British placed all of the African-American prisoners in this prison, along with European Americans whom other prisoners considered undesirable. The African-American prisoners were led by a huge man named Richard Craftus, popularly called King Dick, and were known for holding religious services and theatrical performances in their prison house.

The prisoners were often unruly and challenged the authority of the British guards. Conditions became even more explosive after the TREATY OF GHENT (1814) peace agreement. Without an easy means of accommodating the prisoners and sending them to the United States, and preoccupied by the return of NAPOLEON BONAPARTE to FRANCE in spring 1815, the British did not release their U.S. prisoners of war. On April 4, 1815, the prisoners rioted when the British commissary attempted to serve them hard biscuits instead of the usual soft bread. They actually won that confrontation and were given the appropriate bread.

On April 6, 1815, an incident along the prison wall, where some prisoners were thought to be trying to escape, led to a general alarm. Amid the confusion, and as the pris-

oners began to rush the gate, the British guards opened fire on them, killing six and wounding many more. This event, called the Dartmoor Massacre, remained a searing testimony of British perfidy for the U.S. maritime community. A joint U.S. and British diplomatic commission, however, determined that no officials were at fault, thus defusing a potentially divisive diplomatic incident immediately after the War of 1812.

Further reading: W. Jeffrey Bolster, *Black Jacks: African American Seamen in the Age of Sail* (Cambridge, Mass: Harvard University Press., 1997); Paul A. Gilje, *Liberty on the Waterfront: American Maritime Culture in the Age of Revolution* (Philadelphia: University of Pennsylvania Press, 2004); Reginald Horsman, "The Paradox of Dartmoor Prison," *American Heritage* 26 (1975): 13–17, 85.

Davie, William Richardson (1756–1820) *American militia leader, North Carolina politician*

Born in Egremont, Cumberland, England, William Richardson Davie was sent to South Carolina at the age of seven to be raised by an uncle. Graduating from the College of New Jersey (Princeton) in 1776, he moved to North Carolina, where he served in the revolutionary MILITIA for three months in 1777–78 and became a cavalry officer in 1779, eventually achieving promotion to lieutenant colonel. He saw extensive and sometimes brutal action against local LOYALISTS and was seriously wounded at the BATTLE OF STONO FERRY (June 20, 1779). Enduring a long convalescence, Davie recovered to become an excellent partisan leader in the months after the British captured Charleston on May 12, 1780, following the SIEGE OF CHARLESTON. He nearly wiped out a detachment of BANASTRE TARLETON's legion at WAHAB'S PLANTATION (September 21, 1780) and delayed LORD CORNWALLIS's whole army at the BATTLE OF CHARLOTTE (September 26, 1780) long enough to allow NATHANAEL GREENE's troops to escape an attack. Davie also served as commissary to Greene for several crucial months in 1781.

After the war, Davie became a lawyer and politician, sitting in North Carolina's lower house from 1784 to 1798. Generally conservative in his positions, he opposed paper MONEY schemes and even advocated lenient treatment of Loyalists. He attended the CONSTITUTIONAL CONVENTION of 1787 and lobbied for the ratification of the U.S. CONSTITUTION in North Carolina in 1788. During the 1790s, Davie supported the FEDERALIST PARTY and was elected governor of North Carolina in 1798. Although he was not active on the national political scene, in 1799 President JOHN ADAMS selected Davie as one of three commissioners sent to FRANCE to negotiate a settlement of the QUASI-WAR (1798–1800). After failing in a bid to be elected to Congress in 1803, Davie retired from politics. He died on November 5, 1820.

Perhaps Davie's most lasting achievement was the establishment of the University of North Carolina. He introduced the legislation to found the university in 1789 and was the guiding hand in its creation. Davie County in North Carolina is named after him.

Further reading: *William Richardson Davie: Soldier, Statesman, and Founder of the University of North Carolina: 1756–2006, Semiquincentennial* (Chapel Hill: North Carolina Collection, University Library, 2006).

Davies, Samuel (1723–1761) *Presbyterian minister*
A PRESBYTERIAN clergyman and president of the College of New Jersey (later Princeton University), Samuel Davies was an important spokesman for religious toleration. He was born in Delaware, and after preparing for the Presbyterian ministry under Samuel Blair, he was licensed to preach by the Presbytery of New Castle in 1746. His first wife, Sarah Kirkpatrick, died in 1747 after only a few months of marriage; he married Jean Holt a year later.

In February 1747 Davies was sent to Virginia, where he transformed a few scattered nonconformist families into seven Presbyterian congregations. He became a prominent spokesman for religious toleration and helped encourage acceptance of nonconformists on the part of the established Anglican Church (see ANGLICANS), which had previously subjected other denominations to strict controls. His success was due partly to his demands for action to defend Virginia's boundaries during wars against the French and Indians and partly to his gift for oratory. His sermons were eloquent and popular, influencing the young PATRICK HENRY among others.

Davies owned slaves but also believed he had a duty to teach them to read. He preached to AFRICAN AMERICANS regularly and baptized more than 100 slaves, encouraging others to follow his example in a sermon published in 1754, *The Duty of Christians to Propagate their Religion among the Heathens, Earnestly Recommended to the Masters of Negro Slaves in Virginia.*

In 1753 Davies was commissioned to go to GREAT BRITAIN with Gilbert Tennant on behalf of the College of New Jersey. They raised over £3,000, and Davies gained a reputation as a talented preacher, which led to his introduction to the prominent ministers Jonathan Edwards, JOHN WESLEY, and George Whitefield. In 1759 Davies accepted the presidency of the College of New Jersey. Although he died of pneumonia on February 4, 1761, he had begun to make important changes in the college during his short period in office, including raising the standards for admission and graduation and making improvements to the library.

Further reading: George William Pilcher, *Samuel Davies, Apostle of Dissent in Colonial Virginia* (Nashville: University of Tennessee Press, 1971).

—Alison Stanley

Dayton, Jonathan (1760–1824) *Congressman, Speaker of the House of Representatives, U.S. senator*
Born in Elizabethtown, New Jersey, the son of General Elias Dayton, Jonathan Dayton joined his father's regiment after he graduated from the College of New Jersey (later Princeton University) during the REVOLUTIONARY WAR (1775–83). Beginning as an ensign, he had been promoted to captain by 1783 and fought in several campaigns, including the BATTLE OF BRANDYWINE (September 11, 1777), the BATTLE OF GERMANTOWN (October 4, 1777), the BATTLE OF MONMOUTH (June 28, 1778), the invasion of IROQUOIS territory by General JOHN SULLIVAN in 1779, and the campaign leading to the surrender of YORKTOWN on October 19, 1781.

During the 1780s Dayton became a lawyer, entered the retail business with his father in their hometown of Elizabethtown, bought depreciated government securities, and speculated in western lands. When his father declined to attend the CONSTITUTIONAL CONVENTION, Dayton took his place; at the age of 26, he was the youngest person to attend. He supported the small states' position for equal REPRESENTATION in Congress, and though he opposed the THREE-FIFTHS CLAUSE, he ultimately signed the U.S. CONSTITUTION.

A moderate supporter of the FEDERALIST PARTY, Dayton failed at his first bid for election to the House of Representatives in 1789, but he succeeded two years later, serving as a congressman from 1791 to 1799 and as Speaker of the House from 1795 to 1799. As a speculator in government securities, he made a huge profit from the full funding of the national debt (see DEBT, NATIONAL) proposed by ALEXANDER HAMILTON. He cast the tie-breaking vote in Congress to fund JAY'S TREATY (1794), backed the Sedition Act (see ALIEN AND SEDITION ACTS), and wanted to go to war against FRANCE during the QUASI-WAR (1798–1800) crisis. He also had close ties to AARON BURR. In 1798 he was chosen as a senator, serving from 1799 to 1805.

After 1800 Dayton became an increasingly controversial figure. He was charged with personally benefitting from legislation he sponsored and kept $18,000 of congressional MONEY for personal use (he later paid it back). He was also deeply implicated in the Burr conspiracy, in which Aaron Burr schemed to create an independent nation in the West, and was indicted for treason as a result. After Burr's acquittal, however, the government dropped the charges against Dayton. His political career waned thereafter, although he was elected to the New Jersey lower house in 1812. He died on October 9, 1824, only a few weeks after the MARQUIS DE LAFAYETTE had visited his home. Dayton, Ohio, is named after him.

Deane, Silas (1737–1789) *politician, diplomat*
An active Revolutionary, Silas Deane was the first person sent by the SECOND CONTINENTAL CONGRESS to solicit support from FRANCE during the REVOLUTIONARY WAR (1775–83). Born in Groton, Connecticut, on December 24, 1737, and educated at Yale, Deane became a leading lawyer and merchant during the colonial period. Successful marriages also accelerated his career. During the 1760s and 1770s he became an active supporter of the RESISTANCE MOVEMENT (1764–1775), and was chosen by Connecticut to serve in the FIRST CONTINENTAL CONGRESS and Second Continental Congress. As a member of Congress, he was largely responsible for supporting the attack on FORT TICONDEROGA in 1775. When he was not chosen for another term in Congress, his colleagues in Philadelphia decided to use his talents and sent him to France.

Deane's diplomatic efforts were important to the United States but were troubled by controversy. After arriving in Paris in July 1776, he encouraged the French to provide further assistance to the Revolutionary cause. He arranged for sending over the equipment and supplies that culminated in the British general JOHN BURGOYNE's surrender at SARATOGA (October 17, 1777). Although he worked closely with BENJAMIN FRANKLIN in convincing France to form an alliance with the United States and to provide crucial supplies, he may also have had some contacts with British agents. He subsequently became embroiled in a controversy over the war's finances when several members of Congress accused him of profiteering from his diplomatic mission. This controversy, triggered by the charges of ARTHUR LEE, who served in the diplomatic mission to France, seriously divided the Continental Congress when Deane returned to the United States.

Stripped of official duties, Deane went back to France in 1780 to pursue private business and resuscitate his reputation, efforts in which he was not very successful. In 1781 he began to despair over the war's outcome. Unfortunately for Deane, he expressed his sentiments in several private letters that the British intercepted and published, and as a result, many claimed that he was a traitor. He died in self-imposed exile on September 23, 1789.

See also FRENCH ALLIANCE.

Further reading: James Coy Hilton, *Silas Deane: Patriot or Traitor?* (East Lansing: Michigan State University Press, 1975).

Dearborn, Henry (1751–1829) *U.S. military officer, secretary of war*
Though he practiced MEDICINE as a young man, Henry Dearborn is most noted for his service as secretary of war in the administration of THOMAS JEFFERSON. Born in North Hampton, New Hampshire he studied MEDICINE, starting a practice in Nottingham, New Hampshire. During the REVOLUTIONARY WAR (1775–83), he served as a captain at the BATTLE OF BUNKER HILL (June 17, 1775) and then joined GEORGE WASHINGTON's staff at VALLEY FORGE as a lieutenant colonel in 1777. He became deputy quartermaster general in 1781. After war ended, he became a member of the DEMOCRATIC-REPUBLICAN PARTY and served as a congressman from the District of Maine (1793–97).

In 1801, Thomas Jefferson appointed Dearborn as secretary of war, a position he held until March 1809. As secretary of war, he supported Jefferson's Indian policy, which centered on the assimilation and Americanization of Indians through TRADE centers known as factories. Dearborn hoped that the factories would provide the tools necessary for NATIVE AMERICANS to become civilized without the threat of exploitation, but his policies backfired as nativist Indian leaders united Native American communities by preaching against the destructive effects of European-American products and culture. Many of these communities, in turn, sought support from the British, gaining access to important trade goods and beneficial military alliances. This situation created tension in the Ohio Valley and the North American Southeast as European-American settlers feared the growing pan-Indianism of nativist communities and the increasing influence of the British among Indians.

After resigning as secretary of war, Dearborn served as the senior major general in the U.S. ARMY during the WAR OF 1812 (1812–15). He was later demoted to commander of New York City due to several questionable strategic decisions. His experiences with Native Americans during his tenure as the secretary of war and in the army eventually altered his views on Indian policy, and by 1820 he supported the physical removal of Native Americans, specifically the CHEROKEE. He died in Roxbury, Massachusetts, on June 6, 1829.

Further reading: Bernard W. Sheehan, *Seeds of Extinction: Jeffersonian Philanthropy and the American Indian* (Chapel Hill: University of North Carolina Press, 1973).

—Patrick Bottiger

debt, national
The national debt was one of the most contentious issues in early U.S. politics. The debates that swirled around how to pay the national debt helped to provide the rationale for

the writing and ratification of the U.S. CONSTITUTION and contributed to the development of POLITICAL PARTIES in the 1790s and early 1800s. The debt also remains one of the most difficult subjects to understand. Indeed, few people—perhaps not even ALEXANDER HAMILTON, the first secretary of the treasury—ever fully comprehended all of the debt's intricacies and complications as a result of the REVOLUTIONARY WAR (1775–83). However, Hamilton's policies successfully transformed the national debt from a public liability to a civic asset, and in the process it became a driving force behind the creation of the United States and crucial to the molding of a national identity.

By the mid-18th century, several European states had long become accustomed to some form of national debt. Both GREAT BRITAIN and FRANCE depended on debt as a means of paying for their repeated wars with each another. Armed conflict fought on a global scale had become too expensive to sustain on a pay-as-you-go basis. Debt allowed a country to spread out the cost of a war over many years, including years of peace. The two nations, however, took their debt in different directions. The British government had greater flexibility in raising taxes, encouraged an active capital market in London, and formed an intimate relationship with the Bank of England that allowed for quick infusions of cash. The French government was more antiquated and cumbersome, had a less well-developed capital market, and did not have an equivalent institution to the Bank of England. In the closing decades of the 18th century, Great Britain continued to draw on its capital resources while the French Crown experienced a bankruptcy that contributed to the outbreak of the FRENCH REVOLUTION (1789–99).

British Americans were not only aware of the national debt in Great Britain but also had a more direct experience with government debt within each colony. The victory in the FRENCH AND INDIAN WAR (1754–63) had been funded with deficit spending on both sides of the ATLANTIC OCEAN. Parliament increased its own national debt and reimbursed the colonists for about 40 percent of the £2.5 million spent by the colonial governments. Most of the colonies paid for their share of the fighting with fiat currency—that is, they printed MONEY that could be used to pay taxes in the future. This type of funding was a form of debt since the intention was to eventually withdraw all of the paper MONEY in circulation. The New England colonies—including Massachusetts, which had some of the heaviest expenditures during the conflict—were prohibited from printing money by the Currency Act of 1751 and therefore issued interest-bearing treasury notes, which were a more direct form of state debt. Whether the colony used fiat currency or treasury notes, during the 1760s and into the 1770s almost all of the colonies were successful in withdrawing currency through payment of taxes and thereby retiring their debt.

When the Revolutionary War broke out, the SECOND CONTINENTAL CONGRESS, building on the colonial experience, turned to fiat currency as a means of paying for the conflict. The idea was that the Continental currency would be used for supplies and the army, and then the notes circulate until those notes were used to pay taxes. Once returned to the government through taxation, the money would either be recirculated or, when no longer needed, retired and taken out of circulation. From this perspective, it was all right for the Continental dollars—often popularly known as Continentals—to be a little inflationary, since a decrease in their value would make it cheaper for the money to be redeemed. However, Continental money soon became highly inflationary, creating problems for the U.S. government and for the people who held onto Continental dollars. After about $25 million were printed in 1776, the value of the currency began to slide. With 76 million more Continental dollars placed in circulation in 1777 and 1778, the ratio of paper money to specie fell to 5:1. In 1779 the value of the printed money began a free fall so that by the end of 1780 the ratio had become 100:1, and soon thereafter the Continental money was all but worthless, with the result that in 1781 the government suspended issuing of further notes. From 1775 to 1781 the Continental Congress had authorized $227.8 million to be printed and netted about $47 million in specie value.

Fiat currency did not work for the Continental Congress because the war became more expensive than expected and because the Revolutionaries used a variety of different and conflicting methods to raise money. Under the ARTICLES OF CONFEDERATION, Congress did not have the power to tax directly, and the states were supposed to impose taxes payable in Continental money and then return that money to the national government. Since individual states printed their own fiat currency, most states preferred to take care of their own currency first and therefore did not always meet the requisitions imposed by Congress. State currencies, too, became inflationary, creating a maze of shifting values that made it difficult for anyone to know what their money was worth. Throughout the war, the states printed $210 million in money, which had a specie value of $6 million.

If the existence of multiple fiat currencies was not complicated enough, there were other ways the national and state governments paid for the war. Local MILITIAS and committees, as well as the CONTINENTAL ARMY, issued impressment certificates to pay for goods and services. Really nothing more than formal IOUs, these certificates could be used for taxes, although they were usually redeemed at less than face value. In addition, as head of the treasury, ROBERT MORRIS suspended payment of the army in 1781 and later issued $11 million in interest-bearing certificates to soldiers in lieu of back pay. Both levels of government also floated loans, although the national government did so on a grander scale in the domestic and international market: Individuals within the United States loaned the Continental Congress about $11 million; foreign countries, especially France and The NETHERLANDS, loaned another $12 million.

The situation became even more complex during the 1780s after Morris suspended all interest payments on the domestic debt in 1782. With unpaid interest added to the principle each year, the debt grew. To help deal with the expanding debt, the national government issued indents on the loan certificates held by individuals, which were paper payments for the interest on the debt that also accrued interest. Simultaneously, the states actually began to retire some of the Continental currency through taxation; in the early 1780s states collected about $119 million in bills that had a specie value of $3 million. They also started to work off their individual debt, and by the end of the 1780s some states had begun to assume the interest payments on the national debt.

The Continental Congress was most concerned with maintaining its credit overseas. Even though it suspended interest payments on the French debt in 1786, Congress did everything it could to service the Dutch debt. The capital market in Amsterdam was absolutely essential to the United States's reputation. To maintain that position, the United States continued to borrow money from Dutch investors—who, amazingly, continued to provide loans—even if it was to just pay off the interest on the money that had already been borrowed.

Also during the 1780s, many of the various forms of debt were traded in an open market. Most of the military certificates exchanged hands, as did many of the impressment certificates, sometimes for as little as 10–15 cents on the dollar. Although it may seem as if the original holders of such certificates received a bad deal, that judgment is based on hindsight and does not take into account the risk any purchaser took, nor the years of delay before the government was willing to pay out on the debt. One scholar has calculated that had the original holder turned around and invested the specie he received for the certificate, his returns were not that far from the delayed return of the purchaser. Of course, such calculations overlook the fact that many of the original holders sold their certificates because of POVERTY and quickly spent what they had been paid, nor does it fully take into account the multiple times notes were traded—sometimes for a profit and sometimes for a loss.

The nationalists of the 1780s who wanted to strengthen the central government hoped that a rigorous United States would deal with the debt more effectively. But they did not do so simply, as Progressive historian Charles Beard believed, to ensure profit on their speculation in government securities. Instead, they saw a symbiotic relationship between their NATIONALISM and the debt. As Alexander Hamilton explained as early as 1781: "A national debt, if not excessive, will be to us a national blessing. It will be a powerful cement of our union." In other words, creating a stronger union was not the means to the end of paying the national debt; instead, the national debt would be the means to the end of a stronger United States. The men who gathered at the CONSTITUTIONAL CONVENTION in 1787 included two provisions directly related to the national debt: First, they guaranteed that the new government would stand behind all financial obligations made by the previous government; second, they provided Congress with the power to tax.

After the Constitution was ratified and a new national government was elected, it was left to Hamilton as secretary of the treasury to disentangle the complicated web of financial instruments that comprised the national debt and develop a program to guarantee that the debt would become the "cement of our union." In his *Report on Public Credit* of January 9, 1790, Hamilton embraced the national debt as a positive force and not, as many in the 1780s had believed, a burden. Hamilton argued for the full funding of the debt—that is, he wanted to honor all financial obligations at their full face value regardless of the current market price. He also pushed for the assumption of the states' debts. Although this assumption would increase the debt, by shifting the obligation to the federal government, more creditors would be tied to Congress and want a powerful central government that would be able to support the debt.

Hamilton, however, had no intention of paying off the debt; he merely wanted the United States to pay the interest on it. Built into his program was a regulation limiting final repayment of the debt to 2 percent a year. He believed that a continued debt would create a capital market in government securities similar to the one that existed in England that the United States could tap into in emergencies—such as a war. In other words, the debt would guarantee the republic's independence by ensuring that there would always be eager domestic investors with liquid assets held in government securities, which could facilitate financing of the government through any crisis.

Hamilton set up both full funding and the assumption of state debts to obtain advantageous interest rates, significant profits for the holders of government securities, and low taxes for U.S. citizens. The total debt included $40 million held by the national government ($27 million in original debt and $13 million in interest), $12 million in foreign debt ($8.4 million to France and $3.6 million to the Netherlands), and $18.2 million in assumed state debts. Leaving the terms of the foreign loans the same, Hamilton kept borrowing from the Dutch to pay the interest and even, at first, to sustain his overall financial program. He fully funded the national debt but drove down the interest rate by exchanging outstanding notes for new federal securities, paying 6 percent interest on two-thirds of the notes and delaying payment of that interest on one-third until 1800. He also limited the interest on the outstanding arrears, including the indents issued during the 1780s in lieu of interest, to only 3 percent interest. For the assumed state debts, he came up with an even more complicated formula: 6 percent interest would be paid on four-ninths of the total immediately, 3 percent interest on three-ninths immediately, and 6 percent on the remaining two-ninths after 1800. Taken all together, the payment program lowered the effective interest rate on government bonds to between 4 and 6 percent, the same rate given on the international market to only the strongest of governments. Investors eagerly seized on the program since by 1790 few of them had paid par for the notes, and their effective rate of return was much higher than the face yield. Moreover, they were now guaranteed a return through the government's power to tax. An investment that had been a gamble before the Constitution now became a sure thing.

The financial program also lowered the tax burden. Most of the cost of the program would be carried by an impost duty of 5 percent. Such a tax was invisible since it was paid at the time of importation and would be carried by the most affluent consumers—those people most likely to benefit from the financial program itself. There was also an excise tax imposed on alcoholic beverages. Hamilton wanted this tax more to establish the principle of the federal government's right to impose domestic tax than for the $500,000 in revenue it was expected to generate. The total taxes would raise about $5 million a year, which Hamilton hoped could pay the interest on the debt and carry the government's expenses.

State taxes could be reduced since most states were now relieved of the burden of their debt. Although Hamilton set a $4 million ceiling on the amount assumed from any one state, by the mid-1790s the rest of the state debts were all but wiped out by a final accounting of the expenses from the Revolutionary War. In 1786, in an effort to clarify the level of state debt, the Continental Congress organized a special settlement claims commission to calculate how much each state had spent on the war and how much they should have spent on a per capita basis. The national government under the Constitution continued this work and came to a final accounting in 1794 when the settlement claims commission determined that the 13 states had spent a combined $114.4 million on the Revolutionary War. After subtracting the portion of the state debts assumed by the national government under the Hamiltonian program, and counting the amount of money each state had already paid back, the commission used a zero-sum formula and con-

cluded that six debtor states owed seven creditor states $3.5 million. The national government then issued bonds to be paid to the creditor states, while the debtor states were supposed to pay the national government the difference. The result was that the seven creditor states, and three other states where the balance was nearly even, had almost no debt. Combined, the federal and state taxes were thus reduced to an extremely low 2 percent of the total national income.

Hamilton's efforts concerning the national debt drew opposition and contributed to the organization of the DEMOCRATIC-REPUBLICAN PARTY. THOMAS JEFFERSON did not accept the idea that debt could be a good thing and thought that each generation should be responsible for their own expenditures. He also viewed the creation of a market for capital—something that Hamilton believed strengthened the republic—as anathema. Whereas Hamilton believed that all men were dependent and that a republican government was best served when the people relied on that government, Jefferson believed that a republic could only be composed of independent men divorced from such ephemeral forms of wealth as stocks and bonds.

Regardless of party differences, the United States continued to have a national debt that persisted as "a powerful cement of our union" throughout the 1790s and early 1800s. With the FEDERALIST PARTY in control of the national government during the 1790s, Hamilton's policies predominated. The national debt hovered persistently around $80 million, even though Hamilton encouraged the creation of a small sinking fund to shrink the debt modestly. Once Jefferson took office, however, he and his treasury secretary, ALBERT GALLATIN, reversed government policies and began to erase the national debt, which dwindled to about $45 million by 1811. That debt would have even become smaller without the $15 million LOUISIANA PURCHASE and the dramatic decline in revenues during the EMBARGO OF 1807. The WAR OF 1812 (1812–15), however, reversed the downward trend for the national debt, which ballooned to $127.3 million by the end of 1815.

Further reading: E. James Ferguson, *The Power of the Purse: A History of American Public Finance, 1776–1790* (Chapel Hill: University of North Carolina Press, 1961); Edward J. Perkins, *American Public Finance and Financial Services, 1799–1815* (Columbus: Ohio State University Press, 1994).

Decatur, Stephen (1779–1820) *U.S. naval officer, duelist*

Stephen Decatur was a swashbuckling officer of the U.S. NAVY in the early 19th century. Born in Maryland on January 5, 1779, Decatur grew up in Philadelphia in a seafaring family. He became a midshipman in the U.S. Navy in 1798 and fought in the QUASI-WAR (1798–1800) with FRANCE. He first gained fame in action in the war against Tripoli, by which time he had been promoted to lieutenant. In October 1803 the frigate *Philadelphia* ran aground off Tripoli and was captured. On the night of February 16, 1804, Decatur led a raid into Tripoli harbor to deny the vessel to the Tripolitans. He entered the harbor on a captured schooner named the *Intrepid,* seized and burned the *Philadelphia,* and then made a safe getaway, a success that earned him promotion to captain. He also was involved in several other engagements at Tripoli, including hand-to-hand combat, that captured the imagination of the U.S. public.

The WAR OF 1812 (1812–15) brought both success and failure to Decatur. As captain of the frigate USS *UNITED STATES* on October 15, 1812, he outmaneuvered a slightly less powerful foe, the HMS *Macedonian,* pummeling the British ship with more than 70 broadsides, killing or wounding a third of her crew, and compelling the British captain to strike her colors. This action was one of a series of spectacular single ship victories at the beginning of the war, but Decatur remained trapped in the United States for most of the rest of the conflict, unable to get into the open sea because of the British blockade. On January 15, 1815, unaware of the TREATY OF GHENT of December 24, 1814, he took advantage of weather conditions to slip out of New York harbor in the frigate USS *President.* However, he struck a sandbar off Sandy Hook, damaging the ship, and when winds prevented his reentry to New York harbor, he continued on in his efforts to run the blockade, pursued by several British frigates. He was able to defeat the fastest of these, but his ship was almost crippled from the battle and running aground, and, while dealing with a storm at sea, he was compelled to surrender.

Following the war, Decatur served as commander of the U.S. Mediterranean Squadron. At a dinner during negotiations for a peace treaty with Algiers, he gave the toast for which he remains famous: "Our country! In her intercourse with foreign nations may she always be in the right; but our country, right or wrong!" Upon his return to the United States, he served on the Board of Navy Commissioners, in which role he supported denying JAMES BARRON's application to be reinstated in the navy. (Decatur had been a judge at Barron's court-martial after the *CHESAPEAKE-LEONARD* AFFAIR in 1807.) Barron took exception to comments Decatur made and issued a challenge that Decatur felt honor-bound to accept. On March 22, 1820, the two fought a duel at a field in Bladensburg, Maryland. Decatur wounded Barron in the thigh, but the shot he received in the chest was fatal, and he died 12 hours later.

See also BARBARY WARS; DUELING.

Further reading: Robert J. Allison, *Stephen Decatur: American Naval Hero, 1779–1820* (Amherst: University of Massachusetts Press, 2005); William M. Fowler, Jr., *Jack Tars and Commodores: The American Navy, 1783–1815* (Boston: Houghton Mifflin, 1984).

Declaration of Independence

The Declaration of Independence is the document by which the thirteen colonies proclaimed their independence from GREAT BRITAIN. It was adopted in its final form on July 4, 1776, and signed the following month. The aim of the document was to announce the colonies' independence to the world and to list the reasons why the AMERICAN REVOLUTION was legitimate. Although its statement that "all men are created equal" has received the most historical attention, the majority of the words in the document are devoted to a catalog of what the colonists saw as the transgressions of King GEORGE III.

The delegates to the FIRST CONTINENTAL CONGRESS in no way intended to declare independence from Great Britain; they met simply to discuss forms of resistance to the British imperial regulation and the COERCIVE ACTS (1774). On October 14, 1774, the delegates passed a resolution called the Declaration of Rights and Grievances, which denied the right of Parliament to tax the colonies and presented the king with a list of grievances. Six days later, they agreed to the Continental ASSOCIATION setting up a timetable for banning all imports and exports to Great Britain. The Association also empowered local committees to take charge of the boycott on TRADE with the British. The members of the First Continental Congress were careful to maintain their loyalty to the king and claimed they wanted to restore their relationship to what it had been. When the Congress adjourned, they agreed to meet again in May 1775.

By the time the SECOND CONTINENTAL CONGRESS convened, extralegal provincial assemblies were replacing the legal legislative bodies and royal governors. The outbreak of actual fighting at the BATTLES OF LEXINGTON AND CONCORD (April 19, 1775) altered the Congress's mission: They now had to operate as a governmental body in order to run a war.

Even though the war had begun, it was many months before the Continental Congress issued the Declaration of Independence. On June 7, 1776, RICHARD HENRY LEE of Virginia delivered to Congress a resolution that began: "Resolved: That these United Colonies are, and of right ought to be, free and independent States, that they are absolved from all allegiance to the British crown, and that all political connection between them and the State of Great Britain is, and ought to be, totally dissolved." Lee's sentiments echoed those of a growing number of people. In

Presentation of the Declaration of Independence in Independence Hall, Philadelphia, Pennsylvania. Painting by John Trumbull

August 1775 the king had issued a proclamation declaring the colonies to be in open rebellion. Congress also learned that the king had hired German mercenaries—HESSIANS—to fight in North America. It became increasingly clear that the British government was treating the colonies as a foreign body, and Congress increasingly acted like one. On April 6, 1776, Congress opened North American ports to trade with other nations. At this point many Revolutionary Americans began to think that independence was inevitable. This rise in popular sentiment was partly due to the publication of THOMAS PAINE's COMMON SENSE in January 1776. By May 1776, eight colonies had decided that they would support independence, and there were at least 90 documents declaring independence passed before July 4 by states, committees, and other groups of Revolutionary Americans. However, there were still some members of Congress who wished to continue to seek reconciliation with Britain. Although Congress voted to postpone discussion of the Lee resolution in early June, it also appointed a committee of five—JOHN ADAMS (Massachusetts), BENJAMIN FRANKLIN (Pennsylvania), THOMAS JEFFERSON (Virginia), ROBERT R. LIVINGSTON (New York), and ROGER SHERMAN (Connecticut)—to draft a statement offering the arguments for independence.

The Declaration of Independence presented by the committee to the Congress on June 28 was written almost entirely by Jefferson. The Sage of Monticello had worked on his draft from June 11 to June 28 in Philadelphia; Franklin and Adams had offered adjustments. Congress, meeting as a committee of the whole, resumed debate on Lee's resolution on July 1 and voted for independence the next day. With that done, delegates made some more substantial changes to the wording of the declaration. For example, Jefferson had wanted to blame the king for the SLAVE TRADE, but Congress elected not to address the issue of SLAVERY. Regardless of the changes, the essential language and argument remained the same. The key to Jefferson's eloquence was his combination of lofty principles, drawing on the ideas of JOHN LOCKE and the writings of the COMMONWEALTHMEN, with an indictment of King George for usurping American LIBERTY. The opening sections were especially compelling because they proclaimed that all men were created equal and asserted a social-contract theory of government. However, the list of grievances, while effective propaganda at the time, do not hold up to modern scrutiny as an accurate statements of events. Revolutionary Americans may have interpreted the king's actions as a concerted plan to destroy liberty, but there is little evidence to suggest that the various efforts at imperial regulation passed by Parliament and pursued by several different administrations in Great Britain, reflected anything close to a conspiracy.

People in the United States celebrate the Fourth of July as the holiday of national independence, but the actual timing of events is more complex. On July 2 Congress voted 12 states to none to declare independence (New York was allowed not to vote, since its delegation wanted to have the approval of its state's convention). From July 2 to 4, Congress debated the document's wording, and when this process of revision was over, the Declaration of Independence became official on July 4. The next day, Congress dispatched word of the Declaration to the states and the army, and on July 9 New York approved of the action. Finally, on August 2, 1776, most of the delegates signed the document that has become an icon in the National Archives in WASHINGTON, D.C., including, most famously and conspicuously, the signature of the president of Congress, JOHN HANCOCK.

See also REVOLUTIONARY WAR; RESISTANCE MOVEMENT.

Further reading: Carl L. Becker, *The Declaration of Independence: A Study on the History of Ideas* (New York: Knopf, 1942); Pauline Maier, *The American Scripture: Making the Declaration of Independence* (New York: Knopf, 1997); Garry Wills, *Inventing America: Jefferson's Declaration of Independence* (Garden City, N.Y.: Doubleday, 1978).

Declaration of the Causes and Necessity of Taking up Arms (July 6, 1775)

When the SECOND CONTINENTAL CONGRESS met on May 10, 1775, it confronted an unanticipated problem: war had broken out at the BATTLES OF LEXINGTON AND CONCORD (April 19, 1775). The Congress was divided between radicals and moderates, with the moderates acknowledging the need for defensive measures but still hoping that somehow an accommodation could be reached. The radicals believed that more drastic action was needed—some even thought of independence. To placate the moderates, Congress agreed to send yet another petition to King GEORGE III—the OLIVE BRANCH PETITION—reiterating the points made in the petition sent by the FIRST CONTINENTAL CONGRESS. But the radicals also wanted to have a statement explaining why North American colonists needed to fight the British army. On July 6, 1775, the Congress issued just

such a statement, which could be read to the troops that were then gathered around Boston under the command of GEORGE WASHINGTON and were to become the nucleus of the CONTINENTAL ARMY.

Originally drafted by THOMAS JEFFERSON and then edited and amended by JOHN DICKINSON, who was a moderate, the Declaration of the Causes and Necessity of Taking up Arms fell short of asking for independence but offered a one-sided interpretation of events that emphasized the colonists' defense of LIBERTY.

The document began with a WHIG interpretation of colonial history asserting that the colonists had come to North America for "civil and religious freedom" and had established prosperous colonies that had contributed significantly to the triumph of GREAT BRITAIN in the FRENCH AND INDIAN WAR (1754–63). The document continued by arguing that rather than reward the colonies, Parliament had in 11 years sought to alter the previous mutually beneficial relationship and attempted to take colonial property without the colonists' consent. The declaration stated that the colonists had responded with petitions, which Parliament and the king had ignored. Congress then explained that within this context, General THOMAS GAGE had sent troops into the Massachusetts countryside, making an "unprovoked assault on the inhabitants" and murdering several at Lexington. The British troops then "proceeded in warlike array to the town of Concord, where they set upon another party of inhabitants." From this perspective, not only did the British start the war, but Gage's "troops have butchered our countrymen, have wantonly burnt Charlestown, besides a considerable number of houses in other places; our ships and vessels are seized; the necessary supplies of provisions are intercepted, and he [Gage] is exerting his utmost power to spread destruction and devastation around him."

If this view of events satisfied the radicals in the Continental Congress, there were also words suggesting that reconciliation was still possible. The declaration assured "our friends and fellow-subjects" elsewhere in the empire "that we mean not to dissolve that union which has so long and so happily subsisted between us, and which we sincerely wish to see restored." The document continued: "We fight not for glory or for conquest. We exhibit to mankind the remarkable spectacle of a people attacked by unprovoked enemies, without any imputation or even suspicion of offence." The Revolutionaries needed to take up arms "in defence of the freedom that is our birthright, and which we ever enjoyed till the late violation of it—for the protection of our property, acquired solely by the honest industry of our fore-fathers and ourselves." The declaration ended by invoking the Almighty, while leaving the door open for possible settlement: "With an humble confidence in the mercies of the supreme and impartial Judge and Ruler of the Universe, we most devoutly implore his divine goodness to protect us happily through this great conflict, to dispose our adversaries to reconciliation on reasonable terms, and thereby to relieve the empire from the calamities of civil war."

Declaration of the Rights of Man

The Declaration of the Rights of Man, approved by the French National Assembly on August 26, 1789, was a statement of general principle that helped initiate the FRENCH REVOLUTION (1789–99). Drawn up by the MARQUIS DE LAFAYETTE and other liberals, the Declaration of the Rights of Man began with the statement "Men are born and remain free and equal in rights." The document asserted that sovereignty resided in the nation and that "all political association is the preservation of the natural and imprescriptable rights of man." LIBERTY was thus "the freedom to do everything which injures no one else." The purpose of law was to protect against hurtful actions in society, and "Law is the expression of the general will." No one could be arrested without just cause, and everyone was innocent until proven guilty. Government should ensure a "free communication of ideas and opinions." "All citizens have a right" to participate in government," and since property was inviolable, no one could have property taken away except in public necessity.

Representing the ideas of liberal reformists, including Lafayette, the Declaration of the Rights of Man was heavily influenced by the AMERICAN REVOLUTION. Lafayette had shared drafts of the declaration with THOMAS JEFFERSON—then the U.S. minister to FRANCE—who made several suggestions in wording. Within the United States, many commentators noted the influence of various states' bill of rights on the French declaration and generally responded to the document favorably. Although the French Revolution would become much more radical over the next several years and then turn more conservative by the end of the 1790s, the Declaration of the Rights of Man remained a central document for the Revolution and became a symbol of the ideals of equality and liberty throughout the Atlantic world.

Declaratory Act (1766)

When Parliament passed the repeal of the STAMP ACT (1765) in 1766, it was reacting as much to the petitions of merchants in GREAT BRITAIN as it was to the opposition in the colonies. Based on those petitions, British officials stated that it was expedient at that particular moment to repeal the law, though the government still believed that it had the right to legislate for the colonies. In an effort to assert that authority, they passed the Declaratory Act, which claimed that Parliament had the right to bind the colonies "in all cases whatsoever." In other words, Parliament was saying that it would repeal the law now, but that it reserved the right to pass taxes and other legislation for the colonies in the future. Parliament agreed to this act in early March, and King GEORGE III assented to it on March 18, 1766. While the act ran counter to the beliefs of those colonists who had opposed the Stamp Act, most colonial Americans did not worry too much about this face-saving measure. Amid the jubilation and celebration, the actual passage of the Declaratory Act appeared inconsequential compared to the fact that colonial Americans believed that they had compelled the British government to succumb to their will. The act would form the basis of later parliamentary taxes and would be cited by Revolutionary leaders in the 1770s as an example of arbitrary and tyrannical government.

See also RESISTANCE MOVEMENT.

Further reading: Edmund S. and Helen M. Morgan, *The Stamp Act Crisis: Prologue to Revolution* (Chapel Hill: University of North Carolina Press, 1953).

deism

Growing out of 17th-century English intellectual traditions, and expanding in the 18th century with the spread of the ENLIGHTENMENT, deism retained faith in the idea that God created the world but downplayed the role of Scripture and organized RELIGION. Deism also had an important impact on many leaders in the revolutionary generation.

The political and religious upheaval of 17th-century England caused some individuals to question the relationship between church and state. This questioning led to the beginnings of some toleration for different Protestant groups in England and colonial America. It also led to a general questioning among a few of the role of organized religion. Some individuals held that God was a supreme being—deity—who created the world. It was man's duty to worship this deity, but everyone should do so in a personal manner through a moral and virtuous life. These ideas seemed to fit the new intellectual climate of the 18th century represented by the Enlightenment, which emphasized the relationship between nature and reason, holding that nature was organized according to scientific laws dictated by reason. Within this context, deism became a way to explain the origin of natural law. God created the mechanisms that dictated how nature operated. Humans could study nature and, through reason, discover how those mechanisms operated, but ultimately the basis of nature and reason came from God. A few thinkers held that God was like a great clockmaker who created an elaborate machine—the world—wound it up, and allowed it to continue without his providential hand guiding every move.

Prominent thinkers influenced by deism included JOHN LOCKE in England and Voltaire in FRANCE.

Several Revolutionary leaders flirted with deism. BENJAMIN FRANKLIN wrote a deistic pamphlet as a youth but abandoned his commitment to its tenets and regularly attended religious services later in life. THOMAS JEFFERSON, too, was attracted to deism, and political opponents in the 1790s and early 1800s charged him with being godless, based on earlier statements of his that reflected deism's influence. Even GEORGE WASHINGTON, although always pious and a churchgoer, expressed some support for deist ideas.

The most explicit statements of deism came from the pens of ETHAN ALLEN and THOMAS PAINE. In a long manifesto, *Reason the Only Oracle of God* (1785), Allen argued that the Bible was merely a pasting together of scattered documents without divine inspiration. He believed that morality and religion "as well as all other sciences, is acquired from reason and experience." Denying the divine origin of the Bible and placing reason over the "word of God" did not find a receptive audience in Vermont, and it contributed to the decline of Allen's political career.

Thomas Paine wrote the most famous deistic tract while in Revolutionary France. His *Age of Reason* (1794–96) attacked all biblical revelation as falsehood. Paine, who had used the Bible to such good effect in *COMMON SENSE* (1776), now declared that the Bible was a forgery and packed with contradictions and immorality: "It is a book of lies, wickedness, and blasphemy for what is more blasphemous than to ascribe the wickedness of man to the orders of the Almighty." Paine retained his faith in God as a deity; he merely rejected the Bible and organized religion, asserting that "My own mind is my own church" and that state-sponsored churches were "human institutions set up to terrify and enslave mankind, and monopolize power and profit." Although some readers in the United States, especially ARTISANS, found his arguments convincing, the book was extremely unpopular and led to his being condemned by many as godless.

Further reading: David L. Holmes, *The Faiths of the Founding Fathers* (New York: Oxford University Press, 2006); Henry F. May, *The Enlightenment in America* (New York: Oxford University Press, 1976).

De Lancey, James (James De Lancey the Younger)

(1747–1802) *Loyalist*

A member of a leading New York family in the colonial period and grandson of CADWALLADER COLDEN, James De Lancey—like most of his family—became a Loyalist during the REVOLUTIONARY WAR (1775–83). He is often referred to as James De Lancey the Younger to distinguish him from his uncle, James De Lancey, the Elder. Beginning in 1777, De Lancey organized New York LOYALISTS into a MILITIA company called the Westchester Refugees; they also came to be known as De Lancey's Cowboys because they raided the Westchester countryside for cattle. Based in King's Bridge, the Westchester Refugees became infamous for their activities in the no-man's-land of Westchester County between the British and Revolutionary lines. Besides gaining food for the British army and keeping the road north open for supplies, De Lancey's men also captured as many as 500 Revolutionaries to exchange for imprisoned Loyalists. De Lancey himself was captured in December 1777 and charged with violating an earlier parole that he claimed he had never signed. He was exchanged in 1778, and at the end of the war he resigned his commission—he had become a colonel by then—and moved to NOVA SCOTIA. The state government had seized his lands in New York, and he remained detested by the Revolutionaries who not only blamed him for the internecine partisan war in New York but for countless crimes perpetrated by any ruffian who took advantage of the breakdown in law and order between the lines of the contending armies. In Nova Scotia De Lancey served in the legislature and on the council while reestablishing his economic standing. He died on May 2, 1804.

See also COWBOYS AND SKINNERS; LOYALIST PROPERTY CONFISCATION.

Delaware Indians (Lenape)

Originally inhabiting the Delaware Valley and known as the Lenape Indians, the Delaware had been pushed into western Pennsylvania and present-day Ohio by the time of the REVOLUTIONARY WAR (1775–83). Each of the tribe's three major divisions spoke a somewhat different dialect of the Eastern Algonquian LANGUAGE. Calling themselves the Lenape, they had earned a reputation as intertribal diplomats and were called "grandfathers" by most of their neighbors.

Although spread out and often living among other groups of NATIVE AMERICANS, the Delaware played a central role in the FRONTIER warfare of the late 18th century. During the FRENCH AND INDIAN WAR (1754–63), the Delaware under TEEDYUSCUNG spread terror in the Susquehanna Valley of Pennsylvania before agreeing to a peace in 1757. The Delaware further west, in part inspired by NEOLIN, joined in PONTIAC'S WAR (1763–65). The tribe was divided during the Revolutionary War. Some Delaware agreed to fight against the British after attending councils with U.S. representatives at FORT PITT in 1775 and 1776. A treaty signed in 1778 allowed Revolutionary troops to march through Delaware territory and called for forts to protect Delaware villages. At the main Delaware town of

COSHOCTON, on the Muskingum River, a faction led by GEORGE WHITE EYES and JOHN KILLBUCK, JR., declared its support for the United States; another faction, led by Captain Pipe, supported the British. After White Eyes died under suspicious circumstances—many Delaware believed he was murdered by Revolutionary MILITIA—more Delaware favored the British. Aware of the growing pro-British sentiment, a detachment under General Daniel Brodhead burned Coshocton in 1780. Delaware who still supported the Revolutionaries sought refuge at Fort Pitt, while most others fled to join Captain Pipe's band.

Christian converts among the Delaware also suffered. The British and their Native American allies forced Delaware and other Indians at the MORAVIAN town of Gnadenhutten to abandon the settlement in 1781. Short of food, however, a group of the Moravian converts returned to Gnadenhutten only to be assailed by Revolutionary militia. The pacifist Christians offered no resistance, and 96 people were killed in the GNADENHUTTEN MASSACRE. Outraged by repeated assaults on their villages, the Delaware joined the SHAWNEE and routed an expedition by Pennsylvania militia at the BATTLE OF SANDUSKY (June 4–5, 1782). After the TREATY OF PARIS (1783), many Delaware remained hostile to the United States, fought in the campaigns that defeated JOSIAH HARMAR and ARTHUR ST. CLAIR in the 1790s, and joined in the pan-Indian movement led by TECUMSEH in the early 19th century.

Further reading: Earl P. Olmstead, *Blackcoats among the Delaware: David Zeisberger on the Ohio Frontier* (Kent, Ohio: Kent State University Press, 1991); Amy C. Schutt, *Peoples of the River Valleys: The Odyssey of the Delaware Indians* (Philadelphia: University of Pennsylvania Press, 2007; C. A. Weslager, *The Delaware Indians: A History* (New Brunswick, N.J.: Rutgers University Press, 1972).

—Stephen A. Martin

Delaware River forts

After General WILLIAM HOWE occupied Philadelphia on September 26, 1777, the Revolutionaries still controlled the Delaware River forts and prevented supplies reaching the British army from the sea. The British had the formidable task of clearing the Delaware River of obstructions, defeating a flotilla of warships and gunboats under Captain John Hazelwood, and capturing three forts: Fort Mercer near Red Bank, New Jersey; Fort Mifflin on Mud Island; and an outpost at Billingsport, four miles down the river.

The British campaign began well when they captured the frigate *Delaware* on September 27 after it went aground near Philadelphia, and they occupied Billingsport almost unopposed on October 2. But they ran into difficulties

in clearing the river of obstructions near Billingsport and were harassed by Hazelwood's ships. Establishing batteries on the islands at the mouth of the Schuykill River opposite Fort Mifflin proved difficult because of the marshy and unstable nature of the ground. By October 15 the British had opened up a narrow passage at Billingsport and began an artillery bombardment on Fort Mifflin.

The Revolutionaries had their own problems since they were low on ammunition and had a divided command: Hazelwood was independent of the officers in charge of the forts, and those officers were independent of Hazelwood. These difficulties aside, the defenders scored two big victories in the failed assault by HESSIANS on Fort Mercer in the BATTLE OF RED BANK (October 22, 1777) and the disastrous naval attack on Fort Mifflin on October 23 in which the Royal Navy lost a 64-gun ship, the HMS *Augusta*, and a 20-gun sloop, the *Merlin*. Both vessels had run aground near each other and caught fire, then blew up in huge explosions. The loss in men was minimal since the ships had been evacuated, but the destruction of two warships was significant.

The situation, however, remained difficult for the Revolutionaries. Although GEORGE WASHINGTON finally consolidated the command structure under General James Varnum, supplies remained low, and the situation at Fort Mifflin was exposed. The British built platforms on the marshy ground opposite Mud Island to support big cannon from the navy, and they began a heavy bombardment on November 10. The navy brought additional ships up the river on November 15 and fired on the fort from point-blank range, pounding it into a shambles and forcing the Continentals to abandon it that night. About half of the 500-man garrison was killed or wounded; the British lost only a handful of men.

Washington and Varnum hoped that they could still check the British on the Delaware by holding on to Fort Mercer. But when LORD CORNWALLIS and 4,200 men began to move on the fort on November 20, Varnum considered the situation at Fort Mercer untenable, and he reluctantly ordered its evacuation. Varnum's rearguard left just before Cornwallis's troops arrived on November 21, a move that left Hazelwood's fleet without any land-based support. Some of his galleys were able to row upstream, but because of the wind the sailing ships were unable to escape. Hazelwood ordered all 11 ships burned to prevent their falling into British hands. In the meantime, Washington had sent NATHANAEL GREENE and 7,000 men into New Jersey, hoping to use Fort Mercer as bait to trap Cornwallis. But little came of this effort, and Cornwallis was able to recross the Delaware unobstructed. Washington then had to order Greene to rejoin him before Howe and Cornwallis could strike at his depleted army at Whitemarsh. When Greene returned to Washington's main body on December

1, the campaign for the control of the Delaware River forts was over, and the British were able to resupply their army in Philadelphia.

Further reading: Stephen R. Taffe, *The Philadelphia Campaign, 1777–1778* (Lawrence: University of Kansas Press, 2003).

Democratic-Republican Party

During the 1790s, the opposition to ALEXANDER HAMILTON's program to create a stronger central government gradually coalesced into a political party. Initially, this party took its name from the DEMOCRATIC-REPUBLICAN SOCIETIES of 1794; later, party members were often simply referred to as the Republicans. History textbooks use a variety of labels for the party, including Democratic-Republican, Republican-Democratic, Republican, Democratic, Jeffersonian, Jeffersonian-Republican, and Jeffersonian-Democratic. Whatever the name, the party should not be confused with either the Democratic or Republican Parties that emerged later in U.S. history. Centered on the ideas of JAMES MADISON and THOMAS JEFFERSON, the Democratic-Republicans supported limited government, the extension of democratic rights to the "people" (white adult males), and a strict interpretation of the U.S. CONSTITUTION.

The party began in Congress under Madison's leadership. As secretary of state under GEORGE WASHINGTON, Jefferson encouraged and worked with Madison, but it was Madison who coordinated a caucus in opposition to Hamilton's program. If there were some alliances among legislators in 1791 and 1792, local organization only began to emerge in 1793 and 1794. In fact, it was more the FRENCH REVOLUTION (1789–99) and FRANCE's war with GREAT BRITAIN in 1793—rather than economic policy—that mobilized popular sentiment. Enthusiasm for Republican France spilled onto the streets and became a means of Democratic-Republican identity, but by 1796 the party had only partially developed. The Democratic-Republican caucus in Congress nominated Jefferson for president, individual states had formed groups of alliances that called themselves Democratic-Republican, many newspapers had clear party allegiances, and there were local organizations—but a national party structure hardly existed. The FEDERALIST PARTY helped the Democratic-Republicans along by pushing its policies too hard over the next four years. Increased taxation, expansion of the army and navy, the QUASI-WAR (1798–1800), and the ALIEN AND SEDITION ACTS (1798) all demonstrated to many people in the United States the evils of a strong government run amok. By the ELECTION OF 1800, the Democratic-Republican Party had taken form, even if many of its leaders thought that the party was only a temporary expedient to save the republic.

After 1800, the Democratic-Republicans dominated the national scene but did not control every state and region. New England, in particular, remained a bastion of the Federalist Party. As a political party, the Democratic-Republicans were often divided into factions that vied with one another. In New York, for example, the Burrites (supporters of AARON BURR) contended with the Clintonians (adherents of GEORGE CLINTON and his nephew DEWITT CLINTON) and others for control of the state. Allegiances that centered around a family or individual appeared in other states as well. By the end of the WAR OF 1812 (1812–15), and in the wake of the HARTFORD CONVENTION, the Federalist Party had lost almost all support, and the United States became a single-party democracy. The unity of the Era of Good Feelings lasted only a few years, as different factions competed with each other nationally, eventually giving birth to a new party system in the 1820s and 1830s. By that time, although politicians still claimed a Jeffersonian legacy, the Democratic-Republican Party had also ceased to exist.

See also POLITICAL PARTIES.

Further reading: Richard J. Buel, Jr., *Securing the Revolution: Ideology in American Politics, 1789–1815* (Ithaca, N.Y.: Cornell University Press, 1972); Richard Hofstadter, *The Idea of a Party System: The Rise of Legitimate Opposition in the United States, 1780–1840* (Berkeley: University of California Press, 1972).

Democratic-Republican Societies

Founded during the first half of the 1790s, Democratic-Republican Societies were the first grassroots organizations to oppose President GEORGE WASHINGTON. The societies broadened political participation by attracting men from the lower and middling classes to political action, thus precipitating a debate about the legitimacy of such organized opposition to the government.

In May 1793 a group of Philadelphians founded the first and most prominent Democratic-Republican club; by the end of 1794, there were 42 known clubs. Societies were located in urban centers and the backcountry, and membership ranged from a handful to several hundred. While most leaders of these organizations were prominent men in the community, many societies were led by less prosperous and more humble men. Thus, the Democratic-Republican Societies attracted men of diverse status and, as a result, helped to broaden the scope of political participation in the early republic.

Originally founded as debating societies whose purpose was discussion and dissemination of information, the clubs soon became overtly political. Their immediate models were the SONS OF LIBERTY and COMMITTEES OF CORRESPONDENCE; indeed, several members had been active in these organizations. In addition, Democratic-Republican Societies found a degree of inspiration from the FRENCH REVOLUTION (1789–99) and the Jacobin Clubs of FRANCE. Members of the Democratic-Republican Societies saw the French Revolution as a continuation of the AMERICAN REVOLUTION, believing it their duty, and that of the U.S. government, to support their brother republicans across the ATLANTIC OCEAN. Nevertheless the societies cannot be characterized as tools of the French. Although EDMOND GENÊT did suggest including "democratic" in the name for the Philadelphia society, he did not have undue influence over it or any other society.

In addition to being concerned about U.S. policy toward France and GREAT BRITAIN, the Democratic-Republican Societies were troubled by the consolidating impact of Secretary of the Treasury ALEXANDER HAMILTON's financial schemes, including a national bank and an excise tax. Members believed that the Washington administration had betrayed the American Revolution, and to combat such a betrayal, citizens needed to examine the conduct of all government officers, including Washington. Only a vigilant and virtuous citizenry could save the republican experiment, and the societies hoped to fulfill this purpose.

By 1796, almost all of the societies had disappeared. Several reasons explain their decline, which was almost as fast as their ascent. First, as the French Revolution deteriorated into the Reign of Terror and the war between Great Britain and France intensified, more people in the United States feared rather than celebrated the events in Europe; hence, Democratic-Republicans Societies lost support. Second and more important, in November 1794 Washington denounced the societies for what he believed was their role in the WHISKEY REBELLION. Despite efforts by individual societies outside of western Pennsylvania to distance themselves from the rebels, the societies could not recover from Washington's public condemnation and challenge to their legitimacy. Significantly, Washington's comments precipitated a debate within the House of Representatives about whether to officially agree with him. Although Democratic-Republican Party leaders JAMES MADISON and THOMAS JEFFERSON never condoned the societies, they were not ready to denounce them either. The Democratic-Republican Societies were one step in the growing acceptance of the legitimacy of a vocal opposition to the sitting administration.

Further reading: Eugene Perry Link, *Democratic-Republican Societies, 1790–1800* (New York: Columbia University Press, 1942).

Denmark

During the years 1754–1815, Denmark was a minor northern European power that controlled Norway (until 1814) and maintained a presence in the WEST INDIES with small but profitable colonies in what is now the Virgin Islands. The outbreak of the FRENCH REVOLUTION (1789–99) and the subsequent wars in Europe had a dramatic and negative impact on Denmark.

The Danish West Indies came under direct royal control in 1754 and thereafter expanded the amount of sugar produced on the islands and increased their slave population from almost 9,000 in 1755 to almost 17,000 in 1766. The Danish West Indies had close economic ties to both the British West Indies colonies nearby and the British North American colonies. ALEXANDER HAMILTON spent much of his youth working in a countinghouse in the Danish West Indies, which even had an English-language newspaper. Denmark opened TRADE in the West Indies to other European colonies in 1764 and allowed direct trade to Europe in non-Danish ships in 1767. Between 1770 and 1775, more ships from the British mainland colonies entered St. Croix than did ships sailing from Denmark. Worried by the problems of trade caused by the REVOLUTIONARY WAR (1775–83), the Danish government reasserted mercantilist principles in the early 1780s, only to open trade permanently in 1782. After 1783, the United States became an important trading partner of the Danish West Indies. In 1790 about one-fourth of all the ships arriving in the area came from the United States. However, because Denmark aligned itself with NAPOLEON BONAPARTE, the British occupied the Danish West Indies from April 1801 to February 1802 and again from 1807 to 1815, when the islands were handed back to Denmark.

During the Revolutionary War, Denmark joined other European powers in the LEAGUE OF ARMED NEUTRALITY to assert its right to participate in trade with all belligerents. U.S. efforts in the 1780s to set up a trade accord with Denmark failed, although commercial contacts between merchants in the two countries expanded into the 1790s. In the opening decade of the 19th century, Denmark suffered greatly as it was caught in the fighting between FRANCE and GREAT BRITAIN. The British bombarded Copenhagen in 1801 and 1807, and most of the Danish navy was captured or destroyed. After the BERLIN DECREE and MILAN DECREE were issued, the Danish government also seized shipping from the United States in its ports as part of Napoleon's Continental System. At the end of the Napoleonic Wars, Denmark had to transfer Norway to the king of SWEDEN, although the British returned the Danish West Indies as part of the final peace agreement. The United States and Denmark had a number of exchanges about seizures of ships and trade, and there was some representative of the

U.S. government in Denmark beginning in 1801, although formal diplomatic relations between the two countries did not begin until 1827.

Dennie, Joseph (1768–1812) *journalist*

Born in Boston, Massachusetts, Joseph Dennie became an influential journalist and literary proponent of the FED-ERALIST PARTY. Dennie graduated from Harvard in 1790 and, after considering entering the ministry, he decided on a career in law. For three years he worked as a clerk in New Hampshire, and he was admitted to the bar in 1794. His law practice, however, proved to be transient and unproductive, and he quit the legal profession, turning to his literary talents for his livelihood. From 1792 to 1802, Dennie wrote a column, "Farrago," which was printed in several New Hampshire journals. His "Farrago" essays were also reprinted in his short-lived weekly paper called the *Tablet* (published May 19–August 11, 1795, in Boston). It was during this period that Dennie joined with ROYALL TYLER and produced short essays under the pseudonyms "Colin and Spondee."

The *Tablet* folded after 13 issues, and Dennie relocated to Walpole, where he wrote prolifically for the *Farmer's Weekly Museum*. In his most popular essays, entitled "The Lay Preacher," he used a pro–Federalist Party rhetoric and gained a large readership across the nation. As a result of his partisan allegiance, Dennie was appointed personal secretary to U.S. Secretary of State TIMOTHY PICKERING in 1799 and moved to Philadelphia, only to lose his position after Pickering was removed from the cabinet in 1800. In 1801 Dennie and Asbury Dickins began a new periodical called *The Port Folio*. He exerted a tremendous influence on the LITERATURE of the period, encouraging writers such as WASHINGTON IRVING, JOEL BARLOW, CHARLES BROCKDEN BROWN, and PHILIP FRENEAU—some of whom did not agree with Dennie's politics.

Despite his evenhandedness when dealing with literature, Dennie's political positions were clear as he stridently supported the Federalist Party in the pages of the *Port Folio*. One essay he authored in 1803 denounced democracy as "scarcely tolerable in any period of national history," declaring that it "was weak and wicked in Athens. It was bad in Sparta, and worse in Rome. It has been tried in France, and has terminated in despotism. It was tried in England, and rejected with the utmost loathing and abhorrence." He then continued by stating that democracy was "on trial" in the United States "and the issue will be civil war, desolation, and anarchy." Dennie also established the Tuesday Club, a group consisting of the most talented writers in Philadelphia. Dennie continued his distinguished literary career until his death on January 7, 1812.

See also JOURNALISM.

Further reading: William C. Dowling, *Literary Federalism in the Age of Jefferson: Joseph Dennie and The Port Folio, 1801–1812* (Columbia: University of South Carolina Press, 1999); Annie Russell Marble, *Heralds of American Literature: A Group of Patriot Writers of the Revolutionary and National Periods* (Chicago: University of Chicago Press, 1907).

—William R. Smith

Deslondes Revolt (1811)

Beginning with the murder of a white plantation owner in St. John the Baptist Parish in Orleans Territory (the modern-day state of Louisiana) on January 8, 1811, at least 200 slaves engaged in a revolt. Although there is a limited information on the rebels, they were well-organized since they launched their attack when many of the U.S. ARMY units in the area had been dispatched to secure sections of West FLORIDA. Several of the slaves involved in the revolt had come from Saint Domingue and were familiar with the successful overthrow of SLAVERY that had led to the establishment of the independent country of HAITI. The rebels marched toward New Orleans and were intercepted by white MILITIA and some soldiers on January 11, 1811. The poorly armed AFRICAN AMERICANS were overwhelmed, and 29 were captured while the rest scattered into the countryside. A hastily convened tribunal quickly convicted and executed 20 of the rebels, placing some of the heads on poles and mutilating the body of a ringleader named Charles. Since Charles, like many slaves, did not have a last name, the revolt has been named after the owner of the plantation where Charles lived—the widow of Jean-Baptiste Deslondes.

Further reading: Peter J. Kastor, *The Nation's Crucible: The Louisiana Purchase and the Creation of America* (New Haven, Conn.: Yale University Press, 2004).

Dessalines, Jean-Jacques (1758–1806) *Saint Domingue rebel, founder of Haiti*

Founder of the nation of HAITI, Jean-Jacques Dessalines was born into SLAVERY when the French controlled the western third of the island of Hispaniola—the future Haiti—as the colony called Saint Domingue. Dessalines joined the slave revolt that began in Saint Domingue in 1791. In the confused wars that followed, he fought for the Spanish in 1793 and then switched sides after the French abolished slavery in 1794. He rose through the ranks and became a general under TOUSSAINT LOUVERTURE. Dessalines's soldiers were some of the most efficient and brutal in the wars that followed, often mutilating and executing prisoners taken in battle. From 1799 to 1801, Dessalines led the troops that defeated—occasionally with the aid of the U.S. NAVY—dissidents in southern Saint Domingue. He remained loyal to Louverture and resisted the French attempt to regain control of the colony in 1802 with an army under General Charles Victor Emmanuel Leclerc.

In May 1802 Louverture made peace with the French, and Dessalines once again agreed to serve under the French flag. However, the alliance between FRANCE and the ex-slave troops was fragile, and after the French deported Louverture in June 1802 and killed black soldiers suspected of disloyalty, a large number of "colonial" (black) troops deserted the French, and racial warfare again erupted on the island. The French killed colonial troops they believed disloyal, and the rebels massacred white soldiers they captured. In 1803 Dessalines joined the rebels and became the leader of a movement that led to a declaration of independence on January 1, 1804. The words of that document were stark and threatening, stating that the ex-slaves were "innocent before the tribunal of Providence" in resisting "so harsh and shameful a servitude" even if they were "to cause rivers and torrents of blood to run; were they, in order to maintain their liberty, to conflagrate seven-eighths of the globe." A few months after the declaration, Dessalines became governor-for-life in Haiti and later declared himself emperor. Fearing a conspiracy by whites to overthrow his regime, he ordered mass executions of the French remaining in Haiti. In turn, Dessalines was assassinated by some of his own followers on October 26, 1806.

See also LIBERTY.

Further reading: Laurent Dubois, *Avengers of the New World: The Story of the Haitian Revolution* (Cambridge, Mass.: Harvard University Press, 2004).

Detroit

Located on the Detroit River between Lake Huron and Lake Erie, Detroit was a crucial military and trading outpost in the 1754–1815 period. The French established Detroit in 1701 in a successful effort to extend their influence throughout the Great Lakes region in the first half of the 18th century. During the early years of the FRENCH AND INDIAN WAR (1754–63) the French used Detroit to recruit NATIVE AMERICANS to fight the British. However, after the British seizure of FORT NIAGARA in 1759, Detroit became isolated from the rest of CANADA. The British gained control of Detroit as part of the capitulation agreement of MONTREAL in 1760, and a British garrison took possession of the fort on November 29, 1760. During PONTIAC'S WAR (1763–65) Detroit remained one of the few British posts in the West not captured by the Indians, despite a five-month siege led by Pontiac.

During the REVOLUTIONARY WAR (1775–83), Detroit became a crucial staging area for British operations throughout the region. GEORGE ROGERS CLARK launched his famous expedition in 1779 in the hope of eventually seizing Detroit, but despite capturing VINCENNES (February 25, 1779), he did not get within a hundred miles of his real objective. Revolutionary troops marched into Ohio country aiming to take Detroit several times during the war, but they either withdrew far short of their goal or suffered disaster at the hands of British troops and Native Americans, as occurred at the BATTLE OF SANDUSKY (June 4–5, 1782).

Although Detroit lay on the west bank of the Detroit River and was technically ceded to the United States as part of the TREATY OF PARIS (1783), GREAT BRITAIN retained possession of the outpost. The British insisted that they would evacuate neither Detroit nor several other FRONTIER forts until the United States abided by the Treaty of Paris by compensating LOYALISTS and permitting the collection of pre-war debts. Detroit was also important to British fur-trading interests (see FUR TRADE) and allowed them to continue to exert influence on Native Americans throughout the region. However, as a result of JAY'S TREATY (1794), the British agreed to withdraw from all forts in the United States, abandoning their Indian allies. This action helped to open up much of Ohio to European-American settlement. The United States finally occupied Detroit on July 11, 1796.

Detroit's strategic location meant that it would become the scene of conflict in the WAR OF 1812 (1812–15). General WILLIAM HULL, who had command of more than 2,000 soldiers at Detroit at the beginning of the war, crossed the river and tentatively advanced into Canada. Losing his nerve, he retreated back to Detroit, where he was surrounded by a smaller British and Indian army. Fearing a massacre, he surrendered his entire garrison to the British on August 16, 1812, a military disaster for the United States that led to Hull's court-martial. The United States could only reoccupy Detroit after the BATTLE OF LAKE ERIE (September 10, 1813).

Dexter, Samuel (1761–1816) *congressman, senator, secretary of war, secretary of the treasury*

Born in Boston, educated at Harvard, and trained as a lawyer, Samuel Dexter became a prominent, if somewhat independent, member of the Massachusetts FEDERALIST PARTY in the 1790s and early 1800s. Dexter began his political career in 1788 in the Massachusetts House of Representatives and was elected to Congress in 1792. He left Congress in March 1795 but became a senator in December 1799. His Senate career was cut short after President JOHN ADAMS purged his cabinet of those loyal to ALEXAN-

DER HAMILTON and appointed Dexter to become secretary of war on May 13, 1800. A few months later, Dexter left the War Department and became secretary of the Treasury on December 31, 1800. He remained in that position under President THOMAS JEFFERSON until ALBERT GALLATIN replaced him on January 26, 1802.

After leaving the cabinet, Dexter returned to Massachusetts and pursued a lucrative legal career. Although he opposed the restrictions on TRADE imposed by the Jefferson administration, unlike many members of the Federalist Party, he supported the WAR OF 1812 (1812–15). He twice turned down diplomatic posts and ran for governor of Massachusetts unsuccessfully in 1814 and 1815. Dexter died on May 4, 1816.

Dickinson, John (1732–1808) *lawyer, essayist, politician*

A conservative Revolutionary leader, John Dickinson was born on November 8, 1732, in Talbot County, Maryland, and he lived most of his life in Delaware and Pennsylvania. He studied law in London, practiced law in Philadelphia, and served in the legislatures of both Delaware and Pennsylvania. Dickinson opposed the SUGAR ACT (1764) and STAMP ACT (1765), writing a pamphlet that advocated enlisting the support of British merchants to aid the colonies. In recognition of his vocal position, Pennsylvania sent him to the STAMP ACT CONGRESS in 1765. He objected to the use of force during the RESISTANCE MOVEMENT (1764–1775).

Sometimes called the "penman of the revolution," Dickinson gained fame for writing a series of essays that were later published as a pamphlet entitled *Letters from a Farmer in Pennsylvania to the Inhabitants of the British Colonies* (1768) in opposition to the TOWNSHEND DUTIES (1767). Although Dickinson was not really from Pennsylvania nor a farmer, his "letters" demonstrated a broad command of English history and the legal principles underpinning Anglo-American notions of LIBERTY, expressing a fear of corruption and a necessity to resist arbitrary law. He stopped short of calling for force, although he implied that it might someday become necessary. Dickinson remained active in politics in the early 1770s in Pennsylvania but lost some influence in 1774 when he hesitated to support the radical measures that followed the COERCIVE ACTS (1774). He believed that New Englanders had acted rashly in the BOSTON TEA PARTY (December 16, 1773), and he was afraid of taking any step that might prevent reconciliation with GREAT BRITAIN.

Dickinson became a delegate to the FIRST CONTINENTAL CONGRESS in late 1774 and led the movement to petition King GEORGE III for a peaceful resolution to the crisis. As a member of the SECOND CONTINENTAL CON-GRESS, he continued to seek reconciliation with the king while simultaneously joining in the preparations for war. He pursued the same policies in 1776 and even voted against the DECLARATION OF INDEPENDENCE. During the war, however, he served for a time in the military fighting the British, was elected to Congress from Delaware in 1779, and served as the president of Delaware from November 13, 1781, to November 7, 1782. He also became president of Pennsylvania in 1782, and in 1783 he founded Dickinson College in Carlisle, Pennsylvania. Dickinson advocated the creation of a stronger national government in the late 1780s; was president of the ANNAPOLIS CONVENTION; and was a delegate for Delaware at the 1787 CONSTITUTIONAL CONVENTION, where he took an active role in its debates to draw up the U.S. CONSTITUTION. He also wrote several essays, signed "Fabius," strongly supporting the Constitution's adoption. Thereafter, he retired from public life and died on February 14, 1808, in Wilmington, Delaware.

Further reading: Milton Embick Flower, *John Dickinson: Conservative Revolutionary* (Charlottesville: University Press of Virginia, 1983).

Dickinson, Philemon (1739–1809) *militia officer, U.S. senator*

Philemon Dickinson was born in Maryland and grew up on his family's estate near Trenton, New Jersey. The son of a judge, Dickinson began his EDUCATION under the tutelage of a law student in his father's office and graduated from the College of Philadelphia (now the University of Pennsylvania) in 1759. He studied law with his brother, JOHN DICKINSON, in Philadelphia where he signed a nonimportation agreement in opposition to the STAMP ACT in November 1765.

Returning to New Jersey, Dickinson was appointed a colonel in the Hunterdon County Battalion in 1775. In October that year, he was commissioned a brigadier general in the New Jersey MILITIA, and he subsequently earned praise from General GEORGE WASHINGTON for defeating a British foraging party near Somerset Court House in January 1777. Six months later, he became a major general and commander in chief of the New Jersey militia. His destruction of bridges and obstruction of roads slowed the British army's retreat from Philadelphia, allowing the CONTINENTAL ARMY to catch up. From December 1778 to November 1779, Dickinson acted as signal officer for the 150-mile chain of towers between the army headquarters at Newburgh and the Delaware River. He then returned to the New Jersey militia and earned praise for his actions at the BATTLE OF SPRINGFIELD (June 23, 1780).

Dickinson served in the Provincial Congress of New Jersey in 1776 and represented Delaware in 1782–83 as a delegate in the SECOND CONTINENTAL CONGRESS. He was elected vice president of the New Jersey Council for two terms, in 1783 and 1784, and was one of three commissioners named to select a location for the new U.S. capital. WILLIAM LIVINGSTON defeated him in three attempts to become governor of New Jersey (1778, 1779, and 1780), and WILLIAM PATERSON also defeated him in a bid to become a U.S. senator. However, when Livingston died in 1790, Paterson resigned from the Senate to finish out his term as governor, and Dickinson was appointed to fill the rest of Paterson's senatorial term. He served from 1790 to 1793, after which he returned to Trenton, where he died on February 4, 1809.

—Stephen A. Martin

Dieskau, Jean-Armand, baron de (1701–1767)
French military officer

Baron de Dieskau was born in Saxony and became an officer in the service of FRANCE. He advanced through the ranks until he became a major general and military governor of Brest in northwestern France. At the beginning of the FRENCH AND INDIAN WAR (1754–63), he was appointed to lead the French armies in CANADA but remained under the general command of the MARQUIS DE VAUDREUIL, governor of New France. Arriving in North America in 1755, Vaudreuil first sent Dieskau to attack OSWEGO but then ordered him to the Lake Champlain region to meet the threat of invasion from Colonel WILLIAM JOHNSON's troops.

Once he arrived on the scene, Dieskau disobeyed his orders not to divide his force and launched a major raid with 1,500 men (220 regulars, 600 Canadian MILITIA, and 700 NATIVE AMERICANS) on Fort Edward to cut the supply line of the British-American forces on the southern shore of Lake George (the future site of Fort William Henry). However, after he led his men to the southern tip of Lake Champlain and then through the woods to the supply road, the Indians refused to attack Fort Edward. Instead, Dieskau headed north toward Lake George. In the BATTLE OF LAKE GEORGE (September 5, 1755), his troops ambushed a column marching to relieve Fort Edward, with his regulars blocking the road and the Canadian militia and Native Americans attacking the flanks from high ground in the woods. Although the attack began a little too early, it drove back the British Americans and their Native American allies, leaving them in disarray. Dieskau pursued them until they reached Johnson's camp on Lake George, where the entrenched British-American troops held their ground. Wounded, Dieskau was left on the battlefield and captured after his men withdrew; he remained a prisoner for the rest of the war.

Although Vaudreuil decried Dieskau's failure to follow orders, his attack prevented any further advance on Canada that year. It also showed Dieskau as a daring and adaptable commander as he recognized the strengths of the Canadian militia and Native-American allies in the North American wilderness, while remaining confident in the fighting abilities of his regular French troops.

Further reading: Fred Anderson, *Crucible of War: The Seven Years' War and the Fate of Empire in British North America, 1754–1766* (New York: Vintage, 2000); Ian K. Steele, *Betrayals: Fort William Henry and the Massacre* (New York: Oxford University Press, 1990).

dinner table bargain

The dinner table bargain of June 1790 was supposedly a deal arranged by THOMAS JEFFERSON between JAMES MADISON and ALEXANDER HAMILTON to locate the U.S. capital on the Potomac River in exchange for the passage of a bill authorizing the national government to assume state debts. Jefferson's recollection of the dinner, which is the only explicit discussion of the "bargain," does not fully explain the ongoing and complicated negotiations surrounding the gathering. In all likelihood, there were several meetings between the different parties and the final resolution went beyond the location of the capital in exchange for the assumption of state debts. Although the U.S. CONSTITUTION empowered Congress to "exercise exclusive Legislation" over "a seat of government" of not more than 10 square miles to be purchased from the state in which it was located, the document did not stipulate where that capital should be. Each region sought to claim the capital for its own. Assumption of state debts also divided the states since some of them—for instance, Virginia and other states had already paid off a significant portion of their debt—objected to Hamilton's plan because it would mean they would have to pay other states' debt.

The "bargain" therefore had to take account of a number of interests. The residency bill sought to placate the middle states by promising to have the capital in Philadelphia for 10 years before it was moved to the Potomac, near the home of GEORGE WASHINGTON. The Pennsylvanians vainly hoped that once the capital was established in their state, it would be almost impossible to move. The assumption part of the deal focused more exclusively on Virginia's concerns and included special consideration of its contribution to paying the state debts. The Virginians believed that originally the Treasury Department would assume $3 million of Virginia's debt but then tax the state $5 million—a net loss of $2 million. Instead, Hamilton agreed to assume $3.5 million in state debt and tax Virginia the same amount, which meant, as Jefferson explained many years later, "Being therefore to receive exactly what she is to pay," Virginia "will neither win nor lose by the measure." With the middle states mollified at least temporarily, and

Virginia's interest guarded, Madison still voted against the debt assumption, but he did not press the case, allowing others to pass the measure into law.

See also POLITICAL PARTIES; FEDERALIST PARTY; DEMOCRATIC-REPUBLICAN PARTY.

Further reading: Joseph J. Ellis, *Founding Brothers: The Revolutionary Generation* (New York: Knopf, 2000).

Direct Tax Act (1798)

In an effort to raise $2 million to pay for the expansion of the army and the navy to meet the threat posed by FRANCE and the QUASI-WAR (1798–99), Congress, then dominated by the FEDERALIST PARTY, passed the Direct Tax Act on July 14, 1798. This onetime measure created a graduated tax on houses, slaves, and land. Although he was not a member of Congress, the direct tax was the idea of ALEXANDER HAMILTON, who hoped to avoid the popular opposition that had surrounded the earlier excise tax and had led to the WHISKEY REBELLION (1794) by ensuring that the rich would pay a larger share than the poor. More than 65 percent of the tax was to come from a levy on dwellings, with a rate that varied, depending on the building's value. The owner of a house worth less than $100 paid no tax, while the assessment on houses would gradually increase from .002 percent per $100 for those homes worth between $100 and $500 to .010 percent per $100 for mansions worth over $30,000. In other words, an individual in a house worth $500 would pay a dollar tax, and a grandee paying the maximum rate on a $30,000 house would owe $300. The slave tax would also fall disproportionately on the rich since they owned more slaves and would have to pay 50 cents per head for every slave able to work between age 12 and 50. The remainder of the revenue would come from a land tax, which would be nonprogressive. The land tax favored land speculators, whose land was worth less per acre than developed agricultural land owned by middling and poorer farmers.

To collect this tax, the federal government had to create a bureaucracy to figure out how much houses and land were worth and to count the number of slaves owned in the United States. Each state was divided into several districts, and the government appointed a commissioner for each district who oversaw assessors and their assistants in their work. Suddenly the federal government was reaching into every community and looking into the lives of the people to a degree not even imagined by the British in their efforts at taxation in the 1760s and 1770s. The assessors were charged with specifying "in respect to dwelling-houses, their situation, their dimensions or area, their number of stories, the number and dimensions of their windows, the materials whereof they are built, whether wood, brick, or stone, the number, description and dimensions of the out-

houses appurtenant to them, and the names of their owners or occupants." The law did not stipulate why the windows were counted, but it was probably one way of determining the value of the building. More important than the number of windows was the house's size and construction materials. Because the assessors counted windows, the direct tax is sometimes mistakenly believed to be a tax on windows and has been called the "window tax."

Although many members of the DEMOCRATIC-REPUBLICAN PARTY decried the tax, and the expansion of federal government power that came with it, only in eastern Pennsylvania did opposition reach a crescendo as German Americans raised LIBERTY poles, created associations, intimidated assessors, and engaged in a jail rescue in a protest that has come to be known as FRIES'S REBELLION (1798–99). The unpopularity of the law also contributed to the success of THOMAS JEFFERSON in the ELECTION OF 1800. Strangely, once in power the Jeffersonians did not repeal the direct tax but, in an effort that took more than a decade, sought to collect the tax to pay for the expenses of the Quasi-War.

The direct tax has had one unexpected benefit: Modern historians can use the assessment records to learn about housing in the United States in the early republic. Scholars know, for instance, that in 1798 about half of the housing was valued at under $100 and had dimensions of about 20 by 24 feet, and that in a settled region like Worcester County in Massachusetts, only about one-third of the houses had more than one floor. Likewise, genealogists and people who own old houses can use the assessment records to learn about ancestors and the condition of their homes in 1798.

Further reading: Paul Douglass Newman, *Fries's Rebellion: The Enduring Struggle for the American Revolution* (Philadelphia: University of Pennsylvania Press, 2004).

discrimination (tariff policy)

Starting in 1789, when the United States passed an impost to provide a national revenue, THOMAS JEFFERSON and JAMES MADISON advocated a policy of discrimination in TARIFFS that would set higher customs duties for those countries that did not have a reciprocal TRADE agreement with the United States. The idea was that these nations would be so hurt economically that they would have to negotiate a commercial treaty. GREAT BRITAIN was the target of the policy since that country became the United States's predominant trading partner after 1783 but refused to agree to a commercial treaty and would not officially open its WEST INDIES possessions to U.S. shipping.

Madison and Jefferson believed that a policy of discrimination would strengthen the United States. As Madison explained in 1789, Great Britain had "bound us in commercial manacles and very nearly defeated the object of our independence." Discrimination would counter these economic restraints by encouraging the development of U.S. shipping and force the British to relax its navigation acts. Jefferson also hoped that it would allow for increased trade with FRANCE, with whom the United States had a commercial agreement. ALEXANDER HAMILTON opposed discrimination because it would hurt the overall revenue raised by the Treasury Department and might lead to British retaliation, which would stifle the export market.

The Tariff Act of 1789 established customs duties without discrimination, but the issue did not go away. As secretary of state, Jefferson advocated a policy of discrimination in a report in 1791 and pushed these ideas even further in his "Report on the Privileges and Restrictions on the Commerce of the United States in Foreign Countries" in 1793. Jefferson wrote: "Should any nation, contrary to our wishes, suppose it may better find its advantage by continuing its system of prohibitions, duties and regulations, it behooves us to protect our citizens, their commerce and navigation, by counter prohibitions, duties and regulations, also." He concluded: "Free commerce and navigation are not to be given in exchange for restrictions and vexations; nor are they likely to produce a relaxation of them." Despite some support in Congress, however, this policy was not implemented. The war between Great Britain and France that began in 1793 altered circumstances dramatically to increase overall trade carried in U.S. ships during the rest of the decade. Moreover, JAY'S TREATY (1794), which established most-favored-nation status in trade with Great Britain but did not open up the British West Indies to uninhibited trade, was a refutation of discrimination. Later policy during the Jefferson and Madison administrations—such as the NON-IMPORTATION ACT (1806), EMBARGO OF 1807, NON-INTERCOURSE ACT (1809), and MACON'S BILL NUMBER 2 (1810)—that sought to use trade as a bargaining chip in diplomacy reflected the basic idea of discrimination.

See also FOREIGN AFFAIRS.

Further reading: Drew R. McCoy, *The Elusive Republic: Political Economy in Jeffersonian Virginia* (Chapel Hill: University of North Carolina Press, 1980).

disease and epidemics

Americans in the revolutionary and early national period were frequently exposed to disease and suffered from several epidemics. As a result, their lives were shorter and often marred by physical debilitation and personal trial. Many of the diseases, which remain unnamed, resulted from poor sanitation, unhealthy drinking water, as well as unidentified microbes. The two most common diseases were malaria and tuberculosis, but the two most devastating were SMALLPOX and YELLOW FEVER.

Malaria, often called intermittent fever, was endemic in much of the South wherever the anopheles mosquito could breed year-round. Creating recurrent bouts of fever, chills, weakness, and the shakes in its victim, malaria did not necessarily kill but left an individual susceptible to other illnesses. Most people with malaria struggled with the disease, attempting to maintain their work routine as well as possible. When there was no fever, they might function normally enough. If their hands started shaking or if they had an "ague fit," they had to persevere and move on. Because many AFRICAN AMERICANS had a hereditary sickle-cell trait in their blood, they were less susceptible to malaria.

Tuberculosis—or, as it was called at the time, consumption—was transferred by close contact when a sick person coughed or sneezed. The disease was prevalent in cities with crowded housing and workplaces. Consumption acted slowly, destroying its victim's lungs over the course of years. Although consumption became romanticized in the 19th century as a disease that struck young women, supposedly making them pallidly beautiful even as it stole their lives, the reality was often harsh. Tuberculosis had a devastating impact on poor families, removing breadwinners from gainful employment as one family member after another caught the disease and slowly died.

If malaria and tuberculosis were persistent and worked their harm over time, smallpox and yellow fever were episodic and virulent. Smallpox as a disease was on the decline by the end of the 18th century because of the practice of variolation—inoculation by purposefully exposing the blood of an individual to infected matter. A mild form of the disease produced with a much lower mortality rate than if the person had caught the disease naturally. There was some popular opposition to this method since it favored the affluent over the poor: Those with money could afford both the medical expense and the time away from work to effect the treatment. Moreover, poorer folk tended to fear that a person who was inoculated became a carrier of the disease to the rest of the community. By the end of the REVOLUTIONARY WAR (1775–83), with many men in the CONTINENTAL ARMY inoculated, objections decreased. In 1796 the English physician Edward Jenner found a safer vaccination based on cowpox. Within a decade, this form of inoculation had become widespread in the United States, leading to a further decline in smallpox.

Yellow fever, which had appeared occasionally in the colonial period, replaced smallpox as the disease most dreaded in the early national era. Like malaria, yellow fever was transmitted by a mosquito, but it was not endemic. Instead, the disease and the mosquito had to travel from hotter climates, usually the WEST INDIES. In the 1790s, yellow fever appeared in several U.S. cities with horrific results. Philadelphia in 1793, the worst year for the epidemic, lost about 10 percent of its population. The onset of the disease was sudden, and the affected person would feel ill, run a fever, vomit black material, and turn a telltale jaundice yellow. Mortality was high: Within days, sometimes hours, the victim was dead. No one connected the disease with the mosquito, but everyone knew that it struck only in the summertime and lasted until the first frost. Each June and July, urban denizens began to watch for reports of yellow fever, and at the first sign of trouble, masses of people exited the city. The poor, who often lived close to the waterfront, were left to suffer. Not every year brought yellow fever, but the experience became seared into popular memory. For decades after the outbreak of 1793, the people of Philadelphia would remember the call "Bring out your dead" and the procession of coffins in the streets.

See also MEDICINE.

Further reading: Jack Larkin, *The Reshaping of Everyday Life, 1790–1840* (New York, 1988); J. H. Powell, *Bring Out Your Dead: The Great Plague of Yellow Fever in Philadelphia in 1793* (Philadelphia: University of Pennsylvania Press, 1949).

Dismal Swamp Company

Twelve leading Virginia planters, including GEORGE WASHINGTON, organized the Dismal Swamp Company in 1763. The partners used their political influence and social prominence to convince the colony's council to grant them 151,000 acres of swampland—the Dismal Swamp—in southeastern Virginia near the North Carolina border. The Dismal Swamp Company planned to drain the swamp to make the land suitable for farming. However, the partners drained their own resources more quickly than they drained the swamp. The partners tried to grow hemp in the area, again meeting with little success, though some MONEY could be earned by cutting timber for shingles. The partners were also distracted by other land speculation schemes, especially in the West. In the meantime, the years of turmoil that accompanied the AMERICAN REVOLUTION scattered the partners and their heirs, with some becoming LOYALISTS and others WHIGS, leaving them spread across the Atlantic world. Yet the company persisted, selling timber and beginning a canal so that it finally paid a limited dividend in 1810. The old Dismal Swamp Company, which was a limited partnership, ended in 1814 when the Virginia legislature incorporated the Dismal Swamp Land Company.

Further reading: Charles Royster, *The Fabulous History of the Dismal Swamp Company: A Story of George Washington's Times* (New York: Random House, 1999).

divorce

During the 60-year period of the AMERICAN REVOLUTION, divorce was difficult to obtain in most of what became the United States, but by 1815 there were a few changes in law that eased some of the restrictions concerning divorce. Following English tradition, most colonial Americans believed that marriage was sanctified by God and that disrupting a family through divorce was a threat to social order. However, before independence, several colonies allowed their courts of chancery to issue legal separations for a variety of causes, including adultery; bigamy; desertion; and, in some instances, cruelty. These separations often included a support payment but did not allow either party to remarry. New England, a major exception to this trend, had laws allowing divorce that ran counter to English precedent and law. Massachusetts and Connecticut courts granted full divorces with the possibility for remarriage in large part because of the Puritan view of marriage as a legal contract rather than as religious agreement marked by ceremony. Despite Connecticut's liberal divorce practices and the possibility of divorce elsewhere in New England, the total number of divorce cases remained limited, with at most only a handful granted by the courts each year.

Shortly before the outbreak of the REVOLUTIONARY WAR (1775–83), the Pennsylvania assembly attempted to expand its power by authorizing itself to grant divorces in response to a petition to the legislature. Since previously this power had been wielded only by Parliament in England, the Privy Council guarding parliamentary prerogative nullified the law. The Privy Council also instructed all royal governors to veto any future colonial laws concerning divorce.

Independence altered the situation as each state legislature no longer needed to seek the approval of any outside power, and theoretically, legislative petition for divorce was now legal. Although permissible, several state legislatures hesitated to take any action, especially in the South, where, for example, South Carolina refused to pass any divorce decrees during this era. Other southern states acted only in the most extreme circumstances. Maryland in 1790 and Virginia in 1803 passed their first bills for divorce. In both cases the divorce was granted upon the petition of the husband after the wife had an interracial sexual relationship—something slaveholding males did frequently—and gave birth to a mulatto child.

Northern states were more willing to consider divorce laws. In 1785 Pennsylvania passed a statute that gave the state supreme court jurisdiction over divorce with the right to remarry for adultery. Other causes for divorce included willful desertion lasting four years, bigamy, and awareness before marriage of sexual incapacity. Legal separations could be granted for the same reason and also for cruelty. In 1787 New York passed a law that allowed the

Court of Chancery to grant a divorce for adultery, and in 1813 the state legalized the practice of granting separations for cruelty and abandonment. Massachusetts regularized its divorce procedure in 1786, allowing divorce for adultery and conviction of a crime with a prison sentence of seven years. Separations were still legal for desertion and nonsupport of the wife. Connecticut continued to have the most liberal divorce policies in the United States but passed a three-year residency requirement in 1797 to prevent people from out of state flooding their courts with divorce cases.

Further reading: Linda K. Kerber, *Women of the Republic: Intellect and Ideology in Revolutionary America* (Chapel Hill: University of North Carolina Press, 1980); Marylynn Salmon, *Women and the Law of Property in Early America* (Chapel Hill: University of North Carolina Press, 1986).

Doctor's Riot (April 13–14, 1788)

The Doctor's Riot in New York City was the largest urban disturbance between the REVOLUTIONARY WAR (1775–83) and the WAR OF 1812 (1812–15) in the United States. The riot began in response to public concern that the medical profession was using cadavers stolen from graves for dissection at Columbia College. When one boy peeked into the window of the medical school and later told his father he thought he saw the body of his recently dead mother among the cadavers, a crowd quickly formed and marched on the medical school. (One story holds that a student waved the arm of a dead body when he saw the boy at the window and, unaware that the boy had been orphaned, jokingly told him it was his mother.) The crowd stormed the college and destroyed medical instruments, captured and roughed up some medical students, and took the dead bodies kept in the school and buried them. When confronted by some officials, the mob surrendered their prisoners on the promise that they would be jailed and prosecuted. The next morning a crowd of several hundred reassembled and threatened more violence. The governor, mayor, and other officials sought to placate the people in the street by escorting some of the crowd on searches for more cadavers in the medical school and the homes of doctors. Popular rage, however, continued to build during the day, and the crowd threatened an assault on the jail. Officials called out the MILITIA, but not many men reported for duty, and several of them were quickly intimidated by the rioters. Supported by many community leaders, including JOHN JAY and BARON FREDERICK VON STEUBEN, 20–30 militia stood ready to protect the student prisoners. The militia fired on the crowd when it began throwing stones and attacked the jail defenders. In the melee that followed, three rioters were killed before the crowd dispersed. The next day militia arrived from the countryside, but by then the rioting had ended.

See also RIOTS.

Further reading: Paul A. Gilje, *The Road to Mobocracy: Popular Disorder in New York City, 1763–1834* (Chapel Hill: University of North Carolina Press, 1987).

Doolittle, Amos (1754–1832) engraver

Amos Doolittle was one of the most prominent engravers of the early republic. Born in Cheshire, Connecticut, he was trained as a silversmith and gained fame for engraving four scenes from the BATTLES OF LEXINGTON AND CONCORD (April 17, 1775). He and painter RALPH EARLE were part of a Connecticut MILITIA company to arrive in the Boston area shortly after the fighting. To fill spare time, the two went to the battle locations, and Earle captured the scenes in paintings, which Doolittle subsequently engraved. Later, Doolittle did engravings of most of the leaders of the AMERICAN REVOLUTION and several patriotic subjects, as well as maps and illustrations for books. He falsely claimed that he was the first engraver in the United States. While that was not true, he was an important engraver who helped to mold the popular image of the Revolution. He died on February 2, 1832.

Dorchester, Guy Carleton, first baron (1724–1808) British military officer, governor of Canada

An able administrator and brave soldier, Guy Carleton, first baron Dorchester, defended Quebec in the face of a Revolutionary American invasion in 1775 and 1776; he also served as governor of CANADA. Born on September 3, 1724, to a middle-class Protestant family in Strabane, Ireland, Carleton entered the British army at a young age and quickly advanced through the ranks through his courage in battle and use of good political connections. In 1758 and 1759 Carleton served under General JAMES WOLFE in the siege of French-held Quebec and was wounded in battle. He also took part in two other campaigns during the FRENCH AND INDIAN WAR (1754–63), at Belle Isle en Mer in the Bay of Biscay and at the SIEGE OF HAVANA in 1762, serving with distinction and being wounded in both campaigns. For his service he was made a permanent colonel in the British army, and after the war he was appointed lieutenant governor of the new British province of Quebec. Since the governor had been recalled, Carleton became the de facto chief administrator of Quebec in 1766. He was also made a brigadier general, and in 1768 he became governor outright. In Quebec he consolidated power in his own hands and sought to incorporate the French-speaking inhabitants into the British Empire. He supported the

Guy Carleton, first baron Dorchester, British military officer and governor-general of Quebec *(National Archives of Canada)*

QUEBEC ACT (1774) tolerating CATHOLICS, recognized French civil law in the province, and confirmed the land system that had been established under French rule. As the crisis with the North American colonies intensified in 1774–75, Carleton hoped that these policies would ally the French-speaking population to the British government. It may not have done so, but at least it convinced many Canadians to remain neutral.

When the REVOLUTIONARY WAR (1775–1783) broke out, Carleton had only about 800 regulars to defend Canada. Efforts to raise a MILITIA among the French Canadians failed, and MONTREAL quickly fell in November 1775 to a force under General RICHARD MONTGOMERY, who then marched his small army of 300 men to join BENEDICT ARNOLD on the outskirts of Quebec. In the BATTLE OF QUEBEC, Carleton beat back their combined assault on December 31, 1775: Montgomery was killed, Arnold wounded, and almost 500 Revolutionaries captured. Having sustained great losses, the Revolutionaries settled in for a siege. Carleton drove off the remainder of the Revolutionary army in spring 1776, then pursued the retreating soldiers, beating them again in the BATTLE OF TROIS-RIVIÈRES (June 8, 1776). He hesitated at Lake Champlain in his pursuit, waiting for the dismantling of a fleet on the St. Lawrence and having it rebuilt it on the lake. With these

forces, which had been greatly reinforced with troops under General JOHN BURGOYNE, Carleton gained control of Lake Champlain at the BATTLE OF VALCOUR ISLAND (October 11, 1776). However, he did not take FORT TICONDEROGA, at the southern end of the lake, and instead withdrew to Canada to await the spring for a renewed offensive.

Despite Carleton's victories, command of the army destined to invade New York—and ultimately to surrender at SARATOGA (October 17, 1777)—fell to Burgoyne. Up until this point Carleton, who was knighted and promoted to lieutenant general for his defense of Canada, had enjoyed strong political support in GREAT BRITAIN. But a political enemy, LORD GERMAIN, who had become colonial secretary in 1775, forced Carleton to resign as governor of Canada (June 27, 1777), and the general returned to England in summer 1778. Once in Great Britain he avoided any blame for the Saratoga disaster and was provided a government position in Ireland. He lived quietly until 1781, when he was called to return to North America and, as commander in chief, handle the negotiations for the removal of British troops and LOYALISTS at the end of the REVOLUTIONARY WAR (1775–83). Once again Carleton's administrative talents came to the fore. Having succeeded in this difficult and awkward task, he became governor of all of Canada in 1786. At the same time he was ennobled as first baron Dorchester. He remained governor of Canada until 1796, when he retired from public life. He returned to England and died on November 10, 1808, in Stubbings, Berkshire.

Further reading: George Athan Billias, *George Washington's Opponents: British Generals and Admirals in the American Revolution* (New York: Morrow, 1969).

Dorchester Heights, fortification of (March 4–5, 1776)

The Dorchester Heights is a series of hills lying to the south of Boston from which one can command a clear view of Boston Harbor. In 1775, after the British forced the Revolutionary army from Bunker Hill to the north of Boston (see BUNKER HILL, BATTLE OF), neither side fortified Dorchester Heights. During the winter of 1775–76, General GEORGE WASHINGTON, who had taken command of the armed forces surrounding Boston the previous summer, determined that the best way to force the British to evacuate Boston was to capture Dorchester Heights and establish batteries there.

Two problems confronted Washington. First, he needed artillery. This difficulty was overcome by bringing an artillery train across the snow and ice from the recently captured FORT TICONDEROGA in New York. Second, he needed to occupy the heights in one night to prevent

British interference. Since the ground was frozen, the troops could not dig regular earthworks. Instead, the Revolutionary soldiers prepared to build fortifications with logs and other materials and bring them to the top of the hills in one night. This maneuver was carried out the night of March 4–5, 1776.

When the British awoke in the morning, they discovered that their position was untenable in Boston. They either had to attack the entrenched Continentals, with possible results similar to the Pyrrhic victory at Bunker Hill, or evacuate. General WILLIAM HOWE had already determined to evacuate Boston. While he first contemplated an attack, he quickly gave up on the idea and merely accelerated his schedule for departure. On March 17, 1776, the last British ship left Boston harbor, providing an important victory for Washington and the CONTINENTAL ARMY.

Dow, Lorenzo (1777–1834) Methodist preacher

A successful transatlantic evangelical known for his eccentric behavior and appearance, Lorenzo Dow preached for the METHODISTS and espoused radical democratic ideas. Dow was born in Coventry, Connecticut, and raised as a strict Calvinist. A sickly youth, he had a conversion experience when he was 17 years old and began to espouse the idea that an individual had to open his or her heart up to God to achieve salvation. Dow started his career as an itinerant preacher in 1796. Over the next two decades he traveled the length and breadth of the United States, holding CAMP MEETINGS and converting thousands of people during the era known as the Second Great Awakening. He also made several trips to GREAT BRITAIN, beginning with a visit to Ireland in 1798. This journey antagonized Methodist leaders on both sides of the Atlantic and demonstrated Dow's own independent streak. His camp meetings in Ireland unleashed a debate in Great Britain over the value of using such events to find converts.

Dow had a radical faith in democracy. Taking THOMAS JEFFERSON's words to heart, he exclaimed that "if all men are 'BORN EQUAL,' and endowed with unalienable RIGHTS by their CREATOR, in the blessings of life, liberty, and the pursuit of happiness—then there can be no just reason . . . why he may or should not think, and judge, and act for himself in matters of religion, opinion, and private judgement." Combined with Dow's wild looks—he had long straggly hair and a great beard, worn-out and disheveled clothes, and a crazed gaze in his eyes—such ideas attracted audiences.

Dow would often begin a sermon by quoting THOMAS PAINE, and he would rail against more formal clergy, LAWYERS, and doctors. A formidable storyteller, he used gimmicks to reach his audience, including a hidden trumpet to echo the sounds of Gabriel, and he would feign his own collapse and death in front of the assembled crowds. In 1804, at the height of his preaching, he spoke between 500 and 800 times, and in 1805 he traveled 10,000 miles. His books and pamphlets went into countless editions. After 1820 he remained largely in Connecticut, living off the profit of his publications while also peddling "Lorenzo Dow's Family Medicine." He died in Georgetown, D.C., on February 2, 1834.

See also GREAT AWAKENING, SECOND.

Further reading: Nathan Hatch, *Democratization of American Christianity* (New Haven, Conn.: Yale University Press, 1989).

Dragging Canoe (1751?–1792) Cherokee chief

Dragging Canoe led a Native American resistance movement during and after the REVOLUTIONARY WAR (1775–83) in the rugged region of what is now the Georgia-Tennessee border. He was born a CHEROKEE while they were still a powerful force in the southern colonies, but little is known about his early life.

In 1774 a group of investors called the Transylvania Company bought a large tract in Kentucky from the Cherokee. This act infuriated the young Dragging Canoe, who told DANIEL BOONE that although the company had purchased the land, the white settlers would find that their new lands would be "a dark and bloody ground." He refused to recognize the sale and vowed to kill any European American who tried to move into the region. When the Revolutionary War began, he immediately sided with GREAT BRITAIN.

During the early part of the war, Dragging Canoe led raids on settlements in Kentucky and gathered a large band of nearly 600 men to attack the Revolutionary Americans living along the Watauga River. A MILITIA detachment foiled the assault, and Dragging Canoe received a leg wound. Realizing that his men could do better if they broke into small war parties rather than fighting in the European-American style, he ordered raids all along the central and southern FRONTIER. When he perceived that he needed to establish a secure base, he moved to the Chickamauga River Valley, where many warriors from different nations flocked to his cause; thereafter, the Cherokee of this branch were sometimes referred to as the Chickamaugans.

By 1778, as many as 1,000 SHAWNEE, Cherokee, CREEK, and MIAMI warriors fought under Dragging Canoe's leadership. When the CONTINENTAL ARMY sent a force under the command of Colonel Isaac Shelby to put an end to the raids, Dragging Canoe merely shifted his people to Chattanooga, and the raids continued in their intensity. The end of the war did not mean peace since he still considered the Revolutionary Americans to be invaders, and he sent men to attack the settlers flooding into Kentucky and Tennessee through the Cumberland Valley. The U.S. military eventually curbed some of his raids but never managed to stop them. He attracted the allegiance of many warriors who would later become famous, including TECUMSEH, who allegedly fought alongside Dragging Canoe at this time period.

Dragging Canoe died on March 1, 1792, undefeated. After his death, his followers joined forces with the Miami in Ohio and suffered defeat at the BATTLE OF FALLEN TIMBERS (August 20, 1794). In the years after the battle, Chickamaugans moved into Spanish LOUISIANA and joined their relatives, the Western Cherokee, in what is modern Arkansas.

Further reading: Thomas M. Hatley, *The Dividing Paths: Cherokees and South Carolinians though the Era of Revolution* (New York: Oxford University Press, 1995).

—George Milne

Drayton, William Henry (1743–1779) *South Carolina politician*

Scion of a prominent South Carolina family, William Henry Drayton was educated in England and seemed to be heading for a leading role in the colony after he returned home in 1763. However, his defense of the British government during the STAMP ACT (1765) controversy led to the loss of a seat in the colonial assembly. He became even more unpopular in 1769 for opposing nonimportation against the TOWNSHEND DUTIES (1767). Disgusted with being ostracized politically and economically, Drayton went to England, where he was introduced at court as a supporter of royal prerogative. He was soon appointed to the South Carolina Council, and it looked like he was on the path of preferment as a dedicated LOYALIST.

Once Drayton returned to South Carolina, however, he soon became disappointed when more offices did not come his way. Contributing to his change of heart was the Crown's Indian superintendent, JOHN STUART, who prevented Drayton's attempt to gain control of 144,000 acres of CATAWBA land. In 1774 he announced a complete turnaround in his position by publishing *A Letter from Freeman of South Carolina to the Deputies of North America in the High Court of Congress at Philadelphia,* in which he declared that "liberty and property of the American [were] at the pleasure of a despotic power." Opposing the COERCIVE ACTS (1774), advocating near-independence for the colonies, and supporting nonimportation, he was dismissed from the South Carolina Council in 1775. With even more enthusiasm than he had displayed in defending the king, he now attacked royal government. Drayton was elected to the provincial congress, became a member of the local committee of safety in Charleston, and advocated radical action. As president of the provincial congress, he called for independence as early as February 6, 1776.

In 1778 Drayton played a central role in drafting the relatively conservative South Carolina state constitution. That same year, South Carolina sent him to the SECOND CONTINENTAL CONGRESS, where he quickly became a workhorse, serving on more than 90 committees. In Congress he adamantly opposed any reconciliation with GREAT BRITAIN and fought to protect the interests of the southern states. Drayton died of typhoid fever in Philadelphia on September 3, 1779.

Further reading: Keith Krawczynski, *William Henry Drayton: South Carolina Revolutionary Patriot* (Baton Rouge: Louisiana State University Press, 2001).

Drinker, Elizabeth Sandwith (1735–1807) *diarist*

Elizabeth Sandwith Drinker was a well-educated, affluent Quaker who lived in Philadelphia during the revolutionary period. She is best noted for having kept a journal for 47 years that provides insight into society, culture, MEDICINE, politics, RELIGION, and the military presence in Philadelphia. Moreover, Drinker offered an account of a woman's place in society in the 18th century.

Raised in a family that encouraged intellectual growth, Elizabeth Sandwith lost her parents at a young age and in 1761 married Henry Drinker; they had nine children, only four of whom lived to adulthood. The REVOLUTIONARY WAR (1775–83) proved to be a hardship for Drinker and her family. In September 1777 her husband, along with several other QUAKERS who refused to support the war, was arrested and sent to Staunton, Virginia. After the British occupied Philadelphia, and while her husband was gone, Drinker was forced to quarter a British officer in her house. In April 1778 she and some other Quaker women journeyed to Lancaster to petition for the release of their husbands. To do so, they had to pass across British and Continental lines. They also stopped at VALLEY FORGE (1777–78) to meet General GEORGE WASHINGTON and his wife. Although he could not directly offer assistance, General Washington provided the women with a pass to Lancaster. In part as a result of this effort the Quaker men were released.

Drinker continued to keep her diary after the war, providing wonderful insights into the experience of women in this period and social conditions in Philadelphia during the early republic. Her descriptions of the YELLOW FEVER that struck that city offer a glimpse into the harsh realities of the shattering impact of disease. Drinker's ideas reflected the upper echelon of Philadelphia society and her Quaker upbringing. But her diary has proven an invaluable source for generations of historians. She died after a long and rich life on November 24, 1807.

Further reading: Elizabeth Sandwith Drinker, *The Diary of Elizabeth Drinker: The Life Cycle of an Eighteenth-Century Woman,* edited by Elaine Forman Crane (Boston: Northeastern University Press, 1994).

—Elizabeth Simpson

Drummond, Sir Gordon (1772–1854) *British military officer*

Gordon Drummond was born in Quebec but moved to GREAT BRITAIN when he was four years old. He entered the British army in 1789 and rose quickly through the ranks, seeing combat in Europe and Egypt. He served in CANADA from 1808 to 1811 and was in Ireland at the outbreak of the WAR OF 1812 (1812–15). In 1813 he again went to North America as the general in charge of the troops in Upper Canada and president of the provincial legislature. By the time he assumed this command, the British position had deteriorated with U.S. victories in the BATTLE OF LAKE ERIE (September 10, 1813), the BATTLE OF THE THAMES (October 5, 1813), and along the Niagara corridor. Drummond began to reverse the situation when he captured FORT NIAGARA on December 18, 1813. He centered most of his activities in 1814 around the Niagara River and beat back an invasion in the BATTLE OF LUNDY'S LANE (July 25, 1814). His effort to capture FORT ERIE on the Canadian side of the border where Lake Ontario empties into the Niagara River, however, ended in disaster when a powder magazine exploded just as his troops breached the fort's defenses. Subsequent fighting around Fort Erie led to more casualties and Drummond's withdrawal. The war along the Niagara ended in a stalemate.

In early 1815 Drummond became civil administrator and commander of all armies in Canada, a position he held until he left Quebec in May 1816. Knighted and promoted for his services, he remained in the military the rest of his life but did not see any further active combat. He died in London on October 10, 1854.

Duane, James (1733–1797) *New York politician*

A member of a prominent New York family, James Duane became a lawyer and land speculator during the colonial period. He invested heavily in land in the Mohawk Valley and in the area claimed by New York in what would eventually become the state of Vermont. Duane opposed the imperial regulation that began with the STAMP ACT (1765) but was a moderate in his position and did not countenance the mob activity in support of the RESISTANCE MOVEMENT (1764–75). Although he urged caution and measured steps,

he became a member of New York's COMMITTEE OF COR-RESPONDENCE in May 1774 and participated in the major Revolutionary committees formed in New York thereafter. He attended the FIRST CONTINENTAL CONGRESS and supported efforts at reconciliation, but he agreed to the ASSOCIATION, which set up a timetable for nonimportation, nonexportation, and nonconsumption. Duane was also a delegate to the SECOND CONTINENTAL CONGRESS from 1775 to 1781. He was not in attendance during the final deliberations resulting in the DECLARATION OF INDEPENDENCE, but he ultimately supported the break from GREAT BRITAIN. As he explained: "I resolved to share the fortune of my country; to be buried in her ruins, or at every hazard to shake off the fetters which were forged for her bondage." In Congress he worked on financing the government and supplying the CONTINENTAL ARMY. He also sought to protect his and New York's interest by blocking statehood for Vermont.

Having left New York City in summer 1776, Duane returned in 1783 to find that much of his property in the city had been destroyed during the war. In 1784 he became the city's mayor, a position he held for six years as New York began to recover from British occupation. In 1788 he supported ratification of the U.S. CONSTITUTION, and he became a federal judge in 1789. He retired that year and moved to Schenectady, New York, where he died on February 1, 1797.

Further reading: Edward P. Alexander, *A Revolutionary Conservative: James Duane of New York* (New York: Columbia University Press, 1938).

Duane, William (1760–1835) *journalist*

William Duane edited the stridently Jeffersonian *Aurora* newspaper in Philadelphia. He was born to Irish parents near Lake Champlain, New York, but moved to the British Isles at a young age. Trained as a printer, he went to INDIA in 1787 to edit the *Indian World* in Calcutta. Although the paper was successful, his attacks on the East India Company led to his deportation, and he worked as a journalist in London while he sought restitution of his seized property in India. Unsuccessful in this effort, he left for Philadelphia in 1796 and began to work for BENJAMIN FRANKLIN BACHE and the *Aurora*. After the YELLOW FEVER epidemic of 1798 killed both Duane's wife and Bache, Duane took over the editorship of the *Aurora*, and in 1800 he married Bache's widow Margaret, who owned the newspaper.

As editor, Duane made the *Aurora* the most important organ for DEMOCRATIC-REPUBLICAN PARTY (Jeffersonian) politics in the country, using it to attack the JOHN ADAMS administration, the QUASI-WAR (1798–1800) with FRANCE, and the ALIEN AND SEDITION ACTS (1798). As a result, he found himself assaulted by a mob of soldiers in Philadelphia who supported the FEDERALIST PARTY (May 15, 1799), sued for libel by political opponents, prosecuted under the Sedition Act by the courts, accused by the U.S. Senate of "false, scandalous, defamatory, and malicious assertions," and charged with contempt when he failed to appear before the Senate. Neither legal nor illegal actions, however, were able to silence his biting pen. He was a major supporter of THOMAS JEFFERSON in the ELECTION OF 1800, and the Democratic-Republican triumph of that year seemed to guarantee his future. But the removal of the nation's capital to WASHINGTON, D.C., left his paper at a disadvantage, and promised patronage was not immediately forthcoming. Duane remained active in local Pennsylvania politics, and eventually obtained a variety of government posts to supplement his income. He retired from the editorship of the *Aurora* in 1822 and traveled to South America. On his return, he became an alderman in Philadelphia and in 1829 became a clerk to the state supreme court, a position he held until his death on November 24, 1835.

See also JOURNALISM.

Further reading: Jeffrey L. Pasley, *"The Tyranny of Printers:" Newspaper Politics in the Early Republic* (Charlottesville: University Press of Virginia, 2001); Kim Tousley Phillips, *William Duane: Radical Journalist in the Age of Jefferson* (New York: Garland, 1989).

Duché, Jacob (1738–1798) *Anglican minister, Loyalist*

Jacob Duché was a member of a wealthy Philadelphia family who was educated at the College of Philadelphia (later the University of Pennsylvania) and Cambridge University in England. He became an ordained ANGLICAN minister in 1771 and was known for his spirituality and eloquent sermons as he preached to the elite members of the Church of England in Philadelphia. When the FIRST CONTINENTAL CONGRESS met, delegates turned to Duché as their chaplain, and he continued in that role for the SECOND CONTINENTAL CONGRESS. On first hearing Duché, JOHN ADAMS wrote his wife ABIGAIL ADAMS that the minister was "one of the most ingenious men, the best characters, and greatest orators in the Episcopal order, upon this continent."

Although sympathetic to colonial grievances, Duché was never really a Revolutionary. He preached to Congress but was torn by his loyalty as an Anglican minister to King GEORGE III. Perhaps he enjoyed the limelight, but he grew disenchanted with the Revolutionary movement and resigned as congressional chaplain in October 1776. As he later explained, he had viewed the DECLARATION OF INDEPENDENCE as an "expedient . . . thrown out in theorem, in order to procure some favourable terms." To his surprise, he later came to see that "independency was the idol" of Congress "and that rather than sacrifice this, they would deluge their country in blood."

Remaining in Philadelphia after the British occupation, Duché was arrested by the British but was then released after only one night in jail. On October 8, 1777, he wrote GEORGE WASHINGTON a letter insulting Congress and urging the general to repudiate the Declaration of Independence and negotiate directly with the British as head of the CONTINENTAL ARMY. Washington sent the letter to Congress, and it became public knowledge. Duché went from being admired to being despised, with John Adams declaring that he had "turned out an apostate and a traitor. Poor man! I pity his weakness and detest his wickedness."

A closer look at Duché's sermons and position before his letter to Washington suggests that he had never fully supported rebellion, and as a spiritual and religious being he hated all bloodshed. Regardless of what scholars can now see as consistencies, however, at the time he appeared a turncoat. He left for England soon after he wrote his letter, and as a traitorous LOYALIST—in the eyes of the Pennsylvania government—he could not return to the United States in 1783. Instead, he remained in GREAT BRITAIN and managed an appointment as chaplain to an orphanage. He also became a convert to the mystical message of Emmanuel Swedenborg. Duché finally returned to Philadelphia in 1793, and he died there five years later.

Further reading: Clarke Garrett, "The Spiritual Odyssey of Jacob Duché," *Proceedings of the American Philosophical Society* 119 (April 1975): 143–155.

dueling

Dueling was a practice in which two men (usually of the "gentleman" class) met at an assigned place and time to either fight with swords or fire pistols at each other in defense of their honor. This practice, only sporadic during the colonial period in British North America, became widespread during the REVOLUTIONARY WAR (1775–83) and continued as an important component of the military and political world during the early republic. The duel followed a set ritual. First there was an insult in which one party intentionally or unintentionally traduced the honor of the other, either through action or words. The insult was followed by communication between the two parties, usually in the form of a note or notes concerning the offense and delivered by a second party. If there was a retraction, the matter was at an end. If not, the exchange continued until the appointed place and time were set when the two participants would meet for the ritualized combat, which in North America was usually with pistols.

Dueling had a long history in Europe, and English law considered any death by dueling murder. Of course neither this English legal tradition nor local statutes prevented duels, though they was relatively infrequent during the colonial period. In 1768 HENRY LAURENS challenged a judge from the vice-admiralty court to a duel after customs officials seized one of Laurens's ships. A duel in 1771 led to the death of Peter Delancy, and a young JOHN JAY was ready to fight a duel in 1773.

What was a relatively rare practice before 1775, however, became almost commonplace in the military once the Revolutionary War broke out and there was the development of a professional officer corps in the CONTINENTAL ARMY. It was not just that these officers sought to model themselves on the behavior of the French and British; it was also that they were seeking some means in a democratic society to assert themselves as "gentlemen" who lived by a special code of honor that set them above the common man. Dueling also entailed bravado and helped to define an officer as both a man and a gentleman. In January 1779 one French observer wrote of the Continental army that "The rage for dueling . . . has reached an incredible and scandalous point . . . This license is regarded as the appanage of liberty". Despite being against the Articles of War, officers high and low fought duels: General John Cadwalader wounded General Thomas Conway in the mouth after the so-called CONWAY CABAL imploded. Lieutenant Colonel JOHN LAURENS fought a duel with General CHARLES LEE after the BATTLE OF MONMOUTH (June 28, 1778).

Dueling persisted after the war in both politics and the military. The most famous political duel was between AARON BURR and ALEXANDER HAMILTON (both had been Continental army officers) at Weehawken, New Jersey, on July 11, 1804. But there were many duels during this period, including one in which HENRY BROCKHOLST LIVINGSTON killed his opponent. ANDREW JACKSON shot Charles Dickinson (who had slandered his wife) to death after Dickinson had fired and Jackson recocked his own gun to shoot—an action that violated the dueling code and many duelists considered murder. Dueling became particularly popular with officers in the U.S. NAVY to the point that it became a serious problem. In 1820 the naval hero STEPHEN DECATUR was shot to death in a duel with JAMES BARRON.

There were many people who decried dueling as a practice, especially after the Burr-Hamilton affair. By the 1810s it had become a less accepted practice in the northern part of the United States, but dueling remained entrenched in the South as a means of defending honor and defining a gentleman.

Further reading: Joanne B. Freeman, *Affairs of Honor: National Politics in the New Republic* (New Haven, Conn.: Yale University Press, 2001).

Duer, William (1743–1799) *merchant, speculator*
Born in Devonshire, England, William Duer briefly served in the British army in INDIA before he inherited property in the WEST INDIES. While managing this estate, he developed contacts in North America who convinced him to purchase land in the Hudson River Valley in 1768. In the early 1770s Duer established himself as a merchant and landowner in the colony of New York. He did not involve himself in the Revolutionary movement until 1776, when he became a delegate to the New York constitutional convention, allied with the moderates. He also served on crucial extralegal Revolutionary committees and became a judge. From 1777 to 1779 he was a member of the SECOND CONTINENTAL CONGRESS, where he was active on many committees and solidified personal and business relationships with many prominent men. Even before he resigned from Congress, Duer used these connections to further his economic interest and garner lucrative contracts with the U.S. government and with FRANCE and SPAIN.

After the war, Duer continued his multiple business enterprises, which included land speculation, government contracts, and the establishment of the Bank of New York. In 1785 the Continental Congress put him in charge of the country's treasury. Duer continued to mix business and government service to his and his associates' benefits. Using insider information on the likelihood of the creation of a stronger national government, Duer purchased state and federal certificates at bargain prices. After the establishment of the new national government, ALEXANDER HAMILTON appointed him as his assistant at the Treasury Department but convinced Duer to resign in 1790 because he found Duer's financial machinations embarrassing.

The ultimate insider, Duer was a great salesman and businessman who was always rushing to the next project to secure his fortune. In 1792 he reached a little too far. While simultaneously investing in a Pennsylvania canal, a Boston bridge, and new banks in five cities, Duer also became governor of the SOCIETY FOR ESTABLISHING USEFUL MANUFACTURES. Convinced that BANK OF THE UNITED STATES (BUS) stock would rise rapidly in 1792, along with government securities used to buy the stock, Duer attempted to corner the market and borrowed MONEY with wild abandon from both rich and poor. William Livingston lent him $800,000, and he paid exorbitant interest rates to anyone who would extend him credit, including "Shopkeepers, widows, orphans, butchers, cartmen, Gardeners, market women, & even the noted bawd Mrs. McCarty." When the government asked Duer for $250,000 in unsettled accounts, and the BUS stock showed some weakness, he went bankrupt. Mobs in the street howled for their money, while Duer was thrown in debtors' jail—where he remained for most of the rest of his life. He died on May 7, 1799.

Not only did Duer's speculation create the first stock-market crash in the United States, but his actions contributed to the deepening political divisions between the FEDERALIST PARTY and the DEMOCRATIC-REPUBLICAN PARTY. It was as the frenzy of investment hit a feverish pitch in March 1792 that PHILIP FRENEAU began his extended newspaper attacks on Hamilton for supporting an alliance between government and the business interests.

Further reading: Robert F. Jones, *"The king of the alley": William Duer, Politician, Entrepreneur, and Speculator, 1768–1799* (Philadelphia: American Philosophical Society, 1992)

Dulany, Daniel (1722–1797) *essayist, Loyalist*
Born into a prominent Maryland family on June 28, 1722, and educated and trained as a lawyer in England, Daniel Dulany gained enduring fame for a pamphlet he wrote against the STAMP ACT (1765). During the colonial period, he served in both Maryland's lower house and its council and held several important offices. In opposition to the Stamp Act, he wrote a pamphlet entitled *Considerations on the Propriety of Imposing Taxes in the British Colonies, for the Purpose of Raising a Revenue, by an Act of Parliament* (1765). This essay attacked the notion that colonial Americans were virtually represented in Parliament. British politicians had argued that although colonial Americans were not directly represented in Parliament and elected no one to that body, members of Parliament virtually represented all subjects in the British Empire because they had the general welfare of everyone in the empire at heart. Dulany denied this claim and asserted that colonial Americans could not effectively be represented in Parliament and that taxation without REPRESENTATION was a violation of English common law.

If Dulany appeared as one of the foremost colonial spokesmen in the 1760s, he faded in visibility in the 1770s. He opposed the radical moves of resistance leaders in 1773 and 1774 and became a LOYALIST after independence was declared. Most of his extensive property holdings were confiscated during the war, and he died in relative obscurity in Baltimore on March 17, 1797.

See also LOYALIST PROPERTY CONFISCATION; RESISTANCE MOVEMENT.

Further reading: Edmund S. and Helen M. Morgan, *The Stamp Act Crisis: Prologue to Revolution,* rev. ed. (Chapel Hill: University of North Carolina Press, 1953).

Dunlap, William (1766–1839) *playwright, historian*
William Dunlap was born in Perth Amboy, New Jersey, on February 19, 1766, and moved to New York as a young boy because of his father's LOYALIST sympathies. Dunlap trained as an artist in New York and London, but he never became as skilled as some of his contemporaries. Having developed a taste for the THEATER in London, he was one of the driving forces behind establishing a theater in New York in the 1790s and early 1800s. He also wrote almost 30 plays and translated about the same number from French and German. Throughout his career he struggled to earn a living. While involved in stage management, he usually operated at a loss. In particularly hard times he returned to painting portraits and miniatures. He also wrote several histories and other books. While never personally successful, he knew many of the leading intellectuals of his age, and played a major part in the early New York stage. He died in New York on September 28, 1839.

Further reading: Joseph J. Ellis, *After the Revolution: Profiles of Early American Culture* (New York: Norton, 1979).

Dunmore, John Murray, fourth earl of (Lord Dunmore) (1732–1809)
At one time a popular Virginia governor, Lord Dunmore (John Murray, fourth earl of Dunmore) became infamous among Revolutionaries for offering freedom to African-American slaves who joined the British to secure their LIBERTY. He was born in Scotland to a noble family, inherited his father's estates in 1756, and became a member of Parliament in 1761. In 1770 he was appointed royal governor of New York, where his lavish entertainments made him popular with the colony's elite. Within a year he gained a better position through his appointment as governor of Virginia and became even more popular, and even named his newborn daughter Virginia (1772). Interested in the colony's welfare, he ordered the construction of Fort Dunmore at the forks of the Ohio (modern-day Pittsburgh). He also engaged in a war against NATIVE AMERICANS in 1774, defeating the SHAWNEE in what is now Ohio in a conflict known as DUNMORE'S WAR.

Despite these successes, however, Dunmore began to have problems with those who supported the RESISTANCE MOVEMENT (1764–75). He dissolved the House of Burgesses in 1773 because of its efforts to set up a COMMITTEE OF CORRESPONDENCE and did so again in 1774 when the burgesses declared a day of fasting and mourning after news of the Boston Port Bill arrived. He precipitated a crisis on April 20, 1775, when he seized powder in Williamsburg belonging to the colony. He was forced to back down and ultimately fled to a British warship for protection. He then began to organize a LOYALIST force to support him against the rebels. As a part of this effort, he declared martial law and fought several small engagements with Revolutionary forces.

On November 7, 1775, Dunmore made a controversial move that had a profound impact on the AMERICAN REVOLUTION when he issued what became known as Dunmore's Proclamation, offering freedom to all slaves and indentured servants who rallied to the king's cause. Many European Americans now felt compelled to join the rebellion to protect their social system and SLAVERY as many AFRICAN AMERICANS escaped from their masters and sought freedom by fighting for the king. Hundreds joined Dunmore, and thousands, in the spirit of the proclamation, escaped to the British lines during the rest of the REVOLUTIONARY WAR (1775–83). Although he had not intended it, Dunmore's proclamation helped to raise the issue of liberty for slaves during these years and contributed to the debate over emancipation that became part of the Revolution.

Dunmore's proclamation did not lead to victory. After being defeated at the BATTLE OF GREAT BRIDGE (December 9, 1775), he again fled to a British ship. After the BURNING OF NORFOLK (January 1–3, 1776), he was unable to gain a permanent foothold in Virginia and left the Chesapeake in July 1776. He later served in Parliament and as governor of the BAHAMAS (1786–96). He died on March 5, 1809, in Ramsgate, England.

See also ABOLITION; ANTISLAVERY; NORFOLK.

Further reading: John E. Shelby, *The Revolution in Virginia, 1775* (Williamsburg: Colonial Williamsburg Foundation, 1988).

Dunmore's War (1774)

In 1774 the colonial governor of Virginia, JOHN MURRAY, FOURTH EARL OF DUNMORE (Lord Dunmore), instigated a war with the SHAWNEE of Kentucky in an effort to secure their lands. Endemic violence between NATIVE AMERICANS and colonists along the Ohio River prevented Virginians from settling in the lands ceded in the TREATY OF FORT STANWIX (1768). Although various Indian groups were responsible for the violence, Dunmore blamed the Shawnee. His instructions to survey the western lands for settlement earned him support from Virginia speculators but also forced the Shawnee to defend their territory. In summer 1774, Dunmore arrived at FORT PITT with nearly 700 volunteers to prepare for war, while his agent, William Christian, organized another 2,500 men under the command of Charles and Andrew Lewis. The only major battle of the war occurred at Point Pleasant on October 10, 1774 (see POINT PLEASANT, BATTLE OF), where the two sides fought to a draw before the Shawnee withdrew, having been unable to mount a strong defense because the DELAWARE, IROQUOIS, and CHEROKEE all refused to help them. CORNSTALK's neutral Shawnee faction then agreed to peace at Chillicothe and signed the Treaty of Camp Char-

lotte, which ended the war and also established the Ohio River as the dividing line between Indians and European Americans. The treaty gave Virginia claim over the lands south of the Ohio. That move greatly upset other colonies, including Pennsylvania and North Carolina, who protested against Dunmore's blatant landgrab.

Further reading: Patrick Griffin, *American Leviathan: Empire, Nation, and Revolutionary Frontier* (New York: Hill and Wang, 2007).

—Patrick Bottiger

du Pont, Éleuthère Irénée (1771–1834) *businessman*

The son of PIERRE-SAMUEL DU PONT DE NEMOURS, Éleuthère Irénée du Pont was born in Paris, worked for a while in the French gunpowder manufacturing industry, and moved with his father to the United States in 1800 to escape the vicissitudes of the FRENCH REVOLUTION (1789–99). After his family arrived in North America, du Pont decided to produce gunpowder in his new country, but before beginning his business, he returned to FRANCE in 1801 to purchase machinery and study the process of powder manufacturing. The French government aided him, believing that an independent gunpowder production in the United States would only hurt the interests of GREAT BRITAIN. Encouraged by THOMAS JEFFERSON, with the assistance of ALEXANDER HAMILTON, and with capital supplied by his father and Peter Bauduy, a French émigré businessman from Saint Domingue, du Pont began building his gunpowder mill in Delaware in 1802 and was able to start selling gunpowder in 1804. With the U.S. government as a guaranteed customer, the new company under du Pont's direction earned an average profit of $7,000 a year, and by 1811 profits had reached in excess of $40,000. The WAR OF 1812 (1812–15) increased sales even further and guaranteed the company's future success. Du Pont became one of the leading businessmen in the United States after 1815. He died on October 15, 1834. In the 21st century, Du Pont de Nemours & Company remains a manufacturing giant, but it has diversified and produces a large variety of products.

du Pont de Nemours, Pierre-Samuel (1739–1817) *French essayist*

A leading intellectual in FRANCE in the second half of the 18th century, Pierre-Samuel du Pont de Nemours was a transatlantic figure. His *Physiocratie, ou, constitution naturelle du gouvernement le plus avantageux au genre humain* (1768) was an influential statement articulating the physiocratic position, which emphasized that "the rights of man, the natural order of society, and the natural law" meant that low tariffs and free trade between nations would be for the benefit of all.

After Louis XV suppressed some of his publications, du Pont de Nemours went to Poland in 1773 to become a tutor to the royal family and to organize the country's educational system. He returned to France when his fellow physiocrat Baron de Laune Anne-Robert-Jacques Turgot (generally known as Turgot) became naval minister of France in 1774. Although Turgot and du Pont de Nemours both fell out of favor at the French court in 1776, du Pont de Nemours continued to exert some influence and supported the independence of the United States. He also was a friend of THOMAS JEFFERSON in Paris during the 1780s and enjoyed an extensive correspondence with the Sage of Monticello.

Throughout the 1780s, du Pont de Nemours held a variety of government positions, and he became a conservative advocate of the FRENCH REVOLUTION (1789–99). In 1790 he was elected as president of the National Assembly, but he attempted to protect the king in 1792 and disagreed with the radical Jacobins; consequently, during the tumultuous 1790s he was imprisoned and almost executed. After the government closed his publishing house, he decided to emigrate to the United States, arriving with his son ÉLEUTHÈRE IRÉNÉE DU PONT at the beginning of 1800. After Jefferson dissuaded him from speculating in land, du Pont de Nemours opened a mercantile house in New York and helped to fund his son's gunpowder enterprise. However, in 1802 he returned to France, where he helped to facilitate the LOUISIANA PURCHASE (1803). He remained in France until 1815, when he again traveled to the United States, remaining until his death on August 7, 1817, in Greenville, Delaware.

Further reading: Gilbert Chinard, *The Correspondence of Jefferson and Du Pont de Neumours* (Baltimore: Johns Hopkins University Press, 1931).

Duportail, Louis (Louis Lebègue Duportail) (1743–1802) *French military officer*

An aristocrat and officer in the French army, Louis Lebègue Duportail agreed to join the CONTINENTAL ARMY as an engineer in January 1777. This arrangement was made in concert with the French government and had to remain a secret because FRANCE and GREAT BRITAIN had not yet gone to war. Along with three other royal engineers, Duportail covertly left Europe for North America. When they arrived in Philadelphia in July 1777, problems over rank and pay arose because of the large number of foreign officers who had been promised commissions by SILAS DEANE in France. However, General GEORGE WASHINGTON recognized Duportail's more official status and even-

French officer Louis Duportail was a key military adviser to General George Washington. *(Independence National Historical Park)*

tually appointed him as chief engineer of the Continental army. Duportail served in North America until 1783. At his urging, the SECOND CONTINENTAL CONGRESS established permanent engineering companies in May 1778, and this development led to the establishment of a Corps of Engineers in March 1779. He was vital to Washington in a number of campaigns, and although he was captured by the British during the SIEGE OF CHARLESTON (April 1–May 12, 1780), he was exchanged in time to command the engineers at YORKTOWN before its surrender on October 19, 1781.

After the war, Duportail returned to France, where he later became a general in the French army and secretary of war after the outbreak of the FRENCH REVOLUTION (1789–99). Closely associated with the MARQUIS DE LAFAYETTE, he had to flee radical revolutionaries and lived on a Pennsylvania farm until 1802, when he decided to return to France. He died at sea while on his way to Europe.

Further reading: Paul K. Walker, *Engineers of Independence: A Documentary History of the Army Engineers in the American Revolution, 1775–1783* (Washington, D.C.:

Historical Division, Office of Administrative Service, Office of the Chief of Engineers, 1981).

Duquesne, Ange Duquesne de Menneville, marquis de (1700?–1778) *French government official and naval officer*

The son of a maritime family in Toulon, FRANCE, Ange Duquesne de Menneville, marquis de Duquesne, was a midshipman in the French navy by 1713. He worked his way up to a senior command by 1752, when he was named governor-general of CANADA. The French government ordered him to drive British traders out of the Ohio Valley and assert the French claim to the region. In an action unpopular with Canadian residents, Duquesne drained the colony's resources to send a 2,000-man army to the West. This expedition solidified the French presence in the Ohio Country, forced the British from the forks of the Ohio, built Fort Duquesne (later FORT PITT), and compelled Colonel GEORGE WASHINGTON to surrender FORT NECESSITY on July 4, 1754—and in the process Duquesne set off the FRENCH AND INDIAN WAR (1754–63). In 1755 he stepped down from his position in Canada and returned to France, where he resumed his naval career. As an admiral he lost a battle with the British in 1758 and was captured. However, he retained the favor of the king and remained on active duty in various important naval posts until his full retirement in 1776. He died on September 17, 1778.

Duvall, Gabriel (1752–1844) *Supreme Court justice*

Born in Prince Georges County, Maryland, Gabriel Duvall grew up in relative affluence, was well educated, and began practicing law in 1778. By that time he had already held a number of important political offices, including clerk of the Maryland colonial assembly, clerk of the Maryland state convention, and clerk of the Maryland house of delegates. Although an active WHIG, Duvall had only limited military experience during the REVOLUTIONARY WAR (1775–83), serving as a muster master and as a private in the MILITIA. In 1782 he was elected to the Maryland state council and became a member of the state legislature in 1787. He declined to attend the CONSTITUTIONAL CONVENTION, although he had been selected as a delegate.

During the 1790s Duvall emerged as a supporter of the DEMOCRATIC-REPUBLICAN PARTY and was a member of Congress from 1794 to 1796 before becoming chief justice of the general court of Maryland. In 1802 President

THOMAS JEFFERSON appointed Duvall comptroller of the treasury, a position he held until 1811, when President JAMES MADISON named him to the U.S. SUPREME COURT. Despite a career on the high court that lasted until 1835, Duvall had an unexceptional record as a justice: For the most part, he voted with Chief Justice JOHN MARSHALL and did not write any notable opinions. For his last 10 years on the bench, Duvall was ineffective because he was ill and nearly deaf. He died on March 6, 1844, age 91.

Dwight, Timothy (1752–1817) *educator, Congregationalist minister*

Timothy Dwight was one of the leading intellectuals of his era, known as a conservative leader and as an important member of the FEDERALIST PARTY. Born on May 14, 1752, to a prominent New England family, he was precocious as a child and graduated from Yale College in 1769. Two years later, he returned to Yale and served as a tutor, but an intensive personal schedule of study ruined his eyes. Although he originally wanted to be a lawyer, Dwight decided to become a minister instead. In October 1777 he became a chaplain in the CONTINENTAL ARMY, but the death of his father compelled him to resign that position in 1779 to settle his family affairs. In 1783 he became pastor of a Congregationalist church at Greenfield Hill, Connecticut, where he also established a school that helped spread his fame as a preacher, author, and educator. He emerged as a prominent conservative spokesman opposing democracy and the DEMOCRATIC-REPUBLICAN PARTY (Jeffersonians) of the 1790s. He thought that writers such as Voltaire advocated infidelity, and he believed that the FRENCH REVOLUTION (1789–99) was a tragedy of global proportions.

In 1795 Dwight became president of Yale, where he remained for the next 21 years, educating New England's elite in his conservative ways. His enemies called him "Pope Dwight," while his followers looked upon him as a saint. A member of the famed CONNECTICUT WITS, he wrote extensively. Although his poetry was greeted positively at the time, it is difficult to read from a modern perspective. His most lasting work is a four-volume book entitled *Travels in New England and New York* (1821–22), which includes wonderful descriptions and insightful commentary on the areas covered. He died of cancer on January 11, 1817.

Further reading: John R. Fitzmier, *New England's Moral Legislator: Timothy Dwight, 1752–1817* (Bloomington: Indiana University Press, 1998).

E

Earl, Ralph (1751–1801) *painter*

Like many of the revolutionary generations's leading portrait artists, Ralph Earl had a transatlantic career. He was born into an established New England farming family in Shrewsbury, Massachusetts, on May 11, 1751, but he was not to be a farmer. By 1774 he had moved to New Haven, Connecticut, and was painting portraits at a time when many affluent New Englanders were interested in having their portraits done. However, Earl had to live an itinerant lifestyle, moving about the countryside seeking new customers. He reportedly visited Lexington and Concord in 1775 and made four paintings that became the basis of AMOS DOOLITTLE's famous engravings of the battles there. Although he married in 1774 and had children, he does not seem to have spent much time with his wife and family, and he apparently abandoned her, moving to England in 1778, probably because of his LOYALIST sympathies. Here he obtained some success, studying in the studio of BENJAMIN WEST, becoming a member of the Royal Academy, and painting a number of important people, including King GEORGE III. He also married for a second time and had more children before deserting his second wife sometime in the 1780s and returning to the United States. Once again he became an itinerant portrait painter, traveling through New York and New England. Despite his skill and reputation—ALEXANDER HAMILTON was one of his patrons—Earl struggled because of habits of intemperance, and at one point he was imprisoned for debt in New York City. He died on August 16, 1801, in Bolton, Connecticut.

See also ART.

Further reading: Neil Harris, *The Artist in American Society: The Formative Years, 1790–1860* (New York: George Braziller, Inc., 1966).

Easton, Treaty of (1758)

The Treaty of Easton marked a major milestone in the FRENCH AND INDIAN WAR (1754–63) since it neutralized many of the NATIVE AMERICANS in the Ohio River Valley who had been allied with the French. The treaty was the result of a council on October 8–26, 1758, hosted by representatives from the colonies of Pennsylvania and New Jersey and attended by about 500 Native Americans from 13 different nations. During the council the IROQUOIS played a central role: Through careful negotiation and subtle use of LANGUAGE, they managed to reassert dominance over the eastern DELAWARE and limit the influence of the Delaware chief TEEDYUSCUNG. This maneuver, in turn, allowed the Pennsylvania delegates to lay claim to the Wyoming Valley of the upper Susquehanna River.

More important for the war was a series of conflicting assertions that provided just enough ambiguity to allow for peace. Agents for Pennsylvania paid lip service to the old Iroquois claim that they "owned" the Ohio River Valley, while simultaneously accepting the right of the western Delaware and the other Ohio River Indians to speak for themselves in all future negotiations. In addition, Pennsylvania asserted that European Americans would not settle lands west of the Appalachian Mountains. This provision contributed to the reasoning behind the British government's later PROCLAMATION OF 1763. Armed with these legal fictions and vague promises, the western Indians agreed to peace. Underpinning the treaty was the fact that the Indians allied with the French had already paid a heavy price in the war and that the French were having an increasingly difficult time in obtaining supplies and gifts for the Native Americans. With the Treaty of Easton clearing the way, British general JOHN FORBES pressed on to the forks of the Ohio River, compelling the French to abandon Fort Duquesne (later FORT PITT) and opening the way for the British to dominate much of the North American continent.

Further reading: Fred Anderson, *Crucible of War: The Seven Years' War and the Fate of Empire in British North America, 1754–1766* (New York: Knoph, 2000);

Francis Jennings, *Empire of Fortune: Crowns, Colonies and Tribes in the Seven Years War in America* (New York: Norton, 1988).

Eaton, William (1764–1811) *diplomat*

William Eaton was an American diplomat in North Africa who sought to end the war with Tripoli by plotting to overthrow YUSUF QARAMANLI, the bashaw of Tripoli, and supporting an invasion in the name of Hamet Qaramanli, the bashaw's exiled and deposed brother. Born in Woodstock, Connecticut, Eaton ran away from home at 16 to join the CONTINENTAL ARMY. He graduated from Dartmouth College in 1790, served in the U.S. ARMY, and by 1792 had earned the rank of captain. In 1798 he was appointed consul of Tunis, where he renegotiated the 1796 U.S.-Tunis treaty pact.

In 1801 Tripoli declared war on the United States. Three years later, Eaton traveled to the United States to present his plan to Congress for a land campaign in North Africa to achieve peace. He hoped to defeat Yusuf Qaramanli in Tripoli and place Hamet Qaramanli back on the throne. According to Eaton, Hamet would be more friendly and easier to deal with than Yusuf, and America's problems with Tripoli would be solved.

Congress sent Eaton to North Africa in September 1804 as "Navy Agent to the Barbary states." He found Hamet Qaramanli in Egypt and gathered an eclectic army of mercenaries and Arabs. This patched-together force marched to Derne in eastern Tripoli (modern Libya) and took the city with the help of eight U.S. MARINES and a few gunboats. However, after the invaders occupied Derne, Eaton was ordered to leave because treaty negotiations had opened. In 1805 Tripoli signed a peace treaty that helped the United States assert its independence in the Atlantic world. The nation abandoned its ally Hamet Qaramanli, and Eaton returned home in 1805 embittered by what he saw as THOMAS JEFFERSON's betrayal of Hamet in favor of paying off a corrupt leader.

In 1807 Eaton was summoned as a witness in the trial of AARON BURR because of their close association, but he was able to clear himself of any wrongdoing. In December 1807 he won a seat in the Massachusetts legislature, but he was not subsequently reelected. He retired to Brimfield, Massachusetts, where he died on June 1, 1811, age 47.

See also BARBARY WARS.

Further reading: Robert J. Allison, *The Crescent Obscured: The United States and the Muslim World, 1776–1815* (Chicago: University of Chicago Press, 1995); Frank Lambert, *The Barbary Wars: American Independence in the Atlantic World* (New York: Hill and Wang, 2005).

—Charles D. Russell

economy

The rhythms of the American economy between 1754 and 1815 were largely dictated by war and revolution. During the FRENCH AND INDIAN WAR (1754–63), prices remained high as long as the British campaigned in North America. Dangers lurked on the high seas as French privateers and warships threatened Anglo-American TRADE, but profits could also be made if the French cruisers could be avoided. After the conquest of CANADA and the end of the war, two economic problems loomed, and both played a role in the RESISTANCE MOVEMENT (1764–75) against imperial regulation. First, and more short-term, there was a postwar recession. Without armies and navies eating up excess production, prices collapsed and jobs became scarce. Unemployment in the port towns led to general discontent and provided manpower for the mobs that opposed the STAMP ACT (1765) and TOWNSHEND DUTIES (1767). The second problem was more long-term. Colonial America produced raw materials such as lumber and naval stores; staple crops such as TOBACCO, RICE, and INDIGO; and imported finished and manufactured products. The result was a trade deficit that drained the colonies of specie and increased the overall level of debt. The specie shortage made exchange of MONEY for goods more difficult. Efforts to remedy this difficulty were stifled by Parliament's passage of the CURRENCY ACT (1764), which prohibited the colonies from printing more money. The debt was a product of colonial affluence: The more the top echelon in colonial society was worth, the more it borrowed to purchase luxuries from merchant connections in GREAT BRITAIN. By the mid-1760s, the debt had climbed to £5 million per year. Colonial Americans resented imperial taxation in part because they already saw their trade deficit and their debt as a form of taxation.

Trade and the economy did not rebound in the 1760s, especially with colonists proclaiming nonimportation as a part of the resistance movement, and the REVOLUTIONARY WAR (1775–83) only made matters worse. While the situation improved in the early 1770s, the conflict that arose after the BOSTON TEA PARTY (December 16, 1773) and the outbreak of war hurt the economy further. The cost of the war was staggering: Per capita net worth actually went down between 1774 and 1805. The decline may have been even more dramatic during the war and its immediate aftermath as trade all but disappeared and millions of dollars' worth of property was destroyed while both sides pillaged each other. Almost every city had been occupied by the British with devastating results. Many towns and villages had been attacked by one side or another, and all along the FRONTIER, from Maine to Georgia, there had been raid and counterraid between NATIVE AMERICANS and European Americans and between WHIGS and Tories. Thousands of slaves had run away from their masters, and millions of acres of LOYALISTS' property had been seized to help pay for the war. Armies devouring food may have driven up prices, but many people now struggled simply to buy enough to eat. Depreciation of the Continental currency did not help. Almost from the printing of the first bills in 1776, the value of the currency began to slide. In 1778 the currency depreciated to about 5 to 1; by 1780 Continental dollars had gone to 100 to 1 against specie, and by 1781 the currency was not worth the paper it was printed on. Compounding these financial woes were ballooning national and state debts from IOUs and money borrowed to help pay the war. It is almost impossible to follow this maze of debt, but the final bill for the war was approximately $165 million in real money—a phenomenal sum for the period.

The immediate postwar period did not bring much relief. The United States was no longer bound by British imperial restrictions, but in a world of mercantilist monarchies, it was difficult to find trading partners. Many Revolutionaries had hoped that FRANCE would replace Great Britain as an outlet for North American products and as a source of manufactured goods, but the French economy had its own problems and complex regulations and restrictions. British merchants, in the meantime, were all too eager to flood the North American market with goods and quickly reestablished the old mercantile networks. While allowing trade with Britain across the ATLANTIC OCEAN, the British closed their WEST INDIES colonies to trade with the United States. These export and import problems compounded a postwar recession where even local markets collapsed, and some people became desperate. Throughout the 1780s there were periodic RIOTS and crowds closed courts in the countryside in New England, Maryland, Virginia, and elsewhere, as debt-ridden farmers sought relief from lawsuits and tax collection. These rural uprisings reached a crescendo when many people in western Massachusetts, unable to pay their taxes or their debts, interrupted legal proceedings and participated in SHAYS'S REBELLION (1786–87). By the time of the CONSTITUTIONAL CONVENTION in summer 1787, the economy was beginning to recover. The new U.S. CONSTITUTION may not have made an immediate difference, but it did provide a framework for national economic policy. Secretary of the Treasury ALEXANDER HAMILTON sought to strengthen the federal government and promote economic development in the early 1790s with his plan for taxes, assumption of state debts, full funding of the national debt, creation of the BANK OF THE UNITED STATES, and effort to encourage manufacturing.

However rough the economic ride appeared, there was also a pervasive economic optimism that had begun to emerge in the 1780s and blossomed during the 1790s, releasing an incredible entrepreneurial spirit. Faith in the future could be seen in the great wave of land specula-

tion in western lands. A man like WILLIAM COOPER could wrangle a legal claim to vast tracts of land in northern New York State, use creative financing to entice settlers to sign contracts to purchase farms, and establish himself as the wealthy local patriarch. Often, such enterprise was built on a fragile foundation, but few people doubted that fortunes could be won by buying and selling land. The greatest of all these speculators was ROBERT MORRIS, who, before his financial bubble burst in 1797, created a spiral of debt and obligations covering millions of acres and left him owing his creditors almost $3 million. This positive vision of the future also spurred inventiveness and a willingness to find new ways to make money. ELI WHITNEY traveled to Georgia in 1792 as a tutor and became an inventor instead. In 1793 he developed a successful COTTON gin. Unfortunately for Whitney, the machine was easy to copy, and he never fully capitalized on it to make much money. Instead, he experimented with manufacturing rifles with interchangeable parts, and when he demonstrated to President THOMAS JEFFERSON the utility of this mode of production in 1801, he was on his way to making his fortune. Immigrant Samuel Slater memorized the workings of textile machinery in England; came to the United States; and, with the backing of merchants Moses Brown and William Almy, built a textile mill in Pawtucket, Rhode Island, in 1793. If Morris's and Cooper's house of cards collapsed, men like Whitney and Slater pointed the way for future economic development in the United States.

Beyond individual efforts, there also developed some important institutions that would have a dramatic impact on the economy. During the opening years of the early republic, investors increasingly turned to acts of incorporation to pool resources as a means to finance a variety of enterprises. One form of corporation was in banking. Besides Hamilton's Bank of the United States, individual states had chartered four other BANKS by 1791. Twenty years later, more than 100 other banks would be incorporated, creating millions of dollars in capital to be invested in the economy.

Although all of this entrepreneurial activity was important, during the 1790s what really turned the economy around was the war that broke out between France and Great Britain in 1793. Suddenly, markets that had been closed were opened. Not only could farmers sell their own products, but merchants could make great profits in the reexport trade. This economy, however, remained vulnerable. War threatened several times, and seizures of merchant ships occurred intermittently. These difficulties culminated in Thomas Jefferson's attempt to use trade as a policy of diplomacy. The EMBARGO OF 1807 began a tailspin in the economy that hardly stopped until the end of the WAR OF 1812 (1812–15). But there was an upside to this economic decline: With imports stopped, industrial production increased as more entrepreneurs built mills like Slater's. The economic ride remained something of a roller coaster throughout the early republic.

See also CORPORATIONS; DEBT, NATIONAL; FOREIGN AFFAIRS; LOYALIST PROPERTY CONFISCATION; PRIVATEERING.

Further reading: Paul A. Gilje, *The Making of the American Republic, 1763–1815* (Englewood Cliffs, N.J.: Prentice Hall, 2006); Alice Hanson Jones, *Wealth of a Nation to Be: The American Colonies on the Eve of the Revolution* (New York: Columbia University Press, 1980); John J. McCusker and Russell R. Menard, *The Economy of British America, 1607–1789* (Chapel Hill: University of North Carolina, 1985); Douglass C. North, *The Economic Growth of the United States, 1790–1860* (Englewood Cliffs, N.J.: Prentice Hall, 1961).

Edenton Ladies

On October 25, 1775, 51 women in Edenton, North Carolina, held a meeting in which they resolved to support their colony's opposition to the COERCIVE ACTS (1774). Forming an association to do the "duty that we owe not only to our near and dear relations and connexions, but to ourselves, who are interested in their welfare," they declared that they would neither drink tea nor wear clothes of English manufacture. This resolution shows the RESISTANCE MOVEMENT (1764–75) brought some women into the world of politics, and that involvement was triggered not only for the interest of their families—a traditional concern for women—but also for themselves. Moreover, the very fact that the women signed a document demonstrates an enhanced political awareness. The Edenton Ladies may have gone almost unnoticed by historians except for two reasons. First, the women had their resolution printed at the time, and second, a British cartoonist lampooned the idea that women would take such an action. In the cartoon of the Edenton Ladies, a dozen caricatures of women from different social ranks appear—including a slave woman. Many are in ridiculous poses, including one woman drinking from a bowl, and another more attractive woman being embraced by a well-dressed man whispering into her ear.

See also WOMEN'S STATUS AND RIGHTS.

education

Throughout the period between 1750 and 1815, education was most notable for its diversity. There was no common schooling system, much less any common experience shared by all children of a certain age. Children and adults were educated in many places, and their experiences differed by region, gender and class. This is not to say that no significant changes occurred during the period; after the REVOLUTIONARY WAR (1775–83), educators directly linked education to CITIZENSHIP and founded new institutions to serve civic needs.

In colonial America, the home was the principal site for education. Boys and girls learned not only the skills attached to running a home or farm, but also received their basic moral and LITERACY education from parents. The Bible and some religious tracts published for children were the primary texts people read; indeed, the Bible was the only book many families owned. In New England, literacy had a larger significance since Calvinists believed that each person should read the Bible individually. For boys, and especially for girls, literacy rates in New England were significantly higher than anywhere else in the British world.

Colonial homes often included people not directly related to the immediate family. In urban areas, ARTISANS—master craftsmen—took on apprentices at young ages. These boys were usually hired out by parents who wanted to provide their child with productive skills. The apprentice lived with the master, who was responsible for general instruction as well as the teaching of a trade.

Outside the home, churches were the primary formal educational institutions in colonial America. Ministers were called "public teachers" and were responsible for the moral instruction of their community. Most New England and southern states had an established church, and the community's attendance and support of the church was mandatory. In the middle colonies, religious diversity prevented domination by a single establishment; nonetheless, most residents gained moral instruction from their particular church. Although not all colonists were members of the established churches, especially in the western regions of the South, most agreed that ministers had a central role to play in educating the public.

Formal academic training was available to a few. Each colony had only one, if any, college, which trained ministers and prepared some children for careers as political leaders. While serving many of the children of elite parents, colleges also recruited children from middling backgrounds who showed particular promise. Apart from ministerial training, a college education was rare, and few students completed a full course of study. However, many students used college as a stepping-stone to a legal apprenticeship. There were no law schools in this period; college graduates had their legal education under the tutelage of established LAWYERS.

The AMERICAN REVOLUTION altered the ways in which individuals thought about education. Most important, Revolutionary leaders believed that access to education for all citizens was necessary for the preservation of LIBERTY. THOMAS JEFFERSON explained that since the people are the "only safe depositories" of power in a repub-

THE
AMERICAN
SPELLING BOOK;

CONTAINING,

THE RUDIMENTS

OF THE

ENGLISH LANGUAGE,

FOR THE

USE OF SCHOOLS

IN THE

UNITED STATES.

By NOAH WEBSTER, Esq.

JOHNSON'S SECOND REVISED IMPRESSION.

PHILADELPHIA:

PUBLISHED BY JACOB JOHNSON & CO.
NO. 147, *MARKET-STREET.*

1804.

Commonly known as the "blue-backed speller," *The American Spelling Book,* written by Noah Webster, was first published in 1783. *(Library of Congress)*

lic, "their minds must be improved to a certain degree." For Jefferson, improvement meant providing a state-supported common schooling system. In Virginia, he proposed a comprehensive school system consisting of different levels and culminating in a university for the best students. Although his plan was rejected, several states did pass mandatory schooling laws. The SECOND CONTINENTAL CONGRESS approved Jefferson's draft of the Northwest Ordinance of 1787, which required every town in the Northwest Territory to set aside some land for schools. Although the state-supported common school system really came into existence after 1815, many private academies were established to educate both boys and girls; these academies proliferated throughout the nation. In addition, many communities developed district schools, supported by tuition or subscriptions. Children ranging in age from four to 18 might attend the same single-room school for a few years to learn the rudiments of reading, arithmetic, and writing. Teachers were poorly trained and often harsh disciplinarians who struggled to control the older students. Since children were an important source of labor, attendance was often better in winter when there was less work at home than in summer.

Education was not limited to formal schooling. Leaders in the United States understood that regular citizens needed to learn less about Latin and more about what was called "practical knowledge." The rejection of formal knowledge was an act of patriotism. European aristocrats may have had the time to learn arcane subjects, but hardworking republicans needed knowledge that they could use. Moreover, idleness was seen as the breeding ground for vice. Agricultural and mechanical societies were established so that ordinary people could spend their leisure time not in idle amusement but learning about their fields of occupation. Educational leaders hoped to provide interesting lectures about SCIENCE that related to the work of artisans and farmers. Such institutions were meant to increase the knowledge of the population as a whole while promoting values associated with republican liberty.

Female education was supported by most leaders in the United States, and many female academies were established during the early republic. Concerned about the values of the next generation, revolutionary Americans understood that women, as mothers, played a vital role in shaping the character of their children. JOHN ADAMS explained that "it is by the female world, that the greatest and best characters among men are formed." As Adams suggested, female education was still centered on the needs of men. If only men could be full citizens in the new republic, at least women could gain access to education and fill an important public function as moral teachers.

College education changed dramatically during the revolutionary era and the early republic. By the mid-18th century, colleges no longer devoted most of their energy to training ministers. Moreover, affected by the ideas of the ENLIGHTENMENT, colleges broadened their curriculum to include more science and mathematics. However, throughout this period, classical languages remained the bedrock of a college education. College life was mainly for the elite before the Revolutionary War, with only nine colleges established in the colonial period, including Brown (Rhode Island, 1764), Dartmouth (New Hampshire, 1769), Rutgers (New Jersey, 1770), King's (later Columbia University, New York, 1754), and the University of Pennsylvania

(1755) in the decades immediately before the war. Like the earlier colleges of Harvard (Massachusetts), New Jersey (later Princeton), and William and Mary (Virginia), most of these institutions had a religious affiliation. The American Revolution led to several key developments. First, a college education took on new meaning as higher education now had the charge of developing leaders with the proper republican virtue. Second, there were many more colleges founded—as many as 15 started up before 1800. Third, this increase meant that a college education was open to more students from a broader spectrum of ages, social positions, and economic status. These developments, in turn, had ramifications that led to some problems. Because of the drift toward secularization in society and the fact that these colleges now had a civic role, there was an effort in several states to transfer control away from religious denominations to civil authorities. Most of the institutions so challenged—including Harvard College, the College of New Jersey, Yale College, Columbia College, the University of Pennsylvania, and the College of William and Mary—defeated these efforts, and after 1800, with the further spread of evangelicalism, the religious base of most colleges was secured, at least from attack by the state. But it was still challenged from below by the students, for whom the growing number of colleges meant greater competition, which in turn had a tendency to lower the standards for education. Moreover, with many older students entering college, and with the difficulty of recruiting qualified faculty, challenges arose in the classroom and on the campus. Student disruptions and even RIOTS broke out with increasing frequency. In other words, the end result of democratization in education did not lead to a better trained leadership, just more rough-and-tumble behavior and inferior education.

Despite the spread of academies and colleges, much education took place outside schools in informal voluntary gatherings of men called "mutual improvement societies." Members of these societies took seriously the need for civic education in a republic, and they would gather to hear lectures or give their own. Unlike the agricultural and mechanical societies, however, mutual improvement societies were subtly radical. By coming together in informal groups outside the established institutions of school and church, members of these societies took control over their own education.

See also REPUBLICANISM; WOMEN'S STATUS AND RIGHTS.

Further reading: Richard D. Brown, *Knowledge Is Power: The Diffusion of Information in Early America, 1700–1865* (New York: Oxford University Press, 1989); Richard D. Brown, *Strength of a People: The Idea of an Informed Citizenry in America, 1650–1870* (Chapel Hill: University of North Carolina Press, 1996); Lawrence Cre-

min, *American Education: The Colonial Experience, 1607–1783* (New York: Harper & Row, 1970); Lawrence Cremin, *American Education: The National Experience, 1783–1876* (New York: Harper & Row, 1980); Jürgen Herbst, *From Crisis to Crisis: American College Government, 1636–1819* (Cambridge, Mass.: Harvard University Press, 1982); Linda K. Kerber, *Women of the Republic: Intellect and Ideology in Revolutionary America* (Chapel Hill: University of North Carolina Press, 1980); Joseph F. Kett, *The Pursuit of Knowledge under Difficulties: From Self-Improvement to Adult Education in America, 1750–1990* (Stanford, Calif.: Stanford University Press, 1994).

election of 1789

There has been no presidential election where the outcome was less in doubt than the election of 1789. As soon as the CONSTITUTIONAL CONVENTION (1787) adjourned, it became common knowledge that the first president would be GEORGE WASHINGTON. Because we know the outcome, however, it is easy to miss both the election's suspense and its significance. In 1787 no one knew for sure if the U.S. CONSTITUTION would be ratified, and as late as July 1788, as New Yorkers debated the document, the future and shape of the United States remained in doubt. Since New York ratified the Constitution with the assurance that there would be a second convention to consider amendments, Washington, who wanted no reconsideration of the Constitution, was afraid that his vice president might represent the ANTI-FEDERALISTS' point of view or that Congress would be packed with men wanting to alter the document. When his friend JAMES MADISON was not elected to Senate, and two men with Anti-Federalist leanings chosen in his stead, Washington's concerns only increased. Ultimately, of course, there was no second convention, and the first 10 amendments, the BILL OF RIGHTS (spearheaded by Madison), brought no drastic changes.

Washington found himself in an awkward position during the election. He was preoccupied with his own affairs in a period where he found himself rich in land and poor in cash. He even had difficulty borrowing MONEY to take care of his immediate debts. On one level, Washington believed that he had already given his country his best years and that he should devote the remainder of his life to putting his own house in order. On another level, the presidency would be a great honor and another opportunity to serve the people, and it would alleviate his day-to-day expenses even if he did not accept the executive's salary (ultimately, Congress insisted that Washington accept a $25,000 salary, which was also to cover his expenses). Furthermore, the last thing that Washington wanted was for anyone to think that he was seeking office. He relished his reputation as the American "Cincinnatus" who had walked away from glory and power to return to his life as a farmer—or, in Washington's case, a planter who had slaves do his farming. Running for office would sully that image, so Washington avoided any semblance of electioneering. As he was inundated with letters from men seeking office once he was elected, he persistently sidestepped making commitments. While refusing to issue a statement that he would accept the presidency, he also made it clear to his friends that if selected as the nation's first chief executive, he wanted an overwhelming mandate from the electoral college.

The peculiarities of the electoral college as originally constructed in the Constitution dictated that each elector had two votes for the presidency, with the individual obtaining the most votes becoming president and the individual with the second-most votes becoming vice president (the TWELFTH AMENDMENT changed this process). Given the possible preference for state and regional candidates, it was difficult to predict the outcome. Moreover, it was possible for the individual whom many in the electoral college intended for vice president to end up with more votes than the man everyone expected to be president. The authors of the Constitution had created this system to ensure that the two most qualified national figures would become president and vice president.

The Founding Fathers also did not anticipate the development of POLITICAL PARTIES with a single ticket for both offices. No real political parties emerged in 1789, although there was division between the FEDERALISTS—those who supported the Constitution—and the Anti-Federalists—those who opposed the Constitution. This division, however, centered on the vice presidency rather than the presidency, which, despite Washington's studied aloofness, nearly everyone conceded to the man most already considered the father of his country. The issue of the vice presidency therefore became of particular importance since Washington was also talking about resigning from office once he got the ship of state successfully under way.

The Federalists, led by ALEXANDER HAMILTON, generally supported JOHN ADAMS for the position. Adams had played a central role in the day-to-day affairs of the SECOND CONTINENTAL CONGRESS early in the REVOLUTIONARY WAR (1775–83), had extensive diplomatic experience in Europe, and was a proponent of strong government. He also came from Massachusetts and would offer regional balance in the executive office, supporting the Virginian from Mount Vernon. However, while in the Continental Congress, he had a testy relationship with Washington, seeking to limit his power in an effort to assert civilian control over the military. Washington knew that Adams had caused him trouble during the war, and many Federalists were concerned that the two would not get along. BENJAMIN LINCOLN, Washington's main contact in Massachusetts, worked to alleviate any questions Washington

had concerning Adams, writing to the general that Adams was fully aware of every "virtue in your character which the most intimate friends have discovered." Washington's initial response was coy at best, stating that he did not want people to think that he was electioneering for office, that he expected the electoral college to select a "true Federalist," and that he would accept whoever was chosen regardless of his own "predilection." Despite such protestations, Washington came to accept the inevitable and, on January 31, 1789, told Lincoln that he had spoken to some electors stating that Adams "would be entirely agreeable" and that having Adams as vice president would "be the only way to prevent the election of an Anti-Federalist."

A few Anti-Federalists emerged as potential candidates. Perhaps the most important candidate for vice president who opposed the ratification of the Constitution was GEORGE CLINTON, the powerful governor of New York. There was also some support for JOHN HANCOCK from Massachusetts, whose position on the Constitution was lukewarm. Perhaps the biggest Federalist fear was that the Anti-Federalists, through some "malignity," would transfer a few votes to Adams and upset Washington's victory.

The selection of the electoral college was set for the first Wednesday in January 1789. Connecticut, Delaware, Georgia, New Jersey, and South Carolina had their legislatures choose the electors; Massachusetts had the legislature select all but two electors, who were voted on at large; New Hampshire allowed nomination of electors by popular vote, but the final selection was left to the legislature; and Virginia, Maryland, and Pennsylvania selected electors by popular vote. Since neither Rhode Island nor North Carolina had ratified the Constitution, these states did not participate in the election, nor did New York since the lower house was Anti-Federalist and supported Clinton while the Senate leaned toward the Federalists. As a result of this disagreement, New York did not select any electors or senators for the First Congress, and Clinton was deprived of 10 electoral votes.

When the Electoral College met on February 4, 1789, the final outcome was gratifying to Washington and distressing to the irritable Adams. Washington received a unanimous 69 votes (in addition to the 10 nonvotes from New York, two electors from Virginia and one from Maryland failed to cast ballots). Adams received a paltry 34 electoral votes since Hamilton had encouraged some electors to vote for other candidates to guarantee Washington's primacy, and other electors supported a wide array of candidates: JOHN JAY had nine votes, BENJAMIN HARRISON had six votes, JOHN RUTLEDGE had six votes, John Hancock had four votes, George Clinton had three votes, SAMUEL HUNTINGTON had two votes, James Armstrong had one vote, Benjamin Lincoln had one vote, and George Telfair had one vote.

The election, however, could not become official until the new Congress could meet to open the ballots. Scheduled to convene on March 4, both houses of Congress did not have a quorum until April 6, at which time the votes could be announced and notification sent to Adams and Washington concerning the election.

If Washington had any doubts about how the public would view his election and his return from retirement, they were laid to rest by his trip from Mount Vernon to New York City, which began on April 16, 1789. It was more of a royal procession than a passage of a civil official as great crowds showed up to greet him in community after community. Companies of horsemen escorted his carriage in such numbers that thick clouds of smoke enshrouded him, coating his clothes and making the passing countryside almost impossible to see. In Philadelphia as many as 20,000 people turned out to catch a glimpse of the new president. Washington was most touched by the display at Trenton, New Jersey—scene of perhaps his greatest and most desperate battle—with an evergreen arch decorating the bridge across Assunpink Creek and 13 young ladies dressed in white under a banner that declared "THE DEFENDER OF THE MOTHERS WILL BE THE PROTECTOR OF THE DAUGHTERS." When he arrived at New York City on April 23, 1789, he was shuttled across New York Bay in a specially built barge, escorted by a huge flotilla with banners waving, and saluted by roaring cannon. A week later, as the new government settled down to business, Washington was inaugurated on a balcony of New York's Federal Hall on Wall Street.

See also CONSTITUTION, RATIFICATION OF THE.

Further reading: Marcus Cunliffe, "Elections of 1789 and 1792," in Arthur M. Schlesinger, Jr., *History of American Presidential Elections, 1789–1968* (New York: McGraw Hill, 1971), 3–58; James Thomas Flexner, *George Washington and the New Nation (1783–1793)* (Boston: Little, Brown, and Company, 1969).

election of 1792

In many ways, the election of 1792 was a replay of the ELECTION OF 1789. GEORGE WASHINGTON was the resounding choice of the U.S. people, but he was reluctant to be seen as interested in the election. As in 1789, then, the real contest was over the vice presidency, although in this case the challenge to JOHN ADAMS was more centered on one candidate. Moreover, unlike in 1789, the incipient development of POLITICAL PARTIES had some impact on the election's outcome.

Congress altered the voting procedure for the election in March 1792, requiring that the electors be chosen in the month preceding the first Wednesday in December. On that day the electors were to meet in their individual states and vote for two individuals, with no preference indicating whom they wanted for president and vice president. This procedure was a concession to the expanding nature of the nation, which now included—in addition to the 10 states that participated in the first presidential election—New York, Rhode Island, North Carolina, and two new states, Vermont and Kentucky. The states would then send a certificate indicating their electoral vote to the presiding officer of the Senate before the first Wednesday of the New Year, and the votes were to be counted on the first Wednesday in February in Congress. The means of choosing electors, who were not pledged to support any candidate, were left to the states and remained a hodgepodge of popular election and state legislative selection.

The first issue concerning the election was whether or not Washington would serve a second term. Personally, he was tired of public office and had become disconcerted with the political wrangling in Congress and within his own cabinet. Washington even prevailed upon JAMES MADISON to begin to drafting a FAREWELL ADDRESS, which ALEXANDER HAMILTON would revise four years later, to serve as Washington's parting advice to his country. All of Washington's advisers urged him to serve another term, especially considering the severe challenges the United States confronted abroad and at home. Indeed, the one thing that rivals Alexander Hamilton and THOMAS JEFFERSON could agree on was how indispensable Washington was as chief executive; they even suggested that he could resign once the political and diplomatic situation had stabilized. When Washington did not announce his retirement by November 1792, everyone concluded he would agree to serve again. The electoral college rewarded him with its unanimous approval by giving him all 132 electoral votes—the maximum available to any one candidate.

The nascent FEDERALIST PARTY supported Adams as vice president. Even Hamilton wrote of Adams's impartial service to the nation and considered him "to be honest firm, faithful, and independent" and "a sincere lover of his country." Adams, of course, did no campaigning but awaited the outcome with some anticipation. The DEMOCRATIC-REPUBLICAN PARTY initially rallied around GEORGE CLINTON, although some flirted with the idea of supporting Senator AARON BURR. The Burr movement, however, never got much traction, and the final voting had Adams reelected with 77 electoral votes, with Clinton winning 50 votes. Jefferson picked up four votes and Burr one. The breakdown of this balloting, however, revealed some regional trends that would play out further as the first political party system developed over the next four years. Except for Rhode Island, which went for Jefferson as vice president, New England was solidly in Adams's camp. New York and Virginia, however, supported Clinton, as did North Carolina and Georgia. Although Kentucky voted for Adams, and he picked up most of the electoral votes in Pennsylvania and South Carolina, a pattern had begun to emerge where New England would identify with the Federalist Party, the South and West would become Democratic-Republican, and the Middle Atlantic states would remain contested ground.

Further reading: Marcus Cunliffe, "Elections of 1789 and 1792," in Arthur M. Schlesinger, Jr., *History of American Presidential Elections, 1789–1968* (New York: McGraw Hill, 1971), 3–58.

election of 1796

The election of 1796 was the first contested presidential election and therefore was a crucial test for the U.S. Constitution. Although there was no rule against being elected for a third term, by 1796 George Washington had had enough of elective office and was ready to step down from the presidency. Partisan bickering between the developing Federalist Party and the Democratic-Republican Party had become so intense that not even Washington was immune from personal attack. Benjamin Franklin Bache wrote: "If ever a nation was debauched by a man, the American Nation has been debauched by Washington" and "If ever a Nation has been deceived by a man, the American Nation has been deceived by Washington." Many Democratic-Republicans also portrayed Washington as a puppet manipulated by Alexander Hamilton and his minions. For Washington, who sought to be seen as above the fray and to claim for himself an Olympian place in history, such attacks cut all too deeply. In keeping with his previous practice, however, Washington maintained a studied silence about his intentions until he issued his Farewell Address on September 17, 1796, in which he cautioned against entangling alliances and warned "in the most solemn manner against the baneful effects of the spirit of party generally."

By that time the wrangling for the presidency had begun between the parties and even within the parties. John Adams recognized that he was a likely choice to succeed Washington, although early in 1796 he feared that both Thomas Jefferson and John Jay would gain more votes than he. However, by autumn most of the Federalist Party supported Adams and decided on South Carolina's Thomas Pinckney for vice president. Alexander Hamilton, however, had another idea. Recognizing that Adams had a strong independent streak, Hamilton developed a scheme to deliver the presidency to Pinckney by having the New England electors vote for both men and then have some South Carolina electors vote for Pinckney and not Adams. Word of the scheme leaked out, and several New England electors voted for Adams and any number of dif-

ferent candidates as their other choice on the ballot. (Each elector voted for two candidates for president, with the winner gaining the presidency and the runner-up the vice presidency). Hamilton's machinations probably cost Pinckney, who refused to countenance the ruse, second place and the vice president's office.

The Democratic-Republicans were less divided. Jefferson was the acknowledged party leader and was named to head the ticket. His supporters backed Aaron Burr for vice president, hoping to lure New York into their column and maybe gain a few dissident votes from New England. When the final votes were tallied, they managed to gain neither.

The election was nasty. Neither Jefferson nor Adams campaigned for office, and throughout the summer and fall, Adams remained ensconced on his farm in Quincy, hoping for the best but resigned to whatever fate might bring him. Like Washington, he wanted to cast an image of being above party politics and running for office. Jefferson stayed at his retreat at Monticello but took a more active, if no less invisible, hand in the campaign by keeping in constant communication with James Madison about political developments. But if the candidates appeared to remain aloof—Adams more so in reality than Jefferson—their surrogates busied themselves with slinging mud. Democratic-Republican newspapers charged that Adams really wanted to establish a monarchy and that he was an "advocate for hereditary power and distinctions," while Jefferson was "a steadfast friend to the Rights of the People." The Federalist Party press was no less sanguine, calling Jefferson a Jacobin and atheist. They also labeled him a coward for running from the British when he was governor of Virginia during the summer of 1781.

The procedure for the election was similar to that in 1792, with states choosing their electors in November and sending their votes by January to Congress, where the votes were counted in early February. Selection of electors also remained varied. Ten states (Tennessee, Vermont, Rhode Island, Connecticut, New York, New Jersey, Delaware, South Carolina, Georgia, and Kentucky) used the state legislatures to pick the electors. In effect, the election for the state legislature, whenever that might be, dictated whom the state would support for the presidency. Six states relied on popular vote (New Hampshire, Massachusetts, Pennsylvania, Maryland, Virginia, and North Carolina). In some of these popular-vote states, the canvassing was intense. In Pennsylvania, for instance, the Democratic-Republicans distributed 30,000 handwritten ballots, although only 24,420 people voted.

The results of the election were close and confusing. Adams won with 71 electoral votes, and Jefferson became vice president with 68 electoral votes. A total of 13 individuals received votes as electors split their ballots in a bewildering number of directions. Pinckney had 59 votes, gaining the support of all eight of South Carolina's electors, who then also voted for Jefferson. But all six of the New Hampshire electors, all four of Rhode Island's, three from Massachusetts, and five of the Connecticut electors supported Adams and then picked another candidate for vice president. These 18 electoral votes would have given Pinckney the presidency as Hamilton had hoped. Other states split their votes: Maryland gave Adams seven votes, Jefferson four, Pinckney four, Burr three, and John Henry two. Jefferson took 20 votes in his home state of Virginia, where Adams and Pinckney each received one vote. But because many Virginians did not trust Burr, the state also gave 15 votes to SAMUEL ADAMS, three to GEORGE CLINTON, one to CHARLES COTESWORTH PINCKNEY, and one diehard vote to Washington. The final tally beyond the top three candidates was: Burr, 30 votes; Samuel Adams, 15 votes; OLIVER ELLSWORTH, 11 votes; Clinton, seven votes; Jay, five votes; JAMES IREDELL, three votes; Washington, two votes (the non-Virginia vote was from North Carolina); Samuel Johnston, two votes; John Henry, two votes; and C. C. Pinckney, one vote.

To the modern eye accustomed to party politics, the results of the 1796 election seem bizarre. Not only were the president and vice president from two different parties, but a vice presidential candidate almost became president, and there were a plethora of candidates who garnered electoral votes. From the perspective of the Constitution's authors, and even from the point of view of Adams and Jefferson, the election was not so strange. The Founding Fathers did not want to see the development of POLITICAL PARTIES, and they hoped they had created a system that would guarantee the best and most talented men would be selected for high office. Adams and Jefferson probably were the two best men for the presidency, and the also-rans largely reflected a constellation of talent that would have pleased the men at the CONSTITUTIONAL CONVENTION.

In 1796 neither Adams nor Jefferson saw themselves as committed to a political party, and both—perhaps Adams more than Jefferson—hoped to remain above partisan politics. Noting later developments, one can see that hopes to avoid party politics were in vain and that this election marked an important signpost on the highway toward the development of a two-party system in the United States. To the participants, however, the election had a different and larger significance: For the first generation in an independent United States, the election marked an important transition from the presidency of an almost godlike figure—the father of his country—to mortal men. This peaceful transition boded well for the future of the republic.

Further reading: Page Smith, "Election of 1796," in Arthur M. Schlesinger, Jr., *History of American Presidential Elections, 1789–1968* (New York: McGraw Hill, 1971), 59–98.

election of 1800

In the election of 1800, Vice President THOMAS JEFFERSON defeated the incumbent president, JOHN ADAMS. It was a campaign and election of many firsts for the new nation as POLITICAL PARTIES dominated a presidential contest for the first time. The House of Representatives decided its first presidential election when the DEMOCRATIC-REPUBLICAN PARTY candidates tied, and it marked the first time in U.S. history that power was peacefully transferred from one party to another. The campaign was also noteworthy for the personal attacks against Jefferson and Adams. Jefferson's opponents charged him with atheism, while Adams was attacked for being a monarchist.

Democratic-Republicans united behind Jefferson as their candidate in the belief that a victory would rescue the principles of the AMERICAN REVOLUTION from the FEDERALIST PARTY. In particular, they argued that JAY'S TREATY (1794), the ALIEN AND SEDITION ACTS (1798), and the QUASI-WAR (1798–1800) with FRANCE proved that the Federalist Party wished to subvert the rights that had been secured by the Revolution.

Under the Constitution, states determined how and when they chose the members of the electoral college. In 10 states—New Hampshire, Vermont, Massachusetts, Connecticut, New York, New Jersey, Pennsylvania, Delaware, South Carolina, and Georgia—the state legislature chose electors. Thus, legislative elections were of particular importance in these states. Voters in Rhode Island and Virginia chose electors on a general ticket. In Maryland, North Carolina, and Kentucky, voters selected the electors by district, and Tennessee employed a combination of the district and legislative methods. The selection of electors for the presidential election took place from May to December 1800.

Federalists felt confident that they would win New England (with the possible exception of Rhode Island) and Delaware, and they believed they had a chance in South Carolina. Democratic-Republicans would safely capture Virginia, Kentucky, Tennessee, and Georgia. They needed to hold onto the South and win some votes in the mid-Atlantic states for victory. Because of the parties' sectional nature, the outcome of the election primarily hinged on the results in the mid-Atlantic states, particularly New York and Pennsylvania.

New York held its legislative elections in May 1800. AARON BURR masterfully assured a Democratic-Republican victory by capturing New York City's seats and thus the legislature for the party. In doing so, he outmaneuvered his longtime rival ALEXANDER HAMILTON and earned a place for himself on the ticket with Jefferson. Because of New York's national importance, Hamilton and others entreated Governor JOHN JAY to call the old legislature, controlled by the Federalist Party, into session to select the electors to ensure Adams's success. Jay, standing above party, rebuffed them and then stated that "I think it would not become me to adopt" such partisan methods. Though the election had hardly begun, New York was in Jefferson's column.

The Federalist Party caucused in early May and selected Adams and CHARLES COTESWORTH PINCKNEY of South Carolina as their candidates. Hamilton, distraught over Adams's peace overtures to France, worked secretly to arrange Pinckney's election as president. Once the electors in New England and the mid-Atlantic states had committed to Adams and Pinckney, Hamilton hoped that South Carolina's legislature would meet and provide an edge to its favorite son. At this time, there was no separate election for president and vice president. Each elector had two ballots, and whoever gained the most electoral votes would become president, while whoever had the second most votes would become vice president. Unfortunately for the Federalist Party, Adams began to suspect Hamilton and decided to purge his cabinet of Hamilton's close political allies. The president called Secretary of War JAMES MCHENRY, who had long had more loyalty to Hamilton than to the president, for a private interview and launched into a vicious attack on Hamilton for losing New York and undermining his authority. He accused Hamilton of leading a "British faction" and proclaimed him "a man devoid of every moral principle," a foreigner, and a bastard. He then forced McHenry into resigning. A few days later, Adams gave Secretary of State TIMOTHY PICKERING, another supporter of Hamilton, a similar dose of invective, and when Pickering refused to resign, Adams fired him.

These actions created an open split in the Federalist Party. Hamilton wrote a "private" letter, which he published to circulate among his friends, that lambasted the president as having "great and intrinsic defects in his character, which unfit him for the office of Chief Magistrate." These defects included unsound judgment, inconsistency, vanity, and "a jealousy capable of discoloring every object." It seemed inevitable that the Democratic-Republicans would get a copy of "Hamilton's precious letter" and publish it for the entire nation to read.

Even with all of this brouhaha, Adams still almost won the election. In Pennsylvania, voting became deadlocked because the Democratic-Republican Party–controlled lower house and the Federalist Party–controlled Senate could not agree on the method for casting the state's electoral votes. Finally, on November 29, the legislature agreed to split its vote by selecting eight electors from the Democratic-Republican Party electors and seven from the Federalist Party. In New Jersey, a legislature dominated by the Federalist Party chose Adams and Pinckney electors despite the fact that Jefferson would probably have won a popular vote. Ultimately, as Hamilton had suspected, the election hinged on South Carolina. Pinckney, however,

refused to allow the legislature to favor him over Adams, and after some strong politicking by the Democratic-Republicans, South Carolina gave its eight electoral votes to Jefferson and Burr.

By December 16, the nation knew the results of the election. Jefferson and Burr each captured 73 votes, Adams received 65, Pinckney won 64 votes, and Jay had one. Leaders of the Federalist Party would later call Jefferson the "Negro President" since the THREE-FIFTHS CLAUSE had contributed to the Democratic-Republican triumph by giving the region more electoral votes than it would have had if REPRESENTATION had been based on the free white population. (The rumors of Jefferson's sexual relationship with a slave, SALLY HEMINGS, gave the charge added meaning.) Even with the three-fifths advantage, the victory in the electoral college was not overwhelming. Moreover, since Jefferson and Burr had tied, the results created a new crisis for the nation. Following the rules of the U.S. CONSTITUTION in the event of two candidates obtaining the same number of electoral votes, the House of Representatives— then controlled by the Federalist Party—would decide the election between Jefferson and Burr, voting by state.

Nine states were needed to win. Eight states were firmly for Jefferson, the Federalist Party controlled six state delegations, and two states were divided. Burr would be crucial to any resolution, but he seemed to hesitate, neither proclaiming that he wanted Federalist Party support and the presidency nor conceding to Jefferson. Some members of the Federalist Party saw the deadlock as an opportunity to keep control of the presidency and deny Jefferson his victory, and hence they courted Burr. The House began balloting on February 11, 1801, and agreed to remain in session until the election was decided. Congressmen were working against the deadline of March 4, when the Constitution required the next president be inaugurated, and no one knew what would happen if there was no president by that date. On the first 35 ballots, the results remained the same: eight states for Jefferson, six for Burr, and two divided. As rumors of violence and the taking up of arms ran rampant, the governors of Virginia and Pennsylvania prepared their MILITIAS for conflict if the Federalist Party seized the national government.

Finally, on February 17, the crisis was resolved. On the 36th ballot, 10 states voted for Jefferson and four for Burr, while two states did not vote. (Federalist Party congressmen from Vermont and Maryland absented themselves so that their states could move to Jefferson's column). The lone representative from Delaware, JAMES BAYARD, who had previously voted for Burr, submitted a blank ballot. South Carolina did the same. There were several reasons for the break to the deadlock. For one, Hamilton, who detested Burr more than he feared Jefferson, prevailed upon other members of the Federalist Party to end their flirtation with Burr. For another, Bayard was convinced that he had received Jefferson's assurances regarding certain policies, appointments, and the removal of Federalist Party supporters from federal offices, although Jefferson later denied agreeing to these accommodations. Most important, representatives did not want to risk civil war and disunion.

On March 4, 1801, in a relatively smooth transition, Democratic-Republicans took control of the national government for the first time. A peaceful revolution had occurred, and in his inaugural address, Jefferson pledged to restore the principles of 1776. In 1804 the TWELFTH AMENDMENT requiring separate ballots for president and vice president was ratified.

Further reading: Stanley Elkins and Eric McKitrick, *The Age of Federalism* (New York: Oxford University Press, 1993); John E. Ferling, *The Tumultuous Election of 1800* (New York: Oxford University Press, 2004); James Roger Sharp, *American Politics in the Early Republic: The New Nation in Crisis* (New Haven, Conn.: Yale University Press 1993); Bernard Weisberger, *America Affire: Jefferson, Adams, and the Revolutionary Election of 1800* (New York: William Morrow, 2000).

—Terri Halperin

election of 1804

After the difficulties of the ELECTION OF 1800, when AARON BURR almost stole the presidency from THOMAS JEFFERSON, the TWELFTH AMENDMENT to the U.S. CONSTITUTION was passed to ensure that there would be separate balloting for the president and vice president. This new method of selecting the president would also avoid some of the confusion that had accompanied elections before 1800, in which a large number of candidates would garner electoral votes and states would split their votes in a wide array of patterns. The separate ballot for president and vice president was also a rejection of the original idea of the Founding Fathers at the CONSTITUTIONAL CONVENTION that the electoral college would guarantee that the best and most talented individuals would be elected regardless of party affiliation, and it marked a tacit acceptance of the development of POLITICAL PARTIES.

In the election of 1804, if the method of balloting represented some acceptance of party, Jefferson's lopsided victory—162 votes to 14—suggested a decline in party opposition. The president's reelection resulted from three main causes, two of which speak to the development, or lack of development in the party system. First, he had a fortunate first term and was therefore very popular with the electorate. Second, the DEMOCRATIC-REPUBLICAN PARTY was well organized for the election.

Third and finally, the FEDERALIST PARTY was disorganized and even considering secession from the union as its best means to survive.

Jefferson was fortunate on both the international and national front. When he took over the presidency, his predecessor, JOHN ADAMS, had settled the QUASI-WAR (1798–1800) with FRANCE. Shortly thereafter, France and GREAT BRITAIN agreed to the PEACE OF AMIENS, which, together with the *POLLY* DECISION in British admiralty courts, allowed the United States's neutral TRADE to prosper. France's inability to suppress the slave rebellion in Saint Domingue (later HAITI) convinced NAPOLEON BONAPARTE to sell LOUISIANA to the United States, thereby doubling the size of the nation. Jefferson was able to reduce spending on all aspects of government and lower taxes. Moreover, he seemed to speak for the common man, trumpeting the farmer and even the ARTISAN. In short, nearly everything went his way during his first term, making him unbeatable in the election.

The Democratic-Republicans, however, were not going to leave the election to chance. As early as February 25, 1804, they held a congressional caucus and nominated Jefferson for president and GEORGE CLINTON for vice president, Burr having been dropped for his role in the near-debacle election of 1800. The Democratic-Republicans also set up a campaign committee, with one congressman from each state, and state committees were organized, as well as some county and even town committees. These committees held local celebrations and parades to demonstrate their loyalty to the Democratic-Republican cause. Newspapers, too, were active trumpeting Jefferson's achievements and disparaging his opposition.

On the other side, the Federalist Party fell into disarray. John Adams, never much of a party man, was in retirement and not involved in politics. ALEXANDER HAMILTON remained active until his death on July 12, 1804, the day after his fatal duel with Burr. The party held no caucus, although in private they seemed to agree on CHARLES COTESWORTH PINCKNEY and RUFUS KING as their candidates for president and vice president. The Federalist Party lacked the local organization of the Democratic-Republicans in most communities, although they had an active press and would commemorate certain holidays, such as GEORGE WASHINGTON's birthday, with partisan celebrations where they had some strength in numbers. But in some sections of the country, their presence was all but invisible, and they had no issue of any significance with which to attack Jefferson. Instead, Federalists like Timothy Pickering discussed secession and the creation of a new country based on New England and New York. Pickering even encouraged the Federalist Party in New York to support Burr for governor in that state's April elections as a first step in this movement. (It was Hamilton's objections to this plot and Burr's candidacy for governor that led to the infamous duel).

As in previous presidential contests, the method of selecting electors varied from state to state, but the number of states with some form of popular voting for electors increased. Only Connecticut, Vermont, New York, Delaware, South Carolina, and Georgia had the legislature select electors. Massachusetts, New Hampshire, Rhode Island, New Jersey, Pennsylvania, Virginia, and Ohio held elections by the state at large, while Maryland, North Carolina, Kentucky, and Tennessee had either popular vote by districts or a mixture of popular vote by districts and at large. Since the Democratic-Republicans generally had their electors commit to a candidate before the vote—something the Federalist Party was reluctant to do—large number of voters actually made a conscious choice on who they wanted to be president, despite the electoral college system.

Jefferson, of course, viewed the election as a mandate for his policies. He also wrongly believed that the election spelled the end of political parties in the United States. As he explained to one correspondent: "The two parties which prevailed with so much violence . . . are almost melted into one."

Further reading: Manning Dauer, "Election of 1804," in Arthur M. Schlesinger, Jr., *History of American Presidential Elections, 1789–1968* (New York: McGraw Hill, 1971), 159–181.

election of 1808

On the surface, the story of the election of 1808 appears straightforward: Despite some resurgence of the FEDERALIST PARTY and the difficulties created by the EMBARGO OF 1807, THOMAS JEFFERSON's chosen DEMOCRATIC-REPUBLICAN PARTY successor, JAMES MADISON, handily won election to the presidency with 122 electoral votes to CHARLES COTESWORTH PINCKNEY's 47. This interpretation misses some key developments in presidential politics in the contest for the Democratic-Republican nomination and minimizes the volatility of the early republic's politics.

On January 23, 1808, the Democratic-Republicans in Congress held a caucus that supported Madison for president. This endorsement, however, represented not the culmination of the nomination process but merely its intensification as Madison, JAMES MONROE, and GEORGE CLINTON jockeyed for advantage and support among the Democratic-Republicans, and Jefferson, rather than anointing his friend Madison, generally remained aloof from the process. JOHN RANDOLPH, who led a faction of the party called the QUIDS, spearheaded Monroe's candidacy as much out of dislike for Madison as

friendship toward Monroe. Two days before the congressional caucus, Democratic-Republicans members of the Virginia legislature held two meetings; one nominated Madison, the other Monroe. Monroe's supporters then engaged in a series of newspaper attacks on Madison and the congressional caucus system. Other states also had multiple meetings of supporters with equally confusing outcomes as the debate over the nomination raged for much of the first half of 1808. Ultimately, Monroe's candidacy floundered when the diplomatic correspondence of his negotiations with GREAT BRITAIN became public and it became clear that the MONROE-PINCKNEY TREATY (1806), which Jefferson had refused to submit to the Senate, had violated Secretary of State Madison's instructions.

Clinton presented more of a stealth candidacy. At age 68, he was already considered by some to be too old for the office, but as he was the sitting vice president and a New Yorker, others thought that the presidency was his due. The two previous presidents had both served as vice president, and many people were already beginning to wonder about a VIRGINIA DYNASTY (GEORGE WASHINGTON, Jefferson, Madison, and Monroe were all from Virginia). Clinton also complained of the caucus system and gained support from his own state, Pennsylvania, and elsewhere. While several newspapers railed against Madison in support of Clinton, the aged New Yorker, with the aid of his capable nephew DEWITT CLINTON, somehow finessed being considered for both the presidency and vice presidency simultaneously. In the final electoral vote count, six New York electors even voted for Clinton for president, dividing their votes for vice president between Madison and Monroe. Clinton, however, won 113 electoral votes to become Madison's vice president.

The Democratic-Republican machinations receded into the background by the end of summer 1808 as the party faced a serious challenge from the Federalist Party, which had regained its control of New England and asserted some strength in several other states. As in 1804, the Federalist Party did not hold a caucus; its leaders simply announced in early September that Pinckney and RUFUS KING would be the Federalist Party ticket. The party's press attacked Madison as pro-French and anti-British, thought that Madison had been a failure as secretary of state, and considered the Embargo of 1807 a disaster. Yet despite the potency of these arguments, once the Democratic-Republicans fell into place behind him, Madison was able to slide into the presidency.

Further reading: Irving Brant, "Election of 1808," in Arthur M. Schlesinger, Jr., *History of American Presidential Elections, 1789–1968* (New York: McGraw Hill, 1971), pp. 185–246.

election of 1812

The WAR OF 1812 (1812–15), which broke out in June 1812, had a tremendous impact on the presidential election in the fall. Rather than attracting patriotic support for President JAMES MADISON and his reelection bid, the war's unpopularity and the United States's ill-preparedness to fight the war strengthened the opposition's appeal. Madison still won the election with 128 electoral votes to DEWITT CLINTON's 89 electoral votes, but had Pennsylvania gone for Clinton, the challenger from New York would have become president. The election also was notable for its impact on the development of POLITICAL PARTIES in the United States. On the one hand, both the FEDERALIST PARTY and the DEMOCRATIC-REPUBLICAN PARTY demonstrated increased efforts at local organization, especially in the mid-Atlantic states where the two parties competed most intensely. On the other, the willingness of most Federalist Party members to support Clinton, who was a dissident Democratic-Republican, indicates the porous political boundaries that retarded full party development.

Virginia Democratic-Republicans moved quickly in 1812, holding a caucus in February to nominate Madison and hoping to prevent a challenge from the Clintonians. (GEORGE CLINTON was still vice president, although he would die on April 20, 1812, leaving his political mantle to his nephew DeWitt.) A Pennsylvania caucus in March supported the Madison nomination, followed on May 18 by a national congressional caucus, which also nominated Madison. Despite the steamroller effect of these actions, New York's legislature met in a caucus on May 29 and nominated DeWitt Clinton, who thought the war was foolish and the Madison administration's waging of the war inept.

In the meantime, the Federalist Party looked for a candidate. Several leaders considered JOHN MARSHALL, believing he might get some votes from Virginia and the South, but this idea did not garner much support. Over the course of the summer, more and more members of the Federalist Party gravitated to the idea of supporting Clinton as a fusion candidate. On September 15, 1812, the Federalist Party met in New York in a convention, which they claimed was more reflective of the people's will than a caucus of legislators, and decided not to name any candidate, though the party urged supporters to work to select electors who would vote for a change. In short, without saying so, the convention was pro-Clinton. Dissident members of the Federalist Party from Virginia held their own meeting on September 21, probably in ignorance of the outcome of the New York convention, and nominated RUFUS KING as their candidate. King, however, received little support outside of Virginia.

As the selection of the electoral college approached in November, there were two Democratic-Republican candidates: the sitting president and Clinton, who was silently endorsed by the Federalist Party. To add to the confusion, Clinton's appeal was Janus-faced: He appeared to be antiwar in New England, where the conflict was extremely unpopular, while appearing pro-war elsewhere as he called for a more vigorous prosecution of the conflict with GREAT BRITAIN.

Electors, of course, were chosen in a variety of ways depending on state laws. Some states, such as New York and North Carolina, even changed their method of choosing electors to guarantee a partisan outcome. In the competitive mid-Atlantic states, local political clubs from both parties sought to organize voters. In the final tally, New England, except for Vermont, went for Clinton. New York, thanks to the machinations of a young and rising political star named Martin Van Buren, also went to Clinton, and last-minute maneuvering brought New Jersey into Clinton's camp. Maryland, in part as a negative reaction to the Democratic-Republican mob in the BALTIMORE RIOTS of that summer, split its vote, with six going for Madison and five for Clinton. However, Clinton, despite hopes to do otherwise, did not even run close in Pennsylvania, which selected electors by popular vote, while the South and West went solidly for Madison.

Further reading: Norman K. Risjord, "Election of 1812," in Arthur M. Schlesinger, Jr., *History of American Presidential Elections, 1789–1968* (New York: McGraw Hill, 1971), 249–296.

electricity

Though electricity in static form had been understood since antiquity (the base word *electricus* means amber-like, from its property of attraction after being rubbed), by the end of the 18th century experimentation had yielded only a few isolated facts about this elemental force. Nonetheless, the subject was regarded as important and potentially useful, if not susceptible to easy comprehension. BENJAMIN FRANKLIN was the principal electrician of his age and made the greatest theoretical discoveries about electricity in the 18th century. His abstract theorizing and concretely applied technology transformed him into an internationally famous man of SCIENCE, and gave North America some standing in the scientific community.

It was not long after the Library Company, a subscription library founded by Franklin in Philadelphia, received pamphlets on electricity and scientific equipment sent by Peter Collinson in 1745 that Franklin admitted to being "immersed in electrical experimentation". He theorized that electricity was a single force, or "fluid," under two different pressures rather than two separate forces, and he was the first to identify positive and negative poles in electricity. Franklin's analyses led him to the crucially important theoretical breakthrough of identifying lightning as electricity, and this allowed him to propose one of the most valuable innovations of the 18th century—the lightning rod. This invention was widely adopted as an effective means of protecting life and property from lightning strikes.

Despite the subject's intractability, and the lack of outright immediate utility for this "subtle fluid," research into electricity's properties remained steady during the second half of the 18th century. Indeed, electrical lectures and demonstrations were enjoyed as fashionable diversions well into the 19th century. Their appeal stemmed in part from the showmanship associated with scientific exhibitions that included parlor tricks such as using electricity to make hair stand on end, shoot sparks from observers' eyes, and disturbing acts of casual cruelty such as the instantaneous electrocution of barnyard animals.

The hope of exploiting electricity's intrinsic promise helped keep interest in it keen. The discovery of naturally electrified animals also contributed to the widespread interest; electric eels were marveled at and imported in large quantities in order to be studied extensively. While the lightning rod was the one truly useful application to emerge from all the experimentation, planters in the WEST INDIES quickly adopted the electrical apparatus as a means of driving and punishing their slaves. On the mainland, electricity came to be viewed less as a punitive force and more as a health cure. In the decades after the REVOLUTIONARY WAR (1775–83), electricity spawned an entire industry of itinerant "electrotherapists" to cure nervous tensions. Practitioners also offered to heal "palsy, rheumatism" as well as to ease "head ache, tooth ache, sore throat, burns and scalds." Promoted as a wholesome, safe, and effective cure for a variety of ailments, courses of electrical shocks were sought as a modern palliative to age-old infirmities.

Well into the 19th century, despite the high hopes vested in the subject by both researchers and consumers, commentators were forced to acknowledge that electricity remained a powerful but ultimately mysterious force.

Further reading: Bernard I. Cohen, *Benjamin Franklin's Science* (Cambridge, Mass.: Harvard University Press, 1990); James Delbourgo, *A Most Amazing Scene of Wonders: Electricity and Enlightenment in Early America* (Cambridge, Mass.: Harvard University Press, 2006); John L. Heilbron, *Electricity in the Seventeenth and Eighteenth Centuries: A Study in Early Modern Physics* (Berkeley: University of California Press, 1979).

—Robyn Davis McMillin

Eleventh Amendment

Many people in the United States considered the SUPREME COURT decision in *CHISHOLM V. GEORGIA* (1793) a viola-

tion of state sovereignty since it allowed an individual in one state to sue another state in federal court without that state's permission. On the same day the Supreme Court rendered this decision, February 19, 1793, an amendment to the U.S. CONSTITUTION against such action was submitted to the House of Representatives. Although this measure did not succeed, the Senate passed a similar amendment on January 14, 1794, which was then agreed to by the House on March 4, 1794. State ratification took less than a year—an amazingly fast time for an amendment—and it was proclaimed a part of the Constitution on January 8, 1798. The short amendment states: "The Judicial power of the United States shall not be construed to extend to any suit in law or equity, commenced or prosecuted against one of the United States by Citizens of another State, or by Citizens or Subjects of any Foreign State." It has also been interpreted as preventing an individual from suing a state in federal court without that state's consent.

Further reading: Doyle Mathis, "*Chisholm v. Georgia:* Background and Settlement," *Journal of American History* 54 (1967): 19–29.

Ellery, William (1727–1820) *Rhode Island politician*

Born in Newport, Rhode Island, William Ellery graduated from Harvard in 1747 and thereafter tried his hand at many ventures. After inheriting a fortune in the 1760s, he devoted himself to politics, and he became a supporter of the RESISTANCE MOVEMENT (1764–75). In 1776 the Rhode Island General Assembly elected Ellery to the SECOND CONTINENTAL CONGRESS, where he signed the DECLARATION OF INDEPENDENCE. He served in Congress for almost 10 years and sat on numerous committees—no less than 14 in 1777 and 1778 alone. His most important work was carried out on the committees for commerce and for the organization of a navy. He was a strong supporter of the CONTINENTAL NAVY, arguing that it should consist of smaller frigates that could disrupt British supply and commercial lines in the ATLANTIC OCEAN—a policy that Congress ultimately accepted.

After his retirement from Congress in 1785, Ellery moved back to Rhode Island, where he had to rebuild his home, which had been destroyed during the British occupation of Newport. Although initially he believed in STATES' RIGHTS, he became disgusted with the factious nature of Rhode Island politics and therefore supported the U.S. CONSTITUTION. In 1790 President GEORGE WASHINGTON appointed him customs collector for the district of Newport. Thomas Jefferson retained Ellery in this position after the ELECTION OF 1800, even though he was affiliated with the FEDERALIST PARTY, and he served as customs collector until his death on February 15, 1820.

Further reading: William M. Fowler, Jr., *William Ellery: A Rhode Island Politico and Lord of Admiralty* (Metuchen, N.J.: Scarecrow Press, 1973).

—Charles D. Russell

Ellsworth, Oliver (1745–1807) *Connecticut politician, third chief justice of the U.S. Supreme Court*
Oliver Ellsworth was a prominent lawyer, legislator, judge, and member of the FEDERALIST PARTY. Born in 1745 to a prosperous Connecticut family, Ellsworth studied at Yale and then the College of New Jersey (later Princeton), from which he graduated in 1766. He abandoned his study of theology for law and was admitted to the Connecticut bar in 1771. With a prospering law practice, he soon became a wealthy and influential member of the community. He was a member of the state general assembly from 1773 to 1776, and in 1777 he was appointed state attorney general for Hartford County.

During the REVOLUTIONARY WAR (1775–83), Ellsworth represented Connecticut in the SECOND CONTINENTAL CONGRESS from 1778 to 1783, and he was one of the five members of the committee in Connecticut that managed the state's wartime finances. He oversaw other military affairs of the state as a member of the governor's council from 1780 to 1785. In 1785 he was appointed a judge of the Connecticut Superior Court, a position he held until 1789. At the CONSTITUTIONAL CONVENTION in 1787, with his fellow delegates ROGER SHERMAN and WILLIAM SAMUEL JOHNSON, Ellsworth developed the Connecticut Compromise, which provided for a bicameral legislature with REPRESENTATION based on population in the lower house and equal representation for each state in the Senate. He was also a member of the committee that prepared the first draft of the U.S. CONSTITUTION; by his amendment, the name *national* government was replaced by *United States.*

Ellsworth's belief in a strong centralized government and his loyalty to the sectional interests of New England drew him to the Federalist Party. As a U.S. senator for Connecticut from 1789 to 1796, he supported ALEXANDER HAMILTON's financial plan. One of Ellsworth's most important works as a legislator was the JUDICIARY ACT OF 1789. In 1796 he became the third chief justice of the U.S. SUPREME COURT, following JOHN RUTLEDGE, and in 1800 he was succeeded by JOHN MARSHALL. From 1799 to 1800, Ellsworth also worked as commissioner to FRANCE. In failing health, he returned to Connecticut, retired from public life, and died seven years later, on November 26, 1807.

Further reading: William Garrott Brown, *The Life of Oliver Ellsworth* (New York: Macmillan Company, 1905).

—Mary Kaszynski

Ely, Samuel Cullick (1740–1797?) *political activist*
Educated at Yale College for the ministry, the Connecticut-born Samuel Cullick Ely became a popular leader opposed to what he saw as the autocratic state governments in New England; he has sometimes been seen as a forerunner of DANIEL SHAYS. Early in 1782 he lambasted the Massachusetts state government, declaring that the state constitution should be thrown out, and he was charged with "treasonable practices" for his outbursts. In April 1782 a club-wielding Ely led an attempted interruption of court proceedings in Northampton, Massachusetts, claiming that he would rather challenge the authority of the state government than King GEORGE III. Officials arrested and imprisoned him, but he remained popular, and on June 13, 1782, about 120 people gathered in Northampton and rescued him from jail. After he escaped, Ely went to Vermont, where in July 1782 he challenged the nascent state government of the GREEN MOUNTAIN BOYS, declaring that "the State of Vermont is a damned State" and that a recent tax was "a cursed act." He also called the assembly "a cursed body of men" and a "pack of villains," and threatened to overturn the government. He was arrested, tried, convicted of "defamation," and banished from Vermont for 18 months. Upon his return to Massachusetts, local authorities arrested him for his earlier rabble-rousing.

After his father put up a bond for his release, asserting that his son was mentally distressed, Ely traveled to Vermont, again ignoring his banishment, and then moved to the District of Maine (which was then a part of the state of Massachusetts). He kept relatively quiet until the mid-1790s, when he took up the cause of the settlers who contested the large landholdings of proprietors such as HENRY KNOX, who had used political connections to gain control over thousands of acres. Ely participated in the disruption of surveyors and threatened greater violence on any who had a patent from the proprietors. An itinerant preacher, he articulated the grievances of the squatters and offered his own interpretation of the AMERICAN REVOLUTION, writing that "We fought for liberty, but despots took it, whose little finger is thicker than George's loins" and proclaiming that the poor settler had more liberty under the king than he did under the new state government. But Ely was no LOYALIST. He was an advocate of revolution, saying that "if rulers make a law to dispossess me of my just property, I have a just right to resist; and if a man comes to trespass my enclosure, I have a right to stop him."

The date of Ely's death remains unknown. Genealogical records indicate that he died in 1795, but his publications and a petition sent to the Massachusetts state house indicate he was alive in 1797.

See also CONSTITUTIONS, STATE; LIBERTY.

Further reading: Robert E. Moody, "Samuel Ely: Forerunner of Shays," *New England Quarterly* 5 (1932); 105–134; Alan Taylor, *Liberty Men and Great Proprietors: The Revolutionary Settlement on the Maine Frontier, 1760–1820* (Chapel Hill: University of North Carolina Press, 1990).

Embargo of 1807

The Embargo Act, passed by Congress on December 22, 1807, stopped almost all exports from the United States. It was a declaration to GREAT BRITAIN and FRANCE that the United States expected free and uninhibited access to the seas. President THOMAS JEFFERSON believed that a prohibition on TRADE with those two countries would lead the European powers to acknowledge neutral maritime rights.

During the wars that accompanied the FRENCH REVOLUTION (1789–99), the United States enjoyed increasing wealth as a "neutral carrier," especially in the reexport trade where merchants would ship goods from the European colonies to the United States and then to Europe to avoid seizure by warring powers, which were blockading direct trade between European countries and their colonies. In the early 19th century the war between Great Britain and France became something of a stalemate as NAPOLEON BONAPARTE dominated the continent of Europe and Great Britain controlled the seas. Both sides decided to engage in economic warfare: With the BERLIN DECREE, Napoleon created the Continental System to exclude the British from European markets, while the British countered by intensifying their blockade issuing ORDERS IN COUNCIL, which said that any nation that wanted to trade with Napoleonic Europe had to first obtain a license from Great Britain. Napoleon then issued the MILAN DECREE, which stipulated that any ship that stopped in a British port or was searched by a British vessel would be seized by France and her allies when they sailed into a European port. Taken together, the British and French regulations created an impossible situation for the United States as a neutral trader.

Compounding this diplomatic gridlock was a crisis with Great Britain precipitated by the *CHESAPEAKE-LEOPARD AFFAIR* (1807), in which a British warship fired upon a U.S. warship and forced it to surrender so that it could be searched for deserters from the Royal Navy. This episode could easily have led to war, and throughout the summer there was a great deal of saber-rattling in the United States. However, Jefferson hoped to avoid war and turned to economic coercion instead. He believed that Europe needed exports from the United States, which were generally food and agricultural products like COTTON and TOBACCO, more than the people of the United States needed the manufactured items of France and Great Britain. From Jefferson's perspective, the imports were mere luxury items that the virtuous republican citizenry did not need. Congress instituted the long-delayed NON-IMPORTATION ACT (1806) on December 14, 1807, and then passed the Embargo Act eight days later, prohibiting U.S. ships from sailing to foreign ports and closing the borders to trade with FLORIDA and CANADA.

Unfortunately for Jefferson, the United States was more dependent on foreign markets than he imagined, and farmers were not as independent as he had thought. The embargo devastated the ECONOMY, and within months the waterfront was a desolate no-man's-land, with grass growing on wharves where once hustling and bustling commerce had thrived. Within a year, exports sank from about $108 million to $22 million and imports from $144 million to $58 million, while the reexport trade almost disappeared entirely. There was a human cost behind these numbers as sailors and the maritime trades went begging for work, and farmers could not sell their produce as WHEAT went from two dollars a bushel to 75 cents a bushel. In the South, growers of tobacco, cotton, and RICE had even greater price drops. Sheriff sales appeared everywhere as virtuous yeomen became bankrupt and their property was foreclosed. To make matters worse, SMUGGLING proliferated along porous borders and in seaports on the coast. Congress had to strengthen the embargo's enforcement procedures several times, and Jefferson even went so far as to declare the people in the area around Lake Champlain to be "combining and confederating" to form "insurrections" so that they could illegally trade with Canada.

There were also political repercussions as Jefferson's second term as president became marked as a failure. The FEDERALIST PARTY rallied in 1808 and reasserted itself in New England, forcing JOHN QUINCY ADAMS out of the Senate and making gains in New York and elsewhere. Federal-

A cartoon about the Embargo Act depicts the embargo as a turtle preventing a smuggler from selling a keg of New England rum to the British. The word *ograbme* is *embargo* spelled backward. *(New York Public Library)*

ist Party leaders including JOSIAH QUINCY and TIMOTHY PICKERING attacked the embargo as a useless instrument that only hurt the United States and had little impact on Great Britain. Mocking the policy further were Federalist Party newspaper editors who jumbled the letters in the word *embargo* and called coast guard vessels "ograbme cutters" and enforcers of the law "Gen. ograbme." They also published cartoons showing anyone willing to trade with the British as being threatened by a sea turtle named "Ograbme." Despite the Federalist Party's growing popularity, the DEMOCRATIC-REPUBLICAN PARTY candidate, JAMES MADISON, still won the presidential election, though the Federalists once again emerged as a national force.

By the time Madison was about to be inaugurated, nearly everyone from both parties recognized the futility of the embargo, and the act was repealed. Congress replaced it with the NON-INTERCOURSE ACT (1809), which eased trading restrictions with the belligerent powers.

See also EMBARGOES; FOREIGN AFFAIRS.

Further reading: Louis Martin Sears, *Jefferson and the Embargo* (Durham, N.C.: Duke University Press, 1927); Burton Spivak, *Jefferson's English Crisis: Commerce, Embargo, and the Republican Revolution* (Charlottesville: University Press of Virginia, 1979).

embargoes

An embargo is a suspension of international TRADE by a government. Although the EMBARGO OF 1807 is well known as an idealistic and misguided policy meant to avoid war and provide economic pressure on European powers to change policies that inhibited the neutral commerce of the United States, there were other embargoes passed during the revolutionary and early republic era. On one level, the nonimportation movements that accompanied the RESISTANCE MOVEMENT (1764–75) in opposition to the STAMP ACT (1765), TOWNSHEND DUTIES (1767), and the TEA ACT (1773) were all forms of an embargo, although these measures were passed by nongovernmental committees and ad hoc extralegal entities. Similarly, the FIRST CONTINENTAL CONGRESS's ASSOCIATION, which set up a timetable for nonimportation, nonexportation, and nonconsumption, was a form of embargo.

After independence, the United States used embargoes several times. During the war crisis with GREAT BRITAIN in 1794, the United States instituted an embargo on all trade leaving North American ports. This measure, passed for 30 days on March 26, 1794, and then extended to 60 days, put pressure on the British since their WEST INDIES colonies were dependent on the United States for foodstuffs. As a result of the embargo, WHEAT prices in JAMAICA more than doubled. The United States repealed the embargo

after two months as tensions with Great Britain eased and JOHN JAY left for England to negotiate a settlement that became known as JAY'S TREATY (1794).

On April 1, 1812, President JAMES MADISON issued a 60-day embargo which Congress extended to 90 days. Expecting the outbreak of war with Great Britain, Madison believed that during the embargo, most of the merchant ships at sea would return to the United States and then be prevented from leaving port. The embargo therefore minimized the exposure of merchant ships to capture by the British navy. During the WAR OF 1812 (1812–15), the president instituted another embargo in December 1813 to break off trade with the British, which had continued despite the fact that the United States was at war with Great Britain. This measure was so sweeping—it literally did not allow any ship to sail from a port except privateers and naval vessels—that it was repealed in April 1814.

Emuckfau Creek, Battle of (January 22, 1814)

The indecisive battle of Emuckfau Creek occurred during the CREEK WAR against the RED STICKS, a hostile faction of the CREEK Indians. After the BATTLE OF TALLEDEGA (November 9, 1813), General ANDREW JACKSON faced logistical difficulties. His forces, reduced to one regiment in December after widespread desertion, had only 60-day enlistments. New recruits arrived on January 14, but most had never seen combat. Enmity between state MILITIAS and the regular U.S. ARMY prevented Jackson and other senior leaders from effectively massing their forces against the Red Stick towns. The result was that Jackson had only about 2,000 men available to fight in January 1814. On January 17 he moved on the village of Emuckfau without further reinforcements; five days later, his men bivouacked 12 miles from Emuckfau. A large contingent of Red Stick warriors camped near the U.S. soldiers and assaulted them at first light, but they were unsuccessful and retreated shortly thereafter. In retaliation, Jackson ordered Brigadier General John R. Coffee, commander of a mounted infantry brigade from Tennessee, to raze the warriors' camp. Coffee paused in his advance after seeing the Red Sticks' fortified positions. Taking advantage of his hesitation, the Red Sticks attacked, forcing Coffee's withdrawal.

Further reading: John K. Mahon, *The War of 1812* (Gainesville: University of Florida Press, 1972).

—Catherine Franklin

Enitachopoco Creek, Battle of (January 24, 1814)

Following the BATTLE OF EMUCKFAU CREEK (January 22, 1814), General ANDREW JACKSON began to move back to Fort Strother to consolidate and reorganize his forces. To avoid crossing Emuckfau Creek at a dangerous junction, he lengthened his route of march. On the morning of January 24, he prepared to cross Enitachopoco Creek, but roving patrols of RED STICKS identified the weaknesses of the U.S. column and attacked Jackson's artillery train just as it began to ford the water. Bogged down by their heavy equipment, the artillery men could not respond quickly enough to the attack. While the rear guard was under fire, the column's advance guard launched a counterattack in hopes of surrounding the Red Sticks. However, the rear guard failed to hold fast, leaving the flanks of the advance guard exposed. Unable to rout the Red Sticks, Jackson withdrew, and he spent the next couple of months at Fort Strother, training his men to prepare them for the campaign ahead.

See CREEK WAR.

Further reading: John K. Mahon, *The War of 1812* (Gainesville: University of Florida Press, 1972).
— Catherine Franklin

Enlightenment

The Enlightenment was a transatlantic intellectual movement that emphasized the relationship between nature and reason. In particular, beginning in the 17th century with the work of Isaac Newton in England and René Descartes in FRANCE, enlightened philosophes (philosophers) held that everything in the world should be organized on the basic principles found in nature and reason. The idea was to study nature by applying reason to understand the fundamental laws of how the world worked. Descartes applied these ideas to philosophy, emphasizing the importance of observation and the scientific method. Newton used a similar approach to study mathematics and thereby discovered calculus and laws of physics such as gravity. Other European philosophes expanded on this approach. England's JOHN LOCKE wrote about natural rights theory and the social contract, and he emphasized the importance of the ability to learn through sensations and the perfectability of humankind. In France, writers such as Voltaire and Jean-Jacques Rousseau developed elaborate critiques of the ancien régime (Old Regime), attacking antiquated laws and urging the creation of a new order based on the simplicity they believed could be found in nature and reason. These ideas spun out in a number of different directions that included the development of DEISM, studies of political science such as MONTESQUIEU's *Spirit of the Laws* (1748), and analysis of economics with the work of the French physiocrats and Scots like ADAM SMITH. The Enlightenment also affected the way people thought about history. Enlightened thinkers saw all societies as organic and following a life cycle that moved through stages from hunting and gathering to pasturage to AGRICULTURE to commerce—and that nations were vigorous and expansive in their youth, powerful and wise in their maturity, but decrepit and dying in their old age.

These ideas had a profound impact on revolutionary Americans. Many of the leading men in North America read deeply in the works of the Enlightenment and embraced the idea of some of the philosophes that the pristine North American continent was a land where nature and reason prevailed. Like the GREAT BRITAIN described by Montesquieu, the colonies, and later the United States, had a balanced form of government with power divided between the executive and two houses of legislature (in most colonies and later states). More important, North America did not seem to have ancient and confusing antiquated laws and was a land where individuals enjoyed a high degree of freedom. Some locales, such as Pennsylvania, which tolerated RELIGIOUS LIBERTY, were trumpeted in Europe by men like Voltaire as ushering in a "golden age" of simplicity and equality. From this perspective, the AMERICAN REVOLUTION became a significant event in world history as an assertion of Enlightenment ideals.

Despite the clarion call for nature and reason, the Enlightenment was not without its ambiguities. Some European philosophes looked upon nature in North America as enervating and debilitating and believed that the Old World was superior to the New World. They claimed that NATIVE AMERICANS were inferior human beings since the men did not have facial hair and, according to their SCIENCE, had milk running from their breasts. They also held that settlers who came to North America were tainted by the ENVIRONMENT, would be of smaller stature, live shorter lives, and were inferior. To the philosophes, proof of these assertions could be found in the fact that the ANIMALS in Western Hemisphere were smaller than the animals in the Eastern Hemisphere. THOMAS JEFFERSON wrote his *Notes on the State of Virginia* (1787) in part to challenge this argument, and he was ecstatic when the bones of a MAMMOTH were discovered, demonstrating that North America had animals larger than any elephant—the largest of the Old World fauna.

Perhaps a more fundamental problem could be found in the philosophes' approach to the ideal of equality. The call for reason in nature led them to trumpet the enlightened simplicity that could be found in the life of the honest farmer. Voltaire proclaimed that Pennsylvania was unique because the "body of citizens" were "absolutely undistinguished but by the public employments" and that neighbors did "not to entertain the least jealousy one against the other." Jefferson was more explicit when he declared that "those who labour in the earth are the chosen people of God, if ever he had a chosen people, whose breasts he has made his peculiar deposit for substantial and genuine virtue." Yet the ideal man of reason was found in the manners and self-possession of gentlemen like Jefferson. The elite in North America strove to fulfill their vision of a balanced and ordered society in all aspects of their lives. They even built their houses following the precepts of the Enlightenment: Georgian homes placed a door at the center, with the windows spaced equally on either side on both the first and second stories. Men like Jefferson packed their libraries with books by Locke, Newton, and David Hume, and they developed their political ideas from reading Algernon Sidney as well as John Trenchard and Thomas Gordon's *Cato's Letters* (1720–23). They studied the classics and the lessons of history for models of behavior, and they sought to examine science and the natural world around them. It is in this spirit that Pennsylvanians established the AMERICAN PHILOSOPHICAL SOCIETY in the 1760s, that DAVID RITTENHOUSE built his orrery, and that BENJAMIN FRANKLIN—the most famous American philosophe—experimented with ELECTRICITY. Yet this rarified world of gentlemen and ideas was a far cry from the hardscrabble life of a farmer who tramped through mud and manure with his plough. Before the American Revolution, the ambiguity implicit in this contrast was not a problem as the natural aristocrat could both assert his superiority as a product of reason and proclaim the virtues of the husbandman. After U.S. independence was achieved, the contradictions between the enlightened ideal that "all men were created equal" and the reality of equality became increasingly apparent.

Revolutionary leaders faced some difficulties even in the RESISTANCE MOVEMENT (1764–75), when they wrote pamphlets based on Enlightenment ideals yet had to rely on the howling crowd on the street to enforce boycotts. Men such as JOHN DICKINSON, who was affluent and a lawyer and who assumed the guise of a Pennsylvania farmer to promote opposition to imperial regulation, were aghast when mobs of common folk got out of control and destroyed property. After independence, JAMES MADISON and others rejected the "mutability" and "multiplicity" of laws created by state legislatures reflecting the fickle will of the people, most of whom were "those who labour in the earth," and proclaimed the need to "extract from the mass of Society the purest and noblest characters who would protect the public interest"—enlightened gentlemen like themselves. The political debates of the 1790s reflected not only contrasting interpretations of the U.S. CONSTITUTION but also competing versions of the Enlightenment. On the one side, the FEDERALIST PARTY clung to the idea that the Constitution had created a balance of orders within society and government with a natural aristocracy—and even a monarch-like figure in the presidency—to offset the impulses of the common people. On the other side, the DEMOCRATIC-REPUBLICAN PARTY increasingly accepted the idea that all elements of the government were mere reflections of the will of the people. Moreover, this drama was acted out against a larger Atlantic stage as revolutions inspired by the Enlightenment took place in France, Saint Domingue (HAITI), and elsewhere.

Similar tensions can be found in other areas of culture and society. Inspired by the ideals of the Enlightenment, many North American philosophes believed that an independent United States would unleash a new age in ART, ARCHITECTURE, and LITERATURE. They were disappointed in all three areas. No great democratic art emerged in this period, despite the efforts of CHARLES WILLSON PEALE and others. While there was some inspired private and public building, such as Jefferson's Monticello and the Virginia state house he designed, most buildings were less impressive, and no new Athens or Rome emerged. Authors, too, struggled. Instead of high-minded literature, the most popular books were either sentimental romances like *Charlotte, a Tale of Truth* (1791) by SUSANNA HASWELL ROWSON or partially fabricated histories like "PARSON" MASON LOCKE WEEMS's biography of GEORGE WASHINGTON. Similarly, when Jefferson's bill for religious freedom finally passed the Virginia legislature in 1785, it did not usher in a period where all citizens agreed with the deist idea that "the Almighty God hath created the mind free" and that "the truth is great and will prevail if left to herself." Instead, the legislation allowed many of the state's common farmers to embrace evangelicalism by becoming BAPTISTS and METHODISTS.

The triumph of these democratic tendencies may have led to the demise of some elements of the Enlightenment, but it also meant the rise of others. One of the Enlightenment's basic premises was the belief in the perfection of all humankind. This tenet triggered a host of reforms in EDUCATION, PRISONS, and treatment of the sick, and it even contributed to the ANTISLAVERY movement. Often overlooked, these and other reforms indicate how the Enlightenment had a practical impact on every level of society in the transatlantic world, not just on the intellectual elite.

See also RELIGION; REPUBLICANISM.

Further reading: Henry Steele Commager, *The Empire of Reason: How Europe Imagined and America Realized the Enlightenment* (Garden City, N.Y.: Doubleday, 1977); Durand Echeverra, *Mirage of the West: A History of the French Image of American Society to 1815* (Princeton, N.J.: Princeton University Press, 1857); Robert A. Ferguson, *The American Enlightenment, 1750–1820* (Cambridge, Mass.: Harvard University Press, 1997); Henry F. May, *The Enlightenment in America* (New York: Oxford University Press, 1976); Donald H. Mayer, *Democratic Enlightenment* (New York: Putnam, 1976); Roy Porter, *The Creation of the Modern World: The Untold Story of the British Enlightenment* (New York: Norton, 2000).

environment

The environment as we think of it in the 21st century—as a complex ecosystem on which we depend and to which we have done measurable harm—was not much on anybody's mind in revolutionary America. Like respectable folks all over Christendom in the 18th century, colonial Americans believed that the world had been created by God specifically to house human beings—the Crown of Creation—and that all of nature conformed to God's elegant designs, which were intricate, perhaps still mysterious, but neither random nor chaotic. Of course, environments came with different attributes: They could be hot or cold, wet or dry, benevolent (that is, "salubrious") or hostile, bountiful or barren. Compared to England, many colonists found the weather in North America more changeable than they were used to. North of New York winters impressed colonists as being more punishing than in most of Europe; in the Chesapeake and points south, summers were more oppressive, verging on tropical (and potentially dangerous). Particular locales proved hopelessly stony or sandy and barren; especially frustrating were the thin soils of coastal South Carolina and Georgia that required large investments in slaves and infrastructure to support RICE cultivation. But in most places the fruits of the environment were at least adequate, often wonderful, and people saw North America as a rich storehouse of material possibilities.

Whatever its local characteristics, people assumed that the natural environment had been placed there for the convenience and benefit of humans who were entitled—even commanded by God—to modify and use it as they would. Two traditional cultural sources supported this conventional understanding of the natural environment. First, the Christian creation stories in Genesis 1–3 gave Adam "dominion" over the garden, a charge that included both permission to exploit and an obligation to name and look out for all the other creatures. Second, empirical SCIENCE, as it developed in the 17th and 18th centuries, portrayed nature as an ingenious complex mechanism, orderly in design, and imbued with a definite purpose. For the pious, that purpose must have been the glory of God, but as the ENLIGHTENMENT matured, more secular-minded observers celebrated orderliness itself and the spectacular, utilitarian linkages that seemed to make all things predators. Among the common people of revolutionary America, both understandings circulated widely and in tandem. No one doubted the virtue of exploiting the environment, nor did they worry that anything so elegant and well-designed as nature could be hurt or altered in a fundamental way. Science and RELIGION together sustained a universal sense of entitlement to whatever the environment offered.

Within this broad cultural framework, British-American colonists could add a sense of extraordinary abundance. Going back to the 16th century, "new Eden" had been a term to describe the New World, and once they survived the initial "starving times," colonists found the new land to be extravagantly rewarding. Rivers and bays teemed with fish, FORESTS with game, and the very air itself with birds (great flocks of doves and pigeons; turkeys weighing 40 pounds). AGRICULTURE blossomed as ancient woods were cleared for fields of corn (maize), WHEAT, barley, oats, and peas. Salt marshes and meadows (the latter often created when beaver dams collapsed, draining shallow ponds) yielded rich grass and hay on which cattle thrived. Pigs, imported from Europe, ranged freely, merrily plowing the forest floor and feasting on roots, grubs, snakes, rodents, and nuts of all kinds (a fare collectively known as "mast"). Swine reproduced so quickly that they were the first newcomers truly to threaten their own environments. (NATIVE AMERICANS loathed pigs for the damage they did to forest systems.) Compared with Europe, where natural resources had been exploited continuously for hundreds of years, North America seemed marked by exuberant bounty.

As a result of this natural abundance, the European population in North America doubled every 25 years—a rate near the biological maximum. Ordinarily such explosive growth would have been disastrous for a community, but in the colonies there was plenty of land to allow for the expansion of agricultural production. In the TOBACCO colonies, abundant land coupled with slave labor made it possible for ambitious men of "mean estate" (not rich gentlemen already) to extract a fortune and adopt the style of aristocrats. Where no tobacco plantations transformed paupers into gentlemen, the rural landscape still seemed the "best poor man's country" because of the ease with which a comfortable living could be had. With his usual flourish, William Byrd II of Virginia characterized North American land as "fresh" from "it's makers hands" compared with Europe's tired and "tortured" farms: "[N]ature is very indulgent to us, and produces it's [sic] good things almost spontaneously. Our men evade the original [Biblical] curse of hard labour, and sweat as much with eating their bread, as with getting it." Time and again Byrd called Virginia his "New Eden."

Most European observers of the colonial environment employed some version of this comparison between European scarcity and North American natural abundance, casting aspersions (at least implicitly) on land-use practices in the Old World. At the same time, the colonizers poured torrents of criticism on the indigenous people of North America for *not* transforming the forests into fields and making the most of God's gifts. Agriculture was the natural occupation of hungry people; only savages could inhabit places of such rich potential and be satisfied with a mere subsistence from hunting, FISHING, and patch gardening. This ambition to name and tame the elements of wild nature was itself an imperialistic act designed to take possession of the North American continent by imposing on it European classifications and scientific understandings that disqualified Indian "knowledge" and with it any prior claims or rights to the real estate. This approach allowed European Americans to tour a forest full of Indian villages, fishing grounds, and cornfields and pronounce it "vacant wilderness," clearing it in their own minds at least for redemption by a more "industrious" (exploitative?) race.

It is remarkable that in discussions of North American natural resources, almost nobody writing between 1750 and 1815 failed to connect the beauty and abundance of this environment with the industry of people required to unlock its potential. The relationship seemed reciprocal. Raw nature untapped by the hands of skillful farmers was valued for its potential only, not for its undeveloped pristine character. European-American eyes did not sparkle until they began to envision the "wilderness" landscape *improved* by neat fences, tidy fields of corn and flax, snug cabins, and pens of livestock. Conversely, too generous a natural environment fostered ease, neglect, and indolence. European Americans stood in danger from such dark, degenerate forces: whenever they strayed too far from markets, they slid back into those savage ways that wild forests seemed to encourage. GEORGE WASHINGTON worried about this problem as he contemplated squatters living at ease (and paying no rents) on his FRONTIER lands on the Ohio River. J. HECTOR ST. JOHN DE CRÈVECOEUR concluded that men, like plants and ANIMALS, picked up the "wildness" of the woods and became "new-made Indians": "Thus our bad people are those who are half cultivators and half hunters; and the worst of them are those who have degenerated altogether into the hunting state."

This association of human traits and aspects of civilization with environmental factors had become popular among Enlightenment writers in Europe and England by the time of the AMERICAN REVOLUTION. Baron MONTESQUIEU, a French writer from whom many European-American elites drew their understanding of natural laws and political development, included in his influential *Spirit of the Laws* (1748) more than 50 pages on the effects of climate on peoples of the world. Montesquieu thought that people in cold climates were naturally brave, vigorous, and able to withstand sensations of pain, while residents of hot climes exhibited temerity, despondency, and acute sensuality. "If we travel towards the North," he continued, "we meet with people who have few vices, many virtues, and a great share of frankness and sincerity. If we draw near the South, we fancy ourselves entirely removed from the verge of morality." Extrapolating a connection between civilization and a challenging environment, Montesquieu further concluded that "barrenness of the earth" rendered men "industrious, sober, inured to hardship, courageous, and fit for war," while "fertility" produced "ease, effemi-

nacy." It stood to reason that North America was populated with "savages" because of the "fertility of the earth, which spontaneously produced many fruits capable of affording them nourishment." Such musings must have rung true for revolutionary Americans as they took pride in the virtues of their hardworking countrymen, who were contrasted on the one hand with indolent savages out in the forests and on the other with decadent English aristocrats lounging across the sea.

Corruption was the central charge in the Revolutionary indictment of British rule. True or not, in the eyes of radical leaders of the independence movement, by the 1760s Britain's ruling classes had become hopelessly corrupt: Addicted to luxury (pinched off the backs of the overseas colonists), they were now determined to snuff out LIBERTY in the provinces as they had in England itself. Blaming class privilege and hereditary power as the roots of this corruption, revolutionary Americans found it easy to conclude that the Old World, with its worn-out landscape and ancient institutions, had decayed beyond repair. Epic forces (Providence) had chosen the New World as a retreat for liberty, a safe repository full of hope and potential, where virtuous people could rekindle the flame of freedom and lead the world out of darkness. Patriotic orators quickly added the trope of "New Israel" to familiar environmental talk about the "New Eden," resulting in a heady ideological mix that graced revolutionary Americans' immediate ambitions with a world-historical mission of salvation through the erection of new republics. Men of the Old World, argued JOEL BARLOW in his epic poem *Columbiad*, had corrupted their dominion over nature and turned their power to war and domination; but on the "regenerate shores" of North America, mankind would find a second birth, seize the "true treasures of the earth and skies," and

> Unfold at last the genuine social plan,
> The mind's full scope, the dignity of man,
> Bold nature bursting thro her long disguise,
> And nations daring to be just and wise.

With independence accomplished, revolutionary Americans turned a sober eye to their own future prospects and began to take new inventories of their environmental resources. Most famously, THOMAS JEFFERSON sought to refute the accusations of European naturalists that North America and its resources were degenerate offspring of the original Creation. His *Notes on the State of Virginia* (1787) combined a catalogue of descriptions with long recitations of his own scientific methodology, "proving" that neither the resources nor the residents of Virginia could be found deficient by European standards. JEREMY BELKNAP filled a volume with descriptions of the climate, landscape, flora, and fauna of then largely unsettled New Hampshire, pronouncing in the end that agriculture would always be its "chief business" and nobody could "conceive" of the quantities of "beef, pork, mutton, poultry, wheat, rye, Indian corn, barley, pulse, butter and cheese" it would produce.

Not everyone saw such abundance in the new nation. Two negative aspects of environmental change produced a contrary refrain to the dominant positive assessment. The first of these was deforestation, which had become truly critical near the larger seaport cities. The relentless pressure of a booming population kept farmers clearing new forest land for agriculture. Firewood for Boston came from ever-wider circles of clear-cut rural landscape. Fuel shortages plagued Philadelphia, driving up the price of firewood to levels that left the poor begging for public relief each winter. BENJAMIN FRANKLIN's famous stove was one of many inventions sparked by this first American energy crisis. Half a century of warfare around the British Empire also had cut deeply into North America's stocks of shipbuilding timber and other raw materials. The Royal Navy took large quantities of oak and pine, not to mention thousands of wooden barrels filled with salted fish to feed sailors at war. Cutting the huge white-pine "mast trees" of New England produced collateral damage because to facilitate the harvest of these 200-foot giants, woodsmen cut dozens of nearby trees as well. Belknap's *History of New Hampshire* (1784–92) contained one of the earliest warnings that deforestation also threatened agricultural land by disrupting the watershed in mountains that sustained fertility in the valleys.

The second, more pervasive, environmental concern in revolutionary America was generally called soil exhaustion. Colonial agriculture thrived on a wealth of soil nutrients built up by centuries of forest growth, burnings, and small-scale Native American patch agriculture. European farming depleted this natural bounty in two ways: First, wholesale clearing exposed fragile topsoil to erosion; second, entire fields of the same crop (monoculture) sucked out nutrients that might be replenished or drawn down more slowly in complex natural ecosystems. Meanwhile, the population grew exponentially. Rocky farms in New England experienced severe declines of fertility even in the 17th century, and by the late 18th century it was understood that younger sons would have to move west or north to find fresh lands to sustain their families. Crèvecoeur complained of similar depletion of coastal resources in the lower Delaware River valley—which "all the art of Man can never repair."

But the real problem was in tobacco-growing regions of the Chesapeake and the plantation sections of the lower South. Tobacco ruined the soil in five to seven years, forcing planters to maintain huge spreads and a rotation cycle that left land fallow (uncultivated) for up to 20 years. Alternative fertilizing strategies—spreading marl, seaweed, or swamp muck—depended on the local availability of such

"manures" and huge investments of slave labor. Virginia's tidewater plantations were all but exhausted by the time of the REVOLUTIONARY WAR (1775–83). Jefferson begged his neighbors to try wheat cultivation (Washington actually did), but the sons of Old Dominion preferred to fix their gaze west of the Blue Ridge and out into the deep wilderness of Kentucky, Alabama, and Mississippi. In North Carolina, where swamps and sandy-pine barrens yielded mostly pitch and turpentine, the woods filled up with human riff-raff (or so said Virginians) who exhibited few ambitions, little breeding, and less personal HYGIENE. Finally, the coastal lowlands of South Carolina and Georgia, also sandy and marginal, served up profits only to the large-scale rice and INDIGO planters who had, after 1750, completely subverted the Georgia proprietors' original dream of a slave-free yeoman's paradise.

Relief for environmental degradation lay, of course, in the untapped interior backlands; but paradoxically, the richness of the frontier threatened to subvert the human impulse to work hard and improve. Travelers through the swamps of the Carolinas or the deep backcountry from Georgia to New York State harped endlessly on the "degraded" residents they encountered. In a verse description of a hike from Philadelphia to Niagara Falls in 1804, time after time ALEXANDER WILSON returned to the theme:

> Here Nature bounteous to excess has been
> Yet loitering hunters scarce a living glean;
> Blest with a soil that even in winter gay,
> Would all their toils a hundred fold repay,
> Few cultured fields of yellow grain appear. . . .

This anxiety over the impact of rich wilderness on human ambition, coupled with concerns about resource depletion, helped to define one of the key objectives for the new United States—the need to *develop* or *improve* these frontier territories and, with them, forge transportation links and strong "chains" of commercial and political friendship, so that this lush environmental inheritance could be made to serve the whole nation and not merely scattered nests of toothless squatters living like the Indians they ventured to displace. From the beginning of colonization, North America's abundant environment had lured Europeans to seize what to their way of thinking were resources going to waste. Now, as the fledgling republic launched its brave experiment in liberty and self-government, the westward movement, the improvement of raw nature, and the "rising glory" of a new kind of empire emerged as central aspects of the national drama.

In the late 18th century and on into the 19th century, scientific and religious explanations for phenomena in the natural world began to diverge. Among ideas about the environment, one casualty of continuing scientific research was the assumed "œconomy of Nature," which had assured gentlemen-naturalists of the Enlightenment that nothing in the world was so fragile as to be disturbed by the actions of another species. As early as 1781, Jefferson was puzzling over anomalies in the fossil record. By 1816 William McClure at Philadelphia's Academy of Natural Sciences frankly discarded the biblical chronology when discussing geology and natural development. Gradually scientists and then nonspecialists recognized the possibility of species extinction and environmental degradation, but their sense of entitlement remained intact. Long before people in the United States saw their landscapes demythologized by natural science, they had learned to value them primarily as commodities: lots for sale, board feet of lumber, bales of COTTON, bushels of corn. And even as they gradually lost confidence in the immutability of nature or its unlimited capacity to meet these escalating human demands, they acquired a newfound certainty that human genius—in the form of technological innovation—would easily counteract any negative effects of human exploitation in the environment. They considered it the birthright of freemen to squeeze ever more wealth and comfort from what was once "God's Creation" and was still an "inexhaustible" storehouse of natural resources.

See also POPULATION TRENDS; RACE AND RACIAL CONFLICT; REPUBLICANISM; SLAVERY.

Further reading: Caroline Merchant, *The Columbia Guide to American Environmental History* (New York: Columbia University Press, 2002).

—John Lauritz Larson

Equiano, Olaudah (Gustavus Vassa) (1745?–1797)
abolitionist, author, sailor

Probably born in West Africa, Olaudah Equiano became one of the leading ANTISLAVERY voices of the Atlantic world before his death. His memoir, entitled *The Interesting Narrative of the Life of Olaudah Equiano, or Gustavus Vassa, the African, Written by Himself,* is generally regarded as one of the canonical slave narratives. First published in 1789 and reprinted several times thereafter both in the United States and England, "the interesting narrative" was the most thorough and engaging document of the emerging genre of former slaves' written experiences. It remains a standard text about SLAVERY, alongside later slave narratives by Frederick Douglass, Harriet Jacobs, and others.

Among other themes, Equiano focused early attention on the horrors of the overseas SLAVE TRADE, or the "Middle Passage," as it became known—the forced migration of Africans to the Americas. Historians now place the number

Etching of Olaudah Equiano *(Hulton/Archive)*

of Africans who endured the Middle Passage at between 12 and 15 million. Although some European and colonial American statesmen, activists, and scholars began critiquing the slave trade by the 1770s, they often did so from philosophical or religious perspectives. While Equiano meditated on such themes too, he also provided firsthand testimony; in one of the most famous passages, he wrote of the Middle Passage: "[T]he stench of the hold [of the ship] while we were on the [African] coast was so intolerably loathsome, that it was dangerous to remain there for any time . . . the closeness of the place, and the heat of the climate, added to the number in the ship, which was so crowded that each had scarcely room to turn himself, almost suffocated us . . . this wretched situation was again aggravated by the galling of the chains . . . the shrieks of the women, and groans of the dying, rendered the whole a scene of horror almost inconceivable." Equiano's book gained immediate notice after first being published in England. The London *Monthly Review* stated that "his publication appears very seasonable, at a time when Negro slavery is the subject of public investigation; it seems calculated to increase the odium that has been excited" against British planters operating in the Caribbean. The book would also become popular in Ireland, where it sold several thousand copies in the early 1790s, and in the United States, where white as well as black abolitionists used it to attack the slave trade.

Equiano's narrative traced his life from freedom to slavery and back to freedom. Both he and his sister were kidnapped and separated while still quite young (he was roughly 11–13 years old). Equiano was then transported to a slave pen on the western coast of AFRICA, and then sent to Barbados. He ended up on a Virginia plantation, then was sold again to an English owner who brought him to GREAT BRITAIN and renamed him Gustavus Vassa. Sold again and brought to the Americas, Equiano worked on merchant ships and eventually bought his own freedom. At his death on March 31, 1797, he was survived by his wife and two children in England.

Equiano was not just a writer but an early transatlantic antislavery activist. In addition to publishing his famous narrative, he presented petitions against the slave trade and gave public lectures about his experiences in bondage. His work was credited with helping stir popular as well as political sentiment against the slave trade, which England prohibited in 1807 and the United States banned in 1808. But Equiano's narrative is also viewed as a means of establishing a proud racial identity through print. As Henry Louis Gates has argued, Equiano, like other black authors of the postrevolutionary era, wrote to challenge stereotypes of African-descended people as savage and unlettered—and thus fit for enslavement. Equiano countered such pernicious views in a manner that remains powerful 200 years later.

See also ABOLITION; AFRICAN AMERICANS.

Further reading: Robert J. Allison, ed., *The Interesting Narrative of the Life of Olaudah Equiano, or Gustavus Vassa, the African, Written by Himself* (Boston: Bedford Books, 1995); Henry Louis Gates, *The Signifyin' Monkey: A Theory of African American Literary Criticism* (New York: Oxford University Press, 1987).

—Richard Newman

Erskine Agreement (1809)

David M. Erskine was the British minister to the United States in 1809 when JAMES MADISON became president, the EMBARGO OF 1807 ended, and the NON-INTERCOURSE ACT (1809) was put into place. Erskine, who was married to an American, was sympathetic to the United States and engaged in negotiations with Secretary of State ROBERT SMITH to end the disagreements concerning neutral TRADE between the United States and GREAT BRITAIN. He had specific guidelines, which should have limited his ability to negotiate a settlement: British foreign secretary GEORGE CANNING had instructed Erskine that he could make some concessions concerning the HMS *Leopard*'s attack on the USS *Chesapeake* (June 22, 1807; see CHESAPEAKE-LEOPARD AFFAIR), but that he should insist on the repeal of a nonintercourse measure against Great Britain, while retaining it against FRANCE, and gain compliance with the RULE OF 1756. Moreover, although Erskine could begin discussions with the United States, Canning wanted to send a special envoy to complete any treaty. Erskine sidestepped most of these instructions and came to an accord in mid-April 1809, which promised that the British would remove the ORDERS IN COUNCIL inhibiting neutral trade with Europe as they related to the United States and that the United States would open trade with Great Britain. The Erskine Agreement was cast in general terms, but it was to take effect almost immediately; the exact details were to be worked out by the special envoy promised by Canning. As a result, on April 19, 1809, Madison ended nonintercourse with Great Britain.

Unfortunately, Canning repudiated the agreement and recalled Erskine from WASHINGTON, D.C. Canning found that Erskine had gone too far by implying that the British admiral who had ordered the search of U.S. naval vessels in 1807 should be punished. More important, the agreement violated his instructions concerning the Rule of 1756 and the right of the British navy to enforce the ban on trade with France imposed by the Non-Intercourse Act. However, since many merchant ships had left the United States loaded with goods on the assumption that trade was now legal, Canning also allowed any vessel that had left port before news of his repudiation had been known to complete its voyage. The United States reinstituted nonintercourse on June 10, 1809, and the difficulties over neutral trade continued. Tension between the United States and Great Britain persisted and eventually led to the outbreak of the WAR OF 1812 (1812–15).

See also FOREIGN AFFAIRS.

Further reading: Bradford Perkins, *Prologue to War, 1805–1812: England and the United States* (Berkeley: University of California Press, 1968).

Essex decision (1805)

In 1805 the British Admiralty Court decision in the case of the U.S. merchant ship *Essex* altered official British policy toward neutral shipping, aggravated diplomatic relations between GREAT BRITAIN and the United States, and set the two nations on a collision course that ultimately led to the outbreak of the WAR OF 1812 (1812–15). With FRANCE and Great Britain at war for most of the time from 1793 to 1815, there was a tremendous opportunity for U.S. merchants to reap profits as long as both belligerents respected neutral rights. Initially, the British wanted to follow the

RULE OF 1756, which stated that any TRADE prohibited before wartime would remain prohibited after a declaration of war. In other words, if France had prohibited neutral ships from carrying goods from its colonies to France before the outbreak of war, then it could not allow such trade to occur after war broke out. Merchants sidestepped this rule by shipping goods to the United States, unloading them, paying a small duty, and then reshipping the goods to France. Although such actions flouted British control of the seas—and allowed France to obtain goods from its colonies that would have been intercepted by the British had they been in French vessels—the British courts had allowed this trade to continue as indicated in the *POLLY* DECISION of 1800. With such favorable circumstances, the reexport trade in the United States rose from $40 million in 1800 to $60 million in 1805.

The *Essex* decision made it more difficult for Americans to evade British regulations. The court case involved the reshipment of wine between SPAIN (at the time an ally of France) and CUBA (a Spanish colony). The British court said that the reshipment of the wine in the United States was meant to deceive the British and did not represent a legitimate mercantile exchange. Since Spain had prohibited other nations from carrying goods to its colonies before it went to war with Great Britain, the trade was illegal and the ship was liable to seizure. Within the next few months, scores of merchantmen from the United States were seized by the British navy. However, clever merchants soon managed to make the reshipment of goods appear more legitimate, and the total amount of the reexport trade did not decline greatly.

Perhaps more important than the exact nature of the ruling was its symbolic significance. The courts put the burden of proof of neutral trade on the merchant owner, instead of the captain of the British warship that seized a vessel. Merchants, in other words, were considered guilty of violating British regulations until they proved themselves innocent, rather than considered innocent until proven guilty. Such an approach showed little or no respect for the U.S. flag. The British government had acted in what many in the United States thought was an arbitrary way, without warning or diplomatic discussion. When JAMES MONROE, the U.S. ambassador to Great Britain, attempted to discuss this ruling with the British government, he was told that it was nothing extraordinary and therefore not an appropriate topic for a special diplomatic meeting. The affront to national pride could hardly have been more direct. From the *Essex* decision until the outbreak of the War of 1812, the United States had an increasingly difficult time gaining the respect of both France and Great Britain, and in continuing its profits as a neutral trader amid a world at war.

See also FOREIGN AFFAIRS.

Further reading: Bradford Perkins, *Prologue to War, 1805–1812: England and the United States* (Berkeley: University of California Press, 1968).

Essex Junto

The Essex Junto has often been portrayed as a cabal that dominated the FEDERALIST PARTY in Massachusetts during the 1790s and early 1800s and that pushed for disunion in 1803–04 and again in 1814. In reality, the junto was little more than a small group of conservative Revolutionaries who shared an ideology that opposed change and sought to restrict the role of the people in the everyday affairs of government. The group included FISHER AMES, George Cabot, Francis Dana, NATHAN DANE, Benjamin Goodhue, Stephen Higginson, Jonathan Jackson, John Lowell, THEOPHILUS PARSONS, TIMOTHY PICKERING, Israel Thorndike, and Nathaneal Tracy. Most of these men were from Essex County and had made much of their MONEY from opportunities offered by the AMERICAN REVOLUTION. They were on the Revolutionary right and believed in a REPUBLICANISM that held that the people might chose the leaders, but those leaders were then to make the decisions without dissent from the people. "In the political ship," Theophilus Parsons explained, "there must be common seamen as well as pilots; and a mutiny of the crew may as effectually destroy her as a division among the officers."

This group became politically active as early as the 1770s but had limited success in electoral politics. They contributed to, but did not dominate, the writing of the Massachusetts constitution of 1780, and they did not send any delegates in 1787 to the Philadelphia CONSTITUTIONAL CONVENTION. Although they did not think the document was conservative enough, they supported ratification of the U.S. CONSTITUTION. By the mid-1790s, many of the junto had begun to retire from politics, and as a group their influence, such as it was, started to wane.

But just as they began to recede from the political landscape, the phrase *Essex Junto* entered the political vocabulary as a pejorative symbol of reaction. John Adams blamed the closeness of the ELECTION OF 1796 on the junto and saw opposition to his policies as being masterminded, at least in part, by this mythical group. The term was also useful to the DEMOCRATIC-REPUBLICAN PARTY as a means of tainting political opponents in the Federalist Party. The fact that Pickering opened discussions concerning secession of a northern confederacy in 1803–04 has led some historians to suggest that the Essex Junto lay behind that movement. Similarly, the junto has been falsely identified with extremists in the Federalist Party, who discussed leaving the union during the WAR OF 1812 (1812–15) even though by then most of the so-called Essex Junto were no longer politically active.

Further reading: David H. Fischer, "The Myth of the Essex Junto," *William and Mary Quarterly*, 3rd ser. 21 (1964): 191–235.

Estaing, Charles-Henri-Théodat, comte d'
(Jean-Baptiste-Charles-Henri-Hector Théodat)
(1729–1794) *French naval officer*

When FRANCE joined the REVOLUTIONARY WAR (1775–83) in 1778, Revolutionaries had high hopes that the conflict would soon be over. Much of the fulfillment of those hopes was placed on the shoulders of Charles-Henri-Théodat, comte d'Estaing. This French aristocrat had fought in the FRENCH AND INDIAN WAR (1754–63) with some distinction, and he was given command of the French forces sent to North America. Unfortunately, d'Estaing, while avoiding a total disaster, never succeeded in fulfilling Revolutionary expectations.

The problems began soon after France went to war with GREAT BRITAIN. The French fleet sailed from Toulon on April 13, 1778, but reached North American waters too late to trap the British fleet in the Chesapeake. Little

In 1778 French naval officer the comte d'Estaing commanded the first French military force to aid the Revolutionary Americans against the British. *(Bridgeman Art Library)*

came of a plan to attack the British at New York. Instead, d'Estaing decided to join up with Continental forces and capture the British army at Newport, Rhode Island. This campaign never gained much momentum. The Revolutionary army under General JOHN SULLIVAN took too long to concentrate on Newport, delaying its attack. D'Estaing managed to bombard Newport and fought an indecisive action with a smaller British fleet from New York. Then nature interceded; A hurricane swept into both fleets, scattering the ships and severely damaging them. D'Estaing decided that he needed to take his fleet to Boston for a refitting, and without French support, Sullivan withdrew from the siege. In Boston d'Estaing repaired his fleet and worked to resolve some differences and build a sense of camaraderie between the French and Revolutionary forces. Then he headed for the WEST INDIES, where he conquered several British possessions, including St. Vincent and Grenada.

Late in 1779 d'Estaing, determined to aid the CONTINENTAL ARMY in the South, launched an attack on Savannah, but again, things did not work out for him as the British managed to reenforce the garrison, despite the French blockade. Then, in an all-out assault on October 9, 1779, the combined Franco-American armies failed to take the British fortification. D'Estaing was wounded twice in the battle, and he subsequently returned to France. This failure allowed General HENRY CLINTON to capture Charleston on May 12, 1780, and extend the war for two more years. It was left to another French admiral, COMTE DE GRASSE, to defeat the British at the BATTLE OF CHESAPEAKE CAPES (September 5, 1781), and for a French general, COMTE DE ROCHAMBEAU, to join GEORGE WASHINGTON in the victory at YORKTOWN (surrendered October 19, 1781). D'Estaing was honored on his return to France, but when the FRENCH REVOLUTION (1789–99) broke out, he tried to play to both sides and ended his life on the guillotine on April 28, 1794.

See also SAVANNAH, SIEGE OF.

Eustis, William (1753–1825) *physician, secretary of war*

Born in Cambridge, Massachusetts, William Eustis was trained as a doctor and served during the REVOLUTIONARY WAR (1775–83) as a military surgeon. After the war he practiced MEDICINE in his home state of Massachusetts and entered politics in 1788. He represented Boston in the state legislature from 1788 to 1794 and then became a member of the state's council for two years. He won two terms in Congress beginning in 1800 but lost to JOHN QUINCY ADAMS in 1804.

A moderate member of the DEMOCRATIC-REPUBLICAN PARTY, Eustis was appointed secretary of war by

President JAMES MADISON in 1809. In the years leading up to the WAR OF 1812 (1812–15), he strove to reform the war department and sought to create a permanent military establishment, but as an administrator he had a tendency of focusing on details, and he lacked efficiency. He also sought to cut costs, argued with several of the military leaders under him, and received much of the blame for the military disasters at the beginning of the war. One congressman complained that as secretary of war Eustis was "a dead weight in our hands" and that "His unfitness is apparent to every body but himself." By December 1812, Eustis had come to the conclusion that he should resign, even though Madison had supported him throughout the fall and the presidential election.

Eustis's career as a public servant was not over, however. In 1814 Madison appointed him as minister plenipotentiary to The NETHERLANDS, a post he held until 1818. He returned to Congress in 1820 and was elected governor of Massachusetts in 1823. Eustis died on February 6, 1825, before the end of his second term as governor.

Eutaw Springs, Battle of (September 8, 1781)

One of the last and bloodiest major battles of the REVOLUTIONARY WAR (1775–83), the clash between the British and Revolutionary armies at Eutaw Springs helped to determine the outcome of the war in the South. After LORD CORNWALLIS fought General NATHANAEL GREENE's Continentals at the BATTLE OF GUILFORD COURTHOUSE (March 15, 1781), the British general marched to Wilmington on the coast and then headed for Virginia. Greene, unaware of Cornwallis's intention, in the meanwhile decided to retake the rest of South Carolina, and in the spring and summer of 1781, almost every British outpost fell to his forces. He received a serious rebuff, however, at the BATTLE OF HOBKIRK'S HILL (April 25, 1781) outside of Camden. The British commander, Lord Rawdon (see HASTINGS, FRANCIS RAWDON, FIRST MARQUIS OF) also successfully relieved the garrison during the SIEGE OF NINETY-SIX (May 22–June 19, 1781). The situation remained difficult for the British, as the support of LOYALISTS within the state evaporated. Rawdon, worn out by years in the field, headed for England, leaving Lieutenant Colonel Alexander Stewart in charge. By September, Stewart was encamped along the Santee River about 30 miles northwest of Charleston, but without much local support, he had no idea about the location of Greene's army. Greene, on the other hand, knew exactly where he could find his opponent.

By the morning of September 8, Greene had brought his army undetected to within a few miles of the British. The two sides each had about 2,200 men. Greene began to advance on the British position and might have caught Stewart entirely by surprise had the British not sent out a scavenging party of 80 men to collect yams for the troops. Greene's army met this small British detachment and soon overwhelmed it, but the noise of the encounter brought a small troop of horse, who alerted the British army. Greene had deployed his men in what was now his usual fashion, with the MILITIA in the front and the Continentals in the rear. The plan was that once the militia provided an initial volley or two, they would fall back and the British would rush ahead, expecting victory but instead meeting well-trained Continentals. The plan almost worked as the militia fell back and the British advanced in disorder. The Continentals broke the British advance and, joined by the militia, pursued the retreating enemy, but the cavalry, waiting in the wings, was unable to dislodge a British regiment in some thick underbrush. Withering fire from the British took its toll; moreover, once the Revolutionaries reached the British encampment, they began looting it, many drinking rum, creating disorder in their ranks. Just behind the camp, the British had drawn up a defensive position behind some walls at Burwell's Plantation. From this protection they broke the Revolutionary advance and compelled Greene's army to retreat. A complete disaster was avoided when a battalion of Maryland Continentals maintained order and delayed the counterattack. Greene's men managed to withdraw with just enough order to prevent a hot pursuit.

The British held the field, but the battle cost both sides dearly. Greene lost one-fourth of his army as missing, killed, or wounded. The British fared worse: They had less dead but lost more than a quarter of their forces, many either missing or captured by the enemy. Soon after the battle, Stewart withdrew to Charleston, surrendering all of the South Carolina countryside. The British held onto that city until they evacuated it after the peace agreement that ended the war.

Further reading: Don Higginbotham, *The War of American Independence: Military Attitudes, Policies, and Practice, 1763–1789* (New York: Macmillan, 1971); Robert Middlekauf, *The Glorious Cause: The American Revolution, 1783–1789* (New York: Oxford University Press, 1982).

Ewald, Johann (1744–1813) *Hessian military officer*

Johann Ewald was a Hessian officer (see HESSIANS) who served the British during the REVOLUTIONARY WAR (1775–83). As a captain of the jägers—elite light infantry troops—he earned the respect of many of his superior officers and developed a friendship with LORD CORNWALLIS. Ewald fought in the war from October 1776 through the October 1781 surrender at YORKTOWN, but he did not return to Hesse until 1784. After the Second World War, an American officer discovered Ewald's diary and subsequently had it published. This diary provides a detailed account of the

Revolutionary War from the perspective of an exceptionally talented Hessian officer. It offers wonderful insight into GEORGE WASHINGTON's strategy during the BATTLES OF TRENTON AND PRINCETON (December 26, 1776, and January 3, 1777), the effort to capture Philadelphia in 1777 (when Ewald led the vanguard in the envelopment of Washington's army at the BATTLE OF BRANDYWINE [September 11, 1777], the capture of Charleston (May 12, 1780), and the Virginia campaign that culminated in the surrender of Yorktown on October 19, 1781.

After returning to Germany, Ewald wrote several treatises on partisan and light infantry warfare and became a noted expert in military science. However, he was frustrated by a lack of promotion because he was not a noble. In 1789 he left the Hessian service and joined the Danish army, as there his abilities led to rapid promotion, ennoblement, and great distinction. Eventually promoted to lieutenant general, he became a national hero for his adopted country during the French Revolutionary and Napoleonic wars.

Further reading: Johann von Ewald, *Diary of the American War: A Hessian Journal,* translated and edited by Joseph P. Tustin (New Haven, Conn.: Yale University Press, 1979).

excise tax (1791)

In 1790 Secretary of the Treasury ALEXANDER HAMILTON proposed an excise tax on distilled ALCOHOL as a part of his financial program. Once the national government assumed the states' debts, Hamilton estimated a shortfall of more than $1 million for the additional interest, and about half of that total could be made up from a tax on distilled liquor. He believed that this tax would have three benefits: It would "discourage the excessive use of Spirits," "promote Agriculture," and "provide the support of the Public Credit." He sought to limit the potential for abuse by allowing country distillers to pay a flat annual fee on the capacity of their stills. In addition, he wanted to prevent indiscriminate searches and permit civil suits against false seizure to be tried by juries. Although the measure did not pass in 1790, it was reintroduced and became law in March 1791. Opponents viewed the tax as "odious, unequal, unpopular, and oppressive" and complained that it would extend the reach of the national government into everyone's home since, as one opponent explained, it would "let loose a swarm of harpies, who under the denominations of revenue officers, will range through the country, prying into every man's house and affairs."

Much of the opposition centered on the FRONTIER and in the South, where it became virtually impossible to collect the tax. When officials made a more concerted effort to enforce the law in western Pennsylvania, the WHISKEY REBELLION (1794) broke out. The tax remained in effect until after the ELECTION OF 1800, when THOMAS JEFFERSON and the DEMOCRATIC-REPUBLICAN PARTY repealed the measure. A new excise tax was passed in 1813 to help fund the WAR OF 1812 (1812–15).

See also DEBT, NATIONAL.

Further reading: William D. Barber, "'Among the Most Techy Articles of Civil Police': Federal Taxation and the Adoption of the Whiskey Excise," *William and Mary Quarterly,* 3rd ser. 25 (1968): 58–84; Thomas P. Slaughter, *The Whiskey Rebellion: Frontier Epilogue to the American Revolution* (New York: Oxford University Press, 1986).

Fairfax, Thomas (1693–1781) *landowner, patron of George Washington*

Thomas Fairfax, sixth baron lord Fairfax of Cameron, and proprietor of the Northern Neck in Virginia, was one of the few colonial Americans with a British title. He was born in Kent, England, but settled permanently in Virginia in 1747, where he held massive land claims and almost feudal rights over the Northern Neck of Virginia. He developed close personal relations with the Washington family and was the father-in-law of Lawrence Washington, who was the older half brother of GEORGE WASHINGTON. Fairfax was also the father-in-law of Sally Fairfax, with whom George Washington may have fallen in love. Whatever the exact relationship between Washington and Sally Fairfax, the future president maintained good relations with Thomas Fairfax and was best of friends with Sally and her husband George William Fairfax. It was the patronage of Thomas Fairfax that gave the young Washington his start in life as a surveyor. Fairfax also influenced Washington's appointment as a MILITIA officer. and he commanded the Virginia militia in the northern section of the colony during the FRENCH AND INDIAN WAR (1754–63). Somehow he remained neutral during the REVOLUTIONARY WAR (1775–83), but his son became a LOYALIST, ending his and Sally's friendship with Washington. He died on December 9, 1781.

fairs, agricultural

In 1810 retired merchant and gentleman farmer Elkanah Watson organized the first agricultural fair in Berkshire County, Massachusetts. This event became the model for a major national tradition: the agricultural fair. Watson had led an eclectic life, making and losing fortunes in a variety of enterprises before accumulating enough wealth to establish himself as a gentleman farmer in the first decade of the 19th century. He became a proponent of new agricultural techniques, importing special breeds of hogs, sheep, and cattle. Gaining support from the Berkshire Agricultural Society, which he spearheaded, Watson created a special "cattle show" in 1810. The idea was to demonstrate the scientific nature of North American AGRICULTURE and to embody the pastoral ideal. From the beginning the fair included more than a display of cattle; it also exhibited of wide range of farm produce and items manufactured domestically. Watson's fair relied on an elaborate ritual to "seize the farmer's heart" as well as his mind. The idea quickly spread, and within a few decades there were hundreds of county fairs each year across the country, offering prizes and premiums and becoming a highlight of agrarian culture in the United States.

See also RURAL LIFE.

Further reading: Catherine E. Kelly, "'The Consummation of Rural Prosperity and Happiness: New England Agricultural Fairs and the Construction of Class and Gender, 1810–1860," *American Quarterly* 49 (1997): 574–602.

Fallen Timbers, Battle of (August 20, 1794)

Fallen Timbers was a major battle in a contest for the Ohio country that began with the FRENCH AND INDIAN WAR (1754–63), ran through the REVOLUTIONARY WAR (1775–83), and continued into the 1790s between European Americans and NATIVE AMERICANS. Until this battle, it looked as if the Indians were winning the war north of the Ohio River despite certain treaties that had ceded some of the territory. A confederacy of SHAWNEE, DELAWARE, MIAMI, WYANDOT, and other Indians under the leadership of LITTLE TURTLE and BLUE JACKET had twice defeated invading armies from the United States: In 1790 the Indians annihilated a force under General JOSIAH HARMAR, and in 1791 they crushed troops under Governor ARTHUR ST. CLAIR. These disasters crippled the U.S. ARMY and led President GEORGE WASHINGTON to appoint General ANTHONY WAYNE to rebuild and train an army to defeat the Indians. Meanwhile, the Indians, who enjoyed a position of dominance, refused to make peace with the United States and demanded that all of the treaties which surrendered land north of the Ohio River be abolished. They would make peace only if the Ohio River was restored as the boundary between Native Americans and European Americans. Throughout 1793 and 1794, General Wayne trained his army—called the Legion of the United States—and marched it into Ohio, destroying many villages and crops along the way.

The campaign culminated in the Battle of Fallen Timbers, in far northwestern Ohio, on August 20, 1794. Fallen Timbers was so named because a recent thunderstorm had knocked down a large numbers of trees. Wayne's army had about 3,000 men; the Indian forces numbered around 1,300, with a small addition of Canadian MILITIA volunteers also in their ranks. Many Indians were absent from the battlefield, however, because they had sought shelter from the storm at their village several miles away. Those who remained had ritually fasted in preparation for the battle. Unfortunately for them, the battle came a day later than anticipated, leaving the Indian warriors famished, and perhaps as few as 400 actually participated in the battle. Early in the action, the Indians provided stiff resistance to the legion's attack, but Wayne's army compelled them to retreat. They fled to nearby Fort Miami, a British post, where they had been assured in the past that they would find a safe haven in times of trouble. In this instance, however, the British would not allow the Indians to enter, wishing to avoid conflict between themselves and the United States. The Indians thus had to retreat farther from the field and lost additional warriors.

Although the casualties in the battle were nearly equal for the legion and Indians, the victory clearly went to Wayne's army, which had displayed its newfound power. The Indians now realized that the United States would not be easily defeated. Due to the Fort Miami incident, the Indians also lost confidence in the British, who they had hoped would join them as allies. As a result, less that a year later the Indian confederacy signed the TREATY OF GREENVILLE (1795).

Further reading: Wiley Sword, *President Washington's Indian War: The Struggle for the Old Northwest* (Norman: University of Oklahoma Press, 1985).

Falmouth, Massachusetts, destruction of (October 18, 1775)

Frustrated by the siege of Boston, the raids of privateers, and the lack of support along the coast in New England during the early phases of the REVOLUTIONARY WAR (1775–83), the British navy decided to intimidate civilians by attacking port towns. On October 18, 1775, Cap-

tain Henry Mowat bombarded what was then Falmouth, Massachusetts (modern-day Portland, Maine) because the local committee had refused to allow a LOYALIST to ship supplies to the British. Mowat gave the people of Falmouth several hours' warning before he began the attack and even promised to spare the town if it surrendered hostages and military equipment. Most of the citizens packed up their furniture and left their homes unprotected, and the local MILITIA offered only minor resistance to the British, even when they sent a shore party to the town. Most of Falmouth was destroyed: 139 dwellings, 278 additional buildings, and 11 vessels were burned. The British also captured four other vessels. This attack outraged many revolutionary Americans and is in part responsible for the line in the DECLARATION OF INDEPENDENCE that charged GEORGE III with having "plundered our seas, ravaged our coasts, burnt our towns, and destroyed the lives of our people."

See also PRIVATEERING.

Fanning, Edmund (1739–1818) *Loyalist*

Edmund Fanning was born in Southold, Long Island, New York, and educated at Yale. He moved to North Carolina in 1762, and there his EDUCATION quickly helped him stand out. He found preferment with Governor WILLIAM TRYON, who appointed him to a number of offices. Unfortunately for Fanning, he soon earned the ire of the North Carolina Regulators (see NORTH CAROLINA REGULATION), who saw him as a government official who took advantage of his connections to obtain ill-gotten wealth at the expense of the public good. One Regulator song lamented that when Fanning first came to North Carolina, "Both man and mare wa"nt worth five pounds . . . But by his civil robberies" he soon "laced his coat with gold." When the Regulators rioted in Hillsborough in September 1770, they broke into his house, demolished his furniture, and destroyed his legal papers.

Fanning left North Carolina in 1771 when Tryon became governor of New York. Again, he was given multiple offices, serving as Tryon's private secretary, a judge, and surveyor general. At the beginning of the REVOLUTIONARY WAR (1775–83), he quickly sided with the LOYALISTS and raised the King's American Regiment (also called the Associated Refugees). He saw extensive military service during the war and enhanced his infamous reputation among many Revolutionaries.

After the war, Fanning left for NOVA SCOTIA, where he served for a short time as lieutenant governor. He subsequently moved to Prince Edward Island, where he again was lieutenant governor. Fanning maintained his status as a British officer and was eventually promoted to the rank of general based on seniority. However, he never saw any further fighting. He retired from public life in 1805 and moved to England in 1813. He died in London on February 28, 1818.

Farewell Address, George Washington's (1796)

In September 1796 President GEORGE WASHINGTON sent his Farewell Address to a Philadelphia newspaper. The address circulated around the nation and served two purposes: It let the public know that Washington would not run for reelection, and it offered the country some final advice. At the end of the first paragraph, he stated he had decided "to decline being considered among the number of those out of whom a choice is to be made." By so doing, he set a precedent that the president would serve no more than eight years, a precedent that would be followed for more than a century.

Washington advised his countrymen that the states' continued union was their greatest hope for sustained independence, but he warned them that to maintain such a union would take vigilance and sacrifice. The dangers that Washington believed could most easily lead to trouble for the young republic were sectionalism, party politics, and foreign influence. He plainly stated that all sections—North, South, East, and West—were connected to each other politically, economically, and culturally, and that only by strengthening those bonds could the new nation survive. In order to form such a bond, citizens would have to recognize their responsibility to the national government. "The very idea of the power and right of the people to establish government presupposes the duty of every individual to obey the established government."

Another very real danger in Washington's view was the emergence of party politics or "factions" of competing visions of how the government should work. He was clear in his warning that partisan differences, especially those based on geography, could weaken the republic: "I have already intimated to you the danger of parties in the State, with particular reference to the founding of them on geographical discriminations." Washington recognized that there were some who believed that parties "in free countries are useful checks upon the administration of government, and serve to keep alive the spirit of liberty." He admitted there was some truth to this but said that in a popularly elected government, the danger of party politics was greater than the possible benefits. "But in those of the popular character, in governments purely elective, it is not to be encouraged."

In perhaps the most famous advice given in the address, Washington warned his fellow citizens to avoid becoming involved with foreign nations. He implored the people of the United States to take advantage of their geographical isolation and to remain out of the affairs of Europe. The interests of the European powers, he argued, were not the interests of the United States. "Hence, therefore, it must be unwise in us too implicate ourselves by artificial ties in the ordinary vicissitudes of her politics or the ordinary combinations and collisions of her friendships or enmities." His advice to the country was: "The great rule of conduct for us in regard to foreign nations is, in extending our commercial relations to have with them as little political connection as possible. So far as we have already formed engagements let them be fulfilled with perfect good faith. Here let us stop." These words would be cited over the course of U.S. history as a model for foreign policy and become the rallying cry for isolationists.

See also ELECTION OF 1796; FOREIGN AFFAIRS; POLITICAL PARTIES.

Further reading: Felix Gilbert, *To the Farewell Address: Ideas of Early American Foreign Policy* (Princeton, N.J.: Princeton University Press, 1970).

Federalist Papers (*The Federalist*) (1787–1788)

The Federalist, more commonly known as the *Federalist Papers,* is a series of 85 newspaper essays on the U.S. CONSTITUTION by ALEXANDER HAMILTON, JAMES MADISON, and JOHN JAY. Written under the pseudonym "Publius," a reference to the great defender of the ancient Roman Republic Publius Valerius Publicola, the *Federalist Papers* were originally published in two New York City newspapers: the *New York Packet* and the *Independent Journal.* The first essay appeared on October 27, 1787, and the series continued until April 2, 1788. Later that year, the collection of essays appeared as a bound book, edited by Hamilton and published by J. and A. McLean. A second edition, with Madison as editor, was published in 1818.

The purpose of the essays was to urge the people of New York to ratify the new Constitution, which had been drafted by the CONSTITUTIONAL CONVENTION and adopted on September 17, 1787. Because of its thriving commerce and central location, New York's acceptance of the proposed document was essential to the viability and success of a new government. The *Federalist* essays were reprinted in other newspapers across New York State and in several other states.

Alexander Hamilton, a member of the Constitutional Convention who strongly supported the proposed government, was the originator of the work. In an effort to win over public opinion in favor of the Constitution, Hamilton decided to write a series of essays that would both defend the Constitution and explain its provisions. To complete the project, he enlisted the support of two prominent collaborators: Madison, a fellow Constitutional Convention delegate and brilliant scholar of political history; and Jay, the secretary of FOREIGN AFFAIRS under the ARTICLES OF CONFEDERATION. Although the authorship of some of the essays was a subject of intense debate for well over a century, modern research suggests that of the 85 essays, Hamilton wrote 51, Madison wrote 29, and Jay wrote five. Collectively, the authors were experienced scholars on a variety of subjects, and their contributions tended to reflect their individual areas of expertise. Hamilton concentrated on military and financial affairs, while Madison addressed the historical experiences of confederacies, and Jay focused on foreign policy.

For the most part, the authors wrote independently, consulting each other infrequently due largely to time constraints imposed by newspaper deadlines. This loose collaboration was possible because despite some minor differences, the authors generally agreed on the fundamental principles concerning the nature of the new government. They believed in the need for a strong central authority to correct what they saw as the political weakness inherent in the Articles of Confederation and thought that a vertical division of power between the central and state governments would provide the best balance. They maintained that separation of the legislative, executive, and judicial functions of government provided a further safeguard and would prevent any single branch from dominating the others.

Furthermore, Madison and Hamilton agreed about the fundamental question of human nature that underpinned all political systems. Like the English philosopher Thomas Hobbes, they believed that humans were inherently wicked beings who lacked self-control; therefore, the purpose of government was to curb the wild passions of people. This defect in human nature provided a constant state of struggle in which men sought their own selfish desires rather than the common good. This human propensity constituted the foundation of faction, which Madison and Hamilton believed should be incorporated into the function of good government. They thought that a strong republican government would recognize the existence of factions and force them to compete against one another to prevent tyranny by the majority. These ideas, as expressed in Madison's essay number 10, constitute one of the most famous defenses of republican government.

The *Federalist* essays addressed almost every objection raised to the Constitution. In the first few numbers, Hamilton argued that there was more to be feared by *not* having a strong central government than by having one since without a powerful union the United States would quickly divide into several regional confederations that would inevitably make war against each other. Hamilton defended the power of the president under the Constitution while denying that he was like a monarch since he was to be elected every four years and Congress could override his

veto. Moreover, if the president violated the Constitution, he could be impeached. *Federalist* Number 62 defended the small size of the Senate as serving as "a constitutional recognition of the portion of sovereignty remaining in the individual states" and noted that it would double "the security of the people" since it served as a check to what otherwise would be a single house of legislature. It would also be immune from the "impulse of sudden and violent passions" exhibited by many of the state legislatures. Similarly, holding a popular election for the House of Representatives every two years would guarantee that the people would have a constant voice in the government. Questions over the power of the SUPREME COURT were dismissed with the assertion that lower courts retained the jury trial and that the higher court did not have juries since knowledge of law and the Constitution was central to its deliberations. Madison defended the NECESSARY AND PROPER CLAUSE in *Federalist* Number 44 with the assertion that without the ability to pass laws to put the powers of the Constitution into effect, "the whole Constitution would be a dead letter." In *Federalist* Number 51 Madison discussed the nature of human existence, quipping, "If men were angels, government would not be necessary."

In the end, the authors of the *Federalist Papers* achieved their goal: The Constitution won eventual ratification in all 13 states. Since that time, the *Federalist Papers* has become an important treatise in U.S. history, evolving into a definitive treatise on government and providing modern scholars and statesmen alike with insight into the political minds of the founding era.

See also ANTI-FEDERALISTS; CONSTITUTION, RATIFICATION OF THE; REPUBLICANISM.

Further reading: Allan Brinkley, *New Federalist Papers: Essays in Defense of the Constitution;* (New York: Norton, 1997); Albert Furtwangler, *The Authority of Publius: A Reading of the Federalist Papers* (Ithaca, N.Y.: Cornell University Press, 1984); George Mace, *Locke, Hobbes, and the Federalist Papers: An Essay on the Genesis of the American Political Heritage* (Carbondale: Southern Illinois Press, 1974).

Federalist Party

The Federalist Party of the 1790s and early 1800s supported a platform that valued order and stability, a powerful national government, and diplomatic and commercial ties with GREAT BRITAIN. The Federalist Party and the FEDERALISTS of 1787–88 should not be confused. The Federalists who advocated the ratification of the U.S. CONSTITUTION in 1787 did not necessarily become members of the Federalist Party. Some men who had supported the U.S. Constitution, notably JAMES MADISON, became members of the DEMOCRATIC-REPUBLICAN PARTY, while others who opposed the Constitution became members of the Federalist Party. The POLITICAL PARTIES of the 1790s formed around the issues that faced the nation created by the Constitution; both sides accepted the new frame of government. The Federalist Party drew its strength from a curious mix of people, ranging from wealthy merchants and large landowners to conservative farmers, and they came largely from the commercial cities and from slowly developing rural areas. The party was strongest in New England.

The Federalist Party developed during the administration of President GEORGE WASHINGTON. Although Washington believed that parties—or factions, as they were often referred to in the period—were a negative force to be avoided, he is usually identified as belonging to the Federalist Party because of his policies and ideals. Under the leadership of Secretary of the Treasury ALEXANDER HAMILTON, the administration proposed several measures that became the core of the Federalist Party platform. Hamilton wanted to strengthen the national government by fully funding the national debt (see DEBT, NATIONAL), assuming state debts, creating the BANK OF THE UNITED STATES, and encouraging manufactures. The underlying theory of this plan was that such economic actions would provide the wealthy with a vested interest in seeing the United States succeed. Opposition to these measures soon formed, with Secretary of State THOMAS JEFFERSON and Congressman James Madison at its center. They believed that Hamilton's plan would give the federal government too much power. The supporters of Hamilton became the Federalist Party; the supporters of Jefferson and Madison organized the Democratic-Republican Party. In the early 1790s each party was little more than a loose coalition of like-minded politicians arguing over the future direction of the nation.

If the differences between the two parties began in a debate over domestic issues in 1791 and 1792, they intensified in 1793 and 1794 over the direction of U.S. foreign policy. Initially, most people in the United States had greeted the FRENCH REVOLUTION (1789–99) with enthusiasm, but opinions became more mixed by 1793 after the French executed their king and war broke out between Great Britain and FRANCE. The Federalist Party wanted to abandon the FRENCH ALLIANCE, while the Democratic-Republicans hoped to support the French. The differences of opinion between the two groups solidified in the controversy over JAY'S TREATY (1794), which angered many Democratic-Republicans who saw it as too conciliatory to the British. Both parties began to become more organized, supporting newspapers and pushing for a slate of candidates. The Federalist Party, however, had a certain edge because of its control over the national government.

Politics in the late 1790s became more heated as the United States entered the QUASI-WAR (1798–1800) crisis. France had also reacted negatively to Jay's Treaty and began seizing U.S. shipping. War fever swept the nation, as many people in the United States wanted to fight the French for their attacks on U.S. commerce and the insult to national prestige in the XYZ AFFAIR (1797–98). The Federalist Party capitalized on popular opinion by expanding the military and passing the DIRECT TAX ACT (1798), and in an effort to stifle their political opponents, they enacted the ALIEN AND SEDITION ACTS (1798). These last measures sought to control criticism of the government and limit the impact of immigrants on politics. Although the navy was dispatched to attack French warships and preparations were made for war, President JOHN ADAMS decided to try to negotiate with the French. By 1800 an agreement was reached that avoided a declared war, but this statesmanlike action helped to lose Adams the ELECTION OF 1800. Members of his own Federalist Party turned on him, while Democratic-Republicans attacked the unpopular Alien and Sedition Acts. Immediately before he left office, Adams created many new positions in the federal judiciary and filled them with Federalist Party appointees. These so-called midnight appointments caused great controversy and eventually led to the groundbreaking U.S. SUPREME COURT case *MARBURY v. MADISON* (1803).

After the election of 1800, the Federalist Party began to organize more effectively on the local level, even though they fought a losing battle for national prominence. Previously, party leaders had clung to older notions of politics and elections, believing that only the well-educated and relatively wealthy knew what was best for society. With Jefferson's victory, the party began to adopt more democratic campaign tactics to compete with the Democratic-Republicans, yet it still became less important nationally and increasingly developed into a sectionally based minority. The party was revived temporarily because of the unpopularity of Jefferson's EMBARGO OF 1807, which devastated the national ECONOMY.

The Federalist Party hoped to gain similar political capital by opposing the WAR OF 1812 (1812–15), but antiwar sentiment was much more regionally based. Many New Englanders believed that their interests were being pushed aside in favor of the South and West, and most were unhappy with the break in commerce that the war brought. After more than two years of futility in the war, Federalist Party leaders in Massachusetts called for the HARTFORD CONVENTION (1814–15), made up of delegates from several New England states. Although there was some talk of secession at the convention, it did not endorse that drastic step; instead, the delegates proposed a series of constitutional amendments that would strengthen New England's role in the national government. The Federalist Party might have made some headway in this effort if its timing had not been so poor. Just as the convention's representatives reached WASHINGTON, D.C., word of ANDREW JACKSON's victory at the BATTLE OF NEW ORLEANS (January 7, 1815) arrived, and then a few days later news of the TREATY OF GHENT (1814) was announced. Despite the fact that the treaty had settled none of the outstanding issues with Great Britain, many people in the United States believed they had triumphed in the war. The Hartford Convention, which the Democratic-Republican newspapers pronounced treasonous, appeared foolish at best and traitorous at worst. It was a political fiasco from which the Federalist Party never recovered. The party continued to run candidates for election, and while they had some local success, they never again were a strong national presence.

Although the Federalist Party's failure was primarily due to its inability to recognize the growing importance of popular democracy, it left an important legacy. The party may have lost, but its principles were preserved in the Supreme Court decisions of Chief Justice JOHN MARSHALL. It was also instrumental in setting up and operating the U.S. government in the 1790s—successfully establishing national institutions, guiding the economy, and shaping the judicial system in the new nation's most formative years.

See also REPUBLICANISM.

Further reading: James M. Banner, Jr., *To the Hartford Convention: The Federalists and the Origins of Party Politics in Massachusetts, 1789–1815* (New York: Knopf, 1970); Stanley Elkins and Eric McKitrick, *The Age of Federalism: The Early American Republic, 1788–1800* (New York: Oxford University Press, 1993); David Hackett Fischer, *The Revolution of American Conservatism; The Federalist Party in the Era of Jeffersonian Democracy* (New York: Harper & Row, 1965).

Federalists

Federalists were those who supported the ratification of the U.S. CONSTITUTION in 1787 and 1788, and should not be confused with the FEDERALIST PARTY, which formed later and did not necessarily include the same people. Earlier in the 1780s, ROBERT MORRIS led a nationalist movement to create a stronger central government under the provisions of the ARTICLES OF CONFEDERATION that would have given the SECOND CONTINENTAL CONGRESS the ability to pass an impost duty on imports. This effort failed since the states determined that granting Congress this power necessitated an amendment to the Articles, which required unanimous consent. In 1782 Rhode Island held up ratification of the tax; in 1785 a second attempt to allow the central government to pass taxes failed when New York refused to go along with the plan.

By the second half of the 1780s, the Federalists had perceived a need for a stronger national government that not only would have the power to tax but could also rein in the excesses of popular government in the states. They believed that the state governments were too close to the people and seemed to change laws at the slightest whim. JAMES MADISON decried what he called the "mutability" and "malleability" of the law under the states. By being too reflective of the people's fickle will, state governments seemed to be encouraging a lack of public virtue as understood within the ideology of REPUBLICANISM. Rather than being willing to sacrifice for the public good, too many people seemed to be willing to manipulate government for their own good. As Virginian CHARLES LEE explained, the legislatures had written laws "tending to efface every principle of virtue and honesty from the minds of its citizens," especially in laws concerning tax relief for debtors and delinquents. From this perspective, without a strong central government "more powerful and independent of the people, the public debts and even private debts will . . . be extinguished by acts of the several Legislatures of the several States."

Because of the state governments' lax laws, Federalists believed that anarchy and crime were increasing, while unrestrained European-American settlers on the FRONTIER had increased the troubles and warfare with NATIVE AMERICANS. Internal revolt, too, seemed to lurk in the wings and when SHAYS'S REBELLION broke out in 1786, many Federalists became convinced that the contagion of civil discord would spread. As HENRY LEE exclaimed, the unrest in Massachusetts "portend[s] extensive national calamity" and "the objects of the malcontents are alluring to the vulgar and the impotency of government is rather an encouragement to, than a restraint on, the licentious."

The answer to these problems for the Federalists was to create a central government somewhat removed from the people, but which was still responsible to them. The system of government would, in Madison's words, guarantee that "the purest and noblest characters" would rule. As Madison explained, these men would be well-educated and rational, "whose enlightened views and virtuous sentiments tender them superior to local prejudices, and to schemes of injustice." Such men would not form POLITICAL PARTIES. Adhering to notions of hierarchy, the Federalists espoused an aristocratic ideal without an inherited and titled aristocracy. In the words of the historian Gordon Wood, "Despite the Federalists' youthful energy, originality, and vision, they still clung to the classical tradition of civic humanism and its patrician code of disinterested public leadership."

The Federalists dominated the CONSTITUTIONAL CONVENTION in Philadelphia in 1787 and then orchestrated the Constitution's ratification. Generally, many of the

Federalist leaders were relatively young men—GEORGE WASHINGTON and BENJAMIN FRANKLIN being the major exceptions—who had experience either in the CONTINENTAL ARMY or with the national government during the REVOLUTIONARY WAR (1775–83). The Federalists had their greatest strength in commercial areas from merchants, LAWYERS, big planters, and master craftsmen. Cities often voted overwhelmingly Federalist; New York City voted 2,735 to 134 for Federalist delegates to the state ratifying convention. Most of the commercial classes supported the Constitution because they believed that it would promote a more positive business environment. The changeability of the laws—Madison's malleability and mutability—led to an unstable business environment where a shift in legislation could make or break a business. A few agrarian areas supported the Federalists. On the frontier, many settlers hoped that a stronger central government could help them against the Indians. Georgia was strongly Federalist because of its problems with Native Americans and because of the proximity of Spanish FLORIDA. Delaware and New Jersey were both small states with many middling farmers—a group that tended to be Anti-Federalist—but they voted overwhelmingly Federalist because the new Constitution provided them with disproportionate REPRESENTATION in the Senate and offered a government that could assist them with their state debt.

The Federalists were also incredibly articulate and had years of leadership experience. They relied heavily on the prestige of both Washington and Franklin as paragons of wisdom and self-sacrifice. Most newspapers, which had a strong commercial orientation, tended to be Federalist and published many arguments in support of the Constitution—most famously the FEDERALIST PAPERS, written by Madison, ALEXANDER HAMILTON, and JOHN JAY. The Federalists were well organized, and the quick ratification of the Constitution in several states provided a momentum that was difficult for the ANTI-FEDERALISTS to oppose. In several state CONVENTIONS the Federalists simply overawed or outmaneuvered their opponents, often making promises they had no intention of keeping. Ultimately, however, the Federalists had to accept a BILL OF RIGHTS to ensure ratification.

Although the Federalists won the political contest, their vision for the republic did not triumph. Despite packing Washington's administration with the kind of talented men they had hoped would serve the national government, party politics quickly emerged. Even more important, however, was that the Federalist vision of elite, disinterested men ruling an obedient and compliant people was illusory. The United States became more democratic, more egalitarian, with each year during the early republic. Moreover, more and more individuals joined the scramble for economic and political power in a capitalist world order that belied the classical vision that had sustained the Federalist movement in 1787 and 1788.

See also CONSTITUTION, RATIFICATION OF THE.

Further reading: Roger H. Brown, *Redeeming the Republic: Federalists, Taxation, and the Origins of the Constitution* (Baltimore: Johns Hopkins University Press, 1993); Forrest McDonald, *Novus Ordo Seclorum: The Intellectual Origins of the Constitution* (Lawrence: University Press of Kansas, 1985); Gordon S. Wood, *The Creation of the American Republic, 1776–1787* (Chapel Hill: University of North Carolina Press, 1969); Gordon S. Wood, "Interest and Disinterest in the Making of the Constitution," in Richard Beeman, Stephen Botein, and Edward C. Carter II, eds., *Beyond Confederation: Origins of the Constitution and American National Identity* (Chapel Hill: University of North Carolina Press, 1987).

Fenno, John (1751–1798) *political journalist*

John Fenno was the editor of the *Gazette of the United States* and an outspoken supporter of ALEXANDER HAMILTON and the FEDERALIST PARTY. Born in Boston, Fenno served briefly as an assistant to General ARTEMAS WARD during the REVOLUTIONARY WAR (1775–83) before entering the import business. When this enterprise failed, he moved to New York City and, in April 1789, founded the *Gazette of the United States* a newspaper that was a vocal supporter of the U.S. CONSTITUTION and the Federalist Party. Though he angered Democratic-Republican editors such as BENJAMIN FRANKLIN BACHE, Fenno's pro–Federalist Party writings attracted the attention of Alexander Hamilton, who helped him by paying him $2,000 a year to publish Treasury Department announcements. When the capital moved to Philadelphia in 1790, Fenno and the *Gazette* also moved, and the newspaper's circulation increased to its highpoint of 1,400 subscribers. In addition, his columns were reprinted in newspapers throughout the country.

Annoyed at Fenno's pro-Federalist Party stance, THOMAS JEFFERSON hired PHILIP FRENEAU as a translator for the State Department. With a salaried sinecure, Freneau was free to edit the rival Democratic-Republican newspaper, the *National Gazette*. For much of the early 1790s, Fenno and Freneau engaged in a fierce political debate that reflected the animosity between the Federalist Party and DEMOCRATIC-REPUBLICAN PARTY. For his part, Hamilton continued to support Fenno and the *Gazette* and even wrote a series of anti-Jefferson columns under a pseudonym. When the paper stopped publishing briefly in 1793, Hamilton secured loans and additional funding for Fenno, and the newspaper resumed as a daily. Fenno died from YELLOW FEVER on September 14, 1798, and his son,

John Ward Fenno, continued to publish the newspaper before he sold it in 1800. The *Gazette of the United States* ended in 1818.

See also JOURNALISM.

Further reading: Jeffrey L. Pasley, *"The Tyranny of the Printers": Newspaper Politics in the Early Republic* (Charlottesville: University of Virginia Press, 2001).

—Tash Smith

Ferguson, Elizabeth Graeme (1737–1801) *Loyalist sympathizer*

The daughter of a prominent Philadelphia family, Elizabeth Graeme was well educated and a proponent of the development of the arts in North America. She translated François Fénelon's *Télémaque;* wrote poetry; visited London from 1764 to 1765; and established one of the first literary salons in Philadelphia, where she entertained many of the colony's most prominent men. In 1772, against her father's wishes, she married Henry Hugh Ferguson, a man at least 10 years her junior. Although she remained devoted to Ferguson, this match would bring her a great deal of trouble.

Henry Hugh Ferguson traveled to GREAT BRITAIN in 1775, and when he returned to Philadelphia in 1777, he was with General WILLIAM HOWE and became the British commissioner of prisoners. Elizabeth was then residing on the estate outside of Philadelphia she had inherited from her father. After obtaining a pass from GEORGE WASHINGTON to visit her husband, she was persuaded to carry a letter back to Washington, urging the general to sue for peace. Despite her earlier support of the Revolutionary cause, this action, which Washington reported to the SECOND CONTINENTAL CONGRESS, brought Ferguson under suspicion. When she acted as an intermediary in the effort to bribe JOSEPH REED during the negotiations of the CARLISLE COMMISSION, her reputation as a WHIG was permanently damaged.

After the British evacuation of Philadelphia, the state of Pennsylvania declared Ferguson's husband, who had returned to England and separated from his wife, a traitor and confiscated his property. Given the prevailing notions of WOMEN'S STATUS AND RIGHTS, and given Ferguson's own questionable actions, Pennsylvania also appropriated the property she had inherited from her father. This seizure left her almost destitute, and for years she sent letters to prominent friends and filed petitions with the state government for the return of her estate. Ferguson repeatedly declared her loyalty to the United States and proclaimed that it was unjust to take away a wife's property because of her husband's actions. In 1781 some of her property was restored, but she eventually had to sell it since she did not have the wealth to maintain her father's grand house and estate. She died on February 23, 1801, near Philadelphia.

See also LOYALIST PROPERTY CONFISCATION.

Ferguson, Patrick (1744–1780) *British military officer, inventor*

The younger son of an aristocratic Scottish family with a strong military tradition, Patrick Ferguson joined the British army in 1759 as a cornet. After serving on the European continent during the FRENCH AND INDIAN WAR (1754–63), he may have been stationed in the WEST INDIES for a time, though details of his life are vague. Whatever his military experience, he had been promoted to captain by 1768 and spent sometime in the early 1760s recuperating from a serious illness. By 1776 he had developed a breech-loading rifle, which he demonstrated to British military officials, who then ordered 100 of the guns and put Ferguson in charge of a small corps of men armed with the weapons. Some scholars have stressed the weapon's potential for revolutionizing warfare—a potential not fulfilled, so the argument goes, because of the small-mindedness of British generals. However, similar weapons had been around for almost a century, and Ferguson's rifles were fragile instruments that became more inaccurate in battle every time they were fired.

Ferguson's unit arrived in New York in May 1777 and participated in some of the fighting around the city as a light infantry company. His company was part of General WILLIAM HOWE's expedition against Philadelphia and fought in the BATTLE OF BRANDYWINE (September 11, 1777). During that engagement, Ferguson claimed he had a CONTINENTAL ARMY officer in his rifle's sights but decided not to shoot the individual since it would be unsporting and ungentlemanly. Supposedly, that officer turned out to be GEORGE WASHINGTON. Ferguson himself had his arm shattered at Brandywine, an injury that took a long time to heal, and his special rifle unit was disbanded after the battle. Some scholars claim that Howe did not recognize the weapon's utility and was piqued that he had not been consulted in the formation of Ferguson's company. Yet by the time of the Battle of Brandywine, Ferguson had only 28 men under his command, with the rest either dead, injured, or ill.

The rifles were placed in storage, and Ferguson became a member of General HENRY CLINTON's staff, coordinating intelligence. A highly capable officer who had become a favorite of Clinton's, he was promoted to major in 1779 and given a battlefield rank of lieutenant colonel in North America. He raised a new unit of LOYALISTS called "Ferguson's Scottish Corps"—sometimes referred to as the "American Volunteers"—and joined Clinton's southern invasion of 1780. Once in South Carolina, Clinton assigned

British military officer Patrick Ferguson developed the breech-loading rifle (six shots per minute) in 1775 and subsequently assembled a team of sharpshooters to serve in North America. *(National Park Service, King's Mountain National Military Park, South Carolina)*

Ferguson the task of recruiting Loyalists to the British cause. By the end of May 1780, Ferguson had command of an additional 800 Loyalist MILITIA and began to operate independently in the South Carolina backcountry. As he sought to suppress resistance along the FRONTIER, he maneuvered himself into an isolated and exposed position encamped on the top of a barren mountain near the border between South and North Carolina. Revolutionary militia attacked this position at the BATTLE OF KING'S MOUNTAIN on October 7, 1780—an engagement that was a disaster for the British. Ferguson was killed, and his force was wiped out: The British had 119 killed, 123 wounded, and 664 captured.

Further reading: Hank Messick, *King's Mountain: The Epic of the Blue Ridge "Mountain Men" in the American Revolution* (Boston: Little Brown, 1976).

Few, William (1748–1828) *Georgia politician, New York banker*

William Few was born into a hardscrabble farming family that moved from Maryland to the North Carolina backcountry when he was only 10 years old. After involvement with the NORTH CAROLINA REGULATION, the family moved again to Georgia, leaving Few in North Carolina to settle affairs. He followed in 1776 and quickly became involved in Georgia's Revolutionary politics, attending the state's constitutional convention in 1777 and serving in the state assembly. He also became a MILITIA officer and saw combat against LOYALISTS and the British invasion in 1778 and 1779. He was a delegate to the SECOND CONTINENTAL CONGRESS from 1780 to 1782 and 1786 to 1788, passed the Georgia bar in 1784, and became a prominent leader in the state. Though he attended the CONSTITUTIONAL CONVENTION, he was not active in its debates. Few supported ratification of the U.S. CONSTITUTION both in the Continental Congress and in Georgia. He was selected as a senator for a four-year term but failed to be reelected in 1793. Few later wrote, "If I had obtained that appointment, I should have most probably spent the remainder of my days in the scorching climate of Georgia under all of the accumulating evils and fevers and negro slavery—those enemies of human felicity." Instead, after serving again in the state assembly, he moved to New York.

In New York, while retaining DEMOCRATIC-REPUBLICAN PARTY sympathies in politics, Few moved his career in new directions. Almost as soon as he arrived in the North, perhaps following in the footsteps of his father-in-law James Nicholson, Few became an investor and then director of the Manhattan Company, which had formed to provide New York City with water but also operated as a bank. In addition, he became an inspector of state prisons and federal commissioner of loans in New York. All of these activities provided a handsome income. After the WAR OF 1812 (1812–15), Few continued as a banker, encouraged manufacturing in the United States, and became involved in philanthropy. He died on July 16, 1828.

Finley, Robert (1772–1817) *Presbyterian minister, reformer*

A PRESBYTERIAN clergyman, teacher, and president of the University of Georgia, Robert Finley was best known for his role in founding the American Colonization Society. He was born in Princeton, New Jersey, and educated at the College of New Jersey (later Princeton University) before becoming a teacher. In 1792 he resigned his teaching post in order to prepare for entry into the Presbyterian ministry, and in June 1795 he was ordained as the pastor of a church in Basking Ridge, New Jersey. Here he published several sermons and established a boy's school that won a national reputation. In May 1798 he married Esther Caldwell, who brought him a large dowry and a wealth of church connections through her guardian ELIAS BOUDINOT.

In 1816 Finley heard of a plan to create colonies on the west coast of AFRICA, where former slaves could settle. Long concerned about the problems faced by free AFRICAN AMERICANS, he began campaigning for the creation of a national society to raise funds and petitioned Congress to act. In December 1816 he published a pamphlet, *Thoughts on the Colonization of Free Blacks,* which caught public attention. In January 1817 the American Colonization Society (ACS) was founded, largely due to his efforts. (Because the ACS was formed in 1817, it is not part of this encyclopedia). Finley was made an honorary vice president in recognition of his work; other early ACS supporters and members included President JAMES MADISON, HENRY CLAY, Daniel Webster, and U.S. SUPREME COURT justice BUSHROD WASHINGTON.

In April 1817 Finley accepted the position of president of the University of Georgia and moved his family to Athens, Georgia. The long journey and new climate weakened him and he died, probably of malaria, on October 3, 1817.

See also COLONIZATION, AFRICAN.

Fish, Mary (Mary Fish Noyes Silliman Dickinson) (1736–1818)

Outliving three husbands, Mary Fish was born and lived in Connecticut. Her life reflected the experiences of many women from the middle to the upper levels of New England society who lived through the AMERICAN REVOLUTION. Fish had five children (only three lived to adulthood) with John Noyes, her first husband, who died in 1767; and two sons with Gold Selleck Silliman, her second husband, who died in 1790. There were no children from her third marriage to John Dickinson. One of the sons from her second marriage was BENJAMIN SILLIMAN, a noted scientist.

During the REVOLUTIONARY WAR (1775–82) Gold Selleck Silliman, then a MILITIA general, was kidnapped on May 2, 1779, by LOYALISTS and not exchanged for almost a year. During that time Fish had to manage their farm alone. A somewhat fictionalized movie of these events, "Mary Silliman's War" (1994), shows the difficulties confronted by women in her position. Fish was less inspired by the Revolutionary movement and more dedicated to her RELIGION. As such, her life was marked by a strong sense of duty to her three husbands and to her family.

See also WOMEN'S STATUS AND RIGHTS.

Further reading: Joy Day Buel and Richard Buel, Jr., *The Way of Duty: A Woman and Her Family in Revolutionary America* (New York: Norton, 1984).

Fishdam Ford, Battle of (November 9, 1780)

During his 1780 campaign in South Carolina, LORD CORNWALLIS received a report that General THOMAS SUMTER and 300 MILITIA were camped at Moore's Mill, about 30 miles from the British army. Cornwallis ordered Major James Wemyss and 140 men to see if they could surprise Sumter. In the meantime, Sumter had moved his men five miles south, closer to the British, and Wemyss therefore stumbled on Sumter at about 1:00 A.M. In the initial clash Wemyss was wounded, and command passed to Lieutenant John Stark, who ordered a calvary charge into the camp. Unfortunately for the British, in the confused melee that followed, the mounted dragoons were easy targets against the backdrop of the campfires. But when the British infantry entered the affray, most of the militia withdrew from the camp. Five British soldiers had been detailed to capture Sumter. As they entered the front of his tent, Sumter exited the rear and disappeared into the darkness. The British captured the camp but had to withdraw the next day, leaving their wounded behind, including Wemyss, with a flag of truce. Despite Sumter narrowly escaping British clutches, the battle added to his reputation and rallied greater popular support for the Revolutionary cause.

fishing

THOMAS JEFFERSON viewed fishermen as somewhat akin to his much-touted farmer: Instead of being "cultivators of the earth," fishermen harvested the bounty of the sea. Moreover, from Jefferson's perspective, fishing was a nursery of SEAMEN whose labor would ensure the continued flow of commerce and the development of the national ECONOMY. In addition, seamen were central to the nation's defense at times of war in the navy and aboard privateers.

There were two different areas of deep-sea fishing crucial to the economy: cod fishing and whale fishing (whales are mammals, but at this time whaling was identified with the fishing industry). Before the REVOLUTIONARY WAR (1775–83), cod fishing had been well established in the British North American colonies, especially in New England, where fishing vessels traveled to the Grand Banks off the coast of NOVA SCOTIA. As many as 4,000 men worked out of Massachusetts alone on about 28,000 tons of shipping, with a catch often worth £250,000 a year. New Englanders exported dried cod across the ATLANTIC OCEAN to GREAT BRITAIN, to the MEDITERRANEAN SEA, and to the WEST INDIES. Life aboard a fishing vessel, which might have a crew of six to eight men, was relatively egalitarian, and pay, which was divided into shares, was determined in part by how much an individual could catch. Unfortunately for the fishermen, merchants who owned the fishing schooners and extended credit to them made most of the profits. The work was also seasonal, running from March through

November, with New England fishing vessels making two to three runs lasting a couple of months. The rest of the year the fishermen found more eclectic shoreside employment and lived a life close to POVERTY.

Beginning in the middle of the 18th century, the whale fishery also expanded and was largely based in Nantucket. Whalers sailed to the North Atlantic in relatively small vessels of about 60 tons and to the South Atlantic on longer voyages in ships of more than twice that size. At the beginning of the Revolutionary War, there were 177 vessels in the northern fishery and 132 in the southern fishery, and the average voyage took about four months. In the first half of the 18th century, many of the crew members had been New England NATIVE AMERICANS who were trapped in almost a form of debt peonage. By the early 1770s, while crews may have still included some Native Americans and AFRICAN AMERICANS, they were made up mostly of young men recruited throughout coastal New England. Debt played some role in the recruitment of these Yankees. Others, facing limited opportunities ashore as New England became more densely populated, sought to either provide support for young families or build up a nest egg with which to begin life ashore. Like in the cod fishery, whalers were paid in shares—called lays—with the lion's portion going to the merchant ship owner and the officers.

The Revolutionary War devastated the fishing and whaling industries. The New England Restraining Act, which Parliament passed in March 1775, barred New Englanders from fishing in Atlantic waters as of July 20, 1775. In Gloucester, Massachusetts, grass was soon "growing upon the wharves, and many of the larger class of fishing vessels were rotting on their moorings." Because of their speed and maneuverability, many fishing schooners were converted to privateering. Fisherman joined in fighting the war, often as seamen and privateers, but suffered many casualties. Gloucester supposedly lost 357 men during the war, and towns like Marblehead and Beverly were filled with widows and orphans in the 1780s.

After the war the cod fishery revived quickly as demand for fish rose across the Atlantic. The TREATY OF PARIS (1783) specifically allowed fisherman from the United States to continue to fish off the Grand Banks. Although Great Britain maintained prohibitions on imported fish, other nations were eager for the New England catch. Between 1786 and 1789 an annual average of 539 fishing vessels went to sea, mostly from New England, representing almost 20,000 tons of shipping and well over 3,200 fishermen. Moreover, conditions of employment were favorable for these men, who, because of the demand for fish, could negotiate better arrangements with merchants and had increased ownership of the fishing vessels. Atlantic fishing continued to expand until the EMBARGO OF 1807, revived a little after the embargo was repealed and suffered

again during the WAR OF 1812 (1812–15). JOHN QUINCY ADAMS, however, made sure that the TREATY OF GHENT (1814) included a provision to allow fishermen from the United States to continue to fish in the waters off Nova Scotia and Newfoundland.

Whaling, however, faced a more difficult time since several nations sought to lure New England whalemen to their own flag, and exports of whale oil faced either prohibitions or high import duties in Great Britain and even FRANCE in some years. From 1787 to 1786, an average of 91 vessels went to sea in the northern whale fishery, while another 31 voyaged to southern waters. This dropped to a mere 17 ships in both categories in 1800. Whaling picked up a little thereafter until the Embargo of 1807 and subsequent restriction on trade, followed by the War of 1812. In the meantime, some whalers from the United States had begun to enter the PACIFIC OCEAN. The halcyon days of whaling for the United States would occur between 1815 and 1860.

Beyond deep-sea fishing for cod and whales, fishing was a part of the way of life for almost every person in North America who lived near a river, lake, or bay, and it provided an important supplemental source of protein to diets. During the spring, streams would often teem with fish from the ocean seeking to spawn in fresh water, and communities might squabble over access to these "runs" of fishes, especially when some property owners built dams or hindered public access to a river. African Americans in cities like New York became known for selling oysters in the streets or from special stands and shops. Slaves in the South often augmented their meager fare with fish caught on a Sunday or at the beginning or end of a day. Native Americans, too, relied heavily on fish throughout North America. Much of the Pacific Northwest Indians' way of life depended on the bountiful supply of fish in the rivers and bays of that region.

Further reading: Thomas Jefferson, *Report of the Secretary of State, on the Subject of the Cod and Whale Fisheries* (Philadelphia: John Fenno, 1791); Daniel Vickers, *Farmers and Fishermen: Two Centuries of Work in Essex County, Massachusetts, 1630–1830* (Chapel Hill: University of North Carolina Press, 1994); Daniel Vickers, "Nantucket Whalemen in the Deep Sea Fishery: The Changing Anatomy of an Early American Labor Force," *Journal of American History* 72 (1985): 277–296.

Fishing Creek, Battle of (August 18, 1780)

After the BATTLE OF CAMDEN (August 15, 1780) during the REVOLUTIONARY WAR (1775–83), the Continental forces were in complete disarray. Warned of the British victory, General THOMAS SUMTER retreated with his 700

MILITIA up the Wateree River, bringing with him more than 100 LOYALISTS and British PRISONERS OF WAR as well as 44 captured wagons of supplies. LORD CORNWALLIS sent Colonel BANASTRE TARLETON in pursuit with 350 men and one cannon. On the afternoon of August 17, 1780, Tarleton's scouts reported that Sumter was on the other side of the Wateree on a parallel course. Tarleton reached the ferry at Rocky Mount that evening and saw Sumter's campfires a mile away. He bivouacked that night without fires, hoping to attack Sumter after he crossed the river. Although Sumter remained ignorant of Tarleton's proximity, he stayed on the other side of the river. Tarleton crossed the river on August 18 and followed Sumter, leaving some of his infantry behind because they could not keep up the pace and pressing forward with 100 dragoons and 60 infantry riding double with the mounted troops. The British troops met two of Sumter's scouts, killing them to prevent any warning from reaching the Revolutionaries. Shortly thereafter, Tarleton's men crested a hill to find Sumter's force at Fishing Creek, also called Catawba Ford, with their arms stacked and the men bathing, sleeping, or cooking, totally unaware of the approaching British. Sumter had not deployed any pickets, so Tarleton could launch his attack as a total surprise. Overwhelmed by the assault, Sumter jumped on the nearest horse and abandoned his men. Some of the militia put up a brief resistance, but the losses were devastating. Out of 700 men, 150 were killed or wounded and 350 were captured. The rest followed Sumter's example and scattered to save their own skins. Tarleton lost only 16 killed and wounded, freed the prisoners, and recaptured the supplies, including 800 horses. This victory brought great acclaim to Tarleton back in GREAT BRITAIN.

Fitch, John (1744–1798) inventor

Inventor of the first successful steamboat, John Fitch was from a poor farming family in Windsor, Connecticut, and served an apprenticeship as a clockmaker, although he was never fully trained by his master. He married in 1767, but, failing in business ventures and trapped in what he claimed was a loveless marriage, he abandoned his wife and infant son in 1768, not knowing that his wife was pregnant with their second child. Between 1769 and 1775, after establishing himself in Trenton, New Jersey, Fitch tried his hand at a variety of trades, including brass-button making, clock repair, and silversmithing. At the outbreak of the REVOLUTIONARY WAR (1775–83), he was a gunsmith and a lieutenant in the local MILITIA. However, he ran into problems with other officers, and his military service ended without distinction. His house was ransacked by the British and HESSIANS during their occupation of Trenton. For part of the war he was a supplier of ALCOHOL and TOBACCO to both the British and Revolutionary armies. Beginning in 1780, he became involved in a variety of land schemes as a surveyor and speculator in Kentucky and the Ohio country, during which he made several trips to the West, was captured by NATIVE AMERICANS, and was imprisoned by the British for nine months. By 1785 his schemes had come to naught.

About 1785 Fitch began to think about building a steamboat. Although he could not get either GEORGE WASHINGTON or the SECOND CONTINENTAL CONGRESS interested in the project, he drew up plans and built a model that had a steam engine driving paddles along the side. He submitted the plans and model to the AMERICAN PHILOSOPHICAL SOCIETY and then obtained enough backing from a variety of sources to construct a working steamboat. He demonstrated the boat in Philadelphia on August 22, 1787, in front of a huge crowd that included many members of the CONSTITUTIONAL CONVENTION. By 1790 he had constructed a steamboat with the paddles at the rear, and it ran a packet service in the summer between New Jersey and Philadelphia on the Delaware River. Despite the boat's ability to travel at eight miles per hour and work for about 2,000 miles, the enterprise was a commercial failure. By 1791 Fitch's supporters had withdrawn their backing.

Part of the difficulty for Fitch was that a Virginia builder, James Rumsey, also claimed to be the creator of the steamboat. The two vied for backers while obtaining patents and endorsements from different states. After the passage of the PATENT LAW (1790), Secretary of State THOMAS JEFFERSON issued both Rumsey and Fitch patents for their STEAMBOATS on the same day (August 26, 1791)—a solomonic act that did little to settle the controversy. In 1788 Rumsey had gone to GREAT BRITAIN to gain support. Fitch headed for Europe in 1793 but returned empty-handed the next year. Distraught over his failure and lack of recognition, Fitch moved to Kentucky and sought to obtain some lands he had surveyed a decade earlier. On July 2, 1798, he apparently committed suicide.

Further reading: Brooke Hindle, *Emulation and Invention* (New York: Norton, 1983); Andrea Sutcliffe, *Steam: The Untold Story of America's First Great Invention* (New York: Palgrave Macmillan, 2004).

Fithian, Philip Vickers (1747–1776) Presbyterian minister, writer

Born in Greenwich, New Jersey, Philip Vickers Fithian was a plantation tutor, PRESBYTERIAN minister and missionary, and a prolific diarist. Fithian graduated from the College of New Jersey (later Princeton University) in 1772 and considered pursuing the ministry but was diverted from this course by the unexpected death of his parents. He traveled back home, where he studied theology under a local minister and at Deerfield, Massachusetts. In 1773 he accepted a tutoring position in Virginia at the request of Robert Carter III, the wealthy owner of a plantation called Nomini Hall. While there, Fithian recorded observations detailing the social, economic, educational, and cultural aspects of pre-revolutionary Virginia life, writing everything down in his journals and letters. Scholars consider his writings to be of particular interest because they provide a glimpse of the social relations between wealthy planters, common folk, and slaves.

Fithian departed from Nomini Hall in 1774 to study for the ministry and was ordained the same year. Following his theological training, he served in 1775 as a Presbyterian missionary in Pennsylvania and Virginia, then enlisted as a chaplain of the New Jersey state MILITIA at the commencement of the REVOLUTIONARY WAR (1775–83). However, he became ill with camp fever and died near FORT WASHINGTON on October 8, 1776.

Further reading: John Fea, *The Way of Improvement Leads Home: Philip Vickers Fithian and the Rural Enlightenment in Early America* (Philadelphia: University of Pennsylvania Press, 2008)

—William R. Smith

Fitzsimons, Thomas (1741–1811) *Pennsylvania politician, businessman*

An Irish immigrant who arrived in Philadelphia in 1760, Thomas Fitzsimons made his way from clerk at a countinghouse to partnership in the merchant firm of George Meade—in part by marrying Catherine Meade, his partner's sister. Fitzsimons supported the RESISTANCE MOVEMENT against British imperial measures and became a member of the Philadelphia COMMITTEE OF CORRESPONDENCE. During the REVOLUTIONARY WAR (1775–83) he organized a MILITIA company and saw combat in New Jersey. But his major contribution to the war effort was political. He sat on a variety of Revolutionary committees during the war and was a delegate to the SECOND CONTINENTAL CONGRESS in 1782 and 1783. By that time he was already identified with the nationalists who wanted to strengthen the central government and empower Congress with the ability to levy taxes directly. He had also been involved with the formation of the BANK OF NORTH AMERICA and was on its board of directors until 1803. He became active in Pennsylvania state politics during the 1780s and was elected to the state assembly in 1785–87. Within the state, he opposed the democratic Pennsylvania state constitution.

Fitzsimons persisted in his elitist and pronationalist politics with the formation of the new U.S. government under the CONSTITUTION. He was a delegate to the CONSTITUTIONAL CONVENTION, where he supported strengthening the central government. He served three terms in the House of Representatives from 1789 to 1794 and became a congressional spokesman for the policies of Secretary of the Treasury ALEXANDER HAMILTON. Defeated in his reelection bid in 1794, Fitzsimons never again held elective office. However, he remained interested in politics, opposing the FRENCH REVOLUTION (1789–99); the DEMOCRATIC-REPUBLICAN SOCIETIES; the WHISKEY REBELLION (1794); and, after 1800, most of the policies of THOMAS JEFFERSON.

Fitzsimons's major interests were in business. He was a founder of the Insurance Company of North America and became president of the Philadelphia chamber of commerce in 1801. He struggled with bankruptcy in 1805, in part because he had been involved with ROBERT MORRIS's speculations, but later regained some of his fortune. He died in Philadelphia on August 26, 1811.

flags

Flags served as powerful, visual political symbols throughout the era of the AMERICAN REVOLUTION. English colonial troops proudly fought under the British Union Jack during the FRENCH AND INDIAN WAR (1754–63) and widely celebrated this symbol in the aftermath of that conflict. However, as tensions between GREAT BRITAIN and the North American colonies escalated over imperial regulation, new flags emerged as symbols of colonial dissent and, ultimately, as symbols of an independent political identity.

The RESISTANCE MOVEMENT (1764–75) spawned many flags of protest. The STAMP ACT (1765) led to the creation of the "Boston Liberty Flag"; this flag had 13 alternating red-and-white stripes and eventually became the base design for the later U.S. national flag. A solitary pine tree on a white background, a symbol that evoked human connections with divinity, was a widely used flag motif in the 1770s. But perhaps the most famous of these political protest flags was the one raised at Taunton, Massachusetts, in 1774: The British Union Jack was placed in the upper left corner on a solid red background, and the words *Liberty and Union* appeared at the bottom (some variations simply read "Liberty"). The flag symbolized colonial frustrations toward parliamentary policy but emphasized loyalty to the Crown.

The REVOLUTIONARY WAR (1775–83) led to the creation of several different military flags. The dominant symbol for military flags was the rattlesnake. The most famous flags crafted from this motif include the Gadsden Flag (a coiled rattlesnake on a yellow background with the phrase *Don't Tread on Me* at the bottom) and the first U.S. Navy Jack (a straight rattlesnake on 13 red and white stripes with the phrase *Don't Tread on Me*). Colonel CHRISTOPHER

GADSDEN formally submitted the coiled-snake design for the MILITIA in the South Carolina legislature, and Commodore ESEK HOPKINS himself sailed under it.

The first national flag was approved by the SECOND CONTINENTAL CONGRESS in June 1777: It had 13 stars on a blue field in the upper left corner (the arrangement of the stars varied between rows and a single circle—the circular star arrangement is associated with BETSY ROSS) and 13 alternating red-and-white stripes in the background. In 1795 two more stars and two more stripes were added to represent Kentucky and Vermont, and the linear arrangement of the stars became standard. However, in 1818 the U.S. Congress decided to return the flag to its original design of 13 stripes (for the original colonies) and simply add additional stars for new states.

Further reading: Kevin and Peter Keim, *A Grand Old Flag: A History of the United States through Its Flags* (New York: DK Publishing, 2007).

—R. Michael Barnett

Fletcher v. Peck (1810)

In 1803, as an outgrowth of the YAZOO CLAIMS, the New England Mississippi Land Company (NEMLC) began a lawsuit that reached the U.S. SUPREME COURT in 1810 as *Fletcher v. Peck*. Since an individual could not sue a state under the provisions of the ELEVENTH AMENDMENT to the U.S. CONSTITUTION, a suit had to be brought by an individual from one state against an individual from another state. In all likelihood, *Fletcher v. Peck* was a collusive suit where both parties agreed to go to court to obtain an end that would be good for both parties. In this case the defendant, John Peck of Massachusetts, was a director of the NEMLC, while Robert Fletcher, who purchased land from Peck, was a known speculator whose expenses were paid by the NEMLC. The suit claimed that the state legislature's repeal of the initial sale to the Georgia Mississippi Company (which had then sold some of the land to the NEMLC) violated the contracts clause of the Constitution, which prevents states from passing laws "impairing the Obligation of Contracts."

The case began in 1803, was delayed at the circuit level for a few years, and then decided in Peck's favor in 1807. The decision was appealed to the Supreme Court and heard in the winter of 1809–10. Peck's LAWYERS included JOHN QUINCY ADAMS, Robert Goodloe Harper, and JOSEPH STORY. Fletcher was represented by LUTHER MARTIN. The Supreme Court, under Chief Justice JOHN MARSHALL, decided in Peck's favor, issuing an opinion on March 16, 1810, asserting that the Georgia legislature's action was unconstitutional. As Marshall explained, "When a law is in its nature a contract, when absolute rights have

vested under that contract, a repeal of the law cannot divest those rights." Marshall also asserted that the repeal law violated the constitutional provisions against bills of attainder and ex-post facto laws. This marked the Supreme Court's first exercise of the judicial review power to invalidate a state's legislative act. This decision angered the anti-Yazooists in Congress, who wondered if the Supreme Court had to be obeyed. Ultimately, the federal legislature decided to abide by the Supreme Court's decision, and in 1814 Congress implemented a plan for providing compensation to the Yazoo speculators.

Further reading: C. Peter Magrath, *Yazoo: Law and Politics in the New Republic* (Providence, R.I.: Brown University Press, 1966).

Floyd, William (1734–1821) *New York politician*

William Floyd was born into a wealthy landholding family in Brookhaven, Suffolk County, on the southern shore of Long Island, New York. He attended both the FIRST CONTINENTAL CONGRESS and SECOND CONTINENTAL CONGRESS and signed the DECLARATION OF INDEPENDENCE. As a supporter of the AMERICAN REVOLUTION, he became a colonel in the Suffolk County MILITIA in 1775 and served as a New York state senator from 1777 to 1779. During the war, the British seized his property on Long Island, and Floyd had to settle his family in Middleport, Connecticut. From 1779 to 1783 he again sat in the Continental Congress. Following the war, he returned to rebuild his estate, but in 1784 he also purchased a tract of land along the Mohawk River (in what later became Oneida County, New York).

After the REVOLUTIONARY WAR (1775–83), Floyd had a modest political career, again serving as a state senator (1784–88). Despite Suffolk County's ANTI-FEDERALIST tendencies, he was an advocate for the U.S. CONSTITUTION. He was elected to the House of Representatives in 1789 but failed to be reelected in 1791. He became a member of the DEMOCRATIC-REPUBLICAN PARTY and was a friend and supporter of THOMAS JEFFERSON. Floyd moved to Westernville, Oneida County, New York, in 1803. His new neighbors elected him to the state senate in 1808, but his involvement in politics at this point was minimal. He died in Westernville on August 4, 1821.

—Daniel Flaherty

Florida

Between 1754 and 1819, Florida changed hands three times: The TREATY OF PARIS (1763) transferred the territory from SPAIN to GREAT BRITAIN, the TREATY OF PARIS (1783) returned it to the Spanish, and between 1795 and

1821 the United States obtained Florida piece by piece through treaties and military action. From before the REVOLUTIONARY WAR (1775–83) to the final acquisition of all of Florida, the territory remained a sparsely settled borderland, often serving as a haven for illegal TRADE, escaped slaves, and NATIVE AMERICANS raiding across the border.

Before 1763, Spain's hold on Florida, centered on St. Augustine, remained weak. The Spanish encouraged slaves from the British North American colonies to escape to Florida, assuring them freedom and using them to help protect the province. At the time, Florida had an ambiguous northern boundary and stretched only as far west as Pensacola. With the British victory in the FRENCH AND INDIAN WAR (1754–63), Florida became part of the British Empire since Spain had allied with FRANCE. After the change in ownership in 1763, many Spanish settlers and their Native American allies left the province for other Spanish colonies. As a part of the PROCLAMATION OF 1763, the British encouraged settlement in the region and organized the territory into two separate colonies: East Florida, which consisted of the swampy peninsula and the land directly south of Georgia; and West Florida, with the eastern boundary at the Apalachicola River and the Mississippi River as its western boundary. West Florida reached as far north as the 31st parallel (extended to 32°28' north in 1764) and included about a third of the present states of Alabama and Mississippi. As British settlers arrived in the two colonies, they sought to establish the slave ECONOMY that predominated in nearby Georgia and South Carolina.

The outbreak of the REVOLUTIONARY WAR (1775–83) left the two Florida colonies in an awkward position. While some of the colonists favored the opposition to British imperial regulation, many remained loyal to King GEORGE III, recognizing their vulnerability on the FRONTIER. The Floridas thus became a base for LOYALISTS and Native Americans during the war. However, that haven was threatened by the Spanish after they went to war against Great Britain in 1779. The Spanish governor of LOUISIANA, BERNARDO DE GÁLVEZ, swept the lower Mississippi River of British forces in 1779. He then captured Mobile on March 12, 1780, and completed the conquest of West Florida by seizing Pensacola on May 10, 1781. Having lost West Florida, the British ceded East Florida to Spain during the peace negotiations in 1783.

At this point, Florida again returned to its borderland status as a haven for escaped slaves and Native Americans. In fact, an influx of CREEK refugees who had sided with the British in the Revolutionary War moved into the area to become the nucleus of the Native American group called the SEMINOLE. Although there was some exodus of British subjects, many chose to stay. Florida's British and Spanish populations, however, were minimal.

Almost from its inception, the United States coveted Florida, whose northern boundary remained in dispute. Spain was not happy with the peace treaty that granted the United States territory as far west as the Mississippi River. To preempt U.S. settlement in the region, the Spanish bribed men such as JAMES WILKINSON in an effort to buy their allegiance and developed positive relations with the major Native American groups in the area. Initially, Spain claimed a northern boundary of 32°28' (which had been the British border of West Florida), but during the 1780s the Spanish king extended that boundary to include the east bank of the Mississippi River to the Ohio River and then along the Ohio River to the Tennessee River to the Appalachian Mountains (comprising almost all of the modern states of Mississippi and Alabama and sections of Kentucky, Tennessee, and Georgia).

The United States chipped away at Florida's expansive boundaries beginning in 1795. That year, the PINCKNEY TREATY set the northern line for West Florida at the 31st parallel. The LOUISIANA PURCHASE (1803) established the next claim for Florida. The negotiators were supposed to buy Florida and New Orleans, not the vast track of land west of the Mississippi. Based on the fact that the purchase treaty with the French had merely stated that the territory that had been ceded from Spain to France was now given to the United States, ROBERT R. LIVINGSTON claimed that most of West Florida was included in the Louisiana Purchase. The Spanish did not agree with this interpretation, nor did the United States push it immediately. But having Spanish control over Florida created problems for the United States, as British traders infiltrated the region and hostile Native Americans used Florida for a base of operations. Moreover, in the 1790s and early 1800s, many settlers from the United States, often debtors and men on the run, crossed into both Floridas. A group of European-American settlers in Baton Rouge, West Florida, declared their independence from Spain on September 23, 1810, and sought to become part of the United States. President JAMES MADISON obliged them by proclaiming on October 27, 1810, that West Florida "has at all times, as is well known, been considered and claimed" as part of the United States and then sent troops to Baton Rouge to back up this assertion. By 1811, U.S. troops were stationed outside Mobile in West Florida, and Madison set the Perdido River as the boundary between Spanish and U.S. territory. When Louisiana entered the union as a state in 1812, it included a section of West Florida on the east bank of the Mississippi. That same year, the United States extended its efforts in Florida. A band of Georgians and soldiers from the U.S. ARMY seized Amelia Island, failed in an attack on St. Augustine, and were ultimately forced to withdraw. However, in 1813 Madison sent General Wilkinson to occupy Mobile using the claim that it had the potential to be a base of operations for the British. Without any basis in international law, another chunk of Florida became part of the United States. The fact that the United States was not at war with Spain seems not to have bothered any of the invaders.

In the years after the TREATY OF GHENT (1814), the United States became even more aggressive in its bid for Florida. When escaped slaves established a fort and a haven for other runaways, a military expedition struck across the border in 1816, blew up the fort, and killed 270 African-American men, women, and children. By 1818 Seminole raids had become serious enough to draw the attention of General ANDREW JACKSON, commander for the southern district of the U.S. Army. He crossed the border, defeated any Native Americans who opposed him, and arrested two British traders, John Ambrister and Alexander Arbuthnot. Convinced that both men had encouraged the Indians and supplied them with arms, Jackson saw to it that Ambrister and Arbuthnot were executed after conviction in an ad hoc court of law. Then, believing that President JAMES MONROE wanted him to drive the Spanish out of Florida, he occupied Pensacola and sent the Spanish governor and his officials to CUBA. These actions created an uproar in Monroe's cabinet and caused an international crisis. Eventually, the controversy subsided. JOHN QUINCY ADAMS persuaded the Spanish to sell Florida for $5 million and, in an effort to concede something to the Spanish, set a western boundary to the Louisiana Territory in the Adams-Onis Treaty of 1819. While the purchase of Florida opened up more area for the expansion of SLAVERY, the Seminole in central Florida were not easily subdued and fought the U.S. government for decades to come.

See also FOREIGN AFFAIRS.

Further reading: Thomas D. Clark and John D. W. Guice, *Frontiers in Conflict: The Old Southwest, 1795–1830* (Albuquerque: University of New Mexico Press, 1989); James G. Cusick, *The Other War of 1812: The Patriot War and the American Invasion of East Florida* (Gainesville: University Press of Florida, 203); Robert L. Gold, *Borderland Empires in Transition: The Triple-Nation Transfer of Florida* (Carbondale: Southern Illinois Press, 1969); David J. Weber, *The Spanish Frontier in North America* (New Haven, Conn.: Yale University Press, 1992); William Earl Weeks, *John Quincy Adams and American Global Empire* (Lexington: University of Kentucky Press, 1992).

food

North Americans probably ate more and better food than any other people in the world in the 1754–1815 period, with more meat and a greater abundance of grains and other staples. As a result of better nutrition, the average height of North Americans was taller than their contemporaries in Europe. Seasonal variations had some impact on all North Americans and some years were more bountiful than others. The REVOLUTIONARY WAR (1775–83), in particular, created hardships for many because of the inflation and destruction that accompanied the conflict. There was a marked difference in food consumption among European Americans based on socioeconomic status and location: The rich ate better than the poor, and people in the countryside ate better than those in the cities. Within the period, there also occurred a "revolution in diet," as Dr. BENJAMIN RUSH commented in 1810, with the introduction of more vegetables and different standards for food presentation among European Americans. In addition, some significant differences in food consumption developed among European Americans, AFRICAN AMERICANS, and NATIVE AMERICANS.

The basic staple of most European Americans was corn and pork. In the North and East, beef, cheese, and butter were more plentiful than in the South and West, but whether it was freshly slaughtered or salted, pork was ubiquitous. Pigs, which could be found in the streets of New York City and the backwoods of Kentucky, were relatively cheap to raise since they were often allowed to roam freely in search of food. Besides corn, which almost every farmer raised, WHEAT and rye were also prevalent. Apples were made into hard cider to drink, and in the 1790s and early 1800s, more and more farmers made whiskey from grains. Game, fowl, and fish supplemented many diets, especially for those people who lived closer to the FRONTIER. In more settled regions, much of the countryside had been denuded of forests to make way for farms, and overhunting had depleted the available game. Harvest time was a season of plenty, but winters and early spring could be periods of shortage as food salted and stored the previous fall might run out.

Wartime always created hardship since armies drained available labor supply and raised prices as contractors sought to acquire enough provisions to feed thousands of mouths. The FRENCH AND INDIAN WAR (1754–63) and the WAR OF 1812 (1812–15) both had an impact on food prices. Because of the difficulty of transportation during the War of 1812, large disparities occurred: In Virginia there was a glut on the market, and it was hardly worth the cost of growing wheat, while in northern New York, where armies from both CANADA and the United States purchased food, wheat was expensive and difficult to obtain. Similarly, sugar was three times the price in Baltimore that it was in New Orleans. Food, however, was a more serious problem during the Revolutionary War. There were at least 30 FOOD RIOTS triggered by inflation and wartime shortages. The official ration for a soldier in the CONTINENTAL ARMY was a pound of bread, a pound of meat, a gill of peas, and a gill of rum a day, but soldiers seldom had this full ration.

On a daily basis, common soldiers such as JOSEPH PLUMB MARTIN were more interested in finding their next meal than anything else. On several occasions, soldiers were so starved that they were driven to mutiny.

In the 1750s most food for European Americans was made into some sort of gruel or mush and served in a wooden bowl. The poorest half of the population ate this single-dish meal with their fingers or a spoon. Many of these people would not have a table or chair in their house and would therefore eat their meal in a makeshift manner. However, the other half of the population, aspiring to greater gentility, had a table and chairs in their house and ate from plates with a knife and fork. Those furthest up the social scale would also eat a greater variety of food served in distinct portions with meats, vegetables, and grains separated. This trend expanded throughout European-American society in the second half of the 18th and early 19th centuries. In addition, as part of Benjamin Rush's diet revolution, many people in the United States liberated themselves from the seasonality of food preparation by growing a variety of vegetables and purchasing other food items at a local store. One important sign of this shift in food preparation was the publication of the cookbook American Cookery (1796), written by Amelia Simmons.

Food for Native Americans varied from tribe to tribe and group to group. Most Native American villages east of the Mississippi River remained centered on growing beans, corn, and squash, supplemented with hunting and fishing. This dependence on AGRICULTURE left Indians vulnerable during wars with European Americans who invaded Native American territory to burn fields and to force them to the brink of starvation. Revolutionary Americans used this tactic repeatedly against the CREEK and CHEROKEE in the South, the Indians in the Ohio country, and most successfully in the incursion into Iroquoia in 1779. Further west, Native Americans of the Great Plains became increasingly involved in hunting BUFFALO in the mid-18th century but also traded for agricultural produce from Indians living along the edges of the Plains. In CALIFORNIA, more and more Indians were being compelled to work at Franciscan missions to obtain food, as their normal resources became depleted due to the introduction of domestic animals that accompanied Spanish intrusion into the region, which destroyed native vegetation. The Pacific Northwest Indians had developed a highly self-sufficient culture based on fish (see FISHING) and agricultural products.

African-American slaves had a limited diet that was similar to the poorest of the European Americans but relied more on corn, with only occasional supplements of meat. Some slaves were able to hunt, fish, and have their own garden plots, but their fare remained meager compared to European Americans. Slaves who worked in the master's house might have access to food left over from their owners' table. Slaves in different parts of the country could also have variations in diet; those in the North ate better than those in the South. Rations in the lowcountry of South Carolina were sparser than in the Chesapeake, forcing many lowcountry slaves to forage and grow a larger proportion of their own food. Lowcountry slaves also raised more different types of vegetables, including many varieties from AFRICA. The free African-American population in both the North and the South had a greater range of diets depending on their economic status, but most free blacks were relatively impoverished.

Further reading: Richard L. Bushman, *The Refinement of America: Persons, Houses, Cities* (New York: Knopf, 1992); E. Wayne Carp, *To Starve the Army at Pleasure: Continental Army Administration and American Political Culture, 1775–1783* (Chapel Hill: University of North Carolina Press, 1984); Jack Larkin, *The Reshaping of Everyday Life, 1790–1830* (New York: Harper & Row, 1988); Philip D. Morgan, *Slave Counterpoint: Black Culture in the Eighteenth-Century Chesapeake and Lowcountry* (Chapel Hill: University of North Carolina Press, 1998).

food riots

Food RIOTS had a long tradition in Anglo-American culture in the 18th century. In England, common folk often rioted when the price of bread or grain became too high because bakers or merchants sent their supplies of food to distant markets to make greater profits. In these popular disturbances the crowd would often seize the contested bread and either distribute it or actually sell it at the "just price"—the normal price accepted by the community. This type of riot occurred only rarely in British North America. Three bread riots broke out in Boston, and a handful of other mob actions regulated market conditions in a few other colonial cities. However, during the REVOLUTIONARY WAR (1775–83) at least 30 food or market riots were triggered by profiteering, an inflationary currency, high demand for foodstuffs, and wartime shortages. Like many similar riots in England and Europe, the revolutionary bread riots included a high level of participation of women in the crowd since women were most directly involved in local produce markets. These crowds would behave in a manner similar to the English bread riots, but they often inserted some political content by charging the monopolizers of foodstuffs with being Tories (LOYALISTS) and would sometimes drive the violators out of the community. These crowds also were concerned with a variety of market items besides bread, including tea, coffee, sugar, meat, and salt. Most of the riots—at least the ones for which historians have found evidence—occurred north of Maryland and took place in cities and smaller towns. After the Revolutionary War there is no record of any other food riots until the 1830s.

Further reading: Paul A. Gilje, *Rioting in America* (Bloomington: Indiana University Press, 1996); Barbara Clark Smith, "Food Rioters and the American Revolution," *William and Mary Quarterly* 3rd ser., 51 (1994): 3–39.

Forbes, John (1707–1759) *British military officer*
A member of a Scottish military family, John Forbes joined the British army in 1735 as a cornet, saw extensive action during the War of Austrian Succession (1740–48) in Europe, and fought at the Battle of Culloden (April 16, 1746) in suppression of the Jacobite uprising. By 1750 he had been promoted to lieutenant colonel in his regiment, the 2nd Royal North British Dragoons, or Scots Greys. After the FRENCH AND INDIAN WAR (1754–63) broke out, he became colonel of the 17th Regiment of Foot in 1757 and was sent to Halifax, NOVA SCOTIA, as adjutant general to JOHN CAMPBELL; FOURTH EARL OF LOUDOUN.

Forbes was promoted to brigadier general in December 1757 and placed in command of the expedition to capture Fort Duquesne. During the spring and summer of 1758, he slowly built an army of almost 2,000 regulars and 5,000 provincial troops. Determined not to repeat the mistakes of General EDWARD BRADDOCK, Forbes sought Native American allies. The CHEROKEE who joined his expedition, however, soon tired of his slow progress and his insistence that they be disciplined like regular soldiers instead of treated as honored allies. Most of the Cherokee abandoned his army and headed back to their home. (It was during their trek south that European-American settlers on the Virginia FRONTIER killed some Cherokee in an action that triggered the CHEROKEE WAR). Forbes was unable to obtain military allies from more local Indians, such as the DELAWARE and SHAWNEE, but through careful diplomacy he was able to neutralize the erstwhile French allies at the TREATY OF EASTON (1758).

Besides dealing with Native Americans, Forbes had several other problems to overcome, including some difficulty with competing colonial authorities and his provincial troops. Virginians wanted him to follow the road that Braddock had built, which ran from the Potomac River. This approach would have solidified Virginian claims to the forks of the Ohio, but Forbes decided to build a new road west through Pennsylvania instead. He also had little respect for his colonial soldiers, calling them a "a gathering from the scum of the worst of people." Despite his bias, he was able to work with them and complete his campaign before the expiration of their enlistments in December. On top of these difficulties, Forbes was desperately ill from a skin disease. He was often so debilitated that he had to be carried in a litter.

Yet through perseverance, careful planning, and a good bit of luck, Forbes succeeded. He proceeded slowly across Pennsylvania, building forts every 40 miles and stocking them with provisions. In September he agreed to send an advance expedition under Major JAMES GRANT in an effort to surprise the French at Fort Duquesne. Instead, on September 14, 1758, the French and Indians surprised Grant, capturing him and decimating his ranks. Forbes still kept on. On November 23, 1758, as his army came within 10 miles of its goal, the undermanned French abandoned and blew up Fort Duquesne. Forbes arrived the next day, ordered a stockade to be built, and renamed the place FORT PITT. He returned to Philadelphia with an inflamed stomach and liver, dying on March 11, 1759.

Besides Forbes's leadership, French problems with supply and difficulties with their Native-American allies were crucial to the success of the expedition. The capture and destruction of FORT FRONTENAC on August 27, 1758, meant that the garrison at Fort Duquesne had to be reduced to just 300 men in the closing phases of the campaign. Such a small force had little chance against the large British-American army under Forbes. Moreover, without gifts from the storehouse at Fort Frontenac the French were unable to sustain Native American support. In an odd twist of fate, some of the early French successes in raiding the British as they advanced, and in defeating Grant, provided those Indian allies who had been at Fort Duquesne with prisoners and booty that enabled them to return to their tribes as triumphant warriors as the French faced defeat. Meanwhile, Forbes's campaign against Fort Duquesne secured much of the Ohio Valley for the British and contributed significantly to the conquest of CANADA.

Further reading: Fred Anderson, *Crucible of War: The Seven Years' War and the Fate of Empire in British North America, 1754–1766* (New York: Knopf, 2000).

foreign affairs
Between 1754 and 1815, colonial British America and then the United States struggled with four major foreign policy problems. First, and most persistent, was defining its relationship with GREAT BRITAIN and FRANCE as those two nations vied for world dominance. Second, there was the declining Spanish power on the southern and, for a while, western boundary. Third, once the United States became independent, it suffered periodic depredations against shipping by the Barbary States of North Africa on the ATLANTIC OCEAN and the MEDITERRANEAN SEA. The fourth issue centered on the question of race and SLAVERY on the international scene. Although these problems persisted for

the United States, by 1815 each had come to some resolution. Great Britain and France no longer opposed one another, SPAIN was losing its grip on its colonies and would soon surrender FLORIDA to the United States, the Barbary States had at last been defeated, and the United States had outlawed the SLAVE TRADE and had decided to ignore the black republic of HAITI. With these problems out of the way or put aside, the United States after 1815 could seek new commercial outlets and eventually expand in the North American continent.

In 1754 colonial Americans knew where they stood: They were Anglo-Britons locked in a death struggle to drive the French from the continent and subdue NATIVE AMERICANS. There can be no doubt about the enthusiasm colonial Americans had for the FRENCH AND INDIAN WAR (1754–63) and the loyalty they felt to the British Crown. Victory on the Plains of Abraham during the BATTLE OF QUEBEC (September 13, 1759) meant peace and security in a world that had been threatened repeatedly by the French and Indians. But if every colonial American was a British patriot, not everyone followed British imperial regulations. Many merchants had earned a fortune trading with the French and others in the WEST INDIES, even during the war. This SMUGGLING meant jobs for SEAMEN and dockside workers. It also provided markets for goods produced by farmers. Efforts to change this illegal way of life were bound to bring opposition. However, colonial Americans, even during the RESISTANCE MOVEMENT (1764–75), were not ready to jump into the arms of the French. The imperial debate was a debate within, not against, the British Empire.

The guns fired at the BATTLES OF LEXINGTON AND CONCORD (April 19, 1775) changed the situation. Once war broke out, the revolutionaries needed outside support. Inspired by the ideals of REPUBLICANISM, the SECOND CONTINENTAL CONGRESS drew up a model treaty it hoped all nations would sign. The treaty offered free and open TRADE with the United States, but in a world of power politics, no one took it seriously. France, still resentful of its defeat, was willing to aid the rebellion but wanted concessions. The two treaties of 1778 provided most-favored-nation trading status to France and promised a defensive alliance. The Spanish and the Dutch joined in the war before the conflict was over, but neither signed a formal alliance with the United States. Both provided loans and support, and with this foreign assistance, the rebellion eventually succeeded.

In the years after the TREATY OF PARIS (1783) the United States did not get much respect. During the 1780s the diplomatic corps consisted mainly of THOMAS JEFFERSON in Paris and JOHN ADAMS in London. Limits were put on U.S. trade, the Barbary States threatened in the Mediterranean, the British occupied FRONTIER outposts, and Spain contested the southern boundary and navigation on the Mississippi River. Ratification of the U.S. CONSTITUTION did not materially change the situation. Only when war broke out in 1793 between France, inspired by its own revolution, and Great Britain did significant changes occur.

Once again, Americans were confronted with a war between France and Great Britain. France wanted the United States to honor its 1778 treaty obligations and sent Citizen EDMOND-CHARLES GENÊT to convince the United States to at least allow the French to issue PRIVATEERING licenses and launch military expeditions from U.S. territory. The administration of GEORGE WASHINGTON hesitated and then issued the NEUTRALITY PROCLAMATION, declaring the nation would not come to the aid of either power. Because of British seizures of merchant ships and the IMPRESSMENT of sailors, Washington sent JOHN JAY to Great Britain. JAY'S TREATY (1794) left several issues unsettled but granted most-favored-nation trading rights to the British. Distraught over this position, the French began to seize U.S. ships, precipitating a crisis. When French agents insisted on a bribe before negotiations could begin in the XYZ AFFAIR (1797–98), the United States entered the QUASI-WAR (1798–1800), an undeclared war in which the U.S. NAVY fought several engagements against the French. After NAPOLEON BONAPARTE seized power in France, peace was restored as the French agreed that their alliance with the United States was void and stopped capturing merchantmen. The United States did not press for reparations and agreed to treat French trade on equal terms with British trade.

No sooner had Napoleon signed the agreement ending the Quasi-War than he secretly had Spain cede the LOUISIANA Territory to France. Spain, recognizing its weakness in the Western Hemisphere, had already granted the United States free navigation of the Mississippi River, access to New Orleans, and a favorable Florida boundary in the PINCKNEY TREATY (1795). Now it surrendered a huge chunk of North America to Napoleon, who hoped to launch a Franco-American empire. Those dreams ended when a French expedition failed to secure the rebellious province of Saint Domingue. In an effort to raise MONEY for his armies, Napoleon offered the opportunity to buy all of Louisiana. Jefferson had sought to obtain New Orleans but capitalized on the chance to double the size of the nation in the LOUISIANA PURCHASE (1803).

The war in Europe continued to create problems for the United States as the British insisted on stopping U.S. ships and impressing seamen. In the *CHESAPEAKE-LEOPARD AFFAIR* (1807), they even fired on and searched a U.S. naval frigate. Compounding the problem of impressment was the issue of neutral rights. U.S. merchants profited greatly as neutral carriers to both belligerents. The British and French sought to stifle each other's economy by putting limits on such trade. In the ORDERS IN COUNCIL the British demanded that all neutral ships stop in Great Britain before trading with the continent to ensure there was no contraband or war materials on board. Napoleon issued the BERLIN DECREE (1806) and the MILAN DECREE (1807), asserting that any vessel that stopped in Great Britain before entering French-controlled Europe would be liable to seizure. Caught between a rock and a hard place, Jefferson opted to use trade as a diplomatic weapon. His DEMOCRATIC-REPUBLICAN PARTY controlled Congress and passed the EMBARGO OF 1807, which prohibited all exports. As this measure devastated the U.S. ECONOMY, President JAMES MADISON offered adjustments to the trade restrictions, first in the NON-INTERCOURSE ACT (1809), which promised not to trade with both powers until they allowed neutral trade; then with MACON'S BILL NO. 2 (1810), which allowed trade but promised to resume nonintercourse with one power if the other lifted its constraints. When, in the CADORE LETTER, Napoleon suggested that he would do so, the United States reinstated nonintercourse with Great Britain. This action precipitated a crisis that led to the outbreak of the WAR OF 1812 (1812–15).

Although the TREATY OF GHENT (1814) settled none of the outstanding issues between the United States and Great Britain, it marked the end of the biggest foreign-policy problem for the young nation during its first 50 years. Since Napoleon was defeated, impressment and neutral rights became moot issues, and henceforth the United States and Great Britain would settle their affairs amicably.

Other foreign-policy issues also moved toward settlement. Spain, ever weaker and facing rebellions in its American colonies, allowed itself to be bullied out of Florida in return for some compensation and a defined boundary between Texas and Louisiana. After the Adams-Onus Treaty (1819), Spain would not present a serious diplomatic challenge until the end of the 19th century. The Barbary States had been a nuisance and embarrassment for the United States since the 1780s. In 1793 Algiers captured 11 U.S. merchant ships and enslaved more than 100 sailors. Although the United States started to build a navy to deal with this problem, negotiations in 1795 led to a settlement that cost nearly $1 million. Then, in 1801, a war broke out with Tripoli that lasted until 1805. The United States agreed to pay $60,000 for the release of naval PRISONERS OF WAR, and Tripoli agreed to forego all tribute. The other Barbary States came to similar terms until the War of 1812 and more seizures by Algiers. With an enlarged U.S. Navy in 1815, STEPHEN DECATUR forced the Barbary States to submit to treaties without any payment.

The conflict with the Barbary States also brought into focus the fourth major issue confronted by the United States—how to deal with race and slavery on the international scene—by providing the odd spectacle of dark-skinned Africans enslaving white-skinned sailors. This issue became particularly salient given the questions raised about slavery during the AMERICAN REVOLUTION. Almost as soon as the revolutionaries began talking about LIBERTY, they were confronted with the contradiction of living in a society that supported slavery. One of the first reactions to this problem was to attack the international SLAVE TRADE, which Jefferson had wanted to blame on King GEORGE III in the DECLARATION OF INDEPENDENCE (1776). Most states passed laws ending the slave trade in the 1770s and 1780s, although the CONSTITUTIONAL CONVENTION (1787) compromised on the issue by preventing the federal government from ending the slave trade for 20 years. In 1807, however, Congress passed legislation that abolished the slave trade on January 1, 1808. This action made an important statement about slavery in international waters; however, in much of the United States, slavery remained legal, and most of the nation's whites continued to look on other races as inferior.

This racism was evident in the relationship between Haiti and the United States. Throughout the upheaval of the 1790s in Saint Domingue, U.S. merchants did business on the troubled island, and the FEDERALIST PARTY under John Adams even worked out an accommodation with TOUSSAINT LOUVERTURE. In 1798 Joseph Bunel, a Haitian of mixed race, came to the United States to represent Louverture, met with Secretary of State TIMOTHY PICKERING, and then had dinner with Adams—the first presidential dinner with a black man. Adams and Pickering sent Dr. Edward Stevens to Saint Dominigue as general consul. Stevens negotiated a deal that guaranteed the neutrality of the rebellious French possession during the QUASI-WAR (1798–1800), while the United States, in turn, provided some naval support for Louverture's troops fighting dissidents. All of these arrangements fell apart once Jefferson took office. From 1801 to 1804, Jefferson seemed to want to placate both the French and the Haitians in their conflict. However, after Haiti succeeded in gaining its independence, Jefferson refused to recognize the new state—a position that would not be changed by subsequent administrations until Abraham Lincoln became president. In short, the United States dealt with the problem of having a black republic in the WEST INDIES by ignoring it.

In part through luck and in part through dint of arms, the United States emerged from this period in a position of relative strength, ready to tell the rest of the world that it would mind its own business if the world kept at arms length—a policy articulated by Secretary of State JOHN QUINCY ADAMS in the Monroe Doctrine (1821).

See also BARBARY WARS; FRENCH ALLIANCE; FRENCH REVOLUTION.

Further reading: Reginald Horsman, *The Causes of the War of 1812* (Philadelphia: University of Pennsylvania Press, 1962); Bradford Perkins, *The Cambridge History of American Foreign Relations: Vol. 1: The Creation of a Republican Empire, 1776–1865* (New York: Cambridge University Press, 1993); Paul A. Varg, *Foreign Policies of the Founding Fathers* (East Lansing: Michigan State University Press, 1963).

forests

Forests were the most important feature of the landscape in revolutionary America. They provided shelter for wild ANIMALS; forage for livestock; and wood, the period's crucial building and heating material. By the mid-18th century, forests still covered nearly half of the present-day United States (excluding Alaska and Hawaii). The majority of forest—roughly 80 percent—blanketed the region between the GREAT PLAINS and ATLANTIC OCEAN, interrupted only by isolated savannahs and prairies created by lightning and Native American fires. The remaining one-fifth of forests were on the coast of the PACIFIC OCEAN and in portions of the Rocky Mountains, especially what became the states of Colorado, Wyoming, and Idaho. Variations in climate, precipitation, and soil composition made the North American forest remarkably complex and diverse. In the East, the forest included several species of pine—loblolly, longleaf, shortleaf, jack, red, and white—in addition to ash, aspen, birch, cottonwood, cypress, elm, fir, gum, hickory, oak, red cedar, and spruce. Douglas fir, lodgepole pine, ponderosa pine, hemlock fir, and Sitka spruce were a few of the dominant species in the West.

Though colonial farmers and NATIVE AMERICANS brought changes to forests, especially near the coast and alongside rivers, their comparatively small populations and limited technologies had a minimal impact. Indeed, by the 1750s, trees had recolonized many of the forest openings produced by Indian fires because SMALLPOX and other DISEASES AND EPIDEMICS had decimated Indian populations, and European Americans initially opposed the use of fire to clear land. However, human pressure on the forest intensified as the United States's population increased—from 1.6 million in 1760 to 7 million in 1810—and its ECONOMY expanded.

Carving a farm out of the forest was a difficult, labor-intensive process. It took the average New England farmer a decade to clear 30–40 acres. A popular way to clear the land was by girdling—the process of killing a tree without toppling it by interrupting its sap flow through slicing the bark. Another method farmers employed was fire. Burning the land was inefficient, however, because it wasted wood, a precious resource used in home and fence construction or sold on the market. Regardless of the clearing technique, newly denuded lands produced prodigious yields: 45 bushels for WHEAT and 35 bushels for corn. Yet intensive monoculture promoted rapid soil exhaustion, and many farmers, expecting their initial good fortune to persist, suffered financial ruin by overextending themselves.

Farmers also depended on the forest to raise livestock, releasing their cattle and swine into it to fatten on its grasses, acorns, beechnuts, chestnuts, roots, and saplings. Foraging animals had a tremendous impact on the forest ecosystem. Cattle and swine devoured young trees, preventing regrowth, and their hooves compressed the topsoil, encouraging water runoff, river sedimentation, and the spread of nonnative weeds. Free-ranging livestock also compelled farmers to construct fences to enclose their crops. The most popular fence design was the worm, or zigzag, fence since it took the least amount of labor; however, though it did not require digging postholes, it did require staggering amounts of trees.

Unlike AGRICULTURE or livestock, urbanization and the emerging market economy dictated widespread—and not just local—deforestation. The expansion of cities like New York, Philadelphia, and Boston created enormous demands for wood, which urban residents needed to cook and to heat their homes in the winter. Responding to this demand, farmers sold wood to fuel dealers, who shipped the commodity to cities on small sloops navigating the Atlantic coast. The European demand for potash put further pressure on northern forests. Made by baking and boiling wood ashes, potash was a key ingredient in bleach, calico, dyes, glass, saltpeter, and soap manufacturing. Potash's ranking as sixth in value amongst North American exports between 1768 and 1772 reveals its economic importance. When settlers cleared their land with fire, they enhanced the soil's fertility by working the potassium-rich ash into the ground. But potash production accelerated soil exhaustion by depriving the land of the ash and exposing it to the wind.

Production of naval stores also took a heavy toll on forests. After the REVOLUTIONARY WAR (1775–83), the production of turpentine, rosin, pitch, and tar expanded in the South. British and New England shipbuilders used tar to preserve ropes and timber; they needed pitch to caulk ships' planks and joints. The manufacture of pitch and tar consumed vast tracts of North Carolina's longleaf pine forests. Merchants in Roanoke, Bathtown, Beauford, and Brunswick, who exported 60 percent of the nation's naval stores, hired plantation owners to deliver the products. African-American slaves performed most of the production tasks, cutting large rectangular notches in longleaf trees (which killed them) to stimulate a flow of turpentine (resin) that collected in buckets and was then rolled in barrels to coastal cities. Though the naval-stores industry boomed in the early 19th century—GREAT BRITAIN imported 40–50,000 barrels annually—it nearly destroyed the southeastern longleaf forest.

The timber required for industrialization—and especially the iron industry—dwarfed all other uses. Iron smelters consumed enormous amounts of charcoal, which came from burning hardwood trees. Eager to turn a quick profit, backcountry farmers chopped down all of their trees and sold them to nearby ironworks facilities. The average facility annually consumed 400 acres of oak, maple, hickory, and birch forests. IRON MANUFACTURING proved so lucrative that, in 1807, North Carolina and Tennessee subsidized the industry, giving 3,000 acres of forest to any entrepreneur who opened an ironworks facility.

Though scholars dispute the amount of forests leveled for agriculture, subsistence, and domestic and international TRADE during the revolutionary era, it is clear that extended tracts of the Atlantic coast, urban hinterlands, river watersheds, and mountain hardwood forests near iron facilities were entirely stripped of trees. Early 19th-century inhabitants of the United States still had good reason to believe that the nation's timber was inexhaustible; forests had not yet felt the effects of STEAMBOATS, railroads, and advanced industrialization. Few people in this period were concerned with the ecological and cultural consequences of deforestation or embraced a conservationist ethic.

See also CITIES AND URBAN LIFE; ENVIRONMENT.

Further reading: Thomas R. Cox, et al., *This Well-Wooded Land: Americans and Their Forests from Colonial Times to the Present* (Lincoln: University of Nebraska Press, 1985); Donald Edward Davis, *Where There Are Mountains: An Environmental History of the Southern Appalachians* (Athens: University of Georgia Press, 2000); Robert B. Outland III, *Tapping the Pines: The Naval Stores Industry in the American South* (Baton Rogue: Louisiana State University Press, 2004); Michael Williams, *Americans and Their Forests: A Historical Geography* (Cambridge: Cambridge University Press, 1989).

—Anthony E. Carlson

Fort Bull

Fort Bull was the outpost built by British-American forces at the beginning of the FRENCH AND INDIAN WAR (1754–63) to guard the west end of the portage from Wood's Creek to the Mohawk Valley in New York. On March 27, 1756, about 350 Canadians and NATIVE AMERICANS destroyed Fort Bull, killing almost all of its approximately 100 defenders and burning the palisades and buildings. This attack left the British-American troops at OSWEGO isolated and vulnerable to attack. In May the British rebuilt the fort, calling it Fort Wood Creek, only to destroy it on August 20, after the fall of Oswego on August 14, 1756.

Fort Cumberland, siege of (November 7–29, 1776)

Early in the REVOLUTIONARY WAR (1775–83), New Englanders hoped to bring NOVA SCOTIA into the rebellion. In autumn 1776 Jonathan Eddy and several other Nova Scotia leaders sympathetic to the cause of independence raised about 500 men in the region and sought to capture Fort Cumberland, near present-day Sackville, New Brunswick (which was then part of Nova Scotia). The outpost was defended by about 200 LOYALISTS in the Royal Fencible Americans, under Colonel Joseph Goreham. Eddy knew he had to capture the fort quickly before relief arrived from Halifax, and he launched assaults on November 13 and 22, 1776, which failed to dislodge Goreham. After being reinforced, Goreham counterattacked and broke the siege. Although Goreham did not pursue Eddy, about 100 men agreed to surrender their weapons to the British when offered a pardon. The Revolutionary failure at Fort Cumberland helped to secure the region north of Maine for the British during the war.

Fort Dearborn

The U.S. ARMY built Fort Dearborn, located at the junction of the Chicago River and Lake Michigan (present-day Chicago), in 1803. This western outpost served mainly as a trading center until the WAR OF 1812 (1812–15). At the beginning of that conflict, General WILLIAM HULL, believing that the fort was untenable after the capture of FORT MICHILMACKINAC, ordered Captain Nathan Heath to abandon it. Heath destroyed many of the supplies in the fort and began a march to Fort Wayne on August 15 with 54 regulars, 12 militia, nine women, and 18 children. Heath did not get very far before a party of several hundred hostile NATIVE AMERICANS attacked his column, killing 26 regulars, all of the militia, two women and 12 children. The rest were taken captive. This massacre was a part of the disastrous beginning of the campaign in the West. The Indians burned the fort, which remained abandoned until after the war when the army rebuilt it.

Fort Edward, Battle of (July 23, 1757)

During the FRENCH AND INDIAN WAR (1754–63), Joseph Marin de la Malgue, an officer in the French army, led a raid of about 400 NATIVE AMERICANS and 80 French and Canadians on the road between Fort William Henry and Fort Edward. This force canoed down Lake Champlain and up Wood Creek, then cut through the forest to the road, where about half of the Native Americans refused to proceed toward Fort Edward. About a half-mile from the fort, Marin and the remainder of the Indians surprised a wood-cutting detail and its guard, killing at least 10. A larger party of British-American troops sallied out of Fort

Edward, and after a short battle, Marin withdrew. In the initial attack the Indians used bows and arrows, a weapon that struck terror into the hearts of many of the British-American soldiers, especially because the soldiers had not recognized the arrow markings since many of the Indians had been recruited from as far as 1,000 miles away. This raid, which demonstrated how deep into British-held territory the French and Indians could strike undetected, was preliminary to the FORT WILLIAM HENRY "MASSACRE."

Further reading: Ian K. Steele, *Betrayals: Fort William Henry and the Massacre* (New York: Oxford University Press, 1990).

Forten, James (1766–1842) *abolitionist*

James Forten was born on September 2, 1766, to a free African-American family in Philadelphia and learned his father's sailmaking trade. While still in his teens, he served on a privateer during the REVOLUTIONARY WAR (1775–83), and after his ship was captured, he refused British offers of EDUCATION in exchange for his service. Following the war, Forten worked at, and then acquired, the sailmaking business of Robert Bridges. He then began to gather a fortune that made him one of the wealthiest people in Philadelphia, not to mention a leading member of the nation's so-called black elite. Regardless of how far he progressed economically, however, Forten faced the obstacle of race. In 1799, for example, an anti-slave-trading petition he and other black Philadelphians signed was rejected by Congress, 84–1. "We the People does not mean them," one southern congressman told Forten and the other petitioners. Forten wrote the lone supporter of the petition, a Massachusetts representative, and thanked him for joining the cause of justice. Throughout his life, Forten participated in other petition campaigns and struggles for racial equality, including opposition to segregated schooling in Pennsylvania and to the Quaker State's disfranchisement of black voters in 1838.

Forten was a model black activist for later figures such as Frederick Douglass. In 1849 Douglass told a New York City audience that "My heart swells with pride" at the mention of Forten's name. Like Douglass, Forten used the nation's political beliefs in constitutional equality to condemn racialist ideologies in the United States. One of his most important pieces of writing was an 1813 pamphlet critiquing a Pennsylvania bill that sought to restrict African-American migration to Pennsylvania (and even threatened to reenslave those AFRICAN AMERICANS who migrated to the state and did not register their name with a local official). Forten's essay, entitled "Series of Letters by a Man of Colour," cited the DECLARATION OF INDEPENDENCE, Pennsylvania's 1780 gradual ABOLITION act, and the state's

1790 constitution (which did not distinguish between so-called black and white rights) as evidence that the nation rested firmly on beliefs of equality for all. "Let not the spirit of the father behold the son robbed of that liberty which he died to establish," Forten wrote, "but let the motto of our legislators be 'The law knows no distinction.'" The law was not passed, but Forten's pamphlet gained prominence among black activists in other parts of the United States. In 1827 *Freedom's Journal*, the first independent African-American newspaper, based in New York City, republished the essay so that younger generations of activists might learn the skill of written protest.

Although initially interested in voluntary emigration schemes to AFRICA, Forten came to oppose the American Colonization Society, which he believed to be an enemy of free African Americans. After the society's formation in 1817, he organized anticolonization protests in Philadelphia and became an advocate of immediate abolition in the 1830s. When he died on March 4, 1842, Forten was eulogized as a founding father of African-American protest in America. His motto remained "America, with thy faults I love thee still."

See also ANTISLAVERY; LIBERTY.

Further reading: Gary B. Nash, *Forging Freedom: The Formation of Philadelphia's Black Community, 1745–1840* (Cambridge, Mass.: Harvard University Press, 1988); Richard Newman, Patrick Rael, and Philip Lapsansky, eds., *Pamphlets of Protest: An Anthology of Early African American Protest Writing* (New York: Routledge, 2001); Julie Winch, *A Gentleman of Color: A Life of James Forten* (New York: Oxford University Press, 2002).

Fort Erie

Located along the eastern edge of Lake Erie on the Canadian side of the Niagara River, Fort Erie was an important outpost in the defense of CANADA during the WAR OF 1812 (1812–15). The French had a trading post on the location, and the British built a fort on the site in 1764. The outpost played a minor role in the REVOLUTIONARY WAR (1775–83) and was heavily damaged by an ice storm in 1800. A new fort, further from the lake, was constructed in 1805. In spring 1813 the British evacuated and destroyed the fort, and it was briefly occupied by the United States. The British reoccupied the fort in December 1813.

Fort Erie was the first target of General Jacob Brown's invasion of Canada in 1814, and the fort surrendered with minimal resistance on July 3. The U.S. ARMY expanded the fortifications and used it as a base throughout July and into August. After the BATTLE OF LUNDY'S LANE (July 25, 1814), General GORDON DRUMMOND determined to recapture the fort, opening up a bombardment on August

13, 1814. Two days later Drummond ordered a direct assault on Fort Erie. The British breached the defenses on the third wave of attacks, but a powder magazine explosion so decimated their advance troops that they had to pull back; the attacks cost them about 1,000 casualties. After Brown reenforced the garrison, he ordered a sortie against the British on September 17, 1814; during the fighting, the United States lost some 500 men and GREAT BRITAIN about 600. The British subsequently abandoned the siege. On November 5 the U.S. Army withdrew from the Canadian side of the river, blowing up the fort so it would be of no use to the British. In 1939 a reconstruction of Fort Erie was opened to the public to commemorate Canadian sacrifices during the War of 1812.

Further reading: Pierre Berton, *Flames across the Border: The Canadian-American Tragedy, 1813–1814* (Boston: Little, Brown, and Company, 1981).

Fort Frontenac

Fort Frontenac, located in CANADA at the conjunction of the Cataraqui River, the St. Lawrence River, and Lake Ontario (present-day Kingston, Ontario), was a major French supply depot. Through this outpost flowed the trade goods and gifts that sustained the French relations with NATIVE AMERICANS throughout the Great Lakes region and the equipment and food that sustained the French military all the way to DETROIT and beyond.

During the FRENCH AND INDIAN WAR (1754–63), after General JAMES ABERCROMBY's disastrous failure at Fort Carillon (FORT TICONDEROGA) in summer 1758, the British needed a victory to help balance the loss. Abercromby, who generally did not show initiative, agreed to Lieutenant Colonel John Bradstreet's ambitious plan for a raid on Fort Frontenac. Bradstreet disguised his campaign, which was officially under the command of General John Stanwix, by appearing to simply rebuild a fort at the portage between the Mohawk River and the Lake Ontario watershed. He advanced with 3,100 men beyond the portage to Lake Ontario and then moved on to Sackets Harbor. From there he crossed the lake in bateaux (flat-bottomed riverboats), arriving at Fort Frontenac on August 25, 1758. The siege did not last long since the French had only 110 soldiers in the fort. After the British Americans brought cannon within 150 yards from the walls, a few hours of bombardment on August 27 brought a French surrender. The garrison may have been small, but the storehouses were brimming with goods worth £35,000. What the attackers could not carry away in vessels seized from the French, they destroyed before a French relief force could arrive.

The full impact of the raid would be felt for the rest of the war as other French forts were under-supplied and relations with the Indians deteriorated without gifts and trade goods to facilitate the Franco-Native-American relationship. Upon his return to Albany, Bradstreet wanted to follow up this success with a broader campaign, convinced that the French western posts were all undermanned since General Montcalm (see MONTCALM-GOZON DE SAINT-VÉRAN, MARQUIS DE) had concentrated his forces at Carillon. Abercromby, however, did not want to press his luck and would not permit a further advance in the Great Lakes that year.

Frontenac remained an abandoned site until the British built another a settlement—Kingston—and a fort there in 1783. During the WAR OF 1812 (1812–15), Kingston would be a vital supply center for the British.

Further reading: Fred Anderson, *Crucible of War: The Seven Years' War and the Fate of Empire in British North America, 1754–1766* (New York: Knopf, 2000).

Fort George

After the British withdrew from FORT NIAGARA in 1796, they began to build Fort George on the Canadian side of the Niagara River. This outpost became the headquarters for the British army in Upper CANADA. During the WAR OF 1812 (1812–15), Fort George became a major military objective. On May 25, 1813, the United States opened the fighting along the Niagara corridor with an artillery bombardment on the fort. Two days later, Colonel WINFIELD SCOTT led an amphibious landing across the Niagara River and then threatened to attack Fort George from the rear. The British counterattack on Scott failed, and the British commander, finding himself outnumbered and outgunned, abandoned the fort after spiking his cannons and blowing up the powder magazine. The British garrison had numbered about 1,100 men, of whom about 350 were killed, wounded, or missing. The United States had almost 5,000 men and lost 39 dead and 150 wounded.

Although the British soon abandoned their other forts in the Niagara area, the United States did not press its advantage. This failure, which was due to the timidity of Scott's superior officers, allowed the British to rally and win several victories before advancing on Fort George in July. Throughout the summer and fall, the U.S. troops in and around Fort George, totaling more than 6,600, were besieged by a smaller British force of around 4,000. This campaign ended in a stalemate in the fall when General JAMES WILKINSON transferred many of the men to the other end of Lake Ontario to join his St. Lawrence River campaign. The British countered by also moving units from around Fort George to oppose Wilkinson.

By December 1813, the United States had only 250 discontented New York MILITIA in Fort George. Believing that his position was untenable and his men unreliable, the militia commander abandoned the fort on December 10, 1813; he also burned the nearby town of Newark to deny its use to the British army. This retreat marked a dismal end to what had seemed in May to be a promising campaign. It also left Fort Niagara vulnerable to an attack on December 18, 1813. The British retained control of both Fort George and Fort Niagara for the rest of the war.

After the TREATY OF GHENT (1814), Fort George was partially rebuilt, but by the 1820s it had began to fall into ruins. During the 1930s the fort was rebuilt, and today it is a Canadian national park.

Further reading: Donald Hickey, *The War of 1812: A Forgotten Conflict* (Urbana: University of Illinois Press, 1989).

Fort Granby, capture of (May 15, 1781)

Fort Granby, South Carolina, was one of several depots held by the British during the closing phases of the REVOLUTIONARY WAR (1775–83) in the South. Major Andrew Maxwell, a LOYALIST from Maryland known more for his enthusiasm for plunder than his eagerness in battle, commanded 352 men, including about 60 HESSIANS, guarding the outpost. The Continental general NATHANAEL GREENE sent Colonel HENRY LEE to capture the fort. During the night of May 14, Lee placed a cannon within 600 yards of the fortified frame building known as Fort Granby, near modern-day Columbia. The next morning he fired the cannon and drove Maxwell's pickets back with his advancing troops. He then began negotiations for the surrender, fearing that if he waited too long, British reinforcements would arrive. Maxwell agreed to give up the post if his men were paroled as PRISONERS OF WAR and allowed to return to the British lines in Charleston where they would be exchanged. Maxwell also wanted his men to be able to keep the booty that they had looted from South Carolina WHIGS. After a few delays, and as soon as Lee heard news of a British relief column on its way, Lee agreed to the conditions, including the provision protecting "private property of every sort, without investigation of title"—a use of language to protect plunder. Lee even allowed the British and Hessians to keep their horses. Maxwell left with two wagonloads full of "private property." Although local South Carolina leaders complained of the deal, Lee captured the fort without loss of life on either side and seized significant quantities of military supplies.

Further reading: Jerome J. Nadelhaft, *The Disorders of War: The Revolution in South Carolina* (Orono: University of Maine at Orono Press, 1981); John S. Pancake, *The Destructive War: The British Campaign in the Carolinas,* *1780–1782* (University, Alabama: University of Alabama Press, 1985).

Fort Harmar Council

On January 9, 1789, representatives of the IROQUOIS, Chippewa, Potawatomi, Sauk, Ottawa, DELAWARE, and WYANDOT, numbering between 1,000 and 3,000, met with the governor of the Northwest Territory, ARTHUR ST. CLAIR, at the Fort Harmar Council in the Ohio Valley to discuss land cessions. Even though several Native American nations had previously ceded their rights to the Ohio Country east of the Cuyahoga and Muskinghum rivers, many people from the United States, specifically REVOLUTIONARY WAR veterans, continued to settle in the Firelands portion of the WESTERN RESERVE that extended beyond these boundaries. HENRY KNOX had instructed St. Clair to trade land unsettled by European Americans for the Firelands. St. Clair ignored these instructions and obtained the Firelands without exchanging any land. The rest of the treaty did little more than reaffirm the Treaty of Fort Stanwix (1784) and the TREATY OF FORT MCINTOSH (1785). Divisions among the NATIVE AMERICANS and St. Clair's disregard for Knox's instructions prevented several accomodationist chiefs from making greater concessions to the United States. St. Clair's duplicity during the negotiations and the willingness of some chiefs to give in to the United States further polarized FRONTIER relationships. More militant NATIVE AMERICANS—namely the SHAWNEE, who refused to participate in the negotiations—increased their influence as many Indians reacted to the Fort Harmar Council. Simultaneously, many Indians in the region looked more favorably on the British, who were a source of goods and arms. The militant Indians in a pan-Indian confederacy defeated U.S. forces under JOSIAH HARMAR in 1790 and St. Clair in 1791, before being beaten in the BATTLE OF FALLEN TIMBERS on August 20, 1794.

Further reading: R. David Edmunds, *The Shawnee Prophet* (Lincoln: University of Nebraska Press, 1983); Richard White, *The Middle Ground: Indians, Empires, and Republics in the Great Lakes Region, 1650–1815* (Cambridge: Cambridge University Press, 1991).

—Patrick Bottiger

Fort Independence, Battle of (January 17–25, 1777)

After his victories in the BATTLES OF TRENTON AND PRINCETON (December 26, 1776, and January 3, 1777), an optimistic GEORGE WASHINGTON ordered General WILLIAM HEATH in command of 6,000 men in the Hudson Highlands to advance on New York City, with the idea of drawing the British completely out of New Jersey to defend the city. Heath directed his men to converge on King's Bridge across the Harlem River. Advancing in three columns on the night of January 17, 1777, the Revolutionaries overwhelmed several outposts the next day and approached Fort Independence, just north of Spuyten Duyvil. Heath's demand for the surrender of the stronghold, which was defended by 2,000 HESSIANS, was greeted by the German commander with an artillery barrage. Rather than attacking, Heath fired his own cannon on the fort, to little effect. The next day, Heath continued to hesitate as he sought to maneuver his troops into a better position. He decided to cut the Germans off from King's Bridge by crossing a frozen stream on January 20, but warmer weather that day made the ice unsafe, and he called the advance off. During the next few days, both armies skirmished but avoided a bigger conflict. On January 25 the British defenders sallied out of their fort and drove the Continentals back from some of the positions they had seized the week before. When a snowstorm began on January 29, Heath withdrew his entire army. Washington, who had risked everything in an attack in a blizzard only the month before, censured Heath for conduct "fraught with too much caution by which the Army has been disappointed and in some degree disgraced."

Fort Jackson, Treaty of (1814)

The Treaty of Fort Jackson, signed on August 9, 1814, signified the end of the CREEK WAR (1813–14). Despite the fact that the conflict began as a civil war among the CREEK and that many Creek had aided ANDREW JACKSON after the United States entered the fray, the entire Creek nation was affected by the treaty's stipulations. According to the treaty, the Creek ceded 23 million acres, which included most of the present-day state of Alabama and western Georgia. The Creek were also forbidden to have contact with either the British or the Spanish and agreed to allow the United States "to establish military posts, roads, and free navigation of waters" in Creek territory.

See also RED STICKS.

Fort Laurens

Built near Bolivar, Ohio, Fort Laurens was the first U.S. military outpost in modern-day Ohio. In autumn 1778 General LACHLAN MCINTOSH left FORT PITT with 1,200 men, hoping to capture Fort DETROIT, but his army moved through the wilderness at a snail's pace, and by the time he reached the Tuscarawas River on November 21, 1778, he decided that they had gone far enough. Before returning to Fort Pitt, McIntosh began to build Fort Laurens, believing that it could be a supply depot and jumping-off point for later operations. He departed on December 9, leaving 150 men under the command of John Gibson to complete the well-designed fort in late December.

Gibson's situation that winter was difficult since he had scanty supplies and was under constant threat of attack from NATIVE AMERICANS. The situation became desperate in February during a siege that lasted almost a month. The Indians abandoned the attack only because they too were short of food and supplies. During the winter, more than 20 men died in the Indian attacks on the fort, supply trains, and foraging expeditions. By the time a relief column arrived in late March, Gibson's men were eating leather and roots found in the woods. Indians, however, continued to threaten the outpost, and in July Colonel Daniel Broadhead, who had replaced McIntosh, decided the fort was untenable and ordered it abandoned. When the troops left Fort Laurens in early August, they did not destroy its fortifications in the belief that it might be useful later in the war. Today Fort Laurens is being rebuilt and is a state historic site.

Fort Mackinac   See FORT MICHILIMACKINAC.

Fort Malden

GREAT BRITAIN began to build Fort Malden, located at Amherstburg, Upper CANADA (modern Ontario), in 1796 after they abandoned DETROIT according to the provisions of JAY'S TREATY (1794). Before the WAR OF 1812 (1812–15), the fort was a major British military outpost that could control the Detroit River and serve as a base for their Lake Erie fleet. In July 1812 General WILLIAM HULL crossed the Detroit River to try to capture Fort Malden, but he withdrew to the Michigan side of the river when he heard that British reinforcements were on their way. The fort was the base for British operations in the capture of Detroit on August 15, 1812.

The British, however, abandoned and destroyed Fort Malden after the defeat at the BATTLE OF LAKE ERIE (September 10, 1813) made its position untenable. For the rest of the war it remained in the hands of the United States, which began to rebuild and extend the fortifications. The rebuilt fort is visible today as a Canadian national park.

Fort McIntosh, Treaty of (1785)

In 1785 the SECOND CONTINENTAL CONGRESS authorised commissioners GEORGE ROGERS CLARK, Richard Butler, and ARTHUR LEE to meet with representatives from the WYANDOT, DELAWARE, Chippewa, and Ottawa nations at Fort McIntosh (present-day Beaver, Pennsylvania) to negotiate a land cession in the Ohio country. The NATIVE AMERICANS who attended the meeting did not fully represent their tribes, and after they were plied with ALCOHOL, they signed the Treaty of Fort McIntosh on January 21, 1785. The treaty not only granted generous boundaries to the United States in Ohio, but it also compelled "The said Indian nations" to "acknowledge themselves and all their tribes to be under the protection of the United States and of no other sovereign whatsoever," thus renouncing the alliance with GREAT BRITAIN that had developed during the REVOLUTIONARY WAR (1775–83). Most Native Americans in the region, including many from the tribes whose supposed representatives had signed the agreement, refused to recognize the treaty. As a result, it was never put into effect, and the Ohio country Indians successfully resisted European-American incursions north of the Ohio River for almost a decade.

Further reading: Francis Paul Prucha, *The Great Father: The United States Government and the American Indians,* abr. ed. (Lincoln: University of Nebraska Press, 1986); Alan Taylor, *The Divided Ground: Indians, Settlers, and the Northern Borderland of the American Revolution* (New York: Knopf, 2006).

—Daniel Flaherty

Fort Meigs

After the defeat at the BATTLE OF FRENCHTOWN (January 22, 1813), General WILLIAM HENRY HARRISON decided to build a fort on the south bank of the Maumee River to guard against further British attacks and to serve as a forward base for later operations. Named after Ohio governor RETURN JONATHAN MEIGS, construction began on February 2, 1813, and included a 10-acre compound with multiple batteries, a large earth-and-timber palisade, and seven blockhouses, with a garrison of 1,200 men.

General HENRY PROCTER invaded Ohio with about 2,000 British regulars and MILITIA and 1,000 NATIVE AMERICANS and began to besiege the fort on May 1, 1813. Procter's artillery barrage had a limited effect against the strong defensive works. When 1,200 Kentucky militia approached in relief on May 5, Harrison ordered them to attack the British batteries as they arrived. Divided into two columns, the Kentucky militia successfully captured the British artillery and spiked the cannon, but an Indian counterattack practically wiped out one of the Kentucky columns, and only a few hundred of the reinforcements made it safely into the fort. The Native Americans soon became disenchanted with the siege and began leaving Procter, while the Canadian militia, made it clear that they needed to return to their farms to plant their crops. Procter therefore lifted the siege on May 9. In this round of fighting, Harrison lost 135 killed, 188 wounded, and 630

captured; the British lost 14 killed, 47 wounded, and 41 captured, while Indian casualties are unknown.

Procter returned to Fort Meigs on July 21, 1813, with an even larger army, which included between 3,000 and 4,000 Indians. However, Fort Meigs still remained too strong to assault directly. In an effort to lure the defenders out, the British and Indians pretended to be fighting a relief column. When that ruse did not work, Procter left Fort Meigs and besieged the smaller Fort Stephenson on the Sanduskey River, where a direct assault on August 2 did not succeed, even though the fort was defended by only 150 men. As a result of these failures, the British gave up their invasion of Ohio.

Fort Meigs remained an outpost for the rest of the war, although on a smaller scale. Reconstructed by the Ohio Historical Society in the 1960s, today Fort Meigs is a historical site open to visitors.

Fort Mercer   See DELAWARE RIVER FORTS; RED BANK, BATTLE OF.

Fort Michilimackinac

Fort Michilimackinac was located near the conjunction of three Great Lakes: Michigan, Huron, and Superior. Originally established around 1715 as an outpost in the French fur-trading network, the fort gained notoriety during PONTIAC'S WAR (1763–65). The British took control of Fort Michilimackinac after the FRENCH AND INDIAN WAR (1754–63). Many Algonquian Indian communities in the Great Lakes region resented British policies and joined the Ottawa chief Pontiac in his war against the British. In early June 1763, the Ottawa and Ojibwa at Michilimackinac feigned a game of lacrosse near the fort in order to gain entrance; they then killed 20 of the 35 British garrison once they were inside. The Indians marched the captured British commander, Captain George Etherington, out of the fort to be burned at the stake, but Charles Langlade, the son of a Frenchman and Indian woman, persuaded them to spare him. Langlade hoped to demonstrate both his influence among the Indians and his value to the British.

The NATIVE AMERICANS held Fort Michilimackinac for over a year. The British eventually recaptured the fort but abandoned it in 1780 after constructing nearby Fort Mackinac on Mackinaw Island; however, they retained possession of the new fort until 1796 when, following the provisions of JAY'S TREATY (1794), they turned it over to the United States. Until the beginning of the WAR OF 1812 (1812–15), Fort Mackinac was an isolated outpost for the United States. The British captured the fort on July 17, 1812, before its commander had even been informed of the declaration of war. An expedition to retake the fort was beaten back in a bloody battle on August 14, 1814. However, as part of peace agreement in the TREATY OF GHENT, the British returned to the fort to the United States

Further reading: Colin Calloway, *The Scratch of a Pen* (New York: Oxford University Press, 2006).

—Patrick Bottiger

Fort Mims Massacre (August 30, 1813)

The Fort Mims Massacre altered the dynamics of the CREEK WAR (1813–14)—itself a part of the WAR OF 1812 (1812–15)—by uniting people in the southeastern United States against the militant and nativist CREEK faction called RED STICKS. Located 40 miles north of Mobile on the eastern side of the Alabama River, Fort Mims housed many European-American settlers and mixed-blood Creek who sought refuge from the civil strife that had erupted among factions of the tribe. In late July 1813, U.S. commanders Major Daniel Beasley and Captain Dixon Bailey fought a group of Red Sticks at the BATTLE OF BURNT CORN (July 23, 1813). The fighting at Burnt Corn expanded what had been an internecine Creek conflict, pushing the Red Sticks into a war with the United States. On August 30, 1813, around 800 Red Sticks, led by Peter McQueen and WILLIAM WEATHERFORD (Chief Red Eagle), attacked Fort Mims and massacred nearly 500 European Americans and métis Creek. The Red Sticks, however, had not attacked the fort simply out of anger, but rather in retaliation for the Battle of Burnt Corn. They also wanted to send a message to wayward Creek whose support of the United States had led to the civil war. The Red Sticks hoped that an attack on Fort Mims would prevent the United States from intervening in their war with accommodationist Creek. But the massacre had the opposite effect as many land-hungry European Americans used the attack at Fort Mims as a rallying cry in the fighting that ensued and as justification to dispossess the Creek of their lands.

Further reading: Karl Davis, "'Remember Fort Mims': Reinterpreting the Origins of the Creek War," *Journal of the Early Republic* 22 (2002): 611–636.

—Patrick Bottiger

Fort Motte, siege of (May 8–10, 1781)

Located where the confluence of the Congaree and Wateree rivers formed the Santee River, Fort Motte was one of the key outposts of the British in South Carolina in 1781 during the REVOLUTIONARY WAR (1775–83). The stronghold was the fortified mansion of a widow—Mrs. Rebecca B. Motte—and was well defended by about 175 men. General NATHANAEL GREENE dispatched 450 men

under General FRANCES MARION and Colonel HENRY LEE to capture the fort. The Revolutionary soldiers arrived on May 8, set up headquarters in a nearby farmhouse, and began to dig trenches near Fort Motte. On May 10 the British refused Lee and Marion's call for surrender. By May 11 the approach of a relief force under Lord Rawdon (see HASTINGS, FRANCIS RAWDON, FIRST MARQUIS OF) encouraged the defenders and created anxiety in the attackers. Lee and Marion decided to use flaming arrows to burn the Motte mansion. On the morning of May 12, the Revolutionaries were close enough to fire two arrows at the building, setting it aflame and compelling the British to surrender. Lee and Marion lost two men in the fighting; the British garrison lost none, and the captives were sent to the British under parole.

Further reading: John S. Pancake, *The Destructive War: The British Campaign in the Carolinas, 1780–1782* (University: University of Alabama Press, 1985).

Fort Necessity

In summer 1754, during the FRENCH AND INDIAN WAR (1754–63), Colonel GEORGE WASHINGTON began construction of a stockade in an area called the Great Meadows in modern southwestern Pennsylvania. This was part of the British-Virginian expedition to build a road to the Monongahela River to supply a fort at the Forks of the Ohio (modern Pittsburgh). Fort Necessity was poorly located, with forest only 60 yards away, and in a low-lying area that became like a marsh in heavy rains. Washington also never completed the fortifications since he expected reinforcements from the east to help drive the French out of the area. After the BATTLE OF JUMONVILLE GLEN (May 28, 1754) and the death of his own superior officer on May 31, the entire command of the British-Virginian forces for the expedition fell upon Washington's inexperienced shoulders.

Washington had his men continue to work on the road until June 28, when Native-American scouts reported that French troops had left Fort Duquesne (later FORT PITT) to punish the British for the murder of Ensign Joseph Coulon Jumonville on May 28. The commander of the powerful French force was Captain Louis Coulon de Villiers, brother of the murdered Jumonville. Knowing he was outnumbered, Washington retreated. With his men already exhausted from laboring on the road, Washington got as far as Fort Necessity on July 1, and the British-Virginians could go no further. On July 2 it began to rain, making the Great Meadow a morass and leaving everyone soaked to the skin. On the morning of July 3, only 300 out of 400 in Washington's command were fit for duty.

The French attacked at about 11 o'clock that morning in the rain. Washington attempted to line up his troops in the meadow, believing that the French would do battle in the conventional European manner. Villiers, however, was a veteran of North American wars and spread out his numerically superior force in the woods near the fort and, from cover, leveled a devastating fire on the British and Virginian soldiers who huddled in shallow trenches half-filled with water or within the poorly constructed stockade. The defenders could hardly return the fire since their inferior muskets were soaked. By evening the hopeless situation became desperate, and many of the men broke into the rum supply and drank themselves into oblivion.

As night fell, with his own ammunition running low and unsure of the political ramifications of the attack, Villiers offered generous surrender terms. Washington's men would be allowed to march out of Fort Necessity with their possessions, muskets, and colors. All they had to do is give up the fort, promise not to return to the region for a year, relinquish their swivel guns, and leave two officers as hostages to ensure that the terms were kept. Unbeknownst to Washington, the terms, written in French, also included a provision indicating that Washington was personally responsible for the "assassination" of Jumonville. Having lost 30 killed and 70 wounded—the French had only three killed—Washington had little choice but to surrender. At 10 A.M. on July 4, 1754, Washington's ragged and hungover troops left Fort Necessity and began the long march back to Virginia.

The French destroyed the fort and returned triumphantly to Fort Duquesne, having secured the Ohio Valley—for at least the time being. Today, Fort Necessity National Battlefield has a reconstructed stockade run by the National Park Service.

Further reading: Fred Anderson, *The Crucible of War: The Seven Years' War and the Fate of the British Empire in North America, 1754–1766* (New York: Knopf, 2000).

Fort Niagara

Established in 1726, Fort Niagara sat astride one of the natural choke points in communication in the Great Lakes region where the Niagara River flows into Lake Ontario. This fort became an essential bastion in the French empire in North America. Fort Niagara was one of the first objectives identified by the British in the FRENCH AND INDIAN WAR (1754–63). However, French and Indian attacks at OSWEGO and elsewhere, combined with British-American ineptitude, delayed any serious strike at Fort Niagara until 1759.

After many delays, a British-American army of 3,200 under John Prideux approached Fort Niagara on July 6, 1759. Crucial to their success was an alliance with the IRO-QUOIS, who had previously limited their aid to the British

but now became active in the war. The British Americans began their first trenches a half-mile from the fort on July 10. For three days, beginning on July 11, the Iroquois allied with French and the Iroquois allied with the British negotiated with each other. Both groups agreed to withdraw from the fight, but the British-allied Iroquois remained in the area, having been promised loot from the fort when it surrendered. The British-American artillery then began to bombard the French as sappers continued to dig parallels closer and closer to the fort. By July 23 the artillery was at point-blank range, and the situation looked hopeless. However, the French chances brightened as a 1,600-strong French and Indian relief force under François Le Marchand de Ligneris approached from Lake Eire. Native American diplomacy again interceded, with the Iroquois convincing the Indians accompanying Ligneris to abandon the French. On July 24 Ligneris, without NATIVE AMERICANS, marched on Niagara with about 600 French and Canadians. At La Belle Famille they were met by about 450 British regulars and New York provincials behind a breastwork of logs and abatis across the road. An equal number of Iroquois waited in the woods on the wings. The British Americans' effective fire shattered the French advance, and Johnson's men captured about 100; the remainder were either killed on the battlefield or fled. Most of the retreating French were massacred by the Iroquois (although some probably became Native American captives). With the defeat of this relief force, Fort Niagara surrendered on July 25.

Fort Niagara then became a major outpost for the British Empire, and it was the site of a crucial conference with Native Americans at the end of PONTIAC'S WAR (1763–65) attended by 2,000 Indians from 24 nations in July and August 1764. During the REVOLUTIONARY WAR (1775–83). Fort Niagara was never seriously threatened by the Revolutionaries and served as a staging ground for repeated raids into the United States. It also became a refuge for Native Americans driven from their homes by the Revolutionaries. As many as 8,000 Indians lived in and around the fort during the war. Maintaining this polyglot world of Native Americans cost as much as £100,000 in 1781. After the TREATY OF PARIS (1783), many of these Indians were resettled in CANADA. The fort itself was technically in the state of New York, but the British continued to occupy it until 1796, when they abandoned the fort as stipulated in JAY'S TREATY (1794).

During the WAR OF 1812 (1812–15), Fort Niagara again became contested ground. In the early part of the war it was an important base for attacks on Canada by the U.S. ARMY. A small New York MILITIA force of 250 men had abandoned FORT GEORGE on the Canadian side of the Niagara River on December 10, 1813, burning the nearby town of Newark as they retreated. Angered by this wanton act of destruction, and recognizing the weakness of the

American defenses that winter, General GORDON DRUM-MOND planned a retaliatory attack. On December 18, 1813, Drummond led 550 British soldiers across the Niagara River; captured some pickets; and then, having obtained the password from their prisoners, surprised the fort's garrison. The defenders had more than 60 men killed, mostly from bayonets, and lost 350 men as prisoners; the British had only six killed and five wounded. Vast quantities of supplies were also captured. The British continued with their winter offensive by attacking and burning Lewiston, Black Rock, and Buffalo. The British held Fort Niagara until the end of the war.

Today, Fort Niagara is a reconstructed state historic site open for visitors.

Further reading: Fred Anderson, *Crucible of War: The Seven Years' War and the Fate of Empire in British North America, 1754–1766* (New York: Knopf, 2000); Colin G. Calloway, *The American Revolution in Indian Country: Crisis and Diversity in Native American Communities* (Cambridge: Cambridge University Press, 1995).

Fort Pitt

Located in an area of Pennsylvania that is now Pittsburgh, Fort Pitt was built by the British during the FRENCH AND INDIAN WAR (1754–63) and was later attacked during PONTIAC'S WAR (1763–65). The fort was constructed next to the demolished Fort Duquesne, a French stronghold that allowed them to ward off a British attack in 1755. However, in 1758, when British general JOHN FORBES came within 12 miles of Fort Duquesne, the French razed their fort, destroyed supplies, and left the area. With the French gone, the British constructed Fort Pitt in anticipation of a French return and attack.

Tensions between the British and DELAWARE and SHAWNEE Indians, however, posed a greater problem for the British than a French counterattack. The Indians had sided with the French, an alliance that aided the French defense of Fort Duquesne in 1755. However, the British, largely through the diplomatic efforts of the MORAVIAN missionary Christian Frederick Post, persuaded the NATIVE AMERICANS to sever their ties with the French and promised that the British would not settle or hunt in the region. Without Indian support, the French realized it would be impossible to defend the region against the advancing British. The British-Indian alliance, however, was short-lived as the British settlement and construction of Fort Pitt violated their prior agreement with Native Americans to leave the area, thus fueling tensions that culminated in Pontiac's War. During the war, the British withstood an Indian attack on Fort Pitt.

After Pontiac's War, the British left the area, and Fort Pitt became a source of contention as both Pennsylvania and Virginia asserted a claim to the region. For a short period in the 1770s, Virginia governor JOHN MURRAY, EARL OF DUNMORE (Lord Dunmore), took possession of Fort Pitt and renamed it after himself. When fighting broke out between England and the colonies, however, Dunmore lost control of the area. The fort was held by the colonists during the REVOLUTIONARY WAR (1775–83) and served as a base of operations in attacking Native Americans who sided with the British

Further reading: Walter O'Meara, *Guns at the Forks* (Englewood Cliffs, N.J.: Prentice-Hall, 1965).

—Lawrence Mastroni

Fort Stanwix, siege of (August 2–23, 1777)

The British army built Fort Stanwix in 1758 at a portage between the Mohawk River and Oneida Lake—and thus protected a crucial link between the Hudson River Valley and the Great Lakes. Fort Stanwix was also the site of an important treaty with the IROQUOIS in 1768 that ceded Kentucky and other territory to the British colonists (see FORT STANWIX, TREATY OF). By the beginning of the REVOLUTIONARY WAR (1775–83) the fort had been abandoned and was run down. The Revolutionaries, in part at the urging of their allies the ONEIDA, began to rebuild the outpost in July 1776, renaming it Fort Schuyler in honor of PHILIP JOHN SCHUYLER. Because of its strategic location, the fort was garrisoned by units from the CONTINENTAL ARMY. During the summer of 1777, Fort Schuyler—with about 750 troops under Colonel Peter Gansevoort—stood in the way of the advance of Colonel BARRY ST. LEGER and his expedition of 2,000 NATIVE AMERICANS, LOYALISTS, and British regulars. After St. Leger surrounded the fort and began his siege on August 2, he had to fight off a relief column under General Nicholas Herkimer at the BATTLE OF ORISKANY on August 6. During the battle, which took place about eight miles away from the fort, Gansevoort's men left the stockade and destroyed much of the Indian camp. This action, plus the heavy losses the Native Americans sustained at Oriskany, disenchanted St. Leger's Indian allies. Although St. Leger's troops made progress in digging parallels and might have captured the fort, the British abandoned the siege on August 23. The Revolutionaries dispatched a new relief column under BENEDICT ARNOLD, who convinced a Loyalist prisoner to save his own life by reporting to St. Leger that Arnold's force was larger than it really was. On hearing this false information, the disgusted Native Americans, who had hoped for easy plunder and minimal fighting, began leaving St. Leger. Without the Indian allies who constituted half his army, St. Leger ordered a retreat.

For the rest of the war the Continental army occupied the fort, which was the location of negotiations for another

Indian treaty in 1784. Today Fort Stanwix is reconstructed and is a national historic monument.

Fort Stanwix, Treaty of (1768)

The Treaty of Fort Stanwix between the British and the IROQUOIS in 1768 ceded much of the land south of the Ohio River to European-American settlement. The treaty was created as a response to further colonial demands for Native American lands west of the Appalachian Mountains. According to the PROCLAMATION OF 1763, British-American settlement had been forbidden beyond the Appalachians, but many people ignored the law and began moving to present-day Kentucky and Tennessee. The British government and the Virginia colonial legislature sought to obtain the lands through treaty and regulate settlement in the West. Pennsylvania wanted more land on its western FRONTIER, while speculators hoped for a new boundary, which would open land for sale.

In 1768 the British superintendent of Indian affairs, SIR WILLIAM JOHNSON, organized a treaty council with the Iroquois at Fort Stanwix, now Rome, New York. The conference began on October 24, 1768, and ended on November 5 with the signing of the Treaty of Fort Stanwix. Under the treaty's terms, the new boundary ran from Fort Stanwix southward to the Delaware River. The line then followed the Western Branch of the Susquehanna River to the Allegheny River in modern Pennsylvania. The largest tract of land acquired by the British extended from Pittsburgh down the length of the Ohio River to the mouth of the Tennessee River. Even though the Iroquois claim to the lands south of the Ohio River was not particularly valid, they received all of the compensation for the lands, which was almost £10,000 worth of MONEY and goods. The Iroquois saw themselves as the "conquerors and protectors" of the Ohio Indians and therefore could speak for the Ohio tribes who actually lived in and hunted in Kentucky, including the DELAWARE, SHAWNEE, and Mingo. These tribes did not recognize Iroquois land rights in Kentucky, but the British decided to use the Iroquois to acquire the land; they therefore did not let the Ohio Indians speak for themselves and only allowed them to observe the treaty council. The British also chose to ignore the claims to lands north of the Tennessee River made by the CHEROKEE, who regarded the area as their hunting grounds. The Ohio Indians were not satisfied with the treaty, and the region would be marked by warfare for decades as the NATIVE AMERICANS in the area resisted European Americans encroaching on their land.

A second Treaty of Fort Stanwix was signed in 1784 between the newly independent United States and the Iroquois, reaffirming the stipulations of the 1768 treaty. It, too, had little basis in the real situation in the Ohio Valley, which remained in turmoil for years to come.

Further reading: Daniel K. Richter, *Facing East from Indian County: A Native History of Early America* (Cambridge, Mass.: Harvard University Press, 2001); Jack M. Sosin, *The Revolutionary Frontier, 1763–1783* (New York: Holt, Rinehart & Winston, 1967).

Fort Ticonderoga (Fort Carillon)

During the FRENCH AND INDIAN WAR (1754–63), Fort Ticonderoga, known as Fort Carillon to the French and located almost on the southern end of Lake Champlain, was one of the most crucial outposts between CANADA and the British North American colonies. The French began to build the fort in 1754 to protect against a British thrust up to Canada through Lake Champlain. In 1757 General Montcalm (see MONTCALM-GOZON DE SAINT-VÉRAN, LOUIS JOSEPH, MARQUIS DE used the fort as the base of his operations in the attack on Fort William Henry. In July 1758 General JAMES ABERCROMBY approached Fort Carillon with 16,000 British and colonial troops. Although this force vastly outnumbered the 3,500 French under Montcalm, on July 8, 1758, Abercromby launched an ill-fated direct assault on entrenched positions with disastrous results: His army lost about 2,000 men, and he retreated in humiliating defeat. The following summer, however, another British army under General JEFFREY AMHERST had more success. After a four-day siege, a much-depleted French garrison abandoned the fort and blew up its ammunition depot. Amherst subsequently rebuilt the fort and named it Fort Ticonderoga.

With the British victory, and with both Canada and the colonies under the British flag, the fort became less important. At the outbreak of the REVOLUTIONARY WAR (1775–83), it was a backwater post with a small garrison. However, after the BATTLES OF LEXINGTON AND CONCORD (April 19, 1775), several Revolutionary leaders recognized its strategic value. Encouraged by Connecticut backers, ETHAN ALLEN led 200 of his followers, called the GREEN MOUNTAIN BOYS, to capture the fort. The same idea had occurred to BENEDICT ARNOLD, who left his own Connecticut regiment to participate in the attack. Though Arnold and Allen argued over who should be in command, both men set out with the Green Mountain Boys and surprised the garrison on the morning of May 11, 1775.

This capture was important. The guns from the fort would be brought to Boston the following winter to be a part of the armament placed on DORCHESTER HEIGHTS, compelling a British withdrawal from the city. Fort Ticonderoga would also be the starting point of a Revolutionary invasion of Canada in late summer 1775 and the centerpiece in the CONTINENTAL ARMY's defense against British invasions of New York in 1776 and 1777.

Fort Ticonderoga, Essex County, New York *(Library of Congress)*

In his most important victory during the invasion of New York in summer 1777, British general JOHN BURGOYNE recaptured the fort on July 6, 1777. The Revolutionaries had prepared elaborate defenses on both sides of the lake, including entrenched positions on Mount Independence on the eastern shore and a boom bridge across the lake to facilitate the movement of troops and to prevent British boats from passing south of the defenses. However, the Continental commanding officer, General ARTHUR ST. CLAIR, did not fortify Mount Defiance, the highest point in the area directly south of Fort Ticonderoga, because he believed it would be impossible for the British to carry heavy guns up its steep incline. Burgoyne recognized the mistake instantly and, landing just north of the fort, slipped units around the Revolutionaries and, with some backbreaking labor on the part of his troops, placed artillery on top of Mount Defiance. From these heights he could lob artillery shells into Fort Ticonderoga and destroy St. Clair's defenses. Seeing that his position was untenable, St. Clair ordered a retreat on the night of July 5, sending his wounded down Lake Champlain to Skenesboro and marching the rest of his army across the boom bridge and down the eastern shore of

the lake. Although the British caught up to the rear guard of the Revolutionary forces at the BATTLE OF HUBBARDTON (July 7, 1777) and captured other soldiers at the BATTLE OF SKENESBORO (July 6, 1777), most of the revolutionary army escaped to fight at the BATTLE OF BENNINGTON (August 16, 1777) and contribute to Burgoyne's surrender at SARATOGA (October 17, 1777).

After Burgoyne was cut off from his supplies in autumn 1777, the British burned and abandoned Fort Ticonderoga, and it was not garrisoned again during the Revolutionary War.

Further reading: Fred Anderson, *Crucible of War: The Seven Years' War and the Fate of Empire in British North America, 1754–1766* (New York: Knopf, 2000); Richard M. Ketchum, *Saratoga: Turning Point of America's Revolutionary War* (New York: Henry Holt and Company, 1997).

Fort Washington, capture of

After British general WILLIAM HOWE had driven GEORGE WASHINGTON out of New York City, the CONTINENTAL

ARMY occupied the northern end of Manhattan Island. This position centered on Fort Washington, which controlled the Hudson River along with Fort Lee on the Palisades in New Jersey. Fort Washington was little more than earthworks but derived its greatest defensive asset from its height 230 feet above the river. Despite this advantage, the revolutionaries confronted a difficult situation: The perimeter entrenchments spread along five miles needed a force of 8,000–10,000 men to be properly defended, while Fort Washington itself could hold a garrison of about 1,400 men. Moreover, just to the north of the fort was a hill of almost the same height which, if occupied by the enemy, could rain deadly fire on the defenders. Washington thought that it might be best to withdraw from Manhattan, but he deferred to General NATHANAEL GREENE, who was closer to the scene at Fort Lee. Greene believed Fort Washington could withstand an attack by the British army and funneled 2,800 men onto Manhattan—too few to successfully man all the outer defenses and too many to be stationed in Fort Washington alone.

Howe decided to attack the Manhattan outpost after the BATTLE OF WHITE PLAINS (October 28, 1776) and Washington's retreat further into New York State. In early November an officer from the fort deserted to the British and provided them with detailed plans of the defensive works. Howe concentrated 8,000 men around northern Manhattan in mid-November and demanded that Colonel Robert McGaw, who commanded the revolutionary troops in and around Fort Washington, surrender. McGaw refused.

On the morning of November 16, 1776, Howe launched a four-pronged attack. In the early morning, General Von Knyphausen (see KNYPHAUSEN, WILHELM, BARON VON) crossed the Harlem River with 3,000 HESSIANS to advance on Fort Washington from the north, while Lord Percy approached with 2,000 men from the south, and LORD CORNWALLIS and General Edward Mathew crossed the Harlem River near Laurel Hill to the west of the Fort with 3,000 soldiers. The fourth prong, a regiment of 800 Highlanders under Colonel Thomas Sterling, landed closer to the Morris Mansion, intending to cut off the Continentals manning the lines to the south. The coordination did not work quite as planned, and both Knyphausen and Percy had to delay their advance until Cornwallis and Mathew were in position. Moreover, most of the revolutionaries were able to withdraw to Fort Washington by late afternoon. But eluding early capture did not help the defenders. Hessian and British troops seized the hill just to the north of the fort, leaving the revolutionaries crowded into the earthworks in a hopeless situation. With the enemy in such a commanding position, and British troops approaching in vastly superior numbers from all directions, McGaw had no choice but to surrender or see his men slaughtered.

In the fighting, which was very intense, the British lost 78 killed and 378 wounded. The Continental army lost 59 killed and 96 wounded (this number probably only counts the seriously wounded), but 230 officers and 2,600 enlisted men surrendered. The British also seized 146 cannons and a great deal of other military equipment and supplies. In addition, they crossed the Hudson and scaled the Palisades on November 20 to capture Fort Lee. To avoid another disaster, however, Washington had ordered the Continentals in the fort to abandon their heavy equipment and withdraw before the British could surround them.

The capture of Fort Washington is also noteworthy because of two incidents. After the fighting began, Washington, Greene, and several other officers crossed the Hudson River to access the situation. They arrived at the Morris Mansion, which had a commanding view of the Harlem River and the advancing British soldiers. Seeing the imminent danger, the officers urged Washington to withdraw, which he did, insisting that they accompany him. Fifteen minutes later, Colonel Sterling's men arrived at the mansion, just missing capturing Washington and several of his general officers. At Fort Washington, a different kind of drama unfolded. After MARGARET "MOLLY" COCHRAN CORBIN's husband was killed by Hessian fire, she replaced him at his cannon and continued fighting until she was wounded in the shoulder.

Further reading: Barnet Schecter, *The Battle for New York: The City at the Heart of the American Revolution* (New York: Walker & Company, 2002).

Fort William Henry "Massacre" (August 10, 1757)

Built at the southern edge of Lake George (called Lac St. Sacrement by the French) in 1756, Fort William Henry was supposed to be the launching point for a British-American invasion of CANADA through the Lake Champlain corridor. Instead, it became the target of a French siege from August 3 to 9, 1757. Although victory at Fort William Henry represented a high point in French success in the FRENCH AND INDIAN WAR (1754–63), it ended in a so-called massacre of the British Americans by NATIVE AMERICANS. The story of this tragedy has been immortalized in James Fenimore Cooper's novel *The Last of the Mohicans* (1826).

General Montcalm (see MONTCALM-GOZON DE SAINT-VÉRAN, LOUIS JOSEPH MARQUIS DE) brought almost 8,000 men, including approximately 1,800 Indians from dozens of tribes and as far away as Lake Superior, to Fort William Henry. He was able to use these Native Americans effectively to screen his preparations for the attack on Fort William Henry, which was defended by 2,372 soldiers under Lieutenant Colonel George Munro. The fort held only about 500 men; the rest of the British regulars and provincial troops fortified high ground nearby. Montcalm pursued a conventional siege and had his men dig parallels and saps to bring his artillery close to the fort. On August 6 the French cannons began to fire on the defenders. By August 8 the French had placed a battery within 250 yards of the fort and the situation had become hopeless, with most of the British-American artillery destroyed and ammunition and supplies depleted. Munro had expected relief from General Daniel Webb, 16 miles away at Fort Edward, but Webb decided that he did not have enough men to take on Montcalm's larger army. On August 9 Munro sought terms, and following European rules of warfare, he was granted the full "honors of war" for his valiant defense. His men would be permitted to march to Fort Edward and keep their arms and equipment and some personal property as long as they promised not to fight the French for 18 months. The British were also supposed to exchange all prisoners currently held in North America.

The Native Americans, who expected that victory would bring them loot, scalps, and prisoners, could not understand such leniency to a defeated enemy. In an effort to avoid a confrontation with the Indians, Munro and Montcalm first agreed that the march would begin at midnight, but they canceled those plans for fear of an Indian attack. The next morning the British Americans began their trek to Fort Edward. After the soldiers left the fort, Native Americans entered it and killed several wounded men too hurt to travel. When the provincials started to leave the fortified camp—the regulars headed the column—Indians began looting supplies and then taking equipment from the soldiers. This activity quickly spread up and down the line, with some Indians physically assaulting anyone who resisted, while others grabbed soldiers and camp followers as captives. Panic spread through the ranks. Some ran down the road, others into the woods, and there was confusion everywhere. A few French soldiers tried to help the soldiers; others just stood by. Montcalm arrived, as did other officers, and although they saved some people, others were snatched away. In the end, hundreds of soldiers escaped down the road or into the woods and made their way to Fort Edward. Perhaps 500 other people were taken away by the Indians, while the French took custody of hundreds more.

Over the next several months the French negotiated and cajoled the Indians into surrendering most of their prisoners, and the majority were returned to the British before the end of the year. No more than 184 were never accounted for, meaning they were either killed that day or were taken into permanent captivity, never to be heard of again. However, the apparent perfidy of the French and the brutality of the Native Americans—at least one captive was eaten in MONTREAL within sight of prisoners, and many

of the killed had been scalped and mutilated—left a searing mark on the British-American war effort. The British would refuse all honors to surrendering French in North America and "Fort William Henry" became a rallying cry for the rest of the war.

The capture of Fort William Henry ultimately gained Montcalm little and cost him dearly. He had seized one outpost on the far FRONTIER of British North America, but he did not proceed to Fort Edward. Instead, he burned his prize and returned north with his army, and his Indian allies, disgusted with the campaign, quickly left him. Never again would Montcalm be able to raise large numbers of Native Americans to fight against the British. He was also left with a public-relations disaster, although he was ultimately able to defend his honor. Finally, he became more convinced than ever that he needed to fight a conventional war against the British Americans, a war in which his enemy's superior numbers and material would ultimately lead to a French defeat.

Further reading: Fred Anderson, *Crucible of War: The Seven Years' War and the Fate of Empire in British North America, 1754–1766* (New York: Knopf, 2000); Ian K. Steele, *Betrayals: Fort William Henry and the Massacre* (New York: Oxford University Press, 1990).

Fort Wilson riot (October 4, 1779)

For much of 1779, two interrelated debates raged in Philadelphia. Constitutionalists defended the extremely democratic Pennsylvania state constitution against reformers who wanted a more conservative form of government. Simultaneously, radicals in the Philadelphia MILITIA who sought PRICE CONTROLS were opposed by men who wanted to allow the market to set prices. The Fort Wilson riot reflected the crosscurrents of these two conflicts. After months of public meetings and calls for price controls, a frustrated militia decided to take the situation into their own hands. On October 4, 1779, a few hundred militia paraded the streets with five captives whom the militia claimed were price gaugers and Tories (LOYALISTS). When they passed the house of JAMES WILSON, who was a leader of the conservatives and opposed price controls, a gun battle broke out between 30–40 merchants in Wilson's house and the militia in the street. It remains unclear who fired first, but both sides had casualties: One defender was killed and three wounded, while five to seven militia died and at least 14 were wounded. After fighting for about 10 minutes, a troop of cavalry supported by Continentals arrived, drove the militia off and arrested about 30 militiamen. The defenders were left in command of the house and the street. Although the militia lost the confrontation, the state constitution was not altered for over a decade, and the state government passed legislation to provide relief for militia families.

See also FOOD RIOTS; RIOTS.

Further reading: John K. Alexander, "The Fort Wilson Incident: A Case Study of the Revolutionary Crowd," *William and Mary Quarterly* 3rd ser., 31 (1974): 589–612; Steven Rosswurm, *Arms, Country, and Class; The Philadelphia Militia and "Lower Sort" during the American Revolution, 1775–1783* (New Bruswick, N.J.: Rutgers University Press, 1987).

Foster, Augustus John (1780–1848) *British diplomat*
Sir Augustus John Foster was the British minister in WASHINGTON, D.C. in 1811 and 1812. An aristocrat by birth, he attended Oxford University and served from 1804 to 1807 as the secretary to ANTHONY MERRY, who was then the British minister to the United States. Foster arrived in Washington in July 1811 and was in a position to defuse an explosive situation. Instead of acting to ease tensions, he followed his instructions and refused to budge on the issue of neutral rights. He also rigorously protested U.S. intervention in FLORIDA and the *LITTLE BELT* INCIDENT (May 16, 1811). The one area where his instructions allowed for flexibility concerned the *CHESAPEAKE-LEOPARD* AFFAIR (1807). However, Foster did not inform the U.S. government about the British willingness for concessions until November 1811, which was too late to heal relations.

Foster was an important presence in Washington and lavishly entertained members of both the FEDERALIST PARTY and the DEMOCRATIC-REPUBLICAN PARTY. Despite his many connections, he remained unconcerned with the threat of war and therefore contributed to the mutual misunderstanding between his country and the United States. After returning to GREAT BRITAIN in 1812, he was elected to Parliament. He subsequently served as the British minister in Copenhagen from 1814 to 1824 and in Turin, Italy, from 1825 to 1840. He was made a baronet in 1831 and killed himself on August 1, 1848. In the 1930s his *Notes on the United States of America* were discovered and published.

See also FOREIGN AFFAIRS.

Further reading: Bradford Perkins, *Prologue to War, 1805–1812: England and the United States* (Berkeley: University of California Press, 1968).

Foster, Hannah (1758–1840) *novelist*
Born Hannah Webster in Massachusetts, Hannah Foster was well-educated and married the Reverend John Foster of Brighton, Massachusetts in 1785; they had six children. Although not much is known about her personal life, Foster wrote one of the most popular novels of the early republic: *The Coquette; or, The History of Eliza Wharton,* published anonymously in 1797 and based loosely on the well-known tale of Elizabeth Whitman, who had died alone in childbirth after having succumbed to seduction and then been abandoned by her lover. The book, however, was no simple sentimental morality tale: It depicted a well-educated woman who had a powerful mind but, as a woman, had few choices in life because of society's restrictions. Readers of the time were attracted to Eliza's strength and her confrontation with social constraints, rather than her ultimate weakness. Foster also wrote *The Boarding School* (1798), based in part on her own experiences. It was not as popular and more didactic, but it also carried a proto-feminist message supporting EDUCATION for women. After her husband's death, Foster moved to MONTREAL, where two of her daughters lived. She died there in 1840, age 81.

See also WOMEN'S STATUS AND RIGHTS.

Further reading: Cathy N. Davidson, *Revolution and the Word: The Rise of the Novel in America* (New York: Oxford University Press, 1986).

France
With a population of over 20 million, France was the most powerful nation in Europe in the mid-18th century and exerted a tremendous influence on the development of the United States during the period of 1754–1815. France occupied a large territory that stretched from the English Channel in the north to the Pyrenees and the MEDITERRANEAN SEA in the South, and from the ATLANTIC OCEAN to the Alps and almost to the Rhine River in the east. But French influence reached much further than its political boundaries. After the reign of Louis XIV, French culture was the envy of the rest of Europe, with almost every monarch seeking to emulate the splendor of Versailles and the absolute power of the French Crown. French was spoken by the aristocracy in most of Europe and was the language of diplomacy. Moreover, the French had a huge overseas empire that included a large area of North America (CANADA and LOUISIANA), valuable islands in the WEST INDIES, and outposts in AFRICA and INDIA. All of this power came at a price: French finances were in a shambles by mid-century, and it found itself in an ever intensifying conflict with other European powers, especially GREAT BRITAIN.

In the mid-18th century, the contest for empire with the British erupted into the FRENCH AND INDIAN WAR (1754–63)—known as the Seven Years' War (1756–63) in Europe. The French lost this war and, while retaining its most valuable possessions in the West Indies, had to cede most of its North American possessions to Great Britain, holding onto a few small islands off the fishing banks of Newfoundland and signing over Louisiana to its ally SPAIN in compensation for other losses. This war had a profound impact on British colonial Americans because they had participated in the conflict with an intensity that made any sustained peaceful connection between the colonists and the French unthinkable. That antipathy aside, colonial merchants had some illegal TRADE contacts with the French West Indies even during the war, and they continued to trade during the 1760s and early 1770s.

The COLONIAL RESISTANCE MOVEMENT (1764–75) that led to the REVOLUTIONARY WAR (1775–83) and U.S. independence altered the situation. France encouraged the rebellion from its inception and agreed to a formal alliance with the Revolutionaries in 1778. Without French military support—including supplies, troops, and a navy—the British might have won the Revolutionary War. The French also opened up trade relations with the United States in 1778, and during the 1780s many Revolutionary leaders hoped that somehow France would be able to replace Great Britain as the new nation's major trading partner. Despite the efforts of Francophiles like THOMAS JEFFERSON, however, this economic relationship never fully developed.

France's involvement in the Revolutionary War was expensive, and it stretched the government coffers to the breaking point. The FRENCH REVOLUTION (1789–99) began as an effort to reform the French government following republican principles similar to the ideals of the United States, but it soon became a radical attempt to transform France and its people. Seeking to export its revolution to other states in Europe, the country quickly found itself embroiled in wars with more reactionary regimes in Austria and elsewhere. On February 1, 1793, shortly after the execution of France's Louis XVI, Great Britain and France went to war in a conflict that would continue with two short breaks until 1815.

The French Revolution had a dramatic effect in the United States, where initially the people greeted the Revolution with enthusiasm. That excitement waned among those who came to be identified with the FEDERALIST PARTY since the French Revolution challenged the order of civil society so cherished by men such as GEORGE WASHINGTON and ALEXANDER HAMILTON. Others—like Jefferson, who was in Paris at the outbreak of the Revolution—continued to support the French. The war between Great Britain and France brought new opportunities and challenges to the United States. If the young nation could maintain neutrality, great profits could be made in carrying goods from French and British colonies to their respective metropolitan centers, but to do so meant potentially violating international law. Efforts in 1793 by Citizen EDMOND-CHARLES GENÉT to get the United States to support the French were frustrated when President GEORGE WASH-

INGTON issued the NEUTRALITY PROCLAMATION. Similarly, the French government believed that JAY'S TREATY (1794) was not only a repudiation of the FRENCH ALLIANCE but also too favorable to the British. This perception led to French seizures of U.S. shipping, the foiled negotiations in the XYZ AFFAIR (1797–98), and the outbreak of the undeclared QUASI-WAR (1798–1800) between France and the United States.

In the meantime, French armies triumphed in Europe, driving SPAIN out of the war and into an alliance with France and humiliating the Austrian and Prussian armies. French ambitions seemed to have no bounds. General NAPOLEON BONAPARTE led a failed expedition to Egypt, and in 1800, after he had seized control of the French government, he planned to build a North American empire centered on the French colony of Saint Domingue (HAITI). To facilitate this North American empire, Napoleon directed his erstwhile ally Spain to secretly retrocede Louisiana to France, a deal that had the potential to threaten the United States. President Jefferson authorized negotiations to purchase New Orleans as an outlet for the produce of the newly settled regions in the Mississippi and Ohio River valleys, but Napoleon, who had temporarily called a halt to the war with the British in the PEACE OF AMIENS, did not expect peace to last. Moreover, his expensive attempt to subdue the revolt in Saint Domingue by ex-slaves had failed. He therefore agreed to sell all of Louisiana to the United States for $15 million.

France and Great Britain resumed their war on May 18, 1803, with greater intensity than ever. Within a few years Napoleon came to dominate the European continent, winning stunning victories against the Austrians at Austerlitz (1805) and against the Prussians at Jena (1806). But if French armies dominated the land, the British navy controlled the seas after the Battle of Trafalgar (1805). As long as the British navy patrolled the English Channel, Napoleon could not launch an invasion of Great Britain. This stalemate led to economic warfare as Napoleon established the Continental System with the BERLIN DECREE and MILAN DECREE, creating a paper blockade on the British Isles and limiting neutral trade. The British retaliated with a series of ORDERS IN COUNCIL that inhibited neutral trade with a Europe dominated by Napoleon. Caught in the middle of the economic crossfire was the United States, which still sought to pursue trade with both nations. Beginning in 1807, the United States resorted to economic coercion of its own by passing the EMBARGO OF 1807, the NON-INTERCOURSE ACT (1809), and MACON'S BILL NO. 2 (1810) to little real effect. When Napoleon suggested in the CADORE LETTER that he would remove his impositions on neutral trade, the United States reinstituted nonintercourse against Great Britain, following the provisions of Macon's Bill No. 2. Napoleon, however, did not remove those restrictions as the United States and Great Britain drifted into the WAR OF 1812 (1812–15). Although the United States and France were cobelligerents against Great Britain, they did not fight as allies.

By 1812 the French Empire was beginning to show signs of being overextended. A revolt broke out in 1808 on the Iberian Peninsula against the French, and a British army under General Arthur Wellesley (later Lord Wellington) began a long campaign against the French there. Napoleon also launched an invasion of RUSSIA in 1812 and captured Moscow, but he was forced to retreat on account of the weather. After losing much of his army to the Russian winter, a coalition of Russian, Prussian, and Austrian forces defeated him at the Battle of Leipzig (1813). Pursued back to Paris, Napoleon abdicated in 1814 and was exiled to the Island of Elba off the coast of Italy. In 1815 he returned to France, seized power, and marched to meet a combined British and Prussian army at the Battle of Waterloo (1815). Defeated again, Napoleon was sent to the island of St. Helena in the middle of the South Atlantic Ocean. The Bourbon dynasty was restored to France, which was allowed to keep the basic outlines of its prewar boundaries and resume its role as one of the great powers of Europe.

Further reading: Owen Connelly, *The Wars of the French Revolution and Napoleon, 1792–1815* (London: Routledge, 2006); Charles J. Esdaille, *The French Wars, 1792–1815* (London: Routledge, 2001); Collin Jones, The *Great Nation: France from Louis XV to Napoleon, 1715–99* (New York: Columbia University, 2002).

Franklin, Benjamin (1706–1790) *scientist, statesman*

Benjamin Franklin, the first American to rise from rags not only to riches but to greatness as a publisher, scientist, and statesman, was born in Boston, Massachusetts on January 17, 1706 (o.s.). At the age of 16 he fled from his brother James, to whom he had been apprenticed as a printer, to Philadelphia, the only other city in the colonies with a printing press. By the time he was 30, Franklin was publishing the *Pennsylvania Gazette,* handling all of the colony's official printing business, and issuing *Poor Richard's Almanac* each year. This annual compilation of information, advice, and stories achieved popularity throughout the British-American colonies.

Franklin's business was so successful that he retired from it at age 41 and quickly became an important citizen of Philadelphia. He organized the Junto, a self-education study group for middling young men like himself who were not able to attend college; the colonies' first lending library, which survives today as the Library Company of Philadelphia; the city's first fire department, the Union Fire Company; and the Hospital for the Sick Poor, the first of its kind

in the colonies. The society he proposed for promoting useful knowledge became the AMERICAN PHILOSOPHICAL SOCIETY, which still flourishes today, and he was among the founders of the College of Philadelphia, which became the University of Pennsylvania. Franklin was an organizer of VOLUNTARY ASSOCIATIONS founded to accomplish civic projects outside government channels. He also shared the position of postmaster for the colonies starting in 1753. At the same time he was involved in these civic activities, he engaged in scientific work, inventing the Franklin stove and bifocal eyeglasses. His electrical experiments, including the dangerous flying of a kite with keys attached, led to the invention of the lightning rod and membership in Britain's Royal Society.

Franklin emerged as an intercolonial statesman when he represented Pennsylvania at the unsuccessful ALBANY CONGRESS of 1754. His plan for a colonial union—consisting of a North American parliament and British governor-general with responsibility for intercolonial defense—was accepted by the delegates but was turned down by both the British Parliament and the colonial assemblies. Franklin proved crucial in organizing supplies and volunteer troops for General EDWARD BRADDOCK's unsuccessful expedition to Fort Duquesne (see FORT PITT) the next year. He became the leader of the QUAKERS in the Pennsylvania Assembly, to which he was elected in 1751. That body sent him to England in 1757 to present the case against the Penn family, who governed Pennsylvania but refused to pay taxes for the common defense.

Franklin spent the years 1757–62 and 1764–75 in England. During much of this time, he sought to ingratiate himself with British officials, hoping for some huge land grant and perhaps even gaining a title, while working to make Pennsylvania a royal colony. His influence peddling was successful to some degree since he managed to get his son WILLIAM FRANKLIN appointed as governor of New Jersey and his political ally John Hughes made Philadelphia's stamp agent in 1765. This second appointment suggests that Franklin was unprepared for the outrage the STAMP ACT (1765) would provoke: Crowds in some 40 or more communities throughout the colonies compelled stamp agents to resign. In Philadelphia, only a hastily organized defense by Franklin's common-law wife DEBORAH READ FRANKLIN—who, almost unknown to history, managed his household during his long absences—prevented his own house from being attacked.

Although Franklin thereafter was less willing to compromise with the British, he still sought ways to patch up the differences between the colonies and GREAT BRITAIN. The most famous British American in Europe, he became the agent for several colonies and presented their case as Parliament passed laws such as the TOWNSHEND DUTIES (1767), TEA ACT (1773), and COERCIVE ACTS (1774);

Benjamin Franklin. Portrait of Charles Willson Peale *(Library of Congress)*

restricted westward settlement; clamped down on illegal TRADE; and sent troops to Boston. In his 1766 examination before the House of Commons concerning the Stamp Act disturbances, Franklin reminded the British that the colonists paid heavy taxes of their own and had supported the mutual cause well during the FRENCH AND INDIAN WAR (1754–63). Colonial Americans, Franklin asserted, were proud to be British, and only infringements of the rights they perceived as theirs (whether correctly so did not matter) would change their minds. Were military forces sent to North America, he predicted, "they will not find a rebellion; they may indeed make one." Yet as late as 1768 he openly hoped for some royal appointment by declaring to LORD NORTH that he would "stay with pleasure" in England if he "could any ways be useful to government."

By 1773, however, Franklin's British prospects had become bleak, and he decided on a desperate gamble to blame the Anglo-American tension on one person; Massachusetts governor THOMAS HUTCHINSON. In doing this, Franklin ended his British career in scandal. He sent copies of letters addressed to the British ministry by Massachusetts royal officials, including Hutchinson, to the Massachusetts Assembly, and although he had specified that they were only to be viewed privately, he could hardly

have been surprised when the letters were published. His hope was that politicians on both sides of the ATLANTIC OCEAN would blame Hutchinson for the mutual misunderstandings, but he miscalculated. Massachusetts leaders were irate and demanded Hutchinson's recall, while in Great Britain, officials screamed foul and hauled Franklin before the king and Privy Council where the British solicitor general, Alexander Wedderburn, making the most of this incident, denounced him as a thief. In January 1775, having been dismissed as the colonies' postmaster, Franklin left for North America in disgrace. His parting gift to the British was a letter of recommendation for a failed excise collector, THOMAS PAINE, who would soon move to Philadelphia and write COMMON SENSE, the pamphlet that persuaded many colonists to favor independence.

Whatever his dreams for a special place in a transatlantic Anglo-American empire, upon Franklin's return from Europe he quickly declared himself on the side of the revolutionaries and became a member of the SECOND CONTINENTAL CONGRESS. He was one of the five-person committee assigned to frame the DECLARATION OF INDEPENDENCE (1776), although he only added a few minor corrections to THOMAS JEFFERSON's draft. That same year, he was one of the peace commissioners chosen by Congress to meet with British general SIR WILLIAM HOWE on Staten Island, and he joined his fellow delegates in refusing any offer save independence. Meanwhile, Franklin became the first president of the Commonwealth of Pennsylvania. Unlike most members of the old Quaker and proprietary factions who became LOYALISTS, he took a leading role among the "radicals" who controlled the new government of Pennsylvania. These radicals disfranchised Quakers and Tories, handed over local rule to MILITIA committees, and gave power at the state level to the prorevolutionary counties and Philadelphia workers from whose ranks Franklin had sprung.

Franklin did not remain long in Pennsylvania. Since he had an international reputation as a man of SCIENCE, in 1777 Congress sent him to FRANCE to negotiate the FRENCH ALLIANCE that would be signed the following year. Franklin fully understood his role and played to the sympathies of a French court enamored with the ideals of the ENLIGHTENMENT: He wore a fur cap to symbolize the "natural man" praised by the philosopher then in vogue, Jean-Jacques Rousseau, and charmed the court and the ladies, although legends of his sexual conquests are greatly exaggerated. Franklin's popularity enabled him not only to negotiate treaties but to deal with the animosity among other diplomats from the United States. JOHN ADAMS, for instance, resented Franklin's standing at court and thought him too pro-French and lacking in caution. (Franklin's private secretary was a British spy.) Throughout the war, Franklin nurtured his relationship with France, worked to obtain loans, assisted stranded SEAMEN in Europe, and smoothed over a host of diplomatic difficulties. Along with Adams, JOHN JAY, and HENRY LAURENS, Franklin negotiated the TREATY OF PARIS (1783), which sidestepped the provision of the French Alliance that had promised not to engage in separate peace negotiations. This diplomatic sleight of hand came about in part because of his friendship with the COMTE DE VERGENNES, who wanted the United States to make a separate treaty to put pressure on the Spanish to accept an end to the war without the conquest of Gibraltar.

Returning to the United States early in 1785, Franklin abandoned the Pennsylvania states-rights radicals. Like most people who had represented the United States as a nation in the army, Congress, or diplomatic service, he became convinced that only a strong national government could save 13 disunited states from disaster. Elected to the 1787 CONSTITUTIONAL CONVENTION, the aged statesman slept a good deal during a stifling Philadelphia summer; his speeches were read by JAMES WILSON. Nevertheless, his final statement—which urged his countrymen to accept the proposed document as the best possible despite reservations that they, like himself, were sure to have—was circulated throughout the states and had some role in achieving ratification of the U.S. CONSTITUTION.

Ill and in pain from gallstones, Franklin spent the final years of his life in Philadelphia, teaching the printing business to his grandson BENJAMIN FRANKLIN BACHE, but he never totally retired. Although he had owned at least six slaves at different times in his life, he became president of the Pennsylvania Abolition Society. In his last published writing in 1790, he impersonated an African Muslim who held U.S. sailors captive, and he parroted the arguments proslavery advocates used to justify SLAVERY (civilize slaves and teach them the true RELIGION). During his last years he frequently sat in his front yard with a model of a bridge designed by Thomas Paine and tried to persuade his countrymen to support its construction over the Schuylkill River to further economic development.

After his death (April 17, 1790), Franklin's reputation grew to mythic proportions. As a public benefactor, he left a substantial amount of MONEY for the EDUCATION of youth, much of which became the endowment of the Franklin Institute. He is best remembered, however, as "Printer Ben," the most down-to-earth of the Founding Fathers—one who, as he described in *The Autobiography of Benjamin Franklin,* appeared in Philadelphia as a youth with a loaf of bread under each arm. Magazines published excerpts of this literary classic first in 1790. The entire book was published in Paris in 1791 and in the United States in 1794. During the next 34 years, some 22 editions were issued carrying the lightning tamer's rags-to-riches story. Franklin became the model of self-improvement in the egalitarian atmosphere of the early republic and offered a blueprint of middle-class values in a burgeoning capitalist economy. Erased from popular memory was the transatlantic parvenu lobbying for land and office in Great Britain. In its place was the poor boy who made good. Franklin became a businessman turned scientist, philanthropist, diplomat, and statesman who stood up to a king, helped guide the new nation toward independence, carried out delicate negotiations with foreign powers, and offered a calming presence at the Constitutional Convention.

See also FOREIGN AFFAIRS; POSTAL SERVICE; SPYING.

Further reading: Benjamin Franklin, *Writings* (New York: Library of America, 1987); Walter Isaacson, *Benjamin Franklin: An American Life* (New York: Simon & Schuster, 2003); J. A. Leo Lemay, ed., *Reappraising Benjamin Franklin* (Newark: University of Delaware Press, 1993); Edmund S. Morgan, *Benjamin Franklin* (New Haven, Conn.: Yale University Press, 2002); Gordon S. Wood, *The Americanization of Benjamin Franklin* (New York: Penguin, 2004); Esmond Wright, *Franklin of Philadelphia* (Cambridge, Mass.: Harvard University Press, 1986).

—William Pencak

Franklin, Deborah Read (1707?–1774) *wife of Benjamin Franklin*

The common-law wife of BENJAMIN FRANKLIN, Deborah Read Franklin was the daughter of carpenter John Read and Sarah White. Neither the date nor place of Deborah Read Franklin's birth is known, though many sources place it in 1707 or 1708. The first time she is mentioned in any written record is from Benjamin Franklin's famous autobiography, in which he related how she spied the runaway apprentice in a Philadelphia street with loaves of bread stuck in his pocket. Franklin became a boarder at the Read residence and courted Deborah before he left for England in 1724. The two wanted to get married, but Deborah's mother, a widow by this time, convinced them to put off any commitment until after Benjamin's return. Once in London, Franklin became preoccupied with his new life, and Deborah Read, at the urging of her mother, married John Rogers, a potter, in 1725. This marriage did not work out—Rogers may have had a wife in England—and Deborah soon left Rogers and began using her maiden name again. This type of self-divorce was not unusual in 18th-century Philadelphia, although it had no standing in law. Rogers moved to the WEST INDIES, where it was rumored he was killed in a brawl.

When, therefore, Benjamin returned to Philadelphia in 1726, Deborah was not available for a legal marriage. After Franklin failed to find a wife who could bring him a dowry, he and Deborah agreed to the common-law marriage, as to marry legally would have left both open to prosecution under the law if Rogers returned somehow. Franklin also had the inconvenience of having fathered an illegitimate son, WILLIAM FRANKLIN, whom Deborah agreed to raise as her own. Whatever the romantic basis of the marriage, and despite the lack of a dowry, Deborah Read Franklin became the ideal helpmate to Benjamin Franklin's enterprises, working in their shop and contributing significantly to his subsequent economic success. As Benjamin himself admitted, "It was lucky for me that I had one as much dispos'd to Industry and Frugality as myself. She assisted me cheerfully in my Business." Deborah gave birth to only two children, one of whom, a son, died in early childhood. Their daughter Sarah "Sally" Franklin married Richard Bache, with whom she had eight children, including BENJAMIN FRANKLIN BACHE.

Benjamin Franklin's early retirement at the age 41 and his devotion to public service and scientific inquiry led the couple to grow apart gradually, although Deborah did participate in some of Benjamin's experiments with ELECTRICITY and helped with his duties in the post office. Deborah, however, remained a women of the ARTISAN class, while Benjamin transformed himself into a gentleman and international celebrity. His long absences—he was in England from 1757 to 1762 and 1764 to 1775—were particularly hard on the marriage. Deborah continued to write him affectionate letters, to which he initially responded in kind. She also stood by him politically and even organized the defense of their Philadelphia house when a mob threatened its destruction during the STAMP ACT (1765) crisis because many Pennsylvanians thought Franklin had not done enough to oppose imperial regulation. By the end of her life, however, as she lay dying after prolonged illness, any letters she received from her famous husband were perfunctory, and he never even mentioned to her the birth of their grandson WILLIAM TEMPLE FRANKLIN—the illegitimate son of William Franklin. She died on December 24, 1774, not having seen her husband for nine years.

Further reading: Claude-Anne Lopez and Eugenia W. Herbert, *The Private Franklin: The Man and His Family* (New York: Norton, 1975).

Franklin, state of

The short-lived state of Franklin in what is now eastern Tennessee demonstrated the confused nature of politics on the western slopes of the Appalachians in the late 18th century. Men and women from the backwoods of the Carolinas, Virginia, and Pennsylvania came to the region in the tumultuous years following the REVOLUTIONARY WAR (1775–83). To the south, the Chickamauga Indians, led by DRAGGING CANOE, fought their advance. These NATIVE AMERICANS also came to the Tennessee Valley to start new lives.

North Carolina had ceded the lands to the federal government, but when the state did not receive payments for its war debt, it reclaimed the territory. Despite this claim, in August 1784 delegates from the far-western counties of North Carolina met in Jonesborough to organize the state of Franklin. In March 1785 JOHN SEVIER accepted the governorship of the infant state. The loyalty of many of the inhabitants of Franklin rested on the fact that they had settled illegally on land that North Carolina had set aside for the Indians, and the Franklinites launched several raids against the CHEROKEE. The situation remained complicated: Sevier represented land speculators from the East and eventually sought to maneuver the region back into North Carolina; he was even elected to the North Carolina Senate in 1789. Conflict over land claims also led to some fighting between individuals holding deeds under the state of Franklin and those who had North Carolina deeds. By 1790 the state of Franklin had ceased to function. North Carolina established control over the area until it became part of the new state of Tennessee in 1796. Sevier served as Tennessee's first governor.

Further reading: Wilma Dykeman, *Tennessee: A Bicentennial History* (New York: Norton, 1975).

Franklin, William (1731–1813) *Loyalist*

A Loyalist and last governor of colonial New Jersey, William Franklin was the son of BENJAMIN FRANKLIN and an unknown mother, though Benjamin and his common-law wife, DEBORAH READ FRANKLIN, always treated him like a legitimate child. He was privately tutored and put to work in Franklin's print shop, but he longed to leave home. When his father prevented him from sailing on a privateer during King George's War (1744–48), Franklin enlisted in the Royal American Regiment. Although only 16, by 1747 he had served with distinction on the New York FRONTIER and was commissioned captain of a company of grenadiers. That year he assisted his father in raising Pennsylvania's volunteer MILITIA. In 1748 he accompanied CONRAD WEISER to the Ohio Valley to negotiate with NATIVE AMERICANS, and in the early 1750s he was sufficiently involved in his father's experiments with ELECTRICITY that when Benjamin received his honorary doctorate from Oxford in 1762, William obtained a master's degree.

A political supporter of his father, William served as the elder Franklin's clerk when he left for GREAT BRITAIN in 1757 in an effort to remove Pennsylvania's proprietary Penn family and replace them with a royal governor. William's behavior in England was as impressive as it had been in Pennsylvania, though he had an illegitimate son, WIL-LIAM TEMPLE FRANKLIN, born in 1760. He became governor of New Jersey in 1762 and at first was successful in that post. He urged the improvement of roads and bridges, supported the colony's college, and punished European Americans who invaded Native American rights. However, when Britain passed the STAMP ACT (1765), Franklin felt it his duty to uphold the law. His father, now an agent for several colonies in England, denounced him as "a thorough government man." When the REVOLUTIONARY WAR (1775–83) broke out, William and New Jersey's Loyalist assembly were overthrown by the SECOND CONTINENTAL CONGRESS. "An enemy to the liberties of this country," William was imprisoned in Connecticut for two years until he was exchanged on November 1, 1778. His wife had died in the meantime, and his health suffered greatly after 250 days served in solitary confinement.

After his release, Franklin immediately went to New York, where he organized the Board of Associated Loyalists, of which he served as first president. The board cared for thousands of refugees while planning military ventures in cooperation with the British army. The guerrilla tactics Franklin urged were responsible for much of the vicious, small-scale warfare in southern New York and northern New Jersey that accompanied the last years of war.

Leaving North America in August 1782, Franklin received a generous pension and compensation for his losses from the British government. In 1785 he briefly met his father on the latter's return from FRANCE to the United States, but after the elder Franklin died, William's inheritance was some worthless land in NOVA SCOTIA to which his father had retained title. Benjamin sarcastically noted in his will that since William remained loyal to England, English land was all he deserved. William helped other LOYALISTS receive reimbursement for sufferings, married Mary D'Evelyn, and lived in London until his death on November 17, 1813.

Further reading: Sheila L. Skemp, *William Franklin: Son of a Patriot, Servant of a King* (New York: Oxford University Press, 1990).

Franklin, William Temple (1760–1823) *U.S. diplomat*
The grandson of BENJAMIN FRANKLIN, William Temple Franklin was born in London and was the illegitimate son of WILLIAM FRANKLIN. He spent much of his youth with his grandfather and traveled with Benjamin to North America in 1775. The REVOLUTIONARY WAR (1775–83) divided the Franklin family: William Franklin joined the LOYALISTS, while Benjamin Franklin and William Temple Franklin supported the WHIGS. When the SECOND CONTINENTAL CONGRESS sent Benjamin to FRANCE to repre-

sent U.S. interests there, he took William Temple with him as his secretary. During their time in Paris, Benjamin tried to help his grandson by giving him important responsibilities and experience in diplomacy, although William Temple gained a reputation as a reckless youth who enjoyed the pleasures of Paris nightlife. Due to his grandfather's influence, William Temple Franklin delivered the Treaty of Amity to the French and later served as secretary of the U.S. Peace Commission, which resulted in the TREATY OF PARIS (1783). But William Temple Franklin's otherwise undistinguished diplomatic career and reputation for carousing angered Benjamin Franklin's critics. As a result, Benjamin was unable to secure a ministerial appointment for his grandson, and the two men returned to the United States in 1785.

William Temple inherited his grandfather's papers after Benjamin's death in 1790. He intended to publish the elder Franklin's autobiography upon returning to England in 1792 but found a French language edition already available. After years of procrastination and involvement in a variety of failed business ventures, William Temple Franklin finally published his edited although incomplete version of Benjamin Franklin's papers, including the autobiography, in 1817. He died in Paris on May 25, 1823.

Further reading: Benjamin Franklin, *The Autobiography of Benjamin Franklin,* 2nd ed., edited by Leonard W. Labaree, et al., (New Haven, Conn.: Yale University Press, 2003).

—Tash Smith

Franks, David Salisbury (1742–1793) *Continental army officer, U.S. diplomat*
David Salisbury Franks was a member of a Philadelphia Jewish family who went to CANADA after the British victory in the FRENCH AND INDIAN WAR (1754–63); they moved from Quebec to MONTREAL in 1774. Franks's outspoken opposition to the QUEBEC ACT (1774)—because it did not provide recognition for JEWS—led to his arrest for 16 days in May 1775. That November the CONTINENTAL ARMY captured Montreal, and Franks expressed sympathy for the revolutionary cause. In 1776 he became paymaster and a supplier for the Continental Army in Montreal, and he retreated to New York with the Revolutionary forces that summer. After joining the army, he fought at SARATOGA (October 17, 1777), and then, because of his fluency in French, became a liaison officer to the COMTE D'ESTAING in early 1778. Promoted to major in July, he became an aide to BENEDICT ARNOLD in Philadelphia. He fought in South Carolina in 1780 but was sent to WEST POINT in the summer, again as an aide to Arnold. Tainted by Arnold's betrayal of the Revolutionary cause, Franks was arrested

and suffered a treason trial and a military court of enquiry, the latter at his own request; he was exonerated with the support of GEORGE WASHINGTON. In 1781 he was promoted to lieutenant colonel and thus became the highest ranking Jew to serve in the Continental army.

During the 1780s Franks became a minor diplomat for the United States as a courier and vice consul in Marseilles, France. On several occasions he was entrusted with diplomatic documents, including the final draft of the TREATY OF PARIS (1783). As an assistant to U.S. diplomat Thomas Barclay, Franks also was involved in writing the treaty with MOROCCO in 1786. He returned to the United States in 1787 and moved to Philadelphia, where ROBERT MORRIS used his influence to gain Franks a position as assistant cashier of the BANK OF NORTH AMERICA. Unmarried, Franks died in the YELLOW FEVER outbreak in 1793.

Fraser, Simon (1729–1777) *British military officer*

The younger son of a Scottish family, Simon Fraser became a career officer in the British army. He served with distinction in the War of Austrian Succession (1740–48) and the FRENCH AND INDIAN WAR (1754–63). He was at the siege of LOUISBOURG and the BATTLE OF QUEBEC (September 13, 1759). At the beginning of the REVOLUTIONARY WAR (1775–83), Fraser was a lieutenant colonel. He arrived in CANADA on May 18, 1776, was placed in command of four battalions at the BATTLE OF TROIS-RIVIÈRES, and defeated an attacking force of Continentals on June 8. Two days later, General GUY CARLETON promoted Fraser to brigadier general. After the British victory at the BATTLE OF VALCOUR ISLAND (October 11, 1776), Fraser advanced to within 14 miles of FORT TICONDEROGA before Carleton ordered him to withdraw for fear of the approaching winter.

Fraser was an important field commander during the invasion of New York by General JOHN BURGOYNE. He participated in the attack that captured Fort Ticonderoga and then, placed in charge of the advance guard, he defeated Revolutionary forces at the BATTLE OF HUBBARDTON, (July 7, 1777). At the Battle of Freeman's Farm (September 19, 1777), he commanded the right wing of the British army. However, at the Battle of Bemis Heights (October 7, 1777), Fraser was shot and mortally wounded by a rifleman. He died the next day.

See also SARATOGA, SURRENDER AT.

British officer Simon Fraser commanded the 24th Regiment, one of the few British formations capable of performing as light infantry. He was renowned as a brave and daring officer. *(Clan Fraser Society of Canada)*

Fraunces Tavern

Built as a residence for the colonial merchant Stephen De Lancey in 1719, Fraunces Tavern at 54 Pearl Street, New York City, was a tavern run by Samuel Fraunces, a free African American, during the revolutionary era. The tavern hosted meetings of the SONS OF LIBERTY before the outbreak of the REVOLUTIONARY WAR (1775–83) and served British soldiers during their long occupation of the city from 1776 to 1783. Perhaps most famously, Fraunces Tavern was the site of the farewell of GEORGE WASHINGTON to his officers at the end of the war. From 1785 to 1790 the building housed the offices of the treasury, state, and war departments of the United States. In the 19th century, 54 Pearl Street became a boardinghouse. In 1904 the New York Sons of Liberty—a patriotic organization whose ancestors fought in the Revolutionary War—purchased the building, and in 1907 it opened as a museum. Today Fraunces's Tavern is both a museum and a restaurant.

Freeman, Elizabeth (Mum Bett, Mumbet) (1742–1829)

Elizabeth Freeman, also known as Mum Bett or Mumbet, was an African-American slave who had been born in New York and moved to Massachusetts sometime in her youth to become the property of John Ashley of Sheffield. In spring 1781 she sued in the county civil court for her freedom. How the case was initiated is shrouded in mystery, in part because of Mum Bett's later association with the famous Sedgwick family, including the novelist Catherine Sedgewick. Some stories highlight how she defended her sister from being struck by her master before running away and refusing to continue in SLAVERY. Another story was that she was inspired by the words of the DECLARATION OF INDEPENDENCE or the Massachusetts Declaration of Rights. At least one historian has suggested that she may have been selected by some prominent local individuals, along with a slave man name Brom, as a convenient and willing participant in the court case. For whatever reason, *Brom and Bett v. Ashley* came to trial in the Berkshire County court in August 1781, with the two slaves represented by THEODORE SEDGWICK and TAPPING REEVE, two of the ablest legal talents in the state. The court ruled that Brom and Bett were not Ashley's slaves. That fall, Ashley dropped his appeal to the state supreme court in the wake of the judgments in the QUOK WALKER CASE.

Mum Bett continued to live in western Massachusetts for the rest of her life, raising a family, acting as a nurse and midwife, and serving the Sedgwick household. She was approximately 87 years old when she died in 1829. One of her descendants was the civil rights activist W. E. B. DuBois.

See also ABOLITION.

Further reading: Arthur Zilversmit, "Quok Walker, Mumbet, and the Abolition of Slavery in Massachusetts, *William and Mary Quarterly* 3rd ser., 25 (1968): 614–624.

Freemasonry

In an era marked by clubs and associations, the Freemasons became one of the most important fraternal organizations in the country. Although Freemasons claimed ancient origins, the movement expanded beyond its guild-like roots in 1717 when a group of four lodges, including craftsmen and noncraftsmen, met in London to create a grand lodge. The Masonic Order's original purpose remains unclear; it reflected both the ENLIGHTENMENT's concern for reason and older notions of the occult. A benevolent group and fraternal brotherhood, the Freemasons quickly became identified with 18th-century notions of gentility. While still clinging to a mythology connected to the craft of working with stone, the Masons became a way for gentlemen to gain social acceptance. As such, the organization spread to Europe and to the colonies: Philadelphia's St. John's Lodge, probably the first in the colonies, began meeting sometime around 1730. The colonial lodges that sprang up in community after community in the 1730s and 1740s were exclusive and a means for the local elite to become more English.

Even before the REVOLUTIONARY WAR (1775–83), however, the Freemasons began to change into something

else—a broader-based organization that included not only those who stood at the top of society, but also those who strove to join them. In North America that second group grew ever larger in the revolutionary and early national periods. A debate over ritual was the basis for this expansion, as Freemasons divided into the Ancients and the Moderns. The Ancient lodges, claiming superiority in the antiquity of their ritual, were newer and had a more open membership. The Ancients allowed ARTISANS in the cities and elites in the backcountry to join, and by sheer force of numbers they gained precedence in the fraternity.

The Revolutionary War created something of a crisis for the Freemasons, since its membership was divided between LOYALISTS and WHIGS. Officers in the CONTINENTAL ARMY, however, organized their own lodges. By the end of the war, Masonry became identified with the ideology of REPUBLICANISM. Citing the example of the officers' sacrifices during the war, Freemasons claimed to be willing to put aside their own interests for the good of the general public.

The early national period was the heyday of Masonry. Lodges appeared in every part of the country, and the membership created elaborate rituals. Now more than just a fraternal organization, the Masons engaged in benevolent activities and charities, and it became increasingly apparent to men on the make that one path to success lay through the Masonic lodge. As an organization that asserted the ideals of mutuality and brotherhood, it was only natural for Freemasons to seek business relationships with each other. Similarly, while the Masonic Order did not espouse any specific political cause, many elected officials were Masons and gained support because of their affiliation.

By the 1820s, the secret nature of the organization, and the apparent political and economic connections of its membership, led to growing popular suspicion. When William Morgan disappeared after threatening to reveal some of the Masonic secrets in 1826, an antimasonic movement erupted that almost destroyed the Masonic Order. The Masonic movement, however, survived the attacks in the 1820s and continues as an important fraternal and charitable organization today.

See also VOLUNTARY ASSOCIATIONS.

Further reading: Steven C. Bullock, *Revolutionary Brotherhood: Freemasonry and the Transformation of the American Social Order* (Chapel Hill: University of North Carolina Press, 1996).

"Free Trade and Sailors' Rights"

The political slogan "Free Trade and Sailors' Rights" became popular as the United States entered the WAR OF 1812 (1812–15). It represented in succinct form the two main maritime grievances that the United States had against GREAT BRITAIN. "Free Trade" referred to the call for unimpeded neutral TRADE by U.S. merchant vessels while Britain and FRANCE were at war. In the years leading up to the War of 1812, both countries had sought to limit this trading with measures such as the *ESSEX* DECISION and the ORDERS IN COUNCIL by the British and the BERLIN DECREE and MILAN DECREE issued by the French. "Sailor's Rights" referred to the right of sailors to contract for themselves as merchant SEAMEN, and that once they did so, they should be protected from being seized and forced to serve in the British navy through IMPRESSMENT.

Captain DAVID PORTER was the first person to use the phrase when he raised a banner with the words *Free Trade and Sailors' Rights* from the masthead of the *Essex* in autumn 1812. Soon it gained widespread use by both the political and maritime community. HENRY CLAY proclaimed "Free Trade and Sailors' Rights" in the halls of Congress, and it appeared in several publications in support of the war. Other warships and privateers also flew a pennant with the slogan from a mast, including Captain JAMES LAWRENCE aboard the ill-fated USS *Chesapeake* when he left Boston in May 1813 to fight the HMS *Shannon*. Common seamen took the slogan and made it their own. When sailor PRISONERS OF WAR at DARTMOOR PRISON heard of the TREATY OF GHENT (1814), they were hopeful that they would soon be released. Confident that both impressment and limitations on U.S. commerce had been ended by the treaty—which officially did not deal with either issue—they raised a U.S. flag and a pennant proclaiming "Free Trade and Sailors' Rights" over the British compound. For many years thereafter, the slogan would appear occasionally as a statement not only of sailors' rights but of the rights of the poor. Day laborers in New York City struck for higher wages in 1816 and used a banner with the slogan on it. Whalers etched the phrase on whalebone for decades. As late as 1840, banners appeared in election campaigns proclaiming "Free Trade and Sailors' Rights."

Further reading: Paul A. Gilje, *Liberty on the Waterfront: American Maritime Culture in the Age of Revolution* (Philadelphia: University of Pennsylvania Press, 2004).

French alliance

Without the support of FRANCE, the REVOLUTIONARY WAR (1775–83) would have been difficult, if not impossible, to win for the United States. The French provided aid in the form of munitions and equipment before a formal treaty of alliance was signed on February 6, 1778. After that agreement, the French supplied troops and a navy that played a crucial role in the conflict, especially in the YORKTOWN campaign that led to the surrender of LORD CORNWALLIS on October 19, 1781.

Almost as soon as hostilities broke out at the BATTLES OF LEXINGTON AND CONCORD (April 19, 1775), some revolutionary Americans began to look to France for help. The French, for their part, had long seen the British crisis in the colonies as an opportunity, hoping that it might lead to armed conflict and the chance to weaken its traditional enemy, GREAT BRITAIN. But there were several factors impeding the relationship. First, colonial Americans had fought for nearly a century against the French when France had controlled CANADA, and such animosities did not easily disappear. Second, the vast majority of colonial Americans were anti-Catholic and viewed the French as agents of the Pope. Finally, even after the first guns were fired, many British Americans hoped for reconciliation with King GEORGE III. The French also hesitated since they, too, remembered that their wars against Great Britain had included the colonies. They feared moving too quickly and forcing the revolutionaries and Britons back together. The lack of a clear goal in the rebellion in 1775 and early 1776 was also cause for concern. The objectives of the SECOND CONTINENTAL CONGRESS became clarified after the DECLARATION OF INDEPENDENCE was affirmed on July 4, 1776. But the war went badly that summer, with one defeat after another for GEORGE WASHINGTON and his CONTINENTAL ARMY.

Regardless of these problems, the French provided 1 million livres for munitions for the colonies as early as May 2, 1776. Negotiations for a more formal relationship began in earnest after the arrival in France of BENJAMIN FRANKLIN in December 1776. But not even his widespread fame as an American genius and philosopher could overcome all the difficulties. News of the victory at SARATOGA on October 17, 1777, dramatically altered the situation. France became fearful that the loss of an entire army would convince the British to reconcile with the revolutionaries. By December 17, 1777, the French foreign minister, the COMTE DE VERGENNES, had agreed to recognize the United States and sign a formal alliance.

Two treaties between the United States and France were signed on February 6, 1778. The first was a commercial treaty that opened TRADE between France and United States and gave France most-favored-nation trading status. The second, was the Treaty of Alliance. Although the alliance was contingent on a declaration of war between France and Great Britain, all parties recognized that the agreements made such a war inevitable. Once that war occurred, the French promised to fight until the independence of the United States was guaranteed. They also renounced all territorial claims in the contested areas of North America. Both sides agreed to make peace only with the consent of the other.

As important as the French alliance was to the U.S. independence movement, it took more than three years for it to pay off in any real military sense. Although France and its Caribbean possessions provided a safe haven for U.S. privateers and warships, from 1778 until summer 1781, the French remained more preoccupied with possibly invading Great Britain and the conflict in the WEST INDIES than with the revolutionaries in North America. The North American war was secondary to the larger conflict, and intermittent French efforts to help the U.S. cause directly came to naught and often caused ill will. In summer 1778 French naval and land forces under the command of Admiral Estaing (see ESTAING, CHARLES-HENRI-THÉODAT, COMTE D') made several mistakes by not trapping a British fleet in the Chesapeake, by not attacking a weaker British fleet in New York harbor, and by failing to coordinate with revolutionary troops in the BATTLE OF RHODE ISLAND (August 29, 1778). This last error left hard feelings on both sides. After a hurricane dispersed the French and British navies off Newport, the French sailed to Boston to regroup. General JOHN SULLIVAN was so disgusted with the Rhode Island campaign that he lambasted the French in print, and thousands of MILITIA, equally disenchanted with the French, simply went home. In Boston, French sailors fought in the streets with civilians, creating further ill will. It took a great deal of work by French and revolutionary officials to patch up these difficulties. After capturing Grenada and St. Vincent in the West Indies, Estaing returned to North America off the coast of Georgia in September 1779. A combined Franco-American SIEGE OF SAVANNAH, however, failed. Following some delays, the French insisted on a costly and unsuccessful direct assault—it was hurricane season and the ships were at risk—rather than a drawn-out siege. Not until July 1780 did the French land a major expeditionary force in the United States for any length of time, and then that army remained at Newport, Rhode Island—which the British had evacuated in autumn 1779—for the better part of a year. Finally, in August 1781, Admiral Grasse (see GRASSE, FRANÇOIS-JOSEPH-PAUL, COMTE DE) and a sizable fleet left the West Indies and appeared off the Chesapeake to coordinate operations with the land forces. By that time the French army under General Rochambeau (see ROCHAMBEAU, JEAN-BAPTISTE-DONATIEN DE VIMEUR, COMTE DE) had joined GEORGE WASHINGTON outside New York. The combined Continental and French armies marched to Virginia, trapping the British at Yorktown in the climactic campaign of the war. Despite repeated missed chances, without the French navy and army, there would have been no British surrender at Yorktown, and independence might never have been achieved.

Not only did the Treaty of Alliance have a tremendous impact on the course of the Revolutionary War, it also affected the politics of the new nation. During the FRENCH REVOLUTION (1789–99), many on both sides of the ATLANTIC OCEAN believed that the United States should join the French in their struggles against the powers of reaction. When Great Britain went to war against France in 1793, Citizen EDMOND-CHARLES GENÊT came to the United States to persuade the Washington administration to help the French. His failure, and the granting of most-favored-nation trading status to Great Britain in JAY'S TREATY (1794), led to a crisis with France and the QUASI-WAR (1798–1800). Ultimately, that conflict was resolved, without formally declaring war, through the CONVENTION OF 1800. Although the convention did not settle any of the outstanding issues that had led to the fighting, it officially marked the end of the alliance between France and the United States.

See also FOREIGN AFFAIRS.

Further reading: Samuel Flagg Bemis, *The Diplomacy of the American Revolution* (Bloomington: Indiana University Press, 1957); Ronald Hoffman and Peter J. Albert, eds., *Diplomacy and the Revolution: The Franco-American Alliance of 1778* (Charlottesville: University Press of Virginia, 1981).

French and Indian War (1754–1763)

Often portrayed as the culmination of the great wars for empire between the British and French for control of North America, the French and Indian War, called the Seven Years' War in Europe, was a worldwide conflict that transformed the map of North America but did not end the struggles between GREAT BRITAIN and FRANCE. In many ways the REVOLUTIONARY WAR (1775–83) after France became an ally of the United States, and the Anglo-French Wars of the FRENCH REVOLUTION (1789–99) were a continuation of the imperial rivalry between the two nations that had been going on for over a century.

The French and Indian War began unofficially in 1754 with a British-Virginian expedition to seek control of the forks of the Ohio River (modern Pittsburgh). This effort not only failed but ended in a military disaster for a young and inexperienced GEORGE WASHINGTON, who achieved a minor victory in what amounted to a massacre at the BATTLE OF JUMONVILLE GLEN (May 28, 1754) but later had to surrender at FORT NECESSITY (July 4, 1754). Although the British government sought to avoid an all-out war, they sent General EDWARD BRADDOCK with two regiments of professional soldiers to march to the forks of the Ohio and assert British control of the region. Unrealistically, Braddock was ordered to seize French forts that the British viewed were in contested territory: Fort Duquesne (at the Ohio forks), FORT NIAGARA, St. Frédéric (CROWN POINT), and two forts on the NOVA SCOTIA peninsula.

Not only were these outposts hundred of miles apart, they were also separated by vast expanses of forest and land occupied by NATIVE AMERICANS. Even the first objective was beyond Braddock, who was surprised in western Pennsylvania by a combined force of French and Indians in a battle that has come to be known as Braddock's Defeat (July 9, 1755).

In the meantime, the French ordered their own regular reinforcements to CANADA under a new governor, the MARQUIS DE VAUDREUIL. The British sent Admiral Edward Boscawen to intercept the French fleet if he could; he missed most of the French ships but captured two vessels packed with 330 soldiers on June 8, 1755. When the French heard of this action, their ambassador left England, and open warfare began.

Before Braddock's defeat, he had transferred responsibility for his other objectives to British North Americans. Governor WILLIAM SHIRLEY of Massachusetts agreed to take an army of provincial troops to seize Fort Niagara, while WILLIAM JOHNSON (ca. 1715–1774), noted for his ties to the IROQUOIS, would lead another provincial army against Fort St. Frédéric, and a third contingent of New England provincials were to move against the Nova Scotia outposts. These plans appeared grand on paper but were impossible to fulfill in reality. Only the New England expedition against the Nova Scotia forts was successful as Johnson and Shirley competed for provincial soldiers and Native American auxillaries. Shirley's advance was delayed, and all he managed to do was set up an advance base at OSWEGO on the southeastern shore of Lake Ontario. Johnson's army crawled toward Lake George on its way to Lake Champlain, established Fort Edward on the Hudson River, and constructed a base at the foot of Lake George. On September 8, 1755, a 1,500-man French raiding party under the BARON DIESKAU struck at Johnson's supply lines along the road between Fort Edward and Lake George. In the BATTLE OF LAKE GEORGE (September 8, 1755), both sides incurred over 300 casualties, and despite the French's initial success, they were driven back to Fort St. Frédéric, and Dieskau was captured. Both sides avoided another battle in the area as the British worked feverishly on building Fort William Henry on Lake George, and the French erected a new bastion called Fort Carillon (later FORT TICONDEROGA) on Lake Champlain.

The next year brought even more problems for the British Americans. In February the French and Indians struck at FORT BULL, an outpost on the portage between the Mohawk River Valley and Lake Ontario, making supply of Oswego more difficult. With the French secure at Fort Duquesne, Native Americans raided almost at will along the FRONTIER from Virginia through New England, sending waves of panic among the British-American colonists. On August 13, 1756, the French attacked Oswego itself,

and in less than a day the entire garrison of more than 1,000 men and hundreds of civilians surrendered. Fear that the French might follow this victory by an attack down the Mohawk River convinced General Daniel Webb to destroy the newly rebuilt Bull's Fort and place obstructions in the water passage to the Mohawk. It also convinced the Earl of Loudoun (see LOUDOUN, JOHN CAMPBELL, FOURTH EARL OF), the newly arrived commander of British forces in North America, to order provincial troops at Lake George to cancel any advance on Lake Champlain.

Both the French and the British struggled with conflicting lines of authority and with pursuing a consistent strategy. On the French side there was a conflict between Vaudreuil and the MARQUIS DE MONTCALM, commander of the regular army in Canada. Vaudreuil believed that the best defense was a good offense and wanted to use Native Americans and Canadian troops to raid frontier settlements and destroy advanced outposts like Oswego. He believed that if the British colonials were preoccupied with defending their homes, they would be unwilling and unable to launch an invasion to the north. Moreover, if the British forward bases were taken out of action, any invasion would be almost impossible. Montcalm, on the other hand, detested the Indians and had no respect for the Canadians. He wanted to withdraw to a defensive perimeter based on the St. Lawrence River and rely on the regular army in a European-style war.

Problems also existed on the British side. The strategy of 1755, which had been dictated in Great Britain and embraced in the colonies, had been unrealistic and ended in the disaster of Braddock's defeat. For the time being, therefore, there was a vacuum in British planning. In 1756 provincial Americans attempted to provide some direction by gathering 7,000 colonial troops at the foot of Lake George hoping to advance north. But the provincial officers soon became embroiled in arguments concerning their relative rank in relation to the regular army. They also claimed that their men would probably not obey orders from British officers. These problems festered during the summer of 1756 and were not fully settled by the time the expedition to Lake Champlain was called off after the loss of Oswego. Loudoun's arrival in North America, with almost vice-regal power over the colonies, was supposed to clarify the situation, but although he was an able administrator, his tendency to dictate to the colonists—at one point he even ordered an embargo of all nonmilitary shipping—did not gain much support. It would take a dramatic shift in British policy to change the course of the war.

Given the problems confronted by both sides, the war followed much the same course in 1757 as it had in 1756. The British decided to concentrate on a massive expedition to capture the fortress of LOUISBOURG. But Loudoun's careful plans came to naught while his army waited the entire month of July in Halifax as the royal navy sought to measure the strength of Louisbourg's defense. In early August they found a powerful French fleet at anchor in Louisbourg, and with the campaign season getting shorter, Loudoun called off the attack.

In the meantime, the British-American effort on Lake George ended in disaster. Following Vaudreuil's strategy of striking at forward bases, Montcalm concentrated 8,000 men, including 1,800 Native Americans from scores of tribes, against Fort William Henry. Pursuing standard European siege tactics, Montcalm captured the fort in less than a week, and again following European rules, he granted the garrison the "honors of war," allowing it to march to Fort Edward under arms. Outraged by this leniency, his Indian allies attacked the defeated column, killing, maiming, looting, and seizing captives—all legitimate objects of war in Native American eyes. Perhaps as many as 180 were murdered, and maybe another 500 were captured out of more than 2,000. The FORT WILLIAM HENRY "MASSACRE" (August 10, 1757) represented a low point in the war for the British, but it also provided a rallying cry for the rest of the conflict. Although a great victory for the French, the battle had some negative impact on their war effort: Montcalm became even more convinced that Native Americans were a liability in war, and Vaudreuil was angry that Montcalm did not follow his orders to also capture Fort Edward; he was also irate that Montcalm wanted him to gain the release of the Indian captives from Fort William Henry. The Indians decided that they had been betrayed by Montcalm in the surrender and would never again rally in large numbers for Canada's defense.

By the next campaigning season, the British began to turn things around. WILLIAM PITT, who was the king's chief minister, determined that Great Britain and its colonies needed to put all of their resources together to win the war, which had spread to Europe and beyond. In particular, Pitt decided that he would strive to hold the line in Europe, where the French were stronger, and seek to conquer New France, where the French were weaker. To do so, he wanted the colonies to contribute more than they ever had to the manpower needed in the war. Thus, instead of dictating to the colonies, as Loudoun and even Braddock had done, Pitt now treated the colonists more as allies. To get colonial assemblies to open up their coffers, he offered subsidies to help pay for the war. He also changed the rules for officer rank: Instead of every regular officer outranking even the highest provincial officer, colonial majors, colonels, and generals would have the same status as their regular counterparts, with the exception of being junior to ranks of equivalent grade.

The French, on the other hand, continued to have problems with their divided leadership, which was exacerbated by poor harvests, corruption in the administration of supplies, and inflation. If there was going to be a war of attrition, New France—which had a population of only about 60,000—was outmatched by British North America, with over 2 million colonists in some of the richest and most prosperous country in the world. Moreover, Great Britain was committed to supporting the war in North America and had a superior navy to bring men and supplies across the ATLANTIC OCEAN, while French Canada remained isolated from a France more focused on Europe and the WEST INDIES.

The British Americans put together three huge expeditions as a result of these changes. Fourteen thousand men and a huge flotilla under General JEFFREY AMHERST, who would replace Loudoun, besieged Louisbourg, capturing what many called the "Gibraltar of the North" on July 26, 1758. The army at Lake George under General JAMES ABERCROMBY had 16,000 men, 10,000 of whom were provincials. Unfortunately for the British Americans, on July 8, 1757, Abercromby launched an ill-advised direct assault on Fort Carillon without bringing up his artillery. Montcalm had only 3,500 men, but, fighting from entrenched positions, they inflicted about 2,000 casualties on Abercromby before the British Americans retreated, ending their thrust at Lake Champlain. As a result of this victory, Montcalm was promoted to lieutenant general and came to outrank Vaudreuil. Also as a result of this battle, Abercromby, desperate for some sort of success, agreed to Lieutenant Colonel John Bradstreet's proposal to raid FORT FRONTENAC, a crucial supply depot near the entrance to the St. Lawrence on Lake Ontario. Bradstreet's success in late August dramatically interrupted the supply of the French forts in the Great Lakes interior and cut off much of the French TRADE with Native Americans, which was crucial for Franco-Indian relations. Meanwhile, a third British-American army of 7,000 men under General JOHN FORBES made its way through the woods of Pennsylvania, methodically building a road and constructing forts as supply depots. Despite having an advance party of 800 men soundly beaten by French and Indians striking from Fort Duquesne on September 11, 1757, Forbes kept pressing on. Bradstreet's raid at Fort Frontenac encouraged him, and Forbes also entered into negotiations with many of the Ohio River Indians who had previously been allied with the French and convinced them to withdraw from the war. The French continued to raid his work parties, but on November 23, 1757, a reduced French garrison abandoned and blew up Fort Duquesne. Forbes occupied the site the next day and began to build FORT PITT.

By the beginning of 1759, despite the defeat at Fort Carillon, Pitt's policy was working, and the British Americans were using their superior numbers and matériel to overwhelm the French in Canada. The British Americans planned a three-pronged attack. First, under the command of General John Prideux, a British-American and Iroquois army of 3,200 marched to Oswego and then sailed on to Fort Niagara in July 1759. Arriving on July 6, Prideux began the usual siege preparations, eventually bringing his guns to within 80 yards of Fort Niagara's defenses. Prideux was killed by one of his own cannon and Sir William Johnson took over command. Before the French surrendered, Johnson had to beat off a relief column under François-Marie Le Marchand de Ligneris, inflicting heavy casualties on the French.

Meanwhile, General JAMES WOLFE moved up the St. Lawrence with 8,500 men escorted by the Royal Navy. For most of the summer Montcalm, who had concentrated between 15,000 and 16,000 men to oppose the British, frustrated him. In a desperate move, Wolfe landed 4,500 men under a cliff on a cove called L'Anse au Foulon and climbed to the Plains of Abraham, where Montcalm foolishly attacked him with an equal number of French troops. Both Wolfe and Moncalm died as a result of the fighting, but the British won the BATTLE OF QUEBEC (September 13, 1759), opening the way to MONTREAL.

A third army of 10,000 provincial and British soldiers moved deliberately toward Lake Champlain under Amherst only to find token resistance at Fort Carillon and Fort St. Frédéric, both of which the French blew up before retreating by August 1. Rather than advancing further, and unsure of the progress and fate of Wolfe's army, Amherst repaired and rebuilt the forts, now named Ticonderoga (Carillon) and Crown Point (St. Frédéric), and waited for the next campaign season.

In 1760 some hope still existed for the French in Canada if they could recapture Quebec; victory would then be possible if their navy could bring some help from France. But the French fleet had been beaten at the BATTLE OF QUIBERON BAY (November 20, 1759), ensuring that there would be no French invasion of Great Britain and giving the British navy command of the Atlantic. Without naval support, the marquis de Lévis (see LÉVIS, FRANÇOIS-GASTON, CHEVALIER DE) almost succeeded, defeating General John Murray in the SECOND BATTLE OF QUEBEC (April 28, 1760) and then laying siege to the city. However, the British navy arrived on May 12, forcing a French withdrawal. For the rest of that spring, all Lévis could do was try to delay the advance that now closed in on him from three directions.

By early September the British had 17,000 men at Montreal, and on September 7, 1760, Vaudreuil asked for terms. Amherst was willing to be lenient with the people of Canada, but, following a policy he began after the Fort William Henry "Massacre," he refused to grant the army the honors of war. Lévis wanted to reject those terms, or at least lead the army to one last battle to defend national honor, but Vaudreuil decided that that approach would end

in reprisals against the Canadians and needless deaths. He surrendered New France to the British without further negotiation.

The French and Indian War was over in North America, but the larger contest continued elsewhere as SPAIN entered the conflict. The British went on to conquer most of the French West Indies, Havana, and Manila, and they made gains in AFRICA and INDIA. The war on the continent in Europe remained something of a stalemate. The TREATY OF PARIS (1763) brought favorable terms to Great Britain, which included Canada and FLORIDA as new possessions. However, victory also convinced the British government that it needed a take a more rational approach to its empire. That approach brought on the RESISTANCE MOVEMENT (1763–75) of the North American colonists and helped to precipitate the AMERICAN REVOLUTION.

Further reading: Fred Anderson, *Crucible of War: The Seven Years' War and the Fate of Empire in British North America, 1754–1766* (New York: Knopf, 2000); W. J. Eccles, *The French in North America, 1500–1783*, rev. ed. (East Lansing: Michigan State University Press, 1998); Francis Jennings, *Empire of Fortune: Crowns, Colonies and Tribes in the Seven Years War in America* (New York: Norton, 1988).

French Revolution (1789–1799)

The French Revolution stands as one of the most significant events of world history, had a major impact on the United States. Driven to the verge of bankruptcy, in part by aiding the United States during the REVOLUTIONARY WAR (1775–83), King Louis XVI called the Estates General (a representative assembly) to meet in spring 1789. This group was unsatisfied with simply discussing the monarchy's financial needs and asked for a host of reforms, including reorganizing itself as a national assembly, demanding control over taxation, and writing a constitution. Efforts by FRANCE's king to oppose these measures led to a popular revolt and, on July 14, 1789, on the storming of the Bastille, a Parisian prison that had come to symbolize the king's absolute power. The National Assembly abolished feudal privileges on August 4 and issued the DECLARATION OF THE RIGHTS OF MAN on August 26. This document asserted that LIBERTY, property, and security, as well as the freedom of the press, opinion, and RELIGION, were "natural rights." The document also proclaimed that sovereignty lay with the nation and not with the king.

The French Revolution began in the spirit of the ENLIGHTENMENT and was in part inspired by the example of the AMERICAN REVOLUTION. Because so many of the ideas pushed by the French Revolution seem to coincide with the REPUBLICANISM shared by most Americans, few people in the United States opposed it at first. The fact that the MARQUIS DE LAFAYETTE emerged as one of the leaders of the Revolution's early period brought more support. But even from its earliest phases, the violence of the rioting that accompanied the revolt raised some concerns. Over the next few years, as the French Revolution became more violent and as the forces of reaction in Europe began to send armies against the revolutionaries, opposition to the French increased. By 1793 radicals had assumed power in France, executing the king on January 21, 1793, and establishing the Reign of Terror (September 1793–July 1794), which killed approximately 40,000 royalists and opponents to the Jacobin regime. Largely as a result of the Revolution's radical turn France declared war on GREAT BRITAIN on February 1, 1793. This war created a diplomatic crisis for the United States.

France called upon the United States to come to the aid of its sister republic and reminded Americans of the FRENCH ALLIANCE that had been so instrumental in winning the Revolutionary War. The government sent Citizen EDMOND-CHARLES GENÊT as ambassador to the United States in 1793. Genêt sought to recruit men for French war vessels and wanted President GEORGE WASHINGTON to commit to supporting the French against Britain. If Genêt's entreaties fell on deaf ears in the Washington administration, many elsewhere in the United States seemed to support him. The French Revolution thus contributed to the emergence of two POLITICAL PARTIES in the United States: The FEDERALIST PARTY supported ALEXANDER HAMILTON's program for a stronger central government and opposed the French Revolution; and the DEMOCRATIC-REPUBLICAN PARTY supported THOMAS JEFFERSON and had strong sympathy for the French.

The radical Jacobins did not remain in power in France for long: In July 1794, conservative reactionaries overthrew Maximilien Robespierre. As the French moved away from the extremist policies of their Revolution, power fell into the hands of a group of leaders known as the Directory, who, from 1795 to 1799, restored order and prosperity to France while conducting wars against Great Britain and several European powers. Eventually, NAPOLEON BONAPARTE emerged as the first consul (1799) and then emperor of the French (1804). Napoleon continued to rule France, conquering much of Europe, until he was forced into exile in 1814. He had a brief return to power in spring 1815 but was defeated by a coalition army at Waterloo on June 18, 1815.

Although the excitement over the republican aspects of the French Revolution declined in the United States as the Thermidorian reaction (conservatives in France overthrowing the Reign of Terror) took over, and then as Napoleon seized control, the ongoing power struggle in Europe continued to exert influence on the United States. Americans remained divided in their sympathies. Perhaps more important was the series of diplomatic crises confronting the United States because of the war between Britain and France. As long as the Americans could remain neutral, great profits could be made by shipping goods to both belligerents. The problem was maintaining neutrality in the face of TRADE restrictions and British IMPRESSMENT of U.S. sailors. Indeed, the United States almost went to war with Great Britain in 1794 because of the seizure of merchant ships, until JAY'S TREATY (1794) settled some outstanding issues. But that treaty, which favored the British over the French, helped to bring on the QUASI-WAR (1798–1800) with France. After 1807, neutral trade became more difficult to sustain as both Britain and France sought to limit access to each other's ports. Ultimately, this problem helped to bring on the WAR OF 1812 (1812–15). Although the United States fought this war with Great Britain while the latter was still engaged in a death struggle with France, the United States never came to a formal alliance with Napoleon. By the close of 1814, and with Napoleon's exile, Britain was willing to agree to the TREATY OF GHENT (1814) to end the war with the United States since the issues of neutral trade and impressment were no longer significant in an era of peace.

The legacy of the French Revolution transcended war and diplomacy in the United States and throughout the world. During the 1790s a set of ideas, first brought into focus in the American Revolution, set the stage for the world's transformation. Revolutionary Americans had fought for liberty; the French added equality and fraternity to the vocabulary of revolution.

See also FOREIGN AFFAIRS.

Further reading: E. J. Hobsbawm, *The Age of Revolution, 1789–1848* (New York: New American Library, 1962); George Lefebvre, *The French Revolution* (London: Routlege, 1964); R. R. Palmer, *The Age of Democratic Revolution*, 2 vols. (Princeton, N.J.: Princeton University Press, 1964).

Frenchtown, Battle of (Battle of the Raisin River) (January 22, 1813)

Hoping to counter the disasters of 1812 and to recapture DETROIT, General WILLIAM HENRY HARRISON launched a winter campaign and ordered General JAMES WINCHESTER to advance to the rapids on the Maumee River in northern Ohio. At the request of local residents, Winchester decided to drive a British garrison out of Frenchtown (modern-day Monroe, Michigan). Although he was able to capture Frenchtown easily on January 18, this action brought him too far from Harrison's main body of troops and too close to Detroit. Occupying Frenchtown also alerted Colonel HENRY PROCTER that Winchester was in the vicinity. Procter gathered about 1,300 NATIVE AMERICANS, Canadian MILITIA and British regulars and attacked Winchester, who had 934 men. Winchester had spread his troops out along the Raisin River and did not have sufficient scouts, so Procter's approach came as a complete surprise. Moreover, Winchester had his headquarters at a house distant from his main camp, and Indians captured him on his way to the battlefield. During the fighting the U.S. right collapsed, and the center began to retreat; however, the left held its own. Fearing a rout and possible massacre, Winchester decided to surrender his entire force. Unfortunately, in the aftermath of the fighting, Indians killed 30–60 prisoners along the Raisin River. The British lost 24 killed and 154 wounded, Winchester's loses were much higher, with 397 killed and 561 wounded. Harrison had to cancel his winter campaign, but when his army did advance later that year, their rallying cry became "Remember the Raisin." The Battle of Frenchtown is sometimes called the Battle of the Raisin River.

Freneau, Philip (1752–1832) *poet, journalist*

One of the most significant poets in U.S. history, Philip Freneau was born into a prosperous family in New York. He was educated by tutors as a young man and at age 15 entered the sophomore class at the College of New Jersey (now Princeton University), where he became good friends with JAMES MADISON. With the collaboration of another of his classmates, HUGH HENRY BRACKENRIDGE, Freneau wrote his first published poem in college. Brackenridge read "The Rising Glory of America" during their 1771 graduation ceremonies, and the poem was issued as a pamphlet the next year in Philadelphia.

Freneau was tied to family duties after graduating from college, which kept him from immediate further publication. Unable to make a living as a clergyman, he taught school for a short while and continued to write poetry on his own time. The coming of the REVOLUTIONARY WAR (1775–83) inspired Freneau to publish "American Liberty" in July 1775. Within a few months he published more than eight pamphlet satires aimed at GREAT BRITAIN. Though his poetry did not earn him much MONEY, his pamphlets were widely reprinted and were most popular among moderate WHIGS.

Freneau soon acquired a job as a secretary for a planter who lived on the island of Santa Cruz in the WEST INDIES. He lived there for three years and wrote some of his most significant poems, including "Santa Cruz," "The Jamaica Funeral," and "The House of Night." He returned home in 1778 after being captured and released by the British. In New Jersey, he joined the MILITIA and continued to publish his poetry.

Freneau loved the sea and took many voyages during his life. When he set out in spring 1780 to return to the West Indies, he was captured by a British man-of-war and sent to the prison ship *Scorpion* in New York Harbor. There he suffered brutal treatment and starvation as a prisoner and was soon sent to the hospital ship *Hunter* before he was able to return home to New Jersey. Based on this experience, he wrote a poem entitled "The British Prison Ship." After his imprisonment, Freneau worked in the Philadelphia post office for three years and continued to write poetry, most of which was published in Francis Bailey's *Freeman's Journal.* His extensive publications earned him the title "Poet of the Revolution."

For the next several years, Freneau took to the sea again as an officer on merchant ships. He settled down in 1789 when he married Eleanor Forman and immediately became involved in newspaper work as editor of the New York *Daily Advertiser.* Despite his later denials, it is likely that in 1791 THOMAS JEFFERSON and Madison asked Freneau to move to Philadelphia to establish a partisan newspaper to counter the pro-Washington administration organ of JOHN FENNO, the *Gazette of the United States.* Jefferson, then secretary of state, offered Freneau a position as a translator in the State Department for $250, provided him with government printing contracts, assured him that he would not personally lose money, and solicited subscribers from his followers. For the first few months after starting the *National Gazette* in October 1791, Freneau was relatively measured in his tone, but starting in March 1792, he began a barrage of attacks on ALEXANDER HAMILTON, claiming that the treasury secretary's financial schemes had "given rise to scenes of speculation calculated to aggrandize the few and the wealthy." He also attacked Hamilton as wanting to establish an aristocracy in the United States. Hamilton struck back in July in Fenno's paper, claiming that Freneau held a sinecure in the State Department and accusing him of partisanship. This exchange initiated a bitter debate filled with invective over Hamilton's financial program that continued up to the ELECTION OF 1792. After the election, the *National Gazette* struggled, especially with Jefferson's retirement and the loss of Freneau's state department job.

By autumn 1793, as YELLOW FEVER raged, Freneau had a difficult time obtaining subscriptions, and he abandoned the newspaper in October. He then retired to his farm in New Jersey, though he tried his hand in a few other newspapers, including the New York *Time Piece and Literary Companion* in 1797 and 1798. Ultimately, Freneau left JOURNALISM entirely, spending the rest of his life alternating between the sea and his farm in New Jersey. He died on December 18, 1832 when he lost his way home during a raging blizzard.

Philip Freneau left an important mark on the development of POLITICAL PARTIES in the 1790s, but "that rascal

Freneau," as Washington called him, is best remembered for his literary legacy. In "The British Prison-Ship" he immortalized the experience of SEAMEN on such ships:

"The various horrors of these hulks to tell,
These Prison Ships where pain and penance dwell,
Where death in tenfold vengeance holds his reign,
And injur'd ghosts, yet unaveng'd, complain.

Freneau also praised Washington when he stepped down as commander in chief at the end of the Revolutionary War:

"O WASHINGTON!—thrice glorious name,
What due rewards can man decree;
Empires are far below thy aim,
And sceptres have no charms for thee;
Virtue alone has your regard,
And she must be your great reward.

Further reading: Mary Weatherspoon Bowden, *Philip Freneau* (Boston: Twayne, 1976); Harry Hayden Clark, *Poems of Freneau* (New York: Hafner, 1960). Lewis G. Leary, *That Rascal Freneau: A Study in Literary Failure* (New York: Octagon Books, 1964); Jeffrey L. Pasley, *"The Tyranny of Printers": Newspaper Politics in the Early Republic* (Charlottesville: University Press of Virginia, 2001).

Fries's Rebellion (1798–1799)

In 1798 President JOHN ADAMS and a Congress dominated by the FEDERALIST PARTY passed the DIRECT TAX ACT to support a military expansion triggered by the QUASI-WAR (1798–1800) with FRANCE. The German-American protest of the tax in eastern Pennsylvania has come to be known as Fries's Rebellion.

The so-called "rebellion" began in July 1798 in the Pennsylvania counties of Northhampton, Montgomery, Berks, and Bucks in the spirit of the AMERICAN REVOLUTION. German Americans, many of whom had fought in the REVOLUTIONARY WAR (1775–83), erected liberty poles (see LIBERTY TREE/POLE), organized associations by which members proclaimed their opposition to the law, and intimidated tax assessors. Primarily small-property owners living all too close to the margin of POVERTY, the protestors believed the direct tax was an assault on their LIBERTY and the first of several taxes aimed at driving them into a tenancy that would be equivalent to the near SLAVERY they or their fathers and grandfathers had experienced in Germany. To the protesters, the direct tax was reminiscent of the STAMP ACT (1765), which had begun the RESISTANCE MOVEMENT (1764–75) that ultimately led to the Revolu-

tion. Aggravating the situation was the fact that many of the tax assessors were relatively affluent QUAKERS and MORAVIANS who had been at best neutral pacifists during the Revolutionary War and were seen by the protestors as "Tories." Additionally, many southeastern Pennsylvanians believed it was no coincidence that the federal government had passed the ALIEN AND SEDITION ACTS (1798) to stifle political opposition.

Remarkably, the protest had few acts of collective violence, and when it was over, DEMOCRATIC-REPUBLICAN PARTY newspapers strove to minimize its seriousness by reporting that the entire rebellion had consisted of a few women dumping hot water on the heads of assessors as they measured homes and counted windows. There is no evidence to substantiate these reports, which have often been repeated. In any events, individuals and families did threaten assessors and seize their records, and these actions led to the federal district court ordering 23 men arrested and jailed in the Sun Tavern at Bethlehem, Pennsylvania. On March 12, 1799, a Bucks county auctioneer and former MILITIA captain named John Fries rode into Bethlehem with several hundred men and, without using any real violence, freed the prisoners. Since Fries led the rescue and was active in several protest meetings, the rebellion became associated with his name.

The federal government reacted quickly to the jailbreak. Amid the war fever of the winter of 1798–99, the Federalist Party viewed any protest as treasonous and French-inspired. President Adams gave the insurgents six days to stand down and sent troops into the region to restore order. But most of the protestors had gone home after the rescue. The military spent three weeks rounding up about 120 "rebels," capturing Fries after he sought to escape into a swamp. Many in the Federalist Party wanted to make an example of Fries and hoped to see him executed for treason. After one mistrial, the case came before Judge SAMUEL CHASE. Fries's LAWYERS argued that while the actions committed by the defendant could be construed as sedition or riot, they were certainly not treason and worthy of the death penalty. Chase would have none of it and simply defined Fries's actions as treasonous, leaving the jury no choice but to convict. Recognizing that they could do no good, the lawyers dropped the case and let Fries defend himself with the idea that he would gain greater public sympathy and a chance for a reprieve on his own. Fries was found guilty and sentenced to hang. President Adams, who had followed the trials closely, became uneasy over the courts' decisions and therefore pardoned Fries and two others of treason, as well as several others of lesser crimes. Adams's action alienated many in the Federalist Party, contributing to his break with ALEXANDER HAMILTON and hurting him in the ELECTION OF 1800.

See also LAND RIOTS; RIOTS.

Further reading: Paul Douglass Newman, *Fries's Rebellion: The Enduring Struggle for the American Revolution* (Philadelphia: University of Pennsylvania Press, 2004).

frontier

Americans have customarily defined the frontier as the limit of European-American agricultural settlement. This definition ignores the fact that many NATIVE AMERICANS farmed and lived in towns. More recently, historians have viewed frontiers less as a boundary and more as a zone of communication between cultures—between European Americans and Native Americans as well as between Anglo-Americans and colonists from other European powers. In particular, scholars have emphasized the role of the individuals who lived along and traveled through the frontier as cultural intermediaries. Whatever definition one uses, the period between 1754 and 1815 witnessed the frontier's pushing back from east of the Appalachians to just beyond the Mississippi River.

Traditional ideas of the frontier were in large part molded by the ENLIGHTENMENT thought of the revolutionary generation, whose republican beliefs held that all societies could be placed on a spectrum from primitive to advanced. A primitive society was one that depended on hunting and gathering; many European Americans falsely assumed that Native Americans were at this level of development. Conservatives also believed that even the European Americans who moved to the frontier adopted the Indian mode of living and became hunters and gatherers as well. As a society moved toward civilization, it became more dependent on AGRICULTURE, and with the addition of new layers of complexity, commerce became more important, CITIES AND URBAN LIFE developed, and industrial production expanded. The revolutionary generation, however, believed that there were cycles in history: The more advanced stages of civilization were symptoms of decay, leading to the society's destruction and the beginning of the cycle all over again. From this perspective, the frontier's expansion was crucial since new areas of settlement promised to sustain the United States as an agricultural nation and put off the end of European-American society.

Concerns with the frontier played a role in the origins of the AMERICAN REVOLUTION. After victory in the FRENCH AND INDIAN WAR (1754–63), colonial Americans hoped that new lands west of the Appalachians would be open to settlement. However, in an effort to protect its Native American subjects, and to reduce military expenditures, the British government issued the PROCLAMATION OF 1763, prohibiting settlement west of the Appalachians. The QUEBEC ACT of 1774 granted this territory to CANADA and also sought to limit colonial American settlement in the West, a barrier to frontier expansion that became an impor-

tant colonial grievance. At the end of the REVOLUTIONARY WAR (1775–83), the TREATY OF PARIS (1783) provided a generous boundary for the United States, stretching to the Mississippi River. During the 1770s, DANIEL BOONE and a few other European Americans had already begun to cross the mountains. Following the war, thousands of European Americans streamed across the Appalachians to settle the new frontier. U.S. government efforts to guide and limit the settlements to below the Ohio River proved fruitless, leading to a series of wars with Native Americans that culminated in the BATTLE OF TIPPECANOE (November 7, 1811) and ANDREW JACKSON's campaign against the CREEK Indians in the WAR OF 1812 (1812–15).

Popular images of the frontier reflect only some of the reality. Men did wear coonskin caps, and the first dwellings erected were often lean-tos or crude log cabins. But as soon as people on the frontier could afford to, they bought CLOTHING in stores and improved their houses. Perhaps equally important in the mythology was the idea that every frontiersman wanted his own piece of land to farm and to raise a family in some agrarian paradise. Few on the frontier had such limited ambitions. Settlers south of the Ohio often hoped someday to own a plantation with slaves; settlers farther north may have simply wanted to produce a cash crop for the market. Speculation was rampant on the frontier. Those with the grandest dreams sought to acquire thousands of acres. More humble men merely wanted to improve the land to sell it for a higher price. Within such an aggressively capitalistic atmosphere, more fortunes were lost than won. The frontier, in other words, was less rough and tumble and more boom and bust.

Further reading: Stephen Aron, *How the West Was Lost: The Transformation of Kentucky from Daniel Boone to Henry Clay* (Baltimore: Johns Hopkins University Press, 1996); Andrew R. L. Cayton and Fredrika J. Teute, eds., *Contact Points: American Frontiers from the Mohawk Valley to the Mississippi, 1750–1830* (Chapel Hill: University of North Carolina Press, 1998); Drew R. McCoy, *The Elusive Republic: Political Economy in Jeffersonian America* (Chapel Hill: University of North Carolina Press, 1980); James H. Merrell, *Into the American Woods: Negotiators on the Pennsylvania Frontier* (New York: Norton, 1999); Alan Taylor, *William Cooper's Town: Power and Persuasion on the Frontier of the Early American Republic* (New York: Knopf, 1995).

Fugitive Slave Law (1793)

When the U.S. CONSTITUTION was written, it included a vaguely worded provision for the return of escaped slaves from one state to another. Article IV, Section 2 states: "No person held to service or labour in one state, under the laws thereof, escaping into another, shall, in consequence of any law or regulation therein, be discharged from such service or labour, but shall be delivered up on claim of the party to whom such service or labour may be due." This clause—which carefully avoided the word *slave*—became a part of the Constitution without much debate in 1787, but it provided little more than a rhetorical commitment to returning escaped slaves without describing the mechanisms for how the process would work. Congress clarified the procedures for returning fugitive slaves in a 1793 law that strengthened the national government and furthered its commitment to the protection of the institution of SLAVERY.

Oddly, the controversy that triggered the law began as an effort to protect a fugitive slave. John Davis was a slave who had lived in what became the western part of the state of Pennsylvania, which both Pennsylvania and Virginia had claimed in the 1770s. Pennsylvania's gradual-emancipation law stipulated that all slaves had to be registered with the state by November 1, 1780; all unregistered slaves would be immediately free. Even though the boundary dispute was technically settled in 1779, some slave owners in the contested area refused to register their slaves because the action would tacitly accept Pennsylvania's SOVEREIGNTY in the region. The state government later amended the law to allow for the registration of slaves as late as January 1, 1783. John Davis's owner, however, never registered him as a slave, thus unwittingly granting him his technical freedom. Nonetheless, Davis remained in bondage and was moved to Virginia in 1788. Several sympathetic Pennsylvanians went to Virginia and brought Davis back to Pennsylvania and freedom. In turn, the owner hired three Virginians to kidnap Davis and bring him back to Virginia. Following the Constitution's extradition clause, which preceded the fugitive-slave clause, the state of Pennsylvania indicted the kidnappers and requested Virginia authorities to arrest the men so they could be sent to Pennsylvania to stand trial.

The case led to a series of exchanges between Governor THOMAS MIFFLIN of Pennsylvania and his Virginia counterpart. In 1791 Mifflin sought redress by contacting GEORGE WASHINGTON and requesting assistance. Washington asked Congress to address the issue of clarifying extradition. After debate and several revisions, Congress passed a bill that came to be known as the Fugitive Slave Law. The law had four sections; two focused on extradition, and two centered on fugitive slaves. The extradition clauses stated that the "executive authority" of one state had to send to the "executive authority" of another state a copy of the indictment or an affidavit from a magistrate indicating that an individual had been charged with a crime. Upon receipt of this legal documentation, the second state's "executive authority" was to arrest the charged individual and hold that person for six months, to be picked up by an official

from the state charging him with the crime. If no one ever came for the suspect, then he or she was released.

The law's fugitive-slave clauses made it easier for the slave owner to obtain a fugitive slave then for state officials to extradite a criminal. No state official had to be directly involved: All the slave owner had to do was to seize the slave—or have his agents seize the slave—and go before a local, state, or federal magistrate in the community where the "slave" was seized and provide proof of ownership. That proof merely had to be "to the satisfaction of such judge or magistrate" and could be as simple as an affidavit from the slaveholder's state or even "oral testimony." No court session was needed, and there was no decision by a jury. Moreover, anyone aiding or hiding a fugitive slave could be fined $500. This law remained the basic legal mechanism for the return of escaped slaves from free territory until Congress passed a stronger law even more favorable to slave owners in 1850.

Neither political party opposed the law. Although the FEDERALIST PARTY included several ANTISLAVERY advocates, since the law increased the power of the national government—an approach that fit into the Federalist Party political philosophy—no party leader challenged the law. The DEMOCRATIC-REPUBLICAN PARTY generally advocated STATES' RIGHTS and might have viewed the measure as an intrusion by the national government, but despite the party's appeal to the common man, Democratic-Republicans tended to be proslavery. Finally, the law also had no impact on the case of John Davis or his kidnappers. Davis remained a slave, and no action was taken against the kidnappers.

Further reading: Paul Finkelman, *Slavery and the Founders: Race and Liberty in the Age of the Founders* (Armonk, N.Y.: M. E. Sharpe, 1996).

Fulton, Robert (1765–1815) *inventor*

Robert Fulton was a U.S. inventor who designed canals, SUBMARINES, mines, and the first commercially successful steamboat to travel on North American waterways. Fulton was born on November 14, 1765, to a SCOTS-IRISH family in southeastern Pennsylvania. He grew up in the town of Lancaster in a family of a modest wealth. As a young man, Fulton became a portrait painter to a number of wealthy Pennsylvania families in the 1780s. He traveled to England in 1787 to advance his artistic career and did not return to the United States for 20 years.

In England, Fulton shifted the direction of his career from portrait painting to canal engineering. With the financial backing of a few landholders and industrialists, he developed sophisticated plans for canals that employed various mechanical devices such as wheels, inclined planes, and aqueducts. Fulton illustrated these features well, using his artistic talents, and in 1796 he published a book on canal design and sent letters to President GEORGE WASHINGTON and Pennsylvania governor THOMAS MIFFLIN advocating canal projects in the United States. Although none of these projects came to fruition, a canal system later constructed in Pennsylvania followed Fulton's basic design.

In 1797 Fulton traveled to FRANCE, where he quickly established connections with the French government. By the end of 1797, he had refocused his energies on naval warfare and proposed a plan for a cigar-shaped submarine that could be used to plant bombs in the water to destroy enemy ships. Between 1797 and 1801, he developed a submarine called the *Nautilus* and experimented with it along the French coast of the English Channel and the Seine River. Though the *Nautilus* proved successful, Fulton declined to present it formally to NAPOLEON BONAPARTE and dismantled it before French naval engineers could investigate and copy the design. He steadfastly considered himself a private entrepreneur with control of his creations independent of the will of the French regime under Napoleon.

Between 1800 and 1802, Fulton developed plans for submerged bombs that he called torpedoes, which would either be released by submarines or anchored on the sea floor. He also initially drew plans for a steamboat that he presented to Napoleon, although these plans were not developed at this time. In 1804 British agents lured Fulton to England to work for the Royal Navy. In two years of service, he designed and launched two torpedo attacks on French ships—and successfully tested a larger mine—before deciding to return to the United States.

Back in his home country, the now-famous Fulton resumed his work on torpedoes for the U.S. NAVY and turned to his steamboat project in partnership with New Yorker ROBERT R. LIVINGSTON. With Livingston's financial support, Fulton completed his steamboat, commonly known as the *Clermont* (officially it was named the *North River Steam Boat*), which caused a national sensation with a trip up the Hudson River in 1807. By 1809 Livingston and Fulton had created another steamboat and established a commercial steamboat line with an exclusive right to operate on New York waters.

During the WAR OF 1812 (1812–15), Fulton contracted with the Captain STEPHEN DECATUR and the U.S. Navy to create the first ever steam warship; unfortunately, it was not completed until mid-1815. He also continued to test mines and more sophisticated torpedo boats, many of which were employed in various naval engagements.

During the war, Fulton became embroiled in legal action, successfully defending his company's patent and monopoly rights to operate STEAMBOATS in New York. He died unexpectedly on February 24, 1815.

See also SCIENCE.

Further reading: Cynthia Owen Phillip, *Robert Fulton: A Biography* (New York: Franklin Watts, 1985).

fur trade

The fur TRADE helped to fuel the competition for empire in North America. Colonists along the coast of the ATLANTIC OCEAN had hoped to profit from victory in the FRENCH AND INDIAN WAR (1754–63) by increasing their share of the fur trade, but with CANADA in the hands of the British, most furs were traded through the St. Lawrence River Valley after 1763. Even after the REVOLUTIONARY WAR (1776–83), GREAT BRITAIN retained posts north of the Ohio River on U.S. territory in part to control the fur trade. By the time the British evacuated those posts after JAY'S TREATY (1794), much of the region had been depleted of furs, and the trade shifted westward across the Mississippi River.

U.S. traders began to compete for western furs from two directions. First, merchant ships in the PACIFIC OCEAN sailed to the Columbia River to obtain furs to trade in China. The LEWIS AND CLARK EXPEDITION in 1803–06 strengthened the U.S. claim to the region of the Pacific Northwest and encouraged the fur trade. JOHN JACOB ASTOR pursued this trade, organizing the American Fur Trading Company in 1808 and the Pacific Fur Company in 1810. He established his trading fort at ASTORIA at the mouth of the Columbia River in 1811 but sold Astoria to the British at the outbreak of the WAR OF 1812 (1812–15). The Hudson Bay Company, the main British agent in the North American trade after 1800, soon controlled the Columbia River basin.

Second, traders from the United States began to move up the Missouri River and into the Rocky Mountains after the LOUISIANA PURCHASE (1803) and the Lewis and Clark Expedition. Based in St. Louis, these fur traders tapped into a huge territory with plenty of beaver. They also explored much of the GREAT PLAINS and Rocky Mountains in their pursuit of furs.

See also CHINA TRADE.

Further reading: David J. Wishart, *The Fur Trade of the American West, 1807–1840: A Geographical Synthesis* (Lincoln: University of Nebraska Press, 1979).

G

Gabriel's Rebellion (1800)

Born a slave in 1776 in Henrico County, Virginia, Gabriel took the name of the biblical prophet. After he planned a slave rebellion in 1800, Gabriel's name became synonymous with the ultimate act of black resistance to enslavement.

Gabriel was the slave of Thomas Prosser, a member of the Virginia gentry and a tobacco farmer who owned one of the largest plantations in Henrico County. The Prosser plantation had more than 50 slaves, and of them, Gabriel stood out: He was literate in a time and place when most AFRICAN AMERICANS were not (and when teaching blacks to read and write was forbidden); he was an ARTISAN, learning his father's smithing trade on the Prosser plantation; and his talent allowed Gabriel's master to hire him out during the 1790s to other masters in need of labor. Thus, Gabriel traveled away from plantation life, often going to the urban environment of Richmond, where he encountered free blacks, some white ANTISLAVERY advocates, and working-class whites, all of whom protested the deferential codes of Virginia politics and society. By the late 1790s, democratic movements had emerged to challenge the Virginia gentry, and these social and political currents established a foundation for Gabriel to begin planning a slave rebellion. His movement was also inspired in part by the AMERICAN REVOLUTION, FRENCH REVOLUTION, and the Haitian Revolution (see HAITI). One slave who was later convicted of involvement in the plot even declared that he had done little more than what GEORGE WASHINGTON had done during the REVOLUTIONARY WAR (1775–83), asserting, "I have adventured my life endeavouring to obtain the liberty of my countrymen, and I am a willing sacrifice in their cause." Gabriel's travels and experience of being hired out further convinced him of SLAVERY's personal oppressiveness: No matter whom he worked for, Gabriel's wages went back to his master. By the autumn 1799, therefore, he had moved toward open rebellion against slavery.

Gabriel planned to marshal forces in late August 1800, capture guns and ammunition from local depots, march to the capital of Richmond (capturing political leaders such as the governor), and demand both an end to slavery and equal treatment. The plot was betrayed by an enslaved person on a nearby plantation and put down before Gabriel's troops could march. A torrential rainstorm had delayed them in any event.

When the rebellion was betrayed, and Gabriel was captured, he refused to speak. But if the details of his plan remain sketchy, its larger import remains clear: He hoped to overthrow bondage and revolutionize Virginia society. Indeed, he demanded that "QUAKERS, METHODISTS, and French people"—generally known as antislavery advocates—be spared. He also hoped that laboring white people who opposed the aristocratic sentiments of Virginia's ruling elite would join him. Unlike South Carolina's Denmark Vesey, a slave rebel who planned to flee the United States, and Virginia's Nat Turner, who sought to wreak as much havoc on the white population as possible in revenge for slavery's brutality, Gabriel sought to radically alter both race and class relations.

For much of the fall of 1800 after Gabriel's capture, white Virginians remained alarmed that other rebellions might occur. Governor JAMES MONROE, who would eventually succeed JAMES MADISON as president of the United States, called out special MILITIA forces to put down any possible revolt. As reports of Gabriel's plot rippled throughout the United States, and even through Europe, Virginia authorities began prosecuting the accused. Although fewer than 100 enslaved people were ever formally deemed part of Gabriel's ranks, trial testimony by some of the rebellion's other leaders put the number at 150–500 strong—perhaps more. More than two dozen black conspirators were eventually put to death, including Gabriel.

The memory of Gabriel's Rebellion, however, was not easily extinguished. In 1802 white Virginians and North

Carolinians unearthed another, even larger, plot by slaves, many of whom had reportedly been involved with Gabriel two years earlier. Twenty-five more African-American slaves were executed for reportedly participating in this second planned revolt, called the Easter Rebellion, and white Virginians also took legislative action to stifle future conspiracies. Virginia's leadership sought to find an outlet to deport troublesome and rebellious slaves and even hoped to ship some back to AFRICA. These discussions, however, came to naught. More successful was the effort by Virginia masters to tighten control over slavery, increasing slave patrols, making it more difficult to manumit slaves, and creating even more difficult living conditions for slaves.

See also LIBERTY.

Further reading: Arna Bontemps, *Black Thunder* (Boston: Beacon Press, 1968); Douglas Egerton, *Gabriel's Rebellion: The Virginia Conspiracies of 1800 and 1802* (Chapel Hill: University of North Carolina Press, 1993); James Sidbury, *Plowshares into Swords: Race, Rebellion, and Identity in Gabriel's Virginia, 1730–1810* (New York: Cambridge University Press, 1998).

—Richard Newman

Gadsden, Christopher (1724–1805) *Continental soldier, statesman*

A radical from South Carolina known as "the Sam Adams of the South," Christopher Gadsden was a leader in the RESISTANCE MOVEMENT (1764–75) against imperial regulation and an important politician and military officer during the REVOLUTIONARY WAR (1775–83). The son of the British collector of customs for Charleston, Gadsden made his own fortune in Charleston as a merchant and developer. When Governor Thomas Boone challenged his reelection to the state assembly in 1762 as fraudulent, Gadsden emerged as a leading critic of British interference in colonial affairs, attending the STAMP ACT CONGRESS and organizing the SONS OF LIBERTY in South Carolina. Later, after the TOWNSHEND DUTIES (1767) were instituted, he promoted the local nonimportation of British goods. He attended both the FIRST CONTINENTAL CONGRESS and SECOND CONTINENTAL CONGRESS and designed a lasting image of the Revolutionary War: a yellow flag featuring a coiled rattlesnake above the words *DON'T TREAD ON ME*.

In 1776 Gadsden returned to South Carolina to serve in the Provincial Congress and state MILITIA before receiving a commission as a brigadier general in the CONTINENTAL ARMY later that year. During the SIEGE OF CHARLESTON (April–May 12, 1780), Gadsden refused to flee and was held captive for 42 weeks in a British prison in St. Augustine, FLORIDA. Although he declined the state assembly's offer to serve as governor in 1781 due to age and ill health,

Gadsden remained active in state politics. As a FEDERALIST, he was a member of the South Carolina convention that ratified the U.S. CONSTITUTION in 1788 and the convention that wrote the state's constitution in 1790. He died in Charleston on September 15, 1805.

Further Reading: Stanly E. Godbold and Robert H. Woody, *Christopher Gadsden and the American Revolution* (Knoxville: University of Tennessee Press, 1982); Daniel J. McDonough, *Christopher Gadsden and Henry Laurens: The Parallel Lives of Two American Patriots* (Sellinsgrove, Pa.: Susquehanna University Press, 2000).

Tash Smith

Gage, Thomas (1719?–1787) *British military officer*

The younger son of an aristocratic English family, Thomas Gage pursued a military career that brought him to the colonies and placed him as a commander in chief of the British army in North America at the outbreak of the REVOLUTIONARY WAR (1775–83). Although he was a capable administrator with a likable personality, he was not a good combat officer. His influence in guiding British imperial policy, and his military missteps, helped shape the crisis that led to the independence of the United States.

Gage's military career had followed a typical and unexceptional path for a member of the British aristocracy before the FRENCH AND INDIAN WAR (1754–63). He saw service in the low countries against FRANCE and fought against the Jacobite invasion in Scotland in 1745. Gage rose through the ranks by purchasing vacant commissions, and by age 30 he was a lieutenant colonel. His regiment was sent to North America when hostilities with the French and Indians broke out in 1754. During that conflict he served in several campaigns with mixed results. He was in command of the vanguard of General EDWARD BRADDOCK's army as it approached Fort Duquesne and was ambushed by the French and Indians. While he did not get blamed for this disaster, he also did not rise to the occasion, showing some bravery but managing to leave the field and escape the disaster with his life. In 1757 he took part in the failed attempt to capture LOUISBOURG on Cape Breton.

Gage was promoted to colonel in 1758 and subsequently developed the concept of using light-infantry companies to replace colonial rangers to reconnoiter and protect the flanks of regiments of regulars. He also participated in another botched campaign, this time before FORT TICONDEROGA, and married Margaret Kemble, daughter of a wealthy New Jersey family. In 1759 he obtained an independent command, was made a brigadier general, and was ordered to take charge of the siege of FORT NIAGARA. After the fall of that French outpost, he was ordered to attack La Galette, at the head of the St. Lawrence River,

Parliament appointed Thomas Gage as royal governor of Massachusetts in 1774 in an attempt to defuse mounting unrest in the colony. Painting by John Singleton Copley *(Yale Center for British Art)*

rial measures, but he hesitated to do anything without firm direction from England, and such direction was not forthcoming. He sought to limit further colonial settlement west of the Appalachians and encouraged the stationing of troops in Boston after the customs RIOTS of 1768, but he also oversaw the withdrawal of British troops from the same city after the BOSTON MASSACRE (March 5, 1770). Even as late as 1774, this middle course kept him relatively popular with both his superiors in England and colonial Americans. After his appointment as governor of Massachusetts to enforce the COERCIVE ACTS (1774) he had the hopes of King GEORGE III and many colonial Americans riding on his shoulders. JOSEPH WARREN believed Gage was "a man of honest, upright principles" who might somehow find "a just and honourable settlement." Unfortunately for the British Empire, Gage's shoulders were not broad enough for this burden.

As the situation deteriorated in autumn and winter 1774, Gage became convinced that dramatic and forceful action was called for to regain control of the colonies. A provincial congress beyond his control or influence replaced the official colonial assembly in Massachusetts, and the SUFFOLK RESOLVES (1774) were put into effect, all but nullifying the Coercive Acts outside of Boston. Gage and the British troops felt isolated in Boston, surrounded by a hostile countryside where MINUTEMEN prepared for war. Gage's reputation in England also declined that winter. Whitehall rejected his recommendations to repeal the Coercive Acts as unenforceable, withdraw from Boston, and set up a naval blockade to shut off all TRADE with the colonies and compel submission. The British government, however, agreed that some action should take place to demonstrate its authority. On April 14, 1775, Gage received orders to use force to suppress what he had previously described as an open rebellion. These orders led to his ill-fated expedition to Concord and the BATTLES OF LEXINGTON AND CONCORD (April 19, 1775). Gage had planned a quick strike to arrest leaders and seize supplies, but he did not catch the colonists by surprise. No leaders were captured, and only a few supplies were destroyed. The column of British regulars suffered dramatic losses.

Gage soon found himself besieged by thousands of minutemen and was all but superseded by the arrival of three new British generals: SIR WILLIAM HOWE, LORD CORNWALLIS, and JOHN BURGOYNE. The idea that the conflict might subside disappeared on June 17, 1775, after the revolutionaries initiated the BATTLE OF BUNKER HILL. With Gage's blessing, the British launched a frontal assault on the entrenched positions in Charlestown, and after three advances, they drove the revolutionaries off but at an appalling cost. Gage was soon recalled to GREAT BRITAIN, and Howe replaced him in command. Gage remained in the army and was promoted to full general

to help relieve pressure on British armies advancing up the St. Lawrence and invading from New York along Lake Champlain. Gage failed at La Galette and was relegated to supervising the rear guard of the invasion of CANADA in 1760. He might have fallen into obscurity at that point, but fate had other plans. Serving as military governor of Canada after 1760, he suddenly found himself commander in chief in North America after Sir JEFFREY AMHERST was recalled because he had miscalculated the Indian threat in 1763. It fell to Gage to supervise the end of PONTIAC'S WAR (1763–65), and once his subordinates crushed the Indians, he remained in the colonies in command of the permanent British army stationed there.

Although the imperial crisis and the RESISTANCE MOVEMENT (1764–75) sorely tested his patience, Gage's strengths were as an administrator. Throughout the 1760s and early 1770s, he was a model of caution. Left to his own devices, he might have pursued a more aggressive policy to put down the street disorder and resistance to impe-

in 1782, though he saw no more active service. He died in London on April 2, 1787.

Further reading: John Richard Alden, *General Gage in America: Being Principally a History of His Role in the American Revolution* (Baton Rouge: Louisiana University Press, 1948); George Athan Billias, ed., *George Washington's Opponents: British Generals and Admirals in the American Revolution* (New York: William Morrow, 1969); David Hackett Fischer, *Paul Revere's Ride* (New York: Oxford University Press, 1994).

Gallatin, Albert (1761–1849) *secretary of the treasury, diplomat*

Albert Gallatin was a transatlantic figure and Swiss immigrant who eventually became a congressman from Pennsylvania, secretary of the treasury under Presidents THOMAS JEFFERSON and JAMES MADISON, and a U.S. diplomat in Europe. Born in Geneva, Switzerland, on January 29, 1761, Gallatin grew up in affluence but lost both his mother and father at an early age. He was raised by close family friends and educated in the best ENLIGHTENMENT tradition. When he graduated from the College of Geneva in 1779, his grandmother arranged for him to obtain a military commission in the army the small German state of Hesse-Cassel, destined for service with the HESSIANS in North America. Gallatin declined that appointment, saying he would not fight for a tyrant. Instead, inspired by the writings of Jean-Jacques Rousseau on the image of the noble savage in North America (NATIVE AMERICANS) and the ideal of an agrarian life, he ran off with a friend to sail to the United States in 1780. His ship landed in Boston, where the two young Swiss men attempted to sell a consignment of tea they had purchased in FRANCE. After that effort brought little profit, Gallatin traveled to the Maine FRONTIER in another mercantile enterprise. This adventure was short-lived, and he traveled back to Boston, where he became a tutor in French at Harvard College in 1782. Soon he moved to western Pennsylvania.

By 1784, Gallatin had become involved in land speculation in the western country and was acting as a land surveyor. He and a partner purchased large tracts in the Ohio River Valley in western Virginia and Pennsylvania, and the following year he began work on a frontier farm and manor that he named Friendship Hill, located on the Monongahela River in Fayette County, Pennsylvania. In 1788 he entered local politics and was elected to represent Fayette County at the state ratifying convention in Harrisburg for the U.S. CONSTITUTION, where he advocated a BILL OF RIGHTS. In 1789 he was an influential participant in the Pennsylvania state constitutional convention, again advocating guaranteed civil liberties.

In the early 1790s, Gallatin established his political reputation as a legislator representing Fayette County in the Pennsylvania General Assembly. There he often voted with a faction loosely aligned with the DEMOCRATIC-REPUBLICAN PARTY in national politics. In 1793 he played an important role in the establishment of the Bank of Pennsylvania. That same year, the Pennsylvania state assembly elected Gallatin to the U.S. Senate. Because there was some confusion as to when he applied for CITIZENSHIP, however, senators from the FEDERALIST PARTY voted to remove him from the nation's upper house in December 1793, asserting that he had not been an "American" for nine years.

Nonetheless, Gallatin remained on the national political stage. In 1794 he acted as an intermediary between western Pennsylvanians involved in the WHISKEY REBELLION (1794) and federal troops sent by President GEORGE WASHINGTON, and he served as a Jeffersonian in Congress between 1795 and 1800. As a result, he was often in the middle of the partisan battles of the era. He openly protested the ALIEN AND SEDITION ACTS (1798) on the House floor and encouraged moderation with regard to France in the wake of the XYZ AFFAIR (1797–98). Simultaneously, he launched a glassworks and a gun factory in the frontier town of New Geneva, Pennsylvania, which he had founded.

Gallatin's national influence increased with his appointment as secretary of the treasury in 1801. In that position he symbolized moderate Democratic-Republican practicality on financial issues and therefore became a lightning rod for political criticism throughout his years as secretary (1801–14). Under President Jefferson, his most important role was as advocate for the BANK OF THE UNITED STATES. Gallatin and Jefferson disagreed over the bank's legitimacy and necessity, and the treasury secretary worked hard to overcome the president's reluctance to accept the bank's status as national repository and lender. Gallatin's understanding of the bank was akin to ALEXANDER HAMILTON's original position on it. Like Hamilton, he believed that the government should maintain some debt and that the bank had clear constitutional legitimacy. In 1804 Jefferson actually signed legislation authorizing new branches of the bank in New Orleans and WASHINGTON, D.C., on Gallatin's recommendation. The treasury secretary also disagreed with Jefferson over the president's controversial EMBARGO OF 1807. In 1808 he presented a comprehensive plan for INTERNAL IMPROVEMENTS that Jefferson rejected on the grounds that the federal government did not have the authority to fund transportation projects. Gallitan's fiscal policies also managed to decrease the national debt (see DEBT, NATIONAL).

Gallatin stayed in the cabinet under James Madison and soon became embroiled in controversy over rechartering the Bank of the United States in 1810 and 1811. He steadfastly defended the bank against Democratic-Republican critics and sought to maintain its existence in the face of impending war with GREAT BRITAIN. But despite his best efforts and Madison's support, Congress voted to kill the bank by a tie-breaking vote cast in the Senate by Vice President GEORGE CLINTON. This action contributed to financial distress during the WAR OF 1812 (1812–15).

In 1813, while still serving in the Treasury Department, Gallatin went to Europe in the hope of beginning peace negotiations. His appointment as a special peace envoy, however, was not confirmed by the Senate because of his position as secretary of the treasury. Gallatin resigned from the cabinet in 1814 and was appointed to the delegation that negotiated the TREATY OF GHENT (1814). Later, he served the nation as Minister to France and then as minister to Great Britain. In the 1830s he wrote and published a number of influential essays on banking, financial policy, and TARIFFS.

Gallatin married twice. He eloped with Sophie Allegre in 1789, but she died a few months later at his home in western Pennsylvania. In 1793 he wed Hannah Nicholson, a city girl who was never comfortable living in the wilds of Friendship Hill and was relieved when Gallitan's political appointments forced the couple to live in the nation's capital. Gallatin had six children in his second marriage, but only three lived to adulthood. He died peacefully at home on August 12, 1849, just a few months after Hannah's death.

See also BANKS.

Further reading: Ray Walters, Jr., *Albert Gallatin: Jeffersonian Financier and Diplomat* (New York, Macmillan, 1957).

James R. Karmel

Galloway, Joseph (1731–1803) *lawyer, Loyalist*

Joseph Galloway was a Philadelphia lawyer who remained loyal to the British Crown during the REVOLUTIONARY WAR (1775–83). Born in Anne Arundel County, Maryland, Galloway came from an affluent family who provided him with an excellent private EDUCATION. In 1747 he moved to Philadelphia, where he became a lawyer, and with a flourishing practice and inherited wealth, he quickly emerged as a force in Philadelphia politics. He and BENJAMIN FRANKLIN developed a warm friendship and close political alliance in the effort to make Pennsylvania a royal colony. Galloway served in the colonial assembly from 1756 to 1775, with the exception of one year, and as speaker from 1766 to 1775.

Despite his concerns over the strength of the RESISTANCE MOVEMENT (1764–75) against imperial regulation,

Galloway attended the FIRST CONTINENTAL CONGRESS in 1774 hoping to find some middle ground. His efforts at compromise led to his drawing up "A Plan of Proposed Union Between Great Britain and the Colonies," which called for a president-general for the colonies appointed by the king and a legislature that would represent all the colonies. Both Parliament and the North American legislature would have to pass on all measures relevant to the British colonies. The Continental Congress rejected the plan. The following year, Galloway attended the SECOND CONTINENTAL CONGRESS, where, distraught over the outbreak of hostilities, he supported JOHN DICKINSON's OLIVE BRANCH PETITION in July 1775. He withdrew from Congress before the DECLARATION OF INDEPENDENCE was issued and sought the protection of General WILLIAM HOWE's British army in New York.

Galloway agreed to serve as a civil administrator for the Crown during the British occupation of Philadelphia in 1777–78. Continuing to hope that the colonies would be reunited with GREAT BRITAIN, he formulated several plans of union that he thought could be used after the rebellion was suppressed. When the British evacuated Philadelphia in June 1778, he went to British-occupied New York until December 1781, when he left for England. Galloway was reviled by the revolutionaries, who considered him a traitor. As punishment for his loyalty to the British Crown, his estates were seized, and when he applied to return to Pennsylvania in 1793, his request was rejected. He died on August 10, 1803, in Watford, England, age 73.

See also LOYALIST PROPERTY CONFISCATION; LOYALISTS.

Further reading: John E. Ferling, *The Loyalist Mind: Joseph Galloway and the American Revolution* (University Park: Pennsylvania State University Press, 1977); Benjamin H. Newcomb, *Franklin and Galloway: A Political Partnership* (New Haven, Conn.: Yale University Press, 1972).

Gálvez, Bernardo de (1746–1786) *Spanish government official*

Born into a prominent family in Málaga, SPAIN, on July 23, 1746, Bernardo de Gálvez served the Spanish Crown in various capacities, including as governor of LOUISIANA from 1777 to 1785. He arrived in North America in 1769 and fought Native American raiders such as the Apaches along New Spain's northern borders. After returning to Spain for a few years, he was sent to Louisiana as the territory's governor.

Early in his tenure as governor of Louisiana, Gálvez formed close friendships with THOMAS JEFFERSON and other revolutionary leaders, and his assistance during

Spanish officer and governor-general of Louisiana Bernardo de Gálvez successfully countered British forces throughout the Mississippi Valley after the Spanish declared war against the British in 1779. *(The Museum of Mobile, Alabama)*

the REVOLUTIONARY WAR (1775–83) proved invaluable. Initially, Gálvez blocked the British from navigation on the Mississippi River, ensuring that only ships allied with the revolutionary cause could pass through. His actions allowed badly needed supplies to flow up the river to the American revolutionaries. When Spain officially declared war on GREAT BRITAIN in the summer of 1779, Gálvez and his army headed east to attack British outposts along the Mississippi and the Gulf Coast. Spanish soldiers under Gálvez captured Baton Rouge, Pensacola, and New Providence, in the Bahamas, earning him accolades from the SECOND CONTINENTAL CONGRESS. In the mid-1780s he took over as viceroy of New Spain (MEXICO) after his father passed away. He spent his remaining years in Mexico City. Gálvez died on November 30, 1786, in Mexico City; some reports suggest he was poisoned by political enemies. A monument to honor him stands in WASHINGTON, D.C., and there is a U.S. postal stamp commemorating his contributions to the United States.

See also NEW SPAIN (MEXICO), NORTHERN FRONTIER OF.

Further reading: Ralph Lee Woodward, *Tribute to Don Bernardo de Gálvez: Royal Patents and an Epic Ballad Honoring the Spanish Governor of Louisiana* (Baton Rouge: Historic New Orleans Collection, 1979).

Michele M. Stephens

gambling

Although gambling faced strong opposition and legal sanctions, it was a favorite pastime of many early Americans. In the backrooms of private residences, at TAVERNS, and at sporting events such as horse races and cockfights, a variety of people tested their luck at games of skill and chance.

Taverns, or "ordinaries," were located in towns and on well-traveled roads throughout early America. These popular establishments offered food, drink, lodging, and entertainment to local residents and travelers. They also provided a place for patrons to gather and enjoy card and dice games, quoits (a British game similar to horseshoes), and an early form of bowling known as skittles, all of which usually involved gambling. Taverns also frequently hosted animal blood-sport events such as cockfighting and animal baiting as well as occasional bare-knuckle prizefights.

The association of taverns with ALCOHOL and gambling often made them the target of reformers seeking to preserve the moral purity of the community or to ensure the productivity of workers. For example, in 1760 the Massachusetts General Court passed legislation outlawing gambling in taverns. This statute, however, and many others like it propagated in other colonies and states, proved ineffective.

In the Chesapeake region of Maryland and Virginia, gambling was a part of the local gentry's social and cultural life. By participating in high-stakes games of cards, billiards, and backgammon, or by owning and training champion horses and fighting cocks, planters demonstrated their elite status and indulged in an enjoyable form of recreation that reflected their financial insouciance. Since the law, if not actual practice, restricted betting to those who owned property, high-stakes gambling also served as a method of emphasizing the region's social hierarchy. Planters with the ability to risk large sums of MONEY at the gambling table or the racetrack demonstrated their elite position in a society where status was highly fluid and financial fortunes could quickly change. Gambling also offered an avenue for planters of lesser influence to prove their social acceptability. Gaming's emphasis on individualism, materialism, and financial risk (it was not unheard-of for a planter to risk an entire year's TOBACCO crop on a single bet) mirrored the values needed to succeed in the highly volatile and ultracompetitive world of the tobacco planter. For the gentry of the Chesapeake, success or failure in the gambling arena helped to reveal a man's true character and his position in the social order.

Further reading: T. H. Breen, "Horses and Gentlemen: The Cultural Significance of Gambling among the Gentry in Virginia," *William and Mary Quarterly* 3rd ser., 34 (1977); 239–257; Benjamin J. Rader, *American Sports: From the Age of Folk Games to the Age of Televised Sports,* 5th ed. (Upper Saddle River, N.J.: Prentice Hall, 2004).

Chris Davis

Gardoqui Arriquibar, Diego María de (Don Diego de Gardoqui) (1735–1798) *Spanish diplomat, politician*

Known generally as Don Diego de Gardoqui, Diego María de Gardoqui Arriquibar was an instrumental figure in Spanish-American relations in the 1770s and 1780s. Born in Bilbao, SPAIN, he was fluent in English, and his Bilbao merchant firm had begun trading with British North America as early as 1765. Once the REVOLUTIONARY WAR (1775–83) broke out, Gardoqui capitalized on these connections, especially with U.S. businessman and politician ELBRIDGE GERRY, and he began to funnel supplies to the revolutionaries in Massachusetts and elsewhere. The Gardoqui firm also aided the CONTINENTAL NAVY and privateers in the port of Bilbao, both as a supplier and purchaser of prize goods. When the Spanish court did not want to deal directly with the U.S. representative, ARTHUR LEE, they sent Gardoqui to intercept him in March 1777 and act as an unofficial contact between Spain and the rebellious North American colonies. In 1780 the Spanish government appointed Gardoqui to negotiate with JOHN JAY, who was in Spain to obtain more MONEY to fight the war. The discussions, however, broke down when Gardoqui insisted that the United States renounce its rights to the Mississippi River in return for £100,000 in aid. In short, although never more than a private subject of the king of Spain, Gardoqui became a pivotal figure in Spain's dealings with the United States during the Revolutionary War.

Gardoqui gained official diplomatic status when he was named Spain's minister to the United States in 1784. Much of his time as minister was devoted to fruitless negotiations with Jay over TRADE, access to the Mississippi River, and boundaries. Although Jay was ready to abandon the right to navigate the Mississippi for a term of years, he was unable to persuade Congress to go along. By the time Gardoqui left the United States, shortly after GEORGE WASHINGTON became president under the new U.S. CONSTITUTION, he had little to show for his diplomatic efforts. He died in Madrid in 1798.

See also JAY-GARDOQUI, TREATY OF.

Further reading: Thomas E. Chavez, *Spain and the Independence of the United States: An Intrinsic Gift* (Albuquerque: University of New Mexico, 2002).

Garrettson, Freeborn (1752–1827) *Methodist minister*

A leading itinerant minister and missionary, Freeborn Garrettson was influential in the early growth of the METHODISTS in North America. He was born in Maryland, and after his father's death in 1773, Garrettson inherited his family's estate, containing a substantial area of land and a number of slaves. In 1775 he underwent a conversion influenced by traveling ministers, including FRANCIS ASBURY, and his religious experience prompted him to free all of his slaves. In 1776 he attended the Baltimore Conference, where he was recognized and licensed as a Methodist minister.

As was common with most Methodist preachers during the REVOLUTIONARY WAR (1775–83), WHIGS suspected Garrettson of being a Loyalist. Despite his support of the revolutionary cause, he suffered intense persecution and imprisonment for his unwillingness to bear arms or take oaths of allegiance. Nevertheless, he persevered and, at Asbury's behest, established and administered a number of Methodist societies throughout Delaware, Pennsylvania, and New Jersey. In 1784 Garrettson was officially ordained at the conference in Baltimore that established the Methodist Episcopal Church in America. The following year, he volunteered to further promote the Methodist movement by traveling to NOVA SCOTIA, where he served as a missionary to exiled LOYALISTS.

In 1799 Garrettson and his wife Catharine built a mansion on an estate situated east of the Hudson River at Rhinecliffe, New York. This property, known as "Traveler's Rest," served as a resort for itinerant preachers. For his remaining years, Garrettson continued to serve the Methodist movement by traveling tirelessly throughout New England as well as attending Methodist conferences until his death in 1827.

Further Reading: Robert D. Simpson, ed., *American Methodist Pioneer: The Life and Journals of the Rev. Freeborn Garrettson, 1752–1827* (Rutland, Vt.: Academy Books, 1984).

William R. Smith

Gaspée affair (June 9, 1772)

In June 1772 a crowd of Rhode Islanders, which probably included the affluent merchant John Brown, boarded a grounded British naval schooner in Narragansett Bay, forced the crew ashore, and burned the vessel. The

Gaspée affair contributed to the sense of mistrust and anger between GREAT BRITAIN and her North American colonies.

After the repeal of most of the TOWNSHEND DUTIES in 1770, relations between the colonies and Great Britain improved, and TRADE grew rapidly. While most merchants carried on legal business dealings, some also continued to trade illegally. Rhode Island was a hotbed of illicit trade. Consequently, several confrontations occurred between smugglers and customs officials in the 1770s. To protect customs officials and to seize smugglers, the Royal Navy stationed a schooner, the HMS *Gaspée* in Narragansett Bay in March 1772. The officer in charge of the vessel, Lieutenant William Dudingston, rigorously pursued smugglers and captured several vessels. In retaliation, the local sheriff threatened to arrest him for false seizure. The British admiral and the Rhode Island governor exchanged threats, further inflaming the situation.

While in pursuit of a suspected smuggler in June 1772, Dudingston ran his vessel aground. Rhode Islanders boarded the *Gaspée,* overwhelmed the crew, examined the ship's papers, and then set fire to the vessel, which they considered a threat to their livelihood. To make matters worse, Dudingston had been wounded during the engagement, and the sheriff arrested him a few days later. After the British admiral paid a stiff fine and obtained Dudingston's release, the British government launched a full-scale investigation into the affair. Although the British could not identify any of the rioters, the investigating commission had been empowered to send those accused of the crime to England for trial, an action that violated the traditional right of an Englishman to a trial by a jury of his peers. Colonial Americans became concerned about this threat to their LIBERTY, and it was in large part in response to the *Gaspée* affair, that the Virginia House of Burgesses organized its COMMITTEE OF CORRESPONDENCE.

See also SMUGGLING.

Gates, Horatio (1727–1806) *Continental army general*

Horatio Gates was an English-born CONTINENTAL ARMY general during the REVOLUTIONARY WAR (1775–83). Born to a lower-class family at Maldon in Essex, England, Gates entered the British army at an early age with a lieutenant's commission and served his first tour of duty in NOVA SCOTIA from 1749 to 1750. After receiving a captaincy, he was seriously wounded in July 1755 when he was a member of General EDWARD BRADDOCK's unsuccessful advance on the French at Fort Duquesne (later FORT PITT) during the FRENCH AND INDIAN WAR (1754–63). He later served in several posts in New York before obtaining a position under General ROBERT MONCKTON.

After participating with Monckton in the expedition that captured Martinique from the French in 1761, Gates was granted a major's commission in 1762. His promotion turned out to be a disappointment, however, and he subsequently returned to England. There, as a major on half pay in GREAT BRITAIN, a lack of further military advancement coupled with social prejudice led Gates to retire from the army and move to Virginia with his family, where he established himself as a planter and lived a life of substantial middle-class comfort.

Although Gates did not initially become involved in Virginia's political affairs, he did accept a position as lieutenant colonel in the local MILITIA. Sympathetic to colonial complaints against the British, he joined the revolutionary cause, was commissioned a brigadier general, and was given the position of adjutant general in the Continental army at Cambridge, Massachusetts, on June 17, 1775.

In May 1776 the SECOND CONTINENTAL CONGRESS promoted Gates to major general and appointed him to command the northern army in CANADA. When he arrived in Albany to assume the new post, however, he learned that the army had retreated out of Canada to

A former British officer, General Horatio Gates became known as the "Hero of Saratoga" owing to his victories at Freeman's Farm and Bemis Heights. *(Independence National Historical Park)*

CROWN POINT, which was under the jurisdiction of General PHILIP JOHN SCHUYLER, commander of the Northern Department. As his superior, Schuyler appointed Gates to command FORT TICONDEROGA. In summer 1777 General JOHN BURGOYNE invaded New York State from Canada. Gates, once again commander of the northern revolutionary army, gained credit for the victory at SARATOGA on October 17, 1777.

After Saratoga, Gates rivaled GEORGE WASHINGTON as the military hero of the revolutionary cause. During the fall and winter of 1777–78, he became involved in the controversy over replacing Washington called the CONWAY CABAL. Although Gates had not been solely responsible for the success of the Saratoga campaign, the victory marked a turning point in the war for which he reaped the glory, and he was named president of the Board of War—a post independent of Washington. Several officers, led by General Thomas Conway, along with some members of the Continental Congress including JOHN ADAMS and SAMUEL ADAMS, feared Washington's popularity and believed his campaign of 1777—in which he lost several battles and was driven out of Philadelphia—paled in comparison to Gates's achievement at Saratoga. But the plot to replace Washington with Gates fell apart as word began to spread that the victory at Saratoga had more to do with the battlefield heroics of BENEDICT ARNOLD than anything Gates had done, and Washington retained the confidence of most of the army and many members of Congress.

In June 1780 Congress appointed Gates as commander of the southern army in the Carolinas without consulting Washington, who had wanted NATHANAEL GREENE to take the post. The Carolina campaign was poorly organized, and a lack of supplies coupled with untrained troops led to a terrible defeat at the BATTLE OF CAMDEN (August 16, 1780) in South Carolina. After this battle, Gates relinquished his command to Greene, and Congress ordered an official investigation of his conduct in the affair, but it was never completed. Gates returned to active service in August 1782, but he never fully recovered his reputation, and he retired to Virginia the following year.

In September 1790 Gates sold his plantation and slaves in Virginia and moved to Rose Hill Farm, an estate in Manhattan, New York. There he renewed an interest in politics, even serving one term in the New York legislature as a member of the DEMOCRATIC-REPUBLICAN PARTY in 1800. He died in New York on April 10, 1806.

Further reading: Max M. Mintz, *The Generals of Saratoga: John Burgoyne and Horatio Gates* (New Haven, Conn.: Yale University Press, 1990); Paul David Nelson, *General Horatio Gates, A Biography* (Baton Rouge: Louisiana State University Press, 1976).

Genêt, Edmond-Charles (Citizen Genêt)
(1763–1834) *French diplomat*

Edmond-Charles Genêt—"Citizen Genêt"—served as the French minister to the United States in 1793. During his short tenure as minister, Genêt managed to antagonize President GEORGE WASHINGTON and members of his cabinet, including Secretary of State THOMAS JEFFERSON, who sympathized with the FRENCH REVOLUTION (1789–99). Thus, Genêt added to a crisis in Franco-American relations as U.S. leaders were trying to maintain neutrality in the war between GREAT BRITAIN and FRANCE.

Genêt was born at Versailles on January 8, 1763. A prodigy, he learned to read English, Swedish, Italian, and Latin by the time he was 12 years old. Previous to his mission in the United States, he served as secretary of legation and chargé d'affaires to RUSSIA. A full convert to the revolutionary cause, Genêt was appointed minister to the United States in late 1792 and set sail for North America in February 1793.

The French government instructed Genêt to negotiate a new treaty with the United States that would expand on the treaty of 1778 (see FRENCH ALLIANCE). He was to use debt payments received from the United States to fund his mission and purchase supplies for French forces in the region. In essence, the government wanted Genêt to use the United States as a base for French operations. In addition, he was instructed to undertake "all measures which comported with his position" to foment rebellion in Spanish LOUISIANA and FLORIDA and in British CANADA.

Genêt landed in Charleston, South Carolina, on April 8, 1793. Upon his arrival, he commissioned four French privateers and established procedures for condemning the British prizes they captured. He then traveled by land to Philadelphia. Almost at every stop, local residents feted Genêt and the French Revolution, causing him to believe that the people of the United States fully supported his cause. Simultaneously, President Washington's cabinet debated how the United States should treat the French Revolution, the new French minister, and the expanding war between France and Great Britain. Genêt became an issue in this increasingly partisan dispute between Secretary of the Treasury ALEXANDER HAMILTON and Secretary of State Jefferson. By the time Genêt arrived in Philadelphia in May, Washington had settled the debate and issued his NEUTRALITY PROCLAMATION asserting that the United States would favor neither belligerent in their war.

Frustrated by this position, and believing that the people of the United States really wanted to help France, Genêt made a direct appeal to the public and ignored the official policy of the Washington administration. He sought to raise an army under GEORGE ROGERS CLARK to invade Spanish Louisiana and commissioned additional privateers. The issue that precipitated a diplomatic crisis was the *Little*

Sarah affair. In June and July 1793, Genêt oversaw the conversion of the captured British ship *Little Sarah* into the privateer *La Petite Democrate* (the *Little Democrat*) in Philadelphia harbor. Upon learning of Genêt's activities, Jefferson demanded the ship remain in port. However, Genêt ordered the ship to sea and consequently alienated his one ally within Washington's administration. Washington was deeply offended by Genêt's actions, and in August the United States requested Genêt's recall.

Because the government in France had changed, Genêt could not go home without endangering his life. In 1794, at the age of 31, he married a daughter of Governor GEORGE CLINTON of New York and settled into the life of a gentleman farmer in New York. He died on his farm on July 14, 1834.

Further reading: Henry Ammon, *The Genêt Mission* (New York: Norton, 1973).

Terri Halperin

George III (1738–1820) *king of Great Britain*

In the DECLARATION OF INDEPENDENCE (passed on July 4, 1776), the SECOND CONTINENTAL CONGRESS asserted, "The history of the present king of GREAT BRITAIN is a history of repeated injuries and usurpations all having in direct object the establishment of an absolute tyranny over these states." There followed a long indictment of more than 20 crimes committed by George III against the rights and liberties of his North American subjects. After a decade of attacking parliamentary authority, revolutionaries had now turned their attention to their monarch, an action that was necessary for propaganda and ideological reasons. If colonial American radicals were to sever their ties with Great Britain, then they had to declare their independence from the king as well as his government and empire. The Declaration of Independence did much to cast an image of George III as a tyrant in the minds of many during and after the REVOLUTIONARY WAR (1775–83). This view, while good politics, was based on a poor understanding of history. The monarch from whom colonists declared independence in 1776 was not a tyrant. Although the titular head of the British state, he was not primarily responsible for the policies adopted in his name which provoked rebellion in colonial America. In many respects he was a sympathetic and tragic figure whose long reign witnessed the collapse of the first British empire and the birth of the second.

George III had the second longest reign in British history. Born on June 4, 1738, he was the son of Frederick, prince of Wales, and Princess Augusta of Saxe-Coburg. He was not a prodigy, experienced educational difficulties as a child, and did not learn to read properly

Painting of King George III *(Library of Congress)*

until he was 11 years old. A year later his father died, and George became prince of Wales, heir to his grandfather King George II, and in 1760 he assumed the throne upon his grandfather's death. He was the third Hanoverian king of Great Britain, and the first who spoke English as his native LANGUAGE.

As a new king, George III oversaw the final stages of the British triumph in the FRENCH AND INDIAN WAR (1754–63), which ended with the TREATY OF PARIS (1763). When he acceded to the throne, he was heavily influenced by JOHN STUART, EARL OF BUTE, who had been his tutor (and was reputed to be his widowed mother's lover). Bute helped to arrange George's marriage to Princess Charlotte of Mecklenburg-Strelitz in 1761, a union that proved to be happy and durable, lasting for more than 50 years and producing nine sons and six daughters. George was a successful family man devoted to his wife and children.

If George III's private life gave him stability and happiness, the same could not be said of his monarchical responsibilities. During the 1760s, a succession of short-lived governments grappled with imperial administration and the fiscal and political problems that came with global empire. George had hoped to recover for the monarchy some of the powers that had been assumed by Parliament since the Glorious Revolution (1688), but he enjoyed little success in this area. He ruled in the style of his Hanoverian predecessors through the extensive use of patronage to establish a group of supporters in Parliament known as the "king's friends." The early part of George III's reign was dominated by the problem of governing Britain's North American colonies. The king favored his minister's policies and supported parliamentary efforts to tax and, later, subdue the rebellious colonies by force. He was not, however, the author of these policies. It is often said that the loss of the North American colonies cost George III his sanity, as he periodically displayed evidence of dementia. But while the strains and stresses of governance took their toll on him, modern research suggests that the king suffered from porphyria, a hereditary nervous disorder, with prolonged bouts of the illness occurring in 1788–89 and in 1801. He was permanently incapacitated by the disease in 1810, and his eldest son—later George IV—acted as prince regent during the last decade of George III's reign.

Apart from his illness, the second half of George III's reign was dominated not by events in North America but by those in Europe, particularly the FRENCH REVOLUTION (1789–99). Between 1793 and 1815, Britain led the successful movement to contain and defeat the French and NAPOLEON BONAPARTE. This effort included the inconclusive WAR OF 1812 (1812–15) with the United States over maritime TRADE and western expansion. Simultaneously, Britain enlarged its colonial holdings in the WEST INDIES and south Asia. Despite the loss of the North American colonies, by the time George III died on January 29, 1820, there had been a great expansion of the British Empire and of trade under his reign. At home the British population had doubled in size, agricultural production had increased, the INDUSTRIAL REVOLUTION had begun, and ENLIGHTENMENT ideas had found wide currency in Britain. Although George III cannot be credited with these developments, he did encourage them. He took a keen interest in SCIENCE and AGRICULTURE—his subjects nicknamed him "Farmer George"—and founded and generously supported the Royal Academy of Arts.

George III could be obstinate. He did not always rule with wisdom or foresight, but he was not, despite the claims of the Declaration of Independence, a tyrant. Rather, he was a good man of limited abilities and considerable health problems who sought to handle massive responsibilities with mixed results.

Further reading: John Brooke, *King George III* (New York: McGraw Hill, 1972).

Francis D. Cogliano

George, David (1742?–1810) *Baptist preacher, African-American Loyalist*

A transatlantic evangelical, David George was born a slave in Virginia but ran away from his cruel master when he was a young man. Pursued by his master, George headed south and was captured by the CREEK, who kept him for a while before returning him to SLAVERY. George escaped again; stayed with another group of NATIVE AMERICANS for several years; and then agreed to work for a white man at Silver Bluff, South Carolina, near Savannah, Georgia. At Silver Bluff, George had a religious experience triggered in part by the preaching of GEORGE LIELE, and he joined the BAPTISTS. Around the beginning of the REVOLUTIONARY WAR (1775–83), he became a Baptist elder, began to preach himself, and taught himself to read with the help of some European-American children. The British invasion of the South, which began in 1778, changed George's life. His master supported the AMERICAN REVOLUTION and left the area, leaving his slaves new opportunities for freedom, whereupon George and his wife moved behind British lines. Despite hardships, including a bout of SMALLPOX, George worked in a butcher stall and continued to preach. By the end of the war he had relocated with his family to Charleston, but they left that city when the British evacuated in 1782.

George joined the African-American and white LOYALISTS who settled in NOVA SCOTIA, where he became a landowner and minister to two churches. He also traveled throughout the province and into nearby New Brunswick as a Baptist minister for almost a decade. Although George served mainly his own race, at times he preached to whites. Early in his ministry his willingness to baptize whites led to a mob attack in Shelburne, which included physical harassment and his house being torn down.

In 1792 George became a leader among the blacks in Nova Scotia who agreed to emigrate to SIERRA LEONE in an effort to escape the white Loyalists' persecution. There he established the first Baptist church in West AFRICA and remained a spokesman for the settlers in the region. He also made a trip to GREAT BRITAIN, where he published a narrative of his life.

Further reading: David George, "Extracts of Letters from Mr. David George . . ." John Rippan, *Baptist Annual Register for . . . 1794;* (London: no pub., 1797), James Sidbury, *Becoming African in America: Race and Nation in the Early Black Republic* (New York: Oxford University Press, 2007).

Georgia expedition (January–July 1782)

As the REVOLUTIONARY WAR (1775–83) drew to a close, the CONTINENTAL ARMY sought to extend its control into

Georgia, which had been devastated by the British occupation and partisan warfare. General NATHANAEL GREENE ordered General ANTHONY WAYNE and a few hundred Continentals into Georgia with the idea that they would be augmented by the local MILITIA to oppose the British, LOYALISTS, and NATIVE AMERICANS in the state. But since many militia units preferred plundering to fighting, and many other local men were afraid to leave their homes and families for service in the military, recruiting militia and obtaining supplies and forage was very difficult. Fortunately for Wayne, the British army began to withdraw from isolated posts and concentrate in Savannah. Moreover, although the British outnumbered Wayne, they did not seek to fight him, though Wayne's troops fought some battles against Indians allied to the British. On the night of January 22–23, 1782, about 300 CREEK attacked his main force and were driven back and pursued with heavy losses.

The British evacuated Savannah on July 11, 1782, but their withdrawal did not end the confusion in the state. There was a severe labor shortage since as many as 5,000 AFRICAN AMERICANS who had been slaves left with the British, and other slaves had escaped to the backcountry. Further, many settlers feared Indian attack. Passions and hatred between Loyalists and WHIGS remained high, while bandits who had fought on both sides continued to roam the countryside.

Further reading: Leslie Hall, *Land & Allegiance in Revolutionary Georgia* (Athens: University of Georgia Press, 2001).

Germain, George, Lord (George Sackville-Germain)

(1716–1785) *British soldier, government minister*
George Sackville—in 1770 he became George Sackville-Germain when he inherited the estate and name of Lady Elizabeth Germain—came from a leading aristocratic family in GREAT BRITAIN and directed British military strategy for most of the REVOLUTIONARY WAR (1775–83). Well educated, Sackville entered the British army in 1737, fought in the War of Austrian Succession (1740–48), and was promoted to colonel by the end of the conflict. He also entered Parliament in 1741. Promoted to major general during the Seven Years' War (see FRENCH AND INDIAN WAR, 1754–1763), Sackville was appointed second in command of the British forces in Germany and then assumed full command after the death of the Duke of Marlborough. However, within the allied armies, Sackville was junior to Prince Ferdinand of Brunswick. At the Battle of Minden (August 1, 1759), poor communication between Ferdinand and Sackville, and Sackville's own hesitance to commit his cavalry to the battle, prevented a complete rout of the French. Sackville received most of the blame for this

failure and had to resign from the army, while George II publicly humiliated him and dismissed him from all government positions.

If Sackville became a political pariah under George II, in part it was because he had already attached himself to the interests of the prince of Wales. When GEORGE III came to the throne, Sackville's political rehabilitation began, and he gradually gained favor at court and was given new offices. During the early 1770s, Germain—his newly adopted name—developed a political alliance with LORD NORTH, who was the king's chief minister, and in November 1775 Germain became secretary of state for the North American colonies, which meant that he was responsible for the management of the Revolutionary War. Although he was an able administrator and developed some sound strategy, he did not push his ideas hard enough on the generals in the field, and he therefore shares in the responsibility for the misdirection in British conduct during the conflict. In particular, his failure to insist that General WILLIAM HOWE operate in concert with General JOHN BURGOYNE's invasion of New York led to the British fiasco at SARATOGA in October 1777. Germain often made decisions based on information he wanted to hear. The result was that he supported the southern strategy that led to the invasion of South Carolina in 1780 because he believed that there were many LOYALISTS in the region. He also favored some generals—LORD CORNWALLIS and Burgoyne—over others—Howe, HENRY CLINTON, and GUY CARLETON.

After Cornwallis's disastrous surrender at YORKTOWN (October 19, 1781), Germain's position became untenable, and he resigned from the government in February 1782. He was then elevated to the peerage as the first viscount Sackville. Retired from politics, he died on August 26, 1785.

German Flats, attack on (September 13, 1778)

During the REVOLUTIONARY WAR (1775–83), JOSEPH BRANT led a party of 150 NATIVE AMERICANS and 300 LOYALISTS in an attack on German Flats (present-day Herkimer, New York), a Mohawk Valley community of about 70 homes. Warned by a scout, most of the settlers found safety in two forts and a church. The raiders killed only three civilians, but they burned 63 homes, 57 barns, three gristmills, and one saw mill. They also destroyed grain and fodder and took away hundreds of horses, cattle, and sheep. This attack was just one in a series of raids and counter raids along the New York–IROQUOIS FRONTIER.

—Catherine Franklin

Germantown, Battle of (October 4, 1777)

After the Continental defeat at the BATTLE OF BRANDYWINE (September 11, 1777) and the British occupation of Philadelphia (September 26, 1777), General GEORGE WASHINGTON sought to make up for the CONTINENTAL ARMY's setbacks and force General WILLIAM HOWE to retreat by launching a surprise attack at Germantown, Pennsylvania. Howe, on his part, may have been too confident because he did not entrench his position and had deployed his troops widely in Pennsylvania and New Jersey near Philadelphia. Washington, however, developed an overly complicated plan: He ordered four separate columns to march on the British position at night for a coordinated assault in the morning. With the best troops, such a maneuver would have been difficult, but with poorly trained Continentals and MILITIA, it was courting disaster.

The first of Washington's men stumbled into British sentries about 4:00 A.M., easily pushing them back. However, it was unusually foggy that morning, and confusion began to reign on both sides. Washington's columns did not attack together, with one division even firing into another, and the militia never came up into position. At a crucial moment in the battle, the disciplined British shored up their line and brought in reinforcements. Confronted with this defense, running out of ammunition, and confused by the smoke and fog, some of Washington's soldiers began to withdraw. The panic spread, and soon the whole army was in retreat. The battle lasted under three hours. Each side had put about 8,000 men in the field: Howe lost about 500 men, Washington lost some 1,000 killed, wounded, and captured. Nonetheless, he was convinced that had they persisted just a little longer, his men would have been victorious.

Gerry, Elbridge (1744–1814) *signer of the Declaration of Independence and the Articles of Confederation, diplomat, U.S. vice president*

One of the revolutionary era's most dedicated politicians and a signer of the DECLARATION OF INDEPENDENCE, Elbridge Gerry was born in Marblehead, Massachusetts, on July 17, 1744. The third of 12 children, Gerry was son of a wealthy, respectable, and politically active father. In 1758 he entered Harvard College, from which he graduated in 1762. He then joined his father's business, exporting dried fish to British colonies in the Caribbean.

Gerry's political career began after the BOSTON MASSACRE (March 5, 1770) when Marblehead residents elected him town inspector to enforce an ongoing boycott of British imports protesting imperial regulation. In 1772 he was elected to the colonial legislature, where SAMUEL ADAMS befriended him. Gerry, who served in the SECOND CONTINENTAL CONGRESS between 1776 and 1785, used the imperial crisis and the REVOLUTIONARY WAR (1775–83) to bolster his political and economic fortunes. During the war he combined public service with private profit, and after a quarrel over the prices paid to military suppliers in which

he had a personal stake as a supplier himself, he walked out of Congress and did not attend for three years. Throughout the contest he invested heavily in privateers and trading ventures.

During the CONSTITUTIONAL CONVENTION in 1787, Gerry participated in many debates. Although at times he appeared inconsistent and, according to some wits, "objected to everything he did not propose," he sought to stifle the effort to create a powerful central government because he believed it would threaten the people's liberties and undermine state independence. He signed the U.S. CONSTITUTION despite his own opposition to it, but then worked against its ratification in Massachusetts. Once the Constitution came into force, Gerry put aside his concerns and served in the House of Representatives from 1789 to 1793. There, too, he reversed himself: At first he seemed to support the strong central government policies of the FEDERALIST PARTY, but he came to back the pro-French and weaker central government policies of the DEMOCRATIC-REPUBLICAN PARTY.

In 1797 President JOHN ADAMS, who was a friend of Gerry's, appointed him as the non–Federalist Party member of the delegation sent to FRANCE to negotiate an end to the seizures of U.S. shipping. Before the negotiations could begin, agents for CHARLES-MAURICE TALLEYRAND-PÉRIGORD demanded a bribe. When news of this diplomatic affront, subsequently called the XYZ AFFAIR (1797–98), reached the United States, the nation began to prepare for war and engaged in a series of naval battles with the French in the QUASI-WAR (1798–1800). In April 1798, Talleyrand ordered the two other U.S. delegates—CHARLES COTESWORTH PINCKNEY and JOHN MARSHALL—to leave France and allowed Gerry to remain, hoping to manipulate him into concessions because of his pro-French sympathies. Gerry did not yield any ground, but he did seek to find some softening in the French position. Fortunately, by the time he returned to the United States in October 1798, he could report to Adams that Talleyrand was ready to negotiate a serious agreement. Receiving similar reports from other U.S. diplomats in Europe, Adams sent a new delegation to France, which ultimately agreed to the CONVENTION OF 1800, ending the Quasi-War.

After the XYZ affair, Gerry became active in partisan politics on the state level and was one of the leaders of the DEMOCRATIC-REPUBLICAN PARTY in Massachusetts. He ran for governor four times before he was finally elected in 1810. During his second term he supported Democratic-Republican redistricting measures, and Federalist opponents coined the term GERRYMANDERING to describe the practice of altering voting district boundaries to favor one party. Although frail in health, Gerry was elected JAMES MADISON's vice president in 1812. He collapsed and died on his way to the Senate on November 23, 1814.

Further reading: George Athan Billias, *Elbridge Gerry: Founding Father and Republican Statesman* (New York: McGraw-Hill, 1976); William Stinchcombe, *The XYZ Affair* (Westport, Conn.: Greenwood Press, 1980).

gerrymandering

Gerrymandering is the practice by which a political party rearranges the boundaries of electoral districts to ensure the future election of party members. Usually it means allowing the opposing political party to have an overwhelming majority in a limited number of election districts and providing for slimmer—but certain—majorities in a larger number of districts. The term *gerrymandering* emerged in 1811 in Massachusetts after the DEMOCRATIC-REPUBLICAN PARTY finally gained control of both houses of the state legislature and the governorship, which was won by ELBRIDGE GERRY. The Democratic-Republican legislature redrew state senate boundaries and congressional boundaries to ensure that candidates from their party would win. Members of the FEDERALIST PARTY were outraged by this practice, although it had existed in some instances since the colonial period. When an artist in the Federalist Party drew a map of an electoral district in Essex County, the twists and turns looked something like a salamander, a description that was quickly altered to "Gerrymander" to mock the Democratic-Republican governor. Although Gerry signed the bill creating the electoral districts into law, he did not draft the bill and actually considered the measure—at least according to his son-in-law—as "exceedingly disagreeable." Whatever Gerry's opinion, the name stuck and has been used in U.S. politics ever since.

Further reading: George Athan Billias, *Elbridge Gerry: Founding Father and Republican Statesman* (New York: McGraw-Hill, 1976).

Ghent, Treaty of (1814)

The Treaty of Ghent was the peace agreement that ended the WAR OF 1812 (1812–15). Although it did not change any boundaries and did not address the issues that triggered the war, it was considered a diplomatic triumph by many in the United States and trumpeted as signaling the success of the republic in not only surviving but persevering in a war with the most powerful nation in the world—GREAT BRITAIN.

The British had agreed to direct negotiations to end the war as early as November 1813, but it took until August 1814 before both sides were ready to talk. In the meantime, the British naval blockade, stalled campaigns in CANADA, British occupation of northern Maine, and the burning of WASHINGTON, D.C., gave the British an advantage. Eager to end this unpopular and unsuccessful conflict, the United States sent major political figures such as JOHN QUINCY ADAMS, JAMES BAYARD, HENRY CLAY, JONATHAN RUSSELL, and ALBERT GALLATIN to Ghent. There they encountered two British unknowns, since the British foreign secretary, Lord Castlereagh (see CASTLEREAGH, ROBERT STEWART, SECOND VISCOUNT) was preoccupied with the preparation for the Congress of Vienna. Confident of their military superiority, the British delegation demanded removal of U.S. FISHING rights off Newfoundland, free British access to the Mississippi River, U.S. demilitarization of the Great Lakes, and finally the establishment of a Native American state northwest of the Ohio River. The U.S. delegation refused these demands, and by October, news of British defeats at Lake Champlain, and Baltimore had undermined the British position. They were therefore willing to settle for keeping all of the territory that each side occupied—a solution that left the British with Fort Niagara, Mackinaw Island, and parts of Maine and gave the United States a few square miles of captured outposts in the Great Lakes region. The British position, however, continued to deteriorate as U.S. privateers and naval vessels attacked their shipping and increased INSURANCE costs. Moreover, there remained the threat of further hostilities in Europe. A final compromise was worked out in December 1814: Boundaries would revert to prewar lines, and the British would give up their demands to control the Great Lakes and to create a Native American state. The U.S. diplomats compromised by omitting the fisheries question, concerns about the IMPRESSMENT of SEAMEN, and the rights of neutral commerce. The treaty also provided for joint commissions to negotiate outstanding boundary issues, making it a diplomatic victory for the United States. It was signed at Ghent on December, 24, 1814, and ratified by the U.S. Senate in February 1815.

The real losers of the agreement were the NATIVE AMERICANS, many of whom had fought as British allies in the hope of being rewarded with an independent country of their own. The treaty did stipulate that any territory taken from Native Americans by the United States during the conflict would be returned to them, but this provision was not complied with. The loss of British support left the Indians between the Appalachians and the Mississippi River little choice but to sign peace treaties with the United States.

News of the treaty did not reach North America quickly. Unaware that the war had ended, General ANDREW JACKSON successfully fought the BATTLE OF NEW ORLEANS (January 8, 1815) against the British in the war's most famous and unnecessary battle. Since the news of the treaty and the victory arrived simultaneously, many people in the United States enthusiastically embraced them both, feeling their national pride and honor were restored.

Further reading: Fred L. Engelman, *The Peace of Christmas Eve* (New York: Harcourt, Brace & World, 1962).

Gibbon, Edward (1737–1794) *British historian, writer*
Edward Gibbon was a member of the propertied class in England, although his family struggled with the loss of much of its fortune. Born in Putnam, Surrey, and educated at Westminster School and Oxford, and in Switzerland, Gibbon served in Parliament, generally supporting LORD NORTH. His real claim to fame, however, was as one of the great figures of the English ENLIGHTENMENT and as the author of *The Decline and Fall of the Roman Empire* (1776–88). ADAM SMITH declared that the book "by the universal assent of every man of taste and learning" placed Gibbon "at the very head of the whole literary tribe at present existing in Europe."

Gibbon's work epitomized enlightened thinking about history. Based on extensive reading tempered with Enlightenment views, the author sought to approach history scientifically and to detect patterns in the development of nations. He famously claimed that his interest in the history of Rome came from his grand tour of Europe and his visit to Italy. While musing on the ruins of the Capitol, Gibbon wanted to learn how a once-great civilization could have succumbed to the ravages of barbarians. Like most Enlightenment thinkers, he believed that cycles of history were governed by scientific laws. Ultimately, Rome's failure came from a corruption born out of its success as an empire.

Gibbon applied to a specific historic example what most European and North American thinkers already believed: that nations rise, decline, and fall, following an inevitable pattern. These ideas underpinned the REPUBLICANISM of the revolutionary movement in the British North American colonies, although Gibbon's first volume appeared in February 1776, after fighting had already begun in the REVOLUTIONARY WAR (1775–83). He died in London on January 16, 1794.

Giles, William Branch (1762–1830) *politician, governor of Virginia*
A Virginia politician, William Branch Giles was a supporter of the DEMOCRATIC-REPUBLICAN PARTY and played an important part into the development of party politics in the 1790s and early 1800s. He was born in Amelia County, Virginia, trained as a lawyer, and was a student of GEORGE WYTHE. Elected to the House of Representatives in 1790, he worked alongside JAMES MADISON in establishing Democratic-Republican opposition to the FEDERALIST PARTY. In one instance, he accused ALEXANDER HAMILTON of misconduct and attempted to bring IMPEACHMENT charges against him. Though this resolution failed, Giles remained a fierce critic of the Federalist Party's government and resigned from Congress in 1798 in protest over the ALIEN AND SEDITION ACTS (1798).

Giles served briefly in Virginia's House of Delegates, where he supported Madison's VIRGINIA RESOLVES (1798), before returning to Congress following the ELECTION OF 1800. From 1803 to 1815, he represented Virginia in the Senate. During the impeachment trial of U.S. SUPREME COURT justice SAMUEL CHASE, Giles argued that Chase no longer represented the will of the people, who now supported Democratic-Republicans, and should be removed as a result. This argument failed to convince Giles's colleagues, and Chase retained his position. Eventually, Giles became even more radical in his political beliefs, joining a minority Democratic-Republican faction that opposed President Madison and heavily criticized the executive branch during the WAR OF 1812 (1812–15).

Giles retired from the Senate in 1815 and returned to Virginia, where he was elected to the House of Delegates and as governor for three terms. Until his death on December 4, 1830, he opposed the extension of federal power overriding states' needs, and he published several political essays.

Further reading: Dice Robins Anderson, *William Branch Giles: A Study in the Politics of Virginia and the Nation from 1790 to 1830* (Menasha, Wis.: G. Banta Publishing Co., 1914).

—Tash Smith

Gill, Joseph-Louis (Magouaovidombaouit) (1719–1798) *Abenaki chief, religious leader*
The child of two European-American captives of the Abenaki Indians, Joseph-Louis Gill became a major Abenaki chief and religious leader in the 18th century. During the FRENCH AND INDIAN WAR (1754–63), he survived an attack on his village near Quebec led by ROBERT ROGERS in 1757, but his wife and one of his sons died after they were captured. By the end of the war he had accepted the British conquest of CANADA and became a mediator between the Abenaki and the British government. Gill remarried and ran a store in the Abenaki country. The REVOLUTIONARY WAR (1775–83) posed new problems for him as he sought to steer the Abenaki on a delicate path of seeming to support the British while not entirely alienating the revolutionaries. Because of his success, he and the Abenaki were able to sustain themselves in British Canada at the end of the war.

Further reading: Colin G. Calloway, *The American Revolution in Indian Country: Crisis and Diversity on Native American Communities* (Cambridge, U.K.: Cambridge University Press, 1995).

Gilman, Nicholas (1755–1814) *New Hampshire politician*

A maverick politician from New Hampshire, Nicholas Gilman was born into a mercantile family, served in the CONTINENTAL ARMY as a junior officer during the REVOLUTIONARY WAR (1775–83), and was a delegate to the SECOND CONTINENTAL CONGRESS from 1786 to 1788. He also attended the CONSTITUTIONAL CONVENTION in Philadelphia, and though he did not actively participate in the convention debates, he supported the creation of a stronger national government. Beginning in 1789, he served four terms in the House of Representatives. During the early 1790s, Gilman generally supported the FEDERALIST PARTY by advocating the creation of the BANK OF THE UNITED STATES and a federal court system, but he opposed the assumption of state debts and JAY'S TREATY (1794). Recognizing that his politics did not always coincide with his constituents' views, he did not seek reelection in 1796. He gradually drifted toward the DEMOCRATIC-REPUBLICAN PARTY, and in 1802 President THOMAS JEFFERSON appointed him a bankruptcy commissioner. In the same year, Gilman failed in his bid for a seat in the Senate, but he was selected as a senator in 1804 and again in 1810. However, he followed his own political path and opposed the EMBARGO OF 1807 as well as the United States's entry into the WAR OF 1812 (1812–15). He also turned his back on JAMES MADISON and supported DeWITT CLINTON for president in 1812. Gilman died on May 2, 1814, before the completion of his second term in the Senate.

Girard, Stephen (1750–1831) *businessman, entrepreneur*

Stephen Girard was a wealthy merchant, banker, investor, and philanthropist in Philadelphia during the early republic. Born on May 20, 1750, in Bordeaux, FRANCE, Girard arrived in New York in 1774 as the son of a successful ship captain and merchant. He quickly established himself in the mercantile field in New York and spent the next few years sailing between New York and the WEST INDIES. During the REVOLUTIONARY WAR (1775–83), he relocated to Philadelphia, where he built a very successful trading business and became one of the wealthiest persons in the United States by 1810. Between 1807 and 1812, he faced financial complications due to the EMBARGO OF 1807 and the escalating tension between the United States and GREAT BRITAIN. However, he successfully liquidated most of his holdings in Europe and turned to domestic banking. In 1812 he opened the Girard Bank in the building that had housed the late BANK OF THE UNITED STATES, using $1.2 million of his own capital. The Girard Bank operated between 1812 and 1832 as a privately owned bank, without a state charter. Nevertheless, it achieved financial parity with the other major Philadelphia BANKS by 1816.

Girard also played a pivotal role in financing the WAR OF 1812 (1812–15). Along with merchants David Parish and JOHN JACOB ASTOR, he invested approximately $10 million in government stock to fund the war effort in 1813. He also used his political influence and financial holdings to support the successful effort to establish a Second Bank of the United States in 1816. Girard distinguished himself in his service to the people of Philadelphia by caring for patients and funding YELLOW FEVER relief efforts in the 1790s. In his will, he left substantial funds for the operation of a home for orphaned boys in Philadelphia, which would become known as Girard College. He died on December 26, 1831, with no immediate family and left most of his $7.5 million estate to the city of Philadelphia.

Further reading: Donald R. Adams, Jr., *Finance and Enterprise in Early America: A Study of Stephen Girard's Bank, 1812–1831* (Philadelphia: University of Pennsylvania Press, 1978); Belden L. Daniels, *Pennsylvania: Birthplace of Banking* (Harrisburg: Pennsylvania Bankers Association, 1976).

Girty, Simon (1741–1818) *soldier, Indian agent*

Simon Girty became one of the most reviled figures in FRONTIER history after deserting to join the British in the REVOLUTIONARY WAR (1775–83). In reality Girty was an individual who served as a cultural broker between the European-American and Native American worlds.

Girty, whose parents were from GREAT BRITAIN, began his life caught between two cultures when NATIVE AMERICANS captured him during the FRENCH AND INDIAN WAR (1754–63) at the surrender of Fort Granville in central Pennsylvania in 1756. For the next three years Girty was an adopted captive of the western SENECA, learning the native language and gaining a reputation as a hunter. After the British victory in the war, Girty returned to the European-American world, living on the Pennsylvania frontier as a hunter, trader, and interpreter. He also gained a working knowledge of the DELAWARE and SHAWNEE language. He thus used his experience with the Indians to serve as a cultural broker.

During the opening years of the War for Independence, he continued his role as an intermediary between two cultures as an Indian agent and sought to maintain the neutrality of the Native Americans in the upper Ohio River Valley. However, by 1778 Girty became disenchanted with the revolutionaries, believing that he had been unfairly treated and poorly rewarded for his services. Along with several other discontent frontiersmen, including two of his brothers, Girty left FORT PITT on March 28, 1778 and headed for DETROIT to join the British.

By switching sides and fighting along side the Indians and British during the remainder of the war, Girty was deemed a traitor. Pennsylvania even placed a bounty on his head. The British, however, valued Girty's efforts with the Indians. Often donning native CLOTHING while with the Indians, Girty was in the thick of the fighting in the Ohio country for the remainder of the war, including the BATTLE OF BLUE LICKS (August 19, 1782). Although blamed for several atrocities, such as the murder of JOHN CRAWFORD, Girty actually came to the aid of a number of European-American captives. He continued to serve as a British agent in the Northwest after 1783, and joined the Indians in the defeat of Gen. ARTHUR ST. CLAIR in 1791. He watched, but did not participate in, the BATTLE OF FALLEN TIMBERS (August 20, 1794).

After the British withdrawal from the Northwest in 1796, Girty settled on land near the mouth of the Detroit River in CANADA. He remained there most of the rest of his life raising his family. Unfortunately he often drank heavily and suffered a variety of ailments until his death on February 18, 1818.

Further reading: Colin G. Calloway, "Simon Girty: Interpreter and Intermediary," in *Being and Becoming Indian: Biographical Studies of North American Frontiers*, edited by James A. Clifton (Chicago: Dorsey, 1989), 38–58.
—Stephen A. Martin

Gist, Christopher (1706–1759) *Colonial American trader, surveyor, guide*
Christopher Gist holds the distinction of being one of the first European-American men to explore the Ohio Country. Born in Baltimore, Gist was one of three sons of Richard and Zipporah Gist. His father was part of the team that surveyed the land for what would soon become the city of Baltimore. Gist himself became a surveyor, and in 1750, while living in North Carolina, he received orders from the OHIO COMPANY OF VIRGINIA to survey the country surrounding the Ohio River between Shannopin's Town (now Pittsburgh) and Louisville, Kentucky. He spent the winter of 1751 exploring, surveying, and mapping the area between the Monogahela and Great Kanawha Rivers in present-day West Virginia. His writings provide some of the first descriptions of the Ohio Country and the NATIVE AMERICANS who lived there.

In November 1751 Governor Robert Dinwiddie of Virginia ordered Major GEORGE WASHINGTON to travel to Fort Le Boeuf and instruct the French to relinquish their posts in the Ohio Country so that British colonists could settle the area. Gist accompanied Washington on this expedition.

Gist continued to act as Washington's personal guide during the first few years of the FRENCH AND INDIAN WAR (1754–63), sharing in Washington's success at the BATTLE OF JUMONVILLE GLEN (May 28, 1754) and his defeat at the surrender of FORT NECESSITY (July 4, 1754). In 1756 he traveled to Eastern Tennessee to ask the CHEROKEE to join the British and fight against the French. Though he failed to gain Cherokee recruits, he stayed on in the area as the regional Indian agent. In 1759 Christopher Gist died of SMALLPOX in either South Carolina or Georgia.

Further reading: Christopher Gist, *Christopher Gist's Journals with Historical, Geographic, and Ethnological Notes and Biographies of His Contemporaries,* edited by William M. Darlington (New York: Argonaut Press, 1966).
—Emily R. Wardrop

Glaize, the (Auglaize) (September 30, 1792–April, 1793)
In late 1792 and early 1793, large delegations of IROQUOIS and Algonquian Indians gathered at Auglaize, on the Miami River of Lake Erie near what is today Defiance, Ohio. Also called "the Glaize," this location was an old buffalo wallow that effectively became the headquarters for a confederacy of NATIVE AMERICANS whose meetings represented a high-water mark in unified Indian opposition to the expansion of the United States. Those who assembled at Auglaize discussed two important matters: continued war against the United States and the possibility of establishing a permanent boundary line between Indian country and the United States. While the SHAWNEE, who were largely in favor of maintaining hostile relations with the U.S. government, took charge of the proceedings, many members of the Iroquois, who favored a peaceful resolution, also participated in the negotiations. The Shawnee were bolstered by victories over Generals JOSIAH HARMAR in 1790 and ARTHUR ST. CLAIR in 1791, and they were confident of aid from the British. Therefore, they rejected RED JACKET's call for a peaceful settlement and instead offered a temporary peace through the winter if the U.S. ARMY withdrew west of the Ohio River.

Even more Indians gathered at a second meeting near the Miami rapids in February 1793, declaring their intention to reject any treaty that did not recognize the Ohio River as the boundary between the United States and Indian country. Many of the Algonquian delegations spoke against the Iroquois's powerful and accomodationist representatives in an attempt to unify all Native Americans against U.S. designs on the Ohio country. Stipulating that the federal commissioners would not be allowed into a spring council without having agreed in writing to the Ohio River boundary, the Indians effectively preempted U.S. participation. This position virtually assured British influence during the deliberations and greatly undercut JOSEPH

BRANT's attempt to reach a compromise between the Indians and the United States.

The debates that raged at Auglaize in 1792 and 1793 ultimately had little permanent impact on Indian relations with the United States. The Native-American defeat at the BATTLE OF FALLEN TIMBERS (August 20, 1794) dramatically changed the military situation, especially when the British army refused to aid or protect Indians after the battle. Subsequently, U.S. negotiators opened up much of Ohio to European-American settlement after the TREATY OF GREENVILLE (1795).

Further reading: Helen Hornbeck Tanuev. "The Glaize in 1792: A Composite Indian Community." *Ethnohistory* 25, no. 1 (Winter 1978): 15–39. Richard White, *The Middle Ground: Indians, Empires, and Republics in the Great Lakes Region, 1650–1815* (New York: Cambridge University Press, 1991).

—Patrick Bottiger

Gloucester, John (1776–1822) *Presbyterian minister*

Beginning his life in SLAVERY in eastern Tennessee, John Gloucester was purchased by Gideon Blackburn, a European-American Presbyterian minister who trained him to preach to slaves. In 1807 Blackburn brought Gloucester with him to Philadelphia, where European-American PRESBYTERIANS, who wanted to reach out to the black community, were impressed with the slave as a preacher. Although it would take two years for the Philadelphia Presbyterians to negotiate Gloucester's freedom, license him, and build a church, he started almost immediately to preach to the African-American community in the city. By 1810 he had become the official minister of the First African Presbyterian Church in Philadelphia, and the next year the congregation had its own building. Gloucester also continued as an itinerant preacher and worked most of the rest of his life to raise enough money to purchase his wife and six children, who were still in Tennessee. He accomplished this goal in 1819.

See also AFRICAN AMERICANS; BLACK CHURCH MOVEMENT.

Further reading: Gary B. Nash, *Forging Freedom: The Formation of Philadelphia's Black Community, 1740–1840* (Cambridge, Mass.: Harvard University Press, 1988).

Glover, John (1732–1797) *Continental army general*

Born in Salem, Massachusetts, on November 5, 1732, and suffering the death of his father when he was only four, John Glover worked his way from being a shoemaker and fisherman in Marblehead, Massachusetts, to being a

Sailor and officer John Glover is considered to have been one of the most accomplished soldiers of the Revolutionary War. *(New York Public Library)*

shipowner and minor merchant by the eve of the REVOLUTIONARY WAR (1775–83). Glover became a member of Marblehead's COMMITTEE OF CORRESPONDENCE in 1772, but in 1773 and 1774 he lost popular support because of his advocacy, along with that of ELBRIDGE GERRY, for establishing a hospital for SMALLPOX inoculation. Only in late 1774 did he once again become active in revolutionary politics by joining the committee of inspection set up under the ASSOCIATION.

Glover was also in the Marblehead MILITIA, and soon after the BATTLES OF LEXINGTON AND CONCORD (April 19, 1775), he was commanding his hometown's regiment. That summer the unit joined the siege of Boston but did not see much action. However, Glover's Marbleheaders formed the nucleus of the small navy that General GEORGE WASHINGTON created to harass the British army's maritime supply lines in Boston. Glover's regiment, which became a regular part of the CONTINENTAL ARMY in January 1776, joined Washington's army in the defense of New York. The Marbleheaders' skill with boats was crucial in the evacuation from Brooklyn Heights after the Continentals' defeat in the BATTLE OF LONG ISLAND (August 27–30, 1776), and the regiment delayed the British effort to cut off Washington's army in Manhattan at the BATTLE OF PELL'S POINT (October 18, 1776). The Marbleheaders' most famous action was in ferrying Washington's army across the ice-choked Delaware on Christmas night, setting up his surprise victories at the BATTLES OF TRENTON AND PRINCETON (December 26, 1776, and January 3, 1777). However, the regiment's enlistment expired a few weeks later, and Glover and his men returned home.

With a sick wife (she would die within a year) and failing personal fortunes, Glover rejected a promotion from colonel to brigadier general in February 1777, though he later accepted the offer after a personal appeal from George Washington. He was given command of a brigade in the fighting at SARATOGA (October 17, 1777) and fought at the BATTLE OF RHODE ISLAND (August 29, 1779) but spent most of the war stationed in the Hudson Highlands. He left the army in 1782 to restore his business interests. At first he struggled because he was cash poor, although he had MONEY invested in real estate and held government securities. By the time of his death on January 30, 1797, Glover was worth about $14,000.

Further reading: George Athan Billias, *General John Glover and His Marblehead Mariners* (New York: Henry Holt and Company, 1960).

Gnadenhutten massacre (March 7–8, 1782)

Gnadenhutten was a town founded in 1772 by MORAVIAN missionaries for NATIVE AMERICANS in eastern Ohio. Its 50–60 cabins housed several hundred DELAWARE and other Christian Indians who farmed and sought to remain neutral during the REVOLUTIONARY WAR (1775–83). These Indians lived better than most European-American frontiersmen and had glass in their windows, pots and pans, and even a piano in their community. If anything, the Christian Indians seemed to favor the United States in the war because they often supplied local officials with information about the activities of the British and their allied Indians. Concerned about these contacts, the British compelled the Gnadenhutten Indians to abandon their prosperous settlement in September 1781 but gave permission to a group of them to return in early 1782 to obtain food and supplies. At about the same time, a party of Pennsylvania MILITIA entered the area in search of Indians who had raided European-American settlements during the summer of 1781. Unable to find the hostile Indians, the Pennsylvania men stumbled into Gnadenhutten on March 7, 1782, and seized its Christian Indians. The militiamen held a mock tribunal to determine the Native Americans' guilt, and since the Indians had kettles, CLOTHING, and various goods that the militia believed only European Americans could own, they concluded that the Gnadenhutten Indians had to be guilty

of the raids on Pennsylvania. Ninety-six Indians—all the men, women, and children in the town—were sentenced to die and locked in their cabins overnight. The next morning was a bloodbath as the Pennsylvania militia took wooden mallets and crushed the Indians' skulls and then scalped them. After the slaughter, the Pennsylvanians burned the town's buildings to the ground. During the same campaign, the militia raided several SHAWNEE towns, raping and killing women and murdering children. This path of destruction further antagonized the Native Americans in the Ohio area, intensifying the war on the FRONTIER.

Further reading: Earl P. Olmsted, *Blackcoats among the Delaware: David Zeisberger on the Ohio Frontier* (Kent, Ohio: Kent University Press, 1991).

Golden Hill, Battle of (January 18, 1770)

In January 1770 a series of confrontations between New York civilians and British soldiers that had taken place over several years culminated in a riot in which the two groups fought each other in the street. This disturbance is popularly known as the Battle of Golden Hill. There were no fatalities, but several on both sides were injured. This disturbance demonstrated how local issues such as competition over jobs could be given a larger ideological meaning within the context of the imperial crisis.

To commemorate the repeal of the STAMP ACT (1765), the New York SONS OF LIBERTY organized a celebration of the birthday of King GEORGE III in June 1766, centered around a flagstaff erected on the city's common and parade ground. Within days of this holiday, the New York assembly refused to comply with the QUARTERING ACT (1765), and suddenly the flagstaff became a symbol of colonial opposition to the presence of British troops. Recognizing the significance of this symbol, British soldiers cut the pole down on the night of August 10, 1766. New Yorkers were outraged by this attack on their "Tree of Liberty" and put up a new pole shortly thereafter. Further confrontations followed through August and September, but the pole remained in place. On March 18, 1767, New Yorkers held their celebration of the anniversary of the Stamp Act repeal around their LIBERTY POLE; the following night, British soldiers chopped it down. New Yorkers erected a new pole, and several more confrontations ensued, but the pole remained in place until January 1770.

That winter there were several major controversies swirling through the colony of New York. Opposition to the TOWNSHEND DUTIES (1767) had finally gained momentum, and a nonimportation movement had begun to succeed. New Yorkers were also agitated over the treatment of ALEXANDER MCDOUGALL, who had been imprisoned for his outspoken opposition to the New York assembly's compliance with the Quartering Act. Furthermore, many workers found it difficult to obtain employment in the middle of the winter with a sluggish ECONOMY. Making matters worse was the fact that off-duty British soldiers competed for jobs, laboring for as little as half the pay of a civilian. On January 16, 1770, New York WHIGS issued broadsides complaining about the presence of the British army and suggesting that merchants and other employers should show "care and benevolence" to their neighbors and not hire any redcoats. Angered by the broadside, British soldiers destroyed the liberty pole that night, and the next day they printed their own handbill. Two New Yorkers seized two soldiers distributing the broadside, intending to turn over their prisoners to the authorities. A group of soldiers came to rescue their comrades, and the confrontation quickly escalated into a riot. Scores of soldiers and civilians fought until officers and local officials parted the two sides. The next day, New Yorkers patrolled the waterfront, beating any soldiers they found working at jobs that should have gone to civilians.

See also RESISTANCE MOVEMENT; RIOTS.

Further reading: Paul A. Gilje, *The Road to Mobocracy: Popular Disorder in New York City, 1763–1834* (Chapel Hill: University of North Carolina Press, 1987).

Gordon, William (1728–1807) *Congregationalist minister, writer*
A dissenting clergyman in England, William Gordon moved in 1770 to Massachusetts, where he became a minister to the Third Congregational Church in Roxbury and an ardent supporter of the AMERICAN REVOLUTION. In 1776 he decided that he would write a history of the REVOLUTIONARY WAR (1775–83), and throughout the conflict he collected documents and interviewed leaders for his project, even traveling to New York to see HORATIO GATES and GEORGE WASHINGTON. In 1786 Gordon left Roxbury and returned to England, where he obtained a new congregation and served as a minister until 1802. His *History of the Rise, Progress, and Establishment of the Independence of the United States of America* appeared in 1788 in GREAT BRITAIN and in 1789 in the United States. Although Gordon strove for impartiality, his book had a prorevolutionary bias and became one of the leading works on the war for over a century. JOHN MARSHALL relied heavily on Gordon's work in his biography of George Washington.

Gore, Christopher (1758–1827) *lawyer, Federalist Party politician, diplomat*
Born in Boston, Massachusetts, Christopher Gore was an influential lawyer, politician, and member of the FEDER-

ALIST PARTY. After graduating from Harvard College in 1776, he supported the AMERICAN REVOLUTION by working as a clerk for the CONTINENTAL ARMY, even though his father was a LOYALIST. During the 1780s and 1790s, Gore became a lawyer with a lucrative practice. He also engaged in shrewd speculation in government securities, bought stock in the BANK OF THE UNITED STATES, and invested in INSURANCE companies. He always feared the radicalism of lower classes and advocated a strong centralized government that would foster Massachusetts's ECONOMY, particularly the interests of merchants, by protecting TRADE with GREAT BRITAIN. His sympathies were shared by his close friend RUFUS KING, Daniel Webster, and others who eventually formed the Federalist Party.

Gore's political career began with his appointment to the state constitutional convention of 1788, where he supported the ratification of the U.S. CONSTITUTION. He was also a member of the Massachusetts House of Representatives in 1788–89. In 1789 GEORGE WASHINGTON appointed him as U.S. district attorney for Massachusetts, and seven years later the president made him commissioner to England. The London Commission, established by JAY'S TREATY (1794), called for great diplomacy in settling disputes between Great Britain and the United States regarding violations of international maritime laws. Gore returned to the United States in 1804 and served in the Massachusetts senate before being elected the state's governor in 1809. He lost the next year's election to ELBRIDGE GERRY but in 1813 was appointed to the U.S. Senate, where he served for three years. He devoted the rest of his life to the study of AGRICULTURE as a gentleman farmer. He died on March 1, 1827, in Waltham, Massachusetts.

Further reading: Helen R. Pinkney, *Christopher Gore, Federalist of Massachusetts* (Portland: Anthoeson Press, 1969); David Hackett Fischer, *The Revolution of American Conservatism, The Federalist Party in the Era of Jeffersonian Democracy* (New York: Harper & Row, 1965).

—Mary Kaszynski

Gorham, Nathaniel (1738–1796) *merchant, politician*
Nathaniel Gorham was born in Charlestown, Massachusetts, on May 27, 1738. The eldest of five children, he left home for six years as an apprentice to a New London, Connecticut, merchant. In his early 20s, Gorham returned to Charlestown and became a successful local businessman. His opposition to British colonial economic policies earned him a seat in the Massachusetts House of Representatives in 1771. He served in various roles in both the colonial and state legislatures throughout the

1770s and 1780s, including as speaker of the house three times (1781, 1782, and 1785).

Starting in 1782, Gorham represented Massachusetts in the Second Continental Congress, where he promoted a strong central government in regard to commerce and banking issues. Under the Articles of Confederation, he served as the eighth president of the United States in Congress Assembled from June 6 to November 5, 1786. Prior to his involvement at the Constitutional Convention in 1787, Gorham advocated states' rights; however, he changed his stance during the convention, favoring compromise with the southern states in regard to slavery.

After failing to win reelection to the Massachusetts legislature in 1788, Gorham retired from public life in 1789. By the late 1780s, he had become deeply involved in land speculation, though the federal government's economic policies thwarted his efforts. He and his partner, Oliver Phelps, contracted to purchase 6 million acres of Massachusetts land in what is now western New York State at depreciated prices, but federal assumption of states' debts resulted in higher prices for the land. Bankrupt, Gorham died in Charlestown on June 11, 1796.

Further reading: John Collier and James Lincoln Collier, *Decision in Philadelphia: The Constitutional Convention of 1787* (New York: Random House, 1986); Merrill T. Jensen, *The Documentary History of the Ratification of the Constitution* (Madison: State Historical Society of Wisconsin, 1976).

—Daniel Flaherty

Graham, Isabella (Isabella Marshall Graham) (1742–1814) *reformer*

Isabella Graham was a leading reformer in early New York City. She was born Isabella Marshall in Scotland on July 29, 1742, married a military doctor in 1765, and went to Canada about a year later. She lived on the frontier at Fort Niagara for several years before moving to the West Indies, where her husband died in 1774. Left largely to her own devices, Graham returned to Great Britain with three young children and established a school there. In 1789 she immigrated to New York and opened another school. She retired in the late 1790s, having made a good real estate investment and after her daughters were all married. At that point, with an adequate income and middle-class respectability, Graham devoted herself full-time to charitable work, hoping not only to aid the poor but also to encourage industry and reform society. In 1797 she helped to organize the Society for the Relief of Poor Widows with Small Children, the first women's benevolent society in the United States. Her work was inspired by her own experience as an impoverished widow and by her strong religious beliefs. As she explained

in an address to her fellow charity workers, destitute women "are also the agents of your God, by whose ministration he is the Father of the fatherless, the Husband of the widow, the stranger's shield and orphan's stay." Graham remained active in charity work until her death in 1814.

Further reading: Paul A. Gilje and Howard B. Rock, *Keepers of the Revolution: New Yorkers at Work in the Early Republic* (Ithaca: Cornell University Press, 1992).

Grant, James (1720–1806) *British general, governor of East Florida*

The younger son of an aristocratic Scots family, James Grant sought a career in the British military and saw service against the French in the War of Austrian Succession (1740–48) on the European continent. Grant was a major at the beginning of the French and Indian War (1754–63), when he was detached to North America. At first he was stationed in South Carolina, but in 1758 he joined General John Forbes's campaign in western Pennsylvania. His first independent command came when he led a reconnaissance force to Fort Duquesne (see Fort Pitt). Unfortunately for Grant, he underestimated the strength of the French position and did not retreat quickly when he lost the element of surprise. Attacked by the French and Indians, most of his men panicked, and in the confusion Grant was captured; he lost about 300 men killed, wounded, and captured out of a force of 850. A little over a year later, he was exchanged as a prisoner of war, and having retained the confidence of his superiors for his efficiency as a military officer, he returned to active duty. He was subsequently detached twice to campaigns in the Cherokee War (1759–61), being the second in command in Colonel Archibald Montgomery's sortie into Cherokee country in 1760 and assuming command of the more successful assault on the Cherokee in 1761, ending the war. In the process he was promoted to lieutenant colonel.

After the war, Grant found employment in 1763 as the first governor of the new colony of East Florida. In this position his strengths as an administrator came to the fore as he had to deal with both civil and military authorities, negotiate with Native Americans, and defend the province. He also had to find ways to encourage settlement of the sparsely settled territory. Between his salary and the proceeds of a successful indigo plantation, he was able to amass a fortune of his own. Perhaps because the colony was so new and underpopulated, there was little upheaval concerning imperial regulations such as the Stamp Act (1765) and Townshend duties (1767), although a few colonists complained that Grant was somewhat autocratic in his governorship because he never organized a representative assembly, as stipulated in his royal instructions.

He left East Florida in 1771 when he inherited his family's estate in Scotland, but he did not resign his governorship until 1773. In that year he entered Parliament, where he was not sympathetic to the North American RESISTANCE MOVEMENT against imperial measures.

The outbreak of the REVOLUTIONARY WAR (1775–83) brought Grant back into military service. Sent to Boston in summer 1775, he developed a close relationship with General WILLIAM HOWE and was promoted to major general after the British army left Massachusetts. He saw combat in the BATTLE OF LONG ISLAND (August 27–30, 1776) and was in charge of British troops in New Jersey when General GEORGE WASHINGTON crossed the Delaware and attacked the HESSIANS at Trenton on December 26, 1776. Grant accompanied Howe's army in his campaign to capture Philadelphia, commanding troops at the BATTLE OF BRANDYWINE (September 11, 1777) and bearing the brunt of Washington's attack at the BATTLE OF GERMANTOWN (October 4, 1777). He also failed to prevent the MARQUIS DE LAFAYETTE's escape from his exposed position at the BATTLE OF BARREN HILL (May 20, 1778). Grant advocated a scorched-earth policy to put down the rebellion in North America, but after the withdrawal from Philadelphia in summer 1778, he became convinced that the war was unwinnable, although he believed that if the revolutionaries were left to themselves, the United States would quickly fall apart and rejoin the British Empire.

Sent to command the British army in the WEST INDIES, Grant captured St. Lucia in December 1778. In spring and early summer 1779, however, he had to scramble to defend several islands once the French established naval superiority in the region. Despite his best efforts, the British lost St. Vincent and Grenada to the French before an ailing Grant sailed for England on August 1, 1779. Upon his return, he concentrated on politics as a member of Parliament. He used his political connections with WILLIAM PITT and his loyalty to King GEORGE III to gain promotion to lieutenant general in 1782 and later to general. In 1789 he also became governor of Stirling Castle, which placed him in command of all the troops in Scotland. He remained in the army until 1796 but did not see any more combat after leaving the West Indies. He died on April 13, 1806, age 86.

Further reading: Paul David Nelson, *General James Grant: Scottish Soldier and Royal Governor of East Florida* (Gainesville: University Press of Florida, 1993).

Grasse, François-Joseph-Paul, comte de (1722–1788) *French admiral in the American Revolution*

The son of a nobleman, François-Joseph-Paul, comte de Grasse, played a vital role in helping to force the British

French naval officer the comte de Grasse commanded forces in the Caribbean and the decisive Yorktown campaign. *(U.S. Naval Institute)*

to surrender at YORKTOWN (October 19, 1781) during the REVOLUTIONARY WAR (1775–83). Born François-Joseph de Grasse, he entered the Garde de la Marine at age 11 to pursue a life in the French navy, becoming a page to the grand master of Malta at 12 and seeing action against corsairs in the MEDITERRANEAN SEA. In 1747 he was captured by the English during the Battle of Cape Finisterre. Upon his release, he resumed his stellar naval career, and by 1781 he was a rear admiral and commander in chief of French naval forces in the WEST INDIES. Contemporaries considered him the finest French admiral of the age, and he was widely admired for his good looks, commanding bearing, and coolness under fire.

Ordered by King Louis XVI to attack British forces in the Caribbean and then assist French and revolutionary armies in North America, Grasse sailed for the West Indies in spring 1781. He defeated a British force commanded by Admiral SAMUEL HOOD, captured SINT EUSTATIUS and St. Kitts, and in August entered Chesapeake Bay with 28 ships and 3,000 French soldiers. He arrived in time to block the seaward escape of the British army, commanded by LORD CORNWALLIS, from Virginia. Combined French and revolutionary armies under GEORGE WASHINGTON and the COMTE DE ROCHAMBEAU had surrounded Cornwallis, and Grasse blocked a British naval attempt to relieve Cornwallis by defeating Admiral THOMAS GRAVES in the BATTLE OF CHESAPEAKE CAPES (September 5, 1781). Graves cautiously decided to retreat to New York for repairs and reinforcements before returning to save Cornwallis, but the delay proved fatal to British interests in North America. Without hope of rescue because of the presence of Grasse's fleet, Cornwallis had to surrender at Yorktown. The British soon began negotiations to end the war, leading to the TREATY OF PARIS (1783).

By then Grasse himself had been decisively defeated and captured by British Admiral GEORGE BRIDGES RODNEY in the famous BATTLE OF THE SAINTES (April 12, 1782), and the Royal Navy reigned supreme as the unquestioned master of the world's oceans. The comte de Grasse died a disappointed man six years later, on January 11, 1788.

Further reading: Barbara Tuchman, *The First Salute: A View of the American Revolution* (New York: Knopf, 1988).

—Lance Janda

Graves, Thomas (1725–1802) *British admiral*

The son of an admiral, Thomas Graves entered the British navy at a young age and quickly moved through the ranks. In the 1740s and 1750s he saw action in several engagements. During the FRENCH AND INDIAN WAR (1754–63), he was briefly governor of Newfoundland (1761 and 1762) and ably defended the province from French attack. By the beginning of the REVOLUTIONARY WAR (1775–83) he was a captain of a ship of the line, and in 1779 he was promoted to rear admiral. Sent to North America in 1780, he took command of the squadron in New York when Admiral MARRIOT ARBUTHNOT headed for England in April 1781.

Graves faced a difficult situation, with his fleet in need of repair; a French force under the COMTE DE BARRAS at Newport, Rhode Island; and the possibility of another French fleet arriving from the WEST INDIES. That possibility became a reality in August when the French admiral the COMTE DE GRASSE headed for Virginia, followed by a smaller British squadron under Admiral SAMUEL HOOD. When Hood arrived in New York, Graves as the senior officer took command of the combined squadron and sailed to intercept the French. On September 5, 1781, he fought the French fleet in the indecisive BATTLE OF CHESAPEAKE CAPES. However, in addition to being outnumbered by the French, he sustained enough damage to his ships that he returned to New York to refit. On the day he left New York to return to the Capes with a larger fleet and reinforce-

ments for LORD CORNWALLIS, however, the British surrendered at YORKTOWN (October 19, 1781).

Because Hood had better political connections, Graves was accused of being timid and was blamed for the failure to defeat the French at the Battle of Chesapeake Capes. Despite several difficult years after the war, he remained in the navy and was even promoted. He was second in command of the Channel Fleet in the British victory over the French on June 1, 1794, and received an Irish baronetcy for his service. However, he was wounded during the fighting and subsequently retired from the navy. He died on February 9, 1802.

Great Awakening, Second

Although in some ways the religious revivals that had begun in the 1740s never really dissipated during the REVOLUTIONARY WAR (1775–83), many historians identify a second wave of evangelicalism that began in the 1790s. This Second Great Awakening, as it is called, swept across the United States and transformed the country's religious and social landscape. The revival reflected tremendous faith in an individual's ability to affect his or her own salvation. In an age when the clarion call for equality gained in strength, suddenly every man was equal before God. All a person had to do, many revivalists declared, was open his or her heart to Jesus, and the individual would be saved. Harsh Calvinism was shunted aside, and learned ministers were no longer needed to guide the lay people. Evangelicals did not write formal and reasoned sermons; instead, they preached as the Lord moved them, threatening sinners with fire and brimstone and speaking in an impassioned voice.

While regular church services were part of the revival, CAMP MEETINGS became its special tool. In rural areas where the population was dispersed, the camp meeting provided a reason for hundreds, sometimes thousands, to assemble together in both a social and religious setting. In summer 1801, more than 12,000 people attended the CANE RIDGE, KENTUCKY, camp meeting. Similar gatherings occurred throughout the early 19th century. The behavior of the participants at such meetings could border on the bizarre, with some barking like dogs, shouting and screaming for the glory of God, and sobbing in the recognition of their own sin.

The enthusiastic RELIGION associated with this revival had its greatest impact on the FRONTIER, both in the North and the South; Kentucky and Tennessee were particularly responsive. Western upstate New York, recently occupied by European Americans, experienced so many revivals that it was known as the "burned-over district" because the fires of religion had repeatedly burned over the area. In newly settled regions, European Americans were looking for some order in an unstructured social environment. The awakening, even with its extravagant behavior, provided individuals with the reassurance that they were guaranteed salvation and had a special relationship with God. Many evangelical denominations also emphasized the need for personal discipline and attacked drinking, gambling, and other forms of misbehavior.

The effects of the Second Great Awakening on society were profound as it brought an ever-increasing number of people into church attendance. It was also at this time that many African-American slaves became Christians, responding to the evangelical currents swirling about them. Denominations such as the METHODISTS and BAPTISTS swelled in numbers, quickly becoming the predominant religious groups in many sections of the nation. Later in the 19th century, new denominations, including the Mormons and the Church of Christ, appeared. The call for self-discipline also helped to encourage a host of reform movements in the United States. With the emphasis on an individual's personal relationship with God, the need to spread the gospel led to Bible and Sunday school societies. In turn, other groups emerged to help the poor and disadvantaged and to reform society. While these reform movements gained their fullest expression in the 1830s and 1840s, they began in the opening decades of the 19th century. Ultimately, however, the greatest impact of the revival was the further impetus it gave to the developing central creed of the American nation, making it increasingly difficult to sustain social distinctions and oppose the rise of equality.

See also AFRICAN AMERICANS; DOW, LORENZO; RELIGIOUS LIBERTY; RURAL LIFE.

Further reading: Whitney R. Cross, *The Burned-Over District: The Social and Intellectual History of Enthusiastic Religion in Western New York, 1800–1850* (Ithaca, N.Y.: Cornell University Press, 1950); Nathan O. Hatch, *The Democratization of Christianity* (New Haven, Conn.: Yale University Press, 1989); Christine Leigh Heyrman, *Southern Cross: The Beginnings of the Bible Belt* (Chapel Hill: University of North Carolina Press, 1997).

Great Bridge, Battle of (December 9, 1775)

During the opening stages of the REVOLUTIONARY WAR (1775–83) in Virginia, Lord Dunmore (see DUNMORE, JOHN MURRAY, EARL OF) left Williamsburg and set up a base in Norfolk, Virginia, the largest city in the colony and believed to be packed with LOYALISTS. With open water on one side, which could be controlled by the British navy, and miles of swampland to the south, Norfolk should have been relatively easy to defend. There was only one practical approach from the south on a road that passed through a town called Great Bridge, which not only contained a bridge (of modest size) but also long, narrow causeways sur-

rounded by tidal swamps. A small detachment defending the bridge could stop a force many times its size. Dunmore ordered a stockade called Fort Murray built on the northern side of the bridge and manned it with less than 100 troops to prevent an advance of revolutionary MILITIA.

In early December 1775, approximately 1,000 revolutionaries gathered in the town of Great Bridge—to the south of the actual bridge. Something of a stalemate emerged as the cautious revolutionary commander, Colonel William Woodford, hesitated to advance on the British position for fear of the carnage that would ensue on the narrow causeway. Dunmore, however, decided to attack Woodford before he was reinforced further and obtained cannon that could destroy Fort Murray. On December 8, 1775, Captain Samuel Leslie marched the 12 miles from Norfolk to Fort Murray with about 200 regulars and Loyalist militia. The plan was to have a diversionary force of African-American Loyalists draw the main body of revolutionaries away from the road, but those troops—recruited after Dunmore's famous proclamation offering freedom to slaves who fought for the king—were too far away to be of much help. Leslie decided to press on with the attack anyway and detailed Captain Charles Fordyce to advance along the causeway with about 80 grenadiers. Amazingly, the British managed to reach the revolutionary pickets before being detected. However, once alerted, the revolutionary advance guard occupied their fortifications and unleashed a devastating fire on the British at close range, breaking up the attack. Fordyce was killed along with at least 14 of his men, and many more were wounded. The British retreated toward the bridge and sustained more casualties from riflemen, whose weapons had a longer and more accurate range than the British. All told, the British lost 17 killed and 44 wounded or captured.

The Battle of Great Bridge may have involved only a few hundred men, but it had important implications for the war. That evening, Leslie abandoned Fort Murray, and a few days later Dunmore evacuated Norfolk, surrendering what could have been a strategic base of operations and a stronghold for the Loyalist cause.

Further reading: John E. Selby, *The Revolution in Virginia, 1775–1783* (Williamsburg, Virginia: Colonial Williamsburg Foundation, 1988); David K. Wilson, *The Southern Strategy: Britain's Conquest of South Carolina and Georgia, 1775–1780* (Columbia: University of South Carolina Press, 2005).

Great Britain

Great Britain as a nation was still in a state of formation in the period of 1754–1815. Many people in the United States look across the ATLANTIC OCEAN and assume that

Great Britain was a single political entity from before the REVOLUTIONARY WAR (1775–83) through the WAR OF 1812 (1812–15). This perception is wrong: In fact, in many ways the break with the North American colonies represented one step in an ongoing process to define British nationhood.

Great Britain as a formal political entity was the result of the Act of Union of 1707, which merged the separate kingdoms of England and Scotland. Wales had been joined with England in 1536, while Ireland remained a possession of Great Britain until 1800, when it too was brought into the union, creating the United Kingdom of Great Britain and Ireland. The Jacobite invasion of Scotland and England in 1745–46 demonstrates the tenuous nature of this union in the mid-18th century.

Great Britain as a nation emerged out of a strong Protestant identity, participation in the development of a commercial empire, a sense of pride in the notion of LIBERTY, and a series of wars against FRANCE. The English had assured themselves a Protestant succession with the Glorious Revolution of 1688. Thereafter, a strident anti-Catholicism marked much of British society and became a cement that bound the somewhat disparate elements of the British Isles—English, Welsh, and Scottish—together in facing a common enemy. Polemical Protestant literature—such as John Foxe's *Book of Martyrs,* which detailed the anti-Protestant atrocities committed during the reign of the Catholic queen Mary Tudor—remained popular throughout the 18th century. Typical of this religious identity were the celebrations of Guy Fawkes Day (known as POPE DAY in the North American colonies), with bonfires spread from one end of Great Britain to the other. From this perspective, Protestantism stood for representative government as embodied in Parliament against popery and absolutism.

As the British Empire spread, the sharing of its commercial benefits helped to shape the emerging nation of Great Britain. On the one hand, all the peoples of Great Britain had access to increased consumer goods, whether it be sugar from the WEST INDIES, tea from INDIA, or TOBACCO from North America, all of which came to symbolize a rising prosperity. On the other hand, an ever-expanding commercial class benefited more directly from their involvement with TRADE. The rising dominance of Glasgow merchants in tobacco imports and the role of Liverpool in the SLAVE TRADE in the mid-18th century reveals that the commerce of empire was not confined to London. Moreover, the INDUSTRIAL REVOLUTION in Great Britain provided manufactured goods on a vastly increased scale.

Although direct political participation remained limited until well into the 19th century, the people of the developing British nation saw themselves as living in the freest country in Europe with a unique form of government. Ideas from the ENLIGHTENMENT only strengthened this faith in British liberty. When MONTESQUIEU praised the supposed balance in the British government between the monarchy (king), aristocracy (House of Lords), and democracy (House of Commons), he was only putting into print that which the British people already knew: Their representative government was superior to all others.

Involvement in wars with FRANCE further enhanced the developing sense of nationhood. Beginning in the late 17th century and continuing until 1815, a series of ANGLO-FRENCH WARS (1754–1815) provided a focus for British national identity. Wars carried out on a global scale entailed the mobilization of people and resources to an unprecedented degree. Before the outbreak of the FRENCH REVOLUTION (1789–99), France represented a Catholic absolutism that competed for commercial superiority. During the 1790s the French exchanged their Catholic and absolutist stance for radical revolutionary and atheist regime. However, with the rise of NAPOLEON BONAPARTE, the British could once again portray the French as an absolutist enemy seeking world domination. Regardless of which government was in power in France, the British people were united as a nation by a century-long series of wars.

It is against this backdrop that the relationship between English-speaking settlers of the North American continent and their cousins in Great Britain should be examined. From this perspective, the independence of the United States can be said to represent Britain's failure to incorporate one segment of its possessions into the new and developing British nationhood, and therefore the Revolutionary War was nothing more than a civil war pitting two groups of British Americans against each other.

By the mid-18th century, colonial North Americans were becoming more rather than less British. Like Britons on the other side of the Atlantic, most colonial Americans were committed to Protestantism and a strident anti-Catholicism. It was at this time that several communities began to have parades celebrating Pope Day, and the same anti-Catholic literature popular in Great Britain was popular in North America. Colonial Americans, too, participated in the spreading commercial empire, eagerly purchasing more consumer goods and trading with the West Indies and other British colonial possessions. With representative governments that had a much broader franchise than in Great Britain, the North American colonists were proud of the British heritage of balanced government and cherished the ideal of British liberty. Moreover, colonial enthusiasm for the FRENCH AND INDIAN WAR (1754–63) remained high throughout that conflict. A young JOHN ADAMS felt his heart pound with patriotism as he watched a column of redcoats march through town on their way to fight in defense of the colonies. Likewise, Britons on both sides of the Atlantic greeted the ascent of GEORGE III to the throne in 1760 with unbridled enthusiasm.

Within this context of growing British national identity, the people of North America and Great Britain confronted a unique situation. The British-American triumph in the French and Indian War had been complete. British control of CANADA provided unprecedented security for the North American colonies, and the Crown began to reexamine its relationship with its overseas possessions. In an effort to redefine that relationship, the government passed imperial regulations that triggered the RESISTANCE MOVEMENT (1764–75). In an odd twist of logic, colonial Americans initially reacted to these measures not out of a nascent sense of American nationality but rather in defense of what they saw as their constitutional rights as Britons, which was a result of their British national identity. British imperial policy at this time was not well thought-out or consistent. Had the British government sought to incorporate the North American colonies into the British nation more fully, the outcome might have been very different. Instead, the British government—or, more properly, governments, as different administrations pursued conflicting policies—passed and repealed measures with a regularity that bordered upon capriciousness.

The lack of consistent policy combined with a host of other problems within the colonies to produce a war that turned into a disaster for Great Britain and left the British having to define a truncated nation without its North American colonies. And yet, for the people of Great Britain, the defeat in the Revolutionary War furthered the development of a sense of nationality. The civil war with the colonies spread to an international war in which the chief enemies were the Catholic and absolutist countries of France and SPAIN. Faced with the threat of invasion, the people of Great Britain had to bind together. Moreover, although defeated in North America, victories elsewhere—in the defense of Gibraltar, with success in INDIA, and in the BATTLE OF THE SAINTES (April 12, 1782)—salvaged some national pride. After the Revolutionary War, confronted with a new nation dedicated to the ideal of liberty, the British had to restake their claim to their own national heritage. Out of this intellectual crisis came increased support for ending the slave trade and the ABOLITION OF SLAVERY. Although these movements would not succeed throughout the British Empire until the early 19th century, Britons drew a sharp contrast between their land of liberty—slavery was outlawed in Great Britain by judicial decree in 1772—compared to the North American land of liberty, which continued to allow both slavery and the slave trade.

In the years after the TREATY OF PARIS (1783), the British acknowledged the independence of the United States but found it difficult to take the new nation seriously. British soldiers continued to occupy posts in the territory it had ceded to the new nation north of the Ohio River and in the Great Lakes region, and British agents encouraged the resistance of NATIVE AMERICANS to the United States. British merchants quickly came to dominate trade with the new republic, while Parliament closed off Britain's West Indies colonies to U.S. merchants (although illegal trade continued). The British king barely recognized John Adams as the new nation's first official representative to Court of St. James. The ratification of the U.S. CONSTITUTION may have created a more powerful union among the former colonies, but it did not alter relations between the two English-speaking countries.

The war that broke out on February 1, 1793, between Revolutionary France and Great Britain had a dramatic impact on the development of the British nation and its relationship with the United States. Once again, the British had an external enemy to help define their nationhood. This war, which continued with only a few short hiatuses until 1815, dominated British life, and whatever they felt concerning the loss of some North American colonies a decade earlier now paled in comparison to the renewed threat across the channel. Repeated invasion threats and mobilization on a massive scale demanded that the British pull together as a nation. Ultimately, they emerged victorious and in command of an empire even greater than the one that had existed before 1776.

This global contest meant that relations with the United States became a minor sideshow. The former North American colonies were important as a market of goods manufactured by the British Industrial Revolution and as a source of agricultural produce and naval stores. U.S. merchant ships might be useful as neutral carriers, but the British also sought to dictate commercial terms to the United States. In 1794 the two nations stood at the brink of war because of the number of ships seized by the Royal Navy for carrying goods between France and its colonies. The British, however, sought to avoid any further distraction with the United States by agreeing to JAY'S TREATY (1794), which established most-favored-nation status between the two countries and effectively ended the 1778 alliance between the United States and France (see FRENCH ALLIANCE). Relations became more heated again in the middle of the first decade of the 19th century as the British navy intensified IMPRESSMENT—the forced recruitment of sailors—and the British government issued ORDERS IN COUNCIL to limit U.S. trade with Napoleonic Europe. War threatened in the wake of the *CHESAPEAKE-LEOPARD affair* and was only avoided when President THOMAS JEFFERSON attempted to use economic coercion with the EMBARGO OF 1807. This policy, along with various adjustments in 1809 and 1810, also failed to pressure the British into concessions. However, with a change of administration in the British government in the first half of 1812, the nation was ready to open trade on terms acceptable to the United States. Unfortunately for both sides, by the time news of this shift in policy arrived in WASHINGTON, D.C., the WAR OF 1812 (1812–15) had already broken out.

Preoccupied with defeating Napoleon, Great Britain fought a largely defensive war in North America until 1814, when it could begin to release forces from the European campaigns to invade the United States. These efforts, however, ran into serious resistance, and after some difficult negotiations, a peace was agreed upon in the TREATY OF GHENT, signed on December 24, 1814. The War of 1812 ended in a stalemate, but neither nation seemed to care. The United States, proclaiming a victory despite the shabby showing of its military, emerged with a new sense of identity. Great Britain, too, felt victorious—more for its European than its North American exploits—and, bathed in the glory of the Battle of Waterloo (June 16–19, 1815) asserted its pride as a great nation that controlled a global empire.

Further reading: John Brewer, *The Sinews of Power: War, Money, and the English State, 1688–1793* (New York: Knopf, 1988); J. C. D. Clark, *English Society 1660–1832: Religion, Ideology and Politics during the Ancien Regime*, 2nd ed. (Cambridge: Cambridge University Press, 2000); Linda Colley, *Britons: Forging the Nation, 1707–1837* (New Haven, Conn.: Yale University Press, 1992); Frank O'Gorman, *The Long Eighteenth Century: British Political and Social History, 1688–1832* (New York: St. Martin's Press, 1997).

Great Plains

The Great Plains, sometimes referred to as the Great American Desert, was teeming with life in the century after 1750. Before 1750, only limited numbers of NATIVE AMERICANS had ventured onto its vast open spaces, but the introduction of the horse in the late 17th century from New Mexico allowed many Indians to alter their culture and pursue the huge herds of BUFFALO that wandered the region. The Comanche trekked onto the Great Plains from the Great Basin area in eastern Utah, and the Sioux moved in from the east and the prairies of Minnesota. This transformation took decades to develop, but by the second half of the 18th century, these and other tribes had created the elaborate Plains Indian culture that was largely dependent on the horse for mobility and the buffalo for almost everything else.

There were several key characteristics of this culture: First, tribal ties grew looser since there was less need for cooperation in a nomadic lifestyle; AGRICULTURE had required greater group organization for labor and for protection. Second, the gender division of labor changed. Women had previously been the primary producers of nourishment by gathering food and growing crops, but now their labor focused on dressing meats and tanning hides. With this shift also came some diminution of the status of women within the tribe. Finally, the Plains Indians developed extensive TRADE networks that reached from New Mexico and the Rio Grande to Hudson's Bay in CANADA, and from beyond the Rockies to the European Americans living along the ATLANTIC OCEAN.

There were also important shifts in the balance of power in this period. The Comanche drove the Apache into the deserts of the Southwest. Further north, the sedentary tribes of the Mandan and Hidatsa, visited during the LEWIS AND CLARK EXPEDITION (1803–06), had been vital as trading centers around 1800 but soon lost ground as they were devastated by DISEASE AND EPIDEMICS. Because of their dispersed conditions, the mobile Plains Indians suffered less from disease at this time. Europeans also claimed the Great Plains as French fur traders traveled throughout the area in the late 18th century. SPAIN held title to most of the plains after 1763 but did not colonize the region beyond southern Texas and the Mississippi outposts established by the French. Shortly after the LOUISIANA PURCHASE (1803), in which the United States acquired the vast territory of LOUISIANA, explorers such as Lewis and Clark and ZEBULON MONTGOMERY PIKE crossed the Great Plains, and fur trading penetrated into the Rockies, but American settlement of the Great Plains would have to wait until later in the 19th century.

See also FRONTIER.

Further reading: Gary Clayton Anderson, *The Indian Southwest, 1580–1830: Ethnogenesis and Reinvention* (Norman: University of Oklahoma Press, 1999); Andrew C. Isenberg, *The Devastation of the Bison: An Environmental History, 1750–1920* (Cambridge: Cambridge University Press, 2000).

Great Savannah/Nelson's Ferry, Battle of (August 20, 1780)

Only a few days after the defeat of HORATIO GATES at the BATTLE OF CAMDEN (August 15, 1780), the Battle of Great Savannah—little more than a skirmish—represented a small bright spot in an otherwise dismal period in the REVOLUTIONARY WAR (1775–83) in South Carolina. In the battle, General FRANCIS MARION led a partisan band of MILITIA in a predawn attack on a British detachment bringing 150 PRISONERS OF WAR from Camden to Charleston. Catching the British by surprise near Nelson's Ferry, Marion captured 22 British soldiers, freed the prisoners, and then withdrew to the swamps before the British army could react. Marion lost only one man killed in the fighting.

Great Wagon Road (Warrior's Path)

Beginning in the early 18th century as the Warrior's Path, which NATIVE AMERICANS used to move north and south on the eastern slopes of the Appalachian Mountains, the Great Wagon Road developed into a significant highway for European-American settlers by the second half of the 18th century. The Great Wagon Road began in Philadelphia and headed west to Lancaster and York, Pennsylvania; then it turned south through Hagerstown, Maryland, and across the Potomac and through the Shenendoah Valley. From Big Lick—later Roanoke, Virginia—the road headed almost straight south into the Carolinas and ended in Augusta, Georgia. Tens of thousands of European Americans, especially German and SCOTS-IRISH immigrants, used the road to populate the backcountry as land in Pennsylvania became too expensive. It also brought consumer goods to the FRONTIER and became an avenue for livestock to be brought to market.

Further reading: Parke Rouse, Jr., *The Great Wagon Road, from Philadelphia to the South* (New York: McGraw-Hill, 1973).

Green Corn Ceremony

The Green Corn Ceremony was an important feast for most southern and eastern NATIVE AMERICANS for whom corn held a central place in society. The ceremony, while similar in its meaning for many different Native American groups, did not have a specific time for its practice. Theoretically, the ritual occurred just as the corn turned from green to yellow. Among the CHEROKEE and CREEK, for example, the ceremony was held in July or August and signaled a time of reflection, cleansing, and rebirth in anticipation of the annual corn harvest. While the southeastern Indian nations celebrated the DANCE during the summer, others began the Green Corn Ceremony at any time between May and October. It is difficult to generalize the activities that comprised the ceremony because each group had its own rituals; nevertheless, its primary function was to celebrate the harvest and good weather, forgive the previous year's transgressions, and purify villages. Highly ritualized, with specific tasks and responsibilities for all of the participants, the Green Corn Ceremony lasted from one to three days.

During the revolutionary era, particularly during the early decades of the 19th century, the ceremony's importance and frequency diminished as government agents and European-American traders often sought to influence the schedule of the ceremonies for times convenient for them to conduct business and TRADE. Rather than succumbing to these pressures on their ceremonies, many NATIVE AMERICANS began holding private dances, with a separate public one for outsiders.

Further reading: Peter C. Mancall and James H. Merrell, eds., *American Encounters: Natives and Newcomers from European Contact to Indian Removal, 1500–1850* (New York: Rutledge, 2000); Theda Perdue, *Cherokee Women: Gender and Culture Change, 1700–1835* (Lincoln: University of Nebraska Press, 1998).

—Michele M. Stephens

Greene, Christopher (1737–1781) *Rhode Island legislator, Continental army officer*

A member of a prominent Rhode Island family, Christopher Greene served in the colonial legislature and supported the revolutionary cause. In May 1775 he was appointed a major in the 1st Rhode Island Regiment, and in June his unit became part of the new CONTINENTAL ARMY. Promoted to lieutenant colonel in autumn 1775, he joined BENEDICT ARNOLD's invasion of CANADA and was captured in the ill-fated BATTLE OF QUEBEC (December 31, 1775). After he was exchanged, he was promoted to full colonel and took command of the 1st Rhode Island, which included several companies of African-American troops and some NATIVE AMERICANS. Greene and 600 Continentals inflicted heavy casualties and beat back an assault from 1,500 HESSIANS at Fort Mercer during the BATTLE OF RED BANK (October 22, 1777). He also participated in the BATTLE OF RHODE ISLAND (August 29, 1778), and in spring 1781 he was placed in command of the troops in Westchester County, New York. On May 14, 1781, some of JAMES DE LANCEY's Westchester Refugees—also known as Cowboys—surprised Greene at his headquarters. As he was surrendering, a few of his own soldiers fired on the LOYALISTS, who then shot back, killing Greene. Revolutionaries subsequently portrayed Greene's death as a wanton act by cutthroat irregulars.

Greene, Nathanael (1742–1786) *Continental army general*

One of General GEORGE WASHINGTON's ablest lieutenants, Nathanael Greene served in the CONTINENTAL ARMY from the siege of Boston (April 19, 1775–Mach 17, 1776) until after the British surrender at YORKTOWN (October 19, 1781). He fought in several battles and took over command of the southern campaign at a critical juncture after the defeat of HORATIO GATES at the BATTLE OF CAMDEN (August 15, 1780).

There was little in Greene's background to suggest that he would become an important military figure. He was born on August 7, 1742, in Warwick, Rhode Island; his parents were QUAKERS, and he was brought up in some comfort. As an adult he became an anchor smith and ironmonger. By the time of the REVOLUTIONARY WAR (1775–83), he had left the Society of Friends and was eager to fight against the British. Somehow the Rhode Island Assembly recognized his greatest assets—tremendous organizational skills and the ability to instill confidence and lead men—by appointing him in May 1775 as the general in command of the Rhode Island Army of Observation, joining the siege of Boston. Once the Rhode Island troops arrived in the Boston area, Greene's talents quickly came to the fore as he helped to organize supplies for the army and ease inter-colonial tensions. On June 22 he was appointed a briga-dier general in the Continental army, and after the British evacuated Boston in spring 1776, he was put in charge of the city's army of occupation.

During the next few years, Greene participated in every major campaign led by General Washington. In April 1775 he brought his Rhode Island regiments to New York City and helped to prepare the defenses against a British attack. He was promoted to major general on June 22, 1776, and although he was ill and did not fight in the BATTLE OF LONG ISLAND (August 27–30, 1776), he recovered in time to take command of the Continental forces in New Jersey in autumn 1776. His attack on Staten Island in October had to be postponed after British general WILLIAM HOWE threatened Washington at the BATTLE OF WHITE PLAINS (October 28, 1776), and Greene had to oversee the retreat from Fort Lee after the disastrous loss of FORT WASH-INGTON (November 16, 1776) on Harlem Heights. He retained Washington's confidence in the face of defeat and had command of one of the columns at the Battle of Tren-ton on December 26, 1776, cutting off the retreat of many HESSIANS and forcing their surrender (see TRENTON AND PRINCETON, BATTLES OF). He was important in setting up the winter camp at MORRISTOWN and in skirmishing with the British in New Jersey in spring 1777. During the BATTLE OF BRANDYWINE (September 11, 1778), Greene's stout defense of the center and careful retreat helped save the Continental army from destruction. However, in the BATTLE OF GERMANTOWN (October 4, 1777), in which the revolutionaries depended on coordinated assaults at dawn and in the fog, he failed to bring his division into play early enough to have an impact on the battle. He was also unable to hold onto the DELAWARE RIVER FORTS in November, after the main Continental forces retreated to VALLEY FORGE (1777–78) and the British occupied Philadelphia.

Recognizing the difficulties of the military situation, Washington did not blame Greene for these reverses, and when the SECOND CONTINENTAL CONGRESS wanted to appoint a new quartermaster general for the army, Wash-ington immediately suggested Greene. As quartermaster from February 25, 1778, to July 15, 1780, Greene once again demonstrated his organizational abilities in supplying the army. He also continued as a field commander, partici-pating in the BATTLE OF MONMOUTH (June 28, 1778) and

General Nathanael Greene assumed command of the Southern Department in 1780 and successfully campaigned against British forces, although he lost every battle. (Independence National Historical Park)

an abortive attack on Newport that led to the BATTLE OF RHODE ISLAND (August 29, 1778). Although often adept at smoothing difference between others, politics ultimately compelled Greene to resign as quartermaster. His greatest service to the cause of independence was yet to come.

In summer 1780, LORD CORNWALLIS's invasion of the southern colonies had almost ended the rebellion in that region. The capture of Charleston on May 12, 1780, after the SIEGE OF CHARLESTON followed by the Battle of Camden all but wiped out the Continental army in South Carolina. At this crucial moment, Washington needed to send someone to the South he could depend on, and he chose the Rhode Island ironmonger Nathanael Greene. As soon as he received his appointment on October 14, 1780, Greene began planning and organizing to make sure that his army would be adequately supplied. As he reformed the Continental army in North Carolina, he made the unorth-odox move of splitting his forces. Cornwallis obliged him by splitting his own army, sending BANASTRE TARLETON after DANIEL MORGAN in the South Carolina backcountry. Morgan so severely trounced Tarleton at the BATTLE OF

Cowpens (January 17, 1781) that Cornwallis abandoned his baggage and set off after Greene in an effort to corner him and regain the initiative. But Greene kept one step ahead of the pursuing British. When Cornwallis at last gave up the chase in northern North Carolina, Greene advanced. Cornwallis's troops were still superior to the Continentals and defeated them at the Battle of Guilford Courthouse (March 15, 1781), but this victory was so costly that Cornwallis marched to Wilmington on the coast and then headed to his ill-fated invasion of Virginia.

Greene did not follow Cornwallis but instead marched into South Carolina and captured several British outposts. He was still no match for concentrated British forces, which, for example, beat back his attack at the Battle of Eutaw Springs (September 8, 1781). Nonetheless, he continued to apply pressure until the British withdrew all their forces except those that held Charleston. As Greene explained, "We rise, get beat, rise, and fight again."

At the end of the war, Greene faced personal difficulties. Although he was granted land by South Carolina and Georgia and made profits from the slaves he purchased, the war had taken a physical toll on him. In the last few years of his life, he divided his time between property he owned in Rhode Island and in Georgia, having moved in his lifetime from being a Quaker to becoming a southern slave owner. He died on June 19, 1786, in Edisto, South Carolina.

Further reading: Theodore Thayer, *Nathanael Greene: Strategist of the American Revolution* (New York: Twayne, 1960).

Green Mountain Boys

The Green Mountain Boys of Vermont began as land rioters, organized themselves as a Whig MILITIA in the opening days of the REVOLUTIONARY WAR (1775–83), and became a regular regiment in the CONTINENTAL ARMY. Starting in 1770, and led by ETHAN ALLEN and several of his relatives, a group of New England settlers formed the Green Mountain Boys. Their aim was to protect their land titles based on New Hampshire grants from landlords whose deeds rested on New York's claim to territory north of Massachusetts and between the Hudson and Connecticut Rivers. Ultimately, the British government sustained the New York right to these lands, but that right became a dead letter in the face of the Green Mountain Boys and their riotous tactics. Calling themselves a militia, the Green Mountain Boys harassed New York sheriffs attempting to evict settlers with New Hampshire deeds, tore down fences, and even destroyed houses built by settlers from New York. Such actions made Allen and his followers outlaws in New York.

The Revolutionary War offered a new opportunity to the Green Mountain Boys. By siding with the WHIGS, they hoped to legitimize their claim and gain recognition. Allen led a group of his followers in a surprise attack on the British, capturing FORT TICONDEROGA (May 10, 1775). SETH WARNER and Allen then persuaded the SECOND CONTINENTAL CONGRESS to incorporate the Green Mountain Boys into the Continental army in June 1775. The new regiment elected Warner its colonel and participated in the invasion of CANADA that winter. After that disaster left the unit devastated, other Vermont regiments were recruited and were also given the Green Mountain label. These units fought in the campaign that led to the British surrender at SARATOGA (October 17, 1777) and in subsequent campaigns along the northern border. This commitment to independence may have strengthened the case of the Green Mountain Boys for secure title of their lands, but it was not until 1791 that Vermont became a separate state.

See also LAND RIOTS.

Further reading: Michael A. Bellesiles, *Revolutionary Outlaws: Ethan Allen and the Struggle for Independence on the Early American Frontier* (Charlottesville: University Press of Virginia, 1993); Robert E. Shalhope, *Bennington and the Green Mountain Boys: The Emergence of Liberal Democracy Vermont, 1760–1850* (Baltimore: Johns Hopkins University Press, 1996).

Green Spring, Battle of (July 6, 1781)

During the summer campaign of 1781, LORD CORNWALLIS could move across Virginia almost at will. All that the MARQUIS DE LAFAYETTE—who had command of the CONTINENTAL ARMY in the state—could do was to shadow Cornwallis's superior army, waiting for an opportunity. In early July, Cornwallis decided to shift his troops from the peninsula between the James and York rivers to the south bank of the James River. This move, Lafayette believed, provided just the opportunity he was looking for, and he decided to attack Cornwallis as the British army was in the middle of the crossing. Cornwallis, however, had anticipated Lafayette's reaction and held back most of his army to surprise the Continentals.

Lafayette ordered General ANTHONY WAYNE to advance cautiously on what he thought was the British army's rear guard. Wayne's men skirmished with some British soldiers, who were constantly pulling back, suggesting that they were engaged in delaying tactics and had no larger support behind them. During the day, Lafayette reinforced Wayne until the latter commanded about 1,000 men. He also scouted along the river and discovered that most of Cornwallis's army was in front of Wayne, but he could not get word of this information to Wayne in time. In the early evening, Cornwallis sprung his trap and suddenly emerged with 3,000 men, whose presence had been covered by some hills and trees. Confronted by a force that outnumbered him three to one, and whose flanks on both the left and right stretched beyond his own, Wayne was in desperate straits. Rather than retreat, which could easily turn into a rout, or stand his ground and be overwhelmed—his left flank composed of riflemen was already dissolving—Wayne attacked. Continental troops advanced to within 70 yards of the British, and an intense 15-minute engagement followed before Wayne withdrew to the main body of Continentals who had formed a line at Green Spring Plantation a mile to the rear. This maneuver bought some crucial minutes, and with dark approaching, the British cavalry did not pursue the battered Continentals. Lafayette's situation remained precarious, and he pulled back further that night.

The British lost 75 killed and wounded; the revolutionaries had 28 killed and 128 wounded. Because of Wayne's brave reaction in attacking in the face of overwhelming odds, and because Cornwallis did not gain the complete triumph for which he had hoped, some commentators claim the revolutionaries won the battle. However, given Cornwallis's superior tactics, fewer casualties, and the fact that his men held the field, the British gained a marginal tactical victory.

Greenville, Treaty of (1795)

The Treaty of Greenville marked a break in the contest for the Ohio Country that had begun in the 1760s between European Americans and NATIVE AMERICANS. Although the treaty opened about half of the present state of Ohio to European-American settlement after 1795, and conflict between the United States and Native Americans in the region decreased for a while, many Indians remained resentful of white incursions into their land and joined a new pan-Indian confederacy under TECUMSEH in the first decade of the 19th century.

The REVOLUTIONARY WAR (1775–83) did not end in the Old Northwest after the TREATY OF PARIS (1783). The Indians of the region had won several battles in the closing years of the war and were not willing to accept the United States's authority north of the Ohio River. This position was reinforced by the presence of several forts in the area that remained garrisoned by the British regardless of treaty stipulations. Although some Indians ceded land in the region to the United States, most Native Americans rejected these concessions, and by the late 1780s and early 1790s a powerful pan-Indian confederacy had emerged to oppose any European-American incursions into the Ohio Country. In the early part of 1790s, this confederacy—under the leadership of LITTLE TURTLE, BLUE JACKET, and others—defeated an army under General JOSIAH HARMAR in 1790 and another army under General ARTHUR ST. CLAIR in 1791. However, they could not defeat a new army, called the Legion of the United States, under ANTHONY WAYNE in the BATTLE OF FALLEN TIMBERS (August 20, 1794).

The next summer General Wayne called for a conference with the Indians at Greenville. Like many such meetings, hundreds of Native Americans attended, and there were speeches and elaborate rituals performed by both sides. However, the Indians recognized that not only had they been defeated militarily, they had also been abandoned politically by the British, who refused to help them after their defeat at Fallen Timbers and who then evacuated their forts in the United States in accordance with the provisions of JAY's TREATY (1794). Within this context the Indians sought the best deal they could, even though they knew they would have to cede land to do so. Consequently, they surrendered southern Ohio and southeastern Indiana in exchange for $20,000 worth of goods and another $9,500 every year thereafter. The United States promised the Native Americans that they could hunt in the region as long as they remained peaceful and assured them of continued TRADE. Perhaps the most important provision for the Indians was a promise to keep settlers and hunters off the land beyond the boundaries marked out in the Treaty of Greenville. The treaty declared: "If any citizen of the United States, or any other white person or persons, shall presume to settle upon the lands now relinquished by the United States, such citizen or other person shall be out of the protection of the United States" and the Indians "may drive off the settler, or punish him in such manner as they shall think fit." With this guarantee of Native American SOVEREIGNTY on their remaining lands—however empty the promise turned out to be—Little Turtle, Blue Jacket and the leaders of the WYANDOT, DELAWARE, MIAMI, SHAWNEE, Potawatamie, Kickapoo, and Weas, signed the document on August 3, 1795.

Further reading: Andrew R. L. Cayton, "'Noble Actors' on 'the Theatre of Honour': Power and Civility in the Treaty of Greenville," in *Contact Points: American Frontiers from the Mohawk Valley to the Mississippi, 1750–1830,* edited by Cayton Teute and Frederika J. Teute, 235–69 (Chapel Hill: University of North Carolina Press, 1998); Richard White, *The Middle Ground: Indians, Empires, and Republics in the Great Lakes Region, 1650–1815* (New York: Cambridge University Press, 1991).

Grenville, George (1712–1770) *British chancellor of the exchequer*

George Grenville was the prime minister of the British government from 1763 to 1765 and is remembered for passing tax reforms in the British Empire that angered the colonists in North America. Born on October 14, 1712, Grenville was educated at Oxford, began his public career as a member of Parliament in 1741, and rose in the political ranks quickly. In 1744 he became Lord of the Admiralty, in 1747 he was appointed a lord of the treasury, and in 1754 he assumed the responsibility of treasurer of the navy and privy councillor. He was given a leadership role in the House of Commons in 1761, appointed secretary of state in May 1762, and gained the top position in the British government in 1763. He inherited a government that was £145 million in debt from fighting the FRENCH AND INDIAN WAR (1754–63). A master of finance, he proposed a plan to put the empire back on a sound financial footing and to ease the tax burden of British subjects.

One element of Grenville's financial plan was to have the king's North American subjects contribute to the costs of the colonies' defense. This effort angered colonial American and incited them to begin the RESISTANCE MOVEMENT (1764–65) against British imperial policy. Despite the fact that the colonists were being asked to pay about half of the cost of the British troops stationed in North America to protect them—the rest of the cost was to come from GREAT BRITAIN—many viewed Grenville's actions as unacceptable impositions on both their wallets and their LIBERTY. Under the Grenville government, Parliament passed the CURRENCY ACT (1764), the SUGAR ACT (1764), and the STAMP ACT (1765). While all three of the acts irritated the colonists, it was the Stamp Act that provoked widespread resistance. The act levied taxes on every newspaper, pamphlet, almanac, legal document, pair of dice, and all other legal and commercial documents in the colonies. RIOTS and other forms of violent protest were extensive, and the tax prompted an intercolonial meeting known as the STAMP ACT CONGRESS, which was attended by delegates from nine colonies.

In part because of the failure of the colonial tax measures, and in part because of the vagaries of the British political-party system, Grenville's ministry was cut short, and he was replaced by Lord Rockingham (see ROCKINGHAM, CHARLES WENTWORTH, MARQUIS OF) in 1765. Grenville continued to defend his policies as a member of Parliament, and he voted against the repeal of the Stamp Act in 1766. He died on November 13, 1770.

Further reading: Allen S. Johnson, *A Prologue to Revolution: The Political Career of George Grenville* (Lanham, Md.: University Press of America, 1997).

—J. Brett Adams

Griswold, Roger (1762–1812) *governor of Connecticut, congressman*
Born into a politically influential family on May 21, 1762, in Lyme, Connecticut, Roger Griswold was an outspoken and fervent supporter of the FEDERALIST PARTY. He attended Yale College from 1776 to 1780, after which he studied law with his father; earned admission to the bar in 1783; and established his practice in Norwich, Connecticut, where he worked for almost 11 years. In 1794 he returned to Lyme and won election to the House of Representatives, where he served from 1795 to 1805.

Despite his youth, Griswold rose to prominence within the Federalist Party. His staunch adherence to the party line during the debates regarding the Sedition Act (see ALIEN AND SEDITION ACTS) led to his 1798 altercation with MATTHEW LYON, a DEMOCRATIC-REPUBLICAN PARTY representative from Vermont. Lyon spat in Griswold's face after the latter insulted him, and Griswold retaliated by attacking Lyon with a cane; the two fought until other Congressmen pulled them apart. The Federalist Party's shift to minority status after the ELECTION OF 1800 further deepened Griswold's partisan tendencies. In 1803 he opposed the LOUISIANA PURCHASE Treaty, believing that the United States was a union of willing participants that should not be forced to accept people from a newly acquired territory on equal terms with the preexisting states. In 1805 he retired from the House of Representatives and returned to Connecticut.

The Connecticut legislature appointed Griswold to the state supreme court in 1807. After serving two years on the court, he became the state's lieutenant governor, serving from 1809 to 1811, and in early 1811 he won election as governor, a position he held until his death on October 25, 1812.

Further reading: Richard J. Purcell, *Connecticut in Transition: 1775–1818*, new ed. (Middletown, Conn.: Wesleyan University Press, 1963).

—Daniel Flaherty

Gronniosaw, James Albert Ukawsaw (1705?–1775) *writer, soldier*
Born in Baurnou in West AFRICA, James Albert Ukawsaw Gronniosaw wrote a narrative of his life that was one of the first autobiographies by a black man published in the 18th century. Although he was mainly concerned with detailing conversion to Christianity, his life story reflected many of the experiences of enslaved Africans in the transatlantic world.

Gronniosaw claimed to be of royal blood and traveled to the Gold Coast with an African merchant to broaden his horizons. On the Gold Coast, the local king threatened him with death and then sold him into SLAVERY. Shipped to the WEST INDIES, he was fortunate to be sold to a man who lived in New York, where he was sold to a minister, converted to Christianity, and obtained his freedom. After the minister and his sons died, Gronniosaw enlisted on a privateer during the FRENCH AND INDIAN WAR (1754–63) to pay off a debt. Cheated out of his prize MONEY, he joined the British army, served in the WEST INDIES, and participated in the SIEGE OF HAVANA in 1762. Dismissed from the army after the war, he traveled to GREAT BRITAIN, where he gained the patronage of some leading evangelicals, including George Whitefield, whom he had previously met in New York. Gronniosaw spent a year in The NETHERLANDS but returned to Great Britain and married an Englishwoman. He died in England in late September 1775. Although Gronniosaw did not dwell on his identity as a black African, the popularity of his narrative demonstrated the hardships faced by people of his race and his own ability to overcome all obstacles through his devotion to Christianity.

See also AFRICAN AMERICANS.

Further reading: James Albert Ukawsaw Gronniosaw, *A Narrative of the Most Remarkable Particulars in the Life of James Albert Ukawsaw Gronniosaw, an African Prince, Written by Himself* (Bath, England: W. Gye [1770]).

Grundy, Felix (1777–1840) *congressman*

Born in Virginia on September 11, 1777, Felix Grundy grew up on the hardscrabble Kentucky FRONTIER. Despite an impoverished youth, he obtained some EDUCATION and was admitted to the bar in 1795. He quickly became a prominent attorney and was elected to the state legislature in 1800. As a politician, he opposed the so-called bluegrass aristocracy led by HENRY CLAY. Grundy became a judge in 1806 and the state's chief justice in spring 1807, but resigned this position and headed for Tennessee late in 1807. In his new state he became active as a lawyer and soon allied himself with ANDREW JACKSON. In 1811 he was elected to the House of Representatives, where he became a leader of the WAR HAWKS urging a war against GREAT BRITAIN. Having had at least three brothers killed by NATIVE AMERICANS, Grundy believed that British "baubles and trinkets" had convinced Indians to attack the United States. However, he also argued that the nation should have "the right of exporting the products of our own soil and industry to foreign markets" without British interference, and he called IMPRESSMENT an "unjust and lawless invasion of personal liberty." He remained a stalwart defender of war measures during the WAR OF 1812 (1812–15) until he resigned from Congress in 1814 because of his wife's health.

Grundy continued to practice law in Tennessee and remained an active politician defending the rights of the common man. He was an avid supporter of Jackson and the emerging Democratic Party in the 1820s and 1830s in the Tennessee legislature and in the Senate, where he served from 1829 to 1838 and from 1839 until his death on December 19, 1840, in Nashville, Tennessee. Between his stints in the Senate, he was President Martin Van Buren's attorney general.

Further reading: Joseph Howard Parks, *Felix Grundy: Champion of Democracy* (University, La.: Louisiana State University Press, 1940).

Guilford Courthouse, Battle of (March 15, 1781)

The Battle of Guilford Courthouse was a defeat for the American revolutionaries, but the heavy price of victory in North Carolina drew the British general LORD CORNWALLIS into Virginia and ultimately to his surrender at YORKTOWN on October 19, 1781. After the BATTLE OF COWPENS (January 17, 1781), the revolutionaries withdrew into North Carolina. Hoping to catch and crush General DANIEL MORGAN, recapture prisoners, and dispel the impression of British vulnerability, Cornwallis followed, destroying all his excess baggage and supplies to increase the army's mobility and speed. Upon learning of the victory at Cowpens, General NATHANAEL GREENE, in turn, maneuvered his forces to reunite with Morgan.

When the two armies finally reached Guilford Courthouse, Greene had approximately 4,400 men to Cornwallis's 2,200. Despite superior numbers, the revolutionaries lacked the experience and training of their enemy. MILITIA units, many of whom had never been in combat, formed the bulk of Greene's army. Generally considered to be highly unreliable on the battlefield, they were not used to formal drills and military discipline, and they carried a mixture of rifles, muskets, and fowling pieces, none of which had bayonets. Meanwhile, though better equipped and trained, the soldiers in the CONTINENTAL ARMY at Greene's disposal were of uneven quality, their ranks continually depleted of veterans as terms of enlistment ended. Nonetheless, the terrain at Guilford Courthouse favored the revolutionaries. The woods, shrubs, and underbrush provided cover for skirmishers and made it difficult for the British to march in their conventional long, tightly formed files. With these factors in mind, Greene deployed his men in three rows, the first two composed of North Carolina and Virginia militia, the third of Continentals.

The redcoats began their approach early in the morning. Greene's first line of militia performed better than expected, but they quickly fell back. As anticipated, the terrain hindered the British advance on the second column, and the redcoats took heavy losses. Exhausted, they engaged the third line, where, quite unexpectedly, a veteran Continental unit bolted and opened a serious breech in their position. Greene was forced to order a retreat. The British carried the day, but they had lost a staggering 27 percent of their engaged forces, compared to only 6 per-

The Battle of Guilford Courthouse, March 15, 1781. *(U.S. Army Center of Military History)*

cent for the revolutionaries. An English parliamentarian later remarked that "another such victory would ruin the British Army."

In the aftermath, Cornwallis considered his options. Having generated little support from LOYALISTS in North Carolina, in desperate need of supplies and rest, and viewing Virginia as the key to victory in the South, he elected to march to the coast at Wilmington to obtain provisions and then move his tattered army north. This course of action allowed Greene to return to South Carolina almost unopposed. With the surrender at Yorktown in October, however, and Greene's reclamation of most of the South, GREAT BRITAIN soon resolved to end the war and relinquish her rebellious colonies.

See also REVOLUTIONARY WAR.

Further reading: Thomas F. Baker, *Another Such Victory: The Story of the American Defeat at Guilford Courthouse That Helped Win the War for Independence* (New York: Eastern Acorn Press, 1981); Robert Leckie, *George Washington's War: The Saga of the American Revolution* (New York: Harper Collins, 1993).

—Rita M. Broyles

gunboats

In an effort to cut down on government expenditures, President THOMAS JEFFERSON reduced the size of military spending and in 1803 began a policy of using gunboats as the mainstay of the U.S. NAVY. There were several different designs for these gunboats, but they were generally small, shallow-draft vessels with fore and aft rigging (as a schooner, sloop, or ketch), and they carried one heavy cannon (a 32-pounder). Intended for coastal defense, they also had sweeps to row the vessel in calms and had crews of approximately 30 men. These vessels were relatively inexpensive, and by the beginning of the WAR OF 1812 (1812–15), Congress had authorized 278 gunboats. However, nowhere near that number were built.

Most naval officers looked down on the gunboats, as did many of the common sailors. Jefferson envisioned a navy comprised almost entirely of gunboats, while naval officers could only accept them as auxiliaries to the larger ships they preferred. Although some gunboats were of use in the BARBARY WARS, they were not effective against the British. The success of the single-ship actions at the beginning of the War of 1812 convinced the navy and Congress to build larger ships and rely less on the gunboats.

Further reading: William M. Fowler, Jr., *Jack Tars and Commodores: The American Navy, 1783–1815* (Boston: Houghton Mifflin, 1984).

Gwinnett, Button (ca. 1735–1777) *Georgia politician, signer of the Declaration of Independence*
A merchant originally from England, Button Gwinnet moved to Savannah, Georgia, in 1765 to run a store. When this business failed, he borrowed extensively to purchase a plantation on St. Catherine's Island. Despite difficulties in making this enterprise a success, Gwinnett entered the fractious politics of colonial Georgia as a member of the lower house in 1769. However, he withdrew from politics in the early 1770s as he dealt with his financial difficulties and was not deeply involved with the RESISTANCE MOVEMENT (1764–75). After the beginning of the REVOLUTIONARY WAR (1775–83), he emerged as an ardent Whig and a leader in the democratic faction within Georgia. Elected to command Georgia's regiment in the CONTINENTAL ARMY in early 1776, he turned down this position to represent the state at the SECOND CONTINENTAL CONGRESS. That summer he voted for and signed the DECLARATION OF INDEPENDENCE; he is often considered one of the most obscure of the document's signers.

Gwinnett did not remain in Philadelphia long and returned to Georgia, where he vied for power with LACHLAN MCINTOSH, who had been given command of the Georgia regiment that Gwinnett had declined, and who supported the Savannah faction of WHIGS in the state. Gwinnett's faction gained control of the assembly, elected him speaker, and wrote a radically democratic state constitution. After becoming president of the state's council of safety and commander of the Georgia MILITIA, Gwinnett launched an invasion of FLORIDA, receiving only half-hearted support from McIntosh. He also briefly became the state's acting governor and arrested McIntosh's brother for treason. When the state assembly absolved Gwinnett of any responsibility for the failed Florida invasion, McIntosh became irate and called him "a Scoundrell & lying Rascal." This denunciation led to a duel between the two rivals in which Gwinnett was mortally wounded. He died near Savannah on May 19, 1777.

See also DUELING.

Further reading: Leslie Hall, *Land & Allegiance in Revolutionary Georgia* (Athens: University of Georgia Press, 2001).